Selected Papers from Nimbus–2003

Compendium

Selected Papers from Nimbus–2003 Compendium

We Solemnly Swear These Papers Were Worth The Wait

Compiled by
The Nimbus-2003 Programming Team
Penny Linsenmayer & Ebony Thomas, Chairs
Lee Hillman, Event Chair
Heidi Howard Tandy, Compilation Coordinator

HP Education Fanon, Inc.
Houston, Texas

To order additional copies of this book, contact:
Xlibris Corporation
1-888-795-4274
www.Xlibris.com
Orders@Xlibris.com
27108

CONTENTS

Moral Development, Philosophy & Religious Studies

Mythology and Magical Systems

Credts & Acknowledgements

The Nimbus—2003 Programming Team was chaired by Penny Linsenmayer and Ebony Elizabeth Thomas, and Lee Hillman was the chair of the overall event. Dr. Philip Nel and Dr. Lana Whited provided helpful advice throughout the process. Team members include Catherine Tosenberger, Emily Balawejder, Stephanie Keener, Jessica Nolam, Kristin McMichael, Carole Estes, Airemay, Carrie Clarady, Barbara Purdom, Heidi Tandy and Lee Hillman.

Special thanks to the 2003-2004 members of the Board of HP Education Fanon, Inc: Lee Hillman, Rob Ihinger, Peg Kerr, Philip Nel, Barbara Purdom, Catherine Schaff-Stump, Steve Vander Ark (AKA "Lexicon Steve"), John Walton, Carlisle Kraft Webber, Debra Duncan, Leeanna Izuel, Penny Linsenmayer and Heidi Tandy.

Emily Balawejder served as copy editor and generated almost all of the papers in PDF form. The art was created by Adrienne Dee, Maggie Bradshaw and Mary Gober. Photographs were supplied by Melissa Anelli of **the-leaky-cauldron.org**, as well as Lauren Kent, Tyler Haas, Mary Gober, Sara Goetz and Hermorrine.

i. Introduction by Gwendolyn Grace

A Look Back at Nimbus—2003

From July 17-20, 2003, 600 eager Harry Potter fans and scholars converged on Walt Disney World for three and a half days of presentations. Amidst the atmosphere of learning, they ate, argued, lived, and breathed Harry Potter. They rejoiced, they mourned, they connected, and they tried their wands at being wizards.

It has been almost a year since that historic occasion: the first dedicated conference on Harry Potter. And here at last are some of the papers from those presentations. Why so long? Why only some? Good questions. I'll take them in reverse order.

Many of our presenters are published authors, and some of them hope to become published soon. A number of presenters were constrained either by their publishers or their institutions to withhold their papers from this compendium. We were unable to record the panel discussions, so unfortunately, there are only a few summaries and transcripts that we were able to reconstruct after the fact. Regrettably, wthout a Pensieve, no amount of going back to our memories can substitute for the experience of having been there. And the longer we waited to reconstruct them, the fuzzier our brains became on the subject.

Which brings us to the second question: Why so long? We could offer up any number of excuses from real life: People moved, changed jobs, resigned, began working on new projects. Truly, in the aftermath of the conference, the Proceedings were a priority no one had time to shoulder. The Board of HP Education Fanon, Inc. was approached in late August with two bids for the next conference—bids which, I'm happy to say, have become the upcoming Witching Hour (**www.hp2005.org**) and Lumos: 2006 (**www.hp2006.org**). We're glad that our plan for an annual event is working, but we're sorry that it delayed our focus on from the final phase of Nimbus—2003. We've accepted our setbacks as well as we can, and we hope you think in the end, this compendium is as "worth the wait" as it claims.

More than half our presentations are represented in this book. We have included the original Summary and Biography sections for all our presenters. If there is a topic that you particularly wanted to see included, and it's not here, I encourage you to contact the author(s) to see if they can provide you with more information.

I once again thank every single one of our presenters for the effort and skill they brought to Nimbus—2003. Without them, we still might have had fun, but we would not have learned nearly as much. Thanks also to the dedicated team of volunteers who have worked many hours to produce this volume of papers—the largest collection of essays and papers on Harry Potter yet printed. Without their labours, we would all still be waiting, impatiently, for the final chapter of Nimbus—2003.

See you in Salem, Vegas, or beyond!

Lee Hillmal, more often known as Gwendolyn Grace
President, HP Education Fanon, Inc.

ii. About HP Education Fanon, Inc.

HP Education Fanon, Inc. ("HPEF") is an educational non-profit corporation founded in 2002 to promote and produce educational Harry Potter themed symposia on an international scale. HPEF draws significant support from members and visitors to such online fandom communities and websites such as FictionAlley, PumpkinPie, HP for Grownups, SugarQuill, the Harry Potter Lexicon, HPANA and the Leaky Cauldron, as well as from academicians from colleges and universities around the world.

HPEF is committed to producing high-quality events that combine a professional and academic focus with the light-hearted spirit of the Harry Potter series for scholar and fan alike. By bringing these two seemingly disparate groups together, HPEF fosters learning and exploration of the Harry Potter novels and phenomenon from the perspectives of a broad spectrum of disciplines. HPEF produced its first event, Nimbus—2003, in July of 2003, at the Walt Disney World Swan and Dolphin hotel. Six hundred people from 12 countries, including the United States, the United Kingdom, New Zealand, Germany, Luxembourg, Malaysia, and Japan, attended two and a half days of programming, including approximately sixty-five formal presentations, a Quidditch tournament, an interactive two-day Quest, informal discussions and creative activities and a charity auction.

The eighty presenters spoke on topics that ranged from legal issues that impact fans, to class and gender issues in the books, examination of the books from a variety of religious perspectives, and much more. This compendium includes papers, transcripts and extensive summaries of about half of the presentations.

The current voting members of the Board of Directors are Lee Hillman (AKA Gwendolyn Grace), Rob Ihinger, Philip Nel, Barbara Purdom, Catherine Schaff-Stump, Steve Vander Ark (AKA "Lexicon Steve"), and Carlisle Kraft Webber. The non-voting advisory directors are Debra Duncan, Leeanna Izuel, Peg Kerr (author of *The Wild Swans* and *Emerald House Rising*), Penny Linsenmayer, Heidi Tandy and John Walton.

For more information about HPEF and our future events, including The Witching Hour (http://www.hp2005.org) and Lumos! (http://www.hp2006.org) please join our mailing list (http://www.yahoogroups.com/group/hpef-events), read our blog on

LiveJournal (**http://www.livejournal.com/~hpef_news**) or visit **http://www.hpeducationfanon.org**.

Highlights of Coverage of Nimbus—2003

"Literary conferences tend to be a long way from wild. For one thing, hardly anyone dresses up in costumes for them. For another, they don't often feature panel discussions of fiction written by fans in which the books' young characters grow up and have really busy sex lives. Nor do they usually feature Quidditch matches. But this is Nimbus 2003, where the official T-shirt bears the slogan, *I solemnly swear that I am up to no good.*"

Colette Bancroft, *The St Petersburg Times*

"Like any smash hit, J.K. Rowling's new Harry Potter book brings a slew of tie-in merchandise. You've got your plastic sword of Gryffindor, your "magical" jelly beans, your wizard chess set. And don't forget your Marxian analysis of the Hogwarts School and class privilege."

ABC News

"[T]he blend of fandom and scholarship on display in Nimbus-2003 has a clear parallel in Rowling's own novels, which celebrate hybrids and outcasts: Hagrid the half-giant, Lupin the werewolf, Hermione the Muggle-born. If there's a clear moral to Rowling's books, it's that through toleration of a little weirdness, we can learn something."

Chris Mooney, *The Washington Post*

"In the hall where my lecture is about to take place, I find a great crowd eager to find out whether we can create three-headed giant dogs, become invisible or whizz around a network of fireplaces with the help of floo powder. (The answer to all of these questions is yes-ish, thanks to genetic modification, adaptive camouflage and quantum teleportation.)"

Roger Highfield, *The Daily Telegraph*

"Different opinions on what is unbreakable truth in JKR's world made way for discussion on inconsistencies in text and the publishing process that ferments them, how to consider the importance of interviews/movies/ancillary texts, treatment of canon in an unfinished series and the assimilation of altered perceptions with the introduction of new canon."

Melissa Anelli, *The Leaky Cauldron*

Education &

Library Studies

Ophelia's Quill Pen:
Empowering Women and Girls Through the
Theory and Practice of Fanfiction

Catherine Danielson

The world of fanfiction has, from some points of view, existed as long as the creative impulse itself. Perhaps it truly does exemplify the idea that there is nothing new under the sun. Various versions of the Biblical flood narratives exist in all cultures extant at that historical period. The storylines of Greek myths were borrowed from older Cretan and Anatolian cultures. None of Shakespeare's plots were new. The rich tradition of commentary on the Torah is based entirely on the idea of over a thousand years' worth of progressive narrative, each author building on the achievements of the last. Or to jump to modern times—and to employ an example pretty close to home for the Nimbus 2003 conference—the empire that is Disney was built on myths that encompass the totality of the history of human storytelling. When it comes to more modern examples, some date the beginning of organized fanfiction, fanfics that were understood as such, to writings based on the work of Arthur Conan Doyle, some to Jane Austen, but most agree that the *Star Trek* was the first that contained the idea of fanfiction in the modern age. And it's significant, too, that this began from a TV series. We'll talk more about that later.

But the world of Harry Potter can be said to have dragged fanfiction from the closet. It is generally agreed to have the most users, both as creators (writers, archivers, Yahoo group and LJ owners, artists, etc.) and readers, as well as the most fanfics (nearly 100,000 on fanfiction.net, and over 60,000 on FictionAlley.org, the largest *Harry Potter* fanfiction site). Anything stemming from the greatest success story in the history of publishing—at least since the Bible—might expect no less.

Yet there is another fascinating fact about the Harry Potter fandom. More than any other, it attracts teenage girls as readers and writers. Why is this so? What are these girls getting out of this particular fandom? What attracts them to it? How do the content, form, and function differ from what is presented to girls in a larger popular culture that is presented for their comsumption, and how is it the same? What is available in it that may not be accessible in their culture at large? How does all of this relate to its meaning for the rest of us? As we will see, a number of factors are coming together at once in the Harry Potter fandom, and it can be argued that this is more true than in any other.

Teenagers have represented not only distinct age group but a distinct cultural group since at least the 1930's. And they've also represented an archetypal fan group for that length of time. Yet they have traditionally been fans of mass cultural icons created by mass media, and as a group, they have not been well represented at all in fandom cultures—until Harry Potter. It's estimated that up to 90% of all HP fanfic writers are female, which is a greater percentage than had ever been represented before. In fact, it might fairly be said that the Harry Potter fandom *created* this preponderance of female fanfic writers in most genres, or at least was concurrent with its rise. So the question that we have to answer, of course, is why.

It's said that women and girls have a much greater need to answer the unanswered questions in a creative work that's presented to them, and the key may lie in how we relate to the mass media that's presented to us. Analyzing fanfic in terms of mass media helps us understand things about fanfiction and where we're going as a culture like nothing else can. What we're really talking about as the basis for fan culture is the mass media that is the visual and auditory wallpaper for all of us. It cannot be otherwise, since the entire idea of forming fandoms is centered around a mass experience that the vast majority of us have had. And in the context of mass culture, boys may be told what to *buy*, but girls are told what to *be*. There is an incredible emphasis on appearance, on creating and presenting the self for the inspection and approval of others in a physical sense, and this is never more true than in commercial girls' culture . . . which is generally thought of as being beneath serious notice.

As Sherri Inness notes in Cultural Delinquents,

> An English major can graduate without ever having read a book written for an audience of girls. A history major can graduate without knowing anything about the culture of girls in the United States over the past centuries. A sociology or anthropology major can get a degree without considering the place of girls in a culture. The belief that girls' culture is no culture at all proves to be remarkably tenacious . . .

When looking at the available resources, whether books, magazines, newspapers, or other sources, it honestly seems as if virtually nobody paid the slightest attention to this issue until Mary Pipher's groundbreaking 1994 work, *Reviving Ophelia: Saving the Selves of Teenage Girls*. Some might argue it's not hard to see why. After all, that which is presented as girls' culture tends to overlap the least respected aspects of culture in general—TV shows, fashion magazines, shopping malls, cheap paperbacks, trendy clothes, Barbie dolls, dumb games. Like a copy of the National Enquirer, girls' culture feels inherently disposable, and impossible to even consider taking seriously. Yet it is the essence of commercial culture as it is marketed to all of us, the ultimate example thereof.

As opposed to media culture, however, fanfiction and fandom culture do not rely on appearance, are interactive, and take place in an interactive community. They provide opportunity for contribution from anyone with a computer and a modem, whereas the greatest truth about mass media, whether print, film, video, or other, is that it is created in a way that is incredibly hierarchical. It's instructive to look at the way film is created in this instance, since it tends to represent the rest of commercial media. The process of film creation is structured like a pyramid with one director at the top, *one* person who creates and shapes the vision presented. The audience coming into a theater has individual opinions and reactions, but they must be overridden and shaped into one predictable reaction. By its very nature, even the greatest film cannot be a two-way street between a director and an audience, because the audience is a passive consumer.

And herein lies the paradox—the Harry Potter fandom came out of what has become an ultimate example of mass culture. There are well over 200 million copies of the five books in the series in print, in 200 countries and 55 languages. There are two major studio films that have already been produced, with several more on the way. There are commercial products from notebooks to Harry-shaped cake pans, from pens to pads of paper, from dolls to calendars, from bubble bath to toothpaste. We see an extraordinary phenomenon going on here, one that is rarely examined. A large group of people has wrested individual control from something that by rights ought to belong exclusively to mass culture, and in this context it makes more sense than ever that so many of these people—the teenage girls—come from the group that has been force-fed mass culture more relentlessly than any other.

Certainly, this helps to explain the *specific* nature of Harry Potter fanfic—why a lot of it is not exactly a stellar example of the writer's art, and why we tend to see the same themes, storylines, and character types over and over again. All of those who write it, but teenage girls in particular, are vastly influenced by the larger commercial culture even as they're trying to break free from it. This helps explain the remarkably strong emphasis on "shipping," or defining and categorizing fics by the relationship pairings involved. It goes a long way towards explaining the preponderance of so-called "Mary Sues," or impossibly perfect female characters that tend to be blatant self-INSERTions on the part of the authors. The perfect girl as represented in films, videos, music, print, and advertising *is* no more nor less than a Mary Sue, and she is presented as the ideal which girls really ought to be able to reach. No wonder girls identify with her, and identify themselves *as* her. This also goes a long way towards explaining the great number of HP fics that end up bearing very little resemblance to anything taking place in the British Isles. Everything about the setting, characters, slang, music, activities, and relationships is resolutely American. I think it's a little too simplistic to say that the teenagers writing these kinds of fics (and they are invariably teenagers) don't feel like putting in the research necessary to convincingly set these fics where they ought to be. It would be more accurate to say that by projecting their own school experiences onto J.K Rowling's character and settings, the authors are exploring problematic areas in their own lives. It's no coincidence that these kinds of fics are most likely to explore issues like rape, unwanted pregnancy, abusive relationships, suicide, and self-injury.

Lastly, the really remarkable aspect of slash writing in the Harry Potter fandom—or the practice of writing same-sex relationships between two characters whose sexuality is not defined as such in the books—is the sheer number of these fics that are being written by very young teenagers. Many of them don't have experience with *any* kind of sex, and while this often results in exactly the kind of literary quality one might expect, it also raises that question of what is attractive about this genre of writing to these authors. From my research, writing about slash at the age of twelve to fifteen seems to be a safe way to explore sexuality in a theoretical sense. It provides the opportunity for girls to imagine and to create what kind of boys they themselves would like to know and relate to. Most importantly, its subversive quality removes sexuality from the commercialized context of mass media. Girls are freed from restricting images of how they should look and behave if they imagine relationships that don't *contain* any girls.

So we see that this fandom community, perhaps more than any other that preceded it, defined itself in opposition to the experience of being a passive consumer of mass culture, even if those involved may never have explicitly thought of their experience in that precise way. One very important point we haven't touched on however, is why the Harry Potter community grew so exponentially after the films. While this community was well established before *Harry Potter and the Sorcerer's Stone* was released by Warner Brothers in 2001, that was the event that caused the explosion.

The HP fandom is special, even unique, specifically in relation to this point. This relation has a great deal to do with the actual structure of the books; its similarities to—and its differences from—the nature of narrative film. And it is a point that provides a vital piece of the puzzle in understanding why this fandom is so very appealing to a group of people that are the targets of mass culture, of which film is such an important part.

All five books in the Harry Potter series utilize the technique of the 3rd person unreliable narrator, which is one most often found in stories with a child protagonist—yet rarely in novels. (Mark Twain's *Huckleberry Finn* is a classic example of the unreliable narrator, yet even it was told in first person.) One reason it's unusual to find this technique used throughout such a long body of work is that none of the wealth of details that are presented in the books can be really explained or followed up on. If a character, setting, spell, backstory, or complexity isn't seen from Harry's point of view, we don't see it, either.

The major difference from other fandoms is that untold stories and background generally do get explored. *Lord of the Rings* is a perfect example. In the sections that are told from the third-person unreliable narrator viewpoint of the hobbits, we catch glimpses of incredibly complicated backstories that are not explained in the narrative. In his appendices and other works (such as the *Silmarillion*) however, Tolkien did choose to explain them at great length. There are officially sanctioned books in the *Star Trek* and *Star Wars* universes that explore every detail of worlds casually mentioned in the films and TV shows. None of this happens with the Harry Potter series.

A curious result ensues—we really don't know how the series will end. It's not likely that any reader could seriously believe at any point of *The Lord of the Rings* that Frodo wasn't going to succeed in throwing the One Ring into the fires of Mount Doom. But we really don't know if Harry is going to make it to the seventh book. We don't know if the characters we love most are going to be killed off. We don't even know if they'll end up defeating Voldemort. This quality is emphasized more than ever in *Order of the Phoenix,* and we feel more strongly than before that for all its whimsical qualities, this magical universe is not predictable. In short, there is an incredible amount of free space in the narrative that invites the group of people who are most likely to be attracted to it to create their own narratives based on it.

Now as I've said, film by its very nature isn't like that. There's a reason why out of the unbelievable number of fandoms, relatively very few are based simply and purely on movies. TV shows provide a lot more of that free mental space to begin with simply due to the cumulative length of universes they create, a total of dozens of hours for each season, as opposed to two or at the most three for film. However, the thing that struck me about Harry Potter in this context is that although the books aren't cinematic— there's far too much dialogue, exposition, and explanation—they do have the same POV presented by film, that of the unreliable narrator. The difference is that in film, video, commercials, time and money and manpower and resources and studios and energy are spent in hiding the fact that the technique used is that one. The illusion is created that we're experiencing what we're being shown, that we're going on an emotional journey ourselves—without the intervention of media.

What good visual media does, in fact, is to remove you from your own everyday life and catch you up in a different reality. In and of itself, this isn't necessarily good or bad. But mass commercial media is by its very nature manipulative. It was never meant to be two-way. This also explains some of the problems that critics feel both Harry Potter films have had. The books, as I've said previously, have a great deal of open space in their narrative, and a tremendous wealth of complexity that is never explained or explored. These are exactly the types of themes that film does not handle well.

However, when the Harry Potter books were translated to film, they entered the world of visual media, which attracted a tremendously large new audience. Because the books themselves were so popular, however, a strange situation was created—people who'd seen the film were unusually likely to also read or have read the books. But there was a gap between the books and the films in a very fundamental way, because we expect our unanswered questions to be answered on film in a way that is emotionally satisfying. I would argue that whatever the merits of the films may have been, they did not provide that satisfying experience. It was a situation tailor-made for the creation of one's own version of the answers to the unanswered questions in the narrative . . . for the creation of fanfiction and an exponentially larger fandom. And since this fandom actually already existed, the rest was easy.

Yet none of this would have been possible without the presence of the internet, and it coincided with the exact period when usership among females and especially teenage girls skyrocketed. The reason it was so vital wasn't just because it made it so much easier for people with similar interests to meet and engage in dialogue, although that certainly was a large part of it. The freedom of movement of teenage girls has always been restricted far beyond that of boys, and they found that it wasn't necessary to leave their schools or living rooms in order to participate in an exciting new community of others who were interested in Harry Potter culture and fiction.

No, as important as that aspect is, what's even more important is that the internet made it all possible through its very nature, which is utterly opposed to commercial mass culture and always will be. The net is fundamentally disorganized—not in access, but in content. It is not based on hierarchical control of theaters, print outlets, and airwaves, but on peer to peer file sharing and the free exchange of information. No matter how much corporations use it commercially, which of course they do, it always follows Tim Berners-Lee's vision of the free exchange of information. Nothing could be a greater contrast to mass culture, its values, its nature, and its ideals. Nothing could have been more tailor-made for the experience of fandoms and fanfiction, which tacitly define themselves in opposition to mass culture. And ironically, this is happening at the same time that traditional media gets concentrated in fewer and fewer and fewer hands. Understanding all of this helps us to understand what the media will not tell us, will not show us, and will not share with us. In a world saturated by advertising and corporate media, girls and women are told that their self-worth depends on what expensive clothing they buy, what exclusive makeup they wear, how many boys they can attract, and how closely they toe the line of the mass standards of beauty. But in fanfiction, they rule. Excluded from control of so many aspects of the outside world, girls have made their own. And through fanfiction writing, reading, and fandom culture, they, and we, have the rare opportunity to assert their identities as creators, not just consumers. No matter how loudly and relentlessly a lifetime of mass culture has screamed in our ears, we can find our own voices. This is how it happens—for teenage girls, and for all of us.

With the help of this unique world, we just may save Ophelia after all.

To view an accompanying short film, please visit:
http://www.nashvilleinsanity.com/myfilms/OpheliasQuillPen.wmv

---

Works Cited

Brown, Lyn Mikel and Carol Gilligan. *Meeting at the Crossroads: Women's Psychology and Girls' Development.*Harvard College, 1992

Cain, Chelsea, ed. *Wild Child: Girlhoods in the Counterculture.* Canada: 1999.

Gates, Catherine. "The Sexy Fandoms: Slash Fiction." In *Deviant Desires.* Juno Books: New York, 2000.

Fraser, Laura. *Losing It: False Hopes and Fat Profits in the Diet Industry.* Penguin Group: New York, 1998.

Greenberg, Judith E. *A Girl's Guide to Growing Up: Making the Right Choices.* Canada: Grolier Publishing, 2000.

Harper, Suzanne, ed. *Hands On! 33 More Things Every Girl Should Know.* New York: Crown Publishers, 2001.

Inness, Sherri A. *Delinquents and Debutantes: Twentieth-Century American Girls' Cultures.* New York University Press: New York, 1998.

Tedesco, Laureen. "Making a Girl Into a Scout: Americanizing Scouting for Girls."

McComb, Mary. "Rate Your Date: Young Women and the Commodification of Depression-Era Courtship."

Justice-Malloy, Rhona. "Little Girls Bound: Costume and Coming of Age in the Sears Catalog, 1906-1927."

Schrum, Kelly. 'Teena Means Business" "Teenage Girls' Culture and 'Seventeen' Magazine, 1944-1950.

Inness, Sherri. "Anti-Barbies"—The American Girls Collection and Political Ideologies.

Scalon, Jennifer. "Boys R Us—Board Games and the Socialization of Young Adolescent Girls."

Gardner, Julia D: "No Place For a Girl Dick:Mabel Maney and the Queering of Girls' Detective Fiction."

Hubler, Angela E. "Can Anne Shirley Help 'Revive Ophelia"?" Listening to Girl Readers."

Inness, Sherry. *Tough Girls: Women Warriors and Wonder Women in Popular Culture.* Philadelphia: University of Pennsylvania Press, 1999.

Mann, Judy. *The Difference: Discovering the Hidden Ways We Silence Girls.* New York: Warner Books, 1994.

Pipher, Mary, Ph.D. *Reviving Ophelia: Saving the Selves of Adolescent Girls.* New York: J.Putman's Sons, 1994.

Rimm, Sylvia, M.D. *See Jane Win: The Rimm Report on How 1,000 Girls Became Successful Women.* New York: Crown Publishers, 1999.

Tannenbaum, Leora. *Slut! Growing Up Female With a Bad Reputation.* New York: Seven Stories Press, 1999.

Yoe, Craig. *The Art of Barbie: Artists Celebrate the World's Favorite Doll.* Workman Publishing Co: N.Y., 1994.

"A Summing Up of Fandom Experiences." Online Questionaire. Conducted March-July 2003.

Various posters.—:

"Looking for Utterly Cliched Fics"—
http://www.fictionalley.org/fictionalleypark/forums/
showthread.php?threadid=32224&goto=newpost

—"Combining Slash and Het—A Fic Sin or Not?"
http://www.fictionalley.org/fictionalleypark/forums/
showthread.php?threadid=13188&goto=newpost

—"How Old Were You When You Started Writing Slash?"
http://www.fictionalley.org/fictionalleypark/forums/
showthread.php?s=&postid=545319#post545319

"Why Do Women Read/Write Slash?"
http://www.fictionalley.org/fictionalleypark/forums/
showthread.php?s=&postid=543673#post543673

January-July 2003

Danielson is an independent filmmaker, editor, and writer in the Nashville, Tennessee area who has received national acclaim for her civil rights work. Her journalism has appeared in many sources, including American Prospect, Southern Exposure *(a publication for the Institute of Southern Studies,) the* Tennessee Tribune, Alternet, Urban Flavor, *and the* Tennessean, *among others. In addition, she's spoken on the subject of voter disenfranchisement in the South at a number of venues. Her work helped to contribute to the U.S. Department of Justice's lawsuit against Tennessee for racially based voting rights violations, and her website tracking voter disenfranchisement nationwide has received over half a million hits. In the arena of the Harry Potter fandom, though, she freely admits to being a relative newbie, since she hasn't been to one of these kinds of seminars since she was dragged to Minicon as a teenager. She's been involved for nearly a year and really enjoys writing her fan fiction epic,* Jewel of the Harem, *as no matter how much controversy there may be in the fandom, it's never really going to measure up to what surrounded her nonfiction work. In addition, she's made and published the first motion graphics HP fanfilms, and is currently working on several other projects, including a Flash fangame and 3D animation.*

The Report of the Inspectors of Schools on the Educational Program at Hogwarts School of Witchcraft and Wizardry

Compiled and edited by Peter Gow
Academic Dean, Beaver Country Day School

SPECIAL PREFACE IN RESPONSE TO RECENT EVENTS AT HOGWARTS SCHOOL

The events of the most recent academic year at Hogwarts School of Witchcraft and Wizardry have distressed and dismayed those responsible for the preparation of the report that follows. Although in many ways the motivations implied by the Ministry of Magic for seizing control of the educational programs at the school echo concerns expressed in this report, the arbitrary and possibly unlawful manner in which these actions were conducted is unacceptable to any legitimate body charged with examining and accrediting institutions of learning in accordance with generally accepted practices.

Although the situation at Hogwarts has now, *prima facie*, reverted to the *status quo ante*, it should be clearly understood that in the event of any further promulgation by the Ministry of Magic of educational decrees affecting Hogwarts School, its administration, and its programs, the inspectorate will categorically withdraw any and all accreditation and certification, stated or implied, from Hogwarts School and those who govern it. It is in the great tradition of independent education that we make this stipulation: The very best education thrives, not when it is to be used as an instrument of power and coercion, but rather when it embraces and encourages a free flow of ideas, a diversity of point of view, and a true exploration of questions intellectual, moral, spiritual, and practical. The actions of the Ministry of Magic *vis-à-vis* Hogwarts School in the academic year just ended run counter to those aims in every respect.

As a recommendation supplementary to those contained in this report, we *strongly* urge that the Ministry of Magic, the governors of Hogwarts School of Witchcraft and Wizardry, and the Headmaster of Hogwarts come to an agreement, to be made public and to serve as a charter for the continuing governance of the school, clarifying the roles of each and affirming the independence of Hogwarts School in its conduct of a highly specialized educational program for a unique student body. Failure to do so will call into question the ability of this inspectorate to continue to recommend the accreditation of Hogwarts.

The situation of Hogwarts at present is grave. The dangers to the well-being of the school and its students are clear and present. For this reason we must underscore two main points of the report that follows: One, we are in every way confident that the administration of the school is in competent hands. Two, we urge the school, its governors, and its administrators to attend to all of our recommendations energetically and expeditiously. We understand the role of Hogwarts in the wizarding world, and we strongly believe that Hogwarts, by proactively and intentionally carrying out its programs in adherence to the highest ideals of its mission and founding purpose, may yet stave off and eradicate those dangers to which the school, its world, and our own are now vulnerable.

METHODOLOGY

The report herein has been prepared based on the observations of the Inspectors of Schools over a period of several years. Most of these observations have been made at Hogwarts School of Witchcraft and Wizardry.

The report and its recommendations are based loosely on the methodologies presented in the *Handbook for the Inspection of Independent Schools Council Schools by [the] Independent Schools Inspectorate* (U.K.; Autumn 2000) and the guidelines for school accreditation reports of the Commission on Independent Schools of the New England Association of Schools and Colleges (U.S.). The editor has previously had the pleasure of participating in the creation of three such reports.

Section I. Characteristics of the School

Hogwarts School of Witchcraft and Wizardry provides a residential learning program for magically endowed boys and girls ages 11 through 18. The program is not intended as preparation for university studies, since in the magical world secondary schooling is the highest attainable level. Instead, Hogwarts is intended to provide both academic and pre-professional preparation for adult life as an active, engaged citizen of the wizarding world.

Occupying extensive grounds, including a lake, a forest, numerous outbuildings, and the castle that houses all residential and most teaching spaces, Hogwarts dates back more than a millennium, having been founded by four accomplished wizards who wished to identify "youngsters who showed signs of magic and [bring] them to the castle to be educated." The school has a distinguished history, and many individuals who have gained prominence in the magical community of the British Isles are graduates of the school. Student life is centered on the school's four houses: Gryffindor, Hufflepuff, Ravenclaw, and Slytherin, each named for a founder. The importance of house membership cannot be overstated, as the intramural athletic program—the Quidditch Cup—and the highly competitive point system leading to the awarding of the house cup at the end of are the focus of spirited, and occasionally problematical, student activity throughout the year.

The Hogwarts curriculum is based on the needs and special circumstances and abilities of students with considerable natural ability in the magical arts. Students are selected with reference only to their abilities in these areas, as identified by school staff; students from both magical and non-magical families are enrolled. The seven-year academic program leads to attainment of Ordinary Wizarding Level proficiency at the end of the fifth year and Nastily Exhausting Wizarding Test professional-level competence by graduation. Hogwarts leavers proceed directly into the workplace in a wide variety of endeavors, ranging from work in the Ministry of Magic to professional sports.

Instruction is characterized by a combination of lecture and hands-on learning experiences. Students regularly produce lengthy pieces of written work, and examinations are held at the end of each year to determine promotion to the next year of study. Members of the Hogwarts staff are selected for their high levels of competence in specific magical arts, although the level of instruction is observed to be uneven in several areas. There is no apparent scheme for regular review and evaluation of curriculum or of individual teachers, and there is no apparent program of professional development. Recent attempts by the Ministry of Magic through the appointment of a "High Inquisitor" to effect the evaluation of curriculum and staff have been discredited in an embarrassing and destructive incident involving serious misuse of authority.

Care of students' welfare and growth is in the hands of the instructional staff, some members of which are attached to houses. Students reside in house dormitories, take classes together by house, and spend much of their free time indoors in the house common room. Student prefects in the fifth year and beyond provide supervision in the houses, although serious disciplinary situations, emergencies, and other special circumstances are managed by the head of house; very serious matters involve the Headmaster. Meals are served in the Great Hall in the castle, with a copious and varied menu prepared by the dining staff, which includes (as does the housekeeping staff) a number of elves bound to the school in involuntary servitude, which, although perfectly legal in the magical world, is in direct contravention of nearly two centuries of British law.

The school is operated by a board of twelve governors acting under the authority of the Ministry of Magic. The Headmaster serves at the pleasure of the governors, whose other responsibilities include stewardship for the health and well-being of students. The governors may choose to act peremptorily in the event of crisis or emergency, and they reserve the right to instruct the Headmaster in all matters pertaining to program and staffing.

The current Headmaster, Albus Dumbledore, Order of Merlin, First Class, etc., has been a member of the school staff for over half a century, and he is generally regarded as a progressive and authoritative voice not only in school affairs but in the magical world at large; he is frequently consulted by the Ministry of Magic on matters of law and custom. Although some of Dumbledore's staff appointments have been controversial, under his tenure Hogwarts has remained among the most highly regarded wizarding schools in the world, ranking with the Salem Witches' Institute, Beauxbatons, and Durmstrang. It is against the latter two schools that Hogwarts has traditionally competed in the Triwizard Tournament, a prestigious 700-year-old event regarded as the highest test of wizarding skill for secondary students in the world.

It should be noted that the nature of education in wizardry and witchcraft presupposes a level of risk that would be considered unacceptable in the non-magical world. Although the professionalism of the Hogwarts staff, including its nurse, and the facilities of the school are without peer in the British Isles, student injuries and profound physical changes are a common fact of Hogwarts life, and student fatalities in the course of study are not unknown. It is in the areas of student health and safety that inspectors have the greatest concern, although the apparent willingness of Hogwarts parents to assume great risks lessens the force of this concern.

In summary, Hogwarts is unique as a school and by all measures its programs continue to produce knowledgeable, skillful, and confident graduates who are well prepared to play leading roles in the magical world. Although the context of its existence creates unusual circumstances and although certain of Hogwarts' policies (admission, financial aid) remain as closely guarded as the school's precise location in southern Scotland, Hogwarts remains an estimable institution that is seen to be carrying out its mission with success. The following report will detail aspects of the school's program and policies and will conclude with commendations, recommendations, and a special section pertaining to the inspectorate's unanswered questions regarding education in the magical world.

Section II. Educational Standards Achieved by Pupils at the School

By all conventional measures the generality of Hogwarts students achieve at a high level against the highest educational standards in the wizarding world of the British Isles. Fifth-year students may begin sitting for their Ordinary Wizarding Level examinations, and students may complete as many as twelve O.W.L.s, although a smaller number is more typical. In the final years students proceed to the N.E.W.T. level in preparation for high-level careers, as in a government ministry or perhaps the financial services industry.

The Hogwarts course of study includes coursework in Arithmancy, Astronomy, Care of Magical Creatures, Charms, Defense Against the Dark Arts, Divination, Herbology, History of Magic, Muggle Studies, Potions, the Study of Ancient Runes, and Transfiguration, as well as (broomstick) flying. Student learning in each subject is assessed by practical exercises as well as year-end examinations (which, like the O.W.L.

examinations themselves, may include practical as well as written sections), and there are lengthy written assignments given during term as well as over holiday breaks. While it is unclear the degree to which instruction and evaluation focus on the improvement of traditional academic skills like reading for information and meaning, writing, and calculation and quantitative analysis, it is quite clear that the leveled course of instruction in the application of the many magical arts provides effective practical training in a broad range of skills and techniques. While not progressive by any measure, the experiential nature of the Hogwarts program seems well designed to give students everything they will need to become contributing and contented members of the wizarding world.

Graduates of the school can be found in such places as the Ministry of Magic, Gringotts Bank, the publishing and retail sales sectors, and the professional Quidditch league. Other graduates pursue scientific or field study, and many achieve eminence. A recent volume on Hogwarts graduates, *Prefects Who Gained Power: A study of Hogwarts prefects and their later careers*, details the successes of a number of graduates who had achieved positions of responsibility at the school. The world of British wizardry is relatively circumscribed, and it is to be noted that the Hogwarts Old Boy and Girl network encompasses the most powerful institutions and offices in the realm. While this situation is of potential benefit to Hogwarts students, it may also suggest a weakness at the core of British wizarding that might be rectified if there were a greater degree of competition from graduates of more schools of Hogwarts' stature.

Section III. Quality of Education Provided

Sub-section A. *Curriculum and Teaching*

Teaching at Hogwarts is observed to be of generally high quality. Classroom methods range from lecture and demonstration to Socratic questioning to practical demonstration. Teacher expectations are universally high, and in-class exercises in virtually all classes encourage students to push the limits of their competence. Teachers are generally held in high regard by students, and the practice of referring to all teachers as "Professor" inculcates a sense of professionalism and respect. Teachers, however, are at times observed to a play favorites, and sarcasm from teachers is not unknown in Hogwarts classrooms.

By discipline, the following observations have been made regarding curriculum and instruction at Hogwarts:

1. **Arithmancy** (Professor Vector). A difficult subject, based on the study of the magical properties of numbers, reserved for third-year students and beyond.
2. **Astronomy** (Professor Sinistra). In the first year the class meets once weekly at midnight. It is not clear whether these younger students are given sufficient rest time either prior to or after class meetings.

3. **Care of Magical Creatures** (Professor Hagrid). A highly practical course involving considerable exposure to magical creatures, some of whom can be quite dangerous. It is possible that the school could take more care to see that when students are working with these creatures, all proper safety procedures are observed. There is some question as to the purpose of having students work with creatures that are apparently unique to the school, such as Blast-ended Skrewts, but instructional practices have recently been improved. The return of Professor Hagrid after an extended absence may signal more change in the nature of instruction and content in this discipline.

4. **Charms** (Professor Flitwick). A core course in wizarding education, the content of this course seems to have been carefully chosen with regard to developmental characteristics of students as well as their skill levels in other areas. Inspectors have been impressed with the teacher's patience in working with students, particular in the early years, of a wide variety of skill levels.

5. **Defense Against the Dark Arts** (various teachers; position currently open). Another core course in wizarding education, and in many ways the weakest point in the Hogwarts program. High turnover in the position of teacher has led to an extreme discontinuity in instructional content, although there have been several highly qualified teachers who have, unfortunately, been dismissed for cause, in particular the danger they may have posed to students. The situation with regard to this teaching position highlights the difficulty encountered by Headmaster Dumbledore and Deputy Headmistress McGonagall in recruiting, screening, hiring, training, and evaluating Hogwarts teachers. The sheer pedagogical incompetence of three other instructors over the past five years (including one who was certified as a Ministry-trained educational expert) suggests some serious potential problems. Furthermore, poor instruction cheats students of the opportunity to learn in a subject that is critical to their well-being as adult witches and wizards.

   That said, it is to the credit of the school and the Headmaster that in a recent year of great unrest in the magical world, it was the decision of the Headmaster to alter the curriculum in this course to teach fourth-year students the nature of—and some defense against—the most dangerous curses that can be encountered, several years before this material is normally covered. This flexibility in meeting a clear need is to be commended. The dismissal of the most recent instructor, who had expressed opposition to practical instruction in any form and who stated that "getting through your [O.W.L.] examination . . . is what school is all about," may mark a signal breakthrough in bringing professionalism and competence to instruction in this discipline.

6. **Divination** (Professors Trelawney and Firenze). Although the subject matter in this course invites disbelief, it remains a part of the Hogwarts program for students in the third year and above. The level of substance in instruction is

uneven, and open skepticism voiced by members of the school administration suggests that the course has not always not had the administration's serious support. It is unclear whether the skepticism is directed at the nature of the course itself or at the senior instructor, and once again the inspectors must question the judgment of the Headmaster in not addressing his own concerns in a more timely fashion before the appointment of Professor Firenze. In addition, some favoritism toward more credulous students has been observed in a Divination classroom.

7. **Herbology** (Professor Sprout). Taught in Hogwarts extensive and well-equipped greenhouses, this course is a central part of the Hogwarts curriculum. Professor Sprout is highly competent, and the practical instruction in the course—and especially the professor's attention to student safety—is to be commended. In this classroom as well, some apparent favoritism was observed.

8. **History of Magic** (Professor Binns). A core course in the wizarding curriculum, this course is almost universally disparaged by students, primarily because of the unchanging instructional approach of Professor Binns. The course is taught exclusively in lecture mode, and only rarely does the teacher digress from his prepared notes. Student learning is assessed by written paper and by examination. The inspectors note that the instructional focus is largely on facts and dates, and in the range of student assignments observed there is little to suggest that there is any attention given to concepts or to the analytical aspects of historical study. The Headmaster is perhaps to be commended for waiving the usual regulations relating to retirement and death, but it is recommended that the instructor be encouraged to seek professional development opportunities that would widen his pedagogical repertoire and focus less on teaching for factual knowledge and more on teaching for understanding. Role-playing exercises, collaborative projects, and more authentic forms of assessment would mirror Hogwarts students' experiences in other disciplines, and they could potentially deepen students' real understanding of their history and culture. Similarly, more coverage of topics from recent history or current events might stimulate increased student interest in this course.

9. **Muggle Studies.** An elective course for students in the third year and above, this course helps students understand the nature of the non-magical world. Observation suggests that instruction in this area could be enhanced considerably, perhaps by bringing in guest speakers (non-magical Hogwarts parents, for example) and expanding the school's collection of non-magical objects and texts.

10. **Potions** (Professor Snape). Yet another core course, Potions at Hogwarts is notable for the extremely high level of competence in the instructor as well as for that individual's unfortunate and egregious tendency to play favorites. The

teacher has been observed to be sarcastic with students in the classroom, threatening in word and manner to students outside the classroom, and even purposely cruel to students at times. Here again, the Headmaster's apparent acquiescence to these behaviors is puzzling, and it is the recommendation of the inspectors that Professor Snape be reprimanded and counseled for these behaviors; a program in anger management would be a first step.

11. **The Study of Ancient Runes.** An elective course in the interpretation of the magical properties of ancient writings for students in the third year and above, known for its high level of difficulty.

12. **Transfiguration** (Professor McGonagall). A core course, offered by the Deputy Headmistress. In this course students not only receive instruction in a critical wizarding skill, but they also have the great good fortune to be exposed to a witch of considerable experience whose willingness to address broader questions relating to wizarding life is a true gift to students. Firm but fair (although inspectors noted a tendency to be somewhat indulgent to members of Gryffindor House's Quidditch team), Professor McGonagall's combination of traditional teaching methods and a profound understanding of and sympathy for young witches and wizards makes this course, as taught by her, a center of excellence in the Hogwarts program.

13. **(Broomstick) Flying** (Madam Hooch). A central part of the Hogwarts program because of the school's great enthusiasm for Quidditch, the program in instruction in flying is not perhaps as well defined as it might be. The instructor's obvious competence as a teacher of flying as well as her knowledge of the nuances of Quidditch make the inspectors wonder whether the program might be expanded to more than one class, or at least that the instructor be raised in grade to the level of "Professor."

It is worth noting that the Hogwarts curriculum seems flexible enough to accommodate a variety of learning styles and ranges of ability. H.G., for example, a student of exceptional ability and engagement, was given a device that made it possible for her to double the number of courses in which she was enrolled, although this was accomplished at some cost to the student; she chose not to repeat the practice the next year. N.L., a student who was apparently developmentally delayed with regard to magical powers, was observed to have been given considerable encouragement by thoughtful teachers (although he was several times publicly excoriated by one), and the acknowledgment of that student's moral courage at a year-end feast was seen to have a positive effect on his self-esteem that bore great fruit in the years following in both academic performance and willingness to participate in community service. It is not known to what extent the school is willing or able to formally accommodate its programs to students with serious physical or known learning disabilities.

Sub-section B. *Non-teaching Staff*

Key members of the non-teaching staff at Hogwarts are the school nurse, Madam Poppy Pomfrey; the caretaker, Argus Filch; and the keeper of keys and gamekeeper, Rubeus Hagrid (who also serves as the instructor in Care of Magical Creatures). In addition, there are ghosts associated with each of the houses and a number of individuals, residing within paintings in the castle, who offer both practical service, some instruction by way of moral example, and even a limited amount of care for students' well-being.

Madam Pomfrey has extraordinary expertise in the magical healing arts, and the well-equipped infirmary is one of the most important and valuable parts of the Hogwarts campus. Mr. Filch's attention to the operation of the castle itself is no less extraordinary, in that he must rely on his own non-magical powers to keep things in working order while also serving as the school's watchman. A poltergeist, although not a member of the staff, serves as a somewhat unreliable adjunct watchman.

Still another category of staff, referred to earlier in this report, are the elves who perform housekeeping and food service work, although there is virtually no authorized contact between the elves and students.

Sub-section C. *Resources for Learning*

The Hogwarts grounds seem eminently suitable for all aspects of instruction. Although classrooms seem to be separated by considerable distances, between turrets and dungeons, classrooms seem to be well equipped, and teachers have individual offices as well as a staff common room. The greenhouses and areas set aside for the Care of Magical Creatures program are in good repair and well equipped. Although off limits to students, the forest provides resources that can be used for instructional purposes.

The school library is admirably administered by Madam Irma Pince, and contains tens of thousands of volumes in open stacks for student use as well as an extensive Restricted Section. Many of the volumes are exceedingly old and rare, and the school is to be commended for keeping such books in good repair and making them available for general use.

Sub-section D. *Premises and Accommodation*

Student living and common areas are all comfortable and well appointed, with sufficient access to water, hot and cold, and fresh air. Student prefects are given the privilege of using a large, well-appointed bathing area. Dormitories are limited to five students (all in the same year), and there is adequate separation between girls' and boys' facilities. The complexity of the Hogwarts castle building and the tendency of the building to change its configuration from minute to minute are potential problems, but students and staff accommodate themselves to these alterations with ease, much as they do with regard to known magical "traps" around the buildings and grounds.

It is to be wished that the castle and grounds were more perfectly mapped than is the case, as potentially dangerous changes in the buildings as well as particular risk factors—a "Chamber of Secrets," believed mythical prior to its being opened and occupied by a creature of lethal menace, for example—could be mitigated if more were known with certainty about the physical nature of the school.

As to security, however, the campus is exceptionally well provided for by a number of powerful spells and charms that have proved generally successful in keeping external dangers at bay. The Headmaster is to be commended for his foresight in expanding the number and nature of these preventive measures designed to ensure student and staff safety.

The school provides all meals, including those for students who must remain at the school for holidays. Food is plentiful and nutritious (although it is observed that sweets and fatty foods occupy perhaps more of a place at the table than they ought) and is served in great variety. School feasts, as at Halloween and Christmas, are truly Lucullan in quantity and quality—as well as good cheer. A school tradition clearly supported by staff as well as students, these feasts provide lasting memories as well as a satisfying repast.

Section IV. Care for Pupils' Personal Development

Hogwarts students are generally well looked-after by teachers, non-teaching staff, and student prefects. The house system allows students to live in units where they can be well known to one another, including older students, and to the heads of house. Even the house ghosts and portrait people (see above) seem attentive to student needs and concerns.

While the house system does encourage students to develop close personal relationships and considerable pride, it is observed that the inter-house competition can lead to levels of passion and even violence that exceed tolerable boundaries. To some degree this seems to be a product of the fierce loyalty of certain teachers, and the degree to which the bias of heads of houses may encourage unacceptable student behavior is a matter to which the school's administration is urged to give attention. Although house placement is out of the hands of faculty, teaching students to interact positively with members of other houses, by modeling as well as by instruction, is an important foundation for the development of students' ability to construct healthy and generous views of their community and their world.

It is to be noted that there is a complete absence of specific instruction or programs devoted to helping students in developmentally appropriate ways to address the common issues of adolescence: sexuality, stress management, maintaining emotional health, bullying, and in general making healthy lifestyle choices. Although much of the instruction in the magical arts addresses ethical issues and effective choice-making and problem-solving, the lack of programs more broadly focused on the lives of adolescents may play some role in the sometimes destructive intensity of student rivalries and house-based "clique-ishness." The inspectors do commend the career counseling sessions offered for fifth-year students by heads of house.

The discipline system seems relatively effective, although corporal punishment is occasionally applied in contravention of modern practice, and some of the sanctions imposed on students can border on the psychologically cruel. More typically, discipline involves rewarding or punishing behavior by a system of added and deducted points keyed to the competition for the annual house cup; by nature such points systems are then related to issues of school-wide importance, in that they have school-wide consequences when points are added up in June. Points may be given or taken away by prefects, teachers, and the Headmaster. It is observed that in many cases the use of points was rather arbitrary, a response to perceived personal affronts or affirmations rather than a measured response to an issue of school-wide significance. Other cases merit detention or expulsion, although the latter has not been used in the past five years (although in the most recent year two students withdrew under threat of expulsion).

There is a generally arbitrary nature to the entire system of discipline at Hogwarts that is both problematical and commendable. The problematical issues are noted above, but the commendable aspect of the system is its flexible nature. The culture of Hogwarts and most of its senior staff encourage and allow students to take great risks in the development not just of wizarding skills but of the judgment that is required to use them well. As a result, students are at least tacitly encouraged to take initiative in many situations, and even where that encouragement is absent, the school must reserve to itself some way of rewarding that initiative and the students who seize it—even if they may violate school rules in the process. The aforementioned exceptional student H.G. and her class—and housemates R.W. and most especially H.P. have on a number of occasions technically violated school rules and policies in attempting, with some success, to remove grave threats from the Hogwarts campus. It is commendable that Headmaster Dumbledore saw fit to overlook the transgressions and in fact to cite these students for meritorious service. Although inconsistent administration of school rules may often have a detrimental effect on student and teacher morale, in the situations observed here there was nearly unanimous approbation for the Headmaster's decisions. It is the inspectors' firm belief that students given the moral example of Professor Dumbledore's leadership (as well as of their fellow students' initiative and courage) are very well served.

Section V. Governance and Management

As noted above, Hogwarts' Board of Governors manages the school and hires and oversees the Headmaster in his work. It was observed that on at least one occasion the influence of a powerful member of the wizarding community was sufficient to bring about the temporary suspension of the Headmaster and the incarceration of a staff member based on circumstantial evidence of malfeasance (a second historical instance of such having a destructive effect in the case of the latter individual), and on another occasion the same individual, who has made clear his opposition to Professor Dumbledore's headmastership, was instrumental in bringing about an intervention from the Committee for the Disposal of Dangerous Creatures against that same staff member— in the context of allegations against the Headmaster's competence. The relatively small size of the "elite" community in the wizarding world may be at least part of the issue here, as are a number of unresolved and potentially explosive issues relating to an serious and violent outbreak of "dark" magic approximately sixteen years ago. The most recent suspension of the Headmaster, an admitted miscarriage of justice on the part of the Minister of Magic, again reveals the vulnerability of the Hogwarts administration to the political vagaries in the ministry; the Special Preface to this report specifically addresses the inspectors' concerns in this area.

There is also some feeling among members of the Hogwarts alumnae/i body that the school should reconsider its admission policy and restrict enrollment to students of known wizarding heritage. Although such policy would fly in the face of current beliefs with regard to the benefits of a diverse student body, indirect pressure is being brought upon the governors. For the moment the wishes of the Headmaster, that qualified students from all backgrounds be welcome at Hogwarts, are being upheld by the board.

In all events, it would appear that the governors provide adequately for the operation and management of the school, and in general the Headmaster and staff carry out the school's programs with the support and cooperation of the governors.

Section VI. Commendations

The governors, administration, and staff of the Hogwarts School of Witchcraft and Wizardry are to be commended in general for the operation of a successful and respected school with a unique mission and purpose and for maintaining a tradition of excellence that dates back over ten centuries.

In particular, the inspectors would like to commend the school for

1. maintaining a high level of instruction in many academic areas, including Charms, Herbology, Potions, and Transfiguration
2. the success of the house system in building student and faculty morale and in encouraging students to achieve at the highest level not only for their individual benefit but for the good of the group
3. the school's success in recent years in repulsing a number of threats to the well-being of its students, including several that nearly resulted in the closing of the school. In this success, the contributions of a number of students were of critical importance.
4. maintaining the campus and grounds as a beautiful and effective environment for living and learning
5. its recent victory on the Triwizard Tournament. Although the tournament involves only a limited number of students, the event serves as a focal point for all the school's energies as well as an opportunity to provide a generous welcome to young wizards from around Europe in the name of fellowship in the wizarding community.
6. its even-handed approach to admission of qualified students from all backgrounds, including non-magical families

Section VII. Recommendations

While the inspectors are more than satisfied that Hogwarts is in general an excellent school with excellent programs and a fine staff, there are areas of concern. The inspectors recommend that Hogwarts

1. immediately review the nominating process for membership on the Board of Governors in order to avoid appearances of favoritism or the application of undue influence on the policies of the school by individual governors or their associates
2. examine current practices with regard to the recruitment and hiring of faculty; it is recommended that a full and comprehensive review of this process be undertaken immediately
3. begin a process of curriculum review, not in response to existing problems but to examine current programs and practices to develop even more effective ways of coordinating and developing the instructional program

4. initiate the development of a consistently applied internal program of professional development and teacher evaluation. This program should include opportunities for teachers to expand their repertoire of pedagogical practice and their understanding of child development.

5. work to find ways of decreasing the unhealthy aspects of inter-house competition, including that which is the product of teacher bias, without sacrificing student pride or enterprise. The point system relating to the house cup should be made less arbitrary and less likely to be used for personal, rather than institutional, reasons.

6. consider the addition of some sort of regular program for students on issues related to adolescent development in general (as opposed to issues relating specifically to wizarding) in order to provide opportunities for students to develop their emotional intelligence

7. free the house-elves and place them on the school payroll with full benefits

8. expand its contacts and relationships with the wizarding world beyond Britain in order to expand its students' awareness and understanding of ways of thinking other than those that are familiar. The prestige of the school would make such outreach potentially of enormous value to both the magical and non-magical worlds.

9. examine all areas of student activity to be clear on associated risks. It is not clear the extent that such risks are communicated to parents, but clear communication in this area is imperative.

While it is not a recommendation to the school, we would further urge the Ministry of Magic, with input from the experienced staff at Hogwarts, to explore the development of a program for the training and certification of teachers in the magical arts.

Section VIII. Inspectors' Further Questions

The inspectors have a number of questions relating to Hogwarts, although some relate to education in the wizarding world at large. Answers to these questions might set the inspectors' minds at ease with respect to certain aspects of the Hogwarts program that have been cited as problematical:

1. How do students from wizarding backgrounds acquire the basic academic skills—reading, writing, mathematics—that allow them to function in the demanding educational environment of Hogwarts? Are there pre-preparatory schools for wizard children? Is there a common primary school experience for wizarding children?

2. To what degree is admission to Hogwarts, which is ostensibly selective, competitive?

3. By what processes are prospective candidates for admission, especially those from non-wizarding families, identified? How are such candidates notified?

4. On what fiscal basis is the operation of Hogwarts sustained? Is there an endowment? Are tuitions collected from student families? If so, is financial aid offered, and if so, on what basis?
5. To what extent is Hogwarts willing or able to accommodate students with physical or learning disabilities?
6. Is it necessary that all students, including those residing in magical communities, be prohibited from the practice of magic except at the school?
7. To what extent is the school indemnified as to injury or death to students relating to the operation of its programs?
8. How outrageously must a teacher behave toward his or her students before such behavior attracts the critical attention of the administration?
9. What is the process for, and who is involved in, the selection of the Headmaster?

Section IX. Summary Remarks

Hogwarts School of Witchcraft and Wizardry is hereby granted continuing certification as a secondary school for the education of witches and wizards. It is stipulated that the school's administration will address all areas noted as recommendations (including those mentioned in the body of this report as well as in Section VII and the Special Preface) and that the school will report specifically on these efforts within three (3) years from the date of issue of this report.

The inspectors have thoroughly enjoyed every aspect of the process of inspection and report, and we have the greatest respect and admiration for the remarkable talents and courage of the administration, staff, and students of Hogwarts. Great Britain can be proud of this unique and wonderful institution, from which we expect to continue to hear great things—great things—in the future.

Peter Gow is a graduate of Yale University and has a Master's in English from Brown. He has worked in independent schools in the northeastern United States for thirty years. He has been a consultant, a teacher, a board member, and an administrator, and he has served on several accreditation committees. He has presented on curriculum and professional development at several national conferences, and he is a frequent contributor to Independent School *magazine. Peter's interest in the educational program at Hogwarts began several years ago when he was reviewing a professional development program and found himself wondering what sort of professional development occurs at Hogwarts. Further questions about Hogwarts' hiring process and school culture led him to begin his in-depth exploration of the topic on which he will be presenting at Nimbus—2003. Peter is currently the academic dean at Beaver Country Day School in Chestnut Hill, Massachusetts, where he also teaches English and serves as an advisor. His spouse and four children (several of whom made important contributions to Peter's research) are all Harry Potter aficionados. Increasingly Peter finds that his professional decisions are mediated by the question, "What would Dumbledore do?"*

Harry Potter: Are They Children's Books?

Evelyn Browne
Mai Pucik
Carlisle Kraft Webber

When the Harry Potter series first came on the market, their appeal to school-age children was unquestioned. *Harry Potter and the Sorcerer's Stone* shared many plot elements with other popular children's fantasy novels, such as Susan Cooper's *The Dark is Rising*. At his coming of age, Harry finds out that he has magical powers, and he will spend his teen years developing his new powers. This classic plot appeals widely to children, but as Harry grows older, the series has taken on many elements of a young adult series. Publishers and booksellers, however, fail to acknowledge the transition.

Often, novels are considered young adult (YA) not just due to the main character's age, but because of their language, the life issues dealt with by the main character, and presence of "controversial" book topics including but not limited to discoveries about family members, first romances, smoking, and bullying. All of these topics are present in *Harry Potter and the Order of the Phoenix*, but Scholastic still regularly markets *Harry Potter* as a children's series, rather than YA. One attendee of the panel, curious as to the book's reading level, called Scholastic and was told that *Harry Potter and the Order of the Phoenix* was the same reading level as *Harry Potter and the Sorcerer's Stone*. This attendee, a fifth-grade teacher, did not agree with Scholastic, and neither did many other attendees of the panel. Any other book with the language and events of *Harry Potter and the Order of the Phoenix*, taking into consideration the book's violence, language, displays of behavior considered inappropriate for children (such as the reference to Dudley Dursley's smoking), and questionable morality, would go straight into the young adult section of a public library or bookstore. *Harry Potter*, however, remains in the children's section. Among other reasons, putting some books in the children's section and some in YA makes a book difficult to sell as a series. Series books are extremely popular with children (as evidenced by Goosebumps, Magic Tree House, Junie B. Jones, and other bestselling children's series), and keeping them all in one section makes them easier for a patron or customer to find.

One damaging effect of Harry Potter's continuous sales as a children's series is the marketing of the idea that fantasy books are solely for children. Since *Harry Potter*, many fantasy series like Eoin Colfer's *Artemis Fowl* books and Philip Pullman's *His Dark Materials* trilogy, which target a teen or adult audience, are being sold as children's books due solely to the age of the protagonist. (Both Artemis Fowl and Lyra Silvertongue, the protagonist of the His Dark Materials trilogy, are twelve when the series begin.) Both of these books appear or have appeared on the New York Times children's bestseller list, which began when publishers protested about *Harry Potter* taking up too many spaces on their standard bestseller list, but they are not children's books. They are young adult books. In the split of the New York Times bestseller lists, YA books are more ignored than ever despite the growth in publication of novels for teens. Young adult books do appear on the children's bestseller list, but this brings us back to the debate over *Harry Potter*'s label as a children's book versus young adult. As the series progresses and Harry ages, it will clearly become more YA, if nothing else due to Harry's age: It is extremely rare to see a book meant to appeal to school-age children with a seventeen-year-old protagonist.

The discussion of *Harry Potter*'s correct place in a bookstore or library, YA versus children's, led to a talk on the changing nature of children's literature and what characteristics separate YA novels from children's. While a book can have a young protagonist, the age of the main character is only one factor. Neil Gaiman's *Coraline* was cited as an example of this. Coraline herself is very young for a YA novel, but the dark themes and scary moments lend the book to a YA audience. Because of Coraline's age and the simpler language of the book, however, *Coraline* is often classified by libraries as a children's novel. *Harry Potter* has passed the point where a novel could be either YA or children's, like Jonathan Stroud's *Bartimaeus* books, but publishers and more importantly, teen readers, still see it as a children's book.

Harry Potter's popularity as a children's series has some distinct advantages. Authors known primarily as writers for adults, such as Carl Hiaasen and Joyce Carol Oates, are now encouraged to write for younger audiences. Children who are waiting for the next *Harry Potter* book, even if they are not avid readers, are going into their local libraries and bookstores and taking fantasy books, books that remind them of their beloved Hogwarts. However, since fantasy books are now marketed heavily for children in the wake of *Harry Potter*, teen fantasy that is intended strictly for a teen audience (as opposed to the best-known adult fantasy series with teen appeal, J.R.R. Tolkien's *The Lord of the Rings*), can get overlooked. If *Harry Potter* is for children and *Lord of the Rings* is for adults, that doesn't leave a lot of middle ground for books like Garth Nix's *Sabriel* series, which was written for teens.

Some younger children, pushed by their parents to read *Harry Potter* at a young age (six, seven, or, eight), are turned off to reading by the complex plot and language of the series. Besides making an argument for the nature of *Harry Potter* as a young adult novel, this can damage not only a child's interest in reading, but also give the mistaken impression that all books that look anything like a children's fantasy series must be for children. Not all children have the same reading ability, and the pressure to read a book as challenging as *Harry Potter* turns the reader off and gives them the impression that the series is "boring," a label commonly given to the books by children who were pushed to read the books and didn't understand them. If the series was marketed as a YA series, many of these problems could be solved.

Right now, there is no resolution to this question. The *Harry Potter* books are marketed and sold as a children's series despite the growing number of criteria they meet for a YA novel. While this is advantageous to talented writers who have an interest in writing for children, due to *Harry Potter*'s success, there is a disadvantage in the idea that most fantasy is written for children. Teen books are often lost in the shuffle between children's and adult fantasy, and some books meet criteria for both children's and YA literature. Even though Harry and his friends are aging and encountering events typical of teen books and teen lives, the series is still marketed to children, presenting the problems of categorizing fantasy, reading levels, age appropriateness, and how marketing the world's most popular book as a children's series affects YA literature.

Ms. Browne is a Ph.D. candidate in linguistics at Cornell University, where she works on the phonology of Icelandic and the sociolinguistics of fandom. Her essay "A Literature of Argument: Slash in the Classroom" will appear in C. Bichler and M.E. Curtin's forthcoming book The Slash Reader: Fan Communities and Fictions of Desire.

Mai Pucik is a rising junior at Swarthmore College, Pennsylvania, her major as yet undetermined. She discovered the Harry Potter books in the fall of 1999, shortly followed by the online community, and has been active in the fandom ever since. Her non-Potter interests include historical naval fiction, paleobiology, and classical music. When not at college she resides in Switzerland with her parents, older brother, and the mortal remains of four gerbils.

Carlisle Elizabeth Kraft holds a Bachelor of Music from Lawrence University, Appleton, Wisconsin, and a Master of Library and Information Science from the University of Pittsburgh, Pittsburgh, Pennsylvania. She is currently the Reference and Teen Librarian for the Kinnelon Public Library in Kinnelon, New Jersey, and a member of the ALA and YALSA. In addition to her librarian duties, she reviews books for America Online's Book Report Network and Voice of Youth Advocates (VOYA) and serves on the Garden State Teen Book Awards Committee; since 2003, she has been a board member of HP Education Fanon, Inc. She writes Harry Potter fan fiction, listens to a lot of classic rock, is a trained percussionist, and has been known to spend the equivalent of a month's car payment in one bookstore transaction.

On-Line Writing Workshops: Fan Fiction as a Springboard into Improving Technique and Original Creative Writing

Dr. Catherine M. Schaff-Stump

During spring semester, 2002, I taught a writing workshop to students at Kirkwood, the college where I work. I felt that by virtue of its nature, a writing workshop would be full of enthusiastic students who wanted to be writers. These eager students would devour fiction, be full of fresh ideas, and work their fingers to the bone to produce work that would be fresh, original, and theirs. Would that were true. My recent experience as a teacher of creative writing was lackluster. Many of my students were dabblers, rather than writers. About half the class lacked motivation to produce work, and the other half lacked ideas to write with. The idea of being creative on demand could have proven part of the difficulty. Certainly but on the rarest of occasions were these students motivated and captivated by the projects they were working on.

At the same time as I was teaching creative writing at Kirkwood, I was also beginning to write creatively myself for the first time in some five years. After working on my doctoral dissertation, I felt that I needed some practice to see if I could still write fiction. My husband and I had read J.K. Rowling's Harry Potter series together, and I found that I was inspired to write about Harry's parents and their friends. Before writing fan fiction, I had written only original fiction, and I felt that fan fiction was well worth my scorn. Fan fiction can be maudlin, overly sentimental, and cliché. I discovered that it could also be interesting, well written and engaging with a little surprising research on the Internet. I decided to write a couple of stories and then get my original novel ideas underway.

That was not meant to be, as my sojourn into fan fiction has proven to be longer than initially intended. I fell in with a crowd of writers on a site called The Sugar Quill. Among the various and sundry fans of Harry Potter and J.K. Rowling at the Quill, I found a core of like-minded writers who wanted to improve their writing. I found myself exchanging emails with about 10 women about our writing projects.

Ironically, at the same time I was having trouble with the motivations of my own students, I was very motivated in pursuing my own creative endeavor. Among these women there was the enthusiasm and creativity that I had expected from my students in the workshop. The Sugar Quill members were motivated to create, had ideas to write about, and were eager and enthusiastic. Here were all the elements of a writing workshop that would succeed! Once the writing workshop that I coordinated in an official capacity ended, I set up SQ Workshop, the writing workshop which I have coordinated for a little over two years.

Many of the qualities necessary for a successful writing group have been evident at SQ Workshop. "It's nice to feel that you are in a group of like-minded people, up to a point" (Bell qtd in Neubauer 9). Bell also suggested some other benefits of writing workshops, rather than writing in isolation. "I also think it is psychologically helpful to people, and strengthening, to feel that they're not freaks, that there are other people who do this, that someone will listen, even in a kind of artificial environment, and that they can try out the effect of their work on a reasonably intelligent audience who will talk back to them and tell them how much they've understood" (Neubauer 9). As you will see from the comments of the writers in SQ Workshop, they find Bell's assertions about writing in a group to be true for them.

SQ Workshop also gives writers a chance to ask each other questions about writing. Shelnutt feels this is important. "My notion, as I tell my students, is that, whatever the creative urge is, it can only be strengthened by questions, and all manner of texts; that it is **not** fragile; indeed that it is bottomless" (Neubauer 200). Members of writing workshops should feel relaxed. "The setting . . . should provide an atmosphere in which the writer can believe that his own thoughts and his own experiences and his own feelings are intensely real and are as important as anything he might read out of a book" (Conrad 23). The accessibility and friendliness of the workshop members produce a level of comfort that shows in the ability to value each other's opinions as we shape both fan fiction and original fiction.

The purpose of this presentation is to talk about SQ Workshop through interviews with its membership, and to talk about how participating in the workshop has in general improved our technique and awareness of writing. For people interested in setting up a writing workshop on line themselves, I'll include information on how I established SQ Workshop. While this isn't a how-to manual per se, it is my hope that writing about the experiences we've had will help other writers form similar workshops and benefit from similar experiences.

Going On-Line

There really wasn't any other choice for SQ Workshop but to go on-line. We originated as friends in an on-line community, and we are spread out all over the globe, in the United States, England, and Australia. Essentially, there were other reasons to have an on-line workshop. SQ Workshop can be accessed 7 days a week, twenty-four hours a day, so writers can participate when they have time.

The trick in establishing SQ Workshop for me is that I am not spectacularly technical. When I conceived of setting up a writing workshop, I went to an accessible free resource,

Yahoo. Setting up any sort of group in Yahoo Groups is very easy. Other reasons that I decided on Yahoo is that it met my criteria for the workshop of free, easy to use, and accessible to all of the participants.

Yahoo Groups have proven to be a good choice. Yahoo offers us a variety of services. We have a message board for posting messages and reviews, a files area for uploading our stories for critique, and a chat room for communicating with each other during our semi-weekly chats. Almost anyone can access Yahoo and set up a free group.

We use the workshop primarily for critiquing and posting stories. Message boards have the option of being checked by members, or having emails sent to members' addresses. The files segment of SQ Workshop is our backbone. In it we post projects that we want to have others read, as well as exercises that we work on for the theme of the week. I also keep a file of notes that I take during our workshops for members that can't make chat sessions due to distance or real life commitments.

The chat room is the feature of Yahoo, which causes us the most difficulty. We use the chat room to get together two times a week. Usually these chats center on a writerly issue, such as writing dialogue or building suspense. Sometimes we will all read and critique one person's story. Yahoo Chat is the one system that I can guarantee everyone has, and even so, one of our members cannot access it due to her hardware. Sometimes Yahoo Chat behaves poorly, so we will switch to conferencing on Yahoo!Messenger, provided everyone in chat at that time has that technology.

Overall, I've been satisfied with using Yahoo for SQ Workshop, with the occasional disgruntled allowance for slow or malfunctioning technology.

Workshop Member Comments

Of course, the most important part of this paper isn't the rhetorical philosophies behind writing workshops, or the technology that is used to run one. The most important part of the workshop is the participants themselves.

Happily, eight of my fellow workshop members consented to be interviewed for this paper. What I wanted to know was how they felt the workshop had helped them to evolve as writers. It wasn't necessarily a pre-requisite that the workshop participants decide to cross over into the realms of original fiction, but surprisingly, a large number of them have plans to.

Some basic statistics about the workshop follow. All of the participants in SQ Workshop are female. We range in age from 20-52. All of the women discussed here use pseudonyms to protect their identities. For those of you cognizant of fan fiction at the Sugar Quill, without fail all of them used their author names.

Writing Experience: Writing backgrounds for the workshop members varied. Six of the eight workshop members interviewed have written professional non-fiction in a variety of employments. Five of them have been writing since they were children. Two mentioned winning awards for their writing. One has been published in small presses and anthologies. Three of the participants have been in face-to-face writing workshops. One has been in a previous on-line workshop.

Previous workshops compared to SQ Workshop: Of the participants that had taken part in writing workshops, an on-line workshop proved very different for them. Clarimonde explained, "SQ Workshop is much smaller, has more commonality of interest, and is more selective of people who **want** to be in it. I think it has much more useful feedback." Yolanda discussed her experience in the workshop. "In the aforementioned three-week course, we learned to diagram ideas in class and read them to each other. I find that the exercises we do for this workshop are more useful because we have a little more time to think about what we're doing. I also know the participants a little better than the four strangers I had to face in that class." Clearly that SQ Workshop is a workshop consisting of commonly interested friends is to the benefit of the members.

Writing Strengths: Assessing writing strengths in the workshop showed that the participants are becoming aware of their various styles. Three of the writers feel that they can weave complex plots. Three feel that they are good at writing setting. Characterization is a strong skill for four of the writers. Yolanda elaborated on this skill. "I enjoy creating characters and exploring emotions. I enjoy writing romantic situations. Because I'm an empathetic person, I think I can portray characters' emotions honestly and believably." Two of the writers said that description and imagery were writerly traits that they felt competent in.

Clarimonde was the only writer that cited dialogue and research as strengths. Alkari suggested, "My ability to tell a story, bring in some of the smaller day to day details, maybe in some respects get inside the heads of certain characters," was a strength. Juliane feels that humor and understated emotions are skills she possesses. Katinka added pacing and "the ability to think up nutty names for sweets and hair potions." Mincot was the only writer who added mechanics.

Writing Improvements: All of the writers in the workshop want to improve certain story telling abilities as well. Axelle said, "I'd like to be able to develop strong character relationships. I'd like to be able to make a reader laugh or cry, but in all cases remain completely unaware that there's an author behind the writing." Mincot similarly added, "Emotional response—it takes a lot of back and forth with friends to get it right."

Five of the writers want to work on plot. JK Rose commented, "My first original fiction tended to the lean and mean side." More dialogue skills are desired by two writers. Juliane wants to work on characterization. Alkari wants to work on writing romance. Katinka wishes to buff up her descriptive abilities.

The reason to discuss both the strengths and the weaknesses of the writers is to suggest a link of awareness to the workshop. As writers practice and receive feedback, certainly they become aware of areas that they need to improve, as well as talents that they already possess.

Fan Fiction Writing Experience: Interestingly, none of the writers in SQ Workshop are fan fiction veterans. Clarimonde proved to be the most experienced fan fiction writer, writing fan fiction for about three years. The newest fan fiction writer is Mincot, who began in the summer of 2002, Most of the writers in the workshop have been writing for 1-2 years. With the exception of Clarimonde, most of the writers were not motivated to write fan fiction until they had read the works of J.K. Rowling.

Why Harry Potter Fan Fiction: The attraction to Harry Potter was the force that united these writers initially, as we all met on the Sugar Quill, a Harry Potter board. Some of the writers were attracted to the content of the book, others to questions concerning the quality of writing in Harry Potter fandom, and still others because they were impatient for more original canon.

Juliane summed up a love for the content of the books briefly. "It seemed like a fun way to start up my creative writing again. I love the world J.K. Rowling created and wanted to play with it." Katinka added, "The Harry Potter fandom was the first in which I'd ever taken part. I think it was the first series of books that entranced me to the point that I'd **want** to seek out a fandom, as such things were only for weirdos."

JK Rose also wrote in part because of the universe. "Once I wrote the first piece, I started seeing different parts of the Harry Potter universe that I wanted to explore—the what-ifs, the what's behind that door or around that corner." Mincot also felt the universe was captivating, "because it was the most appealing fandom I knew as well as being the only one that nagged at me to 'fill in the gaps.' There's something about the world of Harry Potter that tweaked my interest."

Other writers in the workshop wanted to test themselves as writers. Alkari remarked, "I discovered Harry Potter fan fiction and thought, 'Hey! I could do that!' I was more interested in the older characters, and there were just so many gaps to be filled in. I also found that I hated some of the cliché fanfic portrayals of certain characters (Sirius in particular!) and decided that I would write something where Mooney, Wormtail, Padfoot and Prongs were just ordinary kids, not 12 going on 30 in their dialogue and attitudes. I also thought it would be fun to redress the Slut!Sirius and Angsty!Remus stuff, and show that the kids at Hogwarts had more on their minds than just constant romance." Clarimonde simply said, "The stories at the Quill were of such high quality that I felt challenged as a writer to equal them." Yolanda's reasons were similar to Alkari's. "My fan fiction writing in the Harry Potter universe was, in part, a response to all the stories I saw on fan fiction.net pairing adult faculty members with students in romantic situations. It offended me so much that I had to take matters into my own hands."

Axelle typified a writer's impatience for more canon. "I was impatient for Book 5 and I wanted to see the storyline continue. I had my own theories about the mystery J.K. Rowling had set up so nicely and wanted to test them out. At the urging of a friend who'd been reading Harry Potter fan fiction on and off, I wandered online and stumbled onto Harry Potter fan fiction and decided to give it a go since I'd already had a few possible scenarios in my head."

Many of the writers felt inspired by Rowling's books to write. "Being the minor character fanatic that I am," Clarimonde explained, "I wanted to flesh out and create back stories for characters who were not the trio (Harry, Ron, and Hermione), especially the adults. I also wanted to explore different point of views—specifically Slytherin and Hufflepuff as they get dumped on in canon and fanon at large. The books are from Harry's point of view and I think that telling the story from a different point of view is interesting and mind-broadening." Katinka's plot found her. "An idea took hold and proceeded to poke me with a sharp stick until I started to write the story."

Finally, some of the writers began fan fiction for personal reasons. Katinka said, "I desperately needed the intellectual change. I'd just gone through a year filled with challenges—new motherhood, a major move, serious illness in the family, separation due to my husband's career—and I felt like my brain was just about ready to shut down." JK Rose also had personal reasons. "I love the books and the universe and I felt an overwhelming need to express some frustration and emotion going on in my life, and Hermione was a perfect outlet for that."

Regardless of the variety of reasons, the common interest in Harry Potter forged a bond between these writers.

Why Original Fiction: Some of these writers are interested in writing original fiction as well, for a variety of reasons. Axelle and Alkari both enjoy writing fiction as a creative outlet. Many of the writers come from literary homes and received encouragement to write original fiction. JK Rose has just made the switch to original fiction. "I wanted to express myself more fully and wanted to try my hand at developing my own characters and my own universe." Yolanda, like JK Rose, is also new to original fiction. "I'm just starting to develop ideas for original fiction now. I feel like I've developed during my fan fiction experience and I like to create original characters so I have to start branching out." Some of the writers have cited their success in writing fan fiction as giving them confidence enough to try original fiction.

Reason for participating in this workshop: The reasons for participating in SQ Workshop given were varied. Almost all of the participants suggested that participation in a writing community was valuable to them. Respect for other writers in the workshop played a factor. The flexibility of the workshop was also appealing. Another reason stated was that the authors were interested in perfecting their writing.

Juliane commented, "I though a concentrated group of people that were looking for constructive criticism and not just puffs would be a great reciprocal." Yolanda said, "I wanted to work with people who have similar goals and get feedback from people who are seeking some constructive feedback as well." JK Rose also echoed the value of writing community. "I wanted to be in a community with other writers to not only help me improve my writing skills, but to bounce ideas, and to discuss what it means to write and be a writer." Katinka added, "My official Sugar Quill beta reads for dozens more writers, and so we've never been able to have much back and forth about ideas, mechanics, etc. I relished the opportunity to have immediate feedback from writers whose own work I enjoyed and respected."

Respect for the writers in the workshop played a role as well. "I was quite taken aback to be asked, and then I was delighted to be in a group where there were 'mature' writers whose work I already respected," Alkari complimented. Clarimonde agreed. "I thought highly of all the participants and their writing and figured they would give me high-quality feedback. I'm getting real criticism from real writers. Since everyone in the workshop is so gifted I felt rather . . . elite . . . being asked. It was an honor." Axelle stated, "The writers here are simply more seasoned as both readers and writers. They know what they like and they're not afraid to articulate it." Mincot said, "I also respected the other participants as writers and felt that I could definitely learn something!"

The flexible format of SQ Workshop was attractive for some members. "Because the workshop is conducted online, it's easier for members to provide feedback on others' work," said Axelle, "since the workshop is basically open 24 hours, and we benefit from being able to include authors from around the globe."

Finally, perfecting craft was mentioned as an important reason for participating. Mincot commented that she began the workshop, "because it was time for me to think about the reasons for writing, as well as to explore mechanics, with a wide variety of different perspectives. Plus I like the discipline of doing writing exercises every so often; I don't have a lot of time—part of the reason I'm slow at writing—but I like the stimulation of thinking outside of my own particular set of mental paths." Axelle defined the workshop as "a small group of writers who are genuinely interested in perfecting their craft. My impression is that the members contribute more thoughtfully and put more effort into the subject. The weekly topics are quite specialized and focus on areas that are of particular interest and use to the members in their own writing."

How has your writing changed since you participated in this workshop: All of the members of the workshop can see some improvement in their writing since they began writing fan fiction, and since they began participating in the workshop. Many of the writers suggest that the discipline of writing each week has improved them. Confidence was also suggested gained as a result of participation. Katinka said, "Another thing that the workshop has taught me is to trust more in my writing. All the ado about Mary Sue almost kept me from putting pen to paper in the first place." Five of the writers have noticed improvement in their description. Dialogue improvement was noticed by two writers. Characterization improvement was also noticed by two participants.

Individual writers felt that interactions with workshop members had specifically aided their writing in unique ways. "Alkari said, "I think my understanding of certain characters and their motivation has improved, particularly in discussions with other members." JK Rose said, "I'm expanding into different approaches and not being afraid to try different things." Clarimonde mentioned, "I feel inspired to write carefully and well, not churn out something half-assed and dashed off like I sometimes used to." Axelle observed, "I suppose the more you write, as well as the more you read, you are more likely to become aware, almost osmotically, of what rhymes, phraseology, scene shifts, etc, work the best to achieve the effect you want."

Juliane suggested, "It has made me think more about why and how I'm writing a scene. Do I need it, and how does it affect the overall story?" Mincot said that the workshop, "certainly pushed me into thinking about an angle I had not previously considered. I hope that trend continues!" Katinka felt that her stories had become more balanced. "I think I've been able to portray more realistic emotion. My stories have also become more balanced in their structure. I also have a great interest in rewriting."

Clearly, the writers feel that participating in the workshop has had some effect on their writing for its betterment.

Useful about participating in this workshop: Overwhelmingly, the writers felt that feedback from other members was the most useful aspect of participating in the workshop. Camaraderie was a close second. Discussion about writing theory was also considered useful.

Axelle spelled out her thoughts. "Whether or not anything I write gets published is secondary to whether or not I'm happy with it. I knew that this would be a nurturing environment of like-minded individuals pursuing the same goal and I haven't been disappointed. And now I'm proud to call the members friends. How can you **not** become friends when you share so much of yourself with these other wonderful people?"

JK Rose commented, "The camaraderie, the feeling that I am really a writer and connected to a community is very important."

How does feedback help your authoring: Feedback was considered valuable by most of the participants in the workshop. The reasons why it was considered valuable varied. Some of the writers use feedback to reshape entire segments of their story. Yolanda said, "I have re-written some chapters completely after getting feedback. I've found it pretty helpful, especially because I tend to post things in rough draft form." Katinka mentioned that feedback was, "tremendously helpful—I think through my story elements a lot more thoroughly now. Oftentimes, workshop feedback creates the work itself. My current story owes its genesis and about ¾ of its content to Alkari's suggestions." Mincot added, "Certainly informal feedback and discussions with individual workshop members have been invaluable. Some of the best aspects of my stories would not have been there at all if it had not been for questions and observations by workshop members in the draft stages."

For Alkari, one critical plot point was reshaped during the feedback process. "In Jigsaw, one of the writers made a crucial comment in one of the earliest chapters that I was in danger of losing Poppy and just retelling the Prisoner of Azkaban story. That single comment was incredibly valuable, and enabled me to get the whole fic back on track, because I realized that it was all Poppy's little foibles and her attitudes to things that made my story."

Other writers suggest that the feedback works because of the integrity and quality of the authors. "Even if I don't choose to make the changes in accordance with feedback it makes me take a much closer look at my work," Clarimonde commented. "For instance, everyone loved the second chapter of my latest story, but I did some extensive re-writing just because I now have much higher standards for my writing." Axelle said, "I can't think of a better place to get feedback than from a group of authors whose work you're familiar with and whose judgment and opinions you trust implicitly."

Chat: The chat sessions are also useful to workshop participants. Some of the writers like them best. Juliane sees them as sort of a brainstorming session. "I think this may be the most helpful of all. We throw out a lot of interesting thoughts and ideas during the chat." Chats are also mentioned as a useful way of bolstering camaraderie, learning writing theory, and considering other viewpoints. Katinka also said, "They're also a lot of silly fun."

Future plans for fan fiction: Of course, an important aspect of the workshop continuing to support each other in future writing endeavors. I had to ask the participants what they considered would be the future of their fan fiction. Three of the writers suggested that they would continue writing fan fiction. Two said that they would like to see what book 5 had to offer them as story possibilities. Two of the writers said that they have no plans to continue fan fiction at this time.

Future plans for original fiction: Most of the writers suggested that writing original fiction was a possibility for them. Axelle made this comment. "Fan fiction, I think, is the perfect spring board to original fiction. What I learn here, in addition to the use of literary techniques and the group feedback, is also the joy of having completed written work of my own—yes, it utilizes another's characters and setting, but the sense of accomplishment at having completed a project of my own gives me that much more confidence to pursue stories of my own." Clarimonde, Juliane, JK Rose, Mincot, and Yolanda all have ideas for original work, or original works in progress. Alkari and Katinka said that they have no ideas currently, but would try it later if they had ideas. Katinka added that the workshop had given her the confidence to consider original work as an option.

SQ Workshop has proven to be a good experience for these writers. They have managed to assess their abilities as writers, become part of a community, receive valuable feedback, and gain increased confidence in their skills as writers. Regardless of whether their plans are to continue to write fan fiction or to explore their own original worlds and characters, the benefits of banding together with like-minded writers improves the quality of the stories that they write. This involvement will help these writers reap professional and creative benefits. I would like to encourage other writers to set up similar workshops for the benefit of the improvement of their writing, the ability to receive needed feedback, and to feel that they are not writing in a vacuum.

Works Cited

Conrad, Lawrence H. *Teaching Creative Writing*. New York: D. Appleton-Century Company, 1937.

Neubauer, Alexander. *Conversations on Writing Fiction: Interviews with 13 Distinguished Teachers of Fiction Writing in America*. New York: Harper Perennial: 1994.

Dr. Catherine Schaff-Stump is an Assistant Professor of English at Kirkwood Community College in Cedar Rapids, Iowa. She researches second language writing and pop culture, notably anime and the works of J. K. Rowling. Dr. Schaff-Stump is also active in Harry Potter fandom, writing under the name of Catherine, and has posted her stories at SugarQuill.net. Since 2004, she has served on the board of HP Education Fanon, Inc.

The Harry Potter Timeline: The Wizarding World —Past, Present & Future

Steve Vander Ark

AUTHOR'S NOTE: The information in this timeline was current as of July, 2003 and does not incorporate all dates learned in *Order of the Phoenix*. For up-to-date timelines and calendars, visit the Harry Potter Lexicon at http://www.hp-lexicon.org

- **History of Magic**
  - Ancient History 3000 BC—1000 AD
  - Wizards' Council Era 1000—mid-1600s
  - Early Modern Era—1600-1860
  - Modern Era—1860-1945
  - The Rise and Fall of the Dark Arts—1945-present

- **Ancient History**
  - 3000 BC-1000 AD
    - Ancient Egypt
    - Olivanders 382 BC

- **Wizards' Council Era**
  - 1000—mid-1600s
    - Hogwarts founded 993
    - Quidditch first played 1000s
    - Wizard's Council
      - Barbarus Bragge
      - Introduction of Golden Snitch c. 1269
      - Elfrida Clagg
    - Triwizard Tournament est. c. 1294
    - Goblin uprisings 1600s
    - Persecution of Wizarding World

Early Modern Era
- 1600—1860
  - Werewolf Code of Conduct 1637
  - Ministry of Magic est. late 1600s
  - International Statute of Secrecy 1692
  - Dept. of Magical Games and Sports est. 1750
  - Cushioning Charm 1820

• Modern Era
- 1860—present
  - Albus Dumbledore born c. 1840
  - Dumbledore at Hogwarts c. 1851-58
  - McGonagall born c. 1925
  - Tom Riddle born—1926 or 1927
  - Hagrid born—1928
  - Fridwulfa abandons family—1931

• Riddle's School Years
- Death of Hagrid's Father—1941-42 school year
- Myrtle killed and Hagrid expelled—June 13, 1942
- Riddle leaves Hogwarts—Summer 1944
- Tom Riddle kills his father and grandparents—Summer, 1944
- Dumbledore defeats Grindelwald—1945

• The Rise and Fall of the Dark Arts
- Molly and Arthur—speculation
  - Born early 1940s
  - Hogwarts 1950s
  - Married shortly after leaving school?
  - Bill born mid-1960s?
- Riddle pursuing immortality in secret
- Setting the stage
  - Rita Skeeter born 1951
  - Lucius Malfoy born 1954
  - Bertha Jorkins born c. 11958
  - James, Sirius, Remus, Peter, Lily, Severus born c. 1960
  - Barty Crouch Jr. born c. 1962
  - Bill Weasley born mid-1960s?
  - Charlie Weasley born 1967?

• James Potter's School Years
- The First War with Voldemort

- Albus Dumbledore becomes Headmaster of Hogwarts—1970-1971
- James, Sirius, Remus, Peter, Lily, Severus start school—1971
- Whomping Willow planted—Summer 1970
- James, Sirius, Remus, Peter, Lily, Severus done with school—1978
- Harry Potter born—July 31, 1980

• The Rise and Fall of the Dark Arts
- The First Defeat of Voldemort
  - First Order of the Phoenix
    - Mid 1970s through 1981
  - Years of Terror
  - The Potters and the Longbottoms escape Voldemort three times
  - First Prophecy early 1980s
  - Peter Pettigrew begins spying for Voldemort 1979
  - Harry Potter born July 31, 1980
  - Fidelius Charm c. October 24, 1981
  - Defeat of Voldemort October 31, 1981
  - Harry brought to Privet Drive November 1, 1981

• The Next Generation
- 1977 Cedric Diggory, (October) Angelina Johnson
- 1978 (April 1) George and Fred Weasley
- 1979 Cho Chang
- 1980
  - March 19 Ron Weasley
  - June 22 Dudley Dursley
  - July 31 Harry Potter, Neville Longbottom (late July; exact day unclear)
  - Sept 18 Hermione Granger
- 1981 Ginny Weasley

• Post-defeat of Voldemort
- Sirius Black sent to Azkaban
- Longbottoms tortured into insanity
- Barty Crouch Jr. and Lestranges sent to Azkaban
- Barty Crouch Jr. escapes Azkaban
- Peter Pettigrew becomes Percy's pet rat, Scabbers

• Resources

- The Harry Potter Lexicon www.hp-lexicon.org
- detailed timelines
- day-by-day calendars

Steve Vander Ark is a K-8 library media specialist from Grand Rapids, Michigan. He is also a freelance writer and columnist, as well as being the resident director for Caledonia Community Players. Steve is probably best known in fandom as the creator and editor of The Harry Potter Lexicon, a reference web site devoted to the book series; the Lexicon was awarded the Site of the Month award by J.K. Rowling herself in July, 2004. Steve has been involved with fandoms for many years, beginning with his first Star Trek convention back in 1975. He's served as president of various fan clubs and other fan organizations over the years, and currently serves on the Board for HP Education Fanon, Inc. Steve used to be just an inch or two shy of six feet tall, but now he isn't sure if he is shrinking or if his 15-year-old daughter with the long blonde hair is really getting that tall.

Law and Legal Issues

Justice In The
Wizarding World

Susan Hall

I agreed to present this talk well before the release date of *Harry Potter and The Order of the Phoenix ("Phoenix")*. I have to confess that on reading *Phoenix* my immediate response was to contact one of the conference organisers and ask whether I could change the topic of my presentation to one for which there was *some* textual evidence; for example, Lord Voldemort's 50 favourite cake recipes. There appears, on present reading, to be little, if any, notion of justice in the wizarding world, and certainly the procedural safeguards, checks and balances that ought to be present in any legal system to aid it to work effectively and without bias are conspicuous by their absence.

Please note that this presentation will, of necessity, contain spoilers for *Phoenix* and anyone who has not read it may prefer to leave now. There were, however, few surprises in that book so far as my previous analysis of legal themes went, although certain points (such as the absence of any formal notions of separation of powers and the top-to-bottom corruption within the Ministry) were clarified.

What is new is the sheer blatancy of the power struggle that is becoming apparent between different factions of wizarding society, as opposed to the simple struggle of Good against Evil.

One message of the book is not to judge by appearances, or on majority (received) opinion. When, in *Harry Potter and the Philosopher's Stone ("Stone")*, it is made clear that Harry's assumption that the unpleasant, vindictive Professor Snape must therefore be on the side of Voldemort is misguided, the reader is put on notice to be alert for similar future revelations. This lesson has gradually been reinforced, culminating in *Phoenix* with Sirius Black's statement that " . . . the world isn't split into good people and Death Eaters".[1] Evil has its shadings too, and there may well be worse things to be than a vocal supporter of Lord Voldemort's policies. Actions, in the world of Harry Potter, speak louder than words.

The rule of law and other unwarranted expectations about magical society

A useful theological summary states:

> *Justice is getting what you deserve*
> *Mercy is not getting what you deserve*
> *Grace is getting what you don't deserve.*

Fortunately, as a lawyer I only have to cover the first of these propositions, but the list of people who do not get justice in the Harry Potter novels is long and growing. I propose to set out my theory of why this happens below, before examining specific incidents, and discussing the likely authorial intent behind their being highlighted.

One of the key points which should inform a reading of the Harry Potter novels is that the magical world depicted within them is not, and is not intended to be, a modern Western democracy in any sense. Confusing institutions such as the Ministry of Magic, and the wizarding court (the "Wizangemot" as we learn for the first time in *Phoenix* it is properly called) with their apparent equivalents in 20th century English Muggle society is to make a fundamental error about the world we are considering.

Fundamental as the error is, it is one that is initially made both by Harry and by Hermione. Because of their Muggle upbringing, they can function within the text to highlight injustices and dissonances between what the readers, no less than the characters, expect to be "normal". Ron often acts as the mouth-piece of the traditional wizarding position, and it is interesting, given his sympathetic role, how often this comes over as blatant prejudice.[2]

The progress is more jagged and abrupt with Harry, not only because he is less clear-sighted than Hermione, but, because of the sheer awfulness of his home life with the Dursleys he has been led to idealise the magical world into which he escapes each September, and from which he is ritually excluded at the end of every school year.

Because he is the primary point of view character, it is not always easy to distinguish his misconceptions from positions of observed fact about the wizarding world. This has led some readers of *Phoenix* (which is, essentially, the first book in which Harry himself is the victim of wizarding injustice) to describe it as a startling new direction for the storyline. However, the imprisonment of the innocent without trial for political reasons was an issue as early as *Harry Potter and the Chamber of Secrets*[3] *("Chamber")*, as was the slavish subjection of house-elves[4]. The themes are treated with more depth in the succeeding three novels, and more background as to wizarding institutions and their constitutional failings is given, with examples of wizarding trials in *Harry Potter and the Goblet of Fire ("Goblet")* but, in every sense of the word, from *Chamber* onwards the writing is on the wall.

We are now aware of the following points.

First and foremost, the wizarding world is a slave-owning society. Hogwarts itself could not function without the invisible services provided by more than a hundred house-elves[5]. Among witches and wizards there is no, or little, suggestion that house-elf servitude is wrong; even Molly Weasley wishes the Weasleys owned one (the term is used by each of Harry, Fred and George without any consideration of the implications)[6]. It appears that there is no concept of "reasonable chastisement" limiting the punishments that owners may inflict upon house elves or require them to inflict on themselves. Although house-elves can be freed, there is considerable stigma associated with this, and forcible freeing is used as the ultimate penalty to hold over the head of unruly elves. Unlike under Roman law, where freedmen and women could achieve wealth and considerable social status, freeing a house elf appears to confine it to a miserable existence, in which it finds it difficult to establish itself in a new position, where it cannot expect to find paid employment except in extraordinary circumstances.[7] Because house-elves have been conditioned to a life of servitude, sudden removal of that object appears to cause psychological trauma.[8]

Secondly, other magical creatures while not enslaved are the subject of serious restrictions on the powers that they are allowed to use. One of the specific legal provisions of which we are made aware is clause 3 of the *Code of Wand Use: No non-human creature is permitted to carry or use a wand.*[9]

How this legislation is enforced is unclear, given that the other magical beings we meet, apart from house-elves (who are psychologically coerced) appear strong willed and powerful.

This is in particular true of goblins, who occupy a strange and anomalous position; apparently influential (in that they control the wizard bank, Gringotts, one of the few apparently genuinely international institutions in the wizarding world) but still subject to anti-wand restrictions and with an apparently uneasy relationship with wizards.

That force has been used in the past is clear; one of Harry's OWLS questions is "*In your opinion, did wand legislation contribute to, or lead to better control of, goblin riots of the eighteenth century?*"[10]

In earlier books these "riots" are referred to as "rebellions" and even Hermione accepts the received wisdom that goblins do not need their rights protecting and are "quite capable of dealing with wizards".[11]

Tellingly, in *Phoenix* the goblin position is seen as pivotal[12] to the coming struggle against Voldemort with Lupin observing,

> "If they're offered the freedoms we've been denying them for centuries
> they're going to be tempted."

As a werewolf, Lupin has suffered increasingly extreme forms of prejudice and social exclusion, so can be trusted to know what is he talking about. Even more tellingly, the *Quibbler* (a tabloid which is shown, on at least one occasion within *Phoenix*, to exploit its own reputation as the purveyor of sensationalist nonsense so as to allow it to publish a news story which is too politically unpalatable for the "quality" press to touch) runs [13] a story which includes the line,

> "Sources close to the Minister have recently disclosed that Fudge's
> dearest ambition is to seize control of the goblin gold supplies and that
> he will not hesitate to use force if need be."

The story goes on to detail various alleged atrocities committed by the Minister for Magic against goblins; in an act that has chilling echoes Harry dismisses the whole story as nonsense because he cannot imagine that such atrocities could possibly have been committed by the Minister.

Shorn of the sensational details, (which are almost certainly not true of this Minister, at this moment in time) what is described is all too plausible. The goblins are a mistrusted, downtrodden group who have one source of enormous power in the magical world; an apparent monopoly over a key financial institution. So far as we can tell, everyone, regardless of political affiliation, banks at Gringotts. It seems more than likely that the political pressures in a time of increasing instability will force the Ministry of Magic to take expropriatory action against goblin wealth, with potentially disastrous consequences. Certainly if they do it is hard to see where anyone with the vision and political foresight to mount an effective opposition to such a step would come from.

The controversial background to the classification between beasts, beings and spirits is given prominence in *Fantastic Beasts and Where To Find Them ("Beasts")*, which Rowling wrote from the perspective of Newt Scamander, a retired Ministry official from the Department for the Regulation and Control of Magical Creatures (Beast Division).

It is in this work that we learn that the distinctions between beasts, beings and spirits were settled in 1811, though certain classifications remain problematic up to the present day (centaurs and werewolves being, for different reasons, particularly difficult cases).

The basic classification between beast and being (with spirits added as a third category, being dead beings or "has-beens") was,

> *"Any creature that has sufficient intelligence to understand the laws of the magical community and to bear part of the responsibility in shaping those laws"*[14]

Rowling, in her Scamander persona, deplores "the extremists who campaign for the classification of Muggles as 'beasts'" but, on a legal interpretation of the above definition, it is difficult to see them as anything else. Whether Muggles have sufficient intelligence to understand magical law is a moot point, since there exists an insuperable barrier to their taking any part of the responsibility for shaping those laws.

The International Statute of Wizarding Secrecy of 1692 [15] ("the Statute") forms an insuperable barrier to the involvement of Muggles in wizarding law, even those that directly affect them, such as the Muggle Protection Act being promulgated by Arthur Weasley in *Chamber*[16]. Even without the intervention of "extremists" (and we hear, in *Phoenix*, of at least one who campaigned to make Muggle-hunting "legal") Muggles are not treated as beings by the magical world.

Some authors have gone so far as to conclude[17] that the effect of the Statute was almost wholly negative so far as inhibiting the development of wizarding society, because it created as Alec Dossetor puts it,

> "a continuous state of emergency for over three hundred years—ever since the Statute of Wizarding Secrecy was passed: a state of emergency that has lasted so long that it is taken for granted by everyone".

As 20th and 21st century experience has shown, one of the first casualties of any state of emergency is the rule of law, if indeed it existed beforehand. One of the objectives of this presentation will be to show that because the Statute predated any formalised rule of law thinking (it was passed less than a decade after Judge Jeffries infamous "Bloody Assize" in the wake of the Monmouth Rebellion) the notions of checks and balances, concepts of individual liberties, equality before the law and civil rights were, in fact, frozen in the wizard world as they had existed approximately at the end of the seventeenth century (ie rudimentary at best). The wizard world has been largely isolated from the developments which went on in the Muggle world during what that world knew as "the Age of Enlightenment" or "the Age of Reason".

It is also the case that there seems to be very rudimentary notions of the separation of powers in the wizarding world. The Ministry of Magic acts as a law-making body, a judicial body and apparently as a prosecuting authority[18]. It appears to control judicial appointments to the Wizangemot, and the Inquisitors in full sessions also have a vote on acquittal or conviction.[19] In *Goblet* Mr Crouch acts as Inquisitor in a trial of his own son[20] in a clear case of conflict of interest.

Whatever the impact of the Statute both on general magical society and on creating a specific siege mentality among witches and wizards productive of injustice, which will be discussed in more detail below, it has certainly had a profound and almost entirely negative impact on the relations between magical beings and Muggles.

The circumstances that led to its being passed are briefly referred to by Rowling, writing as Scamander, as "the dark days"[21]. At the start of Harry Potter and the Prisoner of Azkaban ("Azkaban") Harry is shown writing a homework essay entitled "Witch-Burning in the Fourteenth Century Was Completely Pointless—discuss"[22]. By this stage we have been sufficient clues to suggest that history, as taught within Hogwarts, is regarded as a second-class subject, taught by a tedious ghost who has almost certainly lied directly to his students about at least one historical fact.[23] The paranoia about the existence of the wizarding world coming to Muggle attention, and the existence of the Statute itself, suggests that the Muggle persecutions—no doubt because of sheer strength of numbers—posed a much higher level of threat than the revisionist history taught within the wizarding world is prepared to admit.

We do not have a full text of the Statute (which has been amended, apparently, on several occasions and has spawned subordinate legislation) but section 13 creates an offence of carrying out magical activity that risks notice by members of the non-magical community[24] and section 73 imposes on relevant ministries obligations of concealment and control of magical beasts, beings and spirits on their territories.[25]

Secrecy, therefore, appears the paramount aim of the Statute. There must logically have been a drive at some point to prohibit miscegenation between witches and wizards on the one hand, and Muggles on the other, not because of the pureblood agenda espoused by the Malfoys and others, but on the purely practical grounds that intermarriage threatens the secrecy of the wizarding world, because Muggle spouses and their relatives must, by virtue of their relationship, learn far more about it than the ordinary Muggle can ever be permitted to know[26].

This can lead to personal and domestic tragedies. While it is popular to equate the family backgrounds of Harry and Lord Voldemort (which Harry himself, Voldemort and Dumbledore all do at one time and another) it is not in fact accurate. Harry's mother was a Muggle-born, not a Muggle, educated at Hogwarts and therefore a witch—a point which Harry forcibly makes to Draco Malfoy in Madam Malkin's Robe Shop[27] even before being aware of the full implications of the question "'But they were our kind, weren't they?' ".

Tom Riddle senior was not only not a wizard, but he was horrified to discover his wife was a witch; a point, it seems, she only revealed to him not only after the marriage but after she had become pregnant.[28] The closest approximation to Voldemort, therefore, in family terms is not Harry, but Seamus who says frankly,

> "'I'm half and half,' said Seamus. 'Me dad's a Muggle. Mam didn't tell
> him she was a witch 'til after they were married. Bit of a nasty shock for
> him.'"[29]

The parallels do not stop there. The future Lord Voldemort is described as being "about sixteen" and a prefect during the school year 1942-3[30]. His parents' marriage must therefore have taken place in 1925 or early 1926 at the latest. Divorce in England and Wales at this date was strictly based upon adultery. If his wife had not died shortly following childbirth,[31] Tom Riddle senior would probably not have had grounds for divorce even under the later and liberalising Matrimonial Causes Act of 1937.[32] His extreme reaction to the false position he was placed in, therefore, seems wholly understandable, even although the familial consequences were nothing short of disastrous. It seems likely that the resentment of the child of the marriage at his abandonment before birth contributed significantly to his dysfunctional relationship with his paternal relatives.

The marriage between the Finnigans must have been a Muggle ceremony also, and on the textually justified assumption that it took place in the 1970s in the Republic of Ireland[33], would have been equally incapable of dissolution under the civil law of the country as it stood at the relevant time. Ironically, the church would probably have granted an annulment on the grounds of Mrs Finnigan's material deception, but this would not have been recognised by the civil power, nor could either party validly have married again.

Fortunately, it appears, Seamus's father became reconciled to the situation rather than abandoning Mrs Finnigan, though one wonders how many other families were tragically split apart by revelations of a similar nature. Unless memory charms were used, the Muggle partners to a failed mixed marriage must have posed the most pressing of dangers to the secrecy upon which the whole wizarding world depends.

There is therefore a secondary aspect to pureblood ideology, which differentiates it from simply racism. A witch marrying a non-wizard (or vice versa) poses a threat to the whole community, much as a recusant marrying a non-Catholic during the Commonwealth, or an ardent Jacobite marrying a fervent Whig might have done during the early 18th century.

Because mixed marriages seem so logically precluded by the objectives of the Statute of Secrecy, the fact that they never seem to have been legally prohibited is a strong indication of the seriousness of the threat of total population collapse in the wizarding community. It seems likely that Ron was saying nothing more than the simple truth when he observed in Chamber[34]

> "If we hadn't married Muggles we'd've died out."

Contrast Between Wizard and Modern 20th Century States Of Emergency In Terms of The Impact On Civil Liberties

"State of emergency" is a powerful mantra towards inhumanity, even now and in our own society. But it *has* not, and, in rule of law based societies, should never be, an overriding force. The rule of law, where operational, should be capable of being invoked to prevent "state of emergency" mutating into "dictatorship".

Before moving on, it is worth paying tribute to what Muggle rule of law thinking can achieve, nevertheless, *even* in the context of a state of emergency. When HMS Submarine *Thetis* sank in Liverpool Bay on 1 June 1939, with the loss of 99 of her crew and one salvage diver, Great Britain and Germany were within three months of war. When the case of **Duncan v Cammell Laird & Co**[35], brought by the relatives of those who had died in the *Thetis* disaster[36], came to trial in 1942 France had fallen, Tobruk had fallen, Singapore had fallen; British cathedral cities burned in the Blitz and the Battle of Midway raged in the Pacific.

Even so, in deciding that the interests of the relatives who brought a negligence suit against the ship-builders were to be subordinated to the interests of national security, and so the plans of the submarine could not be compelled to be disclosed in court, the House of Lords took care to field an unusually full bank of seven judges.[37]

Because it was a civil suit, Viscount Simons allowed the claim of crown privilege made by the Minister in respect of the plans. He went further, and asserted that the Court was not permitted to examine the underlying documents in order to seek to establish whether the certificate that their disclosure was not in the public interest had been validly granted by the relevant minister (the First Lord of the Admiralty in the relevant case). Nevertheless, he observed carefully,

> "the practice, as applied to criminal trials where an individual's life or liberty may be at stake, is not necessarily the same"[38].

Furthermore, he made a point of citing Eyre CJ regarding disclosing the identity of informers, to the effect that,

> "those persons who are the channel by means of which that detection is made, should not unnecessarily be disclosed: if it can be made to appear that really and truly it is necessary to the investigation of the truth of the case that the name of the person should be disclosed, I should be very unwilling to stop it".

Viscount Simons went on to say,

> "In this connection, I do not think it is out of place to indicate the sort of grounds which would not afford to the minister adequate justification for objecting to production. It is not a sufficient ground that the documents are "state documents" or "official" or are marked "confidential". It would not be a good ground that, if they were to be produced, the consequences might involve the department or the government in . . . public criticism . . . Neither would it be a good ground that production might tend to expose a want of efficiency in the administration or tend to lay the department open to claims for compensation. The minister, in deciding whether it is his duty to object . . . ought not to take the responsibility of withholding production except in cases where the public interest would otherwise be damnified . . . . "

It is probable that, notwithstanding the outcome, in judicial terms there have been in English law few finer examples of grace under pressure than the judgment in **Duncan v Cammell Laird & Co.**

However, it appears from the case law in the next twenty-five years that the House of Lords had been optimistic in its assumption about how the relevant ministers would exercise their right to object to the production of documents.

As a result, in **Conway v Rimmer**[39] the House of Lords declined to follow the earlier case, making it clear, as Lord Reid observed, that it applied only where

> "the nature of the injury which would or might be done to the nation or the public service is of so grave a character that no other interest, public or private, can be allowed to prevail over it."

Further, they robustly asserted that the final decision as to whether documents should be produced or not was that of the courts and not that of the ministries who might have a personal interest in their workings being revealed.

Crown privilege (or public interest immunity) represents one aspect of a separation of powers debate. But it also demonstrates why, even in a state of emergency or even of war, rule of law thinking is still important, and why the demands of the situation should not be allowed to eliminate consideration of the rights of the individual.

The entire debate—its structure, expression, forum and freedom—represented by both the above cases, even though their outcomes are opposed, is one that is simply not possible within the public arena upon which the Harry Potter books play themselves out. The underlying assumptions that inform both judgments are as alien to wizarding society as an ability to turn a mouse into a wine glass would be for any of us.

In the remainder of this paper, I hope to show why, in my view, in trying to understand the problems in terms of justice and rule of law faced by the protagonists in the Harry Potter novels of JK Rowling it is not sufficient to excuse the actions of the wizarding world merely by quoting the magnitude of the threat they oppose, nor to go to the opposite extreme, and look at the (admittedly repellent) pronouncements of Lucius and Draco Malfoy about "Mudbloods" as though they were simply racist comments falling to be judged by the values of Western democracies of the late 20th century.

There are, indeed, elements of such concerns when analysing such attitudes that cannot be ignored. However, as my survey of the background has, I hope, demonstrated, the situation is significantly more complicated than that simple equation of values, and even the "good" witches and wizards are steeped in values that are anathema to Western, democratic, rule of law-based societies.

Accordingly, in considering the world of *Harry Potter*, one has to accept that ordinary wizarding society, as a result of the pernicious effects of the Statute, is irrevocably rooted in the past, and that "the past is a foreign country. They do things differently there."[40]

Wizardly Extra-Legal Support Mechanisms; an understandable response to intolerable conditions?

It appears from all five of the books to date that there are also individuals or individual situations that are recognised as above the law, and it is quite clear that there is no generalised principle of respect for law or legal institutions[41]. It is suggested below that the weakness of formalised authority structures in the wizard world, the corruption within the Ministry, the absence of legal protection for the individual and the pernicious influence of the Statute-created state of emergency has led to extra-legal protection mechanisms growing up, with witches and wizards forced to attach themselves as "clients" to powerful "patrons" who can protect them against the threats to life, liberty and property which tend to flourish in such conditions.[42]

The client/patronage system was at its height in the later Roman Republic, where it had a respectability and formality it probably has not subsequently attained. A "patron" had his own network of "clients", the more powerful of whom would also be patrons in their own rights, bringing their own client networks into the power-base of their own patron. Although their general duties involved attending on their patron to emphasis his power and status, it was also expected that a patron could call on his clients for practically any service it was in their power to render him, and also that, in turn, clients could call upon their patron for protection and advancement for them and their families.

In the Roman Republic, it was a recognised part of "how things were" and formed part of, rather than an erosion of, government structures. By contrast, systems of "bastard" patronage have tended to grow up in times of social instability where formal institutions of law or government have broken down, or among groups who, for whatever reason, feel institutionally disadvantaged in society and unable to avail themselves of formal mechanisms to achieve justice.[43]

Formal patronage did play a part both in the France of the Ancien Régime and in seventeenth and eighteenth century England. Its abuses in its British incarnation (and, in particular, the institutional weaknesses it created in bodies such as the Army and Navy) were described at length by Maria Edgeworth in her novel *Patronage*[44].

I use the term "bastard patronage" to distinguish the system in the wizarding world, since it is not a formally acknowledged part of society, though it is a very real one, and there are organs of government and law (specifically, the Ministry) which are supposed to carry out the roles which are, in fact, carried out by the extra-legal system.

Dumbledore, Voldemort, Fudge, Lucius Malfoy and Crouch (senior) all act as patrons at various points within the series, and as their individual power bases wax and wane, so too does their ability to protect their own clients from attack from the rival client/patronage networks. There exist a number of key strategic pieces over which each primary network seeks control or influence, Hogwarts and the Ministry being two, and Harry himself representing a third (others may be Gringotts, The Daily Prophet and possibly St Mungo's). A network not controlling a particular strategic piece has the options either of outright conflict for possession of it, entering into an alliance with the network that does have control of the strategic piece, or working to discredit or eliminate the importance of the piece concerned.

Dumbledore, essentially, appears to be working within the system while very aware of its weaknesses. He does, possibly from his closer touch with and respect for Muggle life and institutions than many wizards, appear to have more respect for rule of law thinking.

It appears likely that, when the network controlling the Ministry is weak and/or sympathetic to Dumbledore, Dumbledore can use his influence to have the laws operated to enhance protection of the individual; in any event, it makes a legal attack on members of his client network unlikely either to be initiated or to succeed. As Fudge grows in confidence in his control of the Ministry and its associated patronage links, so the Ministry turns against Dumbledore, and the capricious impact of its jurisdiction becomes more apparent.

The Ministry, therefore, appears to be an organ of state, but there is no apparent enfranchised public to exercise democratic influence over it. In these circumstances, it becomes a powerful weapon in the hands of any patronage network controlling it, and a prize to be fought for, or a hazard to be circumvented.

In these circumstances the best option may be outright illegality, and where necessary Dumbledore does not scruple to place justice above legality, as with the rescue of Sirius and Buckbeak in *Azkaban*.

It is understandable within the world created by JK Rowling that Harry and Hermione are forced to take matters into their own hands, and their actions are within the best traditions of the school story and even the Golden Age detective story: genres which *Azkaban* in particular draws on more than it draws on fantasy or fairy tale.[45] But it is also symptomatic of how far the conditions prevailing in the wizarding world are from those of our own that a figure in a responsible position such as Dumbledore, who is not only Headmaster of Hogwarts but also, at the relevant time[46] Chairman of the International Confederation of Wizards and Chief Warlock on the Wizengamot [47] regards inciting two thirteen year old children to commit a series of highly illegal and dangerous acts as the *only* way to ensure a just outcome.

Dumbledore is an inveterate lawbreaker (for the best of motives, naturally) but he is far from alone in doing so.

When he is not building in loopholes in the laws he drafts to allow him to pursue his hobbies, Arthur Weasley happily conspires with Amos Diggory to conceal what he believes to be Mad-Eye Moody's misdeeds[48]; Sirius's flying motorcycle seems like an evident breach of the Statute to say nothing of the Misuse of a Muggle Artefact; Hagrid breeds Blast-Ended Skrewts and dragons contrary to applicable law[49], to say nothing of sticking a pig's tail on Dudley which has to be removed in a Muggle hospital;[50] we learn of no less than *four* near contemporaries in age who are unregistered Animagi, notwithstanding that there are only seven *registered* Animagi for the whole of the twentieth century[51]; and *faux*-Mad-Eye (allegedly with Dumbledore's express permission) first tells his class of minors that the use of any one of the Unspeakable Curses on a fellow human being is enough to earn a life sentence in Azkaban[52] and a handful of pages later uses it on every one of them for teaching purposes.

The above list of examples leaves out the curiously erratic enforcement of rules on the practice of magic by underage witches and wizards away from Hogwarts. It is clear that the Hogwarts Express is regarded as Tom Tiddler's Ground, otherwise the Crabbe and Goyle pères, to say nothing of Lucius Malfoy, might have made official representations about the state their respective offspring have reached King's Cross in for two years running. However, these are not the only examples of extra-mural use of magic by minors. The Weasley twins' experiments—particularly the Ton-Tongue Toffee—are certainly under-age magic, and unless the Dursleys are exempted from full "Muggle" status by virtue of their relationship with Harry, performed in clear breach of the Statute. Harry's own blowing up of his Aunt Marge in *Azkaban* is ignored for official purposes[53].

Due Process In the Wizarding World; Flogging a Thestral?

The wizard world is not governed by the rule of law[54]. It is fully apparent that witches and wizards are vulnerable to the capricious exercise of administrative powers by the Ministry, and that imprisonment without trial occurs without apparently exciting adverse comment (suggesting either that it is too common to remark upon, or that critical comment on public affairs is suppressed).

Furthermore, torture and mistreatment of prisoners is a given. Conditions in Azkaban are such that "most of the prisoners in there sit muttering to themselves in the dark, there's no sense in them"[55]. In fact, given what we are told about the effect of Dementors on the human psyche, which is nothing short of inducing severe clinical depression in any witch or wizard within their orbit, even a short prison sentence is likely to result in permanent psychological damage. A society which can tolerate this as the standard punishment for any form of transgression, and which does not even ensure such minor safeguards as legal representation, procedural fairness or an unbiased hearing to those threatened with it, is not a healthy society.

Although some suspensions of civil rights do occur in consequence of emergency conditions in the Muggle world, the examples given above demonstrate that these are expected to be the subject of scrutiny by legal institutions. Most of the examples of treatment of house-elves, legal procedures, penal institutions and the like described in this paper would be flatly contrary to the Universal Declaration of Human Rights and action could be taken if their equivalents occurred in the Muggle world. The wizarding world has none of these sanctions to limit the unfettered abuse of official powers.

Furthermore, the imprisonment of Hagrid in *Chamber* and even that of Sirius in *Azkaban* without trial in either case do not take place under wartime conditions: there is no reason why either of them could not have had a trial had there been any political will to hold one.

When hearings are held, however, the sheer scale of the contempt for procedural safeguards is breathtaking. This section will, of necessity, deal at some length with the legal issues raised by *Phoenix* since it is only once Harry steps outside the protected, above the law, status he has largely enjoyed for the first four books that he experiences first hand the evils to which wizarding disregard of any concept of due process gives rise.

However, as ever, these issues have been prefigured in earlier books in the series.

Prosecutions seem to be instituted on curiously haphazard principles (of which more later) and trials (when conducted) ignore basic rules of procedure or of natural justice.

One good example is the trial of Buckbeak in *Azkaban*. While Buckbeak is a Hippogriff, and therefore legally a beast, he does seem to have some legal rights. Not only does he get a hearing, he is even afforded a notional appeal, although an appeal committee that brings the executioner with it can hardly be supposed to be approaching its job with an open mind. But the preparation of his case is left to three schoolchildren, and to someone whose formal education ceased at the age of fourteen.

Phoenix gives us a closer insight into the working of wizarding "justice" because it affects Harry personally.

His hearing in Chapter Eight is a textbook example of procedural irregularity. He is charged with an offence under section 13 of the Statute and under paragraph C of the Decree for the Reasonable Restriction of Underage Sorcery, 1875. He did in fact commit the offence, but has a complete defence; it was committed to protect himself and another from attack.

The first procedural issue is the presumption of guilt; he is informed by letter within minutes of the offence that he is to be expelled from school and his wand destroyed, and he is *then* to attend a disciplinary hearing. Some minutes later a second letter substitutes suspension for expulsion, and he is permitted to keep his wand.[56] We subsequently learn that the original request was *ultra vires* the Ministry who has no power to expel students from Hogwarts nor to confiscate wands until charges have been successfully proven.[57]

Secondly, although he is a minor he is not only denied legal representation, but he is not even allowed adult accompaniment[58].

Thirdly, he has been led to expect a regulatory hearing by the Department of Magical Law Enforcement; what he is confronted by is a full criminal trial before the Wizangemot[59]. Moreover, the time and place of his hearing is brought forward at exceptionally short notice (it appears likely that official correspondence informing him of the change has been deliberately diverted or delayed), in a move apparently intended to prevent his attending, or calling witnesses on his behalf.

The interrogation by Fudge is carried out in a remarkably prejudiced manner, with direct accusations of lying, and an attempt to prevent witnesses being called on Harry's behalf.

Attention is drawn in court to alleged prior offences for none of which he has been prosecuted (still less, prosecuted successfully) in an obvious effort to prejudice the tribunal.

Finally, we learn that the entire situation has arisen from direct entrapment by one of the interrogators[60] in an effort to discredit Harry; as indicated above, a clear attempt to neutralise him as a strategic resource and thereby weaken Dumbledore's power-base.

Conclusions

One might therefore ask, why bother to draw comparisons between the wizarding legal institutions and those of 20th century Muggle England, when it appears they have so little in common?

The answer, or one answer at least, is because the characters do. Hermione, who is increasingly emerging as the voice of reason within the series, continually does so. Her activities with S.P.E.W. explicitly are set within what she assumes to be legal and political institutions equivalent to the Muggle ones with which she is familiar[61], and her objectives are likewise identifiable within a Muggle context of political activism.

Hermione campaigns in the short term to obtain "fair wages and working conditions" for house-elves. In the long term she seeks to get a house-elf hired within the relevant Ministry department, and to change wand-use laws. For her, using political pressure to achieve increased accountability of state institutions and the empowerment of groups who suffer discrimination is a natural, almost inevitable, response to perceived injustice.

The fact that even sympathetic wizards and witches do not see the necessity of what she is urging is already being flagged up as a danger area. Justice is, of course, desirable on moral grounds. What wizarding society appears to be in the painful process of learning is that it is also desirable on pragmatic grounds, and that injustice produces instability which forces such as Voldemort can exploit. The symbolic shattering of the Fountain of Magical Brethren highlights the fissures that have been created throughout magical society by the institutional oppression of non-human magical beings for a period of centuries. That is a harvest which wizarding society is on the point of reaping.

In fact, it is also a key reason why Voldemort was able to rise again. There was no Truth and Reconciliation Committee examining injustices following the first Voldemort period, nor does there appear to have been any examination as to how he was able to come to power so quickly, and what safeguards needed to be built into society to inhibit such things happening again.

If, despite the structural problems they have already created for themselves, wizarding society does succeed in vanquishing Voldemort,[62] unless the question of justice is properly addressed in the aftermath, there will be little to prevent a similar situation arising in future.

Susan Hall is a partner in Cobbetts Solicitors, England, where she specialises in intellectual property and information technology law. She has a first from Oxford University and an LLM from the University of Toronto, where she was a Commonwealth Scholar. Among numerous other legal publications she is the author of the chapter entitled "Harry Potter and the Rule of Law: the Central Weakness of Legal Concepts in The Wizard World," published in Reading Harry Potter: Critical Essays (ed. Giselle Anatol, Greenwood Press, 2003). She has lectured extensively on legal topics both in the United Kingdom and abroad.

Tanya Grotter: A Russian Harry Potter *Knock-off or Parody?*

Mark T. Hooker

The appearance of the Russian Tanya Grotter books caused a furor as reviewers and lawyers compared them to the Harry Potter books, and threats of legal action filled the air. This presentation considers the question of whether Tanya Grotter is a knock-off or a parody.

The Tanya Grotter books have sold over a million copies. There are five books in the Tanya Grotter series thus far:

- Tanya Grotter and the Magical Double Bass (Moscow: EKSMO, 2002. [MC.xxx])
- Tanya Grotter and the Disappearing Upstairs Floor (Moscow: EKSMO, 2002 [DF.xxx])
- Tanya Grotter and the Golden Leech (Moscow: EKSMO, 2002 [GL.xxx])
- Tanya Grotter and the Throne of Drevnir (Moscow: EKSMO, 2003)
- Tanya Grotter and the Staff of the Magi (Moscow: EKSMO, 2003)

Plans are already in place to continue the series with:

- Tanya Grotter and Noah's Pince-nez formerly announced as Tanya Grotter and Perun's Hammer.

When it became clear that their legal efforts in Russia to obtain a cease and desist order for the Tanya Grotter series would be unsuccessful, J.K. Rowling's lawyers decided on a policy of containment. If they could not stop Tanya Grotter in Russia, they would, at least, stop her from spreading to other markets. They chose the Netherlands—often first to market with translations of internationally successful books—as the test venue for their new strategy. If they could block the publication of the Dutch translation of Tanya Grotter and the Magical Double Bass, it would have a chilling effect on the sale of the foreign language rights in other countries. They filed suit in the district court of Amsterdam on 25 March. On 3 April, just 5 days before the intended release, the court ruled in favor of J.K. Rowling, and issued an injunction against the Dutch publisher Byblos.

The Court Case

The court rejected the argument that the story was a parody, saying that the publication of the translation would violate registered copyrights and trademarks.

The court's ruling summarized the plot lines of the first books of the two series as follows:

- Harry Potter and the Philosopher's Stone
- Harry's parents are killed by the evil wizard Voldemort,
- Harry thinks that they were killed in a fire (sic!),
- Harry has a mysterious scar on his forehead,
- Harry is left on the doorstep of his aunt's and uncle's,
- Harry is poorly treated by his aunt and uncle, who spoil their own son,
- When Harry is 10 years old, he gets a mysterious invitation to go to a school for wizards,
- Until this time he was not aware that he had magical powers,
- The school is in a remote location that can only be reached by a train that leaves from a secret track at the train station;

At the school Harry:

- learns various forms of magic from the teachers,
- makes friends with two of the students in particular,
- becomes an outstanding player of Quidditch, a game played while flying on a broomstick,
- learns the story of the Philosopher's Stone, which is supposedly hidden at the school;
- The climax of the story takes place at the school:
- Voldemort is after the Philosopher's Stone,
- Harry and his two friends fight with Voldemort's henchman, after he has been unmasked for what he is,
- Harry wins the fight,
- The Philosopher's Stone is lost.
- This is the end of Harry's first year at school.

Tanya Grotter and the Magical Double Bass

- Tanya parents are killed by the evil wizard Chuma-del-Tort,
- Tanya thinks that they were killed in an avalanche,

- Tanya has a mysterious birthmark on her nose,
- Tanya is left on the doorstep of her aunt's and uncle's,
- Tanya is poorly treated by her aunt and uncle, who spoil their own daughter,
- When Tanya is 10 years old, she gets a mysterious invitation to go to a school for wizards,
- Until this time she was not aware that she had magical powers,
- The school is on a remote island that can only be reached by flying there;

At the school Tanya:

- learns various forms of magic from the teachers,
- makes friends with two of the students in particular,
- becomes an outstanding player of Dragon Ball, a game played while flying on a vacuum cleaner,
- The climax of the story takes place at the basement of the school:
- Chuma-del-Tort is after Tanya's amulet, which is hidden behind her birthmark,
- Tanya and her friends fight with Chuma-del-Tort,
- Tanya wins the fight,
- The amulet is lost.
- This is the end of Tanya's first semester at school.

Rowling's law suit in the Netherlands stopped publication of the Dutch translation of Tanya Grotter because it allegedly infringes on her right to produce derivative works of her Harry Potter stories. Common examples of derivative works include a translation of a book into another language, a jazz version of a popular tune and a movie based on a book. Rowling certainly has the right to defend her intellectual property, which is the source of her income, but what are the limits on her power to stop others from writing on the same topic? At what point does a story on the same topic add so much new material that it becomes a new story instead of a derivative work? At what point does Romeo and Juliet cease to be a Shakespearean classic that itself was borrowed from an earlier Italian story and become West Side Story? At what point does Cinderella change from a classic children's folk tale and become Pretty Woman? At what point does The Lord of the Rings change from a defining moment in twentieth century literature into the comedic Bored of the Rings? At what point does Gone with the Wind change into the social parody The Wind Done Gone? At what point does copyright cease to be a defense of an author's livelihood based on his or her intellectual property and become the censorship of other authors' efforts at new creative expression? Has Tanya Grotter crossed that line? The purpose of this paper is to present some information about Tanya Grotter that will help the reader make up his or her own mind about this last question.

Welcome to Tibidoxs

The name of Tanya's school is Tibidoxs. It is not an elite English boarding school. It is a reform school. Its official title is School for Behaviorally-Challenged Young Witches and Wizards. (MC.207, DF.22) The way that the students are introduced to the reader enhances the sense that it is a reform school. In prison films and novels, invariably the first question that prisoners ask each other is what are they in for. The first character whom Tanya meets after her arrival at school is a ghost. Pleased to meet a new student, he starts his conversation with this question, but before Tanya can answer, he decides to try his hand at guessing what she has done. "Did you magnetize a purse, like those gypsy sisters? Or are you the one who froze her mathematics teacher? Serves her right, she was such a dry ol' biddy. Let her play Frosty the Snow-woman for a while. Wrong again? Then you set fire to the class grade book with a chance glance and burned down the teachers' lounge to boot? Turned your grandfather into a zombie, because he would not buy you a bike? Changed money into candy wrappers? Put your alcoholic father into a vodka bottle?" (MC.213)

The introductions of other Tibidoxs students also generally include an explanation of what they did that landed them in the school.

- Shurik Chpurikov, a very shy boy, who was sent up to Tibidoxs because instead of blushing, he turned invisible, and his shyness made him 'blush' at lot. (GL.65)
- Katya Lotkova, the most beautiful girl in school, had been removed from the non-magical world to Tibidoxs for her ability to enchant boys. Every flat surface around her apartment building was covered with declarations of love for her, and every evening the line of suitors found one on each step of the staircase leading to her apartment, which would have been tolerable, if it was not for the fact that she lived on the ninth floor. (MC.310, DF.171)
- Verka Popugaeva, a terrible fraidy cat, was taken away to Tibidoxs after she developed the power to see through solid objects while spying on her sister to watch her kissing boys. (MC.236, DF.152)
- Dusya Pupsikova, a girl with plump, round cheeks and a fondness for sweets, found herself in Tibidoxs for turning her girlfriend into a gingerbread cookie. (MC.236, DF.156)
- Sem'-Pen'-Dyr, a senior on the Dragon Ball team, was sent up to Tibidoxs for turning his teacher into a dog (pun intended) out of boredom, after finishing all the questions on a standardized math test in six minutes. (MC.310, DF.166)
- Shurasik, the straight-A, teachers' pet student, was doing time in Tibidoxs for causing the class grade book to burst into flames and making mushrooms grow on the teacher's head when she gave him the first 'D' in his life for some such foolishness as bringing the wrong notebook to class. Not even headmaster

Chernomorov could make the mushrooms on the teacher's head go away. (MC.254)

- Grobynya Sklepova, Tanya's Black-Arts roommate, was doing time at Tibidoxs for her telekinetic abilities, which she used in the non-magical world to steal watches and billfolds on the subway. At Tibidoxs, she used the same trick to steal chocolates from other students. (MC.330)
- Zhora Zhikin, the wearer of the Dragon Ball jersey with the number one, was hauled off to Tibidoxs after he teleported himself to the studio of a popular television program. (MC.309)

Throughout the first part of book I, Tanya's adoptive parents have been threatening to send her off to reform school, so when she first hears the official school title, she thinks to herself that her adoptive sister Pipa would have been happy, if she had known where Tanya had disappeared to. (MC.207, 235) Tanya asks headmaster Chernomorov about the 'reform' aspect of the school and he soft-pedals the issue, saying that Tibidoxs is really "not a prison camp or correctional institution," but rather a place to help young witches and wizards find themselves and get a good start. His explanation of the onset of the ability to use magic makes it sound much like puberty. At the age of 10 or 12 a boy or a girl from a normal family may suddenly discover that they can work magic. Under a certain set of circumstances they may do something that a normal Dumbbelloid— non-magical person—could never do, "like turn a bothersome neighbor into a parrot, or cause a pair of rollerblades to jump through a plate glass store window without breaking the glass. [. . .] They all have their own talents. Some are excellent at teleportation, others can walk through walls, still others can read minds, or have a talent for levitation. Then there are those, who after three years cannot master the simplest incantation, but without any instruction at all can cast such an evil spell that it takes us two weeks of hard work to remove it. [. . .] At Tibidoxs we work with these children to make sure that they do not use their skills to cause harm. [. . .] Magic can be very dangerous if you do not keep it under control." (MC.222-223)

During the two months that the students had to be sent 'home' to the non-magical world after Tibidoxs was laid waste by the Titans in their battle with Chuma-del-Tort (Tanya's archnemesis), every last one of the students did something that they were not supposed to do in the Dumbbelloid world. At the first all-school assembly after the students are allowed back in Tibidoxs, the deputy headmaster has an enchanted quill and stack of parchments in his lap. The quill is scratching away all by itself, writing down the transgressions that each and every student committed while away from school. (DF.143-144) He summarizes them in his 'welcoming' speech: "Some of you—I won't name any names for the time being— took being—took the liberty of flying, others used incantations right and left, yet others tried to apply the higher-level magic of shape shifting. As a result of which several quite law-abiding Dumbbelloids are still . . . ah . . . are displaying certain strange behaviors." (DF.145) The hard-line disciplinarian that he is, the deputy headmaster would like to punish the transgressors by zombification, stripping them of their magical powers and permanent exile to the Dumbbelloid world. "Unfortunately," continues the deputy headmaster, "if we were to use zombification, this auditorium would be completely empty, because there is not one of you, who did not commit at least one serious infraction." (DF.146-147)

In addition to keeping these young delinquents off the street, Tibidoxs is also "a fortress-prison where the old spirits, the pagan gods and forces of chaos are kept imprisoned in the dungeon." (MC.225-226, DF.22) These are the forces that Chuma-del-Tort is always trying to release so that she can take over the world. The location that Emets has chosen for the school fits this characteristic of the school to a 'T'. It is taken straight from Slavic folklore. The school is located on the island of Buyan, which is exactly where—according to legend—the legend—the old pagan gods and spirits should be. The "green oak" on the Isle of Buyan that Pushkin—the Pushkin—the Russian Shakespeare—refers Shakespeare—refers to in his poem about The Emperor Sultan, was the world tree of pagan times, the center of the world, the point from which the four cardinal directions are defined.

Abdulla, the library genie, a proponent of the Black Arts, laments that passing of the days of the spirits of old, with power untold, when Black Magic was in flower. "Modern magicians," he says, "have long forgotten what a really powerful curse is. They are afraid, they are too cowardly to call upon the genuinely powerful spirits. These spirits have to be paid for their services . . . paid a dear price . . . a very dear price. [. . .] It was those drivelling White magicians who spoiled everything. It all started with Drevnir. He wanted, you see, to organize everything. He forbade calling on the powerful spirits, prohibited human sacrifices. Today's Black Magic isn't fit to sole the shoes of the magic that went before it." (DF.219-220)

The duality of good and evil in Tibidoxs on its primordial island at the center of the world is embodied not only in the presence of the old gods and chaos locked in the school dungeon, but also in the fact that the school has Departments of both White and Black Magic. Tanya studies on the faculty of White Magic. Her roommate, however, studies on the faculty of Black Arts. Half the staff of the school is made up of White wizards and witches, and half is made up of Black wizards and witches. Having the forces of White and Black magic in such close proximity ensures that there is always friction between the two, and something for Emets to write about.

Getting to School

Tanya's invitation to attend Tibidoxs and the way that she gets there are more reminiscent of Peter Pan than they are of Harry Potter. Done in the same schematic style as the court brief in the Dutch Tanya Grotter case, the story line of Peter Pan is:

- Young boy flies to a big city from a magical island
- He flies to the window of a young girl
- He invites the girl to come back to the island with him
- He teaches her how to fly
- They fly off to the island, where they meet a group of children
- They have a series of adventures, in which they fight an arch villain
- One of the members of their group betrays the girl to the villain
- They defeat the villain in the end.

The same schematic story line can also be used for Tanya Grotter. In this case, the boy in question is not Peter Pan, but Bob-Yagun, the grandson of the well-known Russian witch Baba Yaga. He flies to Tanya's window and brings her an invitation to Tibidoxs, a book of magic and a magic ring. She has a week's time to learn how to use the ring and how to fly on her magical double bass. When he comes back at the end of the week, she has learned her lessons so well that she is able to show off as they fly back to Tibidoxs, saving her companion from a crash when his jet vacuum cleaner—a 700 series with all the bells and whistlesÑgoes whistles—goes into a stall because the brush attachment, where all the magic is concentrated, comes loose from the hose. (MC.202)

For a native-English-speaking reader, the description of their flight back to Tibidoxs is suggestive of the flight to Never-Never Land: second star on the right and then straight on till morning. At first Tanya and Bob climbed high in the sky to catch the upper-air currents, and then turned south-west. Their long flight took them over the ocean to the island where Tibidoxs was located, arriving just as the sun was coming up. (MC.205, 206)

Some elements from Harry Potter, however, seem to creep back into the story as they enter Tibidoxs. Track 9 3/4 appears to have been relocated, but its use has become more perilous. Entrance into Tibidoxs requires that Tanya execute a sophisticated and dangerous incantation, one which will only work, if she really believes that it will. (More Peter Pan, anyone?) The warning in A White Magician's Handbook said:

> For all its simplicity, the cross-over incantation is an incantation of Higher-Level Magic. When pronouncing the incantation, one needs to be absolutely certain that the cross-over will take place completely. In the worst case, one's consciousness and one's body can become separated: the body will make the transition, but one's consciousness will remain in the previous world. This condition is what the Dumbbelloids call death. (MC.205)

She says the incantation and is shaken and blown, pricked by millions of small sparks, disintegrated and reintegrated again. For a moment she "felt like she was passing through the infinitely narrow gap of an hourglass." (MC.206) It worked, but she is not inside yet. They cannot use the front gate. They have to sneak in, using Bob-Yagun's secret way in and out of school. Tanya has to swear not to tell anyone where it is, because if the school administration finds out about it, they will close it off.

Bob's secret passage is on the back wall of the school castle, where the Black Tower meets the wall. In response to an incantation, a stone in the wall changes colors and Bob flies right through it, a la track 9 3/4. It only lets one person through at a time and Tanya has to repeat the incantation herself to get in. She says it, but is still unsure of herself. Expecting to crash into a solid wall, she flies right at the stone, but to her surprise, she only feels the pricks of lots of tiny sparks as she passes through the wall into the school.

Once they are inside, Bob sends her off on her own to find headmaster Chernomorov's office. Bob cannot go with her because flying spells are blocked inside the school, and he has to go put her double bass and his vacuum cleaner away. (Since Nimbus—2003 is meeting in Disney World, I could not resist a couple of Disney metaphors.) Tanya just left Peter Pan's Flight and is now in The Haunted Mansion. To get to Chernomorov's office, she has to go through the Tower of Ghosts.

No sooner has Bob disappeared from sight, than Tanya hears the scrape of metal on stone behind her. She turns to see a rusty, two-handed sword and a highly polished shield mounted on the walk. Upon seeing her reflection in the shield, Tanya almost screams, because she sees that her body is headless. Her head is lying on the floor at her feet, obviously the work of the sword. The shield lets out a taunting ring as it scrapes against the stone wall, and the sword tries to chop off her head. It is restrained, however, by a chain that holds it fast to the wall. It hangs there on the chain vibrating maliciously and visibly rusting in disappointment. (MC.211)

Bob had gone down the stairs, so she has to follow the red carpet that leads up the stairs. The carpet stirs under her feet and she can hear moans and insane cackles, the sound of cards striking a table, the meowing of a cat. She could have dealt with that, but, at the next landing, she encounters two gravestones. The text engraved on both in Gothic letters says: "Tanya Grotter." Tanya's mouth goes dry, but she does not lose her fighting spirit, and fires off a burst of green sparks at the two gravestones from her magic ring.

The letters on the gravestones begin to move, and jumping around, change places. "What'd ya do that for?" says the first gravestone. "We were just fooling," says the second. Tanya hurls an insult at the gravestones, but then asks them how to get to Chernomorov's office. "Straight," says the first gravestone. "If you don't die along the way," says the second. (MC.211-212)

Tanya starts off down the corridor on the landing, where she runs into the ghost of Lieutenant Rzhevskij and his trademark witty repartee. His parting comment is that it was very foolish of Chernomorov to bring Tanya to Tibidoxs, "unless he wanted to add to his collection of poltergeists." (MC.213)

Tanya quickens her steps down the corridor. The carpet continues to squirm under her feet. The marble busts in the niches move. The side corridors appear to have new and unknown terrors defined as lights and smells and sounds. (You would think that Emets had actually been to The Haunted Mansion.)

A wheelchair from one of the side corridors begins to chase her. A blue plaid coverlet covers the invisible passenger. Tanya starts running. She passes a cactus covered with sadly blinking human eyes. She sees a crystal coffin hung on silver chains from two sympathetic looking gallows. Inside the coffin is a long broom with a sign that says: "A Life Size Model of H.P.'s Broom." (MC.215) Tanya does not have time to study this more closely, as the wheelchair is gaining on her. Tanya rounds a corner to find a large double door. No sooner had the thought enters her mind that this might be the door that she is looking for, than a string of brilliant letters flash on above the door to spell out a message: "That's right. You have not made a mistake. In front of you is the small, humble office of" Sardanapalus Chernomorov. (MC.216)

Tanya begins to pound on the door in fright. The two golden sphinxes painted on the door come to life and are getting ready to pounce on her, when the door opens, and headmaster Chernomorov steps out. Upon seeing Chernomorov, the cowardly wheelchair slinks quickly away, and the sphinxes go back to sleep. Chernomorov takes Tanya into his office and explains that the next time she runs into things like the wheelchair, she should not run away. They are energy-vampires. They feed on fear. All it takes to get rid of them is to say the incantation drygus-brygus and they will go away. (MC.217) Welcome to Tibidoxs!

Meet the Staff

Sardanapalus Chernomorov holds a Ph.D. in the Art of White Magic, is a Laureate of the Magical Suspenders (MC.24, DF.18), and headmaster of Tibidoxs for life and posthumously (MC.216, GL.17). His specialty at Tibidoxs is Other-worldly Studies (MC.227), and one of the classes that he teaches is Conspiracy. (MC.140)

His first name was made famous by Lord Byron in the verse drama Sardanapalus (1821), which inspired Delacroix's painting The Death of Sardanapal (1827, oil on canvas, 392 x 496 cm, The Louvre). His last name refers to the area of the Black Sea (Chernoe More).

Two of his more remarkable characteristics are his long beard and moustache. They are animate. The color of his beard is hard to determine, because it keeps disappearing and reappearing, but its length is monumental. It is wrapped around his waist several times and the end is ultimately stuffed into one of his pockets. While his beard is reserved and sedate, the two ends of his moustache are on a mission to bring some comic relief to the story. When the reader is first introduced to them, they are trying to grab on to his glasses so that they can rip them off. The narrator points out, however, that this will be no mean feat, because Chernomorov's glasses are not held on so much by the arms, which had long ago become wobbly, as by a special incantation. (MC.10)

The two ends of his moustache like to punctuate his conversation with gestures. When Chernomorov says that they went that'a way, his moustache points the way. (MC.18) In a conversation where he mentions the arrival of a cupid (cupids fulfill the role of mailmen in Tanya's world), the two ends of his moustache form two hearts. (MC.22) To keep the two ends of his rebellious moustache out of trouble, Dr. Chernomorov sometimes ties them together in a knot behind his head. (MC.216, GL.23) He is also seen reading a brochure entitled: Training and Calming Beards. The Preparation of Tinctures of Obedience for Animate Moustaches (MC.308), but neither of these approaches is entirely successful. In a later scene, at the opening of an all-school assembly, as an invisible band is playing the school song, the two ends of Chernomorov's moustache are seen vigorously conducting the music, while Chernomorov prepares to address the student body, apparently unaware of what his moustache is doing. (DF.144)

Dr. Chernomorov is, however, not above a little Black legerdemain to win at office politics. When the head of the Black Arts Department, professor Klopp, tries to stage a palace coup, and Chernomorov is hauled off to the Society of Slumbering Magicians— in Russian, an excellent pun on the title of the United Nations (Magshchestvo Prodryglykh Magtsij)—Chernomorov defeats the inquisition by casting a spell on the whole lot of them. They reaffirm his appointment as the head of Tibidoxs, and send him off on a luxurious flying carpet with an ovation, falling over each to award him grand titles and decorations. (GL.215)

While the lampoon hurled at high-handed politics will find its mark in any society, this barb is especially pointed in Russia, where, during the Communist period, the kind of denunciation that Klopp used to get Chernomorov out of the way so that he could take over his job was practically raised to the level of an art form, as people denounced their way to positions of power and into scarce apartments. When considered from that point of view, Chernomorov's escape from the clutches of the system is indeed a bit of high-level magic. The fact that Chernomorov used one of the 100 spells prohibited by Drevnir—the founder of Tibidoxs—to accomplish this feat, leaves the reader contemplating a very Russian paradox of the relationship between truth and justice. It is Dostoevskij with his tongue in his cheek. It may have started as Harry Potter, but when you add Dostoevskij and stir, something happens.

Unlike Steve Jobs, Chernomorov's reality distortion field did not collapse when he left. He added a double fifty-year spell of secrecy. The members of the Society will not figure out what happened for 100 years, but by then it will not be important. "Every piece of information has its 'best if used by' date," Chernomorov says. (GL.215)

Pokl'p Pokl'pych is the deputy headmaster of Tibidoxs. He is a former Black wizard turned White, and he is supposed to be the bridge between the two kinds of magic at Tibidoxs. He is the only one who dares use both White and Black magic at the same time. Before he became a White wizard, he was one of the most powerful of the Black wizards. (DF.155) He is a bald (GL.73), small, lopsided man with colorless, powerful, beady little eyes (DF.10, 31), who resembles a bristling crow. (DF.142)

Emets enhances Pokl'p's 'black' personality with an interesting sartorial detail. At the festive opening of a Dragon Ball game Pokl'p is seen "wearing a brand new SS uniform (a war trophy from 1945, a souvenir of the taking of the Reichstag by Soviet troops)." The sinister implications of his clothing are quickly lampooned by the image of the holster at his side. Instead of a pistol, the unbuckled holster contains a roll of parchment sheets with his welcoming speech for the visiting team. (DF.286) The introduction of the SS uniform, nevertheless, does give one pause. He is, after all, the school's physical security officer, responsible for the intrusion detection spells and the cyclops guard.

Pokl'p's name is a play on the Russian word for aspersions (as in slander, calumny), and he has a disposition that even a mother would find hard to love. He and Dr. Chernomorov form the poles of the debate about how to discipline the students. Pokl'p's responses to the students' transgressions are always the most draconian imaginable: zombification, stripping them of their magical powers, returning them to the non-magical world. Dr. Chernomorov always sides with the students.

The running gag about Pokl'p throughout the books is that he is in love with a mermaid who does not love him. This is the result of an argument with a cupid, in which Pokl'p broke the cupid's bow. In revenge, the cupid shot him with an arrow and made him fall in love with the mermaid. Pokl'p is always covered in fish slime and scales. His daily passwords, 'Mermaid Tail' for example, to be given to the cyclops at the school gate show that the mermaid is ever on his mind. (DF.142)

He teaches the class on Defense from Spirits. The rumor about his class is that, as he is a former Black wizard, he does not so much teach the students how to defend themselves from spirits, as sick the spirits on the students (GL.82), and that leads to one of the major threats to magical life and limb in the third book.

Medusiya Gorgonova is number 3 in the hierarchy of Tibidoxs, after headmaster Chernomorov and deputy headmaster Pokl'p Pokl'pych, and in some things she was number one. (DF.358) She practices White magic (MC.270), and has an obvious crush on Dr. Chernomorov.

Her first and last name are, of course, references to classic Greek mythology, where Medusa was once a beautiful maiden whose hair was her chief glory. Her beauty caught Poseidon's eye, and he had an affair with her. This angered Athena and she turned Medusa into a gorgon, a hideous female monster with snakes for hair. Medusa's appearance was so hideous that all who looked at her were turned to stone. Athena later helped Perseus hunt down Medusa and cut off her head, which even in death retained its fearsome petrifying powers.

Emets takes all these story elements and scrambles them to the reader's comic delight. The first time that Tanya sees Medusiya, it is early morning, and "the snakes on her head have not had time to turn back into hair." She has them tied together in a knot on top of her head. Seeing that she has company, Medusiya quickly throws on a scarf. (MC.228) Not only does she have hair to match her names (MC.20, 361, DF.6, 204,

GL.36), but in her first dialogue with professor Chernomorov she talks about how "an audacious character in winged sandals," cut off her head "while looking into his own shield" (MC.11), which is a veiled reference to Perseus, who was aided in cutting off Medusa's head by the loan of Athena's shield and Hermes' winged shoes. He had to look into Athena's polished shield to see what he was doing when he cut off her head, or he, too, would have been turned to stone. The scene in which Tanya sees the sword and shield in the Tower of Ghosts was another allusion to this. (MC.211)

Medusiya says that she was just a young, behaviorally-challenged witch at the time and that Sardanapalus helped turn her around. Sardanapal demurs that "gluing her head back on" (MC.11) was just a trifle, and that she does not have to keep thanking him for that. She persists, bringing up how she used to turn travelers to stone, grabbing a detail from the Greek myth that Emets skillfully parodies in Sardanapal's reply. "You were just a young girl with a complex about your acne, who happened to enchant the poor fellows who saw you by accident. Frankly, I understand you perfectly. Those ancient Greeks sticking their curious noses into everything. You even retired to an island as far out of sight as possible, and they still kept hanging around waving swords. All I needed to do was to cure your acne. And what a beauty you've become." (MC.12) Medusiya blushes.

She teaches Nezhit'ology at Tibidoxs. (MC.11, 228) Nezhit' is a class of petty Russian spirits like house spirits (domovye), water spirits (vodyanye), forest spirits (leshie) and mermaids (rusalki). Emets offers a good definition of what nezhit' is in book I: "Nezhit' is a slow-witted force that arose out of chaos, a part of which has survived from pagan times. There is more nezhit' than there are of us wizards, both Black and White, but they have never been in a position to get together on anything. In as far as I remember, the nezhit' have always broken the rules, played dirty tricks on the Dumbbelloids, and shaken the balance of things." (MC.18) This is Tanya's second favorite subject, because it ties in so well with her first: Veterinary Magic.

Professor Klopp teaches Applied Magic. He is a Black wizard, whose ring gives off red sparks. His trademark entrance into the classroom is in a hammock lowered from a hatch in the ceiling. He is a small, wrinkled, balding old man, with a head that resembles an overgrown radish. His sour smile is punctuated by a single, crooked tooth. (MC.241) He wears two-inch lifts. (GL.86)

His wardrobe makes a definite fashion statement. The first time we meet him, he is wearing a purple sweater with a worn wool waistcoat haphazardly donned on top of it. (MC.241) On special occasions, his waistcoat sports a large medal, that some say was awarded him by the great Merlin, but which others maintain was one that he had found and had not returned to its owner. (DF.286) He had had this waistcoat on for centuries without taking it off. (GL.60) Magical objects, it seems, become less powerful, if cleaned. (GL.58) His name suggests the Russian word for bug (klop), but Emets fudges the issue by spelling it with two 'PP's instead of one like the real Russian word for bug.

He is a 'Zherman', who has a noticeable accent, that is not helped by the fact that he is grammatical mistakes making, when he is talking being. The stereotypical monocle on a chain associated with German professors has been replaced by a bronze tasting spoon, with which he tests the potions and elixirs that the students make in his class. (MC.244)

Klopp is a student's worst-night-mare teacher. He insists on punctuality, can hear a whisper in the back of the class, and, quite literally, has eyes in the back of his head. Tanya learns all these things by being late on her first day of class, talking in class with Bob-Yagun, and sticking out her tongue at Klopp as he is walking away from her, after giving her a dressing down. His teaching technique is horrible and his methods of keeping order in the class draconian. The question that he asks when he is ready for the students to start a laboratory exercise says it all: "Are zer any stupid kvestions?" (DF.152) Needless to say, the students hate his class, even though the topics he covers are rather interesting.

During one class session the students learn how to make a bravery elixir from stinkbugs (dried dung-beetles will do, if you do not have any stinkbugs handy). In another session, they learn to make a jumping potion.

The bravery elixir is a tricky one. Only the back legs of the stinkbugs can be used, and the mixture has to be stirred counterclockwise, and it cannot boil. Klopp is making the rounds of the class, tasting the brews that the students have produced. Condescending and insulting, he dismisses one after another. He was not even going to taste Tanya's brew—it being her first day of class, he is sure that it is not worth the effort—but he does deign to taste it after one of the students mentions that he has not tried Tanya's yet. He gets out his tasting spoon, raises it to his lips, and the scene that follows is right out of a Saturday-morning cartoon.

> From the expression on his face, it was clear that he was about to say something extremely caustic, but then suddenly a thick jet of steam spouted out of his ears, his face turned red, and he jumped up and down shouting: "What are you all sitting there for, dawdlers!! Get me a mammoth! A hundred mammoths! Two hundred! And some dragons, too! I'll smash 'em barehanded! And not just the dragons! I'll give all the titans a black eye, on both eyes!" (MC.245)

Tanya's elixir is obviously a success.

Emets delivers Klopp's announcement to the class that they will be making the jumping potion with a liberal dose of black humor. "Guten morning, kinder!" says Klopp with glee in his heavy accent. "I zee zat you are all alife und wehl. But zat will not long ze kase be. I am shur zat before ze lesson ends, many of you will be in ze magical aid station." (DF.151) If improperly done, the potion is quite explosive, and, if properly done, it allows the user to jump higher than the ceiling. Klopp sees a lot of potential injuries resulting from those two facts.

The potion is an aromatic one, that will smell like rotten eggs when it is done. If it explodes or does not smell like rotten eggs, the student got it wrong. It takes 3 boa constrictor scales, 4 hairs of a vampire, 7 tails of dead rats and 12 heaping table spoons of gun powder, mixed in fish slime and simmered over a low fire.

As per usual, Klopp walks around the class observing the students and making insulting remarks. According to him, there are only idiots in the class. He is displeased when one of the cauldrons explodes. "How much gun powder did you put in? It would have been better were your stupid, empty head explode! I am giving ze whole klass a bad grade! Ze whole klass! Zat was mein favorite cauldron! It has been hier voor two hundred years!" (DF.154)

By the end of the class everybody has hopelessly messed up the potion, except Verka Popugaeva, who was so scared that she got everything right by mistake. Klopp gave her a 'B.' The curious class dunce, Gunya Glomov, decided to try the potion, and smeared it on his legs, but nothing happened. "Where's the magic in this?" he said disappointedly. Klopp becomes all sweetness and light, and tells Glomov to jump, which he does. The potion works like it is supposed to, Glomov crashes into the ceiling and falls back to the floor unconscious. Klopp smiles in satisfaction. "Zomeone take zis simpleton to the magical aid station. Class dismissed," he says. (DF.158)

Zubod'rikha teaches the Evil Spells class. This is a mixed Black and White Arts class. The Black Arts students are enrolled in Casting Evil Spells and the White Arts students are enrolled in Removing Evil Spells. (DF.28) The two classes meet together. Some of the spells that Tanya and her friends cover are:

- The Chicken curse, which makes you act like a chicken (boy does your nose get sore) [DF.173-175],
- The Hiccup spell, which does what it sounds like (MC.253), and
- The Fateful spell, which is fatal.

Zubod'rikha's name is an uncomplimentary slang word for dentist. It literally means "tooth yanker." Behind her back, the students call her "the big tooth." (DF.350) Her teaching style seems to match the literal meaning of her name. With hardly any introduction at all, she casts a spell on the class and tells them to get out of it, leaving them to writhe in green agony on the floor, while she reads one of her books. At the end of the class, she removes the spell with the comment: "That was your homework assignment! The next time be more responsible about your lessons!" (DF.29) Hers is definitely a class where you don't want to sluff off your homework.

> She is "small, round, and young, with bangs like a pony," and she has a penchant for smelling the flowers. (DF.28) Her trademark idiosyncrasy is reading classical literature, like Horace, the poets of the Silver Age, and Plato's Dialogs, in the original. (MC.252, DF.174, 286) She knew Plato personally. As far as the narrator is concerned, her reading is nothing more than "abstruse poems." (DF.28) Most of Emets' young readers will probably agree with that. Zubod'rikha's books are unique among the books at Tibidoxs because they are not animate. They behave like non-magical books, and just have words on a page that can be read by the literate.

The Books

The books at Tibidoxs—except, of course those belonging to Zubod'rikha—are rikha—are very much alive, and have distinct personalities of their own. The first book in the story is the one that Tanya is given together with her invitation to Tibidoxs. When she is first given it, the title reads: One Thousand Hints for the Young Homemaker. (MC.150) She leafs through the book and sees helpful homemaking hints like:

> Hint 8. Your whites will not get dirty so fast, if you add a drop of lemon juice to the detergent. (MC.151)

Tanya is not real thrilled with this 'wonderful' book and asks herself disappointedly: "What kind of nonsense is this? And what's magical about it? What do they want me to go to Tibidoxs for? To be a cook?" (MC.152)

Sensing her disappointment Bob-Yagun remembers that he forgot to tell her how to really open the book. What she has been seeing is just the way that the book camouflages itself in case it falls into the hands of one of the Dumbbelliods or one of the nezhit'. An incantation and magical gesture reveal that it is really A White Magician's Handbook. (MC.153)

Tanya leafs through the book again and this time finds a handy hint more to her taste:

> Hint 24. To feed domestic harpies, take twelve rotten eggs. Beat carefully with the tail of a frightened young skunk. Add some freshly diced rat meat to the mixture, and season to taste with dried gadfly and bumblebee. Serve chilled in a swamp sauce. (MC.154)

Unlike books that Dumbbelloids use, which are printed in thousands of copies, magical books are unique. There is only one copy. Bob-Yagun had a lot of trouble getting it for Tanya from the librarian, a fearsome genie named Abdulla, of whom even the One-Eyed Terror is rightly afraid. Abdulla wanted Bob-Yagun to pledge his soul for the return of the book, but Bob talked his way out of it. Like any library book, it has a stamp on the title page. It says:

Property of the Tibidoxs Library
Return before the second new moon to avoid a curse (MC.153)

Tanya asks, if they really place a curse on you for not bringing a book back, and no sooner has she said the words, than the stamp changed itself into a hangman's noose with the words Just try it! underneath. Bob tells her that she does not want to try it. Things are pretty strict in the library. Rumor has it that the reason the One-Eyed Terror only has one eye is that he once "erased the thirteenth letter on the thirteenth page of the thirteenth volume of The Secrets of Evil Spells" and had to answer to Abdulla. (MC.151) When Tanya inevitably forgets to return the book on time, the stamp changes to "I warned you . . . " (MC.259)

Emets returns to the threat of the Tibidoxs librarian a short time later, when Tanya's adoptive sister Pipa and one of her girlfriends find the book Bob-Yagun brought her. The book, of course, has its camouflage turned on. All they see is One Thousand Hints for the Young Homemaker. Pipa wants to get Tanya in trouble with whomever loaned her the book, and considers her options: "Tear it up—boring, mark up the pages with a pen—takes too long. Aha! Let's smear it with glue." (MC.164) Pipa's girlfriend volunteers to do the dirty work, so that Pipa won't have to lie, when they ask if she did it. They get out a tube of 'Super Cement' and prepare to go to work on the book.

Tanya overhears the fiendish plot, and rushes to stop it with visions of the enraged Tibidoxs librarian in her mind, but before she can reach the door handle, she hears screams coming from the room. The tube of Super Cement is flying around the room like a dive bomber, coating Pipa's hair with glue. The book has latched on to her girlfriend's arm like a bulldog and will not let go. Tanya tries to rescue them from the book by saying an incantation, but the book is either too excited to hear her, or pretends not to hear her. It only stops reluctantly after she says the incantation for the third time. (MC.65) Pipa's hair was super-glued into helmet-like hardness and her girlfriend's hand was covered with curly red hair where the book had 'bit' her. Magical books, it seems, can look after themselves.

The book not only has to defend itself from Pipa and her girlfriend, but also from Tanya. Tanya decides that all these incantations are just too hard to learn, so she will just write them on her hand as a crib so that she can peek when she needs to. The book will not put up with this nonsense either. No sooner had she picked up the pen to write down the incantations, than she smelled burning plastic. A second later she yelled 'Ouch!' and dropped the pen. Before it hit the floor, it had turned into a smouldering glob of plastic. The smoke from the pen rose up in the air and spelled out a message:

Magical secrets! Copying down incantations is strictly forbidden! (MC.169)

The last exclamation mark maliciously floated up into Tanya's nostrils, making her sneeze, at which time the message dispersed.

When Tanya gets to headmaster Chernomorov's office, she finds even more animate books. These are books on Black Magic that Chernomorov keeps in his office as a reference, in case he needs to remove an evil spell. He explained that he did not want to turn the books over to the library, as the librarian would probably turn them all to dust, or the books would re-educate the librarian to their way of thinking. The books are next to his desk in a cage, and for good reason. The books are angrily ruffling their pages and banging against the bars, trying to get out. One thick book with yellowed parchment pages kept trying to turn into a lizard and sneak through the bars, but the bars kept closing together so that it cannot get out. To make them seem even more like wild creatures in a cage, the narrator remarks that the headmaster feeds them raw meat. (MC.218, 220)

The animate class grade book that Tanya meets in her first day of class would appeal to many a teacher in a less magical school. The class starts with the instructor releasing the grade book to take the roll and check homework. The book hovers over the head of each student for a moment, and the pen accompanying it on its rounds makes a note for each one. The book also lets the students know what it thinks of them. When it is pleased, it gives the student a pet on the head. When it is peeved, it gives the student a thump. It gave one particularly obtuse student, who had exhausted the book's patience, a whap. When the book got to Tanya, it stopped longer than for the other students. Tanya was afraid that the book was going to give her a thump too, because she not only did not have any homework done, but also had no idea what the class was about. Instead, the pen that accompanied the book on its rounds made a rather long note, after which the book and pen flew off to the instructor. When the instructor read the note about Tanya, she looked at her with renewed interest. Tanya would have dearly liked to know what the book had said about her, but after the instructor had read the note, the book snapped shut and closed its two brass clasps. (MC.251-2)

Tanya's visit to the Tibidoxs library is more like a visit to the zoo. There were books in chains, books like armadillos crawling across the floor, flocks of books flying about just under the ceiling, and two thick dictionaries with leather bindings—quite obviously Black Arts books—that were tearing a small magazine apart. Tanya's arrival scared off the dictionaries, and they flew off to their shelf. The frightened magazine jumped into Tanya's arms. (MC.259) Luckily, Tanya finds the librarian before he can finish pronouncing his curse on her for bringing the book back late, and gives him the book. The genie-librarian leafs through he book looking for damage, but finds none, and with a grimace that looked like he has a bad toothache says:

> Oh, most providential of the most foolish! All is in order! Thou hast had good fortune, because I had not finished saying my excellent incantation, especially composed for this occasion. But thou should tremble: the next time I will be implacable, and to the point.

Abdulla would be a lot more terrifying, if it were not for the fact that all his curses are so long that he never seems to be able to finish saying them. As he flies away with the book, he says to himself: "Oh most bothersome of all today's bothers! A day has passed and I have not cursed anyone." (MC.261)

The School Nurse's office is called the "Magical Aid Station" (Magpunkt). This is a play on the Russian word for Medical Aid Station (Medpunkt), a point that

Emets emphasizes to make sure the reader does not think that it is just a spelling mistake. (MC.254) Though Emets tries to soft-pedal the association, the school nurse is immediately recognizable as the most famous witch of Russian folklore: Baba Yaga. Emets tries to throw the reader off the track by spelling her name with a double 'GG', which is normally a marker for a non-Russian name. He calls her Yagge.

The name of her grandson—one of Tanya's best school friends—is Bob-Yagun. In Russian, a language in which men's and women's names have different morphological endings, his name is clearly a masculine version of Baba Yaga. As Bob is taking Tanya to meet his grandmother, he pointedly warns her not to call his grandmother Yaga, but Yagge, adding that her leg is not bony at all. The later caution is intended to further disassociate the school nurse from the witch of Russian folklore, whose poetic epithet is Baba Yaga of the bony leg. (It rhymes in Russian: Baba Yaga, kostyanaya noga.) Yagge's description, however matches the classical drawings of the Russian witch of folklore fame, with a slight nod to Tolkien's Gandalf: "a dried out old woman, dressed like a gypsy, with a red scarf on her head, wrapped in a bright shawl. [She] was smoking a cherry pipe, and exhaling clouds of aromatic smoke, which took the shape of all sorts of exotic animals." (MC.254, DF.270)

In the third book, Emets takes yet another attribute from the real Baba Yaga, and immediately turns it on its head. The Baba Yaga of tale and fable lives in a House on Chicken's Legs. This is an allusion to the houses that the Laps of Finland, whom the Russians long considered witches and warlocks. Because of all the snow in the area where the Laps live, buildings were constructed on stilts so that the door would be above the level of the snow in the dead of winter. In one of his inimitable Dragon Ball commentaries, this one from inside a dragon, Bob-Yagun compares the level of heat in the belly of a dragon to a sauna, a very popular institution in Russia. He says that he has not been in a sauna since "they ran off grandmother's House on Chicken's Legs, and replaced it with a Hovel on Buffalo Wings." (Razvalochka na Brojlernykh Okorochkakh, G.41) The image is irresistibly delicious.

The Nurse's Office is a busy place. The Nurse treats wounds both physical, psychological and magical. When Tanya needs someone to talk to after she has gotten herself into trouble by using a forbidden incantation and firing off three red sparks from her magic ring to break a spell, she turns to Yagge for help, and Yagge has some good advice. (DF.274) She has, after all, been at Tibidoxs long enough to see 300 years of Dragon Ball Championships. (DF.278) (In book III, it is 500 years. [GL.17]) That seems enough time to develop the kind of wisdom you can share with others.

Shurasik, the straight-A teachers' pet makes a mistake in a Removing Evil Spells class and uses a freezing incantation to cure the hiccup spell that had been placed on him during the class lab. He has to be taken to Yagge to be thawed out.

She has them put him on an oilcloth. There will be a puddle when he thaws out. (MC.253, 255)

Dragon Ball injuries are depicted in exaggerated Saturday-morning cartoon style (think Wile E. Coyote), with players falling from great heights, after having been dislodged from their flying vacuum cleaners, propeller driven mops and so forth, and landing in the sand on the playing field up to their ears, or up to their toes, if they go in head first. (DF.319, 327) They are simply dug out of the sand and carried off to the Magical Aid Station, or put back into the game. (GL.19) Bob-Yagun has almost every bone in his body broken at a Dragon Ball match. Yagge wraps him up like a mummy and throws in practically her whole supply of bone regenerators, crawly little bug-like things the size of a coin. According to Bob, they itch like mad when they creep around inside the bandages. (MC.132, 140, DF.270, 274) On the eve of an important Dragon Ball Championship, Gunya Glomov, the school dunce, manages to fall off the castle wall of the school a la Humpty-Dumpty, and gets to experience the itch of the bone regenerators himself. (DF.285) Tanya breaks a leg during a Dragon Ball game in the third book, and likewise gets to share the experience. (GL.51, 54)

The Playing Fields of Tibidoxs

Dragon Ball has it all. It is a high-impact sport, played in grand Saturday-morning-cartoon style, where the hazards to life and limb—like getting swallowed by a dragon—have no effect on the players, who are dug out of the sand, peeled off the stadium dome, drenched in dragon fire, swallowed and regurgitated by dragons with little noticeable effect. A trip to the Magical Aid Station, and they are all right again. Don't try this at home. It seems that the primary risk to being swallowed by a dragon is not being the only one in the dragon's stomach. It is dark in there and the players keep bumping into and stepping on each other, inevitably resulting in cuts and contusions. If Dragon Ball ever makes it to the silver screen, it should be as a cartoon. Nothing else would do all this mock mayhem justice.

Tanya's introduction to Dragon Ball comes while she is still in the non-magical world, when she hears a magical radio broadcast of a game picked up by her very versatile double bass. She joins the game in progress, as the announcer, the irrepressible Bob-Yagun, is filling in a timeout while a fire started by one of the dragons is being extinguished by the Vodyanye, Russian water spirits, whom Emets—very much tongue in cheek—has pressed into service as firemen in the magical world of Tibidoxs. (MC.122, GL.26) It is the Vampires against the all-star team of Bald Mountain Witches. And now we go to Bob-Yagun:

> Today's game has been complicated by gusts of wind from the ocean, regularly knocking the players from their vacuum cleaners. It would seem that one of our sport's ill-wishers has cast a spell that the grounds

keepers have been trying to remove these last three hours. [. . .] If you could just see what is happening in the stands! The vampires are going wild! I am sure that you can hear the sounds of their demoniacal screams and bloodcurdling howls through the microphone. It was certainly a good idea on the part of headmaster Chernomorov and the Dragon Ball Federation to insist that the vampires wear muzzles. Otherwise, blood would certainly be flowing. [. . .] Today's match has been disappointing. The Vampires and the Witches haven't been in top form. There hasn't been a lot of excitement, as the forwards seem to be afraid of flying close to the opposing team's dragon, and have been taking their shots from a distance, completely unable to hit their target. Oh, it looks like I spoke too soon! The defense of the Bald Mountain Witches has broken down. The Vampire team's forward is breaking through with a paralyzing ball, the most dangerous of all the game balls! If he can throw it into the dragon's mouth, the Bald Mountain Witches don't stand a chance. . . . He evades one defender, another. [. . .] Khmyrets throws . . . You can hear the roar of the crowd. It's gonna be a goal! No, wait. The crowd moans. It's the characteristic blood chilling moan of the Vampires. [. . .] The 'Bald Mountain' Dragon has snapped its jaws shut, making the shot impossible . . . The ball hits him in the eye and explodes! The dragon is enraged! He flaps his wings, flails his articulated tail, and takes off. Looking to get even, he is trying to get to the Vampire forward. [. . .] This dragon is not joking! He really means to catch Khmyrets. [. . .] The dragon is getting closer . . . He's opening his terrible jaws . . . Khmyrets screams and takes a swan dive off his vacuum cleaner, hoping to use his handkerchief as a parachute. It's too late! The dragon caught him in his jaws . . . Swallows . . . It's a nightmare. The Vampire team has lost its best player. It's a dangerous time! G-O-A-L! And another one! I can't believe my eyes! Taking advantage of the situation, the Bald Mountain Witches have broken through to the "Vampires'" dragon, and have thrown both the fire-extinguishing and pepper balls at the dragon's mouth. [. . .] The balls explode, releasing their magical charges. The fire goes out. The dragon begins to sneeze, and it's three players from the opposing team that were swallowed earlier and the referee Solovej Razbojnik that fly out of his throat. They don't look good: three hours in the belly of a dragon takes a heavy toll. [. . .] The referee blows his magical whistle! Can it be? Yes, it is. The Bald Mountain Witches win! (MC.121-126)

Bob-Yagun's commentary is a very good parody of a soccer game as heard on the radio. It has just the right rhythm. The commentary is not the only thing that points to Dragon Ball's 'soccer' heritage. Penalty shots are taken from the eleven-meter line in both games (GL.28, 32), and "Red Cards" are handed out just as they are in soccer. (DF.311) The number of players on a team in both gamesÑif games—if you count the dragon as a 'member' of the team, which is clearly the case (GL.28)Ñis—is also eleven. The names of the team positions and of the game officials are also the same.

When Tanya gets to Tibidoxs her excellent flying ability gets her on the team. Her first game is broken off before it finishes when disaster strikes Tibidoxs. In her second game, she wins literally single-handed. In her third, she breaks her leg, which is quickly mended at the MAS.

After the first, short Dragon-Ball radio commentary—interesting because of its fresh, tongue-in-cheek look at the game—the Dragon-Ball sequences become long and tedious. They would film—that is to say, cartoon—well, but fall flat on the printed page.

The Magical broadcasting media offer a glimpse of things that are happening in the magical world outside of Tanya's immediate proximity.

Always ready to pun at the drop of a rat (a common ingredient in many magic potions), Emets goes overboard in creating his broadcast scripts. They seem to have more than their share of puns and lampoons. An excerpt of the news on what might—in translated Emets-speak—best be termed The Magical News Enchantwork offers an excellent example of the kind of thing he does there.

> The economic news. The fall on the world's magical markets continues. Over the last week, European toad warts have climbed two and seven tenths percent. The exchange rate for overseas green toe corns continues to fall. The primary reason being attributed to the fall is the numerous erasures and additions being made by Black magicians and banking goblins with access to the books in which the magiccounts are kept. In the words of our economic expert Kharlampiya Zaviral'nyj, the financial crisis will not have any effect at all on the exchange rate for the holes in domestic doughnuts, which are as strong as ever. 'Our wizards can rest assured that they can continue to work magic! Their holes will continue to be holes!' says Kharlampiya Zaviral'nyj confidently. (GL.100)

That works in the climbing Euro, the falling dollar and the Enron accounting scandal, plus the old saw about the worth of the hole in the doughnut, not to be confused with doughnut holes, which are indeed listed on the commodity market, if memory serves.

To show that he was not biased against the West, the cultural news takes a shot at the pride of Russian ballet repertoire, Swan Lake by Peter Ilyich Tchaikovsky. The premiere of the ballet in Moscow at the Bolshoi Theater (1877) choreographed by Julius

(Wentzel) Reisinger was not a success. The first production of Swan Lake with the Petipa/Ivanov choreography as we know it today, was at the Maryinsky Theater in St. Petersburg (1895).

The ballet Gorgul Lake, staged by Ceasar Djavetov, a magicographer famed well beyond the confines of Bald Mountain, premiered yesterday in the concert cave of Shaitan Mountain. In the words of the critics, the first act went well and earned the thunderous applause of the audience. However, during the second act, there was a mass brawl on stage. The gorgulinas could not come to an agreement as to who among them would be the first to kiss the handsome prince, and kicked him with their pointe shoes, so that none of them got him. The handsome prince has been hospitalized. In addition to this, the concert cave was heavily damaged by the caustic tears of the talented dancers. Ceasar Djavetov is convinced that the reason for the failure of Gorgul Lake is an evil spell cast on it by malicious persons who are jealous of him. (GL.101)

The Mail

In the magical world, mail is delivered by cupids, who had found themselves out of work in the "boring" modern world, in which declarations of love are most often made by telephone. "Cupid's arrows don't penetrate anyone any more—people's skin has become much too thick—so the poor cupids have had to take up delivering the mail. After all, they have to have some way of earning their nectar and ambrosia," explains headmaster Chernomorov. (MC.22)

Emets' treatment of this element in his story line is somewhat mixed. He has a number of episodes in which Cupid's arrow really does work. The deputy headmaster, it seems, once broke the favorite bow of one of the cupids, and the cupid took revenge on him by shooting the deputy headmaster with an arrow and making him fall in love with a mermaid. She cannot stand him. This leads to all sorts of consequences. Much as he would like to, the headmaster is unable to remove the spell of love from his deputy, because, as the narrator explains: "the magic of love is the most subtle and complex magic of all. It can only be removed by the one who cast the spell." (DF.10) In another episode, an arrow falls out of the quiver of a cupid delivering a letter to Tanya, and she hides in the couch. Her uncle Herman sits on it, and falls in love with himself. If, as Chernomorov had explained, people's skins were so thick that cupid's arrow did not work any more, then why do they seem to work so well on the deputy headmaster and uncle Herman?

There is also an episode in which Tanya is listening to a radio broadcast from the magical world, where the hostess says that every day she has thousands of wormograms crawl in, and hundreds of cupids fly in with sacks full of letters, all of which contain the same question from young witches: 'How to get married?' (MC.120) According to the hostess, nothing could be simpler. All they have to do is drink a potion of dinosaur bone, mermaid scales, kikimora nails, white raven feathers and dragon blood. From that point, until the next full moon, they will be irresistibly gorgeous, which should give them more than enough time to get married. There is, however, one unfortunate side effect, notes the hostess. When the potion wears off, they will gain 40 kilos (that is 88 pounds for those who still cannot think metric) and grow sideburns, but since there is no divorce in the magical world, this should not be a problem. Tanya's first thought on hearing this is that her Aunt must have used this potion to catch uncle Herman. (MC.121)

When a cupid delivers a letter or a package, the recipient has to 'tip' the messenger with something good to eat, like chocolates or cookies. When a box is delivered to Tanya, the cupids literally hang around in midair waiting for their tip, but Tanya, being new to all this, does not get the hint. One of the other girls has to clue her in. She warns Tanya that, if she does not give the cupids a tip, they just might just shoot her with one of the arrows that they carry around with them in quivers to make her fall in love with someone out of spite, pointing out Shurasik. Tanya turns beet red at the thought, and borrows some chocolates to 'tip' the cupids with. (MC.364)

Cyclopses

In Tanya Grotter, cyclopses play a role that I rather more associate with trolls. They are large, strong, clumsy and none too bright. The guard at the draw-bridge leading into Tibidoxs is the very same cyclops that Ulysses blinded. Headmaster Chernomorov gave him a new eye, taken from a witch who had so many that she never even missed this one. Unfortunately, it is an 'evil eye,' which can cast a deadly curse. (MC.207-208)

The sinister feeling created by this introduction is swept away in book II, when Tanya encounters the cyclops again on her return from the non-magical world. In this scene, the cyclops has a black eye instead of an 'evil eye.' The narrator surmises that the three mythic Russian heroes who form the Tibidoxs strong-arm squad were too lazy again to learn the new password, and just belted the cyclops one to make him let them in.

The exchange between Tanya and the cyclops that follows sounds like a vaudeville routine. When he asks Tanya for the password she gives him the old one. He says that he wants the new one, and she replies: "Black Eye." The cyclops takes that as an insult and draws back to swat her with his battle-ax, but Tanya is quick on her feet. She says: "You can't hit girls." The cyclops has to think about this for a minute. "Not even with an ax?" he asks. "Especially with an ax," says Tanya. Sad that he cannot hit her with an ax, the cyclops still refuses to let her in without the proper password. Tanya sees that this is getting her nowhere fast, so she asks the cyclops to call one of the teachers to let her in. The cyclops, however, is peeved with her and refuses to call one of the teachers, because

Tanya has been making fun of him. To emphasize how put out he is, he turns his back on her, and here comes the punch line. The password is written on the cyclops' back in big chalk letters. Tanya says the password and the cyclops is so surprised that he sits down right on the ground. "You, too!" he says. "Nobody knows it for some reason, and then they all guess it." He just cannot understand it. (DF140-142)

Somewhat later in book II, the cyclopses do a Three Stooges routine, embellished with a touch of Alice in Wonderland. Tanya and her two friends, Bob and Van'ka, are in a part of the school that they should not be, and three card-playing cyclopses are blocking their exit. From her position above the cyclopses, Tanya can see that one of them is cheating. Pretending to scratch his neck, he is getting rid of his extra cards by dropping them behind his collar. The other two are constantly losing, but cannot figure it out. The game is not for money, but for the chance to thump your opponents on the head. When struck, their heads make a sound like a brass pot. (DF.240) The two losers have some serious bumps on their heads by the time that Tanya figures out what to do.

She says an incantation that shifts the scene to Alice in Wonderland. The cards march up out of the cheater's shirt, climb over his shaved head and flutter around in front of his nose like a bunch of butterflies. The other two cyclopses cannot understand where all these other cards had come from, and everything would have been fine, if the cyclops who was cheating had not started trying to chase the cards away. When he began to tear the Queen of Hearts to pieces, she began to scream, hitting the cyclops with her fan: "Help, murder, police. Get him, boys. He's a cheat!" The same idea dawned on the two other cyclopses at the same time, and they stood up. The cheater reached for his club, and a cartoon ball of fighting cyclopses bounced down the stairs, taking out all the intrusion detection incantations along the way. It was followed closely by Tanya, Bob and Van'ka. (DF.252-253)

The examples above show that Emets adds a considerable amount of original material to the story line. His style is humorous, and his point of view is clearly different. The examples also make it clear that Emets did not borrow exclusively from Rowling to create the tale of Tanya Grotter.

Babylon-5

Another good, though less humorous example of a Emets' borrowing is the parallel between the showdown at the end of the first book, in which Chuma-del-Tort interrogates Tanya about the talisman that Tanya's father gave her and an episode from the second season of Babylon-5, entitled "Comes the Inquisitor," in which Delenn is interrogated by Sebastian. The key moment in this comparison is the scene in which the Inquisitor/Chuma-del-Tort demonstrates how easy it would be to stop Delenn's/Tanya's heart. All that he/she has to do is to close his/her hand, as if it were about Delenn's/Tanya's heart and it will stop. The pain and the shadow of death are palpable as the hand tightens its grip, but then, having made his/her point, the Inquisitor/Chuma-del-Tort releases his/her grip, and the interrogation continues. The images and feel of the two scenes are incredibly similar. (MC.392) Magic, as the Technomage Elric explains in "The Geometry of Shadows," is defined by the perspective of the beholder.

The Munsters

Tanya's guardian, uncle Herman is the great-great-grandson of Count Dracula (MC.148). The combination of his relationship to Dracula with his first name bears a strong resemblance to Herman Munster of the American TV series The Munsters, based on Charles Adams' books about The Adams Family. Marilyn always called Herman Munster uncle Herman.

Meet the Durnevs: Tanya's Adoptive Parents

When the Soviet Union collapsed and market capitalism raised its head, Russia found itself awash in "New Russians." In another time and another place, people like this were called the "Nouveau Riche." In the jargon of twentieth-century America, they would be called "Yuppies." The appearance of the "New Russians" was immediately greeted with a host of jokes, poking fun at the things that defined their newness. For example, there is the joke about the New Russian who went to the Hermitage Museum, the storehouse of Russia's national treasures. He is walking through the galleries, when his cell phone rings. He answers the call and plumps down in a chair to talk. The gallery's guard, and old woman, sees this and runs over full of indignation. "What are you doing?!" she says. "That is Empress Catherine's chair." To which the New Russian replies: "Don't worry, granma. If she comes, I'll get up and let her have it."

Tanya's adoptive parents—her uncle Herman and her aunt Ninel'—are just one big "New Russians" joke. Uncle Herman's talking surname says it all. It is Durnev, which is based on the Russian word durnoj (bad), a quite appropriate appellation for a "New Russian." It is also a quite successful play on the sound envelope of Rowling's name: Dursley. In English, Durnev would be approximated by something like Badsley.

Their life is defined in terms of the English loanwords that are part and parcel of "New-Russian-speak." Uncle Herman runs a business with a name that is just so much alphabet soup for most Russians, but is hilarious in its absurdity for bilingual readers like the author. He is the Director of "Socks Second-hand". (Noski Sekond-khend). (MC.5) He goes to work in an "office", while the real Russian word is "kabinet". (MC.35) He gets mad at a subordinate for not getting him the "price" of used toothbrushes, while the real Russian word is "tsena." (MC.36) Aunt Ninel' has a "Tefal" skillet (MC.41), shops at the "supermarket" (MC.84), goes "bowling" (DF.60), buys "chips" (MC.183), "ketchup" (MC.89) and magazines on "fitness and aerobics" (MC.86). These are all things that did not exist in the Soviet Union. The effect in English is something like saying that Tanya's uncle works in 'le office,' and her aunt shops at 'le supermart,' where she buys 'le chips' and 'le ketchup.'

The "New-Russian-speak" words come and go with the Durnevs. When Tanya arrives at school and sets off in search of the headmaster's office, she says that she is looking for his "kabinet" (MC.212), using the real Russian word for office.

The Durnevs live in a chic modern high-rise apartment on Rublev Boulevard (Rublevskoe Shosse) in the Moscow suburbs where the new elite live, and houses and apartments are listed for sale in dollars instead of Rubles. Jokes abound about all the high-priced imported cars that race up and down Rublev Boulevard: Rolls Royces, Bentleys, Lincoln Continentals, Mercedes and BMWs. One day a 700-series Mercedes stopped on Rublev Road. The driver got out and walked up to a group of "New Russians" standing in front of a huge mansion, and said: "Guys, can I drive through here to such-and-so street?" Silence. You can see that they are all thinking hard. After a while one of them raises his head and says: "I don't know about the rest, but I personally don't have any objection."

As if being a "New Russian" was not enough for Emets, Herman Durnev is a politician, too. Emets plays that angle with great style, in a way that will be immediately recognizable in the West, too. Western-style politics, it seems, have finally arrived in Russia, lock, stock and pork barrel.

In contrast to his office, where every available inch of space was crammed full of "discounted junk" and all kinds of used things, everything in the Badsley's apartment was new. (MC.36) While the Durnevs were rich (they even have a cleaning lady, GL.13), Tanya had to wear used clothes that came from uncle Herman's rag trade. (MC.67) Needless to say, they were not nice to Tanya in other ways, too. They called her "stupid" and said that she was a "degenerate." (MC.58) They lied that she was the daughter of a "thief and an alcoholic mother." (MC.67, 100) Uncle Herman beats her. (MC.102)

The fridge is bursting at the seams with food (MC.86), but Tanya has to eat leftover noodles for breakfast. (MC.78) She had to sleep on the glassed-in balcony until it got so cold that her blanket was covered with frost in the morning; then she could sleep inside, on the couch. (MC.49) They never gave her Christmas presents, let her go to movies, paid for her to go on school excursions, or gave her an allowance. Uncle Herman only paid for her school lunches, because it would look funny, if he did not. (MC.61, 100)

Tanya did not just take this lying down. Aunt Ninel' and uncle Herman always drank filtered water, but made Tanya drink water from the tap, so as not to waste filters on her. To get even Tanya would occasionally fill their teapot with water from the toilet. (MC.53)

When she left to go to Tibidoxs, her aunt and uncle did not know anything about it. She just left in the middle of the night, a la Wendy with Peter Pan, but unlike Wendy, she left a note on the mirror in lipstick. (MC.196)

Harry Potter

Harry Potter makes a cameo appearance in book I, in the Tower of Ghosts, where a life-sized model of his broom is on display in a glass coffin. (MC.215) He returns in book III for a larger role, as a member of the "Invisibles" Dragon Ball team that has come to play Tibidoxs for the World Dragon Ball Championship. (GL.256) It is an "English" (GL.260) team with players whose names are full of puns, like:

- Prince Omelet, a Prince Hamlet pun that gets even worse when he flies through the flame of a fire-breathing dragon during the game and Bob-Yagun puns him onto the breakfast table. (GL.273)
- An Ophelia pun, that in Russian asks the question: "Oh, am I a fairy?" (O-Feya-Li-Ya) The running joke that accompanies this name is based on Russian grammar and will be impossible to replicate in English, which does not change the endings of words like Russian does to show which grammatical case they are. (GL.260) For the English translation, she will have to be something like O'Fee, Lee A., obviously the daughter of an Irish Leprechaun who served in the army for a long time and names all his children last name first, first name, middle initial. Unless done by a translator with the same amount of literary skill and imagination as Emets has, the translations will not be anywhere near as funny as the original.
- Sheik Speer (it sounds more like Shakespeare when pronounced in Russian), who is a real Arabian sheik, playing on an English team. (GL.260) This is not as farfetched as it first sounds. Just remember who owns Harrod's.

Harry's name is not Shakespearean, but English, nevertheless. When he introduces himself, he says: Poopper, Hurry Poopper, the "Invisibles," (GL.242, 244) in the hallmark cadence of a James Bond introduction: Bond, James Bond, Universal Exports. Harry's name is based on the same linguist's sleight of hand as the name of Herman Durnev's company: Socks Second Hand Socks (Noski Sekond-khend). It is English spelled in Russian letters, a trick that will escape monolingual Russian readers, but which will be well appreciated by bilingual readers.

All the girls at Tibidoxs have a crush on Hurry. He is the "dream of any girl under the age of 14," says Bob-Yagun, as he introduces Hurry at the start of the game. (GL.261) Tanya's roommate is really taken by Hurry. She even tries on his last name for size, and likes it. (GL.228) She borrows a book from the library entitled How to Be Irresistible: 500 Potions and Love Charms from Cleopatra of Egypt, (GL.235) so that she can make Hurry fall in love with her. Her first effort is baked into a loaf of bread.

In Russia, if they know you are coming, they do not bake a cake, but a loaf of bread, which they present with a small bowl of salt. It is a very great honor to be met with bread and salt, and the guest so welcomed cannot refuse to break off a piece of the bread, dip it in the salt and eat it. Tanya's roommate is sure that she has Hurry firmly in her sights, but, unfortunately, in a scene reminiscent of a Saturday-morning cartoon, she has put too much exploding spice in the bread and it blows up, when Hurry touches it. The result leaves Hurry looking like he is wearing black-face. (GL.243-4) No American political correctness for Emets.

Emets also makes fun of the fact that Hurry flies on an old-fashioned broom. When Tanya makes her first flight on her double bass, she thinks to herself how terrible it must have been for those old-fashioned witches, who flew on brooms. "What is a broom after all? A stick with a bunch of twigs tied to it, that will probably start to roll and shake when the twigs catch an air pocket or when a sidewind hits it." (MC.178) This line of thinking gets a little bit more upbeat treatment, when Hurry gives a radio interview. The host makes a point of telling the listeners that Hurry "arrived, you won't believe this, on a real curiosity, a broom." (GL.164) Bob-Yagun goes on at great length about what a terrible form of airborne transportation a broom is. It does not have any aerodynamics. It's just a stick with a bunch of twigs on the end. It doesn't have a fuel tank, and "if it doesn't have a fuel tank, where do you put the mermaid scales?" (Yagun's flying vacuum cleaner runs on mermaid scales.) (GL.129-130) At a training session, the Tibidoxs Dragon Ball trainer—with stereotypical sarcasm—tells his team that an old witch on a broom flying to the corner store for yogurt flies better than they do, (DF.165) which is hardly a complimentary thing to say about brooms, if you stop to think about it.

At Tanya's school, they fly on almost anything. Bob-Yagun makes his first flight to deliver Tanya's invitation to school in a flying bed. (Since we are at Disney World, I have to mention Bedknobs and Broomsticks.) His normal airborne transportation is a 700 series vacuum cleaner, a skillful play on the very chic 700 series Mercedes, which is very popular in Russia these days. Tanya, of course, flies on a double bass. Rita Shito-Kryto flies on a guitar. Liza Zalizina flies on a cuckoo clock, with a deranged cuckoo that keeps pecking everybody. There is also an abundance of flying carpets.

For those who did not get the subtlety of his earlier parodies, Emets tries to be a little less subtle in book III. Emets at first makes light of the similarities between Tanya and Hurry, and, in essence, Rowling's court case. One of Tanya's teammates, surprised that Tanya has not read about Hurry in the papers, explains to her that: "Well, this Poopper's story is terribly similar to yours. He is also an orphan, and also lived with some relative or other. In addition to that, he was chased by an evil, dreadful Black wizard, who he fought bravely. [. . .] What he had to live through was a nightmare. You wouldn't wish that on your worst enemy." (GL.259) Tanya is sympathetic, and blows Hurry a kiss. Bob-Yagun's comment on the similarity of their names is simply heavy-handed sarcasm. "Did you hear that? Poopper, that's almost the same as Grotter. Can you imagine such a coincidence! It's just some sort of cheap plagiarism, I'm enraged,' he yelled in disgust.'" (GL.129)

That, however, was just the pre-show. The real show is in the interaction between Tanya and Hurry in the World Championship Dragon Ball game. There is only one ball left in play. The team that scores with this ball wins. Tanya and Hurry are both after the ball. They are on a collision course, but neither of them will swerve to avoid the collision. The crash destroys Tanya's double bass and sends Tanya plummeting to the ground below. It also makes time fold back on itself to the point, at which Chuma-del-Tort killed Tanya's parents.

In the new temporal reality, Chuma-del-tort wins. She gets Tanya's talisman, successfully blames professor Chernomorov for the murder, and locks him away in the dungeons of Tibidoxs, where she is the new headmistress. Everything has been turned on its head. Good is evil. Evil is good. (GL.306) Chuma has changed all the words (GL.359), and the new political correctness of Orwellian newspeak is the order of the day. 'Friend' (drug) has become 'nofriend' (nedrug, GL.306), on the same model that Orwell used for making words with opposite meanings in 1984. Saying 'please' and 'thank you' is impolite. One should instead express their 'nothankfulness.' (GL.355-56)

Orwell did not just make newspeak up out of thin air. It is based on the realities of the Communist Revolution in Russia, and allusions to newspeak in a Russian book have a special resonance, especially since 1984 was a banned book under the Communists, and only appeared in print in Russian in the early 1990s.

Tanya, however, is a paradox in this new time. She has not changed, and it is up to her to restore time to its original path, before Chuma-del-Tort can open the Dreadful Gates, release the ancient spirits, and destroy the Dumbbelloids, giving their bodies to the ancient spirits who have so long hungered for bodies to inhabit. (GL.329) In order to triumph, Tanya has to brave fire and crush the Golden Leech. Needless to say, since this is book III of the series, Tanya saves the day and time is returned to its original path, at a point just a second or two before the collision between Tanya and Hurry that caused the wrinkle in time. This time, Hurry swerves, and Tanya gets the ball. The close of the book, however, hints that there is more trouble ahead. As Tanya sees Hurry flying away from her, it seems to her that the end of his broom is made up not of twigs, but of hundreds of golden leeches. (GL.379)

Not to put too fine a point on it, this segment of the book is an allegory of Rowling's court case. The collision between Tanya and Hurry is really between Emets and Rowling. The fold in time, if applied to the real world, would make 1984 a banned book again, and would also make Tanya Grotter impossible, because of the government monopoly on the publishing industry at that time, which would very likely have not allowed Harry Potter to be published in Russian. The form of address used for Chuma-del-Tort in the new temporal reality is Gospozha. This is the form of address that was applied to capitalists and land owners in pre-Communist Russia. Its use was swept away by the 'newspeak' of the Communist revolution, and its renewed use in this story represents a return to Capitalism, also symbolized by the golden leech of the book's title. While the fall of Communism and the rise of Capitalism brought new freedoms to the Russian people, Emets is discovering that his newly acquired freedom of speech is now being restricted not by Communist censorship, but by declarations in the newspeak of Capitalism that his books are plagiarism. The newspeak of Capitalism is the language of the Durnevs, with office instead of kabinet, price instead of tsena, supermarket, bowling, chips, ketchup plus fitness and aerobics. If Rowling is successful, censorship will have returned to Russia. This will doom Russia's inhabitants to being taken over by the spirits of Capitalism, and becoming "New Russians," like the Durnevs. The end is at hand, unless Emets can save the day, by telling the Russian side of the story. He has to brave the fire of the court case and overcome the power of gold to do it.

In determining if Tanya Grotter is a parody of Harry Potter, the comparison that needs to be made is not so much the one between The Lord of the Rings and Bored of the Rings, as the one between Gone with the Wind and The Wind Done Gone. Who will create the literature of the new age in Russia? The victors or the vanquished?

Mark Hooker is an independent scholar at Indiana University's Russian and East European Institute. His current research project is "Tolkien Through Russian Eyes." It examines the sociological impact of the translation and publication of J.R.R. Tolkien's works in post-Soviet Russia. After 70 years of obligatory State atheism, when the Soviet Union collapsed, Russian society began actively seeking new sets of spiritual values. The Christian-like doctrine of Tolkienism has attracted a substantial following. During the Soviet era, The Lord of the Rings was a banned book, which was translated independently by a number of underground translators. Hooker's book relates the history of the publication of Tolkien's works, examines the philosophical distortions introduced by the competing translations, and attempts to explain their origins and how they will be perceived by the Russian reader. He has been published widely in the Tolkien specialist press, in the United States, in Holland (both in Dutch and in English) and in Russia (in Russian). His interest in Harry Potter and Tanya Grotter is all his daughter's fault.

Harassing Harry: The "Demonizing"
of
The Harry Potter Series

A Keynote Address by Judith Krug, Director, Office of Intellectual Freedom at the American Library Association

I'm delighted to be here today to celebrate Harry Potter! He is a phenomenon— and although a fictional character, he has done what no human being has been able to do, namely, to bring an entire generation of young people back to reading. And in the process of reacquainting young people with reading, Harry dispelled two myths:

1) Kids won't read long books! and
2) Kids don't understand—and, therefore, can't follow—complex plots!

Just reiterating those myths makes me laugh. In fact, I can't think of another book— let alone a series—that has reached so many young people so quickly! This fact alone has made Harry Potter a favorite among most—but not all!—librarians and educators.

But there is another aspect of this story that has touched librarians. Harry Potter, wildly popular among young readers and their parents, has also been the target of the largest censorship effort in recent years. The series has been the most frequently challenged title for four years running! With two books yet to be published in the series, and Harry now fully into his teen years, there's no end in sight.

If history is any guide to the future, however, it won't be Harry's budding romance or his surly teenage attitude that riles the censors. It will be his very existence that they find threatening—and attempt to suppress. The reason Harry Potter is challenged is because he is a wizard and he lives in a world of magic. The danger is Harry Potter will tempt readers to witchcraft and the Occult. Indeed some people believe that just the act of reading Harry will actually automatically convert readers into witches!

Another major complaint is that the books glorify evil. When this charge is hurled, I patiently explain that these books are about *good* and evil. Good and evil is a classic theme in children's books, whether it's "Snow White" or "Charlie and the Chocolate Factory." Fairy tales and other fantasy stories have always been a way to teach children about the difference between good and evil and how to make choices. And children love to be scared—a little. If it's too much, they won't read it.

To date, in Harry Potter, good is winning. Harry's very existence proves that. If the person complaining had actually read the book(s), it would quickly become apparent that the love Harry's mother had for him saved him.

But I digress—and before we get any further into specifics, let me give you some background. Librarians do many things, but we have one primary job, namely, to bring people and information together. We do this by making sure our libraries have information and ideas across the spectrum of social and political thought, so people can choose what they want to read or view or listen to. Since libraries provide information for all of the people in their community, we find, from time to time, that not all of our users agree with all of the material we acquire. Some users find materials in their local library collection to be untrue, offensive, harmful, or even dangerous. Nevertheless, if the material is legal, it can legitimately be in the library. A wide range of ideas and information is imperative because libraries serve the information needs of all the people in the community—not just the loudest, not just the most powerful, not even just the majority. Libraries serve everyone—and their information needs and wants differ vastly.

We call this core concept—or, core value!—intellectual freedom. It is not only based on the First Amendment to the U.S. Constitution, but is also the library profession's interpretation of the First Amendment. It means the right of ever person to hold any belief or ideas in whatever way she considers appropriate. The ability to express an idea or a belief, however, is not very meaningful without an audience on the other end to hear, read, or view that expression. Intellectual freedom then, is the right to express your ideas and the right of others to be able to hear them.

As I said, our concept of intellectual freedom finds its roots in the First Amendment to the U.S. Constitution:

> Congress shall make no law respecting an establishment of religion, or prohibiting the free exercise thereof; or abridging the freedom of speech or of the press; or the right of the people peaceably to assemble, and to petition the Government for a redress of grievances.

That's it—45 words—45 words that go a long way toward making the United States of America unique among the nations of the world.

The uniqueness of the First Amendment lies not only in its guarantees, but also in its lack of proscriptions. For instance, the First Amendment guarantees freedom of speech—but it doesn't mandate that the speech be truthful, honest, equal, sensitive, tasteful, showing good judgment, respectful or any other adjective you can think of. If you want to lie through your teeth, the First Amendment gives you the right to do so. But—you have to live with the consequences of your speech.

The importance of the First Amendment is that it is the mechanism which allows us to be a nation of self-governors. We live in a constitutional republic—a government of the people, by the people, and for the people. But this form of government can only function if its electorate has information available and accessible on which to make its decisions. And because librarianship's fundamental value is intellectual freedom, the nation has available and accessible the information it needs in our nation's libraries.

With that framework in mind, I'd like to tell you about the types of materials we see challenged in schools and libraries.

A book challenge is a formal, written complaint, requesting that library materials be removed from the collection. Books are most frequently challenged in schools and school libraries, and challenges in public libraries most often revolve around materials that are available to minors. A full 75%—or three out of every four challenges—fall in these categories.

OIF maintains a database of challenges and we see the same types of materials come up year after year. In 2002, 515 challenges were reported to OIF. We estimate that for every challenge reported to the office, another four or five go unreported. The most frequently challenged books of 2002 were:

1) J.K. Rowling/ Harry Potter series

Rowling's series follows young wizard Harry Potter through his years at Hogwart's School of Witchcraft and Wizardry. Harry is famous as a survivor of the wizard who tried to kill him. He is left only with a lightning-bolt scar on his forehead, curiously refined sensibilities, and a host of mysterious powers. The novels chronicle his adventure-filled school years with best friends Ron and Hermione.

Challenged for: Occult/Satanism

2) *Phyllis Reynolds Naylor/Alice series*

Naylor's series follows Alice—a girl coping with adolescence after her mother's death. The first book of the series finds Alice longing for a woman's guidance as she enters puberty; subsequent entries show her falling in love for the first time, learning about adult responsibilities, and contending with all the ups and downs of her teenage years.

Challenged for: sexual content, unsuited to age group

3) *Robert Cormier/The Chocolate War*

The masterful account of freshman Jerry Renault's lonely battle against the ruling powers of his school, The Chocolate War is the story of his refusal to participate in his school's fundraiser.

Challenged for: offensive language, sexual content, violence

4) *Maya Angelou/I Know Why the Caged Bird Sings*

I Know Why the Caged Bird Sings is story of Maya Angelou's early life in Arkansas and California. At the age of five, Maya and her brother Bailey are taken to St. Louis to visit their mother, but after Maya is raped they are returned to the rock-hard loving care of their grandmother in Stamps, Arkansas. Maya stops speaking for five years but becomes a keen observer of everything around her, including the racial politics and divisions of her town.

Challenged for: rape, sexual content, racism, offensive language, violence, and being unsuited to age group.

5) *S. E. Hinton/Taming the Star Runner*

A misguided youth is sent to stay with his uncle in a town where his cool city ways don't earn him the respect they did at home. He turns his back on the kids his age, but finds friendship with Casey, who runs a riding school at the ranch. She's the bravest person Travis has ever met, and crazy enough to try to tame the Star Runner, her beautiful, dangerous horse who's always on edge, about to explode. It's clear to Travis that he and the Star Runner are two of a kind—creatures not meant to be tamed.

Challenged for: offensive language.

6) *Dav Pilkey/Captain Underpants*

The adventures of George and Harold, two second graders who hypnotize their school principal and turn him into their own made-up superhero ("Captain Underpants"). The books are full of atrocious schoolboy humor and cartoon-style illustrations that have made the series wildly popular among young readers.

Challenged for: models bad behavior (disrespectful of adults, disobedience)

7) *Mark Twain/The Adventures of Huckleberry Finn*

A complex masterpiece and compelling adventure story, it is the story of Huck, in flight from his murderous father, and Nigger Jim, in flight from slavery, who pilot their raft thrillingly through treacherous waters, surviving a crash with a steamboat, betrayal by rogues, and the final threat from the bourgeoisie. Informing all this is the presence of the River, described in palpable detail by Mark Twain, the former steamboat pilot, who transforms it into a richly metaphoric entity.

Challenged for: racism, insensitivity, and offensive language

8) *Katherine Paterson/Bridge to Terabithia*

Best friends Jess and Leslie create a secret kingdom in the woods named Terabithia, where the only way to get into the castle is by swinging out over a gully on an enchanted rope. Here they reign as king and queen, fighting off imaginary giants and the walking dead, sharing stories and dreams, and plotting against the schoolmates who tease them. Jess and Leslie find solace in the sanctuary of Terabithia until a tragedy strikes and Leslie dies in an accident.

Challenged for: offensive language and Occult/Satanism.

9) *Mildred Taylor/ Roll of Thunder, Hear My Cry*

Newbery Medal-winning *Roll of Thunder, Hear My Cry* tells the story of one African American family, fighting to stay together and strong in the face of brutal racist attacks, illness, poverty, and betrayal in the Deep South of the 1930s. Nine-year-old Cassie Logan, growing up protected by her loving family, has never had reason to suspect that any white person could consider her inferior or wish her harm. But during the course of one devastating year when her community begins to be ripped apart by angry night riders threatening African Americans, she and her three brothers come to understand why the land they own means so much to their Papa. "Look out there, Cassie girl. All that belongs to you. You ain't never had to live on nobody's place but your own and long as I live and the family survives, you'll never have to. That's important. You may not understand that now but one day you will. Then you'll see."

Challenged for: insensitivity, racism, and offensive language.

10) *Jean Craighead George/ Julie of the Wolves*

At 13, an orphan, and unhappily married, Miyax runs away from her husband's parents' home, hoping to reach San Francisco and her pen pal. But she becomes lost in the vast Alaskan tundra, with no food, no shelter, and no idea which is the way to safety. Now, more than ever, she must look hard at who she really is. Is she Miyax, Eskimo girl of the old ways? Or is she Julie (her "gussak"-white people-name), the modernized teenager who must mock the traditional customs? And when a pack of wolves begins to accept her into their community, Miyax must learn to think like a wolf as well.

Challenged for: sexual content, offensive language, being unsuited to age group.

Although the "Top 10" is continuing work in progress, Harry Potter has been stuck at the top of the list since 1999, and the grounds for challenging the series are consistently "witchcraft." While "witchcraft" is not an unusual complaint, the most common reasons giving for challenges to library materials are sexual content and offensive language.

For good measure, some people list as many things as they can on the challenge form. So in addition to witchcraft, we've heard complaints that Harry Potter encourages disrespect for adults and authority, and that the Dursleys are mean. In one case, the complainant alleged that the novels promote drug use—all those portions—and we've seen a handful on the grounds that the series promotes Wicca and, therefore, violates the separation of church and state.

As I said, last year, 515 challenges were reported to OIF. Reports come primarily from librarians and teachers who call or write to our office and voluntarily report the challenges occuring in their communities. Challenges are kept strictly confidential.

While we don't have definite numbers, the good new is that, in most cases, challenged library materials are retained; the books are not removed. The bad news is that every day books are challenged, and ever challenged book is potentially a banned book.

People try to remove materials containing ideas they believe are untrue or harmful in some way. Most people who bring challenges are well meaning. They are primarily concerned about protecting children, and to a lesser extent, society at large, from materials and ideas they consider harmful.

Because challenges to the Harry Potter books have been on the grounds of witchcraft or Satanism, challenges have primarily come from evangelical Christians on the right. As is typical of challenges, most are local and involve an individual or perhaps a small group of people. While we do not have evidence of an organized effort behind the challenges, we do believe that some religious groups have encouraged local action. This is because of the unprecedented volume of challenges and also the fact that so many of the challengers have not actually read the books.

Instead, they have "heard" about their dangers.

A quick aside: we had a slew of cases after *The Onion* reported that Harry Potter was turning children to the Occult and detailed the Satanic practices of several pre-teens. *The Onion*, for those of you who aren't familiar with it, is a satiric news weekly that pokes fun at current events and popular culture. The eleven year old witches it described were, of course, figments of their imagination. The commentary was aimed at the very people who took it seriously. Although the OIF staff thought the article was hilarious, many librarians were put in the difficult position of explaining to irate parents that their "proof" was pure fiction.

Interestingly enough, while we often see challenges to books coming from parents, parents are also the biggest defenders of many of books. This has certainly been true for Harry. While he may face an unparalleled level of criticism, he also received uncommon support. When word gets out that the books have been banned or challenged, supporters come out of the woodwork.

One example of this took place in Zeeland, Michigan when the books were really just beginning to take off. In an effort to avoid controversy, the superintendent restricted access to the books and forbid the local schools from purchasing copies of the titles still forthcoming. Word got out, and the community took action. It was a long, hard fight, but the community demanded the restrictions be rescinded, and got those books back on the shelves! We have seen this story played out again and again throughout the country.

The *Harry Potter* books make an intriguing case study of censorship in schools and libraries. In some ways, it is unusual but in others it's textbook. The first Harry Potter challenge was reported to the Office in October of 1999. In only 3 months time, we received reports of more challenges to Harry Potter then any other book during that entire year. I can only speculate as to why that is, but I believe it has to do with the overwhelming success of the series, and the onslaught of publicity surrounding the publication of the third book in the series. Interestingly, the first two books were published without incident. But, once the challenges began, they were unbelievable. And, tellingly, the novels are usually challenged as a series in its entirety. We rarely receive a challenge to individual titles in the series. With other series, challenges usually focus on one or two specific titles.

This raises an important point, namely, that challenged books are books that are read. This is true with popular books, like *Harry Potter*, and also with books that are widely read because they are mainstays of English classes—*Adventures of Huckleberry Finn, Of Mice and Men, Lord of the Flies.*

Considering this is Nimbus—2003, a symposium on Harry Potter, I'm willing to bet you've enjoyed the books and have probably even shared them with the young people in your lives.

Nonetheless, we must recognize that not every book is for every child. Parents know their children best and should guide their children's reading. If parents think Harry Potter, or any other book for that matter, is inappropriate for their child, they should discuss it with their child. If the book is being used in a class, they should request an alternative selection. (As far as I'm aware, Harry has never been used as a classroom text but has been used as an incentive.) They should not, however, impose their beliefs on every other member of the community. When a book is removed from a school or library, it limits the access of all the members of the community, not just those who dislike the work. Removing the book imposes the will of that one parent, or group of parents, on all the other parents and children in the community.

And that, I think is really the crux of the issue.

Obviously, not everything in the library is suitable for every person. And this is true for adults as well as children. There is not book or magazine or any other piece of library material that is suitable for everyone who walks in. I guarantee that each and every one of us can find something offensive and distasteful in the library!

But the question is, who is going to limit your use—and your children's use—of the library? Who is going to decide what you can and can not read? That is not—and can not be—the responsibility of the librarian. Each individual must make his or her own selections. For children, that right, and responsibility, rests with the parents. And only the parents.

The most common reason given for a book challenge is because of sexual content. Books like Maya Angelou's autobiography *I know Why the Caged Bird Sings* and Robbie Harris's *It's Perfectly Normal: A Book About Changing Bodies, Growing Up, Sex and Sexual Health* fall into this category.

The second most common objection given is offensive language or profanity. *The Chocolate War* by Robert Cormier, *Blubber* by Judy Blume, and *Of Mice and Men* by Steinbeck are just a few of the books frequently challenged because of language.

Other reasons we hear for book challenges include Satanism, which covers the Harry Potter objections, and Sensitivity, which means cultural sensitivity and includes racism and sexism. *Of Mice and Men* falls into this category, which often overlaps with offensive language. *The Adventures of Huckleberry Finn* is also frequently targeted because the language is "insensitive."

These subjects and titles have been fairly consistent over the years. The old standbys remain on the top ten list year after year. And I love that! That means that censors, real and would be, are not making the headway they think they are. Books that matter are still in libraries, whether public or school. For all the effort, Harry Potter is widely available in schools and libraries. Materials that contain messages people¾young and not so young¾can understand, can relate to and that contribute to their growth and their ability to think more clearly—are still our stock in trade.

A library's role never has been, is not currently and will not be in the future to keep people from the information they need and want. I believe our job is more difficult today than it's ever been in my almost 40 year career. Unfortunately, I think it will become ever more difficult. But we cannot govern ourselves without information to enlighten our decisions. If the United States is to continue to be a nation of self-governors, the people must have available and accessible the information they need to make decisions.

James Madison defined it almost 200 years ago: "A popular government, without popular information, or the mean of acquiring it, is but a prologue to a farce or a tragedy; or perhaps both. Knowledge will forever govern ignorance; and a people who mean to be their own governors must arm themselves with the power which knowledge gives."

Judith F. Krug is director of the Office for Intellectual Freedom of the American Library Association (ALA), a position she has held since 1967. In this capacity, Ms. Krug assists libraries and librarians in upholding First Amendment principles and resisting censorship in order to fulfill their responsibilities to bring people together with the information they need and want. Ms. Krug also serves as executive director of the ALA's sister organization, the Freedom to Read Foundation (FTRF), which participates in First Amendment litigation. Ms. Krug is a noted speaker and author in the area of intellectual freedom. In addition to her professional responsibilities, she serves as a Senator of the Phi Beta Kappa Society, chair of the Board of Directors of the Center for Democracy and Technology, chair of Media Coalition, vice-chair of the Internet Education Foundation, and a member of the Advisory Board of GetNetWise.

Harry Potter and the Prisoner of Azkaban:
A Case Against the Death Penalty

Joy Morgenstern

The Harry Potter books are a magical journey through a world we've all come to love, but underlying this journey is a tale of the moral development of a boy approaching adulthood. That this boy will grow to be a moral man of heroic proportions seems, at least in the early books, to be implicit. However, the process is less than certain to Harry himself, who worries about his own worthiness. In an oft-quoted line from *Harry Potter and the Chamber of Secrets*, Dumbledore says, "It is our choices, Harry, that show what we truly are, far more than our abilities." During the course of the Harry Potter series, we see Harry struggling to make decisions that are moral and righteous—he desperately wants to be worthy of Gryffindor house, which he believes represents all that is noble and good, and not Slytherin house, which to him stands for the evil forces that killed his parents. Thanks to the Sorting Hat Harry is only too aware that he carries both of these potentials within him.

In Chapter 17 of *Harry Potter and the Prisoner of Azkaban*, Harry is faced with what is up until then probably the most crucial moral choice he has ever faced:

> *"Harry raised the wand. Now was the moment to do it. Now was the moment to avenge his mother and father. He was going to kill Black. He had to kill Black. This was his chance."* (p. 342, US edition)

In countless literary works the hero, in the same situation as Harry, kills his foe, thus avenging the death of his loved ones. However, Harry Potter does not do so. He *chooses* not to kill Black, and also later chooses not to allow the man who turns out to be the real culprit to be killed. Is this choice made out of weakness? Harry thinks so, at first:

> *"Harry stood there, feeling suddenly empty. He hadn't done it. His nerve had failed him."* (p. 343, US edition)

There is nothing in any of the other characters' attitudes, however, nor anything in the text, that suggests that Harry has acted less than courageously in failing to kill Black. This is a considerable departure from the traditional hero legend. So *why* didn't Harry kill Black? Was it really lack of courage? Or was it because he wasn't truly sure that it was the right thing to do? Or was it because Crookshanks, an innocent bystander who is loved by one of his best friends, would be killed too? Does something about Black himself stop Harry?

We don't know exactly what stops Harry from killing Black (or from trying to; it is the source of much debate by fans whether Harry actually had the ability to kill him, despite the fact that he clearly believes he does). However, we do know why, after learning that Pettigrew is the one guilty of all the crimes attributed to Sirius Black, Harry refuses to allow Remus Lupin and Black to kill *him*. Harry says to Pettigrew:

> *"I'm not doing this for you. I'm doing it because—I don't reckon my dad would've wanted them to become killers—just for you."*

Harry states a clear moral precept—that by killing even the most evil of villains, one becomes a killer oneself. This is reminiscent of the words of anti-death penalty activist Sister Helen Prejean on the execution of Timothy McVeigh, who murdered 169 men, women and children in the 1984 Oklahoma City Federal Building bombing:

> *"Of course, any decent human being cannot but feel outrage at McVeigh's unspeakably evil act. Outrage at the death and suffering of innocent human beings is part of moral sensitivity. Outrage, yes. Imitation, never. In the books of justice, if anyone deserves to die for a horrendous deed, it's Timothy McVeigh, but do we deserve to kill him? What happens to us as we kill him?"* (1)

It is probably not coincidence that Harry Potter expresses similar sentiments, given what is known about author J.K. Rowling's political views. For example, Rowling once worked for Amnesty International, (2) an organization very actively involved in opposition to the death penalty. Many of the arguments articulated by anti-death penalty activists find their parallel in *Harry Potter and the Prisoner of Azkaban*.

Out of eleven more or less discrete arguments against the death penalty, culled from discussions with various people and web sites, including those listed below (3, 4), direct parallels can be found for five of those arguments, and two more of those arguments may be relevant. The remaining four are not applicable.

The first argument has already been discussed—a person who kills for even the most justifiable reason becomes a murderer. This argument is the most clearly articulated by Rowling when Harry states that he will not allow Sirius Black and Remus Lupin to kill Peter Pettigrew because he does not want them to be killers. It is a possible explanation for why Harry fails to kill Sirius Black. Harry is clearly angry enough to do so, but as he is about to (try to) kill Sirius, he may start to realize what it takes to be a killer and ultimately decides that he does not want to be one. Further evidence that Harry believes that those who kill, for any reason, are murderers, is found in *Harry Potter and the*

Order of the Phoenix. Harry's interpretation of the prophecy that either he or Voldemort must die at the hand of the other is that he must be "either murderer or victim" (p. 849, US edition). Harry is greatly affected by this—he feels that "an invisible barrier separated him from the rest of the world. He was—he had always been—a marked man . . . his life must include, or end in, murder" (p. 855-856).

Another argument against the death penalty is that it seems to be primarily motivated by revenge, which is neither healthy nor productive. Harry certainly does want revenge on Sirius Black. By the time Harry meets Sirius in the Shrieking Shack, he is so angry that he cannot see or hear anything else. He desperately wants to avenge the death of his parents and to retaliate for his miserable life with the Dursleys. Death penalty advocates often counter this argument by saying that it's not revenge they are seeking; they are seeking to protect others from the same fate as the killer's victim. But when Harry says to Black, "You killed my parents . . . . You sold them to Voldemort. That's all I need to know," it is clear that Harry was not thinking about protecting others—he was thinking only of revenge.

A third argument against the death penalty is that even the most despicable person has someone, somewhere who cares about him or her, who will suffer from the killer's death. This is symbolized by Hermione's cat, Crookshanks, who sits on Sirius' chest as Harry ponders killing him. In order to kill Sirius, Harry will have to kill Crookshanks as well. This would not only punish Crookshanks for being Sirius' friend, but would also hurt Hermione, who loves Crookshanks.

Another important argument against the death penalty is that the evidence against the accused is rarely totally clear. We can never be sure that we know the truth. This is certainly the case in *Harry Potter and the Prisoner of Azkaban*. From the early chapters of the book until almost the last, the evidence against Sirius Black seems compelling. Everyone in Harry's life, including many adults whom he trusts—Hagrid, his other teachers, Arthur Weasley, and no less an authority than the Minister of Magic himself—has made it clear that they believe Sirius Black is responsible for the deaths of James and Lily Potter. And, as even Dumbledore later points out, "Sirius has not acted like an innocent man." (p. 392).

Of course, it turns out that we do *not* know the truth. We do have a few hints, such as Rosmerta's remark: "Do you know, I still have trouble believing it. Of all the people to go over to the Dark Side, Sirius Black was the last I'd have thought . . . I mean, I remember him when he was a boy at Hogwarts. If you'd told me then what he was going to become, I'd have said you'd had too much mead," (p. 203, US edition) and Lupin's enigmatic comment about Black, "Yes, I know him . . . or I thought I did." (p. 243).

If Harry *had* actually killed Sirius Black, he would have unintentionally destroyed the man who would later become the closest thing to a father to him and added yet another disastrous event to his tragic life. Fortunately, Harry is not able to bring himself to commit murder before he discovers the truth about Sirius Black. His decision to refuse to allow Lupin and Black to kill Pettigrew, the real culprit, may have been colored by his realization of how close he came to making a grave, irrevocable, and horrible error.

The fifth argument often cited by death penalty opponents is that the justice system in many societies is unfair, arbitrary, and tainted by bigotry. In the United States the charge is generally that the justice system is racist and that poor people have an unfair disadvantage because they can not afford to obtain competent counsel. Wizarding society also seems to have a justice system fraught with problems. For example, Sirius Black was never actually given a trial before being sent to Azkaban. The wizarding world's justice system is explored much further the two subsequent books, which make it clear that their legal system is arbitrary, corrupt and devoid of even the most minimum standards of due process.

This is particularly evident in *Harry Potter and the Goblet of Fire*, when the Minister of Magic, Cornelius Fudge, essentially issues a death sentence to Barty Crouch, Jr. without any sort of due process and in clear abuse of his power.

Two more arguments against the death penalty may have some relevance. Many people argue that it is simply wrong to kill under any circumstances. This may be some of Harry's motivation for not killing Black, or for not wanting Pettigrew to be killed. Another argument against the death penalty, although perhaps an argument that is pronounced less often, is that the death penalty is actually an *insufficient* punishment for a crime as terrible as murder—a life sentence in jail is actually worse. People who believe this argue that a murderer should have to live with his/her crime. It is possible that this is some of Harry's motivation for keeping Pettigrew alive, especially considering that Harry does argue that sending Pettigrew to Azkaban is a deserved punishment.

There are four more arguments against the death penalty that do *not*appear in *Harry Potter and the Prisoner of Azkaban*, but may nevertheless form part of Rowling's motivation. One argument is that killing someone amounts to cruel and unusual punishment. This is not really applicable, as we don't know how Harry intended to kill Sirius or how Sirius and Remus intended to kill Pettigrew. We could presume that Sirius and Remus would use *Avada Kedavra*, which seems to be relatively quick and painless. The second non-relevant argument is that people who kill are people with problems such as mental illness or drug addiction, whose problems were generally evident long before they started killing and who should have received treatment. The other two non-relevant arguments are that studies show that the death penalty doesn't actually deter crime (and in fact may increase the crime rate) and that the judicial process required for the death penalty process is very costly.

It seems clear that Rowling has allowed, or even intended, her political views on this issue (and other issues) to influence the plot development of the Harry Potter series. Rowling's strong feelings about moral and political issues have clearly guided her development of Harry himself as a hero. She does not want Harry to be the classic swashbuckling hero, arrogantly dispensing his own arbitrary brand of justice to evildoers. She is insisting that her hero have mercy, compassion, and humility. Harry's moral development is brought to a head in this book by the moral choices he faces in the Shrieking Shack. This may be an important reason why so many Harry Potter fans find *Harry Potter and the Prisoner of Azkaban* to be their favorite book in the series. For example, in a poll on the HP for Grownups Yahoo group, 707 (58%) of 1222 respondents chose it as their favorite of the first four books, and 209 (29%) of 720 respondents picked it as their second favorite.

While the popularity of *Harry Potter and the Prisoner of Azkaban* among fans can likely be attributed to many factors, one is clearly the strength of its plot, which makes a strong moral and political argument against what many people see as a brutal, inhumane, arbitrary, and worthless practice that has been abolished in most of the world.

Works Cited

Statement about the Execution of Timothy McVeigh by Sister Helen Prejean, CSJ. (http://www.prejean.org/Statement.html)

"Who hasn't met Harry?," *Guardian Unlimited*, February 16, 1999. (http://www.the-leaky-cauldron.org/quickquotes/articles/1999/0299-guardian-carey.htm)

http://deathpenaltyinfo.msu.edu/c/about/arguments/contents.htm

Arguments for and against the death penalty in the United States by Robert Lebowitz, Digital Freedom Network. (http://www.dfn.org/focus/death-penalty/arguments.htm)

Dr. Joy Morgenstern is an environmental consultant who lives and works in Washington, D.C. She has been a Harry Potter fan since the summer of 1999.

Gender, Identity,
Race & Class

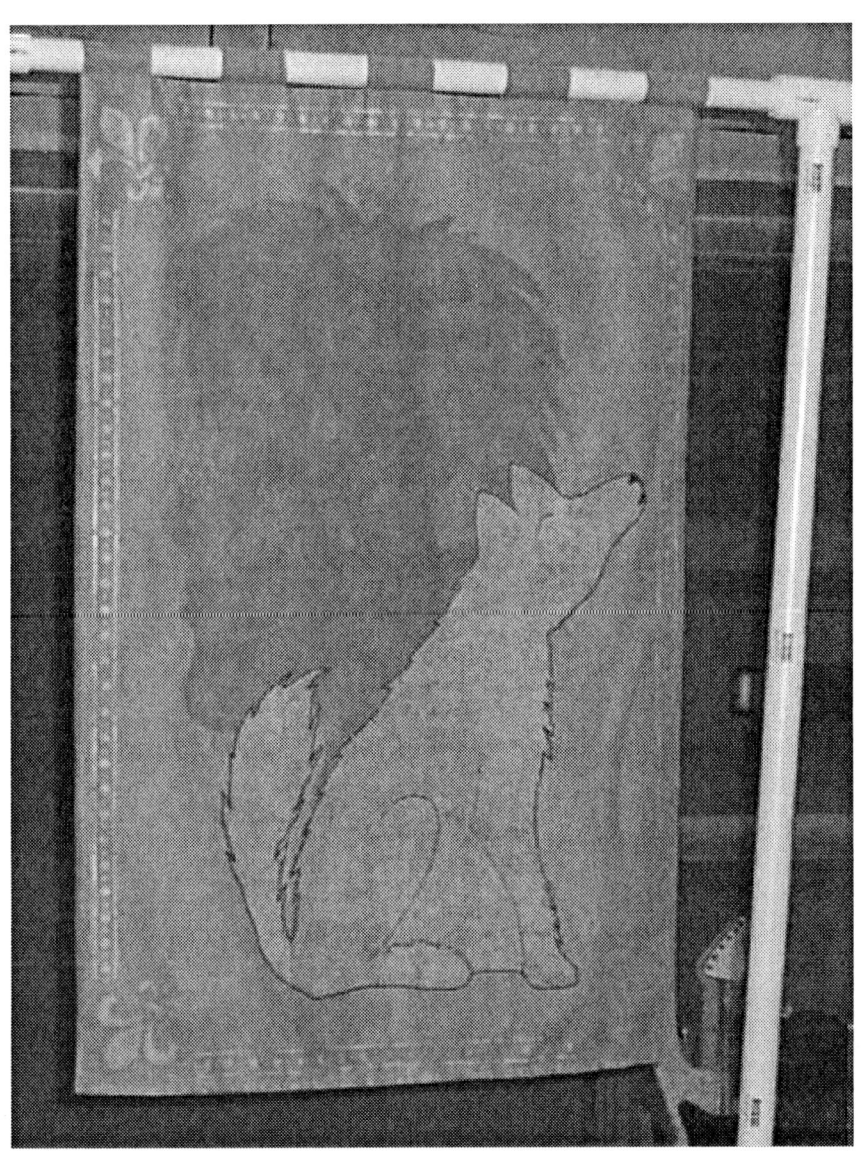

S.P.E.W./spew,
or, *Hermione Spews A Badge*

Bharati Kasibhatla

During one of my class discussions on the house-elves in *Harry Potter and the Goblet Of Fire*, a student insisted that the problem with Hermione's project of promoting elfish welfare is that she attacks the *wrong* people. To this student, an attack on Malfoy's conservative "mudblood" politics is permissible, even desirable; but an attack on Dumbledore's system of liberal slavery is unacceptable. My student argues that Dumbledore is a benevolent force even if this force implies an imposition of power, because such power is "necessary" for the benefit of the house-elves. In *The Goblet Of Fire*, Harry's and Ron's translation of the acronym S.P.E.W. into *spew,* and their accompanying animosity against Hermione's activism parallel my student's resistance to Hermione's radical politics. This paper argues that the rhetorical move from S.P.E.W. to *spew* creates a context within which the ideal of liberalism can be employed in the service of an iniquitous system of power. In other words, Dumbledore's 'liberal' politics allows him to retain his hundred house-elves as slaves, just as it allows Dumbledore to retain Hagrid as his faithful servant. Notably, Harry successfully duplicates this pattern in his relationship with Dobby. The links between Dumbledore and the house-elves, Dumbledore and Hagrid, and Harry and Dobby, are neatly constructed in the text as equitable; a construction that naturalizes some forms of slavery and represents them as benign and desirable. It is precisely this elision of the dominance of the wizards and witches over the house-elves that Hermione challenges in her spirited espousal of elfish welfare. Her protest is read as hysterical and undesirable for the house-elves because it is, in effect, undesirable to the stability of Dumbledore's reign. Hermione's radical potential lies in her challenge to Dumbledore, and concomitantly to Harry's hero narrative, which draws its sustenance from Dumbledore's wisdom.

An important motivation behind the *Harry Potter* series (I use the American version of the texts for this paper) is the maintenance of a locus of benevolent power under Dumbledore's leadership. So, firstly the series undertakes to establish that this power is benevolent by contrasting Dumbledore with a dictatorial and evil alternative. Voldemort functions as the necessary threat to maintain the need for unity and discipline. As the audience begins by identifying with Harry Potter and also Hogwarts as a space that provides Harry with an escape from his 'bad' relatives, the audience is invested in Hogwarts as a positive location. Given that Voldemort threatens the stability of Hogwarts and consequently threatens Harry's happiness, Voldemort's presence reinforces Hogwarts as an ideal space. Presented with the formidable and undesirable alternative that Voldemort represents, the audience prefers the maintenance of Dumbledore's power to any questioning of the internal inequities of the system under Dumbledore's governance.

In his essay "Governmentality," Michel Foucault points to the similar desire to maintaining sovereignty in his analysis of the development of the art of government from the sixteenth to the eighteenth centuries. He describes the 'common good' as obedience to the sovereign.

> 'the common good' refers to a state of affairs where all the subjects without exception obey the laws, accomplish the tasks expected of them, practice the trade to which they are assigned, and respect order so far as this order conforms to the laws imposed by God on nature and men: in other words, 'the common good' means essentially obedience to the law, either that of their earthly sovereign or that of God, the absolute sovereign. In every case, what characterizes the end of sovereignty, this common and general good, is in sum nothing other than submission to sovereignty. This means that the end of sovereignty is circular: the end of sovereignty is the exercise of sovereignty. The good is obedience to law, hence the good for sovereignty is that people should obey it. (Burchell 95)
> [BW_Dobby]

If this is true of the late sixteenth century, Foucault records the changes and development through the next two centuries and points to the triangle of "sovereignty—discipline—government, which has as its primary target the population and as its essential mechanism the apparatuses of security" (102). The "common good" in *The Goblet Of Fire* is the maintenance of Dumbledore's sovereignty by disciplining the population of Hogwarts and clamping down on internal dissent. However it is important to note that the disciplining of Hogwarts cannot be a coercive act, primarily because Dumbledore is a liberal in opposition to Voldemort, the dictator. So any dissent against Dumbledore's system is managed by making an appeal to issues of security and the seriousness of Voldemort's threat to Hogwarts and the entire magical world.

Hermione's dissent is constantly undermined on the pretext of Voldemort's threat. For example, after Mr. Crouch dismissed his house-elf Winky for ostensibly conjuring the death mark, Hermione and Ron argued about Mr. Crouch's indictment of Winky.

> "The way they were treating her!" said Hermione furiously. "Mr. Diggory, calling her 'elf' all the time . . . and Mr. Crouch! He knows she didn't do it and he's still going to sack her! He didn't care how frightened she'd been, or how upset she was—it was like she wasn't even human!"

"Well, she's not," said Ron.

Hermione rounded on him.

"That doesn't mean she hasn't got feelings, Ron. It's disgusting the way-"

"Hermione I agree with you," said Mr. Weasley quickly, beckoning her on, but now's not the time to discuss elf rights." (GOF 139)

There are two ways that Hermione's response is disciplined in this passage—the first is Mr. Weasley's appeal to the larger danger that faces the magic world, which requires him to be active in the fight against Voldemort instead of focusing on the problematic of house-elves. The second way the text indicates that Hermione's reaction is excessive is in its use of words like "furiously" and "rounded." Ron seems to make the obvious point that Winky is not human, and Hermione's argument would have been much more effective were she allowed a more reasoned tone. Instead, Hermione is constantly relegated to the status of the hysteric, which makes it possible for the text to dismiss her position as excessive and tangential, though not entirely incorrect. Also, by rescuing Dobby without challenging Dumbledore's governance, Harry provides the more acceptable alternative, and also proves to be the heir to Dumbledore's power.

Sirus does not dismiss Hermione as easily. He says, "If you want to know what a man's like, take a good look at how he treats his inferiors, not his equals" (525). Even Sirius, however, fails to think beyond the liberal framework of the text. He is not motivated by the condition of the house-elves, but is concerned with defeating Voldemort. His use of the word "inferiors" is telling. In their preoccupation with ensuring the safety of the Dumbledore system, Mr. Weasley and Sirius remain blind to the very structures they are working to protect. Hermione's plea for elf-rights will always be untimely because she opposes the "common good" and challenges the very structure that the others are trying to protect. Her radical demands make it impossible for the wizarding world to maintain an unequal and stratified society that Foucault argues is necessary for sovereignty. The text justifies societal stratification by appealing to 'natural' differences—differences that are not threatened by individual cases of benevolence. So when Dumbledore rescues Hagrid from an unjust fate, and when Harry rescues Dobby from slavery, the text valorizes these acts as acts of benevolence and tolerance since these acts don't challenge the larger framework. On the contrary, they justify the larger framework because, by rescuing Hagrid and Dobby, Dumbledore and Harry respectively prove their capability for doing good and therefore, their capability for leadership. Thus Dobby reiterates his respect for Harry Potter, who excels his own reputation of goodness. On the other hand, Hermione strives to create an atmosphere where the house-elves are equal to the wizards—a desire that directly challenges the naturalized power structure of the text.

The resistance to Hermione's S.P.E.W. takes many forms, ranging from the insistence that the house-elves like being enslaved to the belief that elves are not really enslaved at Hogwarts. Notably, Ron, George, and Hagrid try to convince Hermione to stop demanding elf-rights because, as Hagrid puts it, "it'd be doin' 'em an unkindness, Hermione . . . It's in their nature ter look after humans, that's what they like, see? Yeh'd be makin' 'em unhappy ter take away their work, an' insultin' 'em if yeh tried to pay 'em" (*GOF* 265). Like Hagrid, Fred and George refuse to buy S.P.E.W. badges. George also tries to convince Hermione that the house-elves at Hogwarts are indeed happy. He tells Hermione, "we've met them, and they're *happy*. They think they've got the best job in the world" (239). Harry and Ron, we are told, pay two sickles only to keep Hermione quiet, and "some people, like Neville, had paid up just to stop Hermione from glowering at them. A few seemed mildly interested in what she had to say, but were reluctant to take a more active role in campaigning. Many regarded the whole thing as a joke" (239).

Harry's and Ron's reaction to Hermione's criticism of *Hogwarts, A History* effectively reinforces Hermione's activism as obsessive and thus allows the reader to dismiss her position.

> [Hermione] noticed them all looking at her and said, with her usual air of impatience that nobody else had read all the books she had, "it's all in *Hogwarts, A History*. Though, of course, that book's not *entirely* reliable. *A Revised History of Hogwarts* would be a more accurate title. Or *A Highly Biased and Selective History of Hogwarts, Which Glosses Over the Nastier Aspects of the School.*"
>
> What are you on about?" said Ron, though Harry thought he knew what was coming.
>
> "*House-Elves!*" said Hermione, her eyes flashing. "Not once, in over a thousand pages, does *Hogwarts, A History* mention that we are all colluding in the oppression of a hundred slaves!"
>
> Harry shook his head and applied himself to his scrambled eggs. His and Ron's lack of enthusiasm had done nothing whatsoever to curb Hermione's determination to pursue justice for house-elves. (238)

Harry's and Ron's lack of enthusiasm and in particular, their insistence on referring to her movement as "spew" suggests the venom and verbiage that Hermione is supposedly spewing in her 'obsessive' reaction to the enslavement of house-elves. The adjectives that characterize Hermione's activism are also telling: "eyes flashing," "determination," "vociferous," "badgering," "rattling," "cornering people," "fiercely," and "hotly" (238, 239). Although these adjectives denote her passion, they also imply an *irrational* support for elf-liberation, irrationality that is contrary to Hermione's habitually through research patterns. The text makes it clear that Hermione spends hours in the library conducting research before she emerges with a plan to fight for elf-liberation. Characterizing Hermione as hysterical even though she is least swayed by intuition or emotion points to an anti-intellectual bias in the text that, curiously, exists in contrast with Hermione's deductive brilliance. Even though we are constantly reminded of her visits to the library, and the information she provides is often couched in her research, her plea itself is "impassioned" rather than "reasoned." When Hermione attempts to provide her listeners with her reasons, her arguments are framed by descriptions connoting her emotional hysteria, and are invariably followed by some character's disapproval. Even when Hermione is allowed to provide information, it is followed by adjectives such as "she kept saying fiercely" or with reactions that clearly perceive her position as excessively passionate (239). Therefore Harry applied himself to scrambled eggs, Ron rolled his eyes towards the ceiling and Fred became extremely interested in his bacon (238, 239).

The debate over the 'slavery' of house-elves is played out in terms of passion and objectiveness in the relationship between Hermione, Harry and Ron. Hermione and Ron play the emotional roles in very different yet similar ways—Hermione is intellectual, but is not allowed rationality and Ron is clearly anti-intellectual. Harry is more distanced on the issue of house-elves and adopts the objective standpoint. After all, he has already established his elf-rescuing credentials at the end of the second book. A look at Hermione's introductory comments on S P E W reveals this dynamic between the three friends.

> "'Spew'?" said Harry, picking up a badge and looking at it. "What's this about?"
>
> "Not *spew*," said Hermione impatiently. "It's S-P-E-W. Stands for the Society for the Promotion of Elfish Welfare."
>
> "Never Heard of it," said Ron.
>
> "Well. Of course you haven't," said Hermione briskly, "I've only just started it."
>
> "Yeah?" said Ron in mild surprise. "How many members have you got?"
>
> "Well—if you two join—three," said Hermione.
>
> "And you think we want to walk around wearing badges saying 'spew,' do you?" said Ron.

"S-P-E-W!" said Hermione hotly. "I was going to put Stop the Outrageous Abuse of Our Fellow Magical Creatures in Their Legal Status—but it wouldn't fit. So that's the heading of our manifesto."

She brandished the sheaf of parchment at them.

"I've been researching it thoroughly in the library. Elf enslavement goes back centuries. I can't believe no one's done anything about it before now."

"Hermione—open your ears," said Ron loudly. "They. Like. It. They like being enslaved!"

"Our short-term aims," said Hermione, speaking even more loudly than Ron, and acting as though she hadn't heard a word, "are to secure house-elves fair wages and working conditions. Our long-term aims include changing the law about non-wand use, and trying to get an elf into the Department for the Regulation and Control of Magical Creatures, because they're shockingly underrepresented."

"And how do we do all this?" Harry asked . . .

There was a pause in which Hermione beamed at the pair of them, and Harry sat, torn between exasperation at Hermione and amusement at the look on Ron's face. (224, 225)

If Ron is loud, Hermione is louder. So while Hermione's intellectualism is undercut by the adjectives used to describe her tone or actions, and while Ron's emotional and sarcastic responses belie his suspicion of her research and ideological position; Harry's tone dons the garb of the dispassionate observer. In this instance, like in others, he performs the role of the mediator between the reader, and Hermione and Ron.

To maintain the position of liberalism and tolerance, it is essential for Harry and Dumbledore to refrain from contradicting Hermione directly. In the fifth book, for instance, Harry "had not had the heart to tell her that Dobby was taking everything she made" (451) while Ron confronts Hermione angrily when he sees her conceal hats under garbage, "You're trying to trick them into picking up the hats. You're setting them free when they might not want to be free" (255). While most of the central characters respond to Hermione's S.P.E.W., or at least are confronted with Hermione's plea, Dumbledore does not face Hermione directly in the text. Both Dumbledore and Harry remain supposedly objective and tolerant. Just like

Dumbledore, Harry upholds the liberal value of dissent within limits. Only once does Hermione indicate her problem with Dumbledore, at the conclusion of the welcome feast, "So! Said Dumbledore, smiling around at them all. "Now that we are all fed and watered," ("Hmph!" said Hermione) "I must once more ask for your attention, while I give out a few notices" (183). Unlike Harry, Hermione does not get the opportunity to face Dumbledore directly. While Harry gets the chance to vent his anger at Dumbledore's choices at the end of the fifth book, Hermione can only "Hmph!" her disapproval.

To reiterate my argument, Hermione's S.P.E.W. is a challenge to Dumbledore's liberal politics and Harry's hero narrative. The text creates an opposition between Dumbledore, the benevolent patriarch, who holds command over Hogwarts and Hermione's efforts to disrupt that patriarchal order. To substantiate this, I wish to examine Dumbledore's relationship with the elves at Hogwarts. Dumbledore is aware that house-elves exist at Hogwarts, and in fact, as Nearly-Headless Nick confirms, Hogwarts has "the largest number in any dwelling in Britain" (182). Admittedly, when Dobby asks Dumbledore for a job, Dumbledore offers him a handsome salary and perks. In fact, it is through Dobby's efforts that the salary and perks are considerably reduced. That said Dumbledore does not make any effort to change the situation of the other house-elves. As Hermione points out, "I can't believe no one's done anything about it before now" (224). Who is better equipped to do something than Dumbledore himself, who has complete control over Hogwarts? After all, the *Harry Potter* series reminds us time and time again that Hogwarts is safe (for Harry, and wizarding world) because of Dumbledore's presence.

Hogwarts is indeed under Dumbledore's command, as Harry constantly feels in his interaction with Dumbledore. Just one instance of this is at the end of *The Goblet of Fire* when Harry has a vivid impression of a palpable "aura of power around [Dumbledore]" (708). The final confrontation between Dumbledore and Voldemort in the *The Order of the Phoenix* only confirms this aura of power. So, while it is possible to appreciate Dumbledore's liberal, quasi-democratic set-up where people are given a second chance, it is a setup over which he presides and has complete control. When Lucius Malfoy attempts to destabilize that power in *The Chamber of Secrets*, Dumbledore reminds Harry, "you will find that I will only *truly* have left this school when none here are loyal to me. You will also find that help will always be given at Hogwarts to those who ask for it" (*COS* 263, 264). Truly enough, Harry finds his loyalty rewarded inside the chamber and this loyalty is responsible for Dumbledore's return, which is a matter of form. Dumbledore has never really left, and it is certainly undesirable within the logic of the text to expel him. In this instance, his presence is ratified by Harry's loyalty, and such loyalty is rewarded by Dumbledore's approval. Power and loyalty to power are thus linked in a circular logic.

However, this power is exclusive—Hagrid, who is equally loyal to Dumbledore does not command the same power that Harry, who is clearly grooming to inherit

Dumbledore's power, does. Hedwig and Pig, the owls who are loyal to their masters, or Dobby, who is loyal to Harry, are all excluded from the benefits of this power structure. Such exclusion is necessary for the maintenance of Dumbledore's and Harry's balance of power over the excluded and Dumbledore's control over Howgarts. Dumbledore's system, then, is far from equitable, however apparent the liberal tolerance of his position. In a significant parallel, Dumbledore and Harry both "rescue" Hagrid and Dobby, both of whom end up demonstrating eternal loyalty to their respective "rescuers." Theirs is an unthinking loyalty, unlike Harry who shows the courage and intelligence of a true hero, even as he is grooming to take over from Dumbledore. Hagrid and Dobby are feminized in contrast to their powerful and courageous masters. For instance, Dobby constantly knits socks (a traditionally feminine activity) for Harry, while Harry is largely oblivious to his painstaking efforts to please and save Harry. Hagrid cries very often and mothers Norbert. His slavish dependence on Dumbledore stands in contrast to Harry's loyalty to Dumbledore, which depends on Harry's efforts to prove his courage and capability, and not on dependence. So, within this system of power, the feminine is necessarily subservient.

Hagrid is proud of Dumbledore's trust in him. In the *Sorcerer's Stone*, Hagrid tells Harry that he "'gotta visit Gringotts anyway. Fer Dumbledore. Hogwarts business.' Hagrid drew himself up proudly. 'He usually gets me to do important stuff fer him. Fetchin' you—getting' things from Gringotts—knows he can trust me, see'" (79). Hagrid derives his sense of pride and esteem from Dumbledore's trust in his ability. While the text reinforces the importance and goodness of Dumbledore's trust and his belief in awarding second chances, it also underscores his liberal values with loyalty, which is required from the persons Dumbledore favours. Hagrid repays Dumbledore's trust with unquestioning loyalty, and slavish dependence. The iniquity of Hagrid's expulsion and later reinstatement as gamekeeper is manifest in Harry's fear that he will suffer a similar disadvantage if expelled: "He thought of Hagrid, expelled, but allowed to stay on as gamekeeper. Perhaps he could be Hagrid's assistant. His stomach twisted as he imagined it, watching Ron and the others becoming wizards while he stumped around the grounds carrying Hagrid's bag" (*SS* 186). Significantly, Harry's anxiety of being reduced to Hagrid's position is both his fear of being subservient and his fear of being feminized. While Harry goes on to wizarding glory, particularly in the fourth book with his third triumph over Voldermorte, Hagrid remains the gamekeeper and loyal to Dumbledore, and to Harry.

Dobby is similarly indebted to Harry for his freedom. In *The Chamber of Secrets*, when Dobby is freed, he attacks Malfoy in a vein similar to Hagrid's defense of Dumbledore on many occasions, "'You shall go now,' he said fiercely, pointing down at My. Malfoy. 'You shall not touch Harry Potter. You shall go now" (338). Then Dobby turns to Harry and expresses gratitude, "'Harry Potter freed Dobby!' said the elf shrilly, gazing up at Harry, moonlight from the nearest window reflected in his orb-lie eyes. 'Harry Potter set Dobby free!' 'Least I could do, Dobby' said Harry grinning" (338, 339). Dobby follows this up with his gifts to Harry in the fourth book and his request that he be allowed to visit Harry. Despite the many statements suggesting Harry's desire to treat Dobby as an equal, Harry's position of dominance is reinforced on more than one occasion. Dobby's and Harry's attitude about Christmas gifts in *The Goblet of Fire* is just one example. In *The Order of the Phoneix,* Dobby hangs a hundred golden baubles with Harry's face on them and the legend "HAVE A VERY HARRY CHRISTMAS!" (452). It would not be as convincing were the situation reversed, as it is later when Harry dreams of being back in the DA room, "Harry was protesting that he could not give Cho his Firebolt because Umbridge had it, and anyways the whole thing was ridiculous, he'd only come to the D. A. room to put up some Christmas baubles shaped like Dobby's head" (462).

Dobby maintains that Harry Potter is a great wizard, and funnily enough when he meets Ron at Christmas, he extends the favour to Ron: "'Sir is very kind!' he squeaked, his eyes brimming with tears again, bowing deeply to Ron. 'Dobby knew sir must be a great wizard, for he is Harry Potter's greatest friend, but Dobby did not know that he was also as generous of spirit, as noble, as selfless—" (*GOF* 409). The most significant gift Dobby provides Harry Potter, at considerable risk to himself, is gillyweed, only because "Dobby cannot let Harry Potter lose his Wheezy!" (491). Thus the benevolent feudal structure with Dumbledore in power, and Harry grooming to assume power, thrives on such loyalty from inferiors. The text is implicated in endorsing this system. In *The Chamber of Secrets,* Dumbledore convinces Harry about the importance of choice, but significantly, in the text, choice amounts to the choice to be loyal to either Dumbledore or Voldemort. Harry makes the "right" choices and is loyal to the "right" persons, and is rewarded for his loyalty. Dobby also makes the "right" choice in imparting his loyalty to Harry. Consequently he is positive and helpful, though interestingly strange. On the other hand, Kreacher, in *The Order of the Phoenix,* makes his choice to be loyal to the Dark Lord and Lestrange, and is consequently evil and dark.

In the *Harry Potter* series, there is no precedent for Hermione's S.P.E.W. However, there is the other precedent of Dumbledore's relation to Hagrid. Harry Potter gives Dobby his freedom because this act is allowed within the ideological context of the text. While it is accepted and appropriate for Dumbledore to "give" Hagrid a second chance and earn his lifelong "loyalty;" and following which it is appropriate for Harry to "give" Dobby his freedom and similarly gain Dobby's lifelong "loyalty," it is *not* appropriate for Hermione to make a badge and clamour for the recognition of house-elf rights because this does not follow the established pattern of the hero narrative. Hermione's attempt to shift the subject position from that of the master in an unequal system to that of the house-elves, by raising awareness instead of taking on the mantle of the hero, breaks away from the feudal nature of the hero narrative that the text valorizes. A measure of Hermione's failure to communicate or convince is Dobby's reaction to her efforts to motivate the elves to demand equality (as opposed to his reaction to Harry and Ron).

> "Oh for heaven's sake!" Hermione cried. "Listen to me, all of you! You've got as much right as wizards to be unhappy! You've got the right to wages and holidays and proper clothes, you don't have to do everything you're told—look at Dobby!"

> "Miss will please keep Dobby out of this," Dobby mumbled, looking scared. The cheery smiles had vanished from the faces of the house-elves around the kitchen. They were suddenly looking at Hermione as though she were mad and dangerous." (539)

Hermione's language, as she fights for elf-rights, marks her left leaning politics. She speaks of a "manifesto," "rights," "fair wages and working conditions," "changing the law," and getting representation for "underrepresented" house-elves. Unlike Harry, Hermione does not show loyalty to Dumbledore—quite the contrary. Her S.P.E.W. is a clarion call for revamping the unequal power relation between the wizards and the house-elves and a direct threat to Dumbledore's power structure. It is no wonder then that while Harry is rewarded with Fawkes' help and Griffindor's sword, Hermione is roundly abused for her attempts to question the existing power paradigms.

I would like to end with these lines from *The Order of the Phoenix,* which once again reiterate Hermione's, Harry's and Ron's career choices and ideological positions.

> "Well, it'd be cool to be an Auror," said Ron in an offhand voice.

> "Yeah, it would," said Harry fervently.

> "But they're, like, the elite, said Ron. "You've got to be really good. What about you, Hermione?"

> "I don't know," said Hermione. "I think I'd really like to do something worthwhile."

> "An Auror's worthwhile!" said Harry.

> "Yes, it is, but it's not the only worthwhile thing," said Hermione thoughtfully. "I mean, if I could take S.P.E.W. further . . ."

> Harry and Ron carefully avoided looking at each other. (228)

Works Cited

Burchell, Graham, Colin Gordon and Peter Miller. *The Foucault Effect: Studies in Governmentality*. Chicago: University of Chicago Press, 1991.

Rowling, J. K. *Harry Potter And The Sorcerer's Stone*. New York: Scholastic Press, 1997

Rowling, J. K. *Harry Potter And The Chamber of Secrets*. New York: Scholastic Press, 1999

Rowling, J. K. *Harry Potter And The Goblet Of Fire*. New York: Scholastic Press, 2000.

Rowling, J. K. *Harry Potter and the Order of the Phoenix*. New York: Scholastic Press, 2003

Bharati Kasibhatla completed her Masters in English at the University of Bombay and is currently pursuing her Ph.D. at the University of Florida. Her interests include Victorian literature, Postcolonial theory and South Asian studies.

It's Not Easy Being Hermione:
Harry Potter and the Paradox of Girl Power

Meghan Mercier

" Girl Powers," shouts the headline of *Teen People*'s profile of Emma Watson [the actress who plays Hermione Granger the Harry Potter movies]. "Girl Power" has become a household phrase in the past decade, and even merited a new entry in the Oxford English Dictionary: "spec[ifically]. a self reliant attitude among girls and young women manifested in ambition, assertiveness, and individualism." Hermione seems, as *Teen People*'s title suggests, to be an excellent example of the triumph of girl power. She is a paragon: a bright, responsible overachiever, unintimidated by scholarship, boys, and most monsters. This Ophelia, it appears, needs no reviving. Or does she? While the media coverage of Emma Watson is certainly in line with girl power, anyone familiar with the Spice Girls will agree that the term does not always live up to its dictionary definition. The movies Watson appears in, too, make problematic choices about how Hermione is used on-screen. The simple fact is, Harry Potter's adventures, (as well as his many one-on-one confrontations with ultimate evil) *could not* happen without Hermione Granger's formidable analytical problem solving skills. Yet even J.K. Rowling has been recorded making comments about Hermione that call into question her signal trait: intelligence.

In interviews, J. K. Rowling has made it clear that there is something problematic about Hermione. She chose the character's name, she says, because it was so unusual that she didn't think any contemporary girl would be teased for sharing the name of a know-it-all. To one reporter, Rowling even "confess[ed] that Hermione Granger is a little bit like I was at her age, though I was neither as clever [n]or as annoying," (Sheehan). Just *who* Hermione annoys is a question worth asking. She does raise her hand to answer any question in class, and she does often remind Harry and Ron that they are contemplating breaking school rules. Ron, certainly, finds her trying, pronouncing her a "nightmare" after she succeeds at (and is praised for) a magical task he was unable to perform. But Rowling seems to feel that Hermione grates on the *reader*: "Hermione is a character I understand really, really well. I consciously try to make it clear that underneath the aggravating surface is someone who is actually quite insecure, hence her constant struggle to be the best. . . . It probably is a particularly female characteristic for young girls to cover up their insecurities about feeling plain, or whatever inadequacy, by trying to get the best marks" (Feldman). Hermione is described as having unruly hair and overlarge front teeth, but I wonder if her chore of assimilating into the wizarding world and her lack of female peer support might trouble her more than her appearance. Also, by pronouncing Hermione's drive to excel to be a coping strategy, Rowling implicitly denies the centrality of intelligence in her character. Hermione's insecurity may erupt (and often does) in tears when she is teased, but *surely* it does not determine her intellectual powers. Mary Pipher, in *Reviving Ophelia*, calls adolescence the time "when girls experience social pressure to put aside their authentic selves and to display only a small portion of their gifts" (22). By characterizing academic striving as desperate, Rowling seems to suggest that Hermione is caught up in the culturally-induced dissatisfaction with self Pipher describes. But it is Rowling, and especially Warner Brothers, who limit the quantity and quality of gifts Hermione may display. Pipher paraphrases Simone de Beauvoir on adolescence, saying "Girls who were the subjects of their own lives become the objects of others' lives" (21). This statement, said of reality, is certainly applicable to the film versions of Rowling's novels. Where the novels make it clear that Hermione has a life outside Harry and Ron's presence, referring to her family (and especially in the later books, her initiative: the use of the time-turner, SPEW, and the DA); the two films released so far seem determined to reduce Hermione to literal objecthood of two kinds.

Warner Brothers' *Harry Potter and the Sorcerer's Stone* establishes Hermione as a nerd before it even begins: she is shown clutching a stack of books on the promotional poster. The difference between Hermione in the novel and Hermione in the movie is, not the fact of her intelligence, but the quality of it. In the novel, not all of her information comes from books. She makes connections and comes to conclusions, using her analytical powers as well as her capacious memory. The movie, however, highlights Hermione's rote learning. At the climax of the novel, when Harry, Ron, and Hermione must break a series of enchantments in order to reach Sorcerer's Stone before Voldemort does, there is a challenge suited to each child's talents. Their first challenge requires cooperation. The Devil's Snare entangles Ron and Harry, while Hermione panics because she knows how to repel the plant, but forgets that she can use magic. With some advice from Harry, she calms down enough to get the job done. Next they must capture a key while flying on broomsticks, a task tailored for Harry. They then encounter a monstrous chess set, and Ron, the chess prodigy, directs the game as they play their way across the room. He must let himself be taken, but Harry and Hermione remain in their respective squares and advance to the next challenge, which is not magic at all, but is a logic puzzle in verse. After reading it, "Hermione let out a great sigh and Harry, amazed, saw that she was smiling, which was the last thing he felt like doing"(1-285). After a quick think, she identifies the elixirs that will allow one to move forward to the last challenge and which will allow the drinker to retreat. Because there is only enough of the forward elixir for one person, Harry directs Hermione to go back and get help for Ron and himself. She, momentarily overcome with emotion, hugs him and tells him he's a great wizard. When he protests that he isn't as good as she is, she scoffs "Books! And cleverness! There are more important things—friendship and bravery and—oh, Harry—be careful! (1-287) After this speech, both drink, and go their separate ways, proving her choices to be correct. Steve Kloves, the screenwriter, kept Hermione's self-dismissive speech intact but put it in a decidedly *different* place. The logic puzzle sequence, despite its towering walls of black and purple fire and menacing bottles of poison, wine, and elixir, was cut from the movie. So the Devil's Snare challenge had to be Hermione's moment (remember each kid had to solve some problem, so that they could be awarded enough points for Gryffindor to win the House Cup at the end). There are some extremely significant alterations to the scene. In the book, Hermione scrambles out of the clutches of the plant as soon as she falls into it, while in the movie all three kids are caught up. She calls out to the others to "Relax!" Apparently if you stop struggling and become completely passive, the plant loses interest in you and drops you. Hermione and Harry both achieve total passivity, but Ron remains entangled. This time, instead of knowing what to do but being too panicked to do it immediately, Hermione struggles to recall a mnemonic device: "Devil's Snare, Devil's Snare; It's deadly fun ... but it sulks in the sun." Once the mnemonic is recited, she can take action. This results in fifty house points for "cool use of intellect when others were in grave peril." However, she doesn't actually exercise any intellect here. She meets her challenge with initial passivity and pure rote memory. So after the chess game (the success of which she imperils by threatening to step off her square, requiring Harry to caution her [unlike the novel]), when she gives her self-deprecating speech to the surging, inspirational musical accompaniment, it takes on a different meaning. Instead of a slightly embarrassed disavowal of her obvious talents, it functions as an actual confession—as though Kloves had read Rowling's comments about Hermione's nerd-achievement coping strategy, and wanted her to 'fess up to using facts to conceal imagined personal flaws.

In Rowling's *Chamber of Secrets*, Hermione's planning and problem-solving skills know no bounds. When the trio suspects Malfoy of unleashing the mysterious monster who has been plaguing the school, Hermione takes the lead in formulating a plan to trap him, which involves "breaking about fifty school rules" (2-159). She sneaks into the Restricted Section of the library to get the potion recipe, then steals ingredients from Snape herself, while Ron and Harry are hesitant about all the punishable offenses she's racking up. Despite the fact that her polyjuice potion is botched and only Harry and Ron get to visit the Slytherin Common Room, Hermione continues to put two and two together, finally realizing what the monster is and how it is moving around the school. Unfortunately, she is Petrified before she can sound the alarm, but later, when Harry and Ron visit her in the infirmary, they find the answers on a crumpled up bit of paper in her hand, enabling them to go after the monster. Hermione doesn't appear again until the very end, when (after being un-petrified) she runs towards Harry at the school feast, shouting "You solved it! You solved it!" (2-339). She shouts as though Harry had figured out the solution rather than literally finding her cheat sheet. Rowling (and Dumbledore) overlook her contribution: only Ron and Harry receive House points for their adventure, despite the fact that without Hermione's information on the type and whereabouts of the monster, one little girl would be dead and Voldemort returned to full power.

Yet if the book denies Hermione a share of the credit, Warner Brothers' *Chamber of Secrets* uses her as a tool. Kloves has filled Hermione's mouth with exposition, and she pops out facts like a machine gun, even one about wizarding culture that is out of character for her to know. Nasty Malfoy calls her a "mudblood," tantamount to the ugliest racial slur. In the book, she recognized the insult but turns to Ron, who grew up in wizard culture, for an explanation. In the movie, she lectures the confused Harry on the significance of the term. It seems unlikely that Hermione, who does do most of her research in books in the school library, should know about this word—what sort of books does Kloves suppose Madame Pince buys? After she is finished with exposition, Hermione settles down to spend the rest of the film enabling the boys' fun, while having none herself. She plans the potion, but conspicuously missing is her thrill of stealing from the Potions Master. The encyclopedia-Hermione from the first movie turns to the second film's exposition engine, and though she does solve problems and make connections, she literally becomes an object—a statue—and cannot act on the knowledge she generates.

This diminished Hermione makes me wonder why Emma Watson is so leery of identifying with her. What is so threatening about Hermione? Interviews with Rupert Grint dwell on his large family, love of sweets, and fear of spiders, all hallmarks of his character. Features on Daniel Radcliffe [recount his seeming "Cinderella" discovery by the producer, his maturity and his tears of joy in the bath at being told he had the part, which mark him with a bit of magic, and the genuine emotions of The Boy Who Lived]. Emma Watson, however, when asked "Are you anything like Hermione?" replied "A lot of people have asked this, but I don't think I am, really. She's a total bookworm and will do anything to get top marks. I mean, I enjoy school, but I'm not obsessed with school. Um . . . I hope I have a better fashion sense than she does" (Schwartz). Her other features ring changes on the same tune: "Hermione is a dictionary—she uses long words I don't understand" (Clott), "we're opposites. I love school and I try hard, but I'm not as clever as Hermione" (*16 Magazine*). Even their social lives are fundamentally different: Watson's friends are not like Harry and Ron: "To start with, they are girls," (Girardi). Yet Watson cheerfully owns up to being bossy, announcing that she keeps the boys "in line" (*Teen People*), and that "I do have to keep them on their toes and show them who's boss" (Clott). Other tidbits focus on that dubious girl power, consumption. When asked: "Did you buy yourselves extravagant presents to celebrate the end of the film?" Rupert Grint admitted to buying candy, but Watson 'went on a clothes shopping spree around London. That was my treat'" (Cawthorne). Her "Favourite clothes" she identifies by brand name: "DKNY, Gap for casual, Harvey Nichols"(*16 Magazine*). "I am . . . more obsessed with clothes and shopping whereas Hermione has no fashion sense at all" she says (Girardi). In fact, most of the photos of Watson show her dressed as Hermione, robbing her of the god-given right of girl-power girls to look fabulous. For the *Teen People* article, the 12-year-old does get to don makeup, trendy tight flares, and an off-the-shoulder top, presumably with which to display her powers.

Watson gets the sexualizing treatment in press outside the movies, but Warner Brothers' *Chamber of Secrets* also seems to anticipate more adult relationships between Hermione and Harry (or maybe Ron?). It seems like Kloves is ready to profess a ship, even though the characters are twelve. While the much discussed and highly uncanonical hug at the end of the film can be interpreted either way (H/R or H/H), the discovery of Hermione's paper is less ambiguous. In the novel, Harry sees that she is holding a crumpled paper. In the film, Harry is holding her frozen hand, stroking it with his thumb, and discovers the paper by touch. Fanfic writer Kristin Brown satirized Kloves' screenplays in a mock dialogue between him and Rowling, discussing the *Prisoner of Azkaban* script. Kloves (the character) tells Rowling "I really think I've captured the essence of each character, as well as where you're going with them," and proceeds to horrify her, as she corrects him again and again about Hermione and Harry's relationship, and the fact that Ron, though Kloves can't see it, is not a moron. Rowling particularly objects to the direction "Hermione stands in front of Harry, ripped dress billowing in the breeze . . . in a fruitless but loving attempt to protect her one true love from Sirius Black. Ron crawls under bed, trembling with fear." Though Brown is poking fun, it gives one pause: is cinematic Hermione on the road trodden by Britney Spears and Christina Aguilera from schoolgirl to sexpot?

But sexualization (the typical upshot of "girl power" especially in the music media) may be a kindness: it may distract audiences from the less charming aspects of her character. Watson discloses, for the slow learners, what it is about Hermione that "gets on everyone's nerves. She talks in class all the time, and that is annoying" (Clott). For Rowling, Hermione's achievements are compensatory. For the filmmakers, Hermione's machine-like mind makes her an ideal tool for the advancement of plot. Girl Power might give her the right to speak unpleasant truths, like, "you deserved that detention," as long as she does not reveal her own objectification. Timothy Shary, in an article on "The Nerdly Girl in American Cinema," writes that "smart girl characters are typically shown paying a price for their intellect, in the form of derision, self-contempt, or ostracism" (236). Perhaps Kloves writes Hermione slightly dimmer and decidedly cuter in order to avoid having to mete out that kind of harsh treatment.

But in the end, it is still the smart girl that is threatening, though the threat is disguised by words like "annoying." Rowling and Watson articulate the ways in which Hermione is problematic. Emma Watson ingratiatingly tries to neutralize the threat that even the diminished film Hermione represents by aligning herself with the dominant scripts for girlhood: female friends, disavowal of academic pursuit, and material consumption. But as the novels progress, Rowling shows Hermione as more and more flexible and confident, and no less intellectual . . . her need to achieve, certainly by book five, becomes practical rather than compensatory. [Hermione also uses her intellect to read the subtext of Umbridge's speech, and challenges her as effectively as Harry does (and without the bloody-handed detentions)]. So as book-Hermione moves towards becoming a power with a capital P, girl or no, it remains to be seen how the next film installment will reconcile the jarring roles Warner Brothers has set up for their Hermione: the sex object and the reference object.

Works Cited

Brown, Kristin. "Transcript of Meeting Between S.Kloves and J. K. Rowling." *Sugarquill.com* 8 Dec 2002 **http://www.sugarquill.net/read.php?storyid=1084&chapno=1** (12 Jan 2003).

Clott, Alicia. "Spotlight: Emma Watson" *Girls Life Magazine* Oct/Nov 2002: 46.

Cawthorne, Alec. "Rupert Grint and Emma Watson: *Harry Potter and the Philosopher's Stone.*" *BBC.co.uk* 7 November 2001. **http://www.bbc.co.uk/films/2001/11/07/ rupert_grint_emma_watson_2001_interview.shtml** (17 Nov 2002).

Feldman, Roxanne. "The Truth About Harry." *School Library Journal* Sept 1999: 137-141.

Girardi, Laura C. "WHO-FILES: Emma Watson, movie star." *Time for Kids* **http:// www.timeforkids.com/TFK/emma** (17 Nov 2002).

"Girl Powers." *Teen People.* Nov/Dec 2002.

"Interview." *16 Magazine* Nov/Dec 2001.

Pipher, Mary. *Reviving Ophelia: saving the selves of adolescent girls.* New York : Putnam, 1994.

Rowling, J.K. *Harry Potter and the Sorcerer's Stone.* New York: Arthur A. Levine, 1998.

—. *Harry Potter and the Chamber of Secrets.* New York: Arthur A. Levine, 1999.

Schwartz, Missy. "Season of the Witch" *Entertainment Weekly* http://www.ew.com/ew/ report/0,6115,188388-1-0-harrypottershermionetalks,00.html (17 Nov 2002).

Shary, Timothy. "The Nerdly Girl in American Cinema." In *Sugar and Spice and Everything Nice: Cinemas of Girlhood.* Gateward, Frances and Murray Pomerance, eds. Contemporary Film and Television. New York: Wayne State University, 2002

Sheehan, Paul. "Why Harry Potter is a triumph for women." *Sydney Morning Herald* 29 Nov 2001: 5. Lexis-Nexis. (17 Nov 2002).

Meghan Mercier received her M.A. in English from Syracuse University, and is now pursuing her Ph.D. at George Washington University. She purposely avoided reading the Harry Potter series as long as she could, finally succumbing just before the publication of Harry Potter and the Goblet of Fire. After that midnight purchase, she immediately began pining for the fifth book. Fortunately, she discovered fan fiction, and has been diligently reading it ever since. Now, with both book five and the expanding fan fiction universe, she couldn't be happier.

"That's the Title on the Manifesto": Labor and Class Concerns in Harry Potter

Wendy A. F. G. Stengel

"Class is still essential to a proper understanding of British history and of Britain today. Class is undoubtedly a British preoccupation."—David Cannadine (Wagner)

"There is nothing in the fact of work that degrades; it is only the workers who are degraded" (Linton, Maids).

"It's S.P.E.W. Stands for the Society for the Promotion of Elfish Welfare . . . . I was going to put Stop the Outrageous Abuse of Our Fellow Magical Creatures and Campaign for a Change in Their Legal Status—but it wouldn't fit . . . . I've been researching it thoroughly in the library. Elf enslavement goes back centuries. I can't believe no one's done anything about it before now" (Harry Potter and the Goblet of Fire, p. 224, US version).

Kings and peasants. Masters and servants. In-group and out-group. Class explorations are hardly new in British fiction. However, with the phenomenal interest in J.K. Rowling's *Harry Potter* books, these issues are firmly in the hands of children, teens and adults around the world. While protestors decry the possibility of a mistaken mystical message seeping into children's minds, stronger political messages are coming through. Class conflict is on the rise. Revolution is in the air.

It is tempting to view the major labor conflict of the *Harry Potter* world—the status of house-elves—simplistically: "Slavery is bad." However, the house-elves' exploitation resonates on many more levels. For most of the target audience, slavery itself is seen as an historical, American concern, and is completely indefensible. As many otherwise-sympathetic characters support the use of unpaid house-elf labor, there is clearly more going on. Harry and Hermione have similar Mudblood backgrounds having been raised as Muggles, but have very different levels of political awareness; Harry treats Dobby decently, Hermione becomes a firebrand for labor rights and the Weasley children beg for them not to challenge the status quo. From exploring the status of and reactions to the house-elves, we can extrapolate the production and perpetuation of class in the wizarding world.

Though anyone attending an international symposium on *Harry Potter* is apt to be familiar with elvish basics, it is important to look at just what, exactly, house-elves are. They are "magical brethren" of the wizards (*Harry Potter and the Order of the Phoenix*, p.127, US version), who are bound in service to one family and one house for life (*Harry Potter and the Chamber of Secrets*, p. 16, US version). They have their "own kind of magic," and we are given hints that it is that magic which does the actual binding of elf-to-family (*Harry Potter and the Goblet of Fire*, p. 687, US version). Having a house-elf in your family is a sign of privilege:

> "Well, whoever owns him will be an old wizarding family, and they'll be rich," said Fred.

> "Yeah, Mum's always wishing we had a house-elf to do the ironing," said George. "But all we've got is a lousy old ghoul in the attic and gnomes all over the garden. House-elves come with big old manors and castles and places like that, you wouldn't catch one in our house . . . " (*Chamber of Secrets*, pp.27-28, US version).

Though they are servants, they are not paid; they are not, however, bought or sold as slaves would be. Indeed, dismissing a house-elf requires breaking the magical bond through a ritual of presenting clothing to the elf. When Lucius Malfoy is tricked into throwing a sock to Dobby, he snarls, "You've lost me my servant, boy." (*Chamber of Secrets*, p. 248, US version). In *Harry Potter and the Chamber of Secrets*, at least, the master of the elf is the only one who can free the elf from bondage—otherwise, Harry could have freed Dobby himself.

Though Dobby annoys Harry, and repeatedly attempts to harm (but not kill) him, Harry is sympathetic to Dobby. It is hardly surprising, as Harry views himself as an outsider, and fellow-outsider Dobby frames elf subjugation as part of Voldemort's evil influence, elf redemption by Harry's victory.

> "Dobby remembers how it was when He Who Must Not Be Named was at the height of his powers, sir! We house-elves were treated like vermin, sir! Of course, Dobby is still treated like that, sir," he admitted, drying his face on the pillowcase. "But mostly, sir, life has improved for my kind since you triumphed over He Who Must Not Be Named." (*Chamber of Secrets*, US version)

As early as *Chamber of Secrets*, Dobby seems aware of house-elves as a class, and an exploited one at that. We have no other house-elves to compare him with at this point, however, and we do know that the respectable Weasleys do not seem at all disturbed by the current status of house-elves. If *Chamber of Secrets* were our only exposure to house-elves, we might well take Dobby at his word: house-elves had it very badly before Harry defeated Voldemort, but things have vastly improved for all house-elves not in cruel Malfoy's employ.

In *Harry Potter and the Goblet of Fire*, however, we start to see the system as it really is. At the Quidditch World Cup, we meet a 'proper' house-elf, Winky.

> *"Ah, sir," said Winky, shaking her head, "ah, sir, meaning no disrespect, sir, but I is not sure you did Dobby a favor, sir when you is setting him free."*

> *"Why?" said Harry, taken aback. "What's wrong with him?"*

> *"Freedom is going to Dobby's head, sir," said Winky sadly. "Ideas above his station, sir. Can't get another position, sir."*

> *"Why not?" said Harry.*

> *Winky lowered her voice by a half-octave and whispered, "He's wanting paying for his work, sir."*

> *"Paying?" said Harry blankly. "Well—why shouldn't he be paid?"*

> *Winky looked quite horrified at the idea and closed her fingers slightly so that her face was half-hidden again.*

> *"House-elves is not paid, sir!" she said in a muffled squeak. "No, no, no. I says to Dobby, I says, go find yourself a nice family and settle down, Dobby. He is getting up to all sorts of high jinks, sir, what is unbecoming to a house-elf. You goes racketing around like this, Dobby, I says, and next thing I hear you's up in front of the Department for the Regulation and Control of Magical Creatures, like some common goblin" (Goblet of Fire, p. 98, US version).*

Other than her aversion to being paid for her labor, Winky comes off every bit the proper Victorian house servant. She is unswerving in her loyalty to the family she serves, she suffers abuse and neglect without complaint, and the worst thing she can imagine is being cast aside (*Goblet of Fire*. p.138, US version). The comparison holds up: servants in both systems are status symbols,[1] they are a part of the family much the same way the silver is part of the family, and in the proper execution of their tasks, they are ignored[2]—a fact that gives them more power than their masters may like. "Dobby hears things, sir, he is a house-elf, he goes all over the castle as he lights the fires and mops the floors" (*Goblet of Fire*, p.491, US version). Domestics in both scenarios, were "immured in their basements and attic bedrooms, shut away from private gaze and public conscience . . . remained mute and forgotten" (Burnett in Landow). When they break from the quiet background, they risk their security. As we see by Mr. Crouch's reaction to Mr. Diggory, the family considers the elf an extension of its dignity: "If you accuse my elf, you accuse me, Diggory!" (*Goblet of Fire*, p.137, US version) and can be punished for tarnishing it. A house-elf cast aside faces the same problem as a house-maid who has outlived her usefulness: there is "not only the impossibility of chance of making a solid provision for their future . . . but no length, or fidelity of services constitutes a claim for support when the working-time is over and old age has come on." (Linton, *Maids*).

When Percy justifies Winky's dismissal on the grounds that a wizard "deserves unswerving obedience from his servants," Hermione retorts: "His *slave*, you mean! . . . because he didn't *pay* Winky, did he?" (*Goblet of Fire*, p.154, US version) Hermione, a good little Muggle girl, latches on to a capitalist interpretation of the situation: If Winky is not paid for producing commodities, she must be a commodity herself: a slave. Her reaction to the situation is not that of an abolitionist, however. She does not campaign to free the house-elves from their work. Rather, she wants to bring them into the capitalist system, giving them wages, paid leave, and retirement funds. Hermione is a fledgling trade unionist, a fact not lost on the Weasley twins.

> "Going to try and lead the house-elves out on strike now, are you?" said George. "Going to give up all the leaflet stuff and try and stir them up into rebellion?" . . .

> "Don't you go upsetting them and telling them they've got to take clothes and salaries!" said Fred warningly. "You'll put them off their cooking!"
> (*Goblet of Fire*, p.367, US version)

One can hardly discuss capital and labor issues without discussing Marx and Engels. They cannot fully answer house-elf issues, however, as they focus so closely on wage-labor and capital-producing industrialism. Remove the issue of capital from labor, and their economic arguments lack firm footing. However, we must consider Marx and Engels at least in passing, as Hermione has no doubt been exposed to some of their teachings in her Muggle upbringing—she dubs her S.P.E.W. organizational documents a "manifesto," and shows all the earmarks of a radical campaigning for a new world order.

Central to Marx's labor theories is the notion of class, and the conflict that arises from class differentiation. The house-elves, however, are "pre-class"—they lack class consciousness. "Although an aggregate of people may occupy similar positions in the process of production and their lives may have objectively similar determinants, they become a class as a self-conscious and history-making body only if they become aware of the similarity of their interest through their conflicts with the opposing classes" (Coser). Dobby, as an individual, is becoming aware of the conflict, but cannot as an individual actor give elvish society true class consciousness, as the elves do not see themselves as at war with the wizards. Goblins, on the other hand, are "magical brethren" with strong class consciousness, and have transformed that consciousness into political action through a series of rebellions: "Goblins don't need protection . . . . They're quite capable of dealing with wizards . . . They're very clever. They're not like house-elves, who never stick up for themselves." (Hermione in *Goblet of Fire*, p.449, US version). The other magical brethren, the centaurs, have chosen to live apart from, rather than be oppressed by, the wizards.

Hermione is a product of an industrial, capitalist society, so even though she is now acting in a non-industrial society, she responds to crisis with the tools she understands: political power and ideology, which "serve the same functions for capitalist that class consciousness serves for the working class" (Coser).[3] She wants to lessen the degree of disempowerment of the house-elf workers, which would ultimately give renewed legitimacy to the system as a whole (Ganter). Hermione's need to reform the system is understandable; she has embraced the wizarding world wholeheartedly, and finds that it is supported through the oppression of others. She would suffer too much cognitive dissonance if she took no action, but a truly revolutionary course of action would endanger the world she's come to love. Even so, her progressive stance causes discomfort with those she would "save."

> *"Begging your pardon, miss,"* said the house-elf, bowing deeply again, *"but house-elves has no right to be unhappy when there is work to be done and masters to be served."*

> *"Oh, for heaven's sake!"* Hermione cried. *"Listen to me, all of you! You've got just as much right as wizards to be unhappy! You've got the right to wages and holidays and proper clothes, you don't have to do everything you're told—look at Dobby!"*

> *"Miss will please keep Dobby out of this,"* Dobby mumbled, looking scared. The cheery smiles had vanished from the faces of the house-elves around the kitchen. They were suddenly looking at Hermione as though she were mad and dangerous. (Goblet of Fire, pp.538-539, US version).

Though Hermione's desire to turn the house-elves into wage-laborers is in direct conflict with Marxist goals of abolishing wage-labor, some of the answers to the house-elf problem can be found in Marx, who examined two systems of labor pre-dating wage-labor: slavery and serfdom.

> *"The slave did not sell his labor-power to the slave-owner, any more than the ox sells his labor to the farmer. The slave, together with his labor-power, was sold to his owner once for all. He is a commodity that can pass from the hand of one owner to that of another. He himself is a commodity, but his labor-power is not his commodity. The serf sells only a portion of his labor-power. It is not he who receives wages from the owner of the land; it is rather the owner of the land who receives a tribute from him. The serf belongs to the soil, and to the lord of the soil he brings its fruit."*

The topic of slavery certainly has a place in a discussion of labor and *Harry Potter*, if only because Hermione constantly refers to the house-elves and their labor in slavery terms. However, framing the issue solely—or even, primarily—as one of slavery paralyzes the discussion. Slavery is bad, evil, wicked, not to be tolerated, something all reasonable people abhor. Supporters of slavery are all those things, and more. Consider, then, that the Weasleys are supportive of the use of house-elf labor, and that we are shown over and over how admirable and just the Weasleys are; we must conclude that we can not frame labor in *Harry Potter* strictly as slavery without damaging the text severely.[4] Moreover, in Marx's definition of slavery, the slave is bought and sold as a commodity; we have no evidence of house-elves ever being bought or sold. In fact, when Mr. Crouch wants to get rid of Winky, he has no option but to *free* her (*Goblet of Fire*, p.138, US version).[5]

If we are to move from slavery as an intellectual framework for non-wage labor, we can follow Marx and look at the historical non-wage labor of England: feudal serfs. Serfs were neither bought nor sold. They were bound to the land and their lords through oaths (and extreme financial dependence). Serfs had obligations to toil for the lords above them, but the lords, in return, had obligations to care for their serfs—though the standard of care was negligible. If a lord were to lose his land, or die, the lord who replaced him would carry on the obligations to the land and the serfs. This was deemed to be entirely natural, and, indeed, decreed by God.

> *And since it is ordained from the original and superabounding wisdom of all things, That there should be Degrees and Diversities amongst the sons of men, in acknowledging of a Superiority from Inferiors to Superiors; the*

*Servant with a reverent and befitting Obedience is as liable to this duty
in a measurable performance to him whom he serves, as the loyalest of
Subjects to his Prince (Alsop).*

Serfs had no self-determination, no possibility to act upon self-interest, and no
expectation of class-mobility: serfs lived and died serfs, tied to the land. Kreacher is
the strongest elf-as-serf image we have in *Harry Potter*, yet he does not express the
gushing loyalty to his master that we've seen before; he loathes his master. He tries to
render as little productive service to Sirius as possible, and thwarts Sirius' activities to
the best of his ability. However, he is devoted to the Black house, and bound to it
until his head should join those of his ancestors collecting dust on the wall. Sirius, for
his part, does "not hate Kreacher . . . he regard[s] him as a servant unworthy of much
interest or notice." (*Order of the Phoenix*, p. 833, US version) Serfs are also a distinctly
a pre-industrial labor source, and as such, fit nicely into the non-industrial wizarding
labor scheme.

However, the feudal system parallels break down when you try to include
non-lords and non-serfs; where are "the rest of us?" The rise of the middle class
in post-plague Europe coincided with the *fall* of feudalism; the Weasleys are
decidedly post-feudal. They are, however, part of a strong *caste*, system. A
Victorian reformer said one "might as well talk to a high caste Hindoo [*sic*] of the
common humanity of a Brahmin and a Pariah as to English gentlefolks of the
common humanity of a mistress and her maid" (Linton, *Maids*). And, if one
does consider class, race[6], and caste as equivalent[7], we can discern how the
Weasleys and Hagrid can be sympathetic and yet not be engaged in elf-rights:
brethren or no, they simply do not see a common bond of humanity between
themselves and the house-elves.

> *"The way the were treating her!" said Hermione furiously. "Mr. Diggory,
> calling her 'elf' all the time . . . and Mr. Crouch! He knows she didn't
> do it and he's still going to sack her! He didn't care how frightened
> she'd been, or how upset she was—it was like she wasn't even human!"*
>
> *"Well, she's not," said Ron.*
>
> *Hermione rounded on him.*
>
> *"That doesn't mean she hasn't got feeling, Ron. It's disgusting" (Goblet of
> Fire, p.139, US version).*

Ron, however, is a product of his class, and shares the common class views. The four castes in Indian culture map neatly onto the classes in *Harry Potter*.[8]

Wendy A.F.G. Stengel is a graduate student at Georgetown University in Washington, D.C. Her research interests include gender and friendship in science fiction and fantasy, slash fan fiction, and class issues. She is active in the Popular Culture Association. Though part of the academic track of Nimbus, she is fan enough to have waited in line at Eason's in Dublin to purchase Harry Potter and the Goblet of Fire at midnight on the day of release, and then called everyone she could in the States to gloat about being able to read it hours before them.

Sexuality, Protest, Elves, and White Womanhood: Hermione and S.P.E.W.

Laurie Barth Walczak

To those of us immersed in children's culture right now, it feels as if we could divide the reading world into two categories: those who have read the *Harry Potter* books and those who plan to read them. Now of course, there are those who are too scholarly or too cool for Harry Potter, but they are in the minority. The rest of us realize the importance of Harry. Harry has changed childhood, simple as that, and not only in Britain or America, but indeed, in countries throughout the world. Harry has cast a spell, exactly the spell that parents, teachers, librarians, and other children's culture professionals have been waiting for: Harry makes kids read. Perhaps Harry is exactly what we have all been wishing for. Or perhaps he is not.

We know Harry is reaching children worldwide, but what message does he give them? What system of identification does the series shape or impact in its readers? More specifically, what do children learn about race and identity from Harry Potter? It is not within the scope of this paper to attempt to answer such questions for a worldwide audience, and thus my focus is on Harry's American readers.

Harry Potter began as a distinctly British phenomenon. His creator, Scottish J.K. Rowling, of course utilizes British slang and references. But as Harry's audience grew, the British constructions in the series changed. Indeed, the books were not only translated into different languages but also were specifically edited for an American audience. Thanks to Arthur Levine, the editor of the United States editions at Scholastic, Inc., the language was Americanized. Sara Heiberger, author of "Harry Potter and the Editor's Pen" comments, " . . . Levine has made editorial suggestions on all the books, identifying any Britishisms, for example, whose unfamiliarity might bewilder U.S. readers. In such cases he and Rowling search together for terms that are clearer but still maintain a British flavor." While Heiberger suggests that the American editions have changes "only in instances where Rowling believed ambiguity might be problematic," an examination of the differences between the U.K. editions and the U.S. editions seems to demonstrate a more significant Americanization of the stories. For example, the first book underwent a title change from *Harry Potter and the Philosopher's Stone* to *Harry Potter and the Sorcerer's Stone* because Levine thought the British title "'too esoteric'" (Heiberger). Within this first book itself, "shan't" becomes "won't," "mummy" becomes "mommy," and "letter-box" becomes "mail slot" (Word Gallery). These modifications do not seem to be so much a case of ambiguity or obscurity as they are a case of unfamiliarity or discomfort. American readers are not accustomed to calling "mommy" by the name "mummy," but most likely they would understand the meaning, especially in context.

Perhaps more disturbing is that characters of color are even added to the American editions. An example is when Harry and his fellow first-year students are being sorted into the appropriate house in the first book of the series. In the U.K. edition, Harry's readers see: "And now there were only three people left to be sorted. 'Turpin, Lisa' became a Ravenclaw and then it was Ron's turn" (91). After Ron Weasley is sorted into Gryffindor, Blaise Zabini is placed into Slytherin, and the sorting is complete. However, in the U.S. edition, edited by Levine, American children read: "And now there were only three people left to be sorted. 'Thomas, Dean,' a Black boy even taller than Ron, joined Harry at the Gryffindor table. 'Turpin, Lisa' became a Ravenclaw and then it was Ron's turn" (122). Even though Dean, Ron, and Lisa make up three students left to be sorted, Blaise Zabini still comes last, making it actually four students left. However, the addition of Dean Thomas is not troubling because it makes the count of the students left to be sorted inaccurate. What is troubling is that Dean Thomas, the black boy, is an obvious maneuver of tokenism. He appears to be INSERTed as a token character of color for the American audience. While there are a variety of multicultural characters in the novel—for example the Patil sisters and now Kingsley Shacklebolt—they remain minorities. The addition of one more in the American editions—Dean Thomas—does not significantly impact the presence of people of color in the series.

The American editions seem to be set in Britain not because the author and the characters are British, but because it is a land of wizards and castles and dragons—especially to Americans. Has Harry's American audience exercised its manifest destiny over him, as the American culture tends to do with anything it finds appealing? As Harry's American audience make these books their own, what do they bring to the *Harry Potter* series, and what do they find there? The position of whiteness.

What is whiteness? There is perhaps no definition that encompasses the inevitability, the invisibility, and the omnipresence of whiteness in American culture. Valerie Babb, author of *Whiteness Visible: The Meaning of Whiteness in American Literature and Culture*, describes whiteness as "more than an appearance; it is a system of privileges accorded to those with white skin" (9). Whiteness is a part of the structural and institutional hegemony that assigns privilege to white people. The ubiquity of whiteness exerts power over every American social and cultural construction.

Perhaps the most significant and most unsettling aspect of whiteness is in its invisibility. To begin his book *White*, Richard Dyer explains that in Western thought, non-white people are members of a particular race while white people are "just people," not members of a race at all: "As long as race is something only applied to non-white peoples, as long as white people are not racially seen and named, they/we function as a human norm. Other people are raced, we are just people" (1). White people do not see themselves as members of a race; they see themselves as "just people." Dyer goes on to explain that "Research—into books, museums, the press, advertising, films, television, software—repeatedly shows that in Western representation whites are overwhelmingly and disproportionately predominant, have the central and elaborated roles, and above all are placed as the norm, the ordinary, the standard" (3). The *Harry Potter* series is no exception: all of the major characters are white, and no attention needs to be called to their race at any time. When new characters are introduced, their whiteness is not labeled, but their Otherness is. For example, in *Harry Potter and the Order of the Phoenix*, readers meet two several new characters early on in the book: Nymphadora Tonks is described with "She looked the youngest there; she had a pale heart-shaped face, dark twinkling eyes, and short spiky hair that was a violent shade of violet" (47) but Kinglsey Shacklebolt is "a bald black wizard standing farthest back; he had a deep, slow voice and wore a single gold hoop in his ear" (47). The other witches and wizards are described with "the wheezy-voiced wizard," the "stately looking witch in an emerald-green shawl," the "square-jawed wizard with thick, straw-colored hair," and the "pink-cheeked, black-haired witch" (49). An indicator of race—"black"—is assigned to Shacklebolt, but no one else. White remains the invisible norm, and only deviations from this norm are made visible.

Without any knowledge or awareness and regardless of their own race or ethnicity, American child readers may bring whiteness to the *Harry Potter* books. And whiteness may already exist within their pages. The nature of whiteness itself is its invisibility and its ineffability; it generally only becomes visible and definable in terms of its relationship to an Other. Because whiteness is what it is not, its goodness, its purity, its supremacy, and its power comes from its use of the Other.

Within Harry's world is the established dichotomy of Hogwarts magic vs. the dark arts. Hogwarts magic is defined by what it is not; it is not dark. In this dichotomy, Albus Dumbledore, Headmaster of Hogwarts, becomes the construction of absolute whiteness: he is the core of power, of goodness, and of magic. His skin is pale, and his long, flowing hair and beard are silver. He is extremely revered, and he has an almost godlike power to know and see all at Hogwarts. From his color to his control, he is the model of whiteness that Harry and his readers admire. The greatest threat to Dumbledore and his kind of magic is the aptly-named dark arts. Just as whiteness is defined by its relationship to its Other, Dumbledore and Harry especially are defined by their relationship to the dark arts.

The dark arts is all that Hogwarts magic is not; it is evil, greedy, and cruel. Lord Voldemort epitomizes the dark arts. In his past attempt to rise to power and take over the magic world, Voldemort had killed numerous wizards and witches, including Harry's parents. Indeed, Voldemort also attempted to kill baby Harry, as well, but he could not; his curse backfires on him and obliterates his powers. Over the course of the series, Voldemort attempts to regain his strength, and in the fourth book, he and his followers, called "The Death Eaters," recover their powers, launching an Armageddon-like battle against Dumbledore and Harry. Of course, Harry prevails, but Voldemort establishes that he is now an extremely real, extremely violent force.

The battle between Hogwarts magic and the dark arts is simply the eternal struggle between good and evil, with variations, such as the giants and the house elves, tenuously trapped in the middle. But it is also the struggle between white/light and black/dark. Perhaps the dark arts is the kind of "Africanist presence" Toni Morrison discusses in *Playing in the Dark: Whiteness and the Literary Imagination*. While Morrison examines the black presence in American literature (5), perhaps her theories can be extended usefully to *Harry Potter*. Morrison explains that the presence of a blackness in literature "provides a way of contemplating chaos and civilization, desire and freedom, and a mechanism for testing the problems and blessings of freedom" (7). This role seems to be the one played by the dark arts in the series. The dark arts is the force against which Dumbledore, Harry, and their allies can measure their goodness. By struggling against the dark arts, Harry finds himself and establishes his identity and power. Morrison also discusses the terror that American literature often explores: "and terror's most significant, overweening ingredient: darkness, with all the connotative value it awakened" (37). The dark arts is definitely the source of terror in the series. Harry must attempt to face this terror and overcome it, not only to save himself, but the entire magic world. Voldemort threatens to not only terrorize but subsume the magic world if Harry does not stop him. Thus, Harry's position and purpose is to exert the power of goodness, perhaps the power of whiteness, over the dark arts. Morrison explains that we need to "analyze the strategic use of black characters to define the goals and enhance the qualities of white characters" (52-53). Indeed, we need to analyze the use of the dark arts to define Harry.

Another struggle for definition of one's own identity occurs in the series in Hermione Granger, the muggle-born witch with exceptional intelligence and homework-doing abilities. In the fourth book, Hermione is introduced to the plight of the house-elves. House-elves are slave-creatures that spend their entire lives completely subservient to their masters. If they fail to serve in any way, they inflict physical harm upon themselves, for example, by beating their heads against walls or hitting themselves with various objects. House-elves serve Hogwarts, as well, working in the kitchens and on the grounds. Important to note, though, is that house-elves are supposed to enjoy this life.

Still, Hermione takes on a kind of abolitionist campaign to free the house-elves when she creates "S.P.E.W.," or "the Society for the Promotion of Elfish Welfare"—the acronym itself demonstrates the mocking tone used toward her work (Rowling *Goblet* 224). Hermione comes from the muggle world into the wizarding world and identifies the injustice in the lives of the house-elves. Few, if any, within the magic world consider their enslavement to be in any way wrong: "Some people, like Neville, had paid up just to stop Hermione from glowering at them. A few seemed mildly interested in what she had to say, but were reluctant to take a more active role in campaigning. Many regarded the whole thing as a joke" (Rowling *Goblet* 239). Only Hermione in her position on the outside of the systems of the wizarding world considers the house-elves' situation problematic, and the solution does not seem to be freeing the house-elves but instead convincing Hermione that their service natural and acceptable. For example, when

Hermione protests to Harry and Ron, "'Elf enslavement goes back centuries. I can't believe no one's done anything about it before now,'" Ron responds with, "'Hermione— open your ears .... They. Like. It. They *like* being enslaved'" (Rowling *Goblet* 224).

One house-elf, Dobby, proves differently, however. Dobby was originally the servant of the Malfoy family, but Harry frees him in the third book. Dobby explains that after being set free, he could not find a job because, in his words, "'most wizards doesn't want a house-elf who wants paying, miss. "That's not the point of a house-elf," they says, and they slammed the door in Dobby's face! Dobby likes work, but he wants to wear clothes and he wants to be paid .... Dobby likes being free!'" (Rowling *Goblet* 378). Dobby demonstrates that this enslaved race of creatures is capable of taking pleasure in and benefiting from freedom.

While Dobby plays the freed slave, another house-elf, Winky, plays quite the opposite role; she is the slave who cannot comprehend any other life. Due to what appears at first to be her disobedience, Winky is stripped of her position as the house-elf for the Crouch family early on in the fourth book. She spends the remainder of the story drunk, miserable, and unable to cope with freedom. At the conclusion of the book, readers find that Winky was not disobedient but instead was tying to protect the family she served, despite that this family was entangled with the dark arts. It is her master's son, Barty Crouch, Jr., who in the end of the novel is revealed to be Voldemort's collaborator in returning Voldemort to power and attempting to kill Harry. Winky knows of Crouch's plot; however, she cannot warn anyone. As a house-elf, she is bound to silence. Dobby explains to Harry, "'"Tis part of the house-elf's enslavement, sir. We keeps their secrets and our silence, sir. We upholds the family's honor, and we never speak ill of them" (Rowling *Goblet* 380).

In *Harry Potter and the Order of the Phoenix*, Kreacher, the Black family's house elf, figures more like Winky than like Dobby.

Perhaps like the dark arts, the house-elves act as another kind of Africanist presence in the *Harry Potter* series. Most disturbing is the parallel to the shared belief that slaveowners clung to: slaves enjoyed being enslaved. This belief has been represented before in American children's literature. The daughter-in-law of Joel Chandler Harris, author of the Uncle Remus tales, writes in *Life and Letters of Joel Chandler Harris*, "'imagine that the myth stories of Uncle Remus are told night after night to a little boy by an old negro who appears to be venerable enough to have lived during the period which he describes—who has nothing but pleasant memories of the discipline of slavery'" (qtd. in Walker 236). Most unfortunately, a comparable attitude is presented in the *Harry Potter* series: Hagrid, the Keeper of the Keys and the Care of Magical Creatures instructor at Hogwarts, explains to Hermione, "'It's in their nature ter look after humans, that's what they like, see? Yeh'd be makin' 'em unhappy ter take away their work, an insultin' 'em if yeh tried ter pay 'em'" (Rowling *Goblet* 265).

Moreover, the house-elves may serve as an Africanist presence in the manner in which they observe their masters but do not speak about them. In *Black on White: Black*

Writers on What It Means to Be White, David Roediger explains that scholars such as W.E.B. Du Bois and bell hooks "emphasize the servants' ability to know the families for whom they work" (5). The house-elves' inability to speak out against their masters is possibly a reminder of "What bell hooks describes as the fantastic white ability to imagine 'that black people cannot see them'" (Roediger 6). The house-elves are of course able to view their masters, but the "white illusion," as Roediger calls it, is still in place, for the house-elves cannot tell what they see (6).

The position of the house-elves as Africanist presence in the *Harry Potter* series may help to explain why Hermione's fight for fair wages and working conditions for house-elves seems to fail. At some point in the novel, Hermione's abolitionist cause appears to just simply get dropped. Morrison explains that writers may encounter a "breakdown in the logic and machinery of plot construction," which "implies the powerful impact race has on narrative—and on narrative strategy" (25). Perhaps such is the case in this novel. Hermione's association with the house-elves and S.P.E.W. can no longer be maintained because of its racial implications. In allying herself with the house-elves, an Africanist presence, Hermione herself is darkened; she becomes an embarrassment to even her closest friends as she fights for a cause they feel is wholly worthless. Hermione needs to regain her position in whiteness, and to do so, she needs to abandon S.P.E.W. What is interesting is that the cessation of her efforts also seems to mark her maturity to young womanhood; Hermione deserts the seemingly childish S.P.E.W. in order to grow up, and growing up to young white womanhood means finding a love-interest. Hermione forgets her activism when her time and her mind become occupied with her admirer, Viktor Krum:

> Harry glanced up at Hermione to see how she felt about this new and more complicated method of dining—surely it meant plenty of extra work for the house-elves?—but for once, Hermione didn't seem to be thinking about S.P.E.W. She was deep in talk with Viktor Krum and hardly seemed to notice what she was eating. (Rowling *Goblet* 416-17)

It seems as though the plot of the novel cannot accommodate both positions. Hermione cannot be darkened by her connection to the house-elves and at the same time be a young, white woman. Thus, S.P.E.W. is left behind as Hermione is reinscribed into whiteness and femininity. Such is not a powerfully positive message to send to children regarding slavery or abolition, whiteness or femininity.

It may be challenging for parents, teachers, librarians, and other children's culture professionals to at once love and critique the *Harry Potter* series. Far easier is allowing ourselves to be swept up on a broomstick into the world of Harry Potter, into a world of magic, mystery, and myth. However, that voyage may not be as carefree or escapist as we might think. Instead of flying into a world of make-believe, we may be taking part in a world of all-to-real whiteness, and this world can have definite implications for its adult and, more importantly, its child readers. Thus, perhaps we cannot allow ourselves to completely fall under the spell of Harry Potter; Harry's spell instead should be scrutinized so that we may see exactly what kind of magic he is practicing.

Works Cited

Babb, Valerie. *Whiteness Visible: The Meaning of Whiteness in American Literature and Culture*. New York: New York UP, 1998.

Dyer, Richard. *White*. New York: Routledge, 1997.

Heiberger, Sara. "Harry Potter and the Editor's Pen." *Brown Alumni Magazine Online* Nov./Dec. 2001. 16 Dec. 2001. <http://brownalumnimagazine.com/ storydetail.cfm?ID=421>.

Morrison, Toni. *Playing in the Dark: Whiteness and the Literary Imagination*. New York: Vintage Books, 1993.

Natov, Roni. "Harry Potter and the Extraordinariness of the Ordinary." *The Lion and the Unicorn* 25.2 (2000): 310-27.

Pinsent, Pat. *Children's Literature and the Politics of Equality*. New York: Teachers College P, 1997.

Roediger, David R. Introduction. *Black on White: Black Writers on What It Means to Be White*. Ed. David R. Roediger. New York: Schocken Books, 1998.

Rowling, J.K. *Harry Potter and the Goblet of Fire*. New York: Scholastic P, 2000.

_____. *Harry Potter and the Order of the Phoenix*. New York: Scholastic P, 2003.

_____. *Harry Potter and the Philosopher's Stone*. London: Bloomsbury, 1997.

_____. *Harry Potter and the Prisoner of Azkaban*. New York: Scholastic P, 1999.

_____. *Harry Potter and the Sorcerer's Stone*. New York: Scholastic P, 1997.

Schafer, Elizabeth D. *Exploring Harry Potter*. Beacham's Sourcebooks for Teaching Young Adult Fiction. Osprey, FL: Beacham, 2000.

Walker, Alice. "The Dummy in the Window." *Black on White: Black Writers on What It Means to Be White*. Ed. David R. Roediger. New York: Schocken Books, 1998. 233-39.

"Word Gallery: American English." *HP Galleries: The Harry Potter Phenomenon*. 16 Dec. 2001. <http://www.hpgalleries.com/wordgallery1.htm>.

Laurie Barth Walczak is a Ph.D. candidate in Literary Studies at the University of Wisconsin-Milwaukee. Her areas of interest include young adult literature, critical race theory, and multicultural pedagogy. Laurie also teaches courses on adolescence in literature. Laurie is a devoted Harry Potter fan and celebrated her best birthday ever this year, as it coincided with the release of Harry Potter and the Order of the Phoenix.

Moral Development, Philosophy & Religious Studies

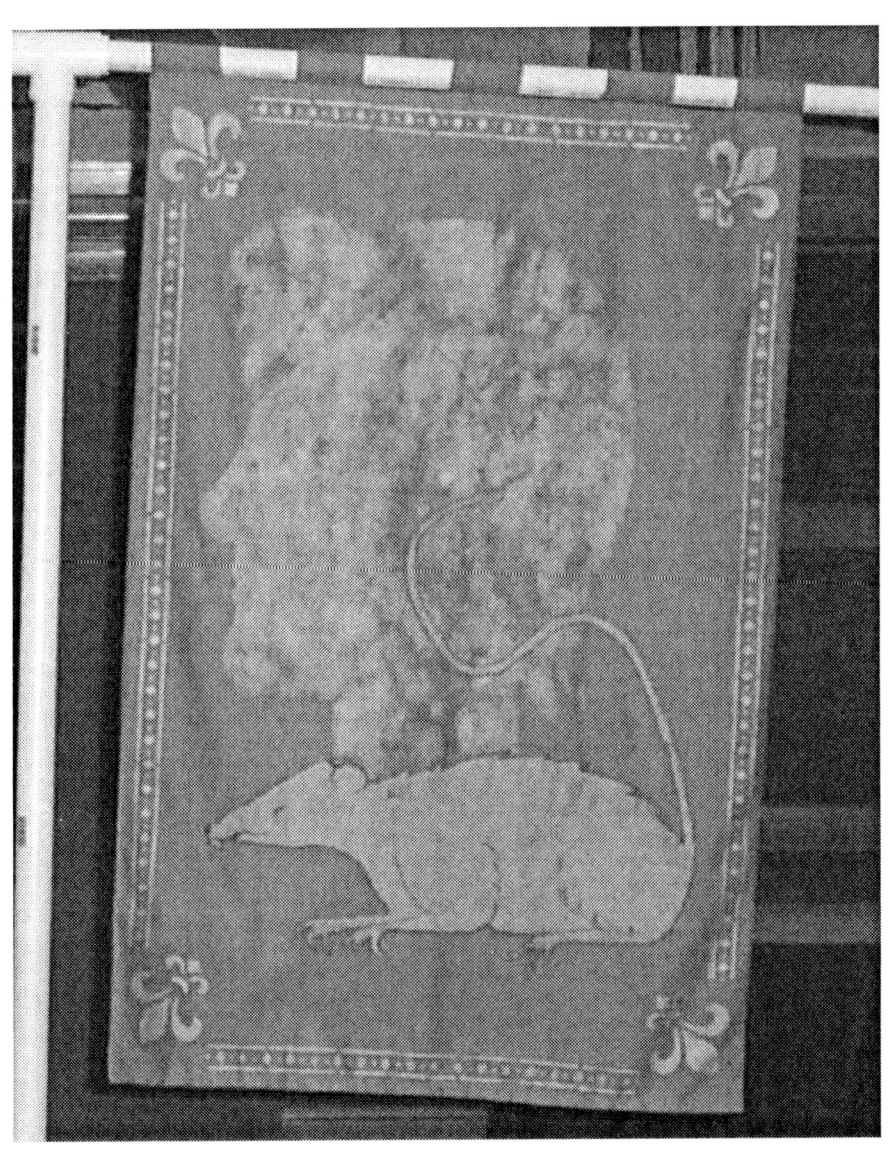

Talking about Harry . . .
The Modern Fairy Tale and Moral Development

Gina Burkart

Ms. Burkart's paper is part of a forthcoming book with InterVarsity Press. The title is still being determined.

Some Christians argue that the Harry Potter books promote witchcraft and have been inspired by Satan. They fear the violent and dangerous scenes. Some extremists are not only pushing to ban the books from schools and libraries, but they are burning the books as well. Harry Potter even tops the American Library Association list of the 100 most challenged books. You wonder "What should I do? Will the books adversely affect my children?" When faced with questions such as these, it is important to remember that as a parent you are the ultimate model for your child(ren). You have the ability to help them build a moral character that will last throughout their lives. And the use of the fantasy world has been used to enchant and teach children moral lessons for centuries. Harry Potter is really nothing new—in fact Harry Potter is essentially a modern fairy tale. By looking at the elements and use of the fairy tale as well as consulting with moral theorists Lawrence Kohlberg, Jean Piaget, and Martin Hoffman, you will not only find the answers to your questions, but you will realize that Harry Potter and this guide, *A Christian Parent's Guide to Harry Potter and the Sorcerer's Stone,* are useful tools for developing moral character in your children.

The Importance of the Fairy Tale

"Once upon a time . . . " children were taught moral lessons from the fairy tale. The phrase "once upon a time" beckoned children to begin a journey of enchantment¾a journey that would whisk them off to a location far away where they would encounter mystery, magic, pain, and amusement. They would meet fairies, witches, villains, and friends. And upon returning they would be refreshed with a new outlook on life and their everyday struggles. They would have a renewed faith in themselves and a better understanding of life and what the human condition entails. The fairy tale was not just an escape or retreat but a moral compass for life.

For example in *The Emperor's New Clothes* children learn that vanity and dishonesty can have negative consequences. The emperor, in his vanity, believes the two swindlers who pretend to make the emperor a magnificent new suit. They profess that anyone who can't see the new suit is not worthy of his or her profession. The emperor follows along and ends up processing in the streets naked because he does not question the swindlers. The courtiers lie and deceive the emperor to protect their offices. The emperor suffers embarrassment because of his vanity and fear that he may be unworthy of his office. His vanity continues the lie; he is too worried about his position and what others think to challenge the courtiers. This story provides children with a great example of the dangers of conformity and peer pressure. And yet it is humorous and allows them to laugh at the emperor's mistakes as well as their own.

But somewhere down the road of life, parents became concerned about the influence of fantasy and imagination on our young children's minds. They feared fantasy would lead our children away to Never-never Land, and our children would not return. Reality and fact was emphasized in education, and imagination was discouraged. And now we are in the middle of a technological era. Scientists strive to uncover the mysteries of the universe and the workings of the biological man. Computers have become common in the household and have replaced many human jobs. Cloning, the Internet, and nuclear power are in the forefront of our technological era. And our children are trained to succeed in this technological era. But what are they being taught about human relationships and the meaning of life? They may know what a human being is, but they have no idea how to form a meaningful relationship with one. And why should they? Today, success is not measured by relationships. In fact, relationships are discouraged because they get in the way of getting to the top of the "corporate ladder." Success is measured by money, title, and materialism. Marriage and children are often put off until career and financial goals are met. Children are raised by day-care workers who are paid minimally and switch jobs frequently. Quality relationships among these children are nearly non-existent. Children turn to children for support and guidance.

And what of nature and the environment? Our children know what nature is made up of, and how natural resources can be used to further our material lifestyles, but they have no idea how to enjoy a sunset. They know how to identify clouds, but they don't find pictures and stories in the sky. Again, nature is a means to an end. Not an end in itself that should be savored and enjoyed, but an end to material resources. In *Functions of Folk and Fairy Tale,* Donald Baker explains

Because science apparently offers factual answers to life on earth and even among the stars, our educational systems have been geared to a world of technology. There is a definite trend to design and develop curricula capable of preparing children for the life they will presumably lead in a technologically based society. The actual value of that technology and the quality of life it supports—in fact, the morality of extracting from the earth all that we need without concern for putting back—are issues we either ignore or do not give nearly as much thought as they deserve or demand. We merely cry out when the oil dries up, not realising that we are responsible for the drought. How to live with nature not off it is a matter of moral, not only of conservation (1).

And now after extracting morality, religion, and imagination from education, we ask "What is wrong with our children?" Columbine shocked and stunned us. "Why are our children killing each other?" Almost daily, the news informs us of school violence, drug and alcohol abuse, delinquency, rebellion, sexual disease, and teen pregnancy. By emphasizing fact and discouraging imagination, our children never learn the value of life. Because we extracted the supernatural and morality from education; our children know what life is but don't understand the meaning of life. We gave our children reality but neglected to give them a means for understanding it. In *The Uses of Enchantment,* Bruno Bettelheim asserts "Before a child can come to grips with reality, he [or she] must have some frame of reference to evaluate it" (117).

Bruno Bettelheim, an educator and therapist of severely disturbed children, found two things imperative in helping children find meaning in their lives: parents (guardians) and literature (4). The relationships of the parents (guardians) with the children and the transmission of the children's heritage through literature in the form of the fairy tale gave meaning to the children's life because the stories

> start where the child really is in his [or her] psychological and emotional well being. They speak about his [or her] severe inner pressures in a way that the child unconsciously understands, and—without belittling the most serious inner struggles which growing up entails—offer examples of both temporary and permanent solutions to pressing difficulties (6).

Bettleheim found that the fairy tales coveyed to children "moral education which subtly, and by implication only, conveys . . . the advantages of moral behavior, not through abstract ethical concepts but through that which seems tangibly right and therefore meaningful" (5). The fairy tale is the ideal literature for moral instruction because it has "access to deeper meaning" and is able to reach children at their stage of moral development. The fairy tale holds children's attention, entertains and arouses curiosity, and enriches life by stimulating the imagination. The fairy tale develops intellect, clarifies emotions, is attuned to childhood anxieties and aspirations, gives recognition to childhood difficulties, and offers solutions to life challenges and problems (Bettleheim 5).

Elements of the Fairy Tale

Fear Factor

The fairy tale passes on lessons of heritage and life in the context of a fantasy world. Its framework relates the fundamental issues of good and evil, life and death, and tasks and journeys that symbolize life. The fairy tale also often contains terrifying and frightening scenes, which modern day parents and educators often object to and strive to protect children from. For example, Hansel and Gretel face a witch that wants to eat them; Cinderella is locked up by a wicked step-mother, and Little Red Riding Hood is pursued by a hungry wolf. But these frightening and terrifying scenes allow children to feel a human emotion—fear—within the security of community and family. They allow the subconscious fears of children to surface and be released. For example Hansel and Gretel deal with the loss of their parents successfully. Loss of parents is one of the greatest fears of children, yet it is often unspoken and hidden—thus causing anxiety. The fairy tale allows the fear to be released and dealt with. Donald Baker in *Functions of Folk and Fairy Tale* argues that

> fairy tales like those of the Brothers Grimm or Hans Christian Anderson, two of the best-known collections, undoubtedly include terrifying elements which, paradoxically, are also potentially therapeutic. In a story dealing with fear . . . the intention is to uncover hidden repressions and to show that to feel fear is normal and truly human. It implies respect for others, borne not of fear for them but of a healthy recognition of their claims upon us. The growing child must recognise the rights of others, just as he or she makes a claim on parents for protection and well-being. Fairy tales are not escapist fantasies; nor do they induce anxiety states. In either case they perform the opposite function; namely, to confront children with reality of their subconscious terrors and nightmares in the guise of a tale told in secure surroundings . . . . Without the fairy tale we should never achieve any kind of humanity (5).

But perhaps we are getting ahead of ourselves by focusing on the fear factor of the fairy tale, and perhaps that is why the fairy tale is often criticized and misinterpreted by parents and educators. The main goal of the fairy tale is not to provoke fear. The fear is only a component of the fairy tale. The fairy tale is meant to "depict processes of development and maturation" (Luthi 139). That process of development and maturation involves a certain amount of risks, journeys, and tasks involving danger that inevitably and naturally evoke fear.

The Hero, Villain, and Triumph of Good over Evil

Thus every fairy tale has a protagonist or hero. This hero begins with a struggle or dilemma. He or she is often shown as weak and being abused by a higher authority or force—like Cinderella. The hero has a problem to solve, task to perform, or a journey to embark on in order to overcome the evil force that is portrayed through a villain. "Evil has to be overcome by faithful service, and there is little doubt that the folk tale represents the psychological need for societies and individuals to engage in certain initiatory rites as they pass from one status to another. The journey in the story is an allegory of everyone's journey through life" (Baker 7). Bettleheim believes this to be one of the vital components of the fairy tale, and thus one of the reasons why the fairy tale is so helpful in teaching children the meaning of life. He explains

> fairy tales get across to the child in manifold form: that a struggle
> against severe difficulties in life in unavoidable, is an intrinsic part of
> human existence—but that if one does not shy away, but steadfastly
> meets unexpected and often unjust hardships, one masters all obstacles
> and at the end emerges victorious (8).

Amidst these struggles the hero must choose between good and evil. The battle of good and evil is a powerful theme as it is "omnipresent in life and . . . in every man. It is this duality which poses the moral problem, and requires the struggle to solve it" (9). Yet in the fairy tale, good and evil are set up as polar opposites. A character is either all good or all evil. Snow White is good, and her step-mother, the witch, is evil. There is no middle ground. This use of polar opposites is effective with children because that is how they reason. Presenting the characters as the child thinks allows the child to easily distinguish between good and evil (Bettleheim 9).

Fantasy

One of the most enchanting aspects of the fairy tale for children is the imaginative, fantasy world that it explores. Children are allowed to enter a world of magical powers, charms, and fascinating characters that are able to escape the boundaries of time and space. Their imaginations are attracted to talking animals, mythological creatures, and recurrent symbols. One of the most recurrent symbols is the number three. Baker explains "Many traditional tales have three characters, three incidents, three tasks, etc. The reason seems to be that 'three' is the basic family unit with father, mother and child" (8). Baker also asserts that the recurrence of three acts as a sort of refrain. Its repetition adds predictability and thus security (9).

But parents are concerned about their children embarking on such imaginative adventures in a fantasy world. They feel that children will not be able to return to reality. Bettleheim addresses this concern that parents have with fantasy in literature such as fairy tales and Harry Potter (the modern fairy tale—discussed later). He explains that "a child needs to understand what is going on within his conscious self so that he [or she] can also cope with that which goes on in the unconscious" (7). Parents and educators often resort to realistic and factual information to offer children an understanding of the conscious self, but this is not enough. Bettleheim has found that children do not find this understanding

> through rational comprehension of the nature and content of [their] unconscious, but by becoming familiar with it through spinning out daydreams—ruminating, rearranging, and fantasizing about suitable story elements in response to unconscious pressures . . . . It is here that fairy tales have unequaled value, because they offer new dimensions to the child's imagination which would be impossible for him [or her] to discover as truly on his own. Even more important, the form and structure of the fairy tales suggest images to the child by which he can structure his daydreams and with them give better direction to his [or her] life (7).

This is vital and contrary information to parents who often discourage or prevent imaginative and fantasy literature. They see the fantasy world as potentially harmful, and fear that children will confuse reality with fantasy and thus seek magical solutions to real problems. Such is often the case made for such stories as Harry Potter. However, Bettleheim warns that when imagination and the unconscious is repressed "eventually the person's conscious mind will be partially overwhelmed by derivatives of these unconscious elements, or else he [or she] is forced to keep such rigid compulsive control over them that his [or her] personality is severely crippled" (7). But when the imagination is allowed to come to awareness and work out problems in the fantasy world of literature or daydreaming, the chances of the unconscious "causing harm— to ourselves or others—is much reduced; some of its forces can then be made to serve positive forces" (7).

So the fantasy world of the fairy tale and Harry Potter provides children with the *necessary* task of working out their unconscious struggles and conflicts in the fantasy world. It allows the unconscious to surface in a setting that reality does not provide. And more importantly the fairy tale encourages parent and child dialogue— thus fostering a parent/child relationship that includes moral discussion. For "the child's enthusiasm for the story becomes contagious," (18) as has been the case with the story of Harry Potter. Adults are just as enthused about the story of Harry Potter (if not more so) than the children. This is the nature of a good moral story— most typically the fairy tale.

Harry Potter—The Modern Fairy Tale

To better understand what to do about Harry Potter, let's look at what we have just learned about the fairy tale¾for Harry Potter not only has all of the elements of the fairy tale, it also has the same controversial issues. In essence, Harry Potter is a modern day fairy tale. Viewing it as such certainly explains why so many children and adults have become enchanted with the series.

Fear Factor

In *Harry Potter and the Sorcerer's Stone,* Harry Potter, like the fairy tale, contains many frightening scenes and battles. And likewise, parents are concerned for their children. For example, Harry battles a three-headed dog, a troll, and the evil Lord Voldemort (notice there are 3 battles—a recurrent symbol of the fairy tale). He comes face to face with death and always emerges victorious. As previously discussed, this is an essential component of the fairy tale as it reflects the journey of development and maturation occurring within the tale. As Harry succeeds in each battle, he gains more confidence in himself and gains a fuller understanding of the battle of good and evil. For example, it isn't until the final battle with Lord Voldermort that Harry understands that it was the love of his mother that saved him. Evil could not touch something that was so good. Professor Dumbledore tells Harry "Your mother died to save you. If there is one thing Voldemort cannot understand, it is love. He didn't realize that love as powerful as your mother's for you leaves its own mark . . . . Quirrell full of hatred, greed, and ambition, sharing his soul with Voldemort could not touch you for this reason. It was agony to touch a person marked by something so good" (Rowling 299). As with the fairy tale, here the terror of the final battle leads to a moral understanding of good and evil—and thus a better understanding of the meaning of life.

This lesson, of course, also allows the Christian parent and child to relate Harry's battle with the battle of Christ, Satan, and humanity. Out of love, Christ died to save us (like Harry's mother died for Harry). Love triumphed over evil. Christ saved us from Satan, as Harry's mother saved Harry from Lord Voldemort. Looking at the Harry Potter series a religious allegory perhaps best answers our questions and concerns about the frightening nature of the Harry Potter story. For the Bible also contains many frightening stories (and perhaps more so because they are true) that teach our children about morality and the meaning of life. For example, Abraham obeys God and takes his son, Isaac, to the top of a mountain with the intent to sacrifice him for God. The situation of a father intending to kill his son is extremely frightening for a child, yet it teaches the moral lesson that obedience to God must come above all else—and God proves to be merciful and loving. God does not have Abraham kill Isaac. Thus, we learn to trust and obey God.

And remember, Bettleheim argues that the experience of fear in the fantasy world is cathartic and therapeutic for the child. It allows the child to come back to reality refreshed and with a better understanding of how to deal with good and evil in the real world. Harry Potter returns from Hogwarts with hope and strength to endure the Dursleys because he has not only defeated the much stronger evil power Lord Voldemort, but he now has found friendship with Ron, Hermione, Hagrid, and the Weasley family. And the readers have a better understanding of friendship, family, relationships, choices, peer pressure, death, and how they all relate to good and evil.

The Hero, Villain, and Truimph of Good over Evil

This connection was briefly touched upon above in the fear factor and is rather obvious to anyone who has read *Harry Potter and the Sorcerer's Stone*. Harry Potter is the hero of the story. His parents have been killed by the villain Lord Voldemort, and Harry has been raised by the mean and abusive Dursleys. In fact the storyline closely resembles that of Cinderella. The Dursleys could easily be equated with Cinderella's evil step-mother. Harry is treated unfairly compared to Dudley, who is showered with praise, love, and material gifts. Harry is ignored, mistreated, and forced to wear rags that don't fit him. Thus Dudley is simlar to Cinderellas's step-sisters. And Harry is rescued from his predicament by Hagrid, who whisks him off to Hogwarts where Harry becomes famous and finds friends. This could compare to the fairy godmother who helps Cinderella go to the ball and gain the admiration of a princess.

However, the story-line of Harry Potter becomes a little more complex as he encounters the evil forces of Lord Voldemort in the wizarding world and embarks on a journey of maturity where he battles Lord Voldemort, and the death eaters. As a modern fairy tale, Harry Potter has been adapted to the complexities that its modern audience expects.

Fantasy

Parallel to the fairy tale, Harry Potter heavily relies on the use of fantasy and magic to enchant its readers—to the dismay of many parents and educators. At Hogwarts, Harry Potter enters a magical world where he uses a magical wand, flies on a broomstick, and learns how to use witchcraft. It is important for us to remember that fantasy is what makes the fairy tale so useful. Children already think imaginatively. They daydream and engage in make-believe play to make sense out of their world. They do not operate on the same level of reasoning and principles of reality that we do, and as Bettleheim (discussed above) warns it can be detrimental to personality development to repress children's use of the fantasy world to make sense out of every day life. Children know that when they open up the Harry Potter books they are about to enter a different world with different rules. And when they close the book, they know that they have returned to reality. Opening the book of a modern fairy tale serves the same purpose as the phrase "Once upon a time . . . " serves in the legendary fairy tale. And keep in mind that as parents, we can ensure that our children understand the difference between reality and fantasy. We can share the stories with our children as they explore the fantasy and reality of Harry Potter. The fantasy world is not something to be feared, rather it is a useful tool for promoting moral growth and development.

In fact, in a world that uses fact to measure truth, the fantasy world of the fairy tale introduces children to a more important truth. Donald Baker labels this "the truth of experience, the intuitive feeling aroused when we contemplate some distant event or try to empathize with another human being" (10). This is the kind of truth that can't be measured, seen, or verified with tangible and concrete proof. However, it is one of the truths by which we make many of our moral decisions because it is the kind of truth that religious faith heavily relies on. So if we don't allow for our children to encounter this "truth of experience" how can we expect them to believe in a supernatural force that we call God? Thus, we should be more concerned about an education system that places all of its emphasis on fact and strives to extract imagination and religion from our children's learning than a system that has fantasy literature in its library.

Rosemary Haughton in *Tales from Eternity* affirms fairy tales are important to faith formation. She argues that in the technological age we lost a way of thinking that was promoted by the fairy tales and the Gospel. Haughton affirms "Fairy tales can open our minds to the human, and make us able to hear more sharply the demand for the transformation of the human into its own completeness in Christ" (15).

Theories of Moral Development

Harry Potter, as the modern fairy tale, provides parents with an opportunity to build the type of relationship that will foster moral development in their children, and my books *A Christian Parent's Guide to Harry Potter* is a resource for building strong parent and child(ren) relationships that foster moral growth and development. The guide offers practical suggestions for applying the principles of the moral development theories of Jean Piaget, Lawrence Kohlberg, and Martin Hoffman to explore Harry Potter, the modern fairy tale.

Piaget's and Kohlberg's theories are often used to develop Christian education programs because Christian education provides a framework for structures that Piaget and Kohlberg identified (Duska and Whelan 83). Thus, it makes sense that this same framework for moral development has also weaved through the stories of the fairy tales. And as a Christian parent, it is essential for you to understand not only how your child progresses through the stages of moral development but also how Christianity and literature work to foster that moral development.

Both Piaget and Kohlberg found that moral development occurs in different stages. While their mapping out of the stages are different, they both agree that moral development begins with an understanding of good and bad. Children realize that there are both bad and good consequences to their actions, and they base their actions on these consequences. In his work *The Moral Judgment of the Child*, Piaget labels this heteronomous morality (111), and Kohlberg in "Stages of Moral Development as a Basis for Moral Education" labels this *State 1: The Punishment and Obedience Orientation* of the *Pre-Conventional Level* (86). At this level of development parents are seen as enforcers of discipline. Parents are authoritarian figures that judge behavior as good or bad and use punishment and reward to help the child decipher what behavior is good and bad. Punishment indicates bad behavior and reward indicates good and desirable behavior. For example, when a child hears "cheating is bad" the child reasons "cheating brings punishment." In this stage, adults are seen as bigger, stronger, and different. Not surprisingly, children in this stage often feel like an outsider against society (Duska and Whelan 52).

Both Piaget and Kohlberg also agree that children must pass through stages of moral development in order to arrive at a higher-level stage of moral reasoning, which Piaget (111) and Kohlberg (87) both call autonomous morality. Autonomous morality is independent of external pressures and "is based on the principles of cooperation and mutual respect and on the notion of subjective responsibility" (111). At this level of reasoning, Kohlberg says in "Continuities and Discontinuities in Childhood and Moral Development" "principles are abstract and ethical and are not concrete moral rules"(416). Kohlberg uses Immanuel Kant's *Categorical Imperative* and Christianity's *The Golden Rule* as examples of autonomous reasoning. Both the *Categorical Imperative* and *The Golden Rule* profess that one should not do to others what he or she would not want done to himself or herself. As parents and educators our goal is to help our children achieve autonomous morality—to grow into critical thinkers that can make moral choices (Duska and Whelan 76).

Piaget found that parents often hinder their children from achieving autonomous morality by reinforcing external rules that focus only on external consequences (Eisenberg 24). He found that when parents don't encourage critical thinking that fosters "participation in formulating morality" (Eisenberg 24) children may never achieve autonomous morality or will likely turn to their peers for morality formation—since peers seldom inflict external laws.

Duska and Whelan in *Moral Development: A Guide to Piaget and Kohlberg* interpret Kohlberg's and Piaget's theories to be proposing that when a parent and child relationship remains at the level of choices reinforced by external consequences,

> the child's experience has been simply that of himself as an individual reacting to an individual reacting to an environment that is other than he is, including things, and to people. To move out of egoism to a state of identifying with a society and its norms, one must develop the ability to role-play, that is, the ability to put oneself in another's place. Until one intellectually puts oneself in another's place, one cannot really comprehend what a society is or feel what it means to be a part of society. And by and large, what it means to be a part of society is to begin to see that the rules have a purpose and are not just arbitrary constraints imposed on a child (Duska and Whelan 52).

In light of this passage, we are brought again to the fairy tale and the story of Harry Potter. For as we discussed earlier, the fairy tale and story of Harry Potter allow our children to do exactly what Kohlberg proposes—"role-play . . . and intellectually put oneself in another's place." By reading and discussing Harry Potter with our children, we help our children understand what it means "to be a part of society." Our children transcend from the outsider of society to an essential part of society—just as Harry Potter transcends from an outcast and orphan to a hero and friend.

Along these same lines of logic and in support of Piaget and Kohlberg, psychologist Martin Hoffman has proposed a developmental theory based on Piagetian principles. "The basis of his theory is the human capacity to experience the inner state of others who are not in the same situation (Peters 173). Like Kohlberg and Piaget, Hoffman claims that the crucial step for moral development growth "is when the child's ego-centricism gives way to role-taking and the child begins to realise that others have different points of view" (Peters 173). Hoffman offers four experiences for fostering this crucial step for moral development: (1) Allow children to have the normal run of distress experiences rather than shield them (2) Provide children with opportunities for role-taking and for giving help and responsible care to others (3) Encourage children to imagine themselves in the place of others (4) Expose children for long periods of time to loved models who behave altruistically (Peters 174).

These explanations about moral development combined with an understanding of the modern fairy tale give us the answers we've been looking for to our questions about how to deal with Harry Potter. By reading *Harry Potter and the Sorcerer's Stone* and similar books with our children, we give our children the opportunity to "role-play," to put themselves "in another's place," and thus feel connected with society. By talking about Harry's struggles, choices, friends, consequences, and morals we form relationships with our children that foster moral development. We encourage our children to think about life and morality through fictional characters. As Hoffman suggests, we should expose our children to experiences rather than shield them so that they can practice making moral judgments with our guidance. Then when our children are faced with tough moral decisions in the real world (and we aren't present), they will know how to respond, because they have already thought it out in a non-threatening and supportive setting.

A Christian Parent's Guide to Harry Potter, founded on the theories of Piaget, Kolberg, Hoffman, and Christ, is a resource for using the Harry Potter books as tools for moral development. As shown through the theories of the fairy tale and moral development, sheltering children from society and reinforcing behavior exclusively with external punishments only retards moral development. Role-playing, imagination, critical thinking, and strong parent-child relationships are crucial for moral development. My guide and Harry Potter can unlock a door that will embark you and your child on a life-long journey of moral growth. So what are you waiting for . . . start talking about Harry!

Works Cited

Baker, Donald. *Functions of Folk and Fairy Tales,* Washington: Association for Childhood Education International, 1981.

Bettleheim, Bruno. *The Uses of Enchantment: The Meaning and Importance of Fairy Tales,* New York: Vintage Books, 1977,

Duska, Ronald, and Mariellen Whelan. *Moral Development: A Guide to Piaget and Kohlberg.* New York: Paulist Press, 1975.

Eisenberg, Nancy. "Self-Attributions, Social Interaction, and Moral Development." *Moral Development Through Social Interaction.* Ed. William M. Kurtines and Jacob L. Gewirtz. New York: John Wiley & Sons, 1987.

Haughton, Rosemary. *Tales from Eternity: The World of Fairytales and the Spiritual Search.* New York: The Seabury Press, 1973.

Kohlberg, Lawrence. "Stages of Moral Development as a Basis for Moral Education." *Moral Education: Interdisciplinary Approaches.* New York: Newman Press, 1975.

Kohlberg, Lawrence. "Continuities and Discontinuities in Childhood and Moral Development." *Moral Education: Interdisciplinary Approaches.* New York: Newman Press, 1975.

Luthi, Max. *Once Upon A Time: On the Nature of Fairy Tales.* Bloomington, Indiana: Indiana University Press, 1970.

Piaget, Jean. *The Moral Development of the Child.* New York: Free Press, 1965.

Peters, R. S. *Moral Development and Moral Education.* London: George, Allen & Unwin, 1981.

Rowling, J.K. *Harry Potter and the Sorcerer's Stone.* New York: Scholastic Inc., 1997.

Smetana, Judith G. "Parenting and the Development of Social Knowledge Reconceptualized: A Social Domain Analysis." *Parenting and Children's Internalization of Values: A Handbook of Contemporary Theory.* Ed. Joan E. Grusec and Leon Kuczynski. New York: John Wiley & Sons, Inc. 1997.

Walker, Lawrence J., et. al. "Reasoning About Morality and Real-life Moral Problems." *Morality in Everyday Life: Developmental Perspectives.* Ed. Melanie Killen and Daniel Hart. New York: Cambridge Press, 1995.

Professor Gina Burkart teaches College Reading and Writing at the University of Northern Iowa where she received her Master's degree in English (with a 4.0) in May 2002. She has published "Why Harry Potter Should Go to School" in Today's Catholic Teacher and presented that same article at the Art & Soul conference at Baylor University in Waco, Texas. With the help of literary agent Peter Rubie, Gina is currently pursuing publication for her book, A Christian Parent's Guide to Harry Potter. Before entering the freelance world, Gina worked as an assistant editor for Harcourt Religion Publishers. She also served on the production team for The North American Review (the oldest literary magazine in America) and has been interviewed by the Northern Iowan, the University of Northern Iowa marketing and public relations department, Radio Iowa, and the Waterloo Courier in regards to the Harry Potter parent guide she has written. As a mother of three children, she is actively involved in her parish as well as her children's Catholic school.

Harry Potter vs. Christians: An Overview of the Debate, Presented as Part of the "Can Any Wisdom Come From Wizardry" Panel

David Isaacs

The purpose of my remarks is to lay out some of the issues raised by those in the Christian, mostly Evangelical, community, regarding Harry Potter (HP). Primarily, I will raise some of the objections offered by those who think HP should not be read either by Christians or by anyone else.

To be simplistic, the detractors of Harry Potter seem to fall into three broad categories: those who are critics but have not read the books, those who have read them but object for religious reasons, and those who have read them but do not appreciate them as quality literature. Of course, these groups may overlap to some extent. In addition, there is a significant number somewhere in the middle who argue that the books may have some problems, but with proper oversight, parents can read and discuss the books with their children. Because of our focus, I will concentrate on the first two groups.

The first group—those who object but haven't read—is typified by Theresa, a soft-spoken grandmother who took my Children's Literature class a year ago. Theresa came the first evening of class an hour early (in fact, she was there before I was!). "Professor," she said, "I have been a good Baptist for over forty years. Why are you making us read that book?" By "that book," I knew she meant the first Harry Potter novel. When I asked what the problem was, she said that she had heard the books were anti-Christian. According to the rumors, they lured unsuspecting children into witchcraft and other unbiblical interests. I assured her that she did not have to like the book, but as a future teacher she should probably at least know what her students were reading; after all, HP is the best selling children's book of all time. This seemed to assuage her for the moment—she did not have to like the book—and Theresa later became the strongest supporter of HP after reading him.

Another student, Saroja, the wife of a pastor, asked if she could give the last word after a class discussion on HP. When she had the floor, she read Deut. 18.10-11: "Let no one be found among you who sacrifices his son or daughter in the fire, who practices divination or sorcery, interprets omens, engages in witchcraft, or casts spells, or who is a medium or spiritist or who consults the dead." She then shut her Bible and sat down and clearly felt there was no more to be said on the subject.

This has occurred enough times in my classes for me to see it as something of a trend. Our colleagues at Azusa Pacific, Emily Griesinger and Jim Hedges, have had similar experiences. In fact, Prof. Hedges has received a pile of rather hateful mail as a result of some positive things he printed on HP (see Hedges "Family"). Here are some samples: (1) "[adult student protesting required reading of H.P.] I have made it a rule in my home not to allow anything of Harry Potter because of the pure evil for which it stands . . . . How do I explain to my two children that it is acceptable for daddy to read and possess a demonic book?"; (2) "Glorifying Satanic worship or approving of it is accepting it. [If] you accept it you are a part of it . . . . How many Christians will think its OK to dabble in black magic from your approval of these books?" [from a pastor]; (3) "I have no doubt [God] hates these books which have created such an interest in witchcraft and the occult in our society" (Hedges "Hating").

And what is the basis of this criticism? Why will some not even read Rowling's works? It primarily stems from their understanding of scripture and its bans on witchcraft. Typically, detractors will quote a few key passages. I've already quoted the most prominent, Deut. 18. However, detractors do not stop there. To Deut. 18, they often add such verses as these:

1. Gal. 5.19-20: "The acts of sinful nature are obvious: sexual immorality, impurity and debauchery; idolatry and witchcraft; . . . ";
2. Phil. 4.8: "Finally, . . . , whatever is true, whatever is noble, whatever is right, whatever is pure, whatever is lovely, whatever is admirable—if anything is excellent or praiseworthy—think about such things";
3. 1 Thess. 5.22: "Avoid every kind of evil";
4. 3 John 11: "Do not imitate what is evil but what is good"; and
5. Romans 12.2: "Do not conform any longer to the pattern of this world, but be transformed by the renewing of your mind."

In addition, we are enjoined to train ourselves to distinguish between what is good and what is evil (Hebrews 5.14), and "hate what is evil; cling to what is good" (Rom. 12.9). Many other verses could be marshaled, but these should suffice as a representative example. One could argue that Rowling's characters are involved in all of the practices condemned in the Bible, and this is enough to keep committed Christians from reading the books.

Before we judge them too quickly, let us acknowledge that an avoidance of evil is healthy and biblical. The Bible's message is very clear—we *are* to abstain from practicing and condoning evil (evil being anything that goes against God's character and activity). I would not, for example, want my children to read Hitler's *Mein Kampf* or *Hustler* magazine because they clearly espouse views contrary to what I want to instill in them (if they read them when they are adults, that's another matter). We do not need to read a book on Satanic rituals to know it goes against Christian beliefs, nor do we need to read pornography to see that it twists God's plans for sexuality. If a book risks leading children into the occult, then why not object? Why bother reading the books at all, and why do people insist that Christians should read HP before condemning it? As occult expert Caryl Matrisciana says,

> My greatest fear is that godly fear that protects mankind [sic] from dabbling in the spirit world is being taken away from children who read these Harry Potter books. The terrors and horrors of black magic and occult practice, ritual, ceremonies and demon possession are being normalized . . . . Alarmingly, the Potter books are engaging in pagan discipleship, disciplining our children to spiritual alternatives and also turning them away from the biblical principles and God's protection. (qtd. in Foster 5).

It is safer, then, not to read these books but rather to encourage children to read other, more spiritually sound books—the Chronicles of Narnia usually come up in this debate as a preferable alternative.

While many will not read the books because of the references to witchcraft and the occult, there is another group that is fairly well-informed yet still objects, many for the reasons mentioned above. There seem to be three primary reasons for objection even after having read the books. First, they contain the aforementioned practices banned by the Bible and may tempt young readers into the occult. Bonta, for instance, argues that the imagery in HP derives from a "sophisticated knowledge of the occult on the part of the author," and these are too close to actual occult practices for comfort (4; see also Montenegro). Perhaps the most vocal and best-known detractor is Richard Abanes, writer of *Harry Potter and the Bible: The Menace Behind the Magick*. In a response to Connie Neal's favorable views of Rowling, Abanes argues,

> There actually exists no difference at all between the so-called "fantasy witchcraft" found in Harry Potter and real world occult practices "forbidden by the Bible." Harry Potter contains positive presentations and accurate depictions of occult practices currently used by Wiccans and other occultists. These practices include: divination, mediumship, arithmancy, numerology, astrology, herbology/potions, crystal-gazing, and charms . . . . (Abanes "A Critique")

Second, the novels contain ambiguous morals. For example, Bonta argues the moral basis in HP is ambiguous at best, with Harry and Voldemort associated with the same imagery and drawing from the same magical sources: "Good and evil," Bonta says, "are never clear-cut, it seems; Harry is part Voldemort and Voldemort part Harry" (5). Abanes goes to great pains to show that "Potterethics" goes against every ideal Christians claim to value. He documents, for instance, all of the times Harry lies, breaks rules, acts disrespectfully towards adults, fights, curses, and does anything of a morally questionable nature (*Harry Potter* 67-71, e.g.; see also Montenegro 11); Abanes also makes similar lists of the other characters' moral faults. Clearly, detractors say, these are not the role models we want our children to emulate. (For a good response to this, see McVeigh.)

Third, the books do not edify in the way "good" fantasy should. For example, Gene Veith, a respected Christian literary critic, argues, "What we fantasize about—as occasioned by literary experience—is spiritually important. Pornographic imaginings and fantasizing about hurting others are indeed harmful, even if they are never acted out, because they corrupt the heart" (21). He goes on to add that "[if] fantasy can be used to teach moral truths and carry them into the imagination, it is also possible for fantasy to desensitize the moral imagination. Just as a tale of chivalry can inspire ideals of courage and honor, the Sword and Sorcery sagas of raping and pillaging, with no moral center, can deaden the heart" (21; see also Kjos 3). Unlike the more Christian, hence "good," fantasy offered by such writers as C.S. Lewis and J.R.R. Tolkien, Rowling's works lead children to fantasize about that which is least noble in humanity; why, then, detractors ask, would we want to encourage this when better works are available?

These are just some of the issues which have swirled around Harry. Other issues include how the books are used in classrooms, the wall of religious separation, censorship, and web sites that connect HP to the occult. Our panel's job is to address some of these. To do so, we really need to keep in mind the most basic question: Should Christians read Harry Potter? To answer this, we need to ask some corollaries: Is the magic in HP the same kind condemned by the Bible? Are there any redeeming qualities in HP that might counter-act the alleged problems? Should Christians read fantasy? Do Christians risk losing more than they gain by attacking the books? For example, if we throw out HP, what do we do about Tolkien, Lewis, Macdonald, L'Engle, and many other accepted Christian writers who have elements similar to Rowling? These issues, among others, will be the focus of our presentation.

Works Cited

Abanes, Richard. "A Critique of Connie Neal, Part 3." Home page. 14 July 2003. <http://www.abanes.com/Neal3.html>.

_____. *Harry Potter and the Bible: The Menace behind the Magick*. Camp Hill, PA: Christian Publications Inc., 2001.

Bonta, Steve. "Harry Potter's Hocus-Pocus." *The New American* 16.18. 28 August 2000. 17 January 2003. <http://www.thenewamerican.com/tna/2000/08-28-2000/vol16no18_potter.htm>.

Foster, Julie. "Potter Books: Wicked Witchcraft? New Documentary Claims Tales Lead Kids to the Occult." *WorldNetDaily* 16 August 2001. 17 January 2003. <http://www.worldnetdaily.com/news/article.asp?ARTICLE_ID=24080>.

Hedges, James L. "Family Matters in the Harry Potter Novels." *APU Life* 15.4 (Winter 2002): 8-9.

_____. "Hating Harry: Christian Complaints Against Potter." from a handout made from personal correspondence.

Holy Bible. *The NIV Study Bible.* Grand Rapids, MI: Zondervan, 1995.

Kjos, Berit. "Bewitched by Harry Potter." 17 January 2003. <http://www.crossroad.to/text/articles/Harry9-99.html>.

McVeigh, Dan. "Is Harry Potter Christian?" *Renascence* 54.3 (Spring 2002): 197-214.

Montenegro, Marcia. "Harry Potter, Sorcery and Fantasy." *CANA.* June 2000. 17 January 2003. <http://www.cana.uderworld.com/cana_harrypotter.html>.

Veith, Gene. "Good Fantasy and Bad Fantasy." *Christian Research Journal* 23.1: 12-22.

David E. Isaacs graduated from Trinity Graduate School with a M.A. in Faith and Culture, and Simon Greenleaf University with a M.A. in Christian Apologetics; and he has done graduate work at California State University, San Bernardino, where he also received a B.A. in English. He has been an Assistant Professor of English for six years at California Baptist University in Riverside, California and has taught for twelve years.

Christianity, Morality, and Harry Potter, Presented as Part of the "Can Any Wisdom Come From Wizardry" Panel

Emily Bytheway

"To allow a child to dwell on Harry Potter books and other occult influences is like feeding them a little bit of spiritual poison each time they read, until they become numb to the things of God. In our day and age a child needs to be protected by discerning parents." (Smith)

This comment is only one of thousands of similar sentiments that can be found all over the internet, in pamphlets, and in books. Most of the world would look at a comment like that and say that it's ridiculous. However, those of us who take the Bible seriously are forced to give real thought to the issue. It is true that the Bible contains warnings against sorcery, witchcraft, fortune telling, and other occult practices. I am not trying to deny that the occult is wrong, and against the will of God. But fantasy novels, especially Harry Potter, and the occult are not the same thing.

The fact that J.K. Rowling chose to label those who could do magic in her world as "witches" and "wizards" should not lead us to jump to conclusions concerning those labels. L. Frank Baum used similar labels in *The Wizard of Oz*. He also made the crucial distinction that J.K. Rowling makes in Harry Potter—that there are good witches and bad witches. J.R.R. Tolkien has characters who can do magic: wizards and elves. David Eddings calls these people sorcerers and sorceresses. Robin McKinley, in her book *Spindle's End*, calls them fairies. James Barrie chose a similar label for those who could do magic in *Peter Pan*, as did Eoin Colfer in his Artemis Fowl books. If J.K. Rowling had chosen to make Harry Potter a fairy or an elf rather than a wizard, would there be as much fuss raised? Somehow I think not.

The important thing is not to look at the label J.K. Rowling chose. Rather, we should look at how magic functions in her world, and how it relates to our own. In the world of Harry Potter witchcraft is more of a quirky talent than a religion. In fact, I think I can be so bold as to say that Harry Potter-style witchcraft isn't a religion at all. There is no book of scripture for witches, no set of philosophies, no rites of initiation[add space here](unless you count the need for training), no selling your soul to the Devil. Rather, magic is something that one can *do*. It comes from inside of you.

It is true that there are similarities in Harry Potter to the occult, and the mythology surrounding it. In Harry Potter, wizards use wands. They ride broomsticks. They use cauldrons, brew potions, gaze into crystal balls, and read palms. J.K. Rowling borrows terms like "Divination" and "Arithmancy" and appropriates myths like dragons, unicorns, and the Philosopher's Stone. But in each case, J.K. Rowling gives them all her own tweak. Most of the potions brewed in Harry Potter require ingredients that don't exist. Divination is portrayed as the most imprecise branch of magic, and those who practice it are buffoons. Most of the things that we would associate with witchcraft, such as curses and killing with magic, are relegated to the Dark Arts, which are pointedly and repeatedly referred to as Bad with a capital B. In fact, anything with a nefarious intent is clearly labeled as "wrong," or at least as underhanded.

Religion is not specifically mentioned in Harry Potter, at least not overtly. But neither is it ridiculed or dismissed. In fact, Hogwarts has both Christmas and Easter vacations. In contrast, they celebrate Halloween, but classes go on normally on that day, with only a feast at night. When discussing the persecutions medieval witches and wizards faced, there is no mention of the Church as the source of these persecutions. Rather, it is blamed on the witches and wizards being "different."

J.K. Rowling herself has spoken out against this kind of thinking, as she did in a recent interview with Katie Couric:

> **Rowling:** "I think that's utter garbage. I absolutely do not believe in the occult, practice the occult. I've never . . . I've met literally thousands of children now. Not one of them has said to me, 'You've really turned me on to the occult,' not one of them. Now I'm convinced that if that's what my books were doing, I would by now have met one child who would have come up to me, covered in pentagrams, and said, 'Can we go and sacrifice a goat later together, will you do that with me?' It's never happened, funnily enough."
>
> **Couric:** "You find it very annoying, I can tell."
>
> **Rowling:** "Well occasionally I do, just occasionally I do. Because I am being accused of something quite horrible. So of course I've got to defend myself."
>
> **Couric:** "What do you believe in? I'm just curious about your belief system—God, heaven?"
>
> **Rowling:** "Oh, I do believe in God."
>
> **Couric:** "You do?"
>
> **Rowling:** "Yeah, which I've said before, but that just seems to annoy them even more for some reason. I don't think they want me on their side at all." (*Dateline*, 20 June 2003)

Probably the biggest concern with the witchcraft of Harry Potter is that is seems too accessible. It's very close to our world. One feels like if you went to Kings' Cross station and ran at the barrier between platforms 9 and 10, you'd be able to board the Hogwarts Express. Magic in Harry Potter isn't far-off and far removed like it is in most fantasy. Tolkien's Middle Earth is supposed to have disappeared thousands and thousands of years ago. David Eddings's books are set on some unknown world completely remote from our own. Even Oz is only reachable in a dream state, and Narnia and this earth never intermingle except in that wardrobe. But in Harry Potter, witches and Muggles live side by side.

I was recently struck by how similar these ideas are to those that circulated at the dawn of the modern Novel. Comparing novels to Romances, which were tales of knights and damsels in distress like the Arthurian legends (which, incidentally, have wizards in them as well), Samuel Johnson wrote in 1750 that "In the romances formerly written, every transaction and sentiment was so remote from all that passes among men, that the reader was in very little danger of making any application to himself; the virtues and crimes were equally beyond his sphere of activity; and he amused himself with heroes and with traitors, deliverers and persecutors, as with beings of another species, whose actions were regulated upon motives of their own, and who had neither faults nor excellences in common with himself." Harry Potter is today what the novel was in the mid-eighteenth century: too close for comfort.

But I think that those who feel that Harry Potter will encourage kids to turn to witchcraft aren't giving those kids enough credit. Those who are old enough to read Harry Potter are certainly old enough to tell make-believe from reality. The fact that Harry Potter is set in contemporary England and Scotland does not make it any more dangerous to a young mind than "Cinderella" or "Beauty and the Beast" or "Hansel and Gretel" are. By and large, you'll find that kids no more believe that Harry Potter is real or that pointing a stick of wood at someone and saying "Avada Kedavra" can kill them, than they believe that pigs can fly. Kids are just smarter than that.

We don't know what religion Dumbledore is, or Harry Potter, or Hermione Granger, or Ron Weasley, or any of the rest of the characters. But I can tell you one thing: they're not Wiccan, and they're not involved in the occult.

If Harry Potter is off-limits to children because of the presence of witches, wizards, and magic, then we can't see Disney movies anymore. We can't read fairy tales. We'll have to avoid *The Lord of the Rings* and the *Chronicles of Narnia* and *Peter Pan* and *The Wizard of Oz* and the tales of King Arthur. Our children can no longer believe in Santa Claus, the Tooth Fairy, and the Easter Bunny. When we rid the world of magic, we also rid the world of wonder, and make it more difficult for children to believe in anything, even miracles and faith. Because when it all comes down to it, Harry Potter isn't about witches and wizards at all. It's about magic and imagination, and loyalty and friendship and love, and all the other good things children can and should believe in.

Works Cited

Johnson, Samuel. *The Rambler* 4 (31 March 1750). Online. <http://www.english.upenn.edu/~mgamer/Etexts/johnson.rambler.html>

Rowling, J.K. "Inside 'Order of the Phoenix.'" Interview with Katie Couric. *Dateline.* NBC. 20 June 2003.

Smith, Kathy A. *Christian Entertainment—Harry Potter: Seduction Into The Dark World Of The Occult—Part Two.* Surf in the Spirit. 16 July 2003. <http://www.surfinthespirit.com/entertainment/harry-potter-2.shtml>

Emily Bytheway is from Murray, Utah. She recently graduated from Brigham Young University with a B.A. in English with an editing emphasis. Now she is desperately trying to figure out what to do with the rest of her life. Emily first read Harry Potter in April 2000 and has been hooked ever since. In September 2001, she started to become involved in the Harry Potter online fandom, including the shipping debates at FictionAlley. Her fan fiction is archived at Sugar Quil and the Astronomy Tower (at FictionAlley). In addition to Harry Potter, Emily enjoys reading Jane Austen, J.R.R. Tolkien, L.M. Montgomery, P.G. Wodehouse and Erle Stanley Gardner. She also enjoys singing and ballroom dancing, although she's not very good at either.

The Need for Honesty and Critical Thinking In Children's Literature, presented as part of the Can Any Wisdom Come From Wizardry? Panel

Helen Huntley

We have gathered together because we have been bewitched by words—Harry Potter books and critics of those books. In fact, so many words whirl by that confusion rather than wisdom may reign. Can wisdom come from wisardry? Indeed! Take a moment and reflect on something you learned from the Harry Potter books . . .

Good. It appears you did learn something.

The chuckles on the left are appreciated, for children demand entertainment from their books. On a more subtle level, children's books provide both honesty and creative critical thinking. The Harry Potter books have both of these elements. Let me elaborate . . .

Harry, our hero, is introduced as "small and skinny with brilliant green eyes and jet-black hair that was always untidy. He wore round glasses, and on his forehead was a thin, lightning-shaped scar" (CHAMBER 4). Young readers identify with the underdog—especially if that underdog is totally ignored on birth dates!

> Harry had never received a birthday card in his life. The Dursleys had completely ignored his last two birthdays, and he had no reason to suppose they would remember this one. (AZKABAN 5-6)

Harry has a horrible home life. The Dursleys are Muggles to the most mundane degree and are intent to "squash the magic out of him" (AZKABAN 2). Such an environment endears Harry to readers, especially the reader who has a less than lovely home life. Remember, too, many children are convinced they were mixed up as infants in a hospital bungling incident.

In each Harry Potter year, honesty surrounds Harry and his plight: his homeliness; his unhappy home life; his heritage. Readers trust Harry; therefore, they follow willingly as Harry guides them into creative, critical thinking. Harry does guide the readers—if somewhat hesitantly.

Harry has every reason to be a hesitant guide. He is thrown into an adult world which is clearly filled with good and evil. This world resembles fairy tales. Bruno Bettelheim writes:

> . . . fairy tales both delight and instruct; their special genius
> is that they do so in terms which speak directly to children.
> At the age when these stories are most meaningful to the
> child, his major problem is to bring some order into the
> inner chaos of his mind so he can better understand himself . . . . (53)

The key word is "chaos." Harry exemplifies chaos as he probes beneath the half-lies and lies adults tell him.

In each year, Harry unravels criptic messages and misinformation. Harry uses his mind to counteract controlling adults. In Harry's creative solutions to chaos, readers also discover possibilities. Dumbledore tells Harry:

> " . . . you happen to have many qualities Salazar Slytherin
> prized in his hand-picked students. His own very rare
> gift Parseltongue—resourcefulness—determination—a
> certain disregard for rules . . . yet the Sorting Hat placed
> you in Gryffindor. You know why that was. Think."
> "It only put me in Gryffindor," said Harry in a
> de feated voice, "because I asked not to be in Slytherin."
> "Exactly," said Dumbledore, "which makes you very
> different from Tom Riddle. It is our choices, Harry,
> that show what we truly are, far more than our abilities."
> (CHAMBER 333)

Children's literature, good children's literature, must give its readers ways to discover new approaches to problems, unique choices to make. Such works guide the young reader into new ways of thinking, new points of view. As a reader reflects on a book, he or she begins to understand a protagonist's behavior. That understanding helps the reader in his or her own behavior and choices. Vicariously, then, the young reader of Harry Potter books gains insights not only into honesty about the world, but he or she also gains an understanding of creative critical thinking.

Critics who insist that the Harry Potter books stimulate and encourage evil in children misunderstand a facet of children's minds. Wonderously vivid blackness lurks in the attic of children's minds. Call them archetypes, hobgobblins, ghosts, phantasmagoria, but by whatever name they are called, to a child they are as real as breakfast, donuts, dinner. Confronting evil through reading with Harry Potter holding the reader's hand and providing creative, directive critical decisions for survival allows the reader to recognize the blackness is universal in the world. This knowledge provides immense relief; it also provides the potential to conquer the blackness.

Lewis Mumford wrote that his decision to eliminate all folk, fairy and fantasy tales from his young son's life was a disaster. After his son, an only child, was killed in war, Mumford realized he had "removed St. George but left the dragon" in his son's mind. For many readers, Harry Potter becomes St. George. With humor, honesty and creative critical thinking, Harry reveals how wisdom comes from wizardry.

Helen Huntley has been a life-long reader; she naturally came into teaching English and specializing in children's literature. She read and wrote her way through a bachelor's degree in home economics and child development; she read and wrote her way through a master's in English. She has been teaching the same number of years as her children's ages; the last thirteen years have been at California Baptist University. Her reading and writing is observed and proofread by five cats, one German Shepherd and three parakeets. Of those in the menagerie, the cats are the most literate and guide her in writing children's stories and novels.

Alchemy, Doppelgangers, and the Irony of Religious Objections to Harry Potter

John Granger

Introduction

L et me begin my talk today by thanking those of you who rose early enough on a Saturday morning to hear a talk on 'Harry Potter, Alchemy and Literature'. When I read that I had been scheduled in this 'slot', I was simultaneously disappointed and relieved: 'disappointed' because I imagined in my vanity that being a featured speaker meant that I would speak to a large audience, 'relieved' because it seemed improbable that anyone outside of friends obliged to make an appearance would be here today. It is flattering and frightening that a few others have joined my friends here this morning instead of catching another half hour's sleep or a bus to Disney World!

I must also thank the Nimbus 2003 gang, especially Penny Linsenmeyer, for flying me here to speak. Certainly I am not an accomplished academic as many of the speakers here are and my thoughts about these books are not popular with many fans, with most of those who dislike the books, or with the inhabitants of the Ivory Tower. I have to acknowledge the act of courage on the part of my sponsors in acting on their conviction to invite me; I will do my best to show they were right in thinking I had something to add to this conversation.

So who am I and what will I be trying to say this early Saturday morning? As you have heard, I am John Granger and I am the author of *The Hidden Key to Harry Potter*. What you don't know is that I am almost certainly less of an authority on these books than most of the people around you, at least with respect to how many times I have read the books or how closely I have studied them. The only thing of value, I think, which I bring to the discussion of these books is a perspective, a perspective that perhaps I share with Mrs. Rowling.

This perspective is that of a classicist. Like Mrs. Rowling, I have an honors degree in Classical Languages and a love of English literature, the Great Books, and even the great ideas. Mrs. Rowling looks at the world diagonally relative to most of us and sees the magic; I believe this diagonal vision springs from her classical education and ideas of truth, love, and beauty—and her consequent discomfort with modernity and disdain for modern ideas and institutions.

In my talk this morning, then, I hope to share with you one classicist's perspective on Mrs. Rowling's use of alchemy in the Harry Potter books. Unless I am much mistaken, understanding these books as alchemical writing—in the tradition of such usage among the English 'Greats'—will explain otherwise bizarre events, plot turns, and names in the novels. I think, too, that a right understanding of alchemy will shine some light on the questions of whence the worldwide popularity of these books, in what way Christian objections to them are ironic, and why the almost uniform approach of scholars to the books as cultural artifacts to be dissected is an exercise in self-parody.

So let's begin.

Socrates' Challenge

Anyone talking to a 21st century group about alchemy finds himself in the position of Socrates in his *Apology* before the Athenian jury. Socrates was charged, you recall, with corrupting the youth of the city and for supplanting the gods of the city with gods of his own invention. He was found guilty, despite his remarkable speech in his own defense, and put to death. He complained in the opening of his defense that he was not so much afraid of the charges brought against him in the trial as he was of his "earliest accusers" who "took hold of so many of [the jurors] when [they] were children and tried to fill [their] minds with untrue accusations against [him]", most notably Aristophanes in his comedy, 'The Clouds.'

Socrates told the jurors his biggest problem was that "I must try, in the short time that I have, to rid your minds of a false impression which is the work of many years" (*Apology*, 19a). As I prepare my notes on alchemy, I recognize Socrates' challenge—and I have to hope for a better or, at least, a less lasting verdict! What modern people know of alchemy in my experience is almost inevitably wrong and, frankly, horribly wrong, so wrong that the use of alchemical imagery in English Literature from Chaucer to Shakespeare, Donne to Blake, from Shelley and Yeats to C. S. Lewis, Joyce, and Robertson Davies—not to mention Mrs. Rowling—must seem absurd.

So I have three tasks before me. First, I must in a very brief time explain what alchemy is and what it isn't (despite what your chemistry teacher, pastor, guru, or Jungian analyst may have told you alchemy was). Next, I must do a hurried survey of the English 'Greats' to document their usage of alchemical imagery through the centuries and explain why the language of this supposedly material or scientific procedure was so fit for expression of grand themes and meaning. And, last, I must explain how and why Mrs. Rowling uses alchemy in the Harry Potter novels—and still have time for my conclusions and your questions. I hope you are all wide awake and had a good breakfast!

Alchemy: What It Is and Isn't

I grew up in 20th century America and was indoctrinated with my peers by inoculation with the popular misconceptions that define our age (as popular ideas, cosmology, and blind-spots define every age). Perhaps the most important spell or charm that entrances us as modern people is the belief that nature, and specifically, matter and energy, are all that exist. This belief, sometimes called 'scientific materialism' or 'naturalism', right or wrong, is what important thinkers like Phillip Johnson have called "the de facto state religion of the United States."

As a good student and child of my era, I was a confirmed naturalist and held the physical sciences—biology, physics, and chemistry—in the highest regard. Though I was a Classics major in Prep School and in College, I also studied AP Chemistry and College chemistry at University. I knew the scientists were the high priests and power brokers, and I struggled to learn their language and their secrets.

One of the first things you learn in chemistry classes, by asides and by osmosis, is that chemistry grew out of a kind of medieval voodoo called alchemy, which pseudo science tried to isolate a philosopher's stone that could turn all metals to gold and bestow immortality on the alchemist. This is still the predominant idea of alchemy in the popular mind; "alchemy is stupid chemistry."

Publicity for a book coming out this November, *The Last Sorcerers: The Path from Alchemy to the Periodic Table* by Richard Morris (Joseph Henry Press, 2003) puts it plainly:

What we now call chemistry began in the fiery cauldrons of mystics and sorcerers seeking not to make a better world through science, but rather to make themselves richer through magic formulas and con games. But among these early magicians, frauds, and con artists were a few far-seeing "alchemists" who, through rigorous experimentation, transformed mysticism into science.

In this picture, too, is the second misconception about alchemy. Not only is it bad science and the way of charlatans, alchemy is also about cauldrons, sorcery, mysticism, and magic. Alchemy certainly was a secret science but not in the sense that its current reputation for being an occult practice would suggest.

The third misconception comes to us via Carl Jung, one of the 20th century's most famous psychoanalysts, who devoted decades of his life to the study of alchemical texts, imagery, and the meaning of these archetypes in the collective consciousness of humanity and the dreams of individuals. Jung and his many followers certainly had a clearer appreciation of alchemy than do disdainful naturalists and those who live in fear of the occult—but their psychological understanding of alchemy and position that the alchemists were 'Gnostics' is a case of historical projection of one's own empiricist and anti-religious beliefs into the past. Or so the accepted authorities on alchemy now say (see especially Titus Burckhardt's discussion of Jung and alchemy in *Alchemy*, Penguin Books, 1972, pp. 8-9 and *Mirror of the Intellect: Essays on Traditional Science and Sacred Art*, Quinta Essentia, 1987, pp. 59-66 and 132-141).

If alchemy wasn't 'chemistry for idiots', witchcraft, or an initiatory path into the archetypes of our unconscious mind, well, what was it? It was **a spiritual path to return fallen man to his Edenic perfection.**

To understand how a science of metallurgy and physical bodies could cause the purification and perfection of the alchemist, body and soul, requires turning the modern world-view upside down. The alchemist, as all traditional people or non-moderns, understood man as essentially spirit (as man is created by the Spirit), then soul, then physical body rather then the reverse. He believed the obvious, i.e., that the lesser thing comes from the greater thing and never greater from lesser. His person-hood or humanity he knew was a joining of soul and body without seam—and his tragedy was that he was 'fallen', i.e., that he had had lost his spiritual capacity or '*intellectus*' by means of which Adam walked and talked with God in the garden. **Alchemy was the means, in conjunction with the Mysteries of the Church (or temple or mosque—there are alchemies in each of the revealed traditions), that he could regain this lost capacity;** the substance changing from lead to gold was his soul and the riches he would glean were spiritual riches (i.e., immortality).

He was able to do this by effecting a similar change in metals. Because the traditional world view does not hold that there is a chasm between subject and object, that is, that objects do not have independent existence from their observers and vice versa, an alchemist understood the substances with which he worked as being related to him as night and day, male and female, sun and moon, and the other complementary antagonistic pairs which reflect the polarity of the Creative Principle or Word (think '*yin* & *yang*'). This relationship amounted to a **correspondence**; as he purified himself in obedience to the work, the work would advance and his soul or bodily consciousness would go through correspondent changes. This was not magic or work independent of nature but an accelerating of the natural work by observance of supernatural, even contranatural Principle.

Titus Burckhardt, who with Mircea Eliade is the authority on the history and meaning of alchemy, wrote:

> Alchemy may be called the art of the transmutations of the soul. In saying this I am not seeking to deny that alchemists also knew and practiced metallurgical procedures such as the purification and alloying of metals; their real work, however, for which all these procedures were merely the outward supports or 'operational' symbols, was the transmutation of the soul. The testimony of the alchemists on this point is unanimous (*Alchemy*, p. 23).

> 'To make of the body a spirit and of the spirit a body': this adage sums up the whole of alchemy. Gold itself, which outwardly represents the fruit of the work, appears as an opaque body become luminous, or as a light become solid. Transposed into the human and spiritual order, gold is bodily consciousness transmuted into spirit or spirit fixed in the body . . . . This transmutation of spirit into body and of body into spirit is to be found in a more or less direct and obvious manner in every method of spiritual realization; alchemy, however, has made of it its principal theme,

in conformity with the metallurgical symbolism that is based on the possibility of changing the state of aggregation of a body (*Mirror of the Intellect*, p.132).

As metals change from rough ores and solid states to more and more pure conditions by change of sates (to liquid and gas and re-condensation) and combination with catalysts and purifying agents, the alchemist affected changes in himself by corespondent changes in his bodily consciousness while attempting the work.

> The Western alchemist by attempting to 'kill' the ingredients, to reduce them to the *materia prima*, provokes a *sympatheia* between the 'pathetic situations' of the substance and his innermost being. In other words, he realizes, as it were, some initiatory experiences which, as the course of the opus proceeds, forge for him a new personality, comparable t the one which is achieved after successfully undergoing the ordeals of initiation (Eliade, *The Forge and the Crucible,* University of Chicago Press, 1978, p. 158-160).

[Eliade points out that Jung was write to have supposed that alchemy had a soteriological role for the alchemist (*The Forge and the Crucible,* p.11) but in Jung's assumption that the alchemist was primarily a gold seeker who experienced *individuation* (by contact with the archetypes of change in the collective unconscious) is 180 degrees off. Jung restricts the work to the psychic or animic sphere and to the unconscious or subconscious part of this sphere; alchemy is essentially a super conscious or spiritual work that happens through correspondence with archetypes that are above not below individual consciousness (cf., Burckhardt, *Alchemy*, pp. 8-9).]

So what was alchemy? It was a traditional or sacred science, ancillary to the work of the revealed tradition and its means of grace, for the purification and perfection of the alchemist's soul in correspondence with the metallurgical perfection of a base metal into gold. It requires a view of man and of creation or cosmology that is opposite and contradictory to that of the physical scientist and chemist of today, of whom alchemists had only disdain; they thought of men who were interested in matter for its manipulation as "charcoal burners" and anything but wise. To an alchemist, the chemist neglects the greater thing in the lesser thing—and in himself.

Alchemy and English Literature

Alchemy as a sacred science was never an American adventure. This science went into precipitous decline and corruption at the time of the Renaissance through the Enlightenment when it was eclipsed by the materialist view and priorities of modern chemistry. Though there was a glut of publication of alchemical work in its decline, this is evidence of its corruption because the work is only passed from master to apprentice and books contain only the most arcane and hidden guides to the work, metallurgical and spiritual.

American readers, consequently, are unaware of alchemy except as the chemists, the illegitimate and disowned children of the alchemists, want us to remember them. This is perhaps no great loss, except for its reinforcement of our naturalist state religion, but it does have one consequence that touches on Harry Potter fans. English Literature is rich in alchemical language, references, themes, and symbols from Chaucer to Rowling; to be ignorant of this language and imagery is to miss out on the depths and heights of Shakespeare, Blake, Donne, Milton, even C. S. Lewis and James Joyce. Mrs. Rowling, as I will demonstrate in a moment, is not ignorant of literary alchemy. The Harry Potter books individually and as a series are built on alchemical structures, written in alchemical language, and have alchemical themes at their core.

Before I just touch on the use of alchemy in English Literature and attempt to explain why an arcane and sacred science plays such a big part in the history of English letters, let me give you three quick references so you can learn more about this on your own.

First, get yourself a copy of Stanton J. Linden's *Darke Hieroglyphicks: Alchemy in English Literature from Chaucer to the Restoration* (University of Kentucky Press, 1998). It is the academic review of all the treatments of alchemy in literature—to include the number of playwrights and writers who satirized and disliked the charcoal burners as well as the adepts—from the late Middle Ages to the sixteenth and seventeenth centuries. [Though he does not discuss this, the writers of the twentieth century who revive alchemical usage, Joyce, the Inklings, Eliot, are the men who revive interest in and appreciation of the writers of this period (C. S. Lewis, for example, writes the 'Oxford History of the English Language' volume for the 16th century, celebrates the world view and intention of its authors in his *Discarded Image*, and, after Charles Williams, writes explicitly alchemical novels in his Space Trilogy).]

Next, find Lyndy Abraham's *A Dictionary of Alchemical Imagery* (Cambridge University Press, 1998). There are several guides and dictionaries of alchemy but Abraham's is the champion and I will refer to it often this morning. In addition to first class entries on stages of the work and specific citations of alchemical references used by authors over many centuries, there is an index for the serious student of, say, Shakespeare or Blake, for easy access to this remarkable resource on alchemy in literature.

And, last, or almost last, ask for a sample copy of '*Cauda Pavonis*' (Latin for 'the peacock's tail'). As they describe themselves, "*Cauda Pavonis* publishes scholarly material on all aspects of alchemy and Hermeticism and their influence on literature, philosophy, art, religion, and the history of science and medicine. Our approach to Hermeticism, is of necessity, interdisciplinary and not limited to any particular historical period, national emphasis, or methodology." For more information, contact the editor Prof. Kate Frost at the University of Texas <Katefrost@mail.utexas.edu> or the assistant editor, Roger Rouland <rrouland@mail.utexas.edu>.

And, while I'm listing resources, here's web site for those of you who may want to learn more about alchemy, with or without literature: **http://www.levity.com/alchemy/ index.html**. The site is a mixed bag but it is a very big bag!

I give you these hurried references because there is not time this morning or this weekend truth be told to do justice to 'Alchemy in English Literature.' If you're familiar with the topic, these resources are a great helps to a deeper appreciation, and, if this is all new to you, they are accessible introductions.

For just a taste, though, of how understanding alchemy opens certain writers, here is an entry from Abraham's *Dictionary of Alchemical Imagery* for 'red tincture'. The 'red tincture' is the red elixir of the philosopher's stone that when thrown upon base metals changes them into gold. As Abraham explains:

> It was thought that just one ounce of the tincture could transmute over a hundred or a thousand times its own weight of weight of base metals into pure gold. Shakespeare used 'tinct' in its alchemical sense in *Anthony and Cleopatra* when Cleopatra says to her 'base' attendant Alexas: 'How much unlike art thou Mark Anthony!/ Yet coming from him, that great Medicine hath/ With his tinct gilded thee' (1.5.34-36). Milton likewise used this metaphor when, in the creation scene in *Paradise Lost*, the stars multiply their light and Venus 'gilds her horns' from the sun's quintessential source, 'By tincture or reflection' (7.364-9) (*Dictionary*, p.169).

William Blake, too, assumes his readers know their alchemy. As Alexander Roob explains in his *Mysticism and Alchemy: The Hermetic Museum* (Taschen, 2001), the two complementary and antagonistic principles of the alchemical work are where he begins his artistry:

> William Blake identified the male principle with time and the female with space. The interpenetration of the two results in diverse reverberations of individual events, all of which, taken as a whole— totality, the micro-macrocosmic body of Christ in the image of the "human and the divine imagination—occur in a state of relative simultaneity. Each individual element opens up, in passing, into the permanent present of this fluctuating organism and in the process attains its "fourfold", complete form, which Blake calls "Jerusalem". This vision generated the kaleidoscopic, narrative structures of his late poems, which reveal themselves to the reader as a multi-layered structure of perspectival relations—aimed against the prevailing idea of a simple location of events in the absolutes of linear time and space (p.25).

Alchemy, then, is key to understanding Blake's last illuminated poem, *Jerusalem*, and his several paintings of Newton whom he singled out for his mechanical and rational view. James Joyce in turn refers to both these works of Blake and other alchemical ideas and images in his *Ulysses* and *Finnegan's Wake* (*Alchemy & Mysticism*, p. 482, 630). These are difficult writers and the best; to understand them requires at least a grounding in alchemy. If I had the two hours I thought I had, you would be hearing about Shakespeare and C. S. Lewis as brothers in letters and in alchemy. Alas. No time for *Taming of the Shrew*, *Romeo & Juliet*, or *That Hideous Strength*!

Even if the alchemy-literature connection is all news to you and you will go the grave believing alchemy is just for New Age nits or Historians of Science, I'm going to ask you to play along with me. Pretend, please, as if you accept it as gospel truth that English Literature from beginning to Rowling is front loaded with alchemical devices and images. **Why, if this is the case, I hope you will ask, should this be so?** What is the connection between alchemy and literature that makes these images the preferred tools of the best writers for centuries?

I think the connection is probably most clear in drama. Eliade even suggests that the alchemical work grew out of initiatory dramas of the Greek Mystery religions (*Forge*, p. 149). Shakespeare doesn't just make asides to alchemy in his plays; many if not most of them are written on alchemical skeletons and themes. *The Tempest, Romeo and Juliet, Anthony and Cleopatra, Two Gentlemen of Verona, The Comedy of Errors, Love's Labours Lost,* & *The Merchant of Venice* come to mind; see Jean Paris' 'The Alchemistic Theatre' (*Shakespeare*, Grove Press, 1960, pp. 87-116), and Martin Lings, *The Secret of Shakespeare* (Aquarian Press, 1984). Frances Yates' *The Art of Memory* (University of Chicago Press, 1974, p. 365) argues persuasively that Shakespeare built the Globe Theatre on Hermetic principles for the proper staging of his alchemical dramas. Why?

If you recall your Aristotle on what happens in a proper tragedy, the audience identifies with the hero in his agony and shares in his passion. This identification and shared passion is effectively the same as the experience of the event and the audience experiences *katharsis* or 'purification' in correspondence. *Shakespeare and Jonson among others use alchemical imagery and themes because they understood that the work of theatre in human transformation was parallel if not identical to the alchemical work.* The alchemical work, of course, claimed to be greater than an imaginative experience but *the idea of purification by identification or correspondence with an object and its transformations* is 'spot on' with the purpose of theatre, to risk a Britishism.

Alchemical language and themes are the shorthand of great English novels, drama, poetry and prose. The success of an artist following this tradition is measured by the edification of their audience. By means of traditional methods and symbols, the alchemical artist provides delight and dramatic release for our souls through archetypal and purifying experiences.

Let me say that again slowly.

Alchemical language and themes are the shorthand of great English novels, drama, poetry and prose. The success of an artist following this tradition is measured by the edification of their audience. By means of traditional methods and symbols, the alchemical artist provides delight and dramatic release for our souls through archetypal and purifying experiences.

That may be harder for some of us than the whole idea of alchemy as a sacred science. If you're like me, you grew up with the idea that entertainment was diversion and anything but life changing. It turns out this 'diversion' idea, really only in currency for the last seventy or eighty years, is a gross misconception. Anthropologists, historians of religion, and professors of literature will tell you that the rule in traditional as well as profane cultures such as ours is that Story, in whatever form, has an instructional or initiatory purpose.

Eliade in his *The Sacred and The Profane* is explicit in saying that, in a profane culture especially, entertainments to include reading fiction serve a religious function; they remove us from our ego-bound consciousness for an experience or immersion in another world or subcreation. C. S. Lewis in *Preface to Paradise Lost* asserts that this is the traditional understanding of the best writers, namely, that their role in culture is "to instruct while delighting." *Alchemy and literature are a match because they both endeavor in their undegenerate or orthodox state to transform the human person.*

Joanne Rowling, Alchemy, and Harry Potter

On Monday of this week I was sent a discussion from 'Harry Potter for Grown-ups' of *The Alchymical Wedding of Christian Rosenkreutz* as a source and model for the Harry Potter series. The authors, Ivan Vlabatsky and William Truderung draw many fascinating parallels between the 7 days of one and the 7 years of the other (HPfGU posts #56254 and 56297). Vlabatsky concludes, astonishingly I think, that Mrs. Rowling probably has **not** read and re-written Andreas' drama but that she was inspired by the same "Masters of Compassion" who inspired Andreas, the authors of "the New Testament, the epic of Gilgamesh, the legend of King Arthur, the Tao Teh Ching, etc." These Masters, I learned Monday, "are the gate keepers who constantly keep the door of liberation open for those seeking freedom."

I cannot answer the question of whether *The Alchymical Wedding* is the source and model of the Harry Potter series. Certainly it bears serious attention, even for those who worship at the altars of the Masters of Compassion. If she did, she won't have been the first to do so. Shakespeare, for example, some have said, writes scenes almost direct from *The Alchymical Wedding* in his *Merchant of Venice* (Paris, op.cit, pp. 98-99). Whatever the answer to this specific alchemical question, however, other larger questions about Mrs. Rowling and alchemy will remain. I'll do my best to answer some of these questions here, specifically:

- How can we tell if Mrs. Rowling is intentionally using alchemical imagery?
- What signs of the alchemical work are evident in the books individually and as a series?
- How does understanding the alchemical themes and images of the series improve our understanding of the books and their power to charm and delight young and old around the world?

Here at last is the part you came for; let's jump in!

How can we tell if Mrs. Rowling is intentionally using alchemical imagery?

A question I am always asked when I say Mrs. Rowling is writing alchemical literature in the tradition of English Literature is how I know she is. The implication, sometimes voiced, is that I have an agenda to show she is doing this in order both to support my thesis that she is writing within the traditions of her genre (rather than being an *ex machina* monster or goddess that fell from the sky) and to demonstrate a side-thesis, that, in being a traditional English writer she is almost certainly a Christian writer, whatever her orthodoxy. These questioners I have found will accept no proof as sufficient reason to accept my common sense observations and alchemical thesis other than Mrs. Rowling's testimony that she is an alchemist, the illegitimate daughter of C. S. Lewis, or a secret Bishop in the Church of Scotland.

As far as I know, and I am far from current on the track of reading Mrs. Rowling's various interviews, she has made no such confessions. She *has* insisted that she is a Christian and that her faith is important in understanding her work (see, for example, 'You can lead a fool to a book but you can't make them think: Author has frank words for the religious right', Max Wyman, Vancouver Sun, 11/25/2001) but I think her fans will need her to walk the stations of the Cross as a *penitente* through the streets of Edinbirgh or on the *via dolorosa* to be convinced she isn't putting on a show.

If the author has not said, though, that alchemy is at least part of the magic of Harry Potter, how can we know or test the books to see if it is or isn't? I suggest the following tests for evidence in support of the alchemical thesis:

- First, the evidence should be fairly clear—we shouldn't have to be practicing alchemists ourselves to see the connections and the evidence shouldn't need to be tortured and twisted to fit the procrustean bed;
- Second, the books should show both a design akin and parallel to the stages of the alchemical work and a bevy of imagery and symbols that are taken from this same work; and
- Third, this evidence should not have another as likely or believable explanation from traditional or conventional literature.

Which three tests takes us to our second question!

What signs of the alchemical work are evident in the books individually and as a series?

Test One: Is the Evidence fairly Obvious or is it Procrustean?

I give you three pieces of evidence to demonstrate that the alchemy connection screams from these books and is not tortured or even teased from them:

1. **Book Titles:**

   a. The title of the first book in the Harry Potter series, as you all know, is *Harry Potter and the Philosopher's Stone*. Only Arthur Levine's brilliant marketing decision—the brilliance of which I'm not sure even he appreciated at the time—to change the title to *Sorcerer's Stone* obscures the alchemical title. If the man in the street knows anything about alchemy, it is that alchemists pursued the Philosopher's Stone to turn lead into gold. Even P. G. Wodehouse wrote a Jeeves novel based on the Philosopher's Stone!

   b. Warner Bros. has reserved the title *Harry Potter and the Alchemist's Cell* for the sixth or seventh novel; again, not hard to see the alchemy in that—it's on the cover of the book.

2. **Alchemical Characters:**

   a. Albus Dumbledore, we learn on the first train ride to Hogwarts by reading his Chocolate Frog card—which distinction we learn in *Order of the Phoenix* he treasures above all his titles—is an alchemist of some reknown, even a partner of the famous Nicolas Flamel. This relationship, it turns out, is the key to unraveling the mystery of what is hidden at Hogwarts in Harry's first year.

   b. Hermione Granger's name, as several of the names in the books as we'll see in a moment, has an especially obvious alchemical reference in it. 'Hermione' is the feminine form of 'Hermes', who beside being the Greek messenger god (Mercury), was also the name of the great alchemist 'Hermes Trismegistos' in whose name countless alchemical works were written through the centuries.

3. **Harry's Transformations from Lead to Gold**

   The alchemical work is about changing the soul from lead to gold, failing to virtue; is this evident in the title character's transformations in each book? Yes, it is.

   a. *Philosopher's Stone*: as the novel opens, Harry is an orphan child who lives in fear of his Aunt and Uncle and without any knowledge or delight in who he is. By book's end, he shows himself a champion of remarkable courage and daring—and reconciled to both his parents' death and destiny as a wizard.

   b. *Chamber of Secrets*: Harry begins the book as a prisoner both of the Dursleys and of his own self-doubts and self pity; at the heroic finish in the morality play acted out in the Chamber, he is the liberator of Ginny and vanquisher of Tom Riddle, who is an incarnation of selfishness and self-importance.

   c. *Prisoner of Azkaban*: Harry blows up Aunt Marge on Privet Drive because he cannot overlook her slights of his parents; in the crucible of the Shrieking

Shack, he rescues the man who betrayed his parents to Voldemort by offering his own life as a shield to him! Unforgiving judgment to Semi-divine Mercy in a year.

d. *Goblet of Fire*: Harry begins the book consumed by thoughts of what others think of him, his external person; by book's end, after trials with Ron, the Hogwarts student body, and a dragon, he is able to shrug off without a dent or tear a *Daily Prophet* hatchet job beaconed to all corners of the wizarding world.

e. *Order of the Phoenix*: Harry is consumed by a desire of news at the beginning of the latest book. He struggles to listen to television reports, agonizes over the lack of reports from friends, and wanders his neighborhood in search of newspapers in trash cans. At the end, he is aware of his need to turn inward and discover and strengthen his inner life; his extroverted dependence on the outer world and events has become his point of vulnerability by which Voldemort manipulates him (and causes Sirius' death).

Test Two: Are both the design and predominant imagery of the books alchemical?

In a word, 'Yes'. This will require some knowledge and reference to details and to stages of the alchemical work the average reader cannot be expected to know but the design and imagery of the Potter series are indeed from the alchemical work.

1. **Design**

a. *Sulfur/Quicksilver—Ron/Hermione*: Let's start with a pretty straightforward one. The Alchemical work is a series of purifications of a base metal from lead into gold that is accomplished by dissolving and recongealing the metal via the action of two principal reagents. These reagents reflect the masculine and feminine polarity of existence; 'alchemical sulfur' represents the masculine, impulsive, and red pole and 'quicksilver' or 'alchemical mercury' the feminine and cool complementary antagonist. Together and separately these reagents and catalysts advance the work from base metal to corporeal light or gold.

Harry's two friends are Ron Weasley and Hermione Granger. Ron, the redhead, passionate boy and Hermione, the brilliant, cool young woman are Harry's never fail companions. They are also living symbols of alchemical sulfur—Ron—and mercury—Hermione, again being the feminine of the Greek name for Mercury. Together, and, more obviously, in their disagreements and separation, Harry's friendship with Ron and Hermione transform him from lead to gold (as discussed above).

For those involved in the 'shipping debate about whether Hermione is meant for Ron or Harry in the end, this point suggests the eventual love match of Ron and Hermione. "Medieval alchemists adopted from the Arabs the theory that all metals were a synthesis of mercury and sulphur, whose union might achieve various degrees of harmony. A perfectly harmonious marriage of the mother and father of metals might produce gold" (Mark Haeffner, *Dictionary of Alchemy*, Aquarian Press, 1994, p. 147). When Ron and Hermione stop quarreling and hook-up, Harry's perfection is near.

b. *The Stages of Alchemy—The Cycle of each book*: Maybe you knew about the action of contraries in alchemy and about mercury and quicksilver; it is the background, after all, to all the twins in Shakespeare and the remarkable pairings of men and women in his better plays (think *Taming of the Shrew!*). Probably fewer people, though, know the stages of the alchemical 'Great Work' and what happens in each. What has often been described as Harry's annual hero journey is in fact the cycle of the alchemical transformation—and each stage of the work, in case you need a road sign, has a character named for it in the Harry Potter books.

The first stage of the alchemical work is dissolution, usually called the **nigredo** or the black stage. In the black, initial stage, "the body of the impure metal, the mater for the Stone, or the old, outmoded state of being is killed, putrefied, and dissolved into the original substance of creation, the *prima materia*, in order that it may be renovated and reborn in a new form" (Abraham, op. cit., p. 135). Sirius Black is named for this stage of the work.

The second stage of alchemical transformation of lead into gold is the **albedo** or white work. It follows the ablution or washing of the calcified matter at the bottom of the alembic, the washing of which causes it show the 'peacock's tail' (*cauda pavonis*) or the colors of the rainbow before turning a brilliant white. "When the matter reaches the albedo it has become pure and spotless" (Abraham, op. cit., p.5). Albus Dumbledore is the character with the 'white' name; '*albus*' is Latin for 'white, resplendent.' Frequently used symbols of the **albedo** stage of the work in pictorial representations and descriptions of it are Luna (Latin for the moon) and a lily.

The third and last stage of the chemical work is the **rubedo** or the red stage. "When the matter of the stone has been purified and made spotless at the **albedo** it is then ready to be re-united with the spirit (or the already united spirit and soul). With the fixation, crystallization or embodiment of the eternal spirit, form is bestowed upon the pure, but as yet formless matter of the Stone. At this union, the supreme chemical wedding, **the body is resurrected into eternal life** [my emphasis]. As the heat of the fire is increased, the divine red tincture flushes the white stone with its rich, red colour . . . The reddening of the white matter is also frequently likened to staining with blood" (Abraham, op.cit, p.174). Rubeus Hagrid has the red name; 'rubeus' is Latin for 'red' (the Latin for 'black', of course is 'niger' so Sirius' name is translated to English for obvious reasons). A common symbol of the red work and the Philosopher's Stone is the red lion.

I offer for your consideration the possibility that the formula for each book thus far is a trip through these stages. Briefly, the black work or dissolution is the work done on Harry at Privet Drive by the Dursleys and in the dungeons by Snape at Hogwarts. The white work is Harry's study time or year at Hogwarts under the watchful eye of the white alchemist, Albus Dumbledore, in combination with and painful separation from Ron, Hermione, or both. The red work is the crucible scene underground or in a graveyard in which Harry always dies a figurative death and is saved by love in the presence of a Christological symbol. **The resurrection at story's end each year** is the culmination of that year's cycle and transformation. The cycle then closes with congratulations and explanations from the master alchemist and a return to the Dursleys for another trip through the cycle. [For more on this, please see Chapter 6 of *The Hidden Key to Harry Potter* and the individual chapters devoted to each of the first four books.]

    c.   *The Alchymical Wedding of Christian Rosenkreutz:* William Truderung has drawn remarkable parallels between the years at Hogwarts that we have and the first four days of Johann Andrea's *Alchymical Wedding,* a drama of the cycles and stages of the alchemical work told as a story. Here, for example, are Truderung's comparisons with the first day of Christian's adventures and Harry's first year at Hogwarts:

First Day:

—*CRC is living in cramped accommodations, with minimal food*

—*a terrible storm arises*

—*during the storm, an 'otherworldly' being appears, and delivers a letter to him*

—*the letter is heavy, sealed with a curious symbol with a Latin phrase, and written in gold letters*

—*upon opening, the message is an invitation to attend a wedding, which CRC was at birth entitled to attend*

—near the end of the first day, CRC descends (in a dream) into a dark dungeon, containing a peculiar stone

—CRC is presented with seven 'challenges'; six inside the dungeon, and one at the entrance above it, and during the final challenge inside the dungeon receives a wound to the head from the stone, but is rescued by his mentor, a wise old man

The seven HP challenges: Fluffy (entrance above the dungeon); the Devil's Snare; the Keys; the Chess Game; the Troll; the Potions; the Mirror (inside the dungeon)
HPfGU, post #56297

I think without much prompting even the casual reader sees the remarkable similarity and story between *Philosopher's Stone* and *The Alchemical Wedding*. The parallels continue through Day and Year 5, to include an injury to Christian's hand in his fifth day adventure (read *The Alchemical Wedding*: **http://www.sacred-texts.com/eso/chemical/chemical.htm**). I cannot vouch for this theory because I have not studied it but I am obliged to mention it as a remarkable possibility when pointing to alchemy as a design for the series. (*The Alchemical Wedding* is a seventeenth century story, be forewarned; even if borderline heretical, I think the unprepared reader will be taken aback by its forthright Christian tone and content.)

d.   *The Nigredo*

Closer to my heart is the possibility that alchemy is the explanation for the structure and bizarre events of *Harry Potter and the Order of the Phoenix*. I went out on a limb in my book and predicted that HP5 would be the white stage of the alchemical work or **albedo** and that it would culminate in the death of Albus Dumbledore after he told all to Harry about his destiny. Need I say I was wrong? I thought that the wizarding world couldn't get much blacker or Harry more burned down than he was in *Goblet of Fire* so that the **nigredo** or black work was over.

Again, need I tell you how wrong I was? *Order of the Phoenix* from its hot and dry beginnings and sojourn in the House of Black to the police state of Dolores Umbridge ('grieving resentment' or 'grievous shadow'—'a woman who blocks the sun'?) and the death of Sirius Black in the Department of Mysteries is the **nigredo** volume of the Harry Potter series. Harry, literally and figuratively, is burnt up, broken down or dissolved, and bled until everything that he thought he was—Quidditch seeker, Ron and Hermione's superior, pet of Dumbledore, lover of Hogwarts, son and spitting image of a great man, victim of the Dursleys, valiant enemy of Snape, even his being the hero and man of action in time of crisis—are taken from him or revealed as falsehoods. The boundaries of his world collapse; the Dementors come to Little Whinging and Aunt Petunia knows about them. Privet Drive is no longer a sanctuary, however miserable, and Hogwarts is no longer edifying or any joy to him. The world is no longer separated into good guys, Muggles, and Death Eaters—and Harry has been reduced to his formless elements.

A kind friend and serious student of alchemy and literature in the United Kingdom, Alison Williams, has written me to say that she thinks the predictions I made in *Hidden Key* are 'spot on'—only a book early. I, of course, think she is brilliant! Whether the white stage is to follow this black novel however (and a climax in book 7 turning on Hagrid the Red), there is little doubt that *Order of the Phoenix* is Rowling's **nigredo** masterpiece; I felt shattered and undone and released from ideas of self and place throughout the book—and a new person at the end, as is our Harry.

2. Imagery and Symbolism

I hope this will suffice at least as an argument, if not a demonstration or proof (which is hardly possible short of Mrs. Rowling's confesion), that the Harry Potter books are built on an alchemical formula or structure. I have to fly on to alchemical imagery and symbolism if I hope to be done by lunch today—unless you all want to continue on the beach? No? Then let's hurry along.

We think of symbolism, after being trained by mechanical teachers and lifeless texts, as cardboard signs; 'this represents that.' "The white whale is a symbol for God, Mrs. Johnson," we al learned to say in 10th grade English. Alchemical and real literary symbolism, however, is a different beastie entirely than what we hated in school. An authentic symbol is a means of passage and of grace between what is real and the shadow world of time and space. As Martin Lings, author of *Symbol and Archetype*, wrote in his book on the mysticism and alchemy in Shakespeare's plays:

> Symbolism is not arbitrary, but is based on the very nature of things, on the make-up of the universe. According to all cosmological and metaphysical doctrines, whether Eastern or Western, earthly phenomena are nothing other than the shadows or reflections of spiritual realities. The symbolism of a thing is its power to recall its higher reality, in the same way that a reflection or shadow can give us a fleeting glimpse of the object that casts it; and the best symbols—the only ones worthy to be used in sacred art—are those things which are most perfect of their kind, for they are the clearest reflections, the sharpest shadows, of the higher reality which is their archetype (*Secret of Shakespeare*, Aquarian Press, 1984).

The great authors of the English tradition are no dummies. Shakespeare, Milton, Herbert, Donne, Blake, Joyce, Lewis, Charles Williams, Tolkien—the reason they write in alchemical symbols is because they are what Lings calls "the best symbols", "the clearest reflections . . . of the higher reality." These symbols do the job literature and drama set out to do.

Joanne Rowling is no dummy either. Her books are quite simply stuffed with alchemical images for our edification and transformation in the alchemy of reading. Here are three quick examples: the images in *Goblet of Fire*, in *Order of the Phoenix*, and the gang of doppelgangers in all the books.

    a.   *Goblet of Fire* images from alchemy:

The events of the Tri-Wizard Tournament and Harry's preparation for each trial by fire, water, or labyrinth are wonderfully engaging and fantastic in the root sense of that word. You should know, too, that each is from the alchemical work. A quick review of the tasks and search of guides to alchemical imagery in literature reveals the role in the Opus Alchymicum of dragons, the egg, the prefect's bath and water trial, the labyrinth and the graveyard resurrection and fight.

      i.   **dragons**: symbols of matter at the beginning of the work being resolved into philosophical sulphur and mercury (Abraham, p. 59)

     ii.   **the egg**: "the alchemist's vessel of transmutation in which the birth of the philosopher's stone takes place . . . ; also known as the griffin's egg" (Abraham, p.66)

   iii.   **the bath**: "the secret, inner, invisible fire which dissolves and kills, cleanses and resurrects the matter of the Stone in the vessel" (Abraham, p. 17)

   iv.   **water immersion/flood**: "One of the alchemist's maxims was, 'Perform no operation until all be made water' (Eliade, *Forge*, p.153). "A symbol of the dissolution and putrefaction of the matter of the Stone during the black nigredo stage" (Abraham, p.78)

    v.   **labyrinth**: "the dangerous journey of the alchemist through the opus alchymicum . . . . While in the labyrinth of the opus, illusion and confusion reign and the alchemist is in danger of losing all connection and clarity" (Abraham, p. 113)

   vi.   **grave**: "the alchemist's vessel during the nigredo" In alchemical lore, frequently a copulating couple are buried and die but, in their death, their spirits are joined and the Hermaphrodite body rises from the grave. This is the alchemical ending of *Romeo & Juliet* and why their deaths resolve their families feud (Abraham, p.90)

All the alchemical images of Harry's four Tri-Wizard tasks are preparatory for the black stage of the great work or **nigredo**, to come in *Order of the Phoenix*. How did I miss it? (It was the reason I thought the **nigredo** was over!)

    b.   *Order of the Phoenix* images from alchemy

Maybe you think I just got lucky with *Goblet of Fire*? Here is a quick look at the alchemical symbols in *Order of the Phoenix*:

i.   **Nigredo** As mentioned above, the real Black work happens in Order of the Phoenix. Harry has been undone by his experiences—he knows his parents aren't gods, he can't play quidditch, his own lack of self-awareness causes his godfather's death, he can't act at will, he can't get information, God/Dumbledore is strangely absent, the world hates him, he suffers privately for the truth ("I will not tell lies"), and his friends are honored before him. This dissolution (nigredo), though, is not his purification (albedo) and so we are left at book's end with only the formless dregs of Harry's character, which, frankly, aren't pretty. **the Black King:** Kingsley Shacklebolt is not a token black character but an alchemical reference to the "black king." The king of the alchemical work must die, usually by drowning, and "at this stage the matter is at its blackest black and is known as the black king" (Abraham, p.111).

ii. **Dung:** Sirius and his friends call Mundungus Fletcher ('world-filth arrow maker') "Dung" as an affectionate nickname. Given the subject of this book, it is also a hoot that dung was the heat source for the first stage of the alchemical work and even "became a name for the matter from which the miraculous, rejuvenating elixir or Stone was made" (Abraham, p. 62). Expect big things from Dung.

iii. **Luna:** "Luna is the bride, the white queen, consort of King Sol. She is the moist, cold, receptive principle which must be united with Sol, the dry, hot, active principle in the chemical wedding" (Abraham, p. 120). A girl friend for hot and dry—burned to a cinder—Harry? Just in time: Luna "symbolizes the attainment of the perfect white stage, the albedo, where the matter of the Stone reaches absolute purity" (Abraham, pp.119-120). Look for Harry and Luna to be a couple in HP6—much to Hermione's and Professor McGonagall's disgust.

iv. **Caput Mortuum:** One of the weirder images of *Order of the Phoenix* is the heads of dead house elves lining the stairway at the House of Black ('house' by the way is alchemical language for alembic or vessel). I first thought Mrs. Rowling was pointing graphically to the sufferings of house elves and their disdainful treatment of these 'Kreachers' (which leads to horrible consequences for everyone). Which she may well be doing—but 'head of the dead' is also symbol for—what else?—"the initial stage of the opus, the black **nigredo**" (Abraham, p. 31). How appropriate for wall hangings in the House of Black!

v.   **James/Lily:** James Potter and Lily Evans at last become three dimensional in *Order of the Phoenix* and we get to see the reason or at least one experience that causes Snape to hate Harry so much. Harry gets to watch his 15 year old father, of whom we are told again he is almost a mirror image, and learns that his dad was something of a conceited bully whom his mother at that age despised. 'Lily' is synonymous in the alchemical work with 'Luna' (see above and

Abraham, p. 117-18). No doubt we will learn in the next books how James was tried in the fire to win the lily that reflects the achievement of the second stage of the work. 'James', incidentally, is an alchemical name; St. James is the patron saint of alchemists (Roob, op. cit., p.700).

vi. **Phoenix**: And how about the title of this book and the sacrificial bird of this title, the loyal hero that prevented my prediction of Dumbledore's death from coming true in HP6? Sure enough, the phoenix is an alchemical "symbol of renewal and resurrection signifying the philosopher's stone, especially the red stone attained at the **rubedo**, capable of transmuting base metals into pure gold" (Abraham, p. 152). The raven, in contrast, is symbol of the **nigredo**, as by now you might have guessed with the several Ravenclaw players featured in *Phoenix*.

And, believe me there are more! A quick run through one Alchemical Imagery dictionary threw light on all the following subjects and symbols featured in the Potter series, each with an alchemical meaning that deepens Rowling's decision to use them in her story:

Others : bee (Dumbledore), blood, bolthead, castle, cervus fugitivus (stag), raven (raven's head), cupid, eagle, griffin, lazy Henry (Harry), house, melancholia, metamorphosis (Tonks), night, orphan, red man and white woman (quarreling couple—Ron and Hermione), king, serpent, ship, Sol, skeleton, sulphur, quicksilver, tears, toad, unicorn, wolf, and worm

c. Doppelgangers

OK, enough about the alchemical imagery. If you think I'm making it up, well, I have sent all the arrows I have from that quiver. Before leaving alchemical imagery, though, I want to mention 'doppelgangers.' This staple of 19th century Gothic and romantic fiction is of a creature or pair of creatures that have complementary figures or shadows, which shadows reveal aspects of their character otherwise invisible. Think of Stevenson's Jekyll & Hyde, Stoker's Count Dracula, Shelley's Dr. Frankenstein and his monster, and the Count of Monte Cristo. Rowling points to these shadows in her principal characters in a variety of ways:

i. As **Animagi**: How many animagi do we know of in the books? James, Sirius, Peter, Minerva, Rita, for starters, and I'll add Albus who certainly as a former Master of Transfiguration at Hogwarts and alchemist has mastered this trick (I bet he's the tawny owl that appears in several places). Nymphadora Tonks as a shape changer (Metamorphmagus) deserves a special mention.

ii. **Half-breeds/mudbloods/monsters**: Half-breeds and mudbloods as well as two natured monsters include Hagrid, Olympe, Fleur, Lily, Tom Riddle, Hermione, Remus, Tonks again and Severus (assuming he is a vampire). Harry, because he grew up as a Muggle, has an honorary membership here.

iii. **Threshhold characters** (the 'Liminal'): these are the folks in Potterworld that live in two worlds or so far to the periphery of their own worlds that they cannot fit into the usual categories (good guy or Death Eater, for instance). Snape leads this group, Dobby is a close second, Firenze, Hagrid, Remus, Peter, Neville, squibs Argus and Arabella, Mundungus, and Percy—if he seems to have crossed the threshhold in *Phoenix*—fill out the set.

iv. **Twins, Pairs, and Brothers**: George and Fred, the Weasley troop, Hagrid and Grawp, the Creevey brothers, Sirius and James, Crabbe and Goyle, Ron and Hermione, Slytherine and Gryffindor, Lily and Petunia, Lily and Narcissa (flowers of the same family), Peter and Neville (a cross-generational pair of look-alikes), Harry and Dudley, and Harry and Neville (joined by the prophecy). And those Parkinsons!

v. **Harry/Voldemort**: *Order of the Phoenix* begins with three mentions of Harry's feeling that his skull has been split in two and one has to imagine it must crack right down that jagged scar. It turns out that Harry's head really is divided and he has an unwelcome guest. He isn't carrying a passenger like Quirrell or possessed as was Ginny but Harry has a double nature or shadow in his link to Voldemort—and his inability to turn inward and confront this shadow is the cause of the tragedy at book's end. Like his dad at 15, he was willingly blind to the 'back' of his 'front.'

vi. **Magical Creatures**: Double natured beasties featured in the Hogwarts Gallery include Centaurs, Griffins, Hippogriffs, and the Sphynx with a special mention due to the phoenix, thestral, and unicorn (because they are not what they seem, namely, bird or horse or even bird/horse/dragon).

That so many characters have a twin who is their likeness or antagonistic complement and so many others who live a double existence between worlds makes this aspect of Potterworld—itself divided between Magic and Muggle domains—oddly invisible to many. It's everywhere and consequently 'nowhere.' I suggest for your consideration that this pairing or unity in division is a central theme of the Harry Potter books and that it has an alchemical meaning.

The activity of alchemy is the chemical marriage of the imbalance "arguing couple" of masculine sulphur and feminine quicksilver. These antipodal qualities have to be reconciled and resolved, 'die' and be 'reborn' after conjunction before recongealing in a perfected golden unity. Certainly the similarity of this language to the Christian spiritual path is a remarkable one—and understandably. The symbols of the completion of the alchemical work are also traditional ciphers for Christ, the God/Man, in whose sinless two natures Christians are called to perfection in His mystical body, the Church.

But the old and the new man cannot live together in the same person or world—and this is Harry's war with his doppelganger or twin-in-spirit, Lord Voldemort. Love has overcome death in each of the books' ending thus far; I expect this will be the series' end as well.

3. Themes

I discuss four principal themes in *Hidden Key*: prejudice, death, choice, and change. How do these themes appear in the light of alchemy? I think Rowling's meaning crystallizes around the alchemical perspective of these ideas.

a. Death

Death is the necessary part of the alchemical work; only in the death of one thing, from the alchemical perspective, is the greater thing born. (Alchemists frequently cite John 12:24 and Christ's Crucifixion and Resurrection, Abraham, p. 28). But Love, the action of contraries and their resolution, transcends death; it is what brings life out of death, even eternal life and spiritual perfection. This is a direct match with Rowling's message about how to understand death and love.

b. Change

Alchemy is about transformation from lead to gold, the spiritual work of human life. Each Harry Potter novel is a depiction of the process by which Harry is transformed—and each time we read and identify with his experience we as readers are changed by this alchemy of literature, too.

c. Choice and Destiny

Harry's changes have always come as consequences of his heroic choices; Dumbledore has never failed to let us know in his farewell talks that it is one's choices that determine who you will be not just your birthright (if you have any). But the complement of choice or free will is fate and destiny—and this complement to choice appears in *Order* via the Prophecy of which Harry (or Neville) is the fulfillment. Rowling is resolving the traditional chestnut of fate and free will alchemically; Harry has a destiny in this prophecy and, I think, as Heir of Gryffindor, but he will only fulfill this destiny through his ability to make right choices. This again echos the Christian/alchemical message that we are created as images of God, but, in order to become His likeness, we must die to the old, fallen man in us, and choose rightly the means to our perfection.

Test Three: Better Explanations available?

So we arrive at long last to the last question of our tests of the evidence for or against Joanne Rowling being an alchemical writer in the tradition of the English 'Greats'. Are there better or *just simpler* explanations than all this arcane imagery from a sacred science not recognizing modern distinctions of subject and object, spirit and matter? I can think of four contenders for an easier way to see it.

1. **Mrs. Rowling's imagination:** This is the simplest alternative and the suggestion of 'Hans from Holland' mentioned above, namely, that Mrs. Rowling's use of alchemical imagery is either a happy coincidence or a case of artists in different places and times being inspired by a the same playful muse. Frankly, I think this perspective is borderline misogynist (I struggle to imagine someone saying it about a man of Mrs. Rowling's educational pedigree) and insulting to her genius as an author. Really, "it just happened"? Why not say she just "got lucky"?

2. **Imaginative literature 'compost':** Mrs. Rowling has said in several interviews that her books' inspirations are drawn from the compost in her mind of all the books she has read. Certainly this includes all the imaginative literature and the Great books, poems, and plays of her native tradition. She did not say, however, that her inspiration went without careful sifting and plotting (some seven years before the first book was written). Her characters, plots, themes, and imagery were not items that she picked from the top of her imaginative pile without discernment. Again, no accidents—and not simpler or better than the argument from alchemy and tradition.

3. **Classical Literary 'compost':** No different than the above compost except that this pile reflects Mrs. Rowling's classical education. Yes, Homer and Virgil are in the pile, too, and other non-Englishmen, but the further back we go in time the more traditional and alchemical the view of the cosmos and the human person. Rowling definitely battles on the side of the Ancients in Swift's *Battle of the Books*.

4. **Inkling and Christian references:** Certainly the argument I like best is the one I made in *Hidden Key to Harry Potter*. The argument there is that Rowling is an Inkling wannna-be and a throwback to the tradition of Greats prior to the twentieth century who wrote edifying Christian entertainments and literature. This, however, is not substantially different than the alchemical argument because the reason writers use the alchemical symbols and imagery is because it so powerfully presents Christian truths for readers to experience imaginatively (as prelude to experiencing them liturgically).

Conclusion: I do not think there is a simpler or better explanation for the preponderance of alchemical references, themes, structures, images and symbols in the Harry Potter books than the common sense notion that she is writing brilliantly alchemical literature. Please note I am not saying alchemy is everything about Harry Potter you need to appreciate to understand what the books are about; that would be ridiculous. I am saying, however, that understanding alchemy and its usage in the tradition and in these books will take one a long way in appreciating the heights and depths of Mrs. Rowling's genius

Conclusions

Let me wrap this up quickly with a challenge for you as you leave here and head off to your other lectures, presentations, and panel discussions. I think the question we must all be asking at every talk we listen to here is this: **Why are these books so popular?** What need do they fill? What longing do they satisfy? No book in our time or any other time that I know of (with the possible exception of Dickens' serials) has ever created such a following and diverse readership. As thinking people, we need to understand why this is so.

I will take up my own challenge and conclude by asking myself: Does the alchemy connection answer the question of **why the books are so popular?** If so, what is the alchemical answer to the many-times $64 million question? I think the alchemical connection does answer the question. It points to the facts that:

1. **Joanne Rowling clearly understands both 'alchemy in literature' and the 'alchemy of literature':** like Harry in Riddle's diary, we fall into her books and are carried through a Magic Mountain roller coaster experience of Harry's alchemical transformation and the kaleidoscope of symbols, themes, and imagery from centuries of literary usage.
2. The reason the books are so popular is that they satisfy the need in us, born in a profane culture without heroes or avenues of transcendent experience—a materialist world in which such experience is not considered possible by "serious people"— of at least an imaginative experience of human transformation and perfection. We get this experience in our identification with Harry and we are better for it, more human even, for having been for a while at least in the alembic vessel changing from spiritual lead to gold, dying and rising from the dead. In brief, **Joanne Rowling's novels are so popular because her works transform human person via imaginative identification, experience, *katharsis*, and resurrection.**

Now, this last note. The great irony of Christian objections to Mrs. Rowling's books because they undermine or violate the tenets of the Christian faith is that the Harry

Potter books offer initiation, not into the occult or worlds of invocational sorcery, but rather into the symbolist world view of revealed faiths (and sacramental religions specifically) and the dominant symbols and doctrines of traditional Christianity (as argued in my book). Ignorance of alchemy and the larger traditions of English literature (not to mention the Christian understanding of the relations of faith and secular culture) have brought many to turn away a great help, perhaps providential, in the trouble and struggle we have to prepare our children for fully human, which is to say 'spiritual' lives.

John Granger, the author of The Hidden Key to Harry Potter and Looking for God in Harry Potter, is a Latin and Greek teacher from the Olympic Peninsula and the Harry Potter Professor at Barnes and Noble University on-line. His background in Classics, the 'Great Books', and traditional philosophy and cosmology mirrors Joanne Rowling's education and reading (they both, for instance, have honors degrees in Classical Languages; John's is from the University of Chicago). This shared eyeglass prescription allows John to speak with unusual authority about the alchemical structure of the Potter novels, the meaning of the spells and the character names, the various references and debts to ancient and modern writers, and about the predominant symbolism employed by Ms. Rowling.

John's book version of his popular lectures, The Hidden Key to Harry Potter (Zossima Press, 2003), is an exploration of Rowling's themes, structures, and meaning. Hidden Key has received critical acclaim in the U.S. and the UK for its insights and style. John argues cogently in Hidden Key that the Potter books are best understood within the context of the English 'Greats' tradition and, specifically, as a throwback to the romantic novelists of the 19th century and to the Inklings of the 20th century. John loves the Potter books as only a daddy of seven young readers can and his lectures—described as earning the 'Three E's': entertaining, enlightening, and edifying—show how much meaning Rowling has rolled into so much fun.

Harry Potter: Witchcraft?
Presented as part of the
Pagan Perspectives Panel

Lee Hillman, Amy Vezza, John Walton

Synopsis: Everyone hears a great deal about the Christian controversy over the Harry Potter books. Occasionally a pagan group pipes up, usually to praise the books, sometimes to criticise them. What is paganism, how does it relate to Harry Potter, and what kinds of things do pagans have to say about the books' take on magic, morals, and myth?

After introductions, all three panelists warned the audience that they are neither scholars nor credentialed religious leaders in their paths, and that the opinions presented in this panel are based on their experience of paganism and their readings of the Harry Potter books, not from any position of "authority" in pagan society. However, it should be noted that an important tenet of paganism is that all pagans are qualified to speak to their individual pathway, and pagans do not require certification as religious teachers, such as deacons, cantors, ministers, or other parallel designations, to be able to speak on behalf of their religion.

Though less than half the attendees to the panel identified themselves as pagan, and a few more than half had an idea of what paganism is, this discussion would be confusing and frustrating if we did not first define paganism for the reader.

Here is a highly simplified definition of paganism: the belief, by and large, that a. divinity resides in all individuals; b. the individual has the power to connect to that which is spiritual, without a go-between like a minister or priest; c. the individual has the power to directly affect the world around them through spiritual and magical concentration and manipulation of energy. Paganism is not, by definition, hedonism. It is not occultist by definition, either. It is important to understand that any group of pagans may follow very different paths in their religion: just as "Protestant" comprises dozens of different types of Christians, so "Pagan" is really an umbrella for any number of traditions, belief systems, and worship patterns. For an excellent and comprehensive discussion of Neo-Paganism and modern witchcraft, we recommend Margot Adler's *Drawing Down the Moon*; for this paper, the above definition will be our working one.

Moving on to the Pagan Perspective on Harry Potter, perhaps the first order of business is to discuss magic. The main difference between pagans and other, especially Judeo-Christian religions, is that many or most Christians attribute magic to the realm of miracle, and credit the divine with any magical working that might occur in the world. Pagans, on the other hand, in general believe that every person is endowed with the ability to tap into the same energy and power as is possessed by the divine, because of our connection to the divine, and therefore *can* manipulate reality in ways that could be called magical. Some Pagans do not even perceive magic as a mystical process at all, but more accurately "a convenient word for a whole collection of techniques, all of which involve the mind . . . . including the mobilization of confidence, will, and emotion brought about by the recognition of necessity; the use of imaginative faculties, particularly the ability to visualize, in order to begin to understand how other beings function in nature so we can use this knowledge to achieve necessary ends" (Adler, 8). Thus, Pagans approach the idea of magic in a series of books like Harry Potter with a predominantly different attitude than many, though by no means all, Christians.

As for this series of books, the panelists assert strongly that there is no relationship in the Harry Potter books between religion and magic. Magic is never portrayed as a mystical or a religious experience, nor is the performance of magic ever infused with any religious overtones—good or bad. Religion does have its place in the world of magic, of course, and we will return to that later. First, however, let us examine the magic itself, as a system, and compare it to pagan practice.

Sympathetic Magic and Harry Potter

From the working definition of paganism established in the panel, the group discussed the type of magic found in the books. There is a marked difference between a direct cause-and-effect relationship between magic and reality, as seen in fantasy and role-playing games, and pagan magic, which, we emphasize, is primarily "sympathetic" in nature. It is worth quoting James Fraser here at length:

> If we analyse the principles of thought on which magic is based, they will probably be found to resolve themselves into two: first, that like produces like, or that an effect resembles its cause; and, second, that things which have once been in contact with each other continue to act on each other at a distance after the physical contact has been severed. The former principle may be called the Law of Similarity, the latter the Law of Contact of Contagion. From the first of these principles, namely the Law of Similarity, the magician infers that he can produce any effect he desires merely by imitating it: from the second he infers that whatever he does to a material object will affect equally the person with whom the object was once in contact, whether it formed part of his body or not. Charms based on the Law of Similarity may be called Homoeopathic or Imitative Magic. Charms based on the Law of Contact of Contagion may be called Contagious Magic. To denote the first of these branches of magic the term Homoeopathic is perhaps preferable, for the alternative term Imitative or Mimetic suggests, if it down not imply, a conscious agent who

imitates, thereby limiting the scope of magic too narrowly . . . . [I]n practice the two branches are often combined; or, to be more exact, while homoeopathic or imitative magic may be practised by itself, contagious magic will generally be found to involve an application of the homoeopathic or imitative principle. Thus generally stated the two things may be a little difficult to grasp, but they . . . readily become intelligible when they are illustrated by particular examples. Both trains of thought are in fact extremely simple and elementary . . . . Both branches of magic, the homoeopathic and the contagious, may conveniently be comprehended under the general name of Sympathetic Magic, since both assume that things act on each other at a distance through a secret sympathy, the impulse being transmitted from one to the other by means of what we may conceive as a kind of invisible ether, not unlike that which is postulated by modern science for a precisely similar purpose, namely, to explain how things can physically affect each other through a space which appears to be empty (Fraser, 12-14).

Sometimes the relationship between these sympathetic causers and their effects are tenuous at best, even impossible to prove, save by belief in the reality of magic. In Harry Potter, the books assume a much more direct, traceable relationship that has little to do with faith. Spells have specific effects and if executed properly, they always produce the same results. In addition, spells are learned by rote, and there very little spellwork in the books that has any type of ceremonial component. In that sense, spells in Harry Potter correspond to a much more "scientific" method than most magic practiced by pagans or by aboriginal cultures. Nevertheless, there are some sympathetic elements that may suggest the need for will or intention in the spell, as well as, for example in the case of Neville Longbottom, self-confidence.

Implements, Foci, and Component Magic

The use of wands is vital to magic practiced in Harry Potter, perhaps more than any other component. The wand itself appears to be a focus. Some pagans use wands in their worship, but naturally, there is never any direct effect, unlike when Harry shoots sparks out of his. Wands are also highly individualized, which suggests that a wand's ability to channel a wizard's magic is very important to the effectiveness of spells cast with that wand. We learn in *Chamber of Secrets* that Ron Weasley's broken wand creates unreliable effects, and this concept is reinforced again in *Order of the Phoenix*, when we learn that all this time, Neville has been using his father's wand. On the other hand, Sirius Black uses Professor Snape's wand quite handily during *Prisoner of Azkaban*, and it seems that many fully qualified wizards can produce desired effects with any wand, not merely one's own wand.

Pagans who possess wands tend to purchase one-of-a-kind items, too, but for different reasons. In fact, one Wiccan author advises: "Don't worry about finding the ideal wand at first; one will come to you . . . . Any stick you use will be infused with energy and power" (Cunningham, 28). Some pagans specialize in different types of magic, and rely on folklore and tradition to tell them that such a school of magic uses such a type of wand. Others find they have an affinity for certain woods or other materials for their wands, again, based either on lore or on personal preferences (for example, John and Lee both like purple heart wood, because it's purple!). In this manner, they are similar to the witches and wizards of Harry Potter's universe. However, there are also a number of pagans who adorn their wands with other elements, such as crystals, semi-precious metals and stones, and other natural materials such as bone. Also, there are pagans who carve or burn their wands to incorporate symbols of power or protection, something which we have never seen in the books. Finally, of course, pagans do not have access to magical creatures, and thus cannot use any of their properties in creating the magical "core" of the wand. In this element, Ms. Rowling irrevocably separates her concept of a wand from that of the pagan practitioner.

Incantations are also an important component in spellwork, but again, they are treated differently depending on the system of magic. The witches and wizards we have seen so far seem to use a predominantly Latin base for their incantations. This makes sense, considering that Rowling, a classics student, seems to have based her system of magic on the historical fact that Latin was the universal language of learning throughout the Middle Ages, and her wizarding world feels decidedly Medieval in many ways. It also makes sense that, in an English-speaking nation, many of those spells have also taken on pidgin qualities, incorporating words from the vernacular. One wonders if all wizards use Latin-based spells—most likely Latin is used only in European schools. Nonetheless, it's also clear that the incantation is secondary to the caster's intent in the Potterverse. For example, Ron uses the spell, '*Wingardium Leviosa*" in the girls' bathroom in *Philosopher's/Sorcerer's Stone* to levitate the troll's club. But "*Wingardium Leviosa*" refers to the *feather* they learned to levitate in class. It seems clear that Ron's desperation and clear focus on his intent overrode the incorrect object from his incantation. Similarly, the spell "*mobili*" is used with a number of different objects throughout the books. Hermione Granger uses the verb root in combination with the word for "tree" to hide herself, Ron, and Harry from the teachers in the Three Broomsticks (*PoA*): "*Mobiliarbus*." Later, Sirius uses the same verb root with the word for "body" to drag Snape's unconscious form with them through the tunnel connecting the Shrieking Shack to the Whomping Willow: "*Mobilicorpus*." There are inconsistencies in this pattern, including some contradictions at times, but that is outside the scope of this investigation. In short, Potteric incantations, thus far, use a Latin base that may or may not be modified to suit the situation. We can only hope that if we are ever fortunate enough to meet a witch or wizard who is not from Europe, we will see a different school of incantation theory altogether.

By contrast, pagan "incantations" tend to fall into several categories. First is more of a meditative chant, similar to a mantra, intended merely to focus the will and free the caster from distraction. Much more common, however, is an incantation either of a short phrase that is repeated (popular in movie magic!), or something that is read once, such as an invocation, prayer, or benediction. Few modern pagans use ancient languages for incantations, though many may use archaic forms of speech, sounding more Shakespearean than Caesarian.

Harry Potter and the Stereotypes

One of the criticisms pagans occasionally have for the Harry Potter books is that they perpetuate the stereotypical witch so demonized in history. As many know, modern pagans, particularly Wiccans and other "organized" branches of pagans, continually meet with objections to their faith based on the notion that "witchcraft" is equivalent to "Satanism." This belief, so exemplified by the witch burnings in Europe and New England up into the 1700's, is perhaps the worst prejudice a modern pagan can face. The images, therefore, of witches flying on broomsticks, eyes of newt and wools of bat in potions, and all the other seemingly dark trappings of witchcraft and wizardry found in the Potterverse, seem to feed this misapprehension, rather than clarify it.

Most intriguingly, on reading the books, it becomes clear that Ms. Rowling made this deliberate choice for several reasons. First, it actually separates modern paganism quite definitively from her brand of witches and wizards. They are much more similar to the classic interpretations of witches in fairy tales and books such as Mary Norton's *Bedknob and Broomstick*, Anna Elizabeth Bennett's *Little Witch*, and Mary Stewart's *Thornyhold*, or television shows and movies like "Bewitched," "Hocus Pocus," and more recently, "Buffy," "Charmed," and "Practical Magic." Without becoming demonic, the witch or wizard's penchant for these "Halloween-esque" elements, including skulls, livers, toads, spiders, and the like, immediately creates a context that Rowling can then play off and against, as she develops her own systems and both upholds and breaks our collective assumptions about literary witchcraft.

Furthermore, this choice reveals its brilliance because it also creates an explanation for the presence of a wizarding world in the first place. It gives us a glimpse of how this entire society can have co-existed alongside our Muggle world for all these centuries, and yet we, the "Muggles" of the real world, have not discovered it until now. The books wink at us and explain, "No, you *have* seen evidence of witches and wizards over the years. You've just taken it out of context and misunderstood what you saw." Using the stereotype, building upon it, acknowledges to the audience that, perhaps, writers like Shakespeare really had seen witches making potions, but didn't know what he saw. Perhaps the Medieval citizens of Paris and London really *did* occasionally see figures riding brooms, but then they went and accused the wrong people (or sometimes, the *right* people) of consorting with the Devil, when they were only playing an innocent match of Quidditch. In short, the choice to use stereotype as a foundation for the wizarding image is one that creates an ironic twist both within, and without, the world of the books, and allows Rowling's readers easy access to their suspension of disbelief.

Wizards and Religion

No discussion of Pagan Perspectives on Harry Potter would be complete without examining religion in the Wizarding World. As some of our Christian colleagues point out, to conclude that Harry Potter's witches are wizards are without religion is preposterous. On the other hand, it's extremely unlikely that the majority of witches and wizards in Harry's universe observe the sabbats and esbats[1] of the Wiccan tradition. Rather, it is much more likely that the majority of British witches and wizards would consider themselves at least nominally Christian—specifically, Anglican.

Rev. Francis Bridger, in his book *A Charmed Life*, offers an excellent and highly perceptive view of the secularized religion seen at Hogwarts and elsewhere in the wizarding world. Rather than produce a pale echo here, the panelists heartily recommend that readers investigate his analysis.

Recall, however, that the panelists are all strongly of the belief that magic and religion have no direct relationship in Harry Potter. Specifically, that "magic is never portrayed as a mystical or a religious experience, nor is the performance of magic ever infused with any religious overtones—good or bad." This, we believe, has been shown through our discussion of the elements of magic and how magic is used in the Potterverse. There is, however, an important area of magic we have not discussed: the ritual, or ceremonial, form.

What is ritual? We speak of our "morning rituals" (coffee and a donut on the way to work), or our "bedtime rituals" (brushing and flossing, reading a bedtime story to the kids, etc.), or the "ritual" of preparing meals. A ritual, then, may be defined in its core as a structured, repetitive approach to doing something. But that by itself, is not really a ritual—it could simply be a pattern or a habit. A *ritual* must also include some infusion of purpose or meaning. A ritual carries with it some acknowledgement or invocation of power, usually a power not limited to that of the participants. A ritual is, at its heart, a systematic application of magic.

It is important to understand that ritual magic is present in nearly every religion known to us. The Mass is a ritual, and the doctrine of transubstantiation is, at its core, every bit as much a piece of ritual magic as the rain dance performed by a medicine man. There is a specific order of events that does not deviate greatly from one time to the next. For example, almost every Sunday morning service in any church uses this or a very similar structure: Invocation, Confession and Forgiveness, Hymn of Praise, Lessons, Psalm, Gospel, Sermon, Prayer, Sharing of Peace, Offertory, Communion, Benediction, Dismissal. Calls and responses are by-and-large fixed and deliberately repetitive, so they can be learned quickly. This is because rituals often pool the collective focus of their observers or celebrants, so that the invocation of power is that much more far-reaching or effective. Thus, rituals, unlike magic itself, have to do with the *application* of that magical power to a specific, established purpose.

For pagans, rituals come in all forms. Many pagans compile "grimoires" or "books of shadows" to record the rituals they use on a regular or semi-regular basis. Some pagans copy or modify rituals already created or researched by others in their order, while other pagans make up their rituals on the spur of the moment or based solely on what they feel to apply to the situation at hand. As for workings by pagans in groups (sometimes called covens, sometimes not), these can be as varied as individuals' ceremonies. However, it's important to note that pagans, as a general rule, only invoke their magic for positive purposes. It's also notable that many pagans prefer to work in loose-fitting robes, much like all Rowling's descriptions and drawings of her wizards, while others feel fettered and confined even by that much clothing, and tend to work "sky-clad"—in other words, nude. Whether this is a true return to our natural beginnings, as some pagans assert, or whether it is merely a backlash against the Judeo-Christian penchant for elaborate ecumenical trappings including stoles, albs, and mitres, we will leave up to the reader.

With this information as a backdrop, we turn back to the Potter books. The closest thing to ritual, ceremonial magic we have yet seen is the graveyard ritual in GoF. It is interesting to note that this is also perhaps the darkest form of magic we have seen to date. The only person without clothes is Voldemort, and he obtains his robes immediately upon completion of the ritual restoring him to his body. It is unclear from this one example, however, whether Ms. Rowling means to equate ritual magic with dark magic, or whether her choice to depict ceremonial magic in this way has more to do with sounding arcane and mysterious.

Nevertheless, given that this is the only sort of mysticism we have seen thus far in five out of seven books, it is overwhelmingly suggestive that religious views, or lack thereof, really do not enter into the magical equation for Harry or his cohorts. By the same token, it cannot be assumed that witches and wizards are, or are not, religious. Dumbledore certainly seems to be more of a moralist than anything else, especially considering his views on death (similar to philosophies in other books, like *Lord of the Rings* and the myths and legends of Celtic traditions)[2]. But it would not be surprising to learn, for example, that some of the Death Eaters view their support of Voldemort partly as a religious conviction that they—pureblood wizards—are more worthy of the Kingdom of Heaven than their Muggleborn counterparts. Of course, it would be equally unsurprising to learn that some of them are corrupted by the Dark Arts they practice and thus have decidedly more sinister religious views. On the other hand, perhaps Ms. Rowling is wise to refrain from letting any additional religious components enter her story, and leave her allegories open to interpretation by her readership.

As for the religious leanings of individual characters, there are a number of possibilities. We know, as Bridger points out in his analysis, that Hogwarts observes Christmas and Easter in addition to Halloween. American readers may find the lack of any other holiday celebrations suspicious, but it is not difficult to understand, given that schools in Britain are not subject to the same expectations of diversity as schools in the United States. There is a strong suggestion in the books that there are non-Christian students at Hogwarts: the Patils are most likely Hindi; Lee Jordan, with his dreadlocks, might or might not be of West Indian descent and faith; and in *Order of the Phoenix*, we met Anthony Goldstein, almost certainly an ethnic Jew. Paganism is a relatively young religion, in that it has gained notoriety and structure on a global scale only within the last half-century, and most of its practitioners are technically "converts"—that is, they were raised as something other than pagan and came to pagan beliefs on their own.

Pagan Symbolism? Not . . . .

With that in mind, it's also unlikely that much of the symbolism in the books is consciously pagan or Christian in nature. For example, someone in the panel asked a question about the correspondence of the cardinal directions and the cardinal elements to the four Houses. The four directions are of course North, South, East, and West. The four elements are Earth, Air, Fire, and Water. These are common both in western ideology and in eastern philosophy. Over the ages, they have been equated with alchemical properties, with the humours of the body, with the energies of mind, body, and spirit, and other comparisons.

However, again possibly as a conscious decision, Ms. Rowling does not correspond these classical interpretations directly with the Houses. Much depends on one's interpretation of the symbols, colours, and characteristics of each. For example, Slytherin's color is green and its symbol is the snake. Does it necessarily correspond that Slytherin represents earth? Not exactly, for "earth" more closely typifies a Hufflepuff: their symbol is the badger, their color could be the yellow of sand or dirt, they are "down to earth" in their willingness to work, etc. A lot may depend on whether one's anchor for the comparison is the color, the totem animal, or something else. It is certain that Gryffindors represent fire: red and hot-tempered, impetuous, brave, etc. But consider the following possible correspondences:

Element	Color	Symbol	Direction
Earth	Green	Snake	West
Air	Blue	Eagle	South
Fire	Red	Lion	North
Water	Yellow	Badger?	East

Color	Element	Symbol	Direction
Green	Earth	Snake?	West
Red	Fire	Lion	North
Blue	Water	Eagle?	East
Yellow	Air	Badger?	South

Symbol	Element	Color	Direction
Lion	Fire	Red	North
Eagle	Air	Blue	South
Badger	Earth	Yellow	West
Snake	Water	Green?	East

None are perfect, but each one can shed different light on each of the three Houses other than Gryffindor. Note that again, while Gryffindor is in the North position consistently, at no time is Slytherin, considered Gryffindor's antithesis, in the South. (Look at a Hogwarts watch face to see this phenomenon in action: Gryffindor is always at twelve o'clock; Ravenclaw at three; Slytherin at six; and Hufflepuff at nine. This corresponds most closely to the third table above, where only the relative positions of Ravenclaw and Slytherin are switched.) It gets more complicated depending on whether one uses "traditional" Wiccan definitions of the directions, Celtic definitions, Eastern philosophy, and so on. There are three likely possibilities here:

1. Ms. Rowling was completely unaware of any pagan symbolism to these elements when she created her House associations;
2. Ms. Rowling, being aware of the associations, deliberately blurred the lines so that they do not correspond perfectly using the most popular classical traditions;
3. Ms. Rowling is using a completely different system to define these symbols.

There's also the fourth possibility: they don't mean anything in particular, save what *she* personally associates with each one. The beauty of a pagan tradition is that depending on the pagan, it could mean one or all of these things. Or nothing. There are other "personal" associations that could have all or nothing to do with paganism: for example, the stag has specific connotations that reach much farther back than Christianity, as does the unicorn. The variety and significance of these links is so myriad, depending on the traditions and beliefs of the individual pagan readers, that we cannot do more than scratch the surface here.

In any event, there is certainly much to explore in Harry Potter's world for pagan non-pagan alike. It would not be fair to read the books in the vacuum of one interpretation over another, ignoring, for example, the overtly Christian traditions permeating the books in favour of a more "earth-based" religiosity for wizard-kind. However, it is also tremendously helpful, and enlightening, to examine the books with an open mind, recognizing that the source of many of the symbols, signs, and themes of the books are not limited to the Judeo-Christian outlook.

Authors' Notes: Important safety tip: If you are running a conference, don't try to be a presenter.

Works Cited

Adler, Margot. *Drawing Down the Moon.* New York: Penguin Books, 1979.

Bennett, Anna Elizabeth. *Little Witch.* New York: Harper & Row, 1953.

Bridger, Francis. *A Charmed Life: The Spirituality of Potterworld.* New York: Random House, 2001.

Cunningham, Scott. *Wicca: A Guide for the Solitary Practitioner.* St. Paul, MN: Llewellyn Publications, 1988.

Fraser, James George. *The Golden Bough.* New York: The MacMillan Company, 1951. (Abridged, one-volume edition)

Norton, Mary. *Bedknob and Broomstick.* Orlando, FL: Harcourt, 1957.

Rowling, J.K. *Harry Potter and the Philosopher's Stone.* London: Bloomsbury, 1997.

Rowling, J.K. *Harry Potter and the Chamber of Secrets.* London: Bloomsbury, 1998.

Rowling, J.K. *Harry Potter and the Prisoner of Azkaban.* London: Bloomsbury, 1999.

Rowling, J.K. *Harry Potter and the Goblet of Fire.* London: Bloomsbury, 2000.

Rowling, J.K. *Quidditch through the Ages.* New York: Bt. Bound, 2001.

Rowling, J.K. *Harry Potter and the Order of the Phoenix.* London: Bloomsbury, 2003.

Stewart, Mary. *Thornyhold.* New York: Morrow, 1988.

Tolkien, J.R.R. *The Lord of the Rings.* Boston: Houghton-Mifflin, 1954.

Lee Hillman, aka Gwendolyn Grace, is a pagan who practices as a solitary witch. She does not identify as Wiccan, though she draws from some of their basic traditions. She has an undergraduate degree in Theatre with a minor in English, and a master's degree in Business Management. In addition to being a life-long pagan who grew up with at least two other religions in the house, she is an active author and moderator on FictionAlley and currently serves as President of HP Education Fanon, Inc.

Amy Vezza, aka Ajes Blue, is also a solitary witch and non-Wiccan. She was born on Thanksgiving Day, which wasn't much of one for her mother. Nothing much of note happened in her life until she was nearly twenty-one and almost lost a couple of fingers to an art project. Must not have learned much from that experience, for although she doesn't use circular saws any more, she is inordinately proud of her growing power tool collection. She holds a B.A. in Theatre, and works as a Web designer for a small company in New England. Amy has walked a Pagan path for much of her life.

John Walton is a Pagan from a generic tradition as well. He 20-something New Yorker with a British accent, and he recently obtained an M.A. in International Relations from the University of St Andrews. John is an educator, specialising in dyslexia, hyperlexia, ADD, ADHD and autistic spectrum students, and recently spent the school year teaching English as a second language in China. He was a moderator of HPforGrownups for nearly three years, and has served as Ombudsman (independent adjudicator) for FictionAlley, and writes under the noms de plume John, Crazy Ivan and Wood's Keeper.

The Seven Deadly Sins / Seven Heavenly Virtues: Moral Development in Harry Potter

Peg Kerr

Abstract: This presentation grows out of a series of essays prepared for HPforGrownups (www.hpfgu.org.uk), tracing the 7 Heavenly Virtues and 7 Deadly Sins in Rowling's work. Critics of the Harry Potter series fault Harry for lying and disobeying authority, but in fact, Harry's story is about the acquisition of a moral education, specifically in learning how to handle an alternate technology (i.e, power (magic)) responsibly. Topics touched upon include the role of the Dursleys in the series, Kohlberg's stages of moral development, and the moral ramifications for Harry and other characters of the tragic events of the Halloween night when Harry's parents died.

Like so many other readers, I first encountered J. K. Rowling's *Harry Potter* novels because I read them to my own children. I certainly enjoyed the books from the very beginning, and as a fantasy novelist myself, I took a keen professional interest in Rowling's work. More than that, however, I quickly became intrigued by the objections toward the books raised by conservative Christian critics. Were the books, in fact, moral in nature, or pernicious as many insisted? Would they harm children? (Interestingly, the objections I read focused entirely on the danger the books presented *for children.* It was not clear whether these critics assumed that adults—who read the books too, of course—were incapable of being influenced by fiction and therefore not a matter of concern, or that the sort of adults who read dangerous works like Harry Potter books had already gone so far down the path of wickedness that they were beyond redemption.)

In the course of my reading of the various critical responses to the Harry Potter books, I encountered an essay by Alan Jacobs entitled "Harry Potter's Magic." Jacobs argues that "Rowling's moral compass throughout the three [at the time] novels is sound—indeed, I would say, acute." He suggests:

> "The place to begin is to invoke one of the great achievements of twentieth—century historical scholarship: the eight volumes Lynn Thorndike published between 1929 and 1941 under the collective title *A History of Magic and Experimental Science*. And it is primarily the title that I wish to reflect upon here. In the thinking of most modern people, there should be two histories here: after all, are not

magic and experimental science opposites? Is not magic governed by superstition, ignorance, and wishful thinking, while experimental science is rigorous, self—critical, and methodological? While it may be true that the two paths have diverged to the point that they no longer have any point of contact, for much of their existence—and this is Lynn Thorndike's chief point—they constituted a single path with a single history. For both magic and experimental science are means of controlling and directing our natural environment (and people insofar as they are part of that environment) . . . . It was not obvious in advance that science would succeed and magic fail: in fact, several centuries of dedicated scientific experiment would have to pass before it was clear to anyone that the 'scientific' physician could do more to cure illness than the old woman of the village with her herbs and potions and muttered charms . . . .

This history provides a key to understanding the role of magic in Joanne Rowling's books, for she begins by positing a counterfactual history, a history in which magic was not a false and incompetent discipline, but rather a means of controlling the physical world at least as potent as experimental science. In Harry Potter's world, scientists think of magic in precisely the same way they do in our world, but they are wrong. The counterfactual "secondary world" that Rowling creates is one in which magic simply works, and works as reliably, in the hands of a trained wizard, as the technology that makes airplanes fly and refrigerators chill the air—those products of applied science being, by the way, sufficiently inscrutable to the people who use them that they might as well be the products of wizardry. As Arthur C. Clarke once wrote, 'Any smoothly functioning technology gives the appearance of magic.'

The fundamental moral framework of the Harry Potter books, then, is a familiar one to all of us: it is the problem of technology . . . . Hogwarts School of Witchcraft and Wizardry is in the business of teaching people how to harness and employ certain powers—that they are powers unrecognized by science is really beside the point—but cannot insure that people will use those powers wisely, responsibly, and for the common good . . . . The educational quandary for Albus Dumbledore, then—though it is never described so overtly—is how to train students not just in the "technology" of magic but also in the moral discernment necessary to avoid the continual reproduction of the few great Dark Lords like Voldemort and their multitudinous followers."[1]

This paper traces the Seven Heavenly Virtues (faith, hope, charity, fortitude, justice, temperance, and prudence) and Seven Deadly Sins (pride, envy, gluttony, lust, anger, greed, and sloth) thematically through Rowling's Harry Potter books, in order to examine a wide array of moral decisions that Harry and his friends must make in order to use their powers ethically.[2]

Rowling uses three structural paths or dimensions to map Harry Potter's personal journey: First, *the past is gradually uncovered.* In many ways, the Harry Potter books are a mystery series. With each book, Rowling reveals more and more about Harry's origins, gradually revealing events which occurred in his parents' generation. The purpose here is to uncover Harry's roots, to answer *Who am I? What led to me being the person I am?* Secondly, *events unfold in the present.* Each book in the Harry Potter series follows a predictable series of happenings in one school year, beginning with Harry's misery at the Dursleys, the arrival at Hogwarts, a precipitating event in the fall, usually taking place around Halloween (*Order of the Phoenix*, interestingly, was an exception to this pattern), accrual of more information at Christmas, a climactic event in June, involving the revelation of a secret of the Defense Against the Dark Arts teacher, the defeat of Voldemort and/or his followers, and the departure from Hogwarts. Questions addressed along this story arc are *What am I learning? What choices am I making?* Thirdly, *events move forward into the future.* With each subsequent book, Harry repeats events that he has experienced before, but *he* is different, because he is growing older and learning from his experiences. The key question under consideration is *Who am I becoming?* Together, these three structural dimensions make each book, and the series as a whole, a journey of *identity.* All of Harry's decisions are a record of his moral choices, and it is choices, as Dumbledore tells Harry in *The Chamber of Secrets* that make us what we are, far more than our abilities. (*CoS*, p. 333)[3]

But how, after all, does a person learn to make moral choices? What is the thinking process involved? And how can an educator like Dumbledore help a child to understand how to make the *right choices*, even if there is no teacher around to offer guidance? It is helpful to look at the work of Lawrence Kohlberg, a developmental psychologist (building initially upon the work of Jean Piaget) who has proposed a stage theory of how people develop moral reasoning:

Kohlberg's Stages of Moral Development[4]

"I. Preconventional Level

> At this level, the child is responsive to cultural rules and labels of good and bad, right or wrong, but he interprets the labels in terms of either the physical or hedonistic consequences of action (punishment, reward, exchange of favors) or the physical power of those who enunciate the rules and labels . . . . [Note: Kohlberg INSERTed an earlier 'Stage 0'

initially, which was eventually removed from later versions of his discussions of the stages of moral reasoning]

Stage 1: The punishment and obedience orientation. The physical consequences of action determine its goodness or badness regardless of the human meaning or value of these consequences. Avoidance of punishment and unquestioning deference to power are values in their own right, not in terms of respect for an underlying moral order supported by punishment and authority (the latter is stage 4).

Stage 2: The instrumental relativist orientation. Right action consists of what instrumentally satisfies one's own needs and occasionally the needs of others. Human relations are viewed in terms such as those of the market place. Elements of fairness, reciprocity, and equal sharing are present, but they are always interpreted in a physical, pragmatic way. Reciprocity is a matter of 'you scratch my back and I'll scratch yours,' not loyalty, gratitude, or justice.

II. Conventional Level

At this level, the individual perceives the maintenance of the expectations of his family, group, or nation as valuable in its own right, regardless of immediate and obvious consequences. The attitude is not only one of conformity to personal expectations and social order, but of loyalty to it, of actively maintaining, supporting, and justifying the order and identifying with the persons or group involved in it. The level consists of the following two stages:

Stage 3: The interpersonal concordance or 'good boy-nice girl' orientation. Good behavior is what pleases or helps others and is approved by them. There is much conformity to stereotypical images of what is majority or 'natural' behavior. Behavior is frequently judged by intention—'he means well' becomes important for the first time. One earns approval by being 'nice.'

Stage 4: The 'law and order' orientation. The individual is oriented toward authority, fixed rules, and the maintenance of the social order. Right behavior consists in doing one's duty, showing respect for authority, and maintaining the given social order for its own sake.

III. Post-Conventional, Autonomous, or Principled Level.

The individual makes a clear effort to define moral values and principles that have validity and application apart from the authority of the groups of persons holding them and apart from the individual's own identification with the group. The level has the two following stages:

Stage 5: The social-contract legalistic orientation (generally with utilitarian overtones). Right action tends to be defined in terms of general individual rights and standards that have been critically examined and agreed upon by the whole society. There is a clear awareness of the relativism of personal values and opinions and a corresponding emphasis upon procedural rules for reaching consensus. Aside from what is constitutionally and democratically agreed upon, right action is a matter of personal values and opinions. The result is an emphasis upon the 'legal point of view,' but with an additional emphasis upon the possibility of changing the law in terms of rational considerations of social utility (rather than freezing it in terms of stage 4 'law and order'). Outside the legal realm, free agreement, and contract, is the binding element of obligation . . . .

Stage 6: The universal ethical-principle orientation. Right is defined by the decision of conscience in accord with self-chosen ethical principles that appeal to logical comprehensiveness, universality, and consistency. These principles are abstract and ethical (the Golden Rule, the categorical imperative); they are not concrete moral rules like the Ten Commandments. At heart, these are universal principles of justice, of the reciprocity and equality of the human rights, and of respect for the dignity of human beings as individual persons."

Critics who object that the Harry Potter books are immoral because Harry does not follow the rules (a point that even Dumbledore admits, *CoS* p. 333) are, by Kohlberg's reasoning, missing the important point. Rowling is concerned with more than the "rightness" of following the rules. This was addressed in the first book, where Harry declares that he must go through the trap door in the third floor corridor to stop (as he believes) Snape. When Hermione objects that they might get expelled (exhibiting fear of punishment, which is Level I thinking), Harry replies:

"SO WHAT? Don't you understand? If Snape gets hold of that Stone, Voldemort's coming back! Haven't you heard what it was like when he was trying to take over? . . . If I get caught before I can get to the Stone, well, I'll have to go back to the

Dursleys and wait for Voldemort to find me there, it's only dying a bit later than I would have, because I'm not going over to the Dark Side! I'm going through that trapdoor tonight and nothing you two say is going to stop me! Voldemort killed my parents, remember?" (SS, p. 270)

This examination of the necessity of making a distinction between simply following the rules versus doing what is right is explored most extensively with Rowling's masterful characterization of Dolores Umbridge in *Order of the Phoenix*. As Umbridge slowly extends her influence over Hogwarts, she creates more and more strictures in her attempts to exert control and force students to ignore the danger posed by Voldemort, but Harry is neither deceived as to her motives nor intimidated into believing that obeying her is the correct thing to do. When she catches him disobeying her, he bears her punishments with stoicism, but punishment does not undercut his determination to oppose her, because he knows what is really at stake: keeping in mind at all times the truth that Voldemort is back and is intent on crushing all resistence. He tutors other students to counter Dark Magic, so they can defend themselves, if need be, against the very real threat that Umbridge refuses to acknowledge. Indeed, Umbridge is probably Rowling's best answer to her critics to the objection that Harry is immoral because he disobeys rules. The Defense Against the Dark Arts teacher serves as a reminder that not all rules *should* be obeyed, and indeed in a totalitarian society (like Hogwarts under the sway of Dolores Umbridge, High Inquisitor), the most moral choice to make is to refuse to go along with the path of least resistance.

The Dursleys

In order to come to a fuller understanding of *how* Harry makes moral choices through Rowling's books, the reader must consider the role the Dursleys play throughout the series. A.S. Byatt argued in a rather dismissive *New York Times* essay that the Harry Potter books are a latency-period fantasy, what Freud would term a "family romance," where a child who is dissatisfied with his ordinary life and family dreams that he is special. Harry is the orphaned child of wizards who were murdered trying to save his life. The horrible Dursleys, then, Byatt suggests, represent his real "real" family.[5] But in fact, the Dursleys' function in the Harry Potter series is arguably more complex. They are an embodiment of the results of making incorrect moral choices, and as such they serve as a warning example to Harry of each of the Seven Deadly Sins (and conversely, what it is like to live without the Seven Heavenly Virtues). Indeed, the Dursleys may be said to signify moral *antimatter*. As terrible as Harry's experience with the Dursleys was, it did have one very real advantage: it seemed to inoculate him against some of the worst temptations that might be presented to him as he struggles to master the ethical use of power. If Voldemort were to say to Harry, "Want to indulge your appetites Harry? Want money? Power? All the coke you can stuff up your nose?" it is easy to imagine

Harry wincing and replying, "No thanks. I saw what that sort of thing did for my cousin. Yuck."

An excellent example of this effect of Harry's miserable upbringing with the Dursleys occurs in the chapter "Snape's Worst Memory" in *Order of the Phoenix*. When he sees for himself in the Pensieve how his father had treated Snape, Harry finds he must question all he has believed up until now about his father, his mother and Snape. Snape is one of his worst enemies, but despite the fact that Harry wants to side with his father, he cannot. Instead, he empathizes with Snape, because "he knew how it felt to be humiliated in the middle of a circle of onlookers, knew exactly how Snape felt as his father taunted him . . . ." (*OotP*, p. 650). His cousin Dudley had taught him that.

The Seven Heavenly Virtues

I. Faith

We will begin the look at the various virtues and vices by examining faith, because faith is the foundation of everything, and is essential to Harry's journey toward becoming a wizard. The concept of *faith* is linked to concepts such as trust, fidelity, loyalty and conviction. What does Harry learn about faith in these books? The fact is, Harry learned nothing about faith from the Dursleys—except, perhaps, in a negative fashion, because he was forced to live without it. It was certainly a miserable existence. Harry has no trust in the Dursleys. He does not confide in them; in fact, all efforts on his attempts to ask questions, to create connections upon which to build trust, are firmly squelched. (For example, the Dursleys refuse to answer his questions about his scar; in fact, they lie about it.) Harry has several hints about his true nature (the incidents where he unexpectedly escapes from Dudley, the haircut that grows back too quickly, the strange people who seem to be keeping an eye on him), but the Dursleys violently reject any hint of whatever-it-is that Harry is sensing (and that something, of course, is magic, and Harry's true history and inner nature).

Then, the letters from Hogwarts appear, and the Dursleys become agitated, especially Vernon, as the mystery deepens. Vernon's instinct is to flee from the truth, forcing Harry to accompany him, but Hagrid catches up with them, with an amazing story to tell. Who should Harry believe? Cold hard facts, the bread and butter of the Dursleys' world? Or something more rich and strange? Vernon argues against Harry's specialness, even as he argues against magic—against faith—but his arguments fail against Hagrid's magical signs (the spell on Dudley, the magical progress of the boat across the lake, etc.) Harry allows himself to believe the magical story more and more as he accompanies Hagrid to London to visit Gringotts and buy his supplies. At this point in the story, however, he is simply a passive follower, merely absorbing information.

The process of growing in faith is often metaphorically described as the undertaking of a journey. The turning point for Harry in terms of faith takes place at the beginning

THE NIMBUS-2003 PROGRAMMING TEAM

of his journey to Hogwarts. The Dursleys take Harry to King's Cross Station, moving him through the mundane, Muggle world that they know. But because they are both faithless and lack faith, they abandon him. They literally think—and tell him—that he is going nowhere.

Now is the point that faith is needed. Harry must be proactive, not just reactive, in order to begin his journey. In order to find out what to do, he turns to a newly introduced character, Mrs. Weasley, to solve his problem, and the encounter is thematically extremely important:

> "'Excuse me,' Harry said to the plump woman.
>
> 'Hello, dear,' she said. 'First time at Hogwarts? Ron's new, too.'
>
> She pointed to the last and youngest of her sons. He was tall, thin, and gangling, with freckles, big hands and feet, and a long nose.
>
> 'Yes,' said Harry. 'The thing is—the thing is, I don't know how to—'
>
> 'How to get onto the platform?' she said kindly, and Harry nodded.
>
> 'Not to worry,' she said, 'All you have to do is walk straight at the barrier between platforms nine and ten. Don't stop and don't be scared you'll crash into it, that's very important. Best do it at a bit of a run if you're nervous. Go on, go now before Ron.'" (SS, p. 93)

The fact that Harry perceives Mrs. Weasley first as a mother in this scene is certainly significant. He lost his own mother at a tender age, a very important blow to his moral development because an infant learns the concept of "trust," the first cornerstone of faith, in the course of interacting with his or her own mother. Over the course of the series Mrs. Weasley will become Harry's surrogate mother, and so it is entirely appropriate that she is the one to give him the instruction that literally starts him on his faith journey.

The Dursleys, of course, would think this advice mad, but then, the Dursleys have no faith. Harry has seen magical signs, first with Hagrid and now watching the Weasleys disappear, one by one, but now he is required to act, to face that wall, even though it makes no rational sense. He trusts, follows Mrs. Weasley's advice—and steps through the wall into the realm of things unseen, to find the Hogwarts Express, waiting to take him into his new life.

Slowly, over the course of the series, Harry builds upon this new understanding, that he can trust other people. He is more wary of adults, which is understandable, given his history with his aunt and uncle. Even when Dumbledore invites him to tell what is on his mind, Harry prefers to keep things to himself. Yet, although he keeps his distance at first, Harry is coming to trust Dumbledore more and more.

He starts to understand loyalty, both in the interaction between the four houses, but even more significantly in his growing friendship with Ron and Hermione. Harry probably experienced for the first time the sensation of standing up for somebody other than himself when he stuck up for Ron to Draco during the train ride in the first book.

And, with trust and loyalty, he begins to define his inner convictions. He rejects Draco's overture of friendship, grounded as it is in an implicit requirement to reject his budding friendship with Ron.

The seminal story arc dealing with faith in the series is the story of the great betrayal of James and Lily Potter by Peter Pettigrew, an act which reverberates still, years later. (Note that the protective spell which the Potters were using was called the Fidelius spell.) As long as Sirius and Peter were faithful, the Potters would be safe. This is the painful thing about faith: sometimes faith is not rewarded as we expect it to be. Peter betrayed James and Lily, and the repercussions—for Harry, for Sirius, for the Muggles who died, for Remus, who lost three of his best friends all in one horror-filled night—were terrible.

In the scene in the Shrieking Shack in *Prisoner of Azkaban*, Harry (and Ron and Hermione) see Remus and Sirius struggle with a profound question, specifically, how do you pick yourself up and go on, rebuilding your faith when trust has been cruelly betrayed? Or even when you yourself have violated a trust? Both Sirius and Remus suffered greatly because of Peter's breach of faith. They each mourn James and Lily, whom they had loved. As a result of Peter's actions, Sirius lost his freedom, and Remus lost his friendship with Sirius. They each probably suffered knowing that they were not in a position to help Harry now that his parents were gone, Sirius because he was wrongfully imprisoned, and Remus because he was a werewolf. Sirius struggled with guilt, thinking he should have known better than to trust Peter—if only he had stuck to the original plan! Remus wrestles with the memory that he had betrayed Dumbledore's trust by running loose at Hogwarts when he had transformed while a student at Hogwarts, a memory which prevents him from telling the truth about how Sirius is getting into Hogwarts again.

Once Remus and Sirius finally face each other—and Peter—in the Shack, they each must decide whether to trust again, to have faith again. Remus does, stepping forward to embrace Sirius like a brother, reclaiming their old relationship of trust. And then, together with Harry, he convinces Sirius to believe, to trust, that he, too, can have a true, faith-based life again—not a orgy of rage, despair and revenge, ending with his murdering Peter, but a real one, rooted in his rightful place in the magical world, where he can relinquish Peter to society's justice, and concentrate instead on reclaiming his role as godfather, providing a home for his spiritual son, Harry.

What Sirius and Remus are doing in this scene is acting out the great drama which has happened again and again throughout the history of Voldemort's rise.

"You don't know who [Voldemort's] supporters are [Sirius tells Harry, Ron and Hermione, trying to help them understand], you don't know who's working for him and who isn't; you know he can control people so that they do terrible things without being able to stop themselves. You're scared for yourself, and your family, and your friends. Every week, news comes of more deaths, more disappearances, more torturing . . . the Ministry of Magic's in disarray, they don't know what to do, they're trying to keep everything hidden from the Muggles, but meanwhile, Muggles are dying, too. Terror everywhere . . . panic . . . confusion . . . that's how it used to be." (*GoF* pp. 526-527).

Indeed—how can faith survive in times like these?

And conversely, how can one survive without it?

All this foreshadows the events of the fourth and fifth books. In the *Goblet of Fire*, like his parents, Harry is betrayed to the enemy by someone he has trusted. Something similar happened with Quirrell in the first book, but the wound goes deeper this time—Harry has blood forcibly removed and knows that it has been used to strengthen his worst enemy; he experiences the Crucio curse; and he suffers the horror and the guilt of watching Cedric's murder. In *Order of the Phoenix*, Voldemort is back and on the rise, and Sirius's description of what it was like in the bad old days seems to be coming true all over again. The Sorting Hat has warned that the Hogwarts houses must all stand together, but Hogwarts under Dolores Umbridge is no longer a haven, and Harry struggles with a growing conviction that Dumbledore has abandoned him. The guilt and shock and remorse Harry felt over Cedric's murder are small compared to the agony of mind he experiences when he loses Sirius. Harry is now in the position that Sirius was in during *Prisoner of Azkaban*. Just as Sirius blamed himself for James and Lily's death, Harry blames himself for what happened to Sirius. And Dumbledore blames himself too, because he failed to trust Harry with the truth about himself, and distanced himself from Harry's struggles, thus giving Voldemort an opening to exploit that in turn led to Sirius's death. Just as Sirius and Remus had to go on after that Halloween night years ago, Harry and Dumbledore will have to learn how to forgive themselves and go on, too.

II. Hope

Faith, it is said, is the essence of things hoped for, the evidence of things unseen. So what, in turn, is hope? And what does it have to do with Harry? What does Harry need to learn about hope on his moral journey?

Hope clusters with the concepts of desire, belief, reliance, expectation.

At the beginning of the first book, we find a paradox: Harry, himself, personifies hope to the wizarding world. He is the Boy Who Lived. Because of him, Voldemort has fled, and wizards everywhere, astounded by this turn of events, arouse themselves from their long nightmare and look around, saying, Is it possible? Could it be? Do you think we could have a normal life again? Can we actually look forward to the future, instead of dreading it?

And yet, simultaneously, Harry must withdraw from the world he has rescued and go into exile to live with the Dursleys. We hear at first from Dumbledore that Harry will be living there because the Dursleys are his only living relatives. He also says it would be best that Harry grow up without being shadowed by his fame. Eventually over the course of the series the reader learns that Dumbledore had another reason for the decision to place Harry with the Dursleys, and particularly his aunt. Because she is a blood relative to his mother, who died for him, his aunt can offer Harry a special kind of protection from Voldemort, despite being only a Muggle. In a way, Harry, the Boy Who Lived, plays the same role as Hope in the Greek myth. He must be sequestered, shut away in a box by Pandora/Dumbledore, to protect him from the evil entities loose in the world.

So Harry stays with the Dursleys. And therein lies the paradox: while Harry is the embodiment of hope for the wizard world, he has absolutely no hope for himself. A trip to the zoo? Birthday presents? A bright future? Harry has been taught by bitter experience not to expect anything pleasant, or to even to hope that things might improve. The language Rowling uses paints him as that archetypal figure without hope, the prisoner. He sleeps in a locked cupboard, where spiders crawl over him; he dresses in ill-fitted clothes (Dudley's cast offs); he is expected to swallow insults without protest; he sometimes goes without meals. This picture of Harry-as-prisoner while with the Dursleys is further fleshed out in later books: during subsequent summers with the Dursleys, it is clear that Harry is supposed to work while Dudley is idle (and doubtless without remuneration); he is locked into his room and has food shoved through a slot; his windows are barred; he is denied access to his books and writing implements.

The day that the first letter from Hogwarts drops through the front door mail slot, however, everything changes. Uncle Vernon's reaction is to tell Harry to move out from the cupboard beneath the stairs up to the second bedroom. The letter from Hogwarts completes the circle, bringing the truth (and thus hope) to Harry, about the hope Harry had brought the entire wizarding world. And as a result, Harry starts to understand that he is not meant to be merely a prisoner, a drudge for the Dursleys and Dudley's punching bag. As the Dursleys sense that Harry is slipping out of their grasp, growing beyond the range of their mundane brutality, they try increasingly to clamp down on him.

But hope, once it has taken root, cannot be denied. The letters will keep coming, and Hagrid, in the end, cannot be prevented from telling the truth. This struggle between repression and rescue continues in subsequent summers: the Dursleys bar Harry's windows; the Weasleys arrive in their flying car to rescue him. The Dursleys threaten Harry, and Harry blows up Aunt Marge, and counters threats with the specter of his fearsome godfather, Sirius. Once the prisoner has hope, he can no longer be cowed into unthinking submission, and eventually, he will be free. (It is instructive to compare Harry's escape from the Dursleys after blowing up Aunt Marge in *Prisoner of Azkaban* with the experience of Sirius, wanted criminal on the run from the Ministry of Magic. The parallel between them is quite deliberate, and yet another hint early in the book that although he has been a prisoner, Sirius, like Harry, is innocent.)

In the same way that Harry is absorbing these new, exciting ideas about the possibility of being able to learn a special kind of power, in a world where he truly belongs, Harry is also learning to place his hope in other people—to believe in them, in other words; to rely on them. Reliance, perhaps, overlaps with faith, or trust; the distinction between these terms is rather slippery. At any rate, Harry is starting to realize that he is not all alone. There are other people besides himself to whom he can turn if he is in need of help or guidance.

The first, of course, are Ron and Hermione. Both of these friendships with Harry were forged with incidents in which the three discovered they could count on each other. Ron and Harry became friends on the train, after Harry refused the opportunity to snub Ron to order to curry favor with Draco. And Harry and Ron became friends with Hermione after the incident with the troll the first Halloween. As Rowling puts it in one of her delightfully wry observations, "There are some things you can't share without ending up liking each other, and knocking out a twelve-foot mountain troll is one of them." (*SS* p. 179)

More warily, Harry starts, quite tentatively, to allow himself to rely upon adults (and we know, after his experiences with the Dursleys, that the idea of trusting and relying on an adult is a very novel sensation for Harry). He takes his time about getting used to the idea. When invited by Dumbledore to share his burdens or concerns, Harry often will refuse, preferring to keep his worries to himself. Again, as he starts to forge a relationship with his godfather, Sirius, Harry is ambivalent. He decides to write to Sirius at the beginning of *Goblet of Fire*, hoping that Sirius might provide an answer about the pain from his scar—but conversely, he scolds himself for endangering Sirius when Sirius reacts to Harry's news by replying that he will fly north immediately.

And yet, almost despite himself, Harry finds that he is growing in his trust and reliance upon other people. In considering his relationship with one of the most important, Dumbledore, we should note Rowling's use of an important symbol of hope: Dumbledore's pet phoenix, Fawkes.

As a symbol for hope, a phoenix is quite appropriate. It dies, but all hope is not lost, for new life springs from the ashes. The first time Harry encountered Fawkes, he was waiting in Dumbledore's office fearing expulsion, or worse: he was found beside a petrified fellow student, Justin Finch Fletchley, and as Harry is a Parselmouth, he is suspected of attacking Justin. As Harry awaits the Headmaster, Fawkes bursts into flames (to Harry's horror). But just as a new reborn Fawkes emerges, Harry will emerge from Dumbledore's office, his academic career not cut short after all.

When Tom Riddle's ghost jeers in the Chamber of Secrets that Dumbledore has been driven from the castle by the mere memory of him (Riddle), Harry counters with a statement that shows how firmly he has placed his hope in Dumbledore:

> "'He's not as gone as you might think,' Harry retorted. He was speaking at random, wanting to scare Riddle, wishing rather than believing it to be true." (*CoS*, p. 315)

And in immediate response to this statement of faith and hope, Fawkes appears, singing his beautiful song, bringing the tool (the Sorting Hat) that will defeat Tom Riddle's ghost, in defiance of "common sense" that all hope is lost.

Another example takes place in *Goblet of Fire*. In the graveyard, crouching behind the gravestone as Voldemort approaches, Harry decides to die standing, defending himself, even though "there was no hope, no help to be had." (*GoF*, p. 662) And yet, when the wizards duel with their wands, the priori incantatem spell is triggered—and suddenly there is hope after all. Harry hears, significantly, phoenix song. "It was the sound of hope to Harry . . . the most beautiful and welcome thing he had ever heard in his life." (*GoF*, p. 664) The ghosts reappear and whisper words support to Harry; his parents' spirits tell him that they will try to help him—and he escapes to fight another day. And it is Fawkes' magical healing tears, falling later in Dumbledore's office, which heal him from the wounds he has suffered.

Goblet of Fire ends somberly, still resonating with the painful memories of what happened when Harry and Cedric seized the cup together in the maze. But Harry is not the same person that he was when he was a child of ten, in thrall to the Dursleys with no hope of rescue. Now, as Dumbledore says, he has shouldered a grown wizard's burden and found himself equal to it. He would not have been able to do what he has done up until now but for the help he has received, that he has come to expect, in his moral journey. He knows he is not alone now. Friends and allies stand shoulder to shoulder with him, all gathered together under Dumbledore's leadership. That is the hope that will sustain him as he steels himself to face the ordeals ahead, in the gathering darkness of Voldemort's new arising.

And yet, as somber as the ending of *Goblet of Fire* is, the ending of *Order of the Phoenix* seems much worse, because Harry's hope that Dumbledore and the Order would protect him proves illusory. The struggle between Harry-as-prisoner and his oppressors, startlingly, now includes his time at Hogwarts, because of Dolores Umbridge. Now Harry is boxed in even where he had previously felt safe and protected, because of a succession of the High Inquisitor's educational decrees. He is banned from Quidditch, and his Firebolt is confiscated and chained up. He must bear the cruel punishment of Umbridge's cutting quill, and Umbridge tries to prevent him from learning the Defense Against the Dark Arts magic he needs to defend himself. The blow delivered at the climax of this book, the loss of Sirius, is an even greater personal shock to bear. The support on which he has come to rely in previous books has failed him; Dumbledore is not infallible. Worst of all is Dumbledore's explanation of the prophecy, which seems to extinguish all hope that he can be anything other than either a murderer or a victim. Harry now seems to be back in the position he was in when crouched behind the tombstone in the graveyard in *Goblet of Fire.* Now when all hope seems lost and he feels entirely alone, how then should he act? How will he conduct himself? The books to come will test him as never before.

III. Charity

The third of the Seven Heavenly Virtues is "charity." Generosity, helpfulness, benevolence, mercy are related to this concept of charity/love. Note that they all have the common component of selflessness.

The first three of the Seven Heavenly Virtues are derived from Christian writings, and St. Paul described charity as the most important one ("so faith, hope and love abide, these three; but the greatest of these is love.") (1 Corinthians 13:13) Charity in this discussion refers to "love," in the sense of the Greek word "Agape." Agape is "pure" love, as between God and man, or selfless love between man and his fellow man (meaning both male and female here when referring to "man" here). Agape love is distinguished from Philos, love between friends, and Eros, erotic love. Charity, besides being the greatest of the virtues, it is perhaps the hardest, the most difficult to achieve, as it is the most antithetical to natural human instinct. As such, achieving the virtue of Charity is a particular challenge to Harry in his moral development.

Again, consider the Dursleys.

Now, the Dursleys are not very reflective people. If asked Vernon and Petunia would probably say that they love Dudley very much. And they would probably characterize themselves as generous—after all, have they not taken Harry in and given him a home?

Neither of these statements hold up very well. The fact is, the Dursleys do not have a scrap of Agape love/charity. Their cruelties against Harry have already been enumerated. Toward Dudley, on the other hand, Vernon and Petunia would say and probably even believe that they feel love, but one must doubt a kind of "love" that manifests itself as blind indulgence that has turned their son into a selfish, sadistic, greedy monster.

The sad truth is that the only experience Harry had with love before he came to Hogwarts was the fifteen months he spent with his parents. And he lost that love, ironically, because they gave their lives to save him. A paradoxical mystery: their love (especially Lily's) led to the sacrifice which saved Harry's life, yet left him bereft of that one thing that would have let him enjoy the life they saved for him: their love. And, as it was self-sacrificing, it can be characterized as charity, Agape love.

And so for the majority of his life, Harry has been without love. A psychologist would say that without it, Harry might be in danger of having great difficulty in building the moral framework he needs to live ethically with others. If you are bonded to no one, why should you care about other people? 'Why not hurt them, use them, discard them—who cares?' a neglected abandoned child might decide, reasoning from his/her innate human selfishness.

That is what fundamentally causes psychopaths.

That is what, in fact, probably caused Voldemort.

Yet, whatever James and Lily gave him, it seems to have been enough to start him down the right road, despite what he suffered with the Dursleys.

He learns to care about Ron and Hermione. And make no mistake, his caring for both of them is tested—for Hermione in *Prisoner of Azkaban* (over the incident with Scabbers and Crookshanks) and for Ron over the Goblet of Fire. Both tests of friendship are tests of Harry's charity, and he nearly gets both wrong. "I gotta tell yeh," Hagrid says, reproving Harry and Ron for the quarrel with Hermione, "I thought you two'd value yer friend more'n broomsticks or rats." (*PoA*, p. 274) Again, with Ron in *Goblet of Fire*, Harry behaves badly—for example, the scene in the common room, where Harry loses his temper and throws the button at Ron. But all comes out in the end—Harry chooses to set those friendships aright, partly because events clarify the things that led to misunderstandings, but partly because he misses the caring and friendship he had with both Ron and Hermione when he was on the outs with them. And that is good; it shows Harry's development. He has gone from someone who lived without either giving or receiving charity, who reacted as coldly toward the Dursleys as they acted toward him, to someone who realizes that something is missing when relationships go awry. He is coming to genuinely care for other people, and not just Ron, Hermione and Hagrid.

Harry sees in *Prisoner of Azkaban* the playing out of the drama from the previous generation's struggle with Voldemort, which foreshadows what he himself will go through, in *Goblet of Fire* and even more clearly in *Order of the Phoenix*. Specifically, he witnesses Sirius's and Remus's confrontation of Peter Pettigrew, which brings this theme of charity right to the foreground:

> "'He [Voldemort] was taking over everywhere!' gasped Pettigrew. 'Wh—what was there to be gained by refusing him?'
>
> 'What was there to be gained by fighting the most evil wizard who has ever existed?' said Black, with a terrible fury in his face. 'Only innocent lives, Peter!'
>
> 'You don't understand!' whined Pettigrew. 'He would have killed me, Sirius!'
>
> 'THEN YOU SHOULD HAVE DIED!' roared Black. 'DIED RATHER THAN BETRAY YOUR FRIENDS, AS WE WOULD HAVE DONE FOR YOU!'

*   *   *

> 'NO!' Harry yelled. He ran forward, placing himself in front of
> Pettigrew, facing the wands. 'You can't kill him,' he said breathlessly.
> 'You can't . . . We'll take him up to the castle. We'll hand him over to
> dementors. He can go to Azkaban . . . but don't kill him.'"

Note Peter's question: "What was there to be gained by resisting him [Voldemort]?"
That is pure selfishness speaking. Peter is stuck at the very first stage of Kohlberg's
stages of moral development, the need to avoid punishment. That is pure humanness
speaking, the natural urge for self-preservation. Sirius's answer is profound: the only
thing to be gained when you lose yourself is the knowledge that your gain is for others,
the ones that you love. Which you can care about only because you love. Because Peter
did not truly love, he did not truly understand the enormity of his crime.

But this points up a very hard thing about charity—if you do it right, you may get
nothing for it (if you look at it from the human selfish point of view). Just as Lily gave
up her life for her son, the true virtue of charity may mean giving up everything for the
one you love. The comfort you have is knowing that the ones you love would be willing
to do the same for you. It is like faith, in that having faith may not mean that you get
what you want. Having charity may gain you nothing but death at the end of Voldemort's
wand . . . and the knowledge that the lives you have saved have gained a few more
seconds, which they will hopefully use to fight on.

Sirius and Remus, although they understand the nature of self-sacrificing love, do
not embody charity perfectly. They would have died for Peter—but since Peter refused
the deal, as far as Sirius and Remus are concerned, the deal is off. "You should have
realized," Lupin said quietly, "that if Voldemort didn't kill you, we would." (*PoA*, p. 375)
This is a higher level of morality than Peter showed—which was pure selfishness and
wish to avoid punishment—but it is not yet pure charity, as it is still based somewhat on
a tit for tat reasoning, what Kohlberg called instrumental relativist orientation (you
scratch my back and I'll scratch yours).

But Harry intervenes and demonstrates something related to charity: he shows
mercy, something that Peter does not deserve. Harry is profoundly insightful at this
moment, because when Peter admits as much, Harry tells Peter that he is not doing it as
much for him but for Sirius and Remus: "I don't reckon my dad would have wanted
them [Sirius and Remus] to become killers—just for you." (*PoA* p. 376)

Rowling raises the stakes in subsequent books so that Harry has to face moral decisions
about charity that come closer and closer to resembling his mother and Peter Pettigrew's
dilemma. He is forced to decide, am I willing to stick my neck out for someone I care
about? In a way he has faced this before to a lesser degree: he did it for Ginny in *Chamber
of Secrets*, and for Ron during the Second Task in *Goblet of Fire*. He took a risk for Ginny,
but when he went down into that tunnel, he still hoped that he would come out alive.

Similarly, when he went down for Ron, he knew that there was a theoretical risk of death, but he really did not think that he would die there at the bottom of the lake (although he was afraid that Ron, Hermione, Cho and Gabrielle might).

In the past books, when Harry has been truly cornered and really looking death in the eye, he has been in situations where he is simply trying to save himself. He was alone at the climax of the first and fourth books, and he was not facing Voldemort directly in the third. In the second, he thought that Ginny might already be dead. But in *Order of the Phoenix*, he must face squarely whether he would willingly risk himself, perhaps even sacrifice himself for someone else: Sirius. Rowling makes the decision even more difficult by having others join Harry, so he is not only risking himself, he is responsible for the safety of his friends as well.

It is not quite clear what exactly has brought Harry to this point in his moral development. Bonds with friends, the bitter experience of the Dursleys to teach him what it was like to live without charity, or perhaps the lingering effects of his mother's sacrifice . . . or something else, who knows? Whatever it is, Harry shows here that he understand charity, and although he wavers and wobbles sometimes, he has chosen his side. Unlike Voldemort, who acts selfishly, Harry acts with a selfless concern for others (i.e., in *Goblet of Fire* helping Cedric with the first task, trying to rescue other hostages with the second task, sharing the cup with Cedric on the third task—and then bringing his body back, and in *Order of the Phoenix*, attempting to rescue Sirius). And even though in *Order of the Phoenix* Voldemort uses Harry's "saving people thing" to trick him, setting off a chain of occurrences that leads to Sirius's death, it is that selflessness that finally drives Voldemort out of Harry's body in the battle at the Ministry. In the conversation with Harry afterwards, Dumbledore speaks of a power Harry has that the Dark Lord does not know.

> "But I don't!" said Harry in a strangled voice. 'I haven't any powers he hasn't got, I couldn't fight the way he did tonight. I can't possess people-or kill them—'

> 'There is a room in the Department of Mysteries,' interrupted Dumbledore, 'that is kept locked at all times. It contains a force that is at once more wonderful and terrible than death, than human intelligence, than forces of nature. It is also, perhaps, the most mysterious of the many subjects of study that reside there. It is the power held within that room that you possess in such quantities and which Voldemort has not at all. That power took you to save Sirius tonight. That power also saved you from possession by Voldemort, because he could not bear to reside in a body so full of the force he detests. In the end it mattered not that you could not close your mind. It was your heart that saved you.'" (*OotP*, pp. 843-844)

IV. Fortitude

Fortitude means strength, courage, endurance and resoluteness. Some might term it "grit" or "guts." This virtue is the first of the Seven Heavenly Virtues derived from what the Greeks termed the cardinal virtues.[6] Note the etymology: the words "fort" and "fortify" are derived from the same Latin root, "fortis," meaning "strong." Like a fort, fortitude is something which shields the hero under siege, like Harry and his friends, all assailed by Lord Voldemort. Fortitude thus is a protective virtue, both for individuals and groups. Groups survive best under siege when they cooperate. The group that Dumbledore gathers around him at the end of *Goblet of Fire*, the "old crowd," are like the blocks in a siege wall, standing together against Voldemort's attack, the last and best hope for protection for the wizarding world. Rowling returns to this thematically again and again in *Order of the Phoenix*, emphasizing in every possible way the necessity for the wizarding world to unite to face Voldemort.

At the beginning of *Sorcerer's Stone*, Harry's powerlessness, living with the Dursleys, is continually emphasized. He sleeps in the worst space in the house, the closet under the stairs; he is continually beat upon by Dudley; he is ordered about and insulted by his aunt and uncle; he has no permission to do as he likes; he is deprived of privileges, decent clothing and food; he is made to work while Dudley loafs, etc., etc. In contrast, Dudley seems to have all the power in the household, even more than his parents, whom he orders around without impunity (note, for example, how quickly Aunt Petunia folds when Dudley discovers that he has received a mere thirty-seven birthday presents).

And yet, the Dursleys' failure to nurture Harry has forced him to develop a core of inner toughness which ironically serves him well in his subsequent adventures. Unlike Dudley, who has had his every whim catered to since birth, Harry has had no one to rely upon but himself since he was fifteen months old.

Fortitude manifests itself both in active and passive forms. Passive fortitude means bearing things (ranging from the merely vexing to the dreadful) without giving up or giving in. For Harry, at a more minor level, this means for example enduring the jibes of classmates who mistakenly think he cheated to get his name in the Goblet of Fire (of course it helps to have Hermione sitting beside him intoning, "ignore them, ignore them, ignore them.") It means stoically bearing the pain of Dolores Umbridge's detentions without breaking. This kind of fortitude, because it is passive, can be easily underestimated or overlooked. A very subtle example of this, perhaps, might be Neville Longbottom, who earns Harry's belated respect once Harry realizes that Neville has lost his parents to Voldemort, too. Neville carries on, nevertheless, trying to conquer his fear of Snape in Potions class, without a murmur of complaint, without even telling anyone. Just quietly going on about his life and humbly doing his best, while continuing to faithfully visit his parents at the hospital on his holidays, although they are unable to even recognize him. Harry is ashamed that he has never truly seen the truth about

Neville before learning it in Dumbledore's Pensieve, but it is understandable why he did not—this kind of fortitude does not draw attention to itself.

Ron, on the other hand, is someone who has a great deal of trouble with this particular virtue. Again and again, he rises to Draco's baiting, utterly losing control of himself in the process. He does not seem to be getting any better at keeping a rein on his temper.

If Ron is an example of someone lacking fortitude in minor matters, then Peter Pettigrew serves as an example of someone who lacked fortitude at a major critical juncture, when life and death hung in the balance: "What was to be gained by refusing him [Voldemort]?" Peter gasps. Sirius's answer is withering: only innocent lives. *That* is what is lost when fortitude fails. (PoA, Ch. 19).

Passive fortitude stands against two of the greatest tools of evil: fear and despair. Voldemort knows this, which is why he leaves the Dark Mark to hang in the sky over the sites of his murders. He knows that this sign awakens terror in the hearts of those who would resist him, weakening their fortitude. And when his enemies' fortitude wavers, Voldemort's job is all the easier.

Consider, too, the dementors. They also act by weakening fortitude, literally sucking it away, leaving only fear and despair behind. The critical importance of fortitude as a virtue is demonstrated by the dread everyone has of Azkaban. Because the dementors rule there, the prisoners' lives are indeed bleak. Stripped of their fortitude, the prisoners are utterly pitiable, screaming until they fall into despairing silence, and many eventually die. The dementors' most concentrated attack (their Kiss) leaves only a soulless husk. They can be fought, Remus tells Harry, but doing so is very advanced magic. Dumbledore is right to argue with Fudge that the dementors should be removed from the protection of Azkaban—the dementors indeed are Voldemort's natural allies.

Here we see that Fortitude's natural ally is Hope. Passive fortitude, the ability to wait out a siege, is strongest when hope is there to sustain. Conversely, then, the strongest fortitude—and perhaps the most critical in resisting evil—is resistance which continues when all hope is gone:

> "Harry crouched behind the headstone and knew the end had come. There was no hope . . . no help to be had. And as he heard Voldemort drawing nearer still, he knew one thing only, and it was beyond fear or reason: He was not going to die crouching here like a child playing hide-and-seek; he was not going to die kneeling at Voldemort's feet . . . he was going to die upright like his father, and he was going to die trying to defend himself, even if no defense was possible . . . . " (GoF, Ch. 34).

The other kind of fortitude, which manifests itself actively, can be called courage. "Courage in the face of the unknown is an important quality in a wizard," as Harry is told when he joins the other Triwizard champions after his name is drawn from the Goblet of Fire. (*GoF*, p. 281) If passive fortitude is the fortress in which the hero waits out the siege, then its active manifestation, courage, is what drives the hero from the safety of the fortress to engage the enemy in the field: "I'm going through that trapdoor tonight," as Harry puts in *Sorcerer's Stone* (*SS*, p. 270) "and nothing you two say is going to stop me!" Fortitude stands resolute in the face of fear and despair; courage keeps moving without giving up. It makes Harry face a dragon in the first task, and keep reaching for the next book on the stack (the next one . . . the next one . . .) while desperately trying to find the answer to how to breathe under water for the second task. Cowardice is fleeing from the task at hand, as Gilderoy Lockhart tries to flee Hogwarts when challenged by the staff to open the Chamber of Secrets to rescue Ginny. Courage instead means facing the unknown and going into the tunnel to face the basilisk, or storming the Ministry of Magic.

I want to make note of one final, special courage which is particularly discussed in *Goblet of Fire* and *Order of the Phoenix*, and that is the courage to face the truth. Again, we see contrasting examples. Dumbledore, speaking to Harry in his office after Harry has returned with Cedric's body, clearly sees this virtue for what it is: "You have shown bravery beyond anything I could have expected of you. I ask you to demonstrate your courage one more time. I ask you to tell us what happened." (*GoF*, p. 695). Facing the terrible truth, bearing witness to it and telling it, is healing: "It was even a relief; he [Harry] felt almost as though something poisonous were being extracted from him. It was costing him every bit of determination he had to keep talking, yet he sensed that once he had finished, he would feel better." (*Id.*) And he does; it is not coincidental that as he finishes speaking, Fawkes' magical tears heal his physical wound.

Harry's example of courage here contrasts with Cornelius Fudge's cowardice. "Take the steps I have suggested," Dumbledore urges him, "and you will be remembered as one of the bravest and greatest Ministers of Magic we have ever seen [note the use of the word "brave," signaling that it is courage we are talking about here]. Fail to act— and history will remember you as the man who stepped aside and allowed Voldemort a second chance to destroy the world we have tried to rebuild!" (*GoF*, p. 708). Despite Dumbledore's urging, however, Cornelius succumbs to his inner fears and rejects the truth, leaving all wizards more vulnerable to Voldemort.

And yet, ironically in *Order of the Phoenix*, Dumbledore himself forgets his own advice to Fudge that the truth has to be faced, no matter how bitter the cost. The result is tragedy, resulting in the death of Sirius.

V. Justice

If the Harry Potter series concerns the conflict of good versus evil, then the point where good and evil clash is the domain of the fifth virtue, justice. Related concepts for purposes of this discussion include fairness, impartiality, equity, rightness and dispassion.

The section on the second virtue, hope, discussed the imagery Rowling uses to depict Harry as a prisoner while he lives with the Dursleys. Of course, if the world is a properly run place, where good triumphs and evil is vanquished, the prisoner *is* a prisoner because of the workings of justice. But in a world where good and evil have become confused, that is, if the prisoner has been wrongfully imprisoned, then hope whispers that when good is restored to its rightful place, justice will eventually set the prisoner free.

When the first book begins, Harry, as a prisoner, has no understanding, no expectation of justice. The Dursleys present themselves as model citizens to the world, but any civility and graciousness they present is merely a facade (see, for example, the elaborate charade planned for the benefit of the builder and his wife Vernon has invited to dinner in Chapter One of *Chamber of Secrets*). The Dursleys' actual cruel and capricious nature is revealed in their treatment of Harry. The philosopher Thomas Hobbes (a pessimist about human nature if there ever was one, who believed that most people at heart were really like the Dursleys) offers a famous summation of what life is like in its natural state, i.e., the life that Harry lives while subject to the Dursleys' tender mercies: "no arts; no letters; no society; and which is worst of all, continual fear . . . solitary, poor, nasty, brutish, and short . . . . "[7] The world of sneers, buffets and torments that Harry has grown up with is the only world he knows. Being treated with fairness feels unreal, unfamiliar, even disorienting. One example is the memorable morning when Henry was unexpectedly allowed to go to the zoo on Dudley's birthday, the day he accidentally sics a boa constrictor on his cousin. The fact that he could go to the zoo at all means "he could hardly believe his luck." (*SS*, p. 23) Being allowed to have a lemon ice and then being allowed to finish Dudley's rejected knickerbocker glory is a strange novelty. When it all ends badly, "Harry felt, afterward, that he should have known it was all too good to last." (*SS*, p. 26)

But after some time at Hogwarts, Harry is starting to develop a sense of what real justice looks like and feels like. And as he does, he is becoming less willing to assume the role of the unjustly punished prisoner. Note, for example, the scene at the end of Chapter Two in *Prisoner of Azkaban*. In his rage at the unfairness of Aunt Marge's sneers at the memory of his parents, he unconsciously uses his magic to "blow her up." His defense? Simple justice. "She deserved it. She deserved what she got." (*PoA*, p. 30).

This sense that some things that are fair and some that are not—a sense of justice, in other words—is something that people understand naturally, according to theologian C.S. Lewis.[8] It is particularly interesting to note the other scene in dealing with justice in Chapter Two of *Prisoner of Azkaban*, the one which begins the chapter, thus "bookending" the scene with Aunt Marge. Together, these two scenes will kick off the theme of justice, which will be broadly dealt with in books three, four and five. Harry learns for the first time of another person, someone who has been held prisoner (like himself), who has escaped—Sirius Black. "No need to tell us he's no good," snorted Uncle Vernon, staring over the top of his newspaper at the prisoner. "Look at the state of him, the filthy layabout! Look at his hair!" . . . [True to type, all the Dursleys concentrate primarily on appearances above all else.] "When will they learn," said Uncle Vernon, pounding on the table with his large purple fist, "that hanging's the only way to deal with these people?" (*PoA*, p. 17) Of course, as Harry will learn, when good and evil collide, justice often is not as easy as Uncle Vernon makes it out to be.

Rowling explores the boundaries of justice by presenting a variety of different kinds of trials. These include the trial of Karkaroff, which Harry sees in the Pensieve, the trial of Ludo Bagman (in the Pensieve), the trial of the torturers of the Longbottoms (including Barty Crouch, Jr.) (also in the Pensieve) (all three of which take place in *Goblet of Fire*); the "trial" of Peter Pettigrew in the Shrieking Shack in *Prisoner of Azkaban*, and the disciplinary hearing that Harry himself undergoes for improper use of magic in *Order of the Phoenix*.

It is a sign of Rowling's skill that none of the trials that Harry sees in the Pensieve feel "right" although on the surface all seem to have reached the right result. Bagman is shown mercy, Karkaroff, an admitted Deatheater, agrees to help the wizarding community, providing helpful information, and the torturers of the Longbottoms are given a harsh sentence.

First: the trial of Ludo Bagman. It is clear from the comments of the onlookers, that Ludo Bagman's status as a Quidditch star has severely hampered the ability of those sitting in judgment of him at this trial to judge him fairly. Ideal justice is often depicted as a blindfolded woman, holding the scales of justice. In Ludo Bagman's case, however, the blindfold is off, and the judges are blinded by Bagman's celebrity. And because Justice is not dispassionately evenhanded, Bagman is allowed to get away with minimizing the crime. "I've been a bit of an idiot," he says, and the onlookers (except for Barty Crouch, Sr. and Alastor Moody) react indulgently. "How was I to know?" Bagman says plaintively, and because he is a sports hero, the wizarding community is willing to give him the benefit of the doubt. Perhaps Bagman deserves mercy, perhaps not. The implication is strong, however, that reason he is being given mercy here is not a fair one, and therefore, justice has not been truly administered here.

There is no indulgence, on the other hand, for Karkaroff. He is condemned, but saves himself by naming others to the investigators. Rowling carefully notes, with references to his facial expression and body language, along with running commentary about his treacherousness supplied by Alastor Moody, that Karkaroff's motivation is not the one he professes. One of the functions of justice is to return rehabilitated wrongdoers to society once they have fully owned up to their crimes, repented of them, made their amends, and endured the punishment that society has meted out. But while Karkaroff has owned up to his crimes, we get the sense that he has done so only because he was caught red-handed. He is not truly repenting and turning his efforts to defeating Voldemort—he is trying to save his own skin. The sense is that his liberty is not being given to him because he has earned it through his innocence. He is not, in fact, innocent. Instead, he has purchased it by trading information about the enemy for it. Purchased justice is suspect. And if Karkaroff has not truly repented, then, Harry and the reader is left to wonder, isn't he fully capable of treachery now—say, treachery toward Harry? Again, the decision reached by Karkaroff's judges does not quite satisfy.

The third trial seen in the Pensieve is that of the group which tortured the Longbottoms, including the Lestranges and Barty Crouch, Jr. Certainly we are convinced that the crime is terrible. The reader is inclined to sympathy toward Neville Longbottom; Dumbledore tells us that his parents were beloved, and anyone who attacks Neville's parents should be caught and punished. Somebody should pay. And yet . . . and yet . . .

Again, this trial feels wrong. First of all, Barty Crouch, Sr. sits in judgment of his own son. For a parent to be in that position in the trial of his own child is a clear conflict of interest. Sirius tells Harry (and the reader) at another point in the book that it was not much of a trial, that Barty Crouch, Sr. simply used it as an opportunity to distance himself from his son, so that his own reputation would not be equally besmirched. This assessment is certainly borne out by Harry's observation. Barty Crouch, Sr. is not dispassionate and impartial in this scene—instead, he is vindictive, even cruel. Barty Crouch, Jr. seems to be merely a frightened innocent—but we do not know for sure, and the implication is that no one knows, because everyone is so angry at the crime that the true question of Barty Crouch, Jr.'s guilt or innocence is not being carefully examined. The question is being swept away in the tidal wave of revulsion at the crime.

The fourth trial is the trial of Peter Pettigrew in the Shrieking Shack. As the whole story is explained to Harry, Ron and Hermione, the reader is struck again by the impression that "our side," meaning the wizarding community fighting Voldemort, in this case too has done a terrible job of administering justice. Sirius, we learn, is actually innocent, and has done thirteen years of time at Azkaban for a crime that he did not actually commit.

And yet, ironically, while the cornered Peter Pettigrew denies his involvement in the murder of James and Lily, Sirius on the other hand willingly accepts blame for his part in their death:

"'You killed my parents," said Harry, his voice shaking slightly, but his wand hand held quite steady.'

> Black stared up at him with those sunken eyes.
>
> "I don't deny it,' he said very quietly, 'But if you know the whole story.'
>
> 'The whole story?' Harry repeated, a furious pounding in his ears. 'You sold them to Voldemort. That's all I need to know.'
>
> 'You've got to listen to me,' Black said, and there was a note of urgency in his voice now. 'You'll regret it if you don't . . . .'"

That is what we need to know, in order for justice to be served. *We need to know the whole story.* It is the only way to know what the correct action should be when we must judge the wrongdoers. I would suggest that Dumbledore is not satisfied with the results of the trials seen in the Pensieve, and he adds more thoughts to the bowl, partly to empty his mind, as he tells Harry—but partly because he is still trying to learn and understand everything that he will need to judge dispassionately and correctly. That is why he administers the Veritaserum to Barty Crouch, Jr.—to learn the rest of the story.

On the other hand, the wizarding world at large, represented at the end of *Goblet of Fire* by Cornelius Fudge, dashes our hopes for equitable justice yet again. Just as Harry almost refused to listen to Sirius Black in the Shrieking Shack (and just as Snape in fact did refuse to listen to Sirius), Cornelius Fudge allows the dementors to administer the Kiss to Barty Crouch, Jr., cutting off any chance that he could tell his story, and he refuses to listen to Dumbledore's warning that Voldemort has returned. This abject failure on Fudge's part is extremely worrisome, and it offers a golden opportunity to Voldemort that the Dark Lord will not be slow to seize.

Cornelius Fudge continues in this same manner when he sits in judgment of Harry in *Order of the Phoenix*. It is extremely evident that he is not interested in justice. The time for the hearing was inexplicably changed at the last moment, and it is evident from Fudge's reactions that this was done because Fudge hoped that Harry and Dumbledore then would not be present to offer a defense. Fudge attempts to cut off Harry's explanations and scoffs at his attempts to defend himself. Fudge is not interested in hearing the whole story.

The dementors themselves are silent. They do not allow stories to be told, and they have no use for rehabilitation. Dumbledore is therefore right—they are not appropriate guardians of justice, at least, not the kind of justice which can properly arbitrate good and evil in the struggle against Voldemort.

We have hope, however, in the figure of Harry Potter. Harry has the thirst to find out the true story, the assistance of Ron and Hermione (among others) in uncovering it, the courage to face it, and the patience to hear it all. And, when given the opportunity, as he was in *Prisoner of Azkaban*, we know that he can temper justice with both dispassion and mercy, as he did when he weighed the fate of Peter Pettigrew.

VI. Temperance

The sixth Heavenly Virtue is Temperance. The first definition offered by the Oxford English dictionary reads: the practice or habit of restraining oneself in provocation, passion, desire, etc., rational self-restraint. Related concepts for purposes of this discussion include moderation, restraint, self-mastery, frugality, and sobriety.

Temperance may be understood in the context of restraining negative impulses. This will be touched upon in the discussion of the individual Seven Deadly sins below. This section, however, will instead focus on how temperance guards against excessive zeal in things that start out for the good, to keep them from spinning out of control.

Take, for example, Barty Crouch, Sr. When Harry, Ron and Hermione meet him at the World Cup, their initial impression is that he is a respected senior member of the wizarding community, an impression strengthened by Percy's almost slavish devotion to him. Hermione figures out quite quickly, however, from his treatment of his house elf, that there is something that is not quite right about Mr. Crouch. Ron scoffs at her suspicions, but as Sirius says later, "If you want to know what a man's like, take a good look at how he treats his inferiors, not his equals." (*GoF*, p. 525). Mr. Crouch shows no restraint, no mercy toward Winky. Mr. Crouch's dismissal of his house elf provides telling insight into his character.

What, then, is Mr. Crouch's passion which he is failing to restrain or moderate? As the (false) Moody says, Barty Crouch, Sr. is obsessed with catching Dark Wizards. A desire for justice should be a virtue, but Mr. Crouch allows his passion to tempt him into the fatal mistake of allowing the ends to justify the means. His principles, Sirius remarks, might have been good in the beginning, but apparently he lost sight of them. He started eliminating protections in the justice systems, allowing the Unforgivable curses to be used against suspects and accused wizards like Sirius to be sent to prison without trial. Mr. Crouch's refusal to moderate his passion for justice means ironically that justice is muddled and twisted, to the point that he sends his own son to Azkaban, not because he was convinced that he was guilty, but to make an example of him. The downfall of both the father and son at Voldemort's hands resulted from the chain of events which proceeded from that decision.

Hermione provides another example, in her use of the time turner. Willingness to study hard in order to excel in school is commendable, but Hermione becomes so obsessed with doing well at school that she resorts to the time turner, actually manipulating time and space to give herself an advantage. Professor McGonagall was, in all probability, giving Hermione enough rope to hang herself. Hermione spends her third year buried in books, and her friendships suffer accordingly. Finally, Hermione comes to her senses and turns the time turner back in ("It was driving me mad." *PoA*, p. 430) She has gained enough perspective to realize that moderation is best.

The final, most poignant example is Harry himself, with his experience with the Mirror of Erised. He goes back to the empty classroom where he found the Mirror to see his parents there again and again. His hunger to see them strains his relationship with Ron, and he begins to lack interest in his own life, longing only to be reunited with these shadows from his past. Dumbledore wisely steps in to counsel temperance.

> "This mirror will give us neither knowledge or truth. Men have wasted away before it, entranced by what they have seen, or been driven mad, not knowing if what it shows is real or even possible. The Mirror will be moved to a new home tomorrow, Harry, and I ask you not to go

looking for it again . . . It does not do to dwell on dreams and forget to live, remember that." (*SS*, pp. 213-214)

In other words, Harry must learn to temper and control the natural love and longing for his own family he feels, in order to move forward to maturation.

Mention must also be made of Harry's study of occlumency in *Order of the Phoenix*. Snape warns Harry that to repel Voldemort's attempts to gain control of his mind, he must master himself and clear himself of emotion:

> "You are not trying, you are making no effort, you are allowing me access to memories you fear, handing me weapons . . . Fools who wear their hearts proudly on their sleeves, who cannot control their emotions, who wallow in sad memories and allow themselves to be provoked easily—weak people in other words—they stand no chance against his powers! He will penetrate your mind with absurd ease, Potter!" (*OotP*, p 536)

Yet, things are not quite as simple as Snape pretends. Snape himself is not master of his emotions. Dumbledore admits that it is Snape's hatred of Harry and the memory of Harry's father that causes the occlumency lessons to fail. In the end, as Dumbledore says, the fact that Harry could not master himself enough to close his mind did not matter, because it was his heart—the heart that Snape scorns so much—that saved him.

VII. Prudence

The last Heavenly Virtue, prudence, suggests caution, foresight, and discretion. One of the most interesting things about prudence is that it is a virtue which must be balanced carefully with fortitude, or courage, and that balancing point, which is explored extensively in *Order of the Phoenix*, is not always easy to see.

Consider, for example, Molly Weasley. One of the most genuinely moving scenes in *Order of the Phoenix* occurs when Harry encounters Mrs. Weasley trying to get rid of a boggart. It manifests itself as her greatest fear: each member of her family, one after the other, dead on the floor. Molly Weasley understands that she needs courage to face that fear, and so begs Remus not to tell Arthur about the episode, attempting to minimize her own fears as "silly." At the same time, her instinct for caution, to protect her family, is what gives the boggart real power. Harry remembers the photograph that Mad-Eye Moody just showed him of the previous generation of the Order of the Phoenix, many of whom have died, and he has to admit that Mrs. Weasley's fears are not silly at all.

It is this underlying caution, based on her assessment of the very real risks involved, which prompts her to argue that Ron, Hermione and Harry should be protected from knowing the doings of the Order of the Phoenix. She also passes on a message to the trio, through Sirius, urging them not to go ahead with their plan form a Defense Against the Dark Arts group, because if they were caught, Dolores Umbridge's wrath would ensure that their futures could be ruined.

Sirius, less cautious than Molly, is inclined to urge that Harry, Ron and Hermione should be told about the Order, and he thinks that forming the D.A. is a good idea. Hermione at least, however, struggles with the question of whether they should follow Sirius's advice. Perhaps Sirius is too rash. And certainly, Molly's fears in part do come to pass. When the existence of the D.A. is discovered, Dumbledore is forced to leave the school. Yet subsequent events prove that forming the D.A. was the right decision, because the skills that the students learned because of Harry's couching proved invaluable when they stormed the Ministry of Magic.

The very painful question, of course, is whether Harry and his friends should have gone to the Ministry at all in the first place. Harry wants to rush right in, but Hermione begs him to exercise prudence and doublecheck to find out whether his vision is real. She warns him that Voldemort knows that he wants to save people, but even with Hermione's warning, and even though they do try to verify on Sirius's whereabouts, Harry is too rash. Disastrously, he fails to remember, before they are caught by Umbridge, that Snape is also a member of the Order of the Phoenix, who could have helped them. Worst of all, he failed to open Sirius's Christmas package and use the mirror, which could have helped him to avoid being fooled by Voldemort in the first place.

Harry had plenty of courage, but it is the memory of his lack of prudence which will torment him the most with regrets in the years to come.

The Seven Deadly Sins

I. Pride

Pride, the first Deadly Sin, is excessive belief in oneself and one's own abilities. Related concepts are arrogance and vanity. Living with the Dursleys, Harry grew up thinking he did not have anything to be proud about, until he got the letter from Hogwarts. He has developed his Quidditch skills, and discovered he has a certain flair for magic in at least some of his classes (but not potions!)

Draco offered Harry his first temptation: will Harry reject certain people because they are poor like Ron, or could be considered odd or oafish like Hagrid, or because they are Muggle-born like Hermione? Gilderoy Lockhart tempts Harry to succumb to self-conceit, and Harry rejects that temptation, too. His experience with the Dursleys undoubtedly had something to do with this. After years living with Dudley, Harry is acutely sensitive to the ridiculousness of people who have overly inflated opinions about their self-worth. It is probably the reason why he also managed to resist the blandishments of Rita Skeeter in *Goblet of Fire*.

Rowling is not so simplistic as to suggest that nothing good ever comes from pride and so it should always be rejected. Much of Harry's drive to succeed and to better his magical abilities springs from his competitive nature. Harry is undoubtedly ambitious: he wants to win at Quidditch, which makes him search for an answer to manage his fear of dementors in *Prisoner of Azkaban*. Harry's pride affects his performance in the Triwizard Tournament. Once his name comes out of the goblet, he wants to win. He realizes from the beginning that whoever had put his name in might very well have nefarious motivations, but he does not struggle very hard to get out of competing. Was this because he believed Dumbledore and the faux Moody, that he had no choice to compete— or did his own ambition make him swallow Voldemort's bait, even though he had his eyes open to the danger? His pride makes him resist accepting help (which almost leads to disaster with the second task—he finally accepts Dobby's help because he has literally run out of time to try to figure the answer out on his own). And then, to compound the complexity of it all, Rowling took one of Harry's noblest moments, his decision to swallow his pride and agree to share the Tournament win and the glory with Cedric— and with that decision sealed Cedric's doom. Now *that's* irony—to take a hero's noblest decision and have it lead directly to a terrible, tragic disaster.

Rowling explores these nuances even further in *Order of the Phoenix*. True, Harry's pride helps him resist Umbridge, as when he endures her punishment with the cutting quill stoically, while still resolving to defy her by continuing to train the members of the D.A. But on the other hand, Harry's faith in his father's memory is shaken when he witnesses his father's arrogant behavior toward Snape in Snape's Pensieve. The danger of pride is that it creates barriers where there should be none. Harry's pride prevents him from going to Dumbledore when he should. It is that failure of communication between Harry, Dumbledore and Sirius that causes Harry to fall into Voldemort's trap, which leads to Sirius's death. Pride on both sides troubles the communication between Harry and Sirius. And in the end, pride comes between Harry and Snape, preventing Harry from learning the occlumency lessons he so urgently needs to take, and this failure is another reason why Voldemort succeeds in fooling Harry into believing that he had kidnapped Sirius.

Many characters at one time or another exhibit truly proud behavior, including Snape, who seems to need to feel superior, Draco and his father, Voldemort, of course, and Ron, to some extent, who is touchy about his poverty, and who is too proud to apologize to Harry for a long time in Goblet of Fire, leading to their painful estrangement.

Characters distinguished by their humility, on the other hand include Hagrid, Dobby, Dumbledore, Neville, and oddly enough, Hermione, who never seems to use her mental superiority to lord it over others. Yes, she is sometimes accused of being a know-it-all and she will correct others when they do not know the subject. But she never preens herself because she has the best grades; she is unfailingly kind to Neville, an often hopeless student; and she is humble enough to think that she cannot coast and so is always trying to study harder.

II. Anger

The prospect of exploring the topic of anger in the Harry Potter books seems almost overwhelming. *Everyone* gets angry in this series at one time or another, heroes and villains both. Dumbledore, Voldemort, McGonagall, Snape (of course), Harry, Ron, Hermione, Sirius, Remus, Draco (of course), Lucius Malfoy, Cornelius Fudge, Amos Diggory, Madam Pomfrey, Madam Hooch—and the list goes on and on. What functions does anger serve in the story in general?

Anger splinters relationships, causing division and conflict between allies—and conflict, of course, is the engine of plot. Think of the fight between Hermione and Ron over Crookshanks and the Firebolt. Think of how Snape's anger over the trick Sirius played on him affected the events in the Shrieking Shack in *Prisoner of Azkaban*—he was not willing to listen to Remus and Sirius because he was still nursing that old grudge—look at all the consequences that followed. Again, it is Snape's anger at Harry's snooping in his Pensieve that causes him to break off the crucial occlumency lessons. Dumbledore understood this danger. Note how he chided Snape and Sirius at the end of *Goblet of Fire* to put their anger aside so that the group as a whole can fight Voldemort. The whole giants subplot in *Order of the Phoenix* is meant to serve as a warning example to the wizarding community, just like the Sorting Hat's song. The giants are dying out because they cannot live together without quarreling.

Anger tests judgment. If a person knows the difference between right and wrong, the test of whether he will stick to his principles often comes when that person is really, really angry. Will you do the right thing even when you have lost your temper? Think of all the times Ron lashes out at Draco because Draco has angered him, even though, logically, he knows Draco's just yanking his chain. Remember how Harry's rage at Aunt Marge made him lose control of himself and break the rules governing minors' use of magic. (This truth, that anger tests judgment, in fact, may be one of the reasons that underage wizards are forbidden to do magic during the summer months. Young people can be particularly impulsive, especially when angry, and their control over their magical powers is still uncertain.) Think of Snape baiting Harry, threatening him with the Veritaserum, and how hard Harry works to control his anger in this scene, knowing that if he loses his temper here, he will ruin everything, getting Hermione and Dobby into trouble. A more serious example is how Sirius is tempted by his anger to murder Pettigrew in cold blood, rather than turn him over to the proper authorities.

Anger can be exploited by the enemy. One example is the way Lucius Malfoy baited Arthur Weasley into an explosion of rage, using the resulting confusion of the fight that followed as an opportunity to plant Tom Riddle's diary on Ginny.

Anger comes when you are backed up against the wall, when you have to decide what is really important to you, what side you stand on when the chips are down. (Remember Harry's anger when he declared to Ron and Hermione, "I'm going through that trap door tonight and nothing you can say is going to stop me! Voldemort killed my parents, remember?")

Anger when channeled correctly, gives power and determination, helps strengthen wavering courage in times of danger. Think of Dumbledore's anger when confronting the false Mad-Eye Moody, or Hermione resolving to uncover how Rita Skeeter is spying on them, simply because she is so angry over the *Daily Prophet* stories. In the same way, Harry uses the force of his anger at Dolores Umbridge to prod him into becoming the best possible teacher that he can be to the students studying Defense Against the Dark Arts with him in the D.A.

III. Envy

Envy is the desire for others' traits, status, abilities, or situations. It should perhaps be remarked that alone among the Deadly Sins envy is the only one which offers no enjoyment to the sinner whatsoever. Harry had plenty of opportunity to learn about envy while living with the Dursleys. Perhaps he had a good, stable foundation with his parents for a year and a quarter, but from that point on, he was stuck in a totally unequal situation. Dudley got everything; Harry got nothing. Dumbledore told Professor McGonagall that Harry should live with the Dursleys because there he could live a normal life, and not grow up being warped by the knowledge he was famous. Things did not turn out quite the way Dumbledore perhaps intended it. But in one respect, Harry's life with the Dursleys helped him understand deep in his bones the nature of inequality that leads to envy. It helped him to understand Ron's jealousy and envy in *Goblet of Fire*—although that understanding does not entirely help Harry to handle the situation with total grace (i.e., throwing the button at Ron and snarling that maybe Ron will have a scar, which is what he always wanted).

Yet, it might be argued that Harry did not exactly envy Dudley. He saw Dudley's privileges, but he does not give the impression that he exactly wanted anything that Dudley had, other than regular food and a sense of belonging (and perhaps an occasional trip to the zoo). He did not seem to long for love from his aunt and uncle, probably because it was so clear to him that they were such awful people, that being loved by them was not much of a prize. Moreover, he saw clearly that the indulgence that Dudley's parents gave their son turned him into something of a monster. Dudley is a loathsome person—a glutton, someone who is not particularly bright, a cruel, sadistic, selfish bully, and so Harry does not exactly look at him and think, "I wish I could be just like him."

His envy toward Cedric, in contrast, is more personal and more real. Cedric is not a loathsome person but a good person, and Harry can see that, and so the feeling, "I want to be like him" is more of a temptation. Moreover, Cedric has things that Harry really does want: a more developed physique, the admiration of Cho, social ease, the undisputed right to compete in the Triwizard Tournament, the acceptance of the other students of his right to be called a Hogwarts champion. This envy of Cedric (as well as

Harry's pride, see above) shapes Harry's response to the temptation to claim the cup alone at the end of the third task. Harry overcomes both pride and envy and invites Cedric to share the cup instead.

In *Order of the Phoenix*, Harry is tested again when Ron is named prefect. In *Goblet of Fire* he knew that according to the rules of the Triwizard tournament he was too young to be properly considered the Hogwarts Triwizard champion. He has much more solid grounds for envy here. Dumbledore's decision to pass over him and give the honor to Ron is painful because Harry knows deep down that the honor could have been—perhaps even should have been his.

Harry anxiously searches his own heart as he struggles with the knowledge that he has been passed over. He does his best to judge the situation as objectively as he can, acknowledging to himself, despite his hurt, that Dumbledore might have quite valid reasons for preferring Ron to himself. In the end, he masters his envy because his friendship to Ron is more important to him.

> "Ron had not asked Dumbledore to give him the prefect badge. This was not Ron's fault. Was he, Harry, Ron's best friend in the world, going to sulk because he didn't have a badge, laugh with the twins behind Ron's back, ruin this for Ron when, for the first time, he had beaten Harry at something?" (GoF 167)

The answer to that is *No*. He turns back to smile at Ron and congratulate him as sincerely as he can. It is a testimony to the strength of their friendship—and indeed, how far Harry has come—that Harry overcomes his envy here.

Other characters struggle with envy, too. Ron, of course, was jealous himself when Harry's name came out of the Goblet of Fire, but again, the strength of the friendship between the two boys overcame the breach in the end. We do not know exactly what Snape's problem is, but we do get the impression that envy is at least part of it. He was jealous of James—he speaks bitterly of James' position as head boy and Quidditch hero and perhaps he might have envied James' relationship with Lily. Questions that remain are: why, exactly, does Snape's hatred of James transfer to James' son, and conversely, why does Snape overcome that hate/envy to save Harry's life in the first book?

Draco seems envious of both Harry and Hermione (Ron he merely seems to scorn). He considers Hermione to be an academic rival, and as for Harry, Draco seems to resent Harry's fame, Quidditch success and general alpha male niche in the school social order.

IV. Gluttony

Gluttony is the inordinate desire to consume more than one requires. Dudley, of course, immediately springs to mind. Dudley is more than merely overweight, someone whose metabolism is a little out of whack; he is a glutton, and as such, he is depicted as a contemptible character. His gluttony leads him to sloth (hey, coming up! Sin No. 7!) and selfishness, almost a kind of solipsism. Dudley believes that the world revolves around him and his appetites, to the extent that nothing *matters* to him unless it has to do with getting his needs met. When Vernon took the family and fled at the beginning of *Sorcerer's Stone* when the letter(s) from Hogwarts started arriving, it did not occur to Dudley to wonder much about this strange adventure the family was having. He could not think past the fact that he was hungry and had missed five of his favorite TV shows.

Note how Dudley's gluttony has skewed the relationships in his family. Dudley's parents totally indulge him, and in doing so, they abdicate their parental roles. Vernon's attitude is fondly indulgent ("Little tyke!") which leads him down the slippery slope of overlooking his son's other faults, i.e., his sadistic bullying. Petunia caters slavishly to Dudley's every whim. Indulging Dudley's gluttony eventually leads to Vernon and Petunia loss of their grip on reality. They cannot see the extra pounds, just as they cannot see that their son is not applying himself in school, and his terrible social relationships.

If the definition of gluttony is considered in a broader sense, applying to more than merely food, then Dudley has several spiritual "twins," characters with a ravenous capacity who suffer all the attendant troubles (selfishness, skewed relationships, inability to recognize that they are not the center of the world).

Lord Voldemort and Dolores Umbridge, for example, are both power gluttons. This, obviously, has given them each an inflated view of their self worth, has skewed relationships, and made both distressingly selfish. This type of gluttony is, of course, particularly dangerous. Voldemort bullies and browbeats his underlings, controlling their actions (Imperius), causing pain (Crucio), and killing (Avada Kedavra). Dolores, too, unbalances all the relationships around herself as she begins assuming the right to inspect other teachers, usurps the headmaster's role, and turns students against students with her Inquisitorial Squad.

The other great glutton in the series is Gilderoy Lockhart. What Lockhart craves is adulation. Again, note how his sense of reality is warped (he twists everything fit his world view that he is universally admired, and that everyone wants to become close to him and imitate him.) The balance in relationships is disrupted: Gilderoy is so hypnotized by his faux-celebrity that he cannot properly teach. He is incapable of focusing his attention on the student where it belongs; instead, he continually tries to yank attention back to himself. Again, the results are disastrous: starting from the point where Lockhart releases the pixies until the point where he tries to turn Ron's wand on Harry and Ron, Lockhart blows it again and again.

Now, if the series is about Harry's moral education, what does it have to say about how to deal with a glutton? Harry actually does quite well. He learned what to do and what *not* to do by observing the Dursleys. And it is this: Don't feed a glutton. Just don't. If you do, they will only want more. And so Harry does all he can to keep from feeding Lockhart's ego. He avoids him, he protests that he did not intend to get a photograph of

Lockhart, ask for his autograph, etc. (Too bad Lockhart is unable to hear what Harry is trying to tell him.)

More importantly, he does all he can to keep Voldemort and Umbridge from feeding on power. In *Goblet of Fire*, Harry resists the Imperius curse; he dodges the Crucio curse. In *Order of the Phoenix* he finds ways to resist Umbridge, too, by giving Rita Skeeter an interview to undercut Umbridge's insistence that the Ministry is doing the right thing by ignoring Voldemort, and most crucially by starting the D.A.

What is Rowling doing with this theme of gluttony? The counter for gluttony (which is/leads to selfishness), is selflessness. Harry has one egregiously self-indulgent episode of gluttony in the series. He broke the rules and left Hogwarts in order to sneak into Honeydukes to buy sweets. Remus saved him from Snape—and then scolded him for it, asking him whether he thinks that Lily's self-sacrifice for him should be jeopardized for such a selfish reason.

V. Lust

Lust is indulging in the gratification of an overwhelming drive of the body. At first glance, there seems to be little about lust in these books, if we are talking about lust in the strictly sexual sense. The kids, best as we can tell, are all virgins, and the teachers do not seem to be involved in sexual relationships (or else they are extremely discreet). One wonders, of course, whether Hagrid and Madame Maxime had two blankets or shared one while camping in giant country, but Hagrid does not talk about it. And Arthur and Molly, judging from the number of their children, seem to have had an active sex life, but they do not seem to do a lot of on-stage snogging.

Well, perhaps not entirely. There are the Veela, of course, first encountered at the Quidditch World Cup in *Goblet of Fire*, those fascinating creatures who seem to inspire ridiculous behavior in any males who happen to wander into their orbit. A more careful look reveals glimmerings of lust, or at least awareness of the opposite sex, in our main characters, starting with *Goblet of Fire*. Exhibit 1 is Harry's uneasiness/excitement around Cho; Exhibit 2 is the peculiar strained conversations swirling around between Hermione and Ron (especially about the Yule Ball) and even between Viktor and Harry, again about Hermione. Hormones are starting to wake up, and the trio is becoming uneasily aware of it. It seems to be a mixed blessing at this point. Harry is suddenly aware that there are a lot of girls at Hogwarts. Lots and lots of girls (and all moving in packs, he thinks fretfully). It is as if his sexual antennae are starting to twitch.

If one effect of gluttony is selfishness, then perhaps an equivalent effect of lust is a certain, well, brainlessness, or loss of judgment. Ron, for example, seems to be suffering a certain disorder in his thinking about Hermione and Viktor going to the Yule Ball together in *Goblet of Fire* (see, for example, the argument between Ron and Hermione at the end of Chapter 23, and Harry's thought that Ron seems to be the one "missing the point"). Rowling develops this further in *Order of the Phoenix*. Harry is hyper self-conscious about what he says to Cho, he doesn't even know what to do with his hands when he is in her presence, and he feels incredibly stupid around her.

Like gluttony, lust can also be considered in broader terms: in other words, lust can also be an overwhelming drive to satisfy any other desire in general (aside from sexual appetite). One character to consider under this broader definition is Remus Lupin. Once a month, a kind of madness seizes Remus (literally, blood lust) coupled with the total loss of all human reason. He has a strong drive to bite other people, the danger being that he could infect them. Remus suffers all the prejudice of the wizarding world blaming him for being a werewolf, but Rowling clearly indicates, and the reader believes, that initially Remus is innocent of any kind of wrongdoing here. He did not ask to be bitten and he tries to protect other people from his malady.

Where Remus goes over the line from innocent victim to someone who commits the sin of lust is when he agrees to let his friends become animagi so that they can release him to run free during his transformations. By doing so, Remus is removing all the restraints that are meant to protect himself and other people during the times that he has no judgment. That is his sin. And for that, he must pay, casting himself out, if you will, from his own personal Garden of Eden, i.e., Hogwarts where he has been so happy, and has been gainfully employed for the first time in his life, all because he has violated the trust of others, most importantly, Dumbledore. For that he must go.

The Mirror of Erised, which shows you your heart's desire (what your heart lusts after the most, if you will) should be mentioned as well. It is useful to know what you desire the most, Dumbledore says, but remember that it may not be attainable or even possible—and thus, you shouldn't let yourself obsess over it, to the exclusion of all else in your life.

VI. Greed

Greed is the ardent desire to possess something belonging to someone else. This aspect of possession makes greed different from, for example, gluttony, which also involves a desire. If you covet something, you want to have it—and your desire, if fulfilled, deprives someone else of that thing, who should rightfully have it.

This is another instance where Harry's upbringing with the Dursleys has perhaps served to "inoculate" him against temptation, because Dudley in particular was such an awful example. Dudley had a multitude of possessions, but Harry saw that they did not give him any particular pleasure. He would get a toy and then break it and forget about it. Rowling speaks specifically about how Dudley coveted things—he would want something if he saw that Harry had it.

The biggest instance of coveting in the series, in my opinion, involves the item which provides the title of the first book: the philosopher's stone. Voldemort wants the philosopher's stone in order to re-incorporate—meant literally, in the sense of the Latin root, corpus for "body." He wants a body back; more than that, he wants eternal life. The stone belongs to Nicolas Flamel, and so Voldemort is determined to steal it.

Voldemort's coveting of the stone leads to a host of other evils. First, he tries theft (attempting to take the stone from Gringotts.) He tricks Hagrid into betraying Dumbledore's trust and revealing the secret of how to get past Fluffy. He ensnares and bullies Quirrell, enslaving him to his will and (eventually) leaving him to die. He kills a unicorn to drink its blood, a terrible sin with a terrible price. So, greed leads to attempted theft, lies, betrayal, and violence.

Harry can defeat him only because he does not want the stone himself. It is that fact that allows him to use the Mirror of Erised to find the stone without giving it away to Voldemort.

There is a more muted example in *Goblet of Fire*. Here, the coveted object is more abstract: it is the position of school champion, picked by the Goblet of Fire, that is desired by many, and eventually, the position of the Triwizard champion. Harry is accused by several students, particularly Draco, of coveting what is rightfully Cedric's ("Support Cedric Diggory—the Real Hogwarts Champion") (*GoF*, p. 297). Harry at first is innocent of this charge. He might instead be called an "anti-covetor." He had thought of what it might be like to be the Hogwarts Champion, but once he had heard about the age line he did not consider entering the competition. But when the Goblet of Fire spits his name out, and he finds himself to be a champion, he really doesn't want the role—even though, and perhaps especially though, everyone thought he did, and thought he was willing to cheat and lie to break the rules to do it. Most hurtfully for Harry, Ron thinks so, and their friendship fractures because Ron reveals that he covets what, ironically, Harry never really wanted in the first place.

Harry, in time, as he works through the tasks, comes to accept his role as champion, to the point that he really does want the Triwizard cup in the maze, just at the point he realizes that Cedric has won it. At that point, the cup represents to Harry everything that Harry thinks Cedric has that Harry wants: the true, unqualified right to be called a champion, the admiration of his peers (especially Cho). And yet, Harry resists temptation here, just as he did in the first book. He does not take what does not truly belong to him. When Cedric refuses the cup, too, Harry suggests that it instead be shared. By doing so, Harry is actually unmaking the sin of coveting; deconstructing it: a possession meant for just one is shared between two.

(Too bad that Voldemort was waiting at the other end.)

VII. Sloth

Slothfulness is laziness, disinclination to work, idleness. Once again, watching Dudley has given Harry an eyeful of the nature (and effects) of slothfulness, up close and personal, which perhaps has warned him against succumbing to the temptation. In general, on the slothfulness continuum, Harry seems to occupy the happy medium niche between

Hermione, the ant, and Ron, the grasshopper. Harry seems to do his homework and study, but he enjoys himself, too, playing Quidditch, for example—he finds that taking Quidditch breaks from his studies helps clear his mind and relax him, so that presumably he is more ready to concentrate when he does get back to the books. He doesn't keep his nose to the grindstone as much as Hermione (especially when she had the time turner) or goof off as much as Ron, or even more, George and Fred Weasley seem to do.

Still, Harry is not perfect. He got a slow start on solving the clue in the dragon's egg for the second task in *Goblet of Fire*, because he was reluctant to start buckling down to work on the problem. He was forced to launch a last minute all-night search through the books in the library, and he would not have managed to complete the task at all if it had not been for Dobby.

At first glance, slothfulness does not seem to be as significant to the story as some of the other sins. Yet by the end of *Order of the Phoenix*, issues surrounding this particular sin become absolutely central.

Rowling approaches this subtly, setting up a subplot contrasting Percy Weasley with his brothers Fred and George, which is initially played entirely for comic effect. In *Goblet of Fire*, Percy works diligently on a report about cauldron bottoms, a ridiculously trivial subject. He busies himself with his job at the Ministry, puffing up his own consequence with his boss, Barty Crouch, Sr., in a manner which is meant to impress onlookers with his busy-ness and importance (an importance which is undercut when his boss cannot even get his name right). His behavior is clearly meant to contrast with that of the Weasley twins, who seems to be frittering their time away on frivolous jokes, to the detriment of their studying—and yet by the end of *Goblet of Fire* it is clear that they are very serious about the joke shop. They have been busy making inventions, they have a business plan, and a venture capitalist (Harry!) and they seem about to make a serious go of it. Percy, on the other hand, has been so busy with various "important" matters that it has entirely escaped his notice that his boss, Barty Crouch, Sr., has become unhinged and is being controlled by Lord Voldemort.

By *Order of the Phoenix*, the contrast between Percy and his brothers has taken an even more serious turn. Percy, the dutiful and hardworking son cruelly rejects his family, ostensibly because of the importance of his work at the Ministry. He does this because he has entirely failed to grasp what is really important, the task which by all rights should be demanding all his immediate attention: the effort to defeat Lord Voldemort. Fred and George, the cut-ups, on the other hand, understand immediately what it truly important, and they apply themselves (with a diligence that probably would have amazed their mother) to the all-important task of baffling Dolores Umbridge in her attempts to derail the Hogwarts educational system from being an effective deterrent to Voldemort.

What Rowling is getting at has to do with the faux Mad-Eye Moody's motto: "Constant vigilance!" Harry had prepared as best as he could for the first and third tasks, and he probably survived his encounter with Voldemort in *Goblet of Fire* only because of the magical lessons he had practiced so assiduously (including the "Accio" and "Impedimenta" spells). The Percy/twins subplot is meant to be a mirror/foil to a parallel plot running through *Goblet of Fire* and *Order of the Phoenix* which gets at the heart of this matter of sloth much more seriously and directly: the battle of wills between Cornelius Fudge and Dumbledore.

Fudge, in his role as Minister of Magic, is refusing to do the work he should be doing at this point. Now, granted, Fudge's refusal to act at the end of Goblet of Fire perhaps cannot be labeled "laziness," exactly. It is definitely a disinclination to do the hard thing, however (to "get up and do what needs to be done," as Garrison Keillor puts it). Fudge adamantly refuses to take the steps necessary to prepare the wizarding world for the change in circumstances resulting from Voldemort's rise.

And really, whatever his reasons, whether it is fear, jealousy of Dumbledore's influence, or disinclination to change the status quo, or something else (even something more sinister, like the possibility that Fudge may secretly already be in Voldemort's camp), the result is the same: because Fudge is refusing to act (to remove the dementors from Azkaban, to send envoys to the giants, to monitor known and suspected Death Eaters, etc.) the wizarding world is not prepared for Voldemort's return. Evil flourishes when good people stand by and do nothing; *that* is the moral danger in slothfulness. And so it is up to Dumbledore—and Harry—to step in and take action.

Conclusion

Analysis and criticism of Rowling's Harry Potter books is complicated at this point in history by the simple fact that the series is still in the process of being written. As such, we are in exactly the same position as Harry himself: we do not know what will happen next. Someday, we hope, the series will be complete, and the reader will have the ability to second guess all of Harry's decisions with the luxury of hindsight, available to anyone who reads the series as a whole. Until then, however, like Harry we can only wonder: has he made the right choice?

In *Order of the Phoenix*, unlike all the other books, all of Harry's coping mechanisms fail him. Hogwarts is not a sanctuary from trouble anymore, and the adults that Harry has learned to trust are forced to admit that they do not have all the answers. It is inevitable: for Harry is moving steadily toward adulthood, where decisions have consequences, some of them searing, and mistakes cannot be wished away. He will need to marshal every possible inner resource to face what lies ahead. The greatest courage is required when hope seems faint, even nonexistent, and indeed things look quite bleak for Harry now. He has demonstrated that courage in the past, showing himself to be a remarkable young man as he struggles to develop an ethical framework for handling his remarkable powers of magic. We can only hope that he will continue to do so in the future. Witnessing Harry's process of ethical decision-making is not a pernicious experience for the reader. Rather, it is an opportunity for Harry's fans to experience vicariously, through these marvelous tales, Rowling's profound and moving examinations of moral behavior.

Peg Kerr was born in a Chicago suburb, moved to Minnesota to attend St. Olaf College, and has stayed in Minnesota ever since. With $50.00 from her first paycheck from her first job out of college, she registered for a science fiction and fantasy writing class. There, she met her husband and wrote the first story she ever sold. In hindsight, this is all quite pleasant consolation for the fact that she was fired from her job the day the class started. She attended the Clarion Writers Workshop in 1988 and has an M.A. in English Literature, specializing in speculative fiction. Her fiction has appeared in various science fiction and fantasy magazines and anthologies. Emerald House Rising is her first novel. The Wild Swans, a stand-alone fantasy based on the Hans Christian Andersen fairy tale, is her second. She presently lives in Minneapolis with her husband, Robert Ihinger, and two daughters, and, until recently, served as President of HP Education Fanon, Inc.

What's A Nice Jewish Boy Like Harry Potter Doing In A Place Like This?

Amy Miller

Harry Potter? A nice Jewish boy? One could make the case that Harry Potter is a mensch[1], and perhaps a "lamed-vovnik,"[2] and that J. K. Rowling is a candidate for membership in the Workman's Circle[3]. Although Harry's story is not specifically a Jewish one, it contains values and lessons that are fundamentally Jewish in their essence. The fact that his is a fantastic story with magic and witchcraft at its core does not preclude its teachings and its morals. Let us first examine the concept of magic in the Bible.[4]

The torah[5] tells us not to divine by sorcery and the commandments are scattered throughout. "You shall not let a sorceress live."[6] "You shall not practice divination or soothsaying."[7] "When you enter the land that HaShem[8] your God is giving you, you shall not learn to imitate the abhorrent practices of those nations. Let no one be found among you who consigns his son or daughter to the fire, or who is an auger, a soothsayer, a diviner, a sorcerer, one who casts spells, or one who consults ghosts or familiar spirits, or one who inquires of the dead."[9] These commandments are also interpreted to include superstitions and astrology. However, as people try to understand the mysteries of the world around them, they attempt to control fate or look into the future, and this also occurs in the Bible.

In Genesis we read about Leah and Rachel, the sisters who were Jacob's wives. Leah's son Reuben brings home some mandrakes, which were thought to have powers of fertility. Since Rachel had no children up till now, she barters with her sister for the mandrakes, hoping they would help her conceive. She ultimately has two sons, Joseph and Benjamin, but it was not the mandrakes that enabled her to have children.

The pharaoh in Exodus has magicians who try to impress Moses and Aaron by turning their staves into snakes, causing locusts and frogs to invade the land, turning the Nile River into blood, trying to demonstrate that they were just as powerful as HaShem (we are told that HaShem made all of these things happen, but to the pharaoh and his court, the magicians were able to perform their own spells). However, when it was time to reverse the spells, the pharaoh has to plead with Moses to ask HaShem reverse them, because the magicians were powerless to do so.

Later in Tanach, I Samuel: 28, the prophet Samuel dies. Since King Saul has decreed the enforcement on the ban of sorcery, no one is permitted to try to contact the spirits of the dead. However, Saul's kingdom is going to be attacked by the Philistines and Saul no longer has Samuel to help and advise him. He prays for guidance, but decides he has not received any answers to his prayers. Saul then asks his courtiers to find him a woman who consults ghosts so he may ask her to speak to Samuel for him (!). They tell him of the witch of En-dor and he disguises himself and visits her. Of course, she realizes who Saul is and asks him if she will be killed if she does this for him. He promises her that she will not be punished, so she summons the ghost of Samuel, who rises from the ground and tells Saul that David has been called by HaShem to be the new king[10].

The occult is not foreign to Judaism. The phrase "mazal tov" is usually thought to mean "congratulations," but it literally means "a good planet." Jews still incorporated astrology into their lives and actions, even if it was strictly forbidden. Gematria,[11] the system of replacing Hebrew letters with their numeric equivalents and then analyzing the numerology, and Kabbalah,[12] the study of the hidden aspects of HaShem and the universe, are other very old and complex attributes of Jewish learning. However, they are only addenda. The knowledge and performance of mitzvot and service to HaShem were (and still are) more important. A solid foundation of Jewish study truly is required for the Kabblah and Gematria to make any sense or to have meaning.

So now that we have seen some examples of Judaism's attitude towards magic and witchcraft, it is evident that these practices are forbidden (but still used). Why, then, should we consider Harry Potter Jewish? Since the magic in the books is simply a vehicle for the story, it is inconsequential and is taken at face value. Therefore, we must look beyond the story's entertainment and examine the value system that J. K. Rowling has established for Harry and his world.

In Harry's new life, he discovers that the magic community does not want to be part of the mainstream of society. Most people do not know that there is an entire sub-culture of witches and wizards.

> "But what does a Ministry of Magic *do*?" [asked Harry].
> "Well, their main job is to keep it from the Muggles that there's still witches an' wizards up an' down the country," [replied Hagrid].
> "Why?"
> "*Why?* Blimey, Harry, eveyone'd be wantin' magic solutions to their problems. Nah, we're best left alone."[13]

Though there have been too many times in Jewish history when Jews wanted or needed to hide, Jews in the modern world usually are open about being Jewish. However, Jews live in the secular world, intersecting with non-Jews openly and freely, but separating from them when necessary; i.e., Jewish religious holiday worship and observance of kashrut[14]. Even when Jews purposely live in separate communities, like in parts of Brooklyn, NY, taxes, the electric bill and public transportation fares must be paid by them just as everyone else. We know that the magic world and the secular one also cross paths, because there is intermarriage among them, and there are many Muggle-born students at Hogwarts. It seems, however, that these occurrences are not to be liberally broadcast. It is interesting to note that the magic world is so hidden, that the witches and wizards have no need for electricity, television, telephones and computers, and many aren't aware of them at all. Magic seems to do everything—it cures disease, connects people, provides heat and light. However, there are problems in the magic world that are identical to the outside world, and Harry (and we, through his eyes) sees them—racism, intolerance, and corruption in politics are a few. We learn that goblins, centaurs and house-elves have especially endured discrimination. Joanne Rowling's personal plea for tolerance and equality shines in her books. Perhaps, if she were Jewish, she would have been interested in the Workman's Circle, mentioned above. This is "a progressive-liberal organization committed to advancing democratic frontiers, eliminating poverty, strengthening civil rights, promoting universal health care and opposing bigotry, tyranny and totalitarianism."[15]

It is worth noting that Harry has had little or no example of proper behavior from the Dursleys. He has been ignored and abused, forced to live in a virtual closet, told not to ask questions or use his imagination, and never been shown any compassion because he is an orphan.[16] These actions contradict the torah's teachings of how to treat others.[17] Yet somehow, somewhere, Harry has acquired a generous spirit, a kind heart, "rachmunos"[18] for others, and a "gitteh neshumeh"[19]. This is why he is a mensch; in spite of his surroundings, Harry has transcended his existence and chosen a different approach to life.

The Talmud teaches us that saving an endangered life[20] is above all else, except for murder, idolatry (which includes incest and human sacrifice) and adultery. (Even the Sabbath laws are to be ignored if there are human lives at stake.[21]) In *Harry Potter and the Order of the Phoenix*, Harry's friend Hermione accuses him of having a "saving-people thing."[22] Harry, she and Ron heatedly discuss Harry's history of rescuing people and the dangers he faces when he does so. And she is correct— Harry embodies this talmudic teaching to the fullest at every turn. When he hears that Ron's sister Ginny has been abducted, he doesn't hesitate before making his decision to rescue her.[23] He follows after Ron when he sees his friend attacked by a large black dog who has dragged him under the Whomping Willow.[24] He waits underwater until he is certain that all the captives will be rescued.[25] He runs to find out what has happened when he hears screaming coming from Cedric while they are in the maze during the Third Task.[26] Saving lives seems to come as second nature to Harry. He cannot ignore anyone, even his repulsive cousin Dudley,[27] when he or she is in mortal peril. Does he endanger himself? Absolutely. However, he does not undertake any rescue without knowing that there are risks involved and acknowledging the threat of his own death. He chooses this risk. This, of course, brings us to the questions of choices in life in general and Harry's choices in particular.

The torah tells us that we have a choice between observing HaShem's mitzvot or not, and that HaShem wants us to live:

"I call heaven and earth to witness against you this day: I have put before you life and death, blessing and curse. Choose life—if you and your offspring would live—by loving HaShem your God, heeding God's commandments and holding fast to God."[28]

The prophet Micah reiterates this:

"[Micah] has told you, O people, what is good, and what HaShem requires of you: Only to do justice, and to love mercy, and to walk modestly with your God."[29]

Rabbi Hillel taught:

"If I am not for myself, who will be for me? If I am for myself alone, what am I? And if not now, when?"[30]

"In a place where there are no human beings, strive to be a human being."[31]

Similarly, Dumbledore exhorts the Hogwarts students:

"Remember Cedric. Remember, if the time should come when you have to make a choice between what is right and what is easy, remember what happened to a boy who was good, and kind, and brave, because he strayed across the path of Lord Voldemort."[32]

The choice of life may be simple, but often it is far from easy. Harry's choice to save Sirius Black was right, even though he discovers too late that Sirius was not in peril.[33] Harry endangers himself because he cannot live knowing someone needs him. This is why his character is so appealing; even without example, he knows the proper thing to do, and does it. He is pure of heart; this is why he would make a good candidate for a lamed-vovnik.

Harry's story, at this writing, is not yet complete. We are hopeful that he will vanquish Lord Voldemort, live to a ripe, old age and have many children. Whatever his fate, his story is one of courage, of hope and of faith, which makes him a good candidate for a "nice Jewish boy." But what's this mishegoss[34] with the wands and the brooms? And what kind of a name is *that* for a school—*Hogwarts*?! Enough with the wizard na-arishkeit![35] Better he should be a doctor, but first maybe eat a little something . . . ?

Works Cited

Hebrew-English Tanakh [Jewish Bible]: *The Traditional Hebrew Text and the New JPS Translation-Second Edition*. Philadelphia: The Jewish Publication Society, 1999.

Rowling, J. K. *Harry Potter and the Philosopher's Stone*. London: Bloomsbury, 1997.

_____. *Harry Potter and the Chamber of Secrets*. London: Bloomsbury, 1998.
_____. *Harry Potter and the Prisoner of Azkaban*. London: Bloomsbury, 1999.
_____. *Harry Potter and the Goblet of Fire*. London: Bloomsbury, 2000.
_____. Harry Potter and the Order of the Phoenix. London: Bloomsbury, 2003.

It was total serendipity that Cantor Amy Miller presented at Nimbus—2003. She replied to a post on the HPforGrownups group citing Jewish sources and was then asked if she would be interested in presenting a Jewish viewpoint of Harry Potter at Nimbus—2003. Although a cantor (the person who leads the chanting in Jewish worship service) and not a rabbi, she has studied Jewish texts concerning mysticism and the occult.

Cantor Miller is a graduate of Smith College, Northampton, Massachusetts and has a diploma as a Certified Cantor from Hebrew Union College, New York, New York. She has served several congregations in New York, Massachusetts and Connecticut, and sang at Tanglewood, Lenox, Massachusetts, in a memorial service for Leonard Bernstein. A lover of Yiddish music, she is the vocalist for the klezmer band "Two Cents Plain." In the fall of 2003, she served with Congregation B'nai Sholom in Huntington, West Virginia for the High Holidays. She has lived in the Berkshires of Massachusetts most of her life and is married to Stephen Miller, with whom she has two daughters and one cat.

Muggle Studies: Where Fandom Culture and Academia Intersect

Canon, Interpretation, and the Alternative Universe:
Navigating the Fandom Safely

Steve VanderArk
Barb Purdom
Peg Kerr

Moderated by Debbie Duncan

Introduction

Only six years have gone by since J.K. Rowling first introduced us to the magical world of Harry Potter. In that short time, millions of fans—children and adults alike—have read and reread the five novels, watched films dramatizing those novels, and purchased large quantities of merchandise ranging from Chocolate Frog cards to action figures to shampoo. Many of those adults—like us—have gone further than that. We have gone online, where we put our thoughts in writing, in the form of essays, role-playing, and fan fiction, as well as reference guides to the magical universe of HP, all based on the Harry Potter "canon."

But what do we mean by "canon"? Whether you're an armchair Auror, an academic studying the books as literature, a writer of HP fan fiction, or a merchandiser developing a product, you need to confront this question. Yet asking a hundred HP fans is likely to result in a hundred different answers.

Before the development of mass media, when an author's works consisted solely of the written word, the answer to that question was simple. Canon was—and still is, if one consults a dictionary—"the authentic works of a writer." For the absolute purists, this means that no source deserves to be called "canon" other than the original U.K. editions published by Bloomsbury (as revised in subsequent editions to correct errors, of course).

Is there something about Harry Potter that changes the traditional definition of canon?

- Is it the huge popularity of the books? Or merely modern times? J.K. Rowling has given many interviews in which she discussed the content of the books, their characters, and the magical world she has created, revealing details and background information that do not appear in the books themselves. Interviews are not new, but transcripts are now posted on the internet, allowing us to parse them line by line to the same extent as the text of the novels.

- Is it Rowling's own control over what bears the *Harry Potter* name? Unlike most authors, she was able to command a remarkable degree of control over adaptations of her works, and derivative products ranging from the Warner Brothers movies to Chocolate Frog cards have received her imprimatur. Does that imprimatur elevate something to the status of canon that normally would be treated as an interpretation or adaptation?

Mass media has made the interpretation of canon more complicated as well. The internet has allowed new sources of interpretation to proliferate, or at least has made these interpretations widely available to the public. We now have hundreds of *Harry Potter* websites and listservs. Just by clicking the send button, fans can publish essays and other commentary, as well as fan fiction and fan art, all of which, at some level, interprets the characters, settings, plots or themes, of the novels. However, they are not all equal in quality, or in faithfulness to the novels. This raises a new challenge: How do we sort through it all? Is fan-written commentary equally worthy of serious consideration as the work of an academic?

Fan fiction raises unique issues. A really good work of fanfiction will seduce the reader into entering the universe that author has created. In many ways, the universe of the fic differs from the world Rowling created. Even if a fanfic writer is 100% true to canon, the work will contain new situations, which create a separate "canon". For this reason, many fans avoid fan fiction on the ground that reading fan fiction would "taint" the reader's understanding of the *Harry Potter* canon. Are such concerns valid? Is it impossible to separate the interpretative aspects of fan fiction from those elements derived from the fanfic author's own imagination? Should we even care?

Questions for the panel include:

1. What standards do you use to decide if something is "canon"?

2. What weight should be given to different source materials?

   a. U.S. and foreign editions of the novels
   b. The "schoolbooks"
   c. J.K. Rowling's interviews
   d. The Warner Bros. films

Debbie Duncan is a tax lawyer with over 15 years' experience in private practice with a firm in Washington, D.C. In addition to her law degree from George Washington University, she has a B.A. in government from The College of William and Mary. A lifelong reader of fiction and nonfiction, she is a list elf at HPforGrownups, as well as a member of the Jane Austen Society. She shares her passion for Harry Potter with her husband and two school-age children.

Peg Kerr was born in a Chicago suburb, moved to Minnesota to attend St. Olaf College, and has stayed in Minnesota ever since. With $50.00 from her first paycheck from her first job out of college, she registered for a science fiction and fantasy writing class. There, she met her husband and wrote the first story she ever sold. In hindsight, this is all quite pleasant consolation for the fact that she was fired from her job the day the class started. She attended the Clarion Writers Workshop in 1988 and has an M.A. in English Literature, specializing in speculative fiction. Her fiction has appeared in various science fiction and fantasy magazines and anthologies. Emerald House Rising is her first novel. The Wild Swans, a stand-alone fantasy based on the Hans Christian Andersen fairy tale, is her second. She presently lives in Minneapolis with her husband, Robert Ihinger, and two daughters, and, until recently, served as President of HP Education Fanon, Inc.

Barb Purdom studied classics and anthropology at Temple University years ago and still lives in her native Philadelphia with her husband and two children, working as a freelance singer (chamber music) and also attending school once more (architecture).

Steve Vander Ark is a K-8 library media specialist from Grand Rapids, Michigan. He is also a freelance writer and columnist, as well as being the resident director for Caledonia Community Players. Steve is probably best known in fandom as the creator and editor of The Harry Potter Lexicon, a reference web site devoted to the book series; the Lexicon was awarded the Site of the Month award by J.K. Rowling herself in July, 2004. Steve has been involved with fandoms for many years, beginning with his first Star Trek convention back in 1975. He's served as president of various fan clubs and other fan organizations over the years. Steve used to be just an inch or two shy of six feet tall, but now he isn't sure if he is shrinking or if his 14-year-old daughter with the long blonde hair is really getting that tall.

Sail on Good Ship:
Shipping Debate

Sarah Goff, Moderator

Emily Bytheway (Wahlee), Susan Faust (Angua) arguing for the Ron/Hermione ship

Sara Goetz (Zorb), Linda McCabe (Athena) arguing for the Harry/Hermione ship

Transcriber's Note:

For those who missed it, we had four debaters, two on each side, as well as a moderator sitting between us and a timekeeper who helped our wonderful mod keep us strictly on schedule. Each debater made a statement for their side and was cross-examined by the other team. Then, we opened the floor to audience questions, two per side. Finally, the debaters each made closing remarks.

My goal in transcribing the debate was to capture what was *really* said. Thus, all of the false starts, self-corrections, and incorrect grammar that are a part of our normal, everyday speech appear in the transcript. I have not edited for accuracy or to make anyone "sound better." I *have* edited in quote marks where it was clear the speaker was quoting directly from a source; the quotations themselves, however, appear as they were spoken.

I used a loose version of the conventions found here: http: //hci.ucsd.edu/102b/ Transcription.htm

Bold italics indicate emphasis
A dash—marks the cutoff of the current sound
A comma, indicates a rising and falling contour or a longer pause without ending the sentence
A ? indicates rising intonation, not necessarily or always in a question
(single parentheses) indicate something unclear in the speaker's speech
((*double parentheses with italics*)) indicate action or transcriber's notes
A [bracket indicates overlapping speech, where the [marks the onset of overlap for both speakers.

Because of the recorder's location in the middle of the table, I could hear the moderator, myself, and Angua the best, followed by Athena, Wahlee and the Chaser, and I could barely hear the audience's comments on the tape at all. They were included where they were audible. Audience actions (applause and laughter) get separate lines.

The tape cut off before the end of the session. I was caught up in the debate at the time and didn't notice it had stopped rolling, so the transcript does not include the end of Wahlee's conclusion and all of Athena's closing statement; Wahlee and Athena were both given an opportunity to review this transcript, as did Angua, and everyone was satisfied by this transcript. For that, I am truly sorry, but it is a testament to how interesting, engaging, and fun the debate was. I'm thankful I was able to participate in a real-time discussion on one of my favorite topics. I'm sure there are things that we all would have done or said differently, given the chance, but thinking on your feet is part of the challenge of live debate, and you have to live with what you actually said. Without further ado . . .

[INSERT BW_SHIP]

SARAH: All right, well, we have to get started cause otherwise we're not gonna get through the whole debate um I'm—hi I'm Sarah and I'm—the mod and—I'm Switzerland so

((*applause*))

SARAH: Uh, I just wanna go over quickly—go over the rules and-

((*muffled business with timekeepers getting the structure*))

SARAH: I just wanna quickly—quickly go over the rules—for the debate um I'd like to emphasize questions are gonna be held until the end where there'll be a question period, okay? ((*timekeeper corrects*)) Yeah, sort of in the middle, I mean before the rebuttal but—th-the questions will be held until a specific time period so: what I'd like everybody to do is to think about what their questions are? and come up with a concise way of stating it because they're no—there'll be no soapboxing. If you go more than a few *seconds* saying your question I will cut you off. Because we have a very very tight time frame and now we've already run into it. Um be concise, don't stall, don't go off on a tangent, don't state your *case*, ask a question, there'll be two questions to each side, um and they'll be evenly distributed, uh what I'll do is I'll ask for a Harry/Hermione question then I'll ask for a Ron/Hermione question, and—we'll give—alternating questions there'll be four of those total. Um, the time frames'll be pretty tight, um I hope everybody can: just stay civil?

((*laughs*))

SARAH: And there'll be a coin toss for—the—to decide who goes first. So—would you like to do the honors?

TIMEKEEPER: ((*groans*))

SARAH: Cause I'm sure that I'll-

((*laughs*))

SARAH: I'm sure that I'll end up with it *(muffled)* ((*laughs*))

TIMEKEEPER: Okay who's calling it.

ZORB: I will.

TIMEKEEPER: In the air? You're team A? and you're team B? Correct?

ZORB: Okay, sure.

TIMEKEEPER: Well I just wanna make sure—*(muffled)*

SARAH: It doesn't matter it's a coin toss—

TIMEKEEPER: ((*tosses*))

ZORB: Heads.

((*coin rolls under table, laughs*))

TIMEKEEPER: It is tails! Here, see, everyone, tails.

((*laughs*))

SARAH: Okay, so—so you're first, you have four minutes.

TIMEKEEPER: And—start.

ANGUA: So Harry Potter has these two wonderful best friends he has Ron who's a boy who's all about emotion and heart, he has Hermione who's a girl who's all about logic and brain, and the question is, is he meant to fall in love with one of these two friends or is he gonna find love—somewhere out*side* the trio—leaving these two friends—uh—leftover? to fall in love with each other. *I*'ve believed since book one—that J.K. Rowling is developing the *Weasley* family—to be Harry's future in-laws the warm wonderful family that he's going to marry into. And I think she's developing Ginny Weasley to grow up—uh the girl that he rescued so heroically in the Chamber of Secrets—to grow up to be the woman of his dreams. So, if—if that's true, then J.K. Rowling must know, that she has a problem, because she's given Harry—one of his two sidekicks—is a *girl*—and—we—we people—are romantics. And what people will do is—is a *lot* of people—she *must* have known that people would see—a hero—and they would see a girl and they would say let's put those together. So—she must have known that and she must have done something—we should see something in the books, where she's trying to steer us away from that conclusion—where she's trying to *show* us, that these are not future lovers, these are friends.

And guess what? that is exactly what we see. Um one of the ways she does this is she sets Hermione up—in a romance—a classic romance plot—that Emily is gonna tell you all about. Another thing she does she was once asked in a chat— uh someone said uh—if—asked if Harry and Hermione would ever develop a love interest and she said, do you really think they're suited? In other words, *no*, they're not, so what do we see in the books—to *show* they're not suited and there's—a lot of things that you could see once you start looking for it. Um, we have Harry's point of view, so we know, that he does not see Hermione that way he does not see her, as a girl to be attracted to he never has—uh—Hermione in the books is *very* bossy with Harry and we see him uh, avoiding her, we see him hiding things from her we see him *lying* to her, to get away from her nagging. He thinks that Hermione talks too much, he thinks that Hermione bickers too much with Ron, and in *five books* we seem him being annoyed by this behavior on her part. She's also—Hermione is a wonderful—focused, driven girl, and when Harry makes jokes—a lot of times they go right past her, or else she says, Harry that's not funny.

So um Harry trusts Hermione, but he doesn't confide in her about his feelings, um he likes her very much, but she's not really good at cheering him up in his dark times, and he has a lot of dark times. Uh in Goblet of Fire for instance, whe—he's-he's been fighting with Ron and he's all down and he's with Hermione all the time, we hear him say uh "'Miss him? I don't miss him!' But this was a downright lie. Harry liked Hermione very much but she just wasn't the same as Ron. There was much less laughter and a lot more hanging around in the library when Hermione was your best friend." So Hermione is a wonderful friend for Harry, a supporter a helper—but uh for his love interest, he needs someone who's lighter, someone who's more sensitive, someone with a sense of humor to cheer him up, and someone he can tell his feelings to and Hermione is just not that person. And JK Rowling *shows* us, that Hermione is not that person, she directly confronts this issue, by having *everyone* do, what people in the real world do, and **assume** that Harry and Hermione must be boyfriend and girlfriend, and uh (*muffled*) there's the articles by Rita Skeeter that say so, and neither Harry or Hermione is at all embarrassed by this idea, um: and then Harry is not jealous of Krum, when Krum comes to him and asks him what's going on between you and Hermione, Harry says "***Nothing*** we're *friends,*" uh Harry's jealousy is shown in what he says to Ron he says, "I don't have a problem with Hermione coming with Krum," and Her**mione** also is not the *sli*ghtest bit jealous of uh Harry's relationship with Cho Chang. She uh tells Harry that Cho likes him, smiling, while she said so, she pushes Harry to da—she suggests that Harry—ask Chum out—uh Cho out, and she ***drags*** Ron away—

TIMEKEEPER: Time.

SARAH: Okay. Now-

((*applause*))

SARAH: Now you have two minutes to respond to that—or cross-examine.

ZORB: You seem to base a lot of your argument on JKR's ***statement***, that Harry and Hermione are just friends what do you make of the quote, from the Chamber of Secrets DVD that says, "Chris in the second film does what I don't until the fourth book, and that is you get hints of certain feelings between ***the three of them*** that belong to a slightly more mature person."

ANGUA: Well of course I relate that to Chris Columbus saying, that he has foreshadowed with the—hug and the non-hug, that there's tension between—Ron and Hermione so Hermione wouldn't hug him, because of the—ro*man*tic tension between them, the feelings between the three of them as you know in Goblet of Fire that—Harry and Hermione are confused they have the feelings of embarrassment and um—uh: dislike of being—confused for a romantic couple while—Ron and Hermione of course have the jealousy and misunderstandings that come from a—romantic couple that's not yet—gotten together.

ZORB: Even though it's *feelings* between the three of them not just—

ANGUA: Right the feelings of—

ZORB:—the feelings *others have* about the three of them.

ANGUA:—the feelings that Harry and Hermione both have of embarrassment—of uh embarrassment and annoyance? the giggling that Hermione does the uh blushing that Harry does it's all—feelings.

ATHENA: Okay, one of your uh regular arguments is that Harry uh ((*tape error*)) that he finds her ugly, in light of direct [evidence to the contrary ((*muffled by the "No"s*)) from Harry's mouth-

A&WAHLEE: [No no no-

ATHENA: Does the R/Hr side concede that the point is no longer valid.

ANGUA: Um no not at all in fact I'm surprised that Hermione **asked** that question, it seems like even Hermione has noticed that Harry is not attracted to her, and she wanted to use that information to help—with the relationship with Cho Chang.

ATHENA: But we know that [she was pretty

WAHLEE: [There is a very big difference between being not ugly and being attractive.

ZORB: She said—

WAHLEE: I think of—I can think of a lot of people who are not ugly? but I'm not attracted to most of them.

((*laughs*))

ZORB: He called her pretty, in Goblet of Fire.

ATHENA: Before he even knew who she was and then when he saw that it was his best friend, his jAngua: w dropped.

ANGUA: Right because he was *so surprised*—

WAHLEE: Because he was so surprised that she looked so incredibly different than she usually does—

ZORB: And *pretty*—

WAHLEE: When she's not—

((*laughs*))

ANGUA: How she normally doesn't look.

SARAH: Okay, that's it. Um I'd—I'd also like to just throw in it—try not to talk over each other cause it's hard to hear—both of you—if you're asking a question (*muffled*) you responded.

((*audience member asks for panelists to introduce themselves*))

SARAH: Sure, quickly?

ATHENA: Uh, Linda McCabe, also known as, Athena.

ZORB: Sara, also known as Zorb.

ANGUA: Susan Faust, also known as Angua?

WAHLEE: Emily Bytheway, also known as Wahlee.

SARAH: Okay. Uh, now your team you have four minutes to state—do your first statement.

ZORB: In the battle of the cli*ch*és that is ship debate, we believe that the hero and heroine paradigm super-cedes that of bickering lovers. Rowling uses a pattern of increasing partnership between Harry and Hermione to demonstrate this trend of growing together. In the first book, the ending sequence is *of*ten seen as a template for the entire series, seven tasks, seven books. Harry and Hermione are the last two standing after Ron sacrifices himself, and it is only because of sheer impossibility that she is unable to follow him all the way. But, before she leaves him, she gives him, the *hug*, the first sign of physical affection within Harry's memory. In the second book, Hermione's intelligence proves *absolutely* crucial and she nearly dies for it. Her struggles are one of Harry's most feared memories. Increasing teamwork is shown when Harry is the *only* person to pick up on her *one-word* clue and solve the mystery. They're beginning to think together. In the third book, the two con*tin*ue to think together, and instinctively turn towards one another, demonstrating both trust and understanding. The ending sequence is all Harry and Hermione, working together and on their own. Again, they are the last two standing when encircled by the dementors. There is some telling imagery in this sequence. They are first chained together, and then they fly off into the night on a hippogriff, a symbol, of love.

((*laugh and applause*))

In the fourth book, Hermione is the only one of his peers to remain loyal to Harry. Rita Skeeter's articles and Viktor Krum's suspicion, are the first time the two are placed together in a romantic context in the books, *and* they show us how the outside world perceives the everyday interactions between these two characters. And of *course*, we end with The *Kiss*. While it's not romantic, this is an important progression from the Hug, at this midway point in the series. In Order of the Phoenix, as one of my Ron/Hermione shipping friends likes to say, it's The *Harry* and Hermione Show. While Ron is a Prefect and a Keeper this year, he remains stuck in that old school mode. Often eh—an—acting as background to Harry and Her*mi*one, who are both transcending, that school mode and leaving it behind to become partners, often seen as, captain and first officer, commander and lieu*ten*ant. Echoing book two they pick up on similar clues like Draco's "dogging" remark. Cho's jealousy is an excellent parallel to Viktor's. *Why* should Rowling show us this same scenario twice if it was supposed to be something we were—supposed to get the first time? She's s-showing us something, that Harry can't yet see. The ending sequence starts with six and narrows to three but it's *not* our beloved *Trio*, as we've come to expect, would be the most important players. It's Harry, Hermione, and *Neville*. If she wanted to show us who would be the most important kids, in the upcoming battle, this was a great time to do it. I'm not talking fate or soul-mates here, these are two characters who are growing together, through experience and understanding, to become the dominant partnership in the books. They're a team. They're looking in the same direction. Love is a recurrent theme in these books, and there is no one closer to Harry than Hermione in his thoughts, in his conscience, and in his heart.

((*applause*))

SARAH: Kay, you have two minutes to cross.

ANGUA: Okay I would like to ask you you're seeing Hermione, as a hero, rather than, as I see them, Ron and Hermione are both Harry's *equal,* friends and supporters. Uh, I was wondering how you reconcile your view of this—this—inequality between the two of them, with quotes like this one from uh, from JK Rowling that she said in 1999, "Harry as a character came fully-formed, as did the idea for his sidekicks, the characters Ron and Hermione."

ZORB: They can still be sidekicks and—have a big role but it just seemed to me like in Order of the Phoenix, Ron was hardly there. Did anyone else think that?

Audience: Yeah.

ZORB: So it may be transcending that they were originally conceived as the sidekicks but they seem to be moving beyond that—growing up into adults.

ANGUA: So she's changed her mind perhaps—

ZORB: [Maybe she has—

ANGUA: [But Harry, has not—does not seem to be aware of that because he— very intr—frequently in Order of the Phoenix refers to Ron and Hermione, as his equal helpers, and he *also several* times, Harry goes into a *boas*tful mode and says, *I'm* the one sent off the dementors, *I'm* the one who faced Voldemort, *I'm* the one who did that, and he uh, why does Harry not seem to realize that there's *any* difference between his two best friends who he seems to value perfectly equally?

ZORB: Typical boy.

((*laugh and applause*))

ZORB: Now in addition—in a—no ((*laugh*)) in—in addition to that, uh he *does,* later— discover, that that little voice in his head who's contradicting him and telling him the truth, is Hermione's voice.

ANGUA: Yes which makes sense because, Hermione and Ron both—represent sides of Harry uh that [rational side and the emotional—

ZORB: [but she's the one who's gotten into his head.

ANGUA: Yeah she's his superego.

WAHLEE: Do you know who—who the voice of my conscience is? My mother.

((*laughs*))

ANGUA: I'd like to ask you—you—

((*applause*))

ANGUA: You are aware that the hippogriff is a symbol of im*poss*ible love.

ZORB: Impossible love that has triumphed [to create this creature.

ANGUA: [Impossible.

ZORB: To create this creature otherwise—

ANGUA: But Harry and Hermione are too convenient, and they still don't see each other.

WAHLEE: And Hermione sure doesn't like riding on the hippogriff.

SARAH: Okay. Stop.

((*laugh and applause*))

SARAH: Okay, you have—four minutes to present your second statement.

WAHLEE: "I had not known you a month before I felt that you were the last man in the world whom I could ever be prevailed on to marry." This passage from Jane Austen's Pride and Prejudice is a prime example of the bickering couple literary convention. Briefly it goes something like this. Boy meets girl. Girl dislikes boy. Boy in*sults* girl. They fight, they bicker, they in-exchange insults. They seem like they are never, ever going to get together. And then they do. This literary convention is so prevalent in fact that whenever we see things like, "Whatever house she's in I hope *I'm* not in it." Or, "She's a nightmare, honestly." Our romance an—our ro-romance antennae begin to twitch. Every insult from "She is tolerable, but not handsome enough to tempt me," to, "You're the most insensitive wart I have ever had the misfortune to meet," Angua: dds to the expect—expectation that the couple will get together. Such is the case with Ron and Hermione. Theirs is not a placid relationship. It gets off to a very, rough st-start, and goes downhill from there. "Are you sure that's a *real* spell," Hermione-

((laughs))

WAHLEE: Inquired of Ron on their first meeting. "Well it's not very good, is it." And yet, even in the very beginning, they care about what the other thinks *of* them. Hermione runs off in tears after Ron insults her, prompting Harry and Ron to rescue her when Quirrell lets in a mountain troll. Hermione *lies* to get her rescuers out of trouble, an action that impresses Ron, and a friendship is born. It's a friendship of fighting, bickering, and backhanded compliments, but it is a friendship. Some have stated that Ron and Hermione would never be friends if it weren't for Harry. But there is ample evidence they genuinely like each other. Hermione reacts strongly to Ron's sacrifice in the chess game, at the end of book one. She screams as he goes down and concernedly asks Harry if he thinks Ron might be seriously hurt. Likewise, Ron is the first to jump to Hermione's defense in Chamber of Secrets when Malfoy calls her a Mudblood. And afterwards, he has to be held back from attacking Malfoy in her defense so often, that it has become almost a reflex for the other two to make a grab for his robes.

((laugh))

WAHLEE: Their fight in Prisoner of Azkaban causes them both a lot of pain, and Hermione sobs unrestrainedly on Ron's shoulder when they make up. And underlying it all is the desire to have the other think well of them. So when does friendship turn to romance. To quote JK Rowling herself, the answer is in Goblet of Fire. Although we have some hints and foreshadowing of a future relationship between Ron and Hermione. It is not until Goblet that it becomes painfully obvious, wher—th—that there is something going on between those two. The notion of who will end up with who is never more important to the plot than in Goblet, for the relationships have a significance in the main plot as well as the subplot, involving as they do all four school champions. Hermione's continued dislike of Fleur and significant scowls whenever Fleur gives Ron attention, are complimented by Ron's sudden turnaround (something?) admiration of Viktor Krum. Hermione expresses hurt and anger when Ron states his preference for a good-looking girl, and Ron's preoccupation with—who Hermione's date is shows he is just as interested, in who Hermione is interested in romantically. The d—the—the debacle that is—*aff*ectionately known as the Yule Brawl—

((laughs))

WAHLEE: Have the most shippy line in all canon. "Next time there's a ball, ask me before someone else does, and not, as a last resort." Ron of course, is firmly planted in a state of denial, about his own feelings, and seems to continue his cluelessness in the Order of the Phoenix, although there is hope. Ron's reaction to Hermione's good luck kiss is extremely encouraging. As is his attempt to give Hermione a meaningful present. Hermione also shows signs of—still being interested in Ron, as in her comment to Harry concerning his complete lack of understanding girl-wise. "Harry, you're worse than Ron. Well, no you're not."

((*laughs*))

WAHLEE: The bickering couple romance lends itself wonderfully to humor, and the Ron/Hermione relationship is no exception. From witty banter such as the bouillabaisse scene, to the backhanded *co*mpliments, the Ron/Hermione relationship provides a humorous subplot, giving all of us a bit of comic relief in the face of such darkness. We look forward to the time when Ron finally gets a clue, and the relationship can proceed from its current state of, wait and see.

((*applause*))

SARAH: Okay okay. You have two minutes to cross.

ZORB: Why, if Hermione is so: desperate for Ron to realize that he likes her, um—uh—does she not react more favorably to his Christmas present, or *e*ven force herself to stay awake the night he is celebrating, making the Quidditch team.

WAHLEE: Well, as for the Christmas present, she—eh—as we see, she doesn't say that she hates it, she states—very clearly that it's an unusual present, trying to keep his feelings from being hurt.

ATHENA: Oh, if she wanted him she'd go oh ((*sniffs wrist*)) smell how it is on me

((*laughs*))

ATHENA: But she doesn't do that, and she d—bAngua: rely mentions it's—yes, "*Har*ry, thanks so: much for the book, I've been wanting the new Theory of th—Numerology for *ages.* And that perfume is really unusual Ron."

WAHLEE: And, what's so unusual about [an Arithmancy book?

ATHENA: [It's a personal gift.

WAHLEE: And how romantic is that?

ATHENA: It's something she really wanted, this is a personal gift of perfume, she could've at least said, that was very thoughtful Ron, [thank you.

WAHLEE: [Yes, but—but think about how clueless Ron is. He—I mean this is a humor subplot he is—uh—every time JK Rowling wants us to know that someone likes someone else it's humorous ((*tape error*)) they—um—put on too much cologne they—um—get combs in their hair by trying to comb it out, it's the *fu*nny thing to her—trying to have couples get together, and uh Ron's cluelessness and Ron's um, lack of um, ideas for a suitable present, adds to the humor.

ATHENA: But why, if she wanted to get together with him did she not even stay awake on a night that he was celebrating.

WAHLEE: She wants, to—let him—[be-

ATHENA: [That would be-

WAHLEE: th—the—the—the um the im—the impetus. [(*muffled*)

ATHENA: [Well to get together you have to be alone and she could've stayed up and forced herself on a night that he was excited.

WAHLEE: At a party? Hey when has Hermione ever partied. [She doesn't.

ATHENA: [She stays awake, she can force herself to stay awake and help Harry do some [of-

ZORB: [If she really really likes Ron, [she would've stayed awake.

ATHENA: [she would have forced herself to stay awake she does drink coffee in this book she could have done it.

WAHLEE: I don't know I really really like people and I couldn't stay awake for most-

SARAH: Okay. Stop. 'Kay, uh you have—four minutes to present your—second statement.

ATHENA: Okay. First of all, I am here to have fun and to entertain you.

((*laughs and applause*))

There are many reasons that we think that Harry and Hermione will be romantically linked—in the *full*ness, of *time*. For brevity's sake I will concentrate on two recurrent themes by those two principal characters, as seen in the Order of the Phoenix. One. Hermione paid *very* close attention to Cho, more than Harry did, which demonstrates her *siz*ing up a romantic rival. Hermione's jealousy towards Cho, is not shown by, scowls, anger or, semi-colons, *it* is through the repeated and almost ob*sess*ive interest in watching and analyzing the competition, as well as assessing its progress.

((*laughs*))

> This is shown, by every discussion between the Trio regarding Harry's relationship to Cho, being initiated, *by Hermione*. If she had been interested in *help*ing Harry hook up with Cho, then her tone of voice would be *ea*ger and, awaiting juicy *de*tails, rather than "brisk," and "business-like."

((*laughs*))

Hermione knew that Harry had been interested in Cho, for a long time, while Ron? was seemingly ignorant of this fact. Now Jo Rowling violated the old dictum, of *show*, don't: *tell*, with Harry's first kiss. We are simply, *told* of it afterwards. We do not get to *see* or potentially empathize with Cho's emotional vulnerability, nor do we see Harry's awkward response. Instead, we are *told* of Cho's tumultuous emotional state by, Hermione, who obviously has done a *lot* of thinking on the matter.

((*laughs*))

Now repeatedly, throughout the story we hear about Cho's feelings, *af*ter they are filtered through the, Her*mi*one lens. Never, did Hermione offer Harry advice, to help him establish a relationship with Cho, but she was however, more than happy, to explain to Harry after his dating fiasco, what went wrong.

((*laughs*))

She also did not encourage him to try and make *up* with Cho either. And she seemed to be fishing for compliments, when she brought up the idea that Harry thought she was ugly. Now *Ha*rry. His loyalty to Her*mi*one, causes him to side re*pea*tedly with her, over, Cho. The first time he chose Hermione over Cho, was during the Second Task of the Triwizard Tournament. Then, on his *Va*lentine's Day date with Cho, he agreed and followed through on his promise to meet with Hermione, rather than blowing her off, and staying with Cho. This promise to meet Hermione, is the cause of his date going horribly wrong. After the, post-mortem discussion with Hermione of his disastrous date with Cho, Harry did not go and try to smooth things over with her. Even when she came up to him after the publication of the Quibbler, Harry did not take that opportunity to say, "That's why I met with Hermione that day at the Three Broomsticks. She arranged the Interview. It didn't have anything to do with what, *you* thought." And when *Cho* tried to make excuses for Marietta's betrayal, they argued once again over *Hermione*. Harry defended the jinxing of the parchment by saying it was brilliant, to which Cho responded, "Oh yes, I forgot—of course, if it was darling *Hermione*'s idea." And that was the end of their relationship of sorts. The moral of that story is that when *push* comes to shove, Harry would rather give up a girlfriend than his best female friend. No other female will ever eclipse Hermione's importance, to Harry Potter.

((*applause*))

SARAH: Okay, you have—you have two minutes to cross, and then—we'll go to the challenge questions so everybody, be thinking.

((*laughs*))

ANGUA: I know you're aware of the importance of friendship and the existence of platonic love, you understand that Ron has platonic love with Harry I'm sure. *What* in the world is it about Hermione's love for Harry that's in any way different—from Ron's love for Harry, *or*, vice versa, Harry's for them?

ATHENA: Yeah, I'm remembered of the immortal words from that famous philosopher Kenny Loggins. ((*sings*)) "Whenever I call you 'friend', / I believe I've come to understand, / Everywhere we are, / You and I were meant to be, / Forever and Ever . . . "

((*laughs*))

ANGUA: But—but Hermione is—is—is strikingly *un*able to understand Harry's feelings on many occasions, such as after the s—the first task, the dragon task, when uh Ron—when he and Ron are having an ecstatic [reunion-

ATHENA: [Well you know, Harry seems to think that she's good with feelings and stuff she just doesn't understand Quidditch *out of his mouth* she is good with feelings and stuff.

ANGUA: Harry does seem to think that except for *his* feelings that she misses again and again, for instance when—Ron says uh—oh Harry let's go play Quidditch, after he—tells the two of them about Sirius Black, uh, in the—in the fourth book, and Hermione's *no*, Harry doesn't want to play Quidditch he wants to rest quietly, and

R—Harry says oh I'll go play Quidditch. Uh that happens again and again throughout the books. Um but—uh—I wanted to ask—I wanted to read a couple of passages to you. This is Hermione, talking about Cho. Um. She says, "'You just had to be nice to her,' said Hermione, looking up anxiously. 'You were, weren't you?' 'Well . . . ' said Harry, an unpleasant heat creeping up on his face. Hermione looked as though she was restraining herself from rolling her eyes with extreme difficulty. 'Well, I suppose it could have been worse,' she said. 'Are you going to see her again?' 'I'll have to, won't I?' said Harry. 'I've got DA meetings, haven't we?' 'You *know* what I mean,' said Hermione impatiently. Harry said nothing." Um. And it goes on his t—his thoughts. "'Oh well,' said Hermione distantly, buried in her letter once more. 'You'll have plenty of opportunities to ask her.'" Why is she an*noy*ed with Harry for not asking the girl out, you would think-

ATHENA: I don't have time to answer, thank you.

SARAH: Okay folks, it's time.

((*laughs*))

SARAH: For you all to get to ask your questions. Um, so—I'm gonna take—the first question, will be—to—the—this side, cause they started, um, so I want a question to the Ron/Hermione side, a challenge question. In the back, keep it short.

((*Transcriber's Note: Not only could I barely make out what was asked on the tape, I remember the lot of us having trouble deciphering it **during** the debate. The audience member rambled on about his beliefs for a while, until the mod cut him off.*))

SARAH: Okay. S-so the—the outstanding question is, did—do they feel that it sealed it, in Order of the Phoenix?

((*more questioner ramblings*))

ANGUA: What we feel is that

SARAH: [Two minutes.

ANGUA: The Order of the Phoenix was—was for uh, for—Ron, much like—uh the Goblet of Fire was for uh Hermione, in the Goblet of Fire Hermione was very, anxious about, her looks her desirability as a female, and Ron just *killed* that, I mean he—he made the troll remark, he didn't ask her to the ball, he made all these—these horribly insulting things implying that—Viktor only asked her, to get close to Harry, and *every* one of them was just like a stab to the heart of her—of her female insecurities. and then in—Order of the Phoenix it was the opposite way. Uh, Ron's insecurities are of course about his accomplishments, he gets a Prefect's badge, and—Hermione comes in is like *"Ron? Prefect?"*

((*laughs*))

ANGUA: you know, and—and then she criticizes him repeatedly for his performance as Prefect and then Quidditch comes along and you know, that he hopes to prove himself, and—and probably by the end of the book hoping that he'll win the girl, and instead he's *awful*, just horrible, and he comes in, and she says that line you know, oh well it's just your first time, and—he's all—he takes it—he takes it wrong, just like Hermione took the troll remark wrong, uh so it's—it's kind of a turnabout, she got humiliated in Goblet of Fire and he got humiliated in Order of the Phoenix, but they've both worked through it now, so we have great hopes for, the next book.

((*applause*))

SARAH: 'Kay. You have—you have one minute to respond.

ZORB: Yeah that shows they really understand each other really well, they know each other just *back* of their hand, and they can *really* empathize, can't they.

ANGUA: ((*muffled, but it was short*))

SARAH: Okay, if that's all, then we'll move onto: a question for—the—Harry/Hermione team. Um, the woman with yellow—lanyard I saw your hand go up first yeah, you.

((*Question asking the H/Hr team for their reasons why Ron and Hermione would not be a good couple.*))

SARAH: Okay. Did everybody hear the question? Okay, you have two minutes to respond.

ZORB: Well, first of all, uh, I think we can all agree at this point that Hermione is perfectly aware of how Ron feels about her because he's made it perfectly clear. And she doesn't seem to be responding to that. Why should they get together, why should she—*be* with him if she obviously *does not want* to be with him. That's a primary reason.

ATHENA: Yeah, just like I don't think she likes him in that way. I think she likes Harry that way and is keeping her feelings close to her vest, because she knows that at this point in time, Harry does not fancy her and she doesn't want to lose his friendship.

And since H—since *Ron* seems to have a crush on Hermione, if sh—if he were to find out that she—didn't *like* him, and like Harry instead she'd lose both her friends.

SARAH: Anything else? You have one minute to respond.

WAHLEE: Do you really think that Hermione is such a witch that she would deliberately sabotage a relationship that she worked so hard to bring about? Not only that but do you honestly think that she is so much of a—of a bad person that she would deliberately, um kiss Ron on the cheek knowing how he felt about her, um simply to an—an—wound his—his feelings and um excite um—harmful feelings and hopes perhaps, *knowing* that she know—that she know—that she knows that he likes her. Would she really do that? How—I mean—that—that just makes her an awful cruel person who I wouldn't want to see with either of the boys.

ZORB: Well first of all, we never said that she sabotaged the relationship. She-

WAHLEE: She [deliberately sabot-

ZORB: [She gave him advice, *after*wards, she did not—give him advice be*fore* he went to [(*muffled*) not sabotage.

ANGUA: [But Cho came back and *kissed him*, and she understood with*out* being told that Harry had to go to that interview because she could put two and two together she's a *Raven*claw, uh, and she forgave Harry *freely*, and Harry chose not to pursue it because frankly Cho is not the person for him.

ZORB: Uh despite the—still jealous remarks made by Cho about *darling* Hermione? [She *really* forgave him?

ANGUA: [Right, right, which makes Har—which makes Harry *laugh*.

SARAH: Stop. Question to the Ron/Hermione—in the back.

((*Question asking something like, "You've said that Hermione isn't the right girl for Harry because she's bossy, she's a know-it-all, and so on. So how come the same reasoning doesn't apply to Ron?"*))

SARAH: Okay. [Okay, thank you. You have two minutes.

ANGUA: [That's an excellent—excellent question. Uh, the thing is that Harry and Ron are very different people. Ron was brought up being bossed around by Molly, he understands that is love? Harry was brought up being bossed around by Petunia and Vernon, he understands that as—not love. And—th—the bossy thing with Hermione, it's *class*ic for the male-female bickering relationship you have—bossy Leia, you have—bossy uh—*Darc*y. It's—it's just part of the cliché, but for—Harry and Hermione it would be a best friend, *harmony* relationship it's com*plete*ly unsuited for that and it's very one-sided. Harry does not have the—wherewithal to respond he prefers to—avoid it instead, while Ron, steps up to the mic every time, and answers her right back. That's the difference between them.

((*applause*))

SARAH: Okay. Uh one minute to respond.

ZORB: In Order of the Phoenix we re*pea*tedly see Harry and Hermione arguing but not only do they argue, as Ron and Hermione do, but they apologize, to one another, at the end.

((*applause*))

ANGUA: But we don't see Harry calling uh Hermione honestly the most wonderful person who he's ever met in the world, and h—h—having cute little banter, like uh where Ron says "And if I'm ever rude to you again" and Hermione saying "I'll know we're back to normal."

ZORB: [Well yeah, she's doing his homework for him, I'd say ((*laugh*)) he'd say that.

[((*applause*))

SARAH: Finished? I think we're—I think we're done. I'm sorry did you-

TIMEKEEPER: They have one minute.

SARAH: One minute?

ATHENA: Harry jumped on Hermione, at one point, and then she turned around and said, if you don't—stop jumping on my back, (*muffled*) I—I'm on your side and—then he realized and he said, I'm sorry, you *don't* see any resolution between Ron and Hermione. Harry winds up even leaving the room because he can't stand their bickering and sniping at one another.

SARAH: Question to this side?

((*Two questions—the first was about JKR's interviews, and second was asking for an explanation of the summer, with Ron and Hermione alone for a month at Grimmauld Place.*))

ZORB: Well, for the second one, they spent the month cleaning.

((*laughs*))

ZORB: And for the first one, how—how would it make sense for her [JKR] to *also* tell us, that she wants to keep things close to her chest, and to talk about feelings between the *three* of them, and—somehow also at the same time be giving straight answers *which* by the way she is not, when she gives straight answers, she says things like, "Her maiden name was Evans, and she was in Gryffindor," "Yep, James, after his dad." She doesn't answer things with a question and we all know, that answering questions with a question is avoidance.

((*applause*))

ATHENA: She *dodges* things, this page is a list of quotes, from chat sessions in which things are contradicted in canon. And, one of which, was a question, "People on the internet want to know if Gilderoy Lockhart is going to come back." Her answer, "Gilderoy Lockhart, bless him, is currently residing in St. Mungo's Hospital for Magical Maladies and Injuries and his memory is still gone. So at the moment, he's in no fit state to go anywhere which I think serves him right." The questioner, unlike Katie Couric, um said, "You didn't quite answer the question as to whether or not he will be back or not." "Yeah, well, you know, you've got to sometimes dodge these things." She never answered Katie Couric. She went, and dodged, and Katie Couric never followed through.

WAHLEE: She—she never answered Katie Couric when she said, "Do you really think so? No, Ron and Hermione, that's—there's more tension there."

((*applause*))

ZORB: That's—she did not say no.

ATHENA: No-

ZORB: She said-

WAHLEE: Do you want me to play it I have it on my computer.

((*applause*))

ANGUA: I would like to mention a different occasion when someone said "Do, Harry and Hermione have a date," and she said, "No. [They're very platonic friends."

ZORB: [In that book.

ATHENA: And they may never *have* a date but they may still get together and never have a date.

ANGUA: But no is not an avoidance or a quest—uh answering with uh—a question. She said "No, they're *very*, platonic, friends."

ZORB: In that book.

ANGUA: She didn't say that.

WAHLEE: And in the next book, too. [The time limit-

ZORB: [She didn't say-

WAHLEE: The time limit that you've been giving on these has been gradually getting longer.

ZORB: Yeah just like [Ron and Hermione's kiss.

SARAH: [Okay, stop, stop. Okay. Was that four questions? Okay. We're gonna move on now to the closing statements uh—first to you.

ANGUA: All right, *we*, as human beings-

SARAH: Three minutes.

ANGUA: Are—are romantic. We're—we're shippers here, we put everyone together we put Dobby and the Giant Squid together.

((*laughs*))

ANGUA: We have in these books—we have Harry and Hermione who *love* each other deeply, and they're both wonderful people, the main—the main ma—fe—male, in the book and the main female in the book. And, the m-mistake—of thinking—of mistaking their, platonic love, for romantic love, is the easiest one in the world to make. Uh, *that's* why, it's one of the few things, that J.K. Rowling, will tell us about in an interview. *Three* separate times, she's g—four really a negative, type of response, to questions about whether, Harry and Hermione get together because, she understands, that—that is a natural mistake to make. Now, *in the books*, if you look, all the evidence is, w—what—what Wahlee showed us, Ron and Hermione have long discussions about boy-girl stuff, they get together, and argue about who Ron should go to balls with whether Hermione should hang around with Krum, they show—she shows tenderness—between them as she shows—the classic signs of romantic attachment in fiction which she follows to the letter, *blushes, tears, staring*, I have a list of seventeen times in the book where she mentions that—Ron is staring at Hermione, and I used to have problems because—Harry didn't stare back at Ron that much, un*til* we get to *this* book, and she's always, H—Hermione looked up at Ron and her frostiness seemed to melt, or Hermione jumped up when he—he comes in the door. Hermione watches him, uh, and tells Harry, th—you know, to keep Ron from looking at the Slytherin badges th—the girl is watching the boy in this book, and you're not gonna find, if you look through this book, quotes like that about, Harry, staring at Hermione or Hermione staring at Harry, it just doesn't occur. Um.

SARAH: (*muffled*)

ANGUA: So, um. The other side likes to talk about Harry and Hermione's relationship which I think is a wonderful frienship, as if they read each other—each other's minds. Th—th—the problem is, that once you start, with the as*sum*ption, that they're romantic you start re-interpreting everything as romantic actually, Harry and Ron read each other's minds constantly in Order of the Phoenix, it's happening all the time, they looked at each other, Harry knew that Ron was thinking what he was thinking. Ron and Hermione read each other's minds, all the time they work together, when uh— Harry is hurt they—they—you know one instinctively takes one side, one instinctively takes the other, it's—um—it's friendship. The thing about—the—the evidence that the other side gives for—Harry and Hermione being—such—such soul-mates as they sometimes say—it's *friend*ship evidence, you can always say, yeah, as Harry does, to Viktor Krum, yeah, because we're *friends*.

((*applause*))

SARAH: You have three minutes for your first closing.

ZORB: I don't presume to know JKR's *thoughts*, but, I'd say, that this woman who has been *so*: adept, at hiding clues from us, throughout these books, has *got* to know, that she is making an equal case, fo—with the bickering cliché, as she is, with the best friends turned lovers cliché. And it seems to me that the other side has been trying to de*bunk* us as a cliché, that's too common, everyone ex*pects* the hero and heroine to get together, but they're making the case that their cliché is somehow right, and there's no—evidence saying that that's somehow better. If it's invalid for us, why isn't in—it—why isn't it invalid for them. The one thing I do: want to address is that notion of, mothering, that she *does*, as a questioner said, do the same thing to Ron. It's really not that different and you can make that *just friends* case for exactly, the same, Ron-Hermione interactions that is tried to make in Harry-Hermione interactions. The trick, with ship debating, is *not* so say, oh that's just friends, oh that's just friends, not to ignore the other side's evidence, but to ac*cept* it, and try to move beyond that, and find things that prove, your s—case, in more favor, than something that can be explained away, as just friends, and what we believe, is that Hermione has shown distinct, evidence, that she does *not*, want Ron's affections, she is trying to a*void*, being alone with him and trying to, uh—brush off his gestures. Her *sole* focus in these books is on Harry, and making sure that *Harry* is happy, and making sure that *Harry* is safe. And that is—for the moment, that is her goal, aside from—becoming Head Girl, presumably.

((*laughs*))

ZORB: But even that, even *that* is not as important to her now, she's willing to completely *blow off* this Prefect status, in order to—come up with and be second in command, of Dumbledore's Army. Which, if you read—reread all those scenes, you see Harry and Hermione and Harry and Hermione and Harry and Hermione, and then maybe a little Ron, Harry and Hermione-

((*laughs*))

ZORB: Harry and Hermione, Harry and Hermione, and maybe Ron, sometimes there's a little bit of Luna, too, how about some Neville? And it's just them over and over and over again, the—showing that that's where she's thinking, her thoughts are tending towards Harry, and—*we* think that—this is a crafty girl, and she's gonna get what she wants in the end.

((*applause*))

SARAH: Okay, you have three minutes for your second closing statement.

WAHLEE: We talk about the dueling clichés, the girl next door, versus the bickering couple. And—um—it often seems like we're saying one is more valid than the other. But in fact, it seems as though JK Rowling is developing them both. You get the bickering couple with Ron and Hermione. And then you get, crush, best friend's little sister turned romantic interest in Harry/Ginny. Um-

((applause))

WAHLEE: Um our—our esteemed—opponents—um mentioned that in Order of the Phoenix, we see a lot of Harry and Hermione Harry and Hermione Harry and Hermione with—a little bit of Ron thrown in, actually, we did a search of the books and found out that the phrase "Ron and Hermione" is used a hundred and seventy-five times in Order of the Phoenix. The phrase "Harry and Hermione" is used, forty-one.

((audience murmurs, shushed))

WAHLEE: And, it—and even though it is compared to the fact that the book is also in third-person, which means that any interaction between Harry and Hermione, (will?) usually be ref—referenced by—Harry and Hermione, the—the—the fact is that—um—Ro—that Harry comes back from Quidditch practices, Harry comes back from detentions, and Ron and Hermione are together. If Hermione was so anxious to avoid Ron's—company, she should have gone to her parents' for the summer, instead of staying for a month with him, at Grimmauld Place. In addition to that, they say that Hermione has—a—a sole focus on Harry, but the fact is that Hermione's focused also on Ron. She pays very much attention to not only, his feelings, and um being very concerned about he feels about his Quidditch performance, and being just as happy for **Ron** when he wins the Quidditch Cup, as she was for Harry, they both beamed up at him which is a direct parallel, to when Harry and Her—Harry—Hermione and Ron beamed up at Harry at the Quidditch Cup. But also, Hermione is very anxious about what Ron thinks of her, and—very anxious about, um, what Ron—how Ron per*ceives* her as if he per*ceives* her as a girl, he per*ceives* her as intelligent. She's always extremely proud of when he—when he—gives her compliments, even the backhanded ones. And speaking of backhanded compliments, they're **all over** in the bickering couple relationship people say when someone says something like, you know, "You—you're *really* good at it, why do you try and rub it in," type of-

((The tape cut off here. I was caught up in the debate at the time and didn't notice it had stopped rolling. All that it missed was the end of Wahlee's conclusion and all of Athena's closing statement, which Athena has attempted to reconstruct. Keep in mind that the following is not verbatim from the debate; it is based on Athena's notes taken at the time.))

ATHENA: First off I wanted to respond to the idea of Hermione *choosing* to spend her summer at Number 12 Grimmauld Place. Maybe I'm just being paranoid and channeling Mad-Eye Moody here with *"Constant Vigilance!"*, but I think she was there for security purposes. I would think that shortly after the Fidelius Charm was performed that she and the Weasleys were taken there to protect them from becoming targets due to their close relationship with Harry. That being said, I wanted to go back to the Couric interview and explain why I don't think that you should take it at face value. I believe that Rowling was playing poker with us. Because it doesn't make any sense for her to freely give away her romantic pairings *in one interview* when there was another one on BBC where she was totally different. "JEREMY PAXMAN: So there will be some pairing up will there in this book? JK ROWLING: Well *in the fullness of time.* JEREMY PAXMAN: Unlikely pairings? Not Hermione and Draco Malfoy or anything like that?

((*cheers*))

ATHENA: "JK ROWLING: I don't really want to say as it will ruin all the fan sites. They have such fun with their theories . . . and it is fun, it is fun. And some of them even get quite close. No-one has ever—I have gone and looked at some of it and no-one's ever . . . There is one thing that if anyone guessed I would be really annoyed as it is kind of the heart of it all. And it kind of explains everything and no-one's quite got there but a couple of people have skirted it. So you know, I would be pretty miffed after thirteen or fourteen years of writing the books if someone just came along and said I think this will happen in book seven. Because it is too late, I couldn't divert now, everything has been building up to it, and I've laid all my clues." *Exactly.* She doesn't want to spoil our fun and she doesn't want us to know what is going to happen at the end. *So why* would she freely offer shipping info to Katie Couric? It doesn't follow logically, unless she was trying to *avoid the question*, which is what I think she was doing. Because I think that Love is going to play a big role in the resolution of the series. At the end of the Order of Phoenix, Dumbledore told Harry about the permanently locked room in the Department of Mysteries that holds a force "more wonderful and terrible than death, than human intelligence, than forces of nature." That would have to be *the Power of Love.* And there is no other female character that comes close to showing that kind of loyalty, dedication and love for Harry than Hermione. And to close, I would like to say that ovaries *are not* trivial in shipping debates.

Emily Bytheway is from Murray, Utah. She recently graduated from Brigham Young University with a B.A. in English with an editing emphasis. Now she is desperately trying to figure out what to do with the rest of her life. Emily first read Harry Potter in April 2000 and has been hooked ever since. In September 2001, she started to become involved in the Harry Potter online fandom, including the shipping debates at FictionAlley. Her fan fiction is archived at Sugar Quill, Gryffindor Tower, and the Astronomy Tower (at FictionAlley). In addition to Harry Potter, Emily enjoys reading Jane Austen, J.R.R. Tolkien, L.M. Montgomery, P.G. Wodehouse and Erle Stanley Gardner. She also enjoys singing and ballroom dancing, although she's not very good at either.

Susan Faust lives in Houston with her husband, two children, two cats and a dog. She grew up in Alabama and Florida, and acquired all three of her degrees—a Bachelor of Arts, a Bachelor of Architecture, and a Master of Business Administration—from Rice University in Houston, Texas. After a longish career as an architect and a shorter one as a commodities trading risk manager, Susan left the working world in 2000 to become a stay-at-home mom. An avid Harry Potter reader since the summer of 1999, Susan entered the online fandom as 'Angua' or 'Angua9'. She participates in discussions at FictionAlley, HPforGrownups, and Sugar Quill (where she is a 'Forum Ghost'). Her novel-length fan fiction, Harry Potter and the Fifth Year from Hell, is posted at FictionAlley and Sugar Quill.

Sara Goetz is an undergraduate student at the University of California, San Diego, working towards a B.S. degree in Cognitive Science, with a specialization in Human-Computer Interaction. To feed her liberal arts side, she also has a minor in Theatre, and her involvement in the Harry Potter fandom is encouraging her to take one in Literatures of the World as well. Online, she has written for the Star Trek, X-Files, and Harry Potter fandoms under the penname Zorb, and is currently a FictionAlley coder and eMentor. Offline, she enjoys science fiction and fantasy movies and books, as well as acting and stage managing. Her post-graduation goals are as yet unknown, but as long as she can have an Internet connection and live in close proximity to the beach, she'll be happy.

Sarah Goff is a degree student in English Literature at Baruch College of the City University of New York, focusing on the intersection of history and gender studies. She holds a B.S. from Cornell University and a M.B.A. in Information Systems from Rensselaer Polytechnic Institute, and recently delivered a paper on representations of single women in the fiction and journals of LM Montgomery at the fifth international biennial conference on Life Writing. Ms. Goff currently works as a project manager in the consulting industry and lives in Manhattan.

Linda McCabe has been a political activist with the National Organization for Women since 1989 and is currently the chair of the California NOW's hate crimes task force. She's been a speaker at California NOW and National NOW conferences as well as a speaker at a Northern California ACLU conference. She wrote and recorded a series of the top 25 Most Censored News Stories in a joint effort between Project Censored and KRCB public radio. This series was made available to public radio stations nationwide and was broadcast in dozens of radio markets. She is a clinical laboratory scientist by profession and received a Master's degree from Sonoma State University as an historian of science. She presented the findings of her thesis: The Evolution of the Cultural Image of the Cave Man at a joint meeting between an American, British and Canadian history of science organizations. She wrote her first novel as a Harry Potter fan fiction and is currently writing her own original novel as well as pursuing opportunities to publish her master's thesis. She is a member of the California Writer's Club and has over twenty-five years' public speaking experience.

Publishing on Potter: Dodging the Bludgers

A Panel Discussion
M. Katherine Grimes, Moderator

Six authors and editors of books about the Harry Potter series discussed their experiences in publishing on J. K. Rowling's works at Nimbus 2003: A Harry Potter Symposium in Orlando July 19, 2003. The session, entitled "Publishing on Potter: Dodging the Bludgers," was proposed and organized by Lana A. Whited of Ferrum College (Ferrum, Va.); Dr. Whited edited a collection of essays, *The Ivory Tower and Harry Potter: Perspectives on a Literary Phenomenon* (University of Missouri Press, 2002).

Joining Dr. Whited on the panel were the following authors and editors:

- **Giselle Liza Anatol** of University of Kansas, Lawrence, editor of *Reading Harry Potter: Critical Essays* (Greenwood Press, 2003);
- **John Granger**, author of *The Hidden Key to Harry Potter* (Zossima Press, 2003);
- **Edmund M. Kern** of Lawrence University, Appleton, Wisconsin, author of *The Wisdom of Harry Potter: What Our Favorite Hero Teaches Us About Moral Choices* (Prometheus Books, 2003);
- **Connie Neal**, author of *What's a Christian to Do with Harry Potter?* (WaterBrook Press, 2001) and *The Gospel According to Harry Potter* (Westminster John Knox Press, 2002); and
- **Philip Nel**, Kansas State University, author of *J. K. Rowling's Harry Potter Novels: A Reader's Guide* (2001).

Dr. Nel and the moderator, M. Katherine Grimes of Ferrum College, both have essays in Dr. Whited's book.

In addition to the six panelists, Penny Linsenmayer, Esq., co-chair of the Programming Committee for Nimbus 2003, was invited to discuss legal issues surrounding the organization of the conference.

Panelists responded to questions from the moderator and from the audience. Much of the discussion centered on obstacles the authors and editors encountered in their dealings with J. K. Rowling's agents at the Christopher Little Agency; with her publishers, Bloomsbury in the United Kingdom and Scholastic in the United States; and with Warner Brothers, which owns the movie and merchandising rights to Rowling's work.

For most of the panelists, their book on Harry Potter was their first foray into the publishing field. Because of interactions with Rowling's representatives, these novice writers and editors of books felt baptized by fire. Philip Nel let Warner Brothers read his entire manuscript and altered a sentence about a legal issue to suit that company. The Christopher Little Agency denied Lana Whited the right to quote from any of Rowling's works and advised that the title she originally proposed, "Harry Potter and the Ivory Tower," might constitute "false designation of origin," a trademark infringement. Dr. Whited asked each of her contributors to cut most quotations so that no more than 500 words, generally considered fair use, was quoted from any one Rowling work. She also reversed the nouns in her title to avoid the possibility of a reader's thinking that her work was the next Rowling novel.

Giselle Anatol exclaimed that she would have been grateful to quote 500 words from each novel, as a representative from Scholastic had originally told her that 100 words per work was maximum, then, apparently having forgotten what she had said, subsequently allowed 300 words from each Rowling book. Dr. Anatol also read from letters she had received from Scholastic, including a statement that the publisher did not approve of "spin-offs" of the Potter series and an explanation that the author herself should write any potential "companion books" to her own series.

Edmund Kern, author of the latest Potter book published by any member of the panel, said that his experience had been less difficult. His theory about the apparent lack of concern from Rowling's representatives is that there have now been so many books on the Potter series with no apparent deleterious effects on book and box office sales that Rowling's agents and publishers are expending less energy in trying to stifle scholarly works.

Connie Neal, the panelist with the most publishing experience, said that her publishers advised her not to ask permission to quote, as it would probably be denied. Because her books look at the Potter series from a distinctly Christian perspective, Ms. Neal presumes that Rowling's representatives are grateful that she is defending the series against attacks from many in Christian media. Ms. Neal's publishers did have attorneys examine her books before publication to ensure that Rowling's agent and publishers would have no grounds for legal action.

John Granger explained that his book was published with money lent him by generous and supportive friends. Therefore, he did not work through a publisher, who might have been more cautious than he was himself. He explained that a lawsuit would have gained those who sued him nothing, as his primary assets are his seven children, whom a judge would probably never award to Rowling and her agents.

Penny Linsenmayer, an attorney, discussed contacts that she and other members of the Nimbus 2003 planning group made with Rowling's representatives, whom she had found relatively agreeable. Nimbus 2003 was careful not to used logos created or owned by Warner Brothers, Scholastic, or Bloomsbury; instead, the program, web site, t-shirts, and other materials used graphics suggested by the Harry Potter series but created especially for the conference. Because Nimbus 2003 drew attention to Rowling's books and the Warner Brothers movies and could not be perceived as competing with them, it was apparently perceived as less threatening.

One of the common requests of Rowling's representatives is that authors and editors post a disclaimer, preferably on the front of each book, stating that J. K. Rowling is not affiliated with the project. All the authors and editors on the panel, with the exception of Dr. Whited, included that disclaimer, either on the front of the book or on the copyright page. Dr. Whited explained that neither she nor her publisher found the disclaimer necessary. In most other cases, the publishers made the decisions about posting the statement, and the panel members did not object. The conference program also carries the disclaimer.

Members of the audience were interested in the sales records of the books written or edited by the panelists. Connie Neal replied that she has sold 40,000 copies of her Harry Potter books, a number that elicited gasps from other panelists. Phil Nel's book has been lucrative, as well, providing income that has allowed him to work on books that he knows will be less popular. John Granger also reported fairly high sales of his book and videotapes of the lectures from which the book grew. Lana Whited's book is somewhat more typical of an academic work, although its first printing of 1200 copies was 150% of the regular run, and even that sold out in the first five months. Giselle Anatol's and Edmund Kerns's books are too new for sales figures to be relevant.

Panelists and members of the audience discussed at length the question of whether Rowling's representatives' attitudes toward scholarship about the Harry Potter series would affect the longevity of the books' popularity, their critical acclaim, and their entry into the literary canon, especially the canon of children's literature.

The letters read by Dr. Anatol, which used the words "spin-off" and "companion books," generated the most discussion, prompting panelists and audience members to speculate on the ignorance of some mainstream publishers about scholarly criticism. As the term "spin-off" is usually used in television to indicate a series involving a character or characters who first appeared on another show (for example, *The Jeffersons* and *Maude* spun off from *All in the Family*), that term might apply to fan fiction, but certainly not to critical volumes or even to companion guides. In addition, that a publisher cannot distinguish between a companion book or reader's guide, such as Dr. Nel's, and a collection of essays about the series, such as Dr. Anatol's, indicates a lack of understanding of scholarship. It is also extremely uncommon for an author to write companion books to his or her own novels. In addition, the Christopher Little Agency had asserted that Dr. Whited's use of the term "Ivory Tower" was derogatory; as Dr. Whited explained, if the term criticizes anyone, it is the community of scholars and neither the Harry Potter series nor J. K. Rowling. Phil Nel and others pointed out that Neil Blair of the Christopher Little Agency formerly worked for Warner Brothers.

The group generally agreed that the misunderstanding of and apparent disdain for scholarship among Rowling's agents would create an obstacle for her works, although probably not as large an obstacle as the commercialization and merchandising of the series. When the Harry Potter books first became popular, children advertised them by word of mouth. When rights were sold to Warner Brothers and trinkets flooded discount stores, literary purists were repelled. Many children's literature scholars became resentful that these works were receiving so much attention while books they find superior are virtually unknown outside the academy.

Panelists suggested and audience members agreed that the hubbub will have to die down before the works can receive the serious critical attention that will determine their place in the canon of children's literature, and Rowling's agents must understand that in the realm of literature, copyright, not trademark, is the important legal issue. It was generally agreed that the attitude of Warner Brothers and Rowling's publishers and agent might not be the author's, as J. K. Rowling is probably too busy writing to micromanage her property. Perhaps when she finishes her series and considers her place in the future of children's literature, she will encourage the kind of scholarly attention being given her work by panelists in "Publishing on Potter: Dodging the Bludgers" and by other presenters at Nimbus 2003.

Dr. Nel is an Assistant Professor of English at Kansas State University, where he teaches courses in children's literature, including one devoted to Harry Potter. He is the author of J.K. Rowling's Harry Potter Novels: A Reader's Guide (2001) and The Avant-Garde and American Postmodernity: Small Incisive Shocks (2002). His next book will be Dr. Seuss: American Icon (forthcoming in 2004).

Dr. Anatol is an Assistant Professor of English at the University of Kansas, where she teaches classes on Caribbean literature, writing by women of the African diaspora, and children's literature. Her collection of essays entitled Reading Harry Potter: Critical Essays was recently published by Greenwood Press.

Once Upon a Time-Turner:
A History of the Harry Potter Fandom

Mai Pucik (Moderator), Amy Gordanier, Maddy Klink

This panel served both as a trip down nostalgia lane for those familiar with the online Harry Potter fan community, and an outline of its activities for those not so familiar. Starting in August 1999, the month in which the first widely known fan stories were posted and before The Prisoner of Azkaban was even published in the US, we went on an overview of the fandom trend by trend and wave by wave, from the first wave, when everyone knew everyone else and had read all of everyone else's stories, to the fifth wave of the Summer of 2003, where thousands of fans were debating, drawing, and writing about all aspects of the five novels, two movies, and plethora of supplemental modes and texts that then made up the universe J.K. Rowling created.

Among the trends discussed was the tendency for fan stories (otherwise known as "fanfiction") to get longer and longer, the rise and fall in popularity of various fan authors and theorists, the affect the movies had on changing the way characters were viewed, and the increasing reliance on minor character information and other supplemental materials to create new theories and stories as more aspects of the main storyline were explored.

In the brief question-and-answer session at the end of the panel, brief discussions between panelists and the mostly fandom-familiar audience members expanded the issues of terminology, chronology and categorization that the panelists had used.

Amy Gordanier was too old for Harry Potter until the summer of 1999—when, at age 14, she read the first two books out of self-defense. So, of course, she read Harry Potter and the Prisoner of Azkaban as soon as it came out, and discovered online fandom (such as it was) very shortly afterward. She got the Mary Sues out of her system early on thanks to a role-playing message board, and has since written a handful of fan fiction and much more wild speculation. Amy lives in Massachusetts, but in Fall, 2003, fall she'll be embarking on the Great College Adventure at Reed College, in Oregon.

Madeline Klink, known as "Flourish" in the Harry Potter online community, has been studying the Harry Potter books and writing Harry Potter fan fiction since November 1999. A rising freshman at Reed College in Oregon, she is currently writing her first non-fiction book, a guide to the weird world of online fandoms.

Mai Pucik is a rising junior at Swarthmore College, Pennsylvania, her major as yet undetermined. She discovered the Harry Potter books in the fall of 1999, shortly followed by the online community, and has been active in the fandom ever since. Her non-Potter interests include historical naval fiction, paleobiology, and classical music. When not at college she resides in Switzerland with her parents, older brother, and the mortal remains of four gerbils.

Fanwords:
The Evolution of Vernacular in the Harry Potter Fandom

Mai Pucik

Every hobby that involves socializing among its hobbyists will eventually evolve its own distinctive vocabulary. In fandoms such as that of Harry Potter, the development and turnover of such words takes place more rapidly than ever due to the wide-ranging and frequent contact allowed between large numbers of fans by the Internet setting.

This vernacular of fandom words or "fanwords" can be divided into two categories. The first consists of conversational slang, playful in meaning and ephemeral in use. The second category is tied to the writing of fanfiction, stories which as their name indicates are written by fans to take place within the universe they love. Such fanwords are technical terms which refer to constructs and techniques in fanfiction that are either less frequent or nonexistent in original fiction. These words evolve slowly, and are more likely to be borrowed from other fandoms than to be reinvented entirely.

Until recently, the Harry Potter fandom was so large that its vocabulary was segmented; many parts of the community only rarely affiliated with each other, and you could identify a fan's normal online hangout by listening to his—or more usually her—words. Universal terms were rare and usually belonged to the second group of fanwords, as the writing of fanfiction was the main form of community intersection.

However, the increased popularity of LiveJournal.org and other online diary sites in early 2002 caused the fandom to consider itself increasingly in terms of one large group of individuals linked, journal to journal, and less in the sense of multiple congregations of fans loosely connected by a common interest. This transformation led to individual fanwords becoming more widespread among Harry Potter fans, but the change is not complete and future developments remain to be seen.

Mai Pucik is a rising junior at Swarthmore College, Pennsylvania, her major as yet undetermined. She discovered the Harry Potter books in the fall of 1999, shortly followed by the online community, and has been active in the fandom ever since. Her non-Potter interests include historical naval fiction, paleobiology, and classical music. When not at college she resides in Switzerland with her parents, older brother, and the mortal remains of four gerbils.

Don't Tell the Grownups:
Subversion in the Harry Potter Fandom

Catherine Tosenberger

J.K. Rowling's Harry Potter series is a worldwide publishing phenomena, a bestseller of gargantuan proportions. As the release of *Harry Potter and the Order of the Phoenix*, the fifth book in the series, drew near, excited readers prepared to let out the collective breath they'd been holding for the past three years. However, a great many of the most devoted aficionados of Harry Potter had not been content merely to wait for the next book to further their enjoyment of the series; they had gone online in great droves to swap gossip and speculation, draw pictures, and, most especially, create new stories based in the Harry Potter universe. At last count, there were approximately 150,000 individual Harry Potter (hereafter abbreviated as HP) stories written by fans, concerning the continuing adventures of Harry, Ron, Hermione, Snape, and other favorite characters.

Many of these narratives (termed "fanfiction," "fics," or "fanfics") are being produced by the children and young adults whom the series is marketed to; however, an enormous volume of stories are produced by adults, who have likewise been captivated by the series. While the production of fanfiction is not a new phenomena, the immense depth and breadth of the HP fandom's literary activity, inextricably intertwined with the technology of the World Wide Web that fostered and distributed the activities of the fandom, is unique. The high speed nature of Internet communication, as well as the comparatively long wait between books, has engendered a body of fan literature that covers every imaginable permutation of genre and romantic pairing, with semi-literate net-speak atrocities tumbled into fic archives next to sophisticated examinations of intertextuality; in addition, HP fanfiction has made considerable inroads into traditionally taboo areas of discourse, particularly incest, and created thoughtful and intelligent explorations of difficult topics, through the medium of recursive literature. HP fanfiction constitutes, I will argue, a thriving and legitimate literary genre that is ripe for scholarly examination, particularly at this time of simultaneous excitement and crisis regarding the arrival of new canon.

Media fandom is a relatively new arena of cultural and literary studies, but several scholars have already contributed important texts to further general understanding of that much-maligned subgroup of media consumers. Henry Jenkins is one of the most important commentators on fan practices and production, not only for his brilliant elucidation of the structuralist and postmodernist theories that underpin the practice of fandom, but also for his unabashed participation in and celebration of fan culture, which he chronicles in *Textual Poachers: Television Fans and Participatory Culture* (1992).

Following and refining the theories of Michel de Certeau, Jenkins has articulated a conception of fans as "readers who appropriate popular texts and reread them in a fashion that serves different interests, as spectators who transform the experience of watching television into a rich and complex participatory culture" (Jenkins 23). Fans are not simply Adorno's passive consumers of the culture industry, but active participants in an

"interpretive community"—indeed, fannish responses can be a site of resistance to the induced readings of the culture brokers, as fans have a multiplicity of ironic, transformative, and occasionally irreverent responses to their chosen texts.

Intertextuality

So what makes HP so appealing as a source-text for fanfiction? A major component of the appeal is, I believe, that Rowling's text is a mishmash of genres, both straight and parodied: school story, fantasy, Gothic, sports story, fairy tale, bildungsroman, romance, horror, mystery, et cetera. John Fiske calls this horizontal intertextuality: "relations . . . between primary texts that are more or less explicitly linked, usually along the axes of genre, character, or content." One of the simplest methods of writing an HP fanfic is to take a narrative thread—say, Harry's relationship to Draco, which follows the coding of school-story rivals—and switch it to romance. Many fans have spoken intelligently and articulately on the subject of intertextuality, and there are several writers who enjoy experimenting with specific literary genres and styles; Silvia Kundera's love of magical realism, as well as her Harry/Draco (hereinafter H/D) stories done in the style of Kurt Vonnegut and Milan Kundera, are especially well-known, as are Cassandra Claire's Symbolist-inflected shorts "A Season in Hell" and "After the Flood." Fanfic itself, under Fiske's schema, displays vertical intertextuality, which is "that between a primary text, such as a television program or series, and other texts of a different type that explicitly refer to it" (Fiske 219). Even more in keeping with Fiske's notion of intertextuality is the extensive and wide-ranging fanon. However, the true nature of the HP fandom is far more complex than Fiske's model will allow for; witness the concomitant tendency for fanfiction to not only interact with the canon, and with outside literary texts, but also with *other fan stories*. Silvia Kundera is again one of the foremost examples: her characterization of Draco is a witty, and conscious, subversion of the suave, sexy, impossibly brilliant and cool Draco of fanon, as enshrined in countless other fics (most (most famously, Cassandra Claire's "Draco Trilogy").

The concept of genre and intertextuality ties into Eco's ideas about closed and open texts. Closed texts are:

> Those texts that obsessively aim at arousing a precise response on the
> part of more or less precise empirical readers (be they children, soap-

> opera addicts, doctors, law-abiding citizens, swingers, Presbyterians,
> farmers, middle-class women, scuba divers, effete snobs, or any other
> imaginable sociopsychological category) are in fact open to any possible
> "aberrant" decoding. (Eco 8)

There is a link here to the semiotic overcoding that Janice Radway notes is a feature of the romance, and indeed, of any number of genre texts. The HP books would seem, on the surface, to be closed, as they are classed and marketed as children's fantasy, a hybrid genre with a very specific set of conventions, not to mention the fact that the presence of such an enormous amount of fanfiction testifies to the series' ability to support

"'aberrant' decodings." Although the gleefully intertextual nature of the series does complicate this reading, by providing a cacophony of sometimes mutually contradictory generic codes, in general, HP canon seems to qualify as a more-or-less "closed" text. Much of the fanfiction, especially that which is aiming at simple genre inscription (such as many of the "traditional" Harry/Ginny romance/marriage fics), also follow this pattern of precise coding for precise readership, but available and comprehensible to all.

However, there exist a number of fanfics, particularly among the more sophisticated writers, that complicate their texts further, and approach or achieve what

Eco calls "open" texts:

> You cannot use the text as you want, but only as the text wants you to
> use it. An open text, however "open" it be, cannot afford whatever
> interpretation. An open text outlines a "closed" project of its Model
> Reader as a component of its structural strategy. (9)

Many of Silvia Kundera's stories utilize a combination of her typically minimalist style and a loose narrative structure to make her fic rather difficult for a non-Model Reader that is, one not familiar with the fanon characterization of Draco, the vast range of HP fanfiction clichés, and Silvia's own conflicted readings of canon. In her "Double Dare," Draco's anarchistic sense of camp—a major component of fanon Draco that Silvia harnesses to her own ends—disrupts and derails not only the other character's expectations, but the narrative structure itself. "And Now for Something Completely Different" is an examination of the boy-turns-into-a-girl trope that was extremely popular in popslash (the N'Sync/Backstreet Boys fandom) about three years ago; here, Harry's transformation and affair with Draco is surreally sidelined, and the focus shifts to Ron and Hermione, whose own relationship is proceeding in a far more conflicted manner.

Marvolo, Rhoddlet, and Ravenchel are also known for their oblique and multilayered stories, which are virtually incomprehensible to "outsiders" unfamiliar with their fanon readings of *Chamber of Secrets*, particularly the relationships among Ginny, Percy, Tom, and Harry. The characterization of Ginny is especially affected by these authors; what

James Kincaid calls the "Gothic" cultural narrative of child molestation is rendered literally, well, Gothic. Tom's possession of Ginny, which can be read as metaphorical rape in canon, has often been figured as literal rape in fanon. A great deal of the more thoughtful and interesting Ginny stories are haunted by Tom Riddle, whether he actually appears or not; there is much speculation on the emotional aftermath of that experience, and how Ginny's relationships with Harry and her family will be affected, and how what Kincaid calls our cultural narrative of molestation applies. An enormous number of fics show her being (implicitly) healed by the love of a good man (usually Harry); some show her seeking out increasingly self-destructive relationships, particularly with Draco, and perhaps even becoming a Death Eater herself (Holographis' "A Thousand Words"); still others argue that Ginny's susceptibility to Tom Riddle stems from her having been abused in the past, usually by one or more of her brothers (Ivy's "Your Darkest Voice" and Ravenchel's "Repetition" series). Marvolo and Rhoddlet were among the first to point out Percy's status as a) sole defender of Ginny throughout the majority of CoS, and b) red herring, and to elaborate upon that relationship.

Slash

No discussion of subversion would be complete without a mention of slash. Probably the most important subgenre of HP fanfic, it is concerned with a romantic or sexual relationship between members of the same sex. As the most visible and intriguing "site of rupture" (textually and sexually) it is an area of great interest to critics. Much of the scholarship on the subject has focused upon the seeming incongruity between the fact that most writers of male/male slash are female—though not all, as is usually asserted, straight; one of the better-known articles on slash is entitled, after a direct quote from a fan, "Normal Female Interest in Men Bonking" (Green, Jenkins, and Jenkins). Constance Penley's studies have proved most influential; citing de Certeau, Penley characterizes slash as a radical act, as a guerilla action involving "hit-and-run acts" of cultural seizure, enacted by the powerless in order to claim a share in the dominant discourse (Penley 139). It's an explicitly political and liberatory reading of slash fandom, and slash fans and writers argue for and against the merits of this interpretation of their actions. Slash would appear to reinscribe the distance between the reader and the text that fanfiction partially collapses, but according to many fans, it's an assertion of a different kind of power, a different kind of control over the text than a self-INSERTion fantasy. Harry Potter is unique among slash fandoms as the only major fandom whose canon is entirely woman-authored. Much of the scholarship on slash fiction (Jenkins, Penley, Joanna Russ) has praised slash as an alternative to male-dominated discourse of pornography; since a great many slash stories, especially for the pairing of Remus/Sirius, are predicated on a particular reading of (perceived) existing subtext,

HP fandom contains several interesting layers of interpretation between the female author and the female fan concerning the male body.

Pornography

Regarding fanfiction and pornography, they are not one and the same, although a great deal of fanfiction is concerned with romantic relationships. But likewise, they are also both maligned genres looked upon with suspicion. Angela Carter, in her seminal text *The Sadeian Woman*, asserts that pornographic representation is an artistic reduction of Individual human beings into "primordial" male and female:

> The act does not acknowledge the participation of the individual, bringing to it a life of which the act is only a part. The man and woman, in their particularity, their being, are absent from these representations of themselves as male and female. (8)

But fanfic provides porn with a built-in context, and while the execution of specific stories may hew close to Carter's sense of reductionism, even the most shameless PWP

("Plot? What Plot?") story is predicated upon the fan reader's understanding of the individual characters involved, which is where a great deal of the enjoyment comes from.

Fanfiction is not about the "universal male and female," it is about Ron and Hermione, and that's why it's being read.

Also, according to Carter, pornography "can never be art for art's sake.

Honorably enough, it is always art with work to do" (Carter 12). The same could be said of fanfiction. Fanfiction is predicated upon the desires of its audience, who are seeking a further experience with characters and a universe they have grown to love; the source material has provoked in fans a "cerebral insatiability" (Carter 14) that cannot be satisfied by the canon alone.

However, pornography "always throws the reader back on his own resources, since it convinces him of the impotence of his own desire that the book cannot in itself assuage, at the same time as he solaces that loneliness through the medium of the fantasy extracted from the fiction" (Carter 14). Pornography is a solitary act, that arouses and denies desire; it is reductionist and distancing, and an eternal tease—gaps in the text substituting for the gaps in the body of the absent partner. But if pornography is the textual embodiment of *lack*—of identity, of character, of satisfaction—fanfiction is about *abundance*. Fanfiction fills in gaps, explicates subtext, invents and affirms connections and character dynamics, and creates a multiplicity of stories that interpret and sometimes override the original one provided. The writer of fanfiction is doing what the reader of pornography cannot: entering into the text, filling the text with her own desires, and seizing control of the satisfaction of those desires. Moreover, fan writers and readers are a community, and as a community, they claim interpretive power over the texts. Fanfiction is not a solitary, but a communal activity; and pornographic fanfiction is passed around and recommended and discussed in public forums, and fans are encouraged to share their reactions with each other and the author.

Children's Literature and Sexuality

While there isn't space here for more than a quick overview of this particular topic, which could easily fill a book or three on its own, the issue of children's and adolescent sexuality as portrayed in fanfiction is an interesting one. acusations of

"pedophilia" occasionally get leveled at the fandom by outsiders, those who are appalled—appalled!—that anyone would dare to sully the "innocence" of "children's books" by writing stories where Hermione and Ron or Harry and Draco or Fred and

George get down and dirty. Leaving aside the fact that many authors of erotic fanfiction writers are themselves teenagers, what about the fact that a great many of the HP characters are, in fact, underage? And does it make a difference that the HP books are. At least in part, marketed to children? Debate about the desirability of writing explicit fanfiction for HP because of its status as children's text tend, for the most part, not to be undertaken with excessive heat. Many fans note that not only are the main characters not small children, but "horny teenagers" who will be seventeen or eighteen at the series' end (and thus over the age of consent, which in the UK is currently sixteen, and presumably of age in the wizarding world, where one comes of age at 17), but the very idea of the HP texts as "children's literature" is open to question. At the same time, certain general patterns seem to hold for the portrayal of underage sexuality in the fandom; in particular, many stories that concern Harry and his classmates have, over the past few years, tended to "age up" the characters to fifteen or sixteen. While this has served the purpose of rendering the characters' engagement in sexual activity more palatable or "defensible," it's important to note that this "aging up" no longer can be considered as such, as it is now simply an act of "picking up where the books left off"; at the end of *Order of the Phoenix*, as the twins are already eighteen, Ron is sixteen, Percy is pushing twenty and Harry will turn sixteen, it is expected, in the first pages of Book Six (*Harry Potter and the Half Blood Prince*). Also, as has been pointed out by a number of fans, graphic depictions of teenage sexuality are hardly unusual in published literature, and even in literature marketed as "Young Adult" and therefore fanfiction is not doing anything intrinsically outré in that regard.

Fanfiction, by the very nature of its existence, is subversive of dominant ideologies of text and authorship. Within the boundaries of HP fanfiction, more subtle subversions are taking place—of literary genre, of the concept of pornography, of heteronormative sexuality, of the discourse of "children's literature." Accordingly, fanfiction serves a prominent and important role as a means of discource about the book, the characters, the wild and multifaceted universe that J.K. Rowling has created, and what could be more stimulating—intellectually—than that?

Works Cited

Allen, Robert C. "On Reading Soaps: A Semiotic Primer." *Popular Culture: Production and Consumption*. Ed. C. Lee Harrington and Denise Bielby. Oxford: Blackwell, 2000. 234-42.

Bacon-Smith, Camille. *Enterprising Women : Television Fandom and the Creation of Popular Myth*. Philadelphia: University of Pennsylvania Press, 1992.

Baym, Nancy K. *Tune in, Log On: Soaps, Fandom, and On-Line Community*. Thousand Oaks, CA: Sage Publications, 2000.

Becker, Howard S. "Art as Collective Action." *Popular Culture: Production and Consumption*. Ed. C. Lee Harrington and Denise Bielby. Oxford: Blackwell, 2000. 67-79.

Bourdieu, Pierre. *Distinction: A Social Critique of the Judgment of Taste*. Tr. Richard Nice. Cambridge, MA: Harvard University Press, 1984.

Butler, Judith. *Bodies That Matter: On the Discursive Limits of "Sex"*. New York: Routledge, 1993.

Carter, Angela. *The Sadeian Woman: An Exercise in Cultural History*. London: Penguin, 1979.

Cawelti, John G. "The Concept of Formula in the Study of Popular Literature." *Popular Culture: Production and Consumption*. Ed. C. Lee Harrington and Denise Bielby. Oxford: Blackwell, 2000. 203-209.

Certeau, Michel de. *The Practice of Everyday Life*. Berkeley, CA: University of California Press, 1984.

Cicioni, Mima. "Male Pair-Bonds and Female Desire in Slash Writing." *Theorizing Fandom: Fans, Subculture, and Identity*. Ed. Cheryl Harris and Alison Alexander. Cresskill, NJ: Hampton Press, 1998. 153-78.

Eco, Umberto. *The Role of the Reader: Explorations in the Semiotics of Texts*. Bloomington, IN: Indiana University Press, 1979.

Fiske, John. "Intertextuality." *Popular Culture: Production and Consumption*. Ed. C. Lee Harrington and Denise Bielby. Oxford: Blackwell, 2000. 219-33.

Green, Shoshanna, Cynthia Jenkins, and Henry Jenkins. "Normal Femal Interest in Men Bonking: Selections from *the Terra Nostra Underground* and *Strange Bedfellows*." *Theorizing Fandom: Fans, Subculture, and Identity*. Ed. Cheryl Harris and Alison Alexander. Cresskill, NJ: Hampton Press, 1998. 9-40.

Hall, Stuart. "Encoding/Decoding." *Popular Culture: Production and Consumption*. Ed. C. Lee Harrington and Denise Bielby. Oxford: Blackwell, 2000. 123-32.

Jenkins, Henry. *Textual Poachers : Television Fans & Participatory Culture*. Studies in Culture and Communication. New York: Routledge, 1992.

Jensen, Joli. "Fandom as Pathology: The Consequences of Characterization." *Popular Culture: Production and Consumption*. Ed. C. Lee Harrington and Denise Bielby. Oxford: Blackwell, 2000. 301-14.

Kincaid, James R. *Erotic Innocence: The Culture of Child Molesting.* Durham, NC: Duke University Press, 1998.

Medhurst, Andy. "Batman, Deviance, and Camp." *Popular Culture: Production and Consumption.* Ed. C. Lee Harrington and Denise Bielby. Oxford: Blackwell, 2000. 24-35.

Penley, Constance. "Brownian Motion: Women, Tactics, and Technology." *Technoculture.* Ed. Constance Penley and Andrew Ross. Minneapolis: University of Minnesota Press, 1991. 135-62.

Radway, Janice A. *Reading the Romance: Women, Patriarchy, and Popular Culture.* Chapel Hill, NC: University of North Carolina Press, 1984.

Turkle, Sherry. *Life on the Screen: Identity in the Age of the Internet.* New York: Touchstone, 1995.

Catherine Tosenberger is a Ph.D. candidate in children's literature and folklore at the University of Florida; she is in the process of writing her dissertation, on Harry Potter fan fiction, under the direction of Dr. Kenneth Kidd. She has an M.A. in folklore from Ohio State University, and currently serves as the chair of the Programming Committee for HP Education Fanon's 2005 event, The Witching Hour.

Scriptwriting for Pleasure and Profit: The Power of the Written Word in Harry Potter

Bonnie May a.k.a. Dicentra spectabilis

I n Spring 2002, a new posting style emerged on the Harry Potter for Grownups (HPfGU) discussion group. Following the lead of the shippers, some list members began to christen imaginary ships and other flotation devices after theories not related to relationships. These list members began to fictionalize themselves and fellow list members when discussing canon, using dialog, realized metaphors, and a fictional universe that soon came to be known as Theory Bay.

Theory Bay was awash with dozens of vessels of varying degrees of seaworthiness, including a hovercraft, a destroyer, a barge, and majestic sailing vessels. Theorists also sprawled onto the shore, populating it with a canon museum, a psychiatric treatment facility, a castle, a safe house, a volleyball court, a canon college, and a tavern. Some theories were personified so that they could turn up at odd moments—the odder the better. Since the advent of Hurricane Jo, however, much of the content of Theory Bay has been reduced to rubble.

The following presentation has been written in the Theory Bay presentation style. Use of the characters Elkins, Captain Cindy, and Stoned!Harry is, of course, by their express permission.

Dicentra stood anxiously on the shore of Theory Bay, her toes curling in the sand. With her hand over her eyes, she scanned the water, looking for the familiar stumbling gait of Stoned!Harry amid the flotilla of theories that had survived the latest ravages of Hurricane Jo. To her left was the perennially seaworthy destroyer Big Bang, which represents the theory that JKR prefers to use highly dramatic, cinematic, or even melodramatic events to serve as catalytic turning points in her characters' lives.

Farther out was the popular ship LOLLIPOPS, which posits that Snape once had a crush on Lily. Barely visible on the shore, a few meters away, was the wreckage of the Fourth Man hovercraft, which once postulated that the fourth man convicted with Barty Crouch Jr. was none other than the hapless Avery from the graveyard scene.

Finally, Dicentra saw someone emerge from behind the Big Bang, trip on his robes and fall face-first onto the water's surface. Stoned!Harry—the personification of the theory that Harry is the living embodiment of the Philosopher's Stone and therefore has the potential for immortality—is able to walk on water, but because he's, well, stoned, he tends to be a little clumsy.

As Harry stumbled toward the shore, Dicentra glared at him, hands on hips. He swerved to avoid running straight into her.

"Hey!" she said, grabbing a handful of Stoned!Harry's robes. "You promised you'd help."

"Wha . . . ?" He turned around and stared at her blankly.

"Just come with me," she said, dragging Stoned!Harry up toward the Canon Museum, the only structure in Theory Bay that grows every time Hurricane Jo sweeps through. Its shiny new fifth story glinted in the sunlight.

Once at the museum, Dicentra took Stoned!Harry straight down into the basement and stopped expectantly at a door marked "Prop Room."

"I don't have the key," she explained. Stoned!Harry obliged with a quick Alohomora and they went inside. They entered an enormous room filled with shelves from floor to ceiling, all of them populated with objects found in canon.

"See, I promised I'd put up a new exhibit in that dusty display case near the men's room," Dicentra explained. "So I have to go through all this stuff and find some things that have a common thread. Put that down . . . !" Stoned!Harry had found a half-filled box of Bertie Bott's Every Flavour Beans and was poking through it. "You don't know where those have been. Now help me find something interesting."

Dicentra began to walk slowly down the aisles, looking at the objects on the shelves. She saw neatly folded school uniforms, hedgehogs in various stages of becoming pincushions, stacks of golden dishes, telescopes, glass vials . . .

"Ah, here's something." She plucked at something fluid and silvery gray, which slithered to the floor and lay there in gleaming folds.

"That's my invisibility cloak," whispered Stoned!Harry. "Dumbledore gave it to me."

Dicentra stowed it back on the shelf. "You're not the real Harry," she said under her breath, and not for the first time. She had tried to explain to Stoned!Harry that he was only a theory, not a canonical character, but he was always too dazed to understand the difference.

Dicentra continued down to the end of that aisle, then up the next. Stoned!Harry wandered off into another aisle. She found broomsticks, cages, cauldrons, candlesticks, inkpots, quills. Just as she was lifting the visor on a suit of armor, she heard a loud crash.

"What have you done now?" she called out as she strode off toward the noise.

A muffled voice answered, "puhfuh."

Dicentra stopped at the end of the aisle whence the noise came and saw an enormous pile of paper, some of it moving slightly. It appeared that at least a dozen boxes had tumbled from the shelves and emptied themselves directly on top of him. She hurried over and began to dig through the papers until Stoned!Harry's head emerged from the pile.

"Papers!" he cried out.

"You don't say," Dicentra said, lips pursed. "Now we're going to have to put all these back where they belong. Not that way!" She grabbed the wand that Stoned!Harry had just begun to wave. "You don't even know where they all belong. We're going to have to sort through them by hand."

Pouting slightly, Stoned!Harry climbed out of the pile and plopped down on the floor. He poked at the paper with his wand, causing an avalanche of envelopes.

"Don't do that either!" Dicentra protested. "Just look through them and see where they go."

"They're all the same," said Stoned!Harry, petulantly. "They all go in the same place."

"What do you mean they're all the same?" Dicentra said, looking up.

"They're all like this." He held up an envelope and passed it to her. The envelope was unopened, but Dicentra knew immediately what was inside. It was thick and heavy, made of yellowish parchment, and the address was written in emerald-green ink. There was no stamp. On the other side of the envelope was a purple wax seal bearing a coat of arms: a lion, an eagle, a badger, and a snake surrounding a large letter H. The address read:

Mr. Harry Potter
The Cupboard under the Stairs
4 Privet Drive
Little Whinging
Surrey

"Those are all my letters," said Stoned!Harry. "The first letters I ever got."

"Of course," mused Dicentra. "These are the Letters From No One, from *Philosopher's Stone*."

"I didn't even know I was a wizard then," added Stoned!Harry. "Hey!" He reached up into the pile and plucked out a small slip of paper from near the top. "I bet there's only one of these."

Dicentra took the paper from his hand. It was small strip of parchment, slightly singed at the edges, with the words "Harry Potter" scrawled on one side.

"That's the one that came out of the goblet of fire, isn't it?" he said. "I sure wish I never saw that one. It caused nothing but trouble for me."

"Everything causes Harry nothing but trouble," said Dicentra absently, staring hard at the envelope and the parchment. "Wait a minute," she said slowly. "Both of these papers cause something awfully big to happen, don't they?"

"I suppose so," Stoned!Harry shrugged.

"I wonder how many other of these papers make something big happen." She immediately grabbed a sheaf of papers off the pile and began to rifle through them. "Come on, help me find more important papers. I think I've got an idea for the display."

As Dicentra sorted through a stack of Transfiguration exams, third-year class schedules, and History of Magic essays, another piece of paper fell into her lap. It was a clipping from the *Daily Prophet*, folded neatly, but the paper was dirty and worn thin at the folds. Gingerly, she opened it up. It was a photo of an Egyptian pyramid. The headline beneath it read, "Ministry of Magic Employee Scoops Grand Prize."

"Hey, isn't this the clipping Ron sends to Harry?" she asked Stoned!Harry.

"No," he said, squinting at it. "The one Ron gave me wasn't all icky like that. And you could see Ron's family."

Dicentra looked at the photo again. The head of Percy Weasley poked into the frame from the left side of the picture. He frowned and disappeared from view, only to return a moment later dragging George and Ron with him. Fred soon followed, and Molly, Arthur, and Ginny hurried in from the right side of the frame. They posed again for their group photo, Percy donning his fez and Ron placing Scabbers on his shoulder.

"You mean like this," she said, holding up the clipping again.

"Yeah," said Stoned!Harry, "but it still looks too old."

"Oh, I know!" she exclaimed. "This is the clipping that Sirius Black carries with him all through *Prisoner of Azkaban*." She cradled it reverently in her hands. "I think this one most definitely qualifies as causing something big to happen. I mean, if it weren't for this, Sirius never would have found it in him to escape." She set it down beside the parchment scrap and the admission letter.

Stoned!Harry leaned over the pile to look at the papers in front of Dicentra. "One from the first year, one from the third year, and one from the fourth year," he observed.

"Hey, you're right," she said. And then after a moment, "Galloping gargoyles, do you know what these three pieces of paper have in common? They're what kick off the action of each novel. Look," she said, picking up the envelope. "The plot of *Philosopher's Stone* doesn't really start until Harry gets his letter from Hogwarts. The central mystery of *Prisoner of Azkaban* begins when Sirius sees this article in the *Daily Prophet*. And when this scrap of paper pops out, that's when the action of *Goblet of Fire* really starts."

Stoned!Harry stared blankly at her. "So?"

"So? Don't you get it? This is a pattern! Pieces of paper are the catalyst for all of Harry's adventures!"

"What about my second year?"

"Oh. Yeah," Dicentra said, frowning. "Let's see. When does the action of *Chamber of Secrets* start?"

"With the pudding," said Stoned!Harry, a wistful look on his face.

"Not with the pudding," sighed Dicentra.

"I got a letter because of the pudding," he persisted.

"That's right—the letter from Mafalda Hopkirk warning him about the use of magic outside of school. But I don't think that really kicks off the action. I mean, the central mystery of the novel is who is the Heir of Slytherin and where is the Chamber of Secrets. That letter has nothing to do with it."

Stoned!Harry stood suddenly and jabbed his wand in the air, shouting, "The Chamber of Secrets has been opened! Enemies of the Heir, Beware!" Some purple sparks shot out of his wand.

"Oh, sit down," said Dicentra, annoyed. She resumed digging through the pile of papers, but stopped. "Wait," she said. "That *is* when the action began in *Chamber of Secrets*. When they see the handwriting on the wall. That's what kicks off the central mystery."

"It's not paper," Stoned!Harry said cheekily.

"No, but it *is* writing," said Dicentra. "*That's* it then. It's not the paper that kicks off the action, but the writing. Writing is the key, regardless of whether it's on paper or not. Writing is what makes things happen in the Potterverse."

An hour later, Dicentra sat surrounded by neat stacks of parchment. "OK," she said to herself, "I think I've got it all figured out. Hey!" she kicked Stoned!Harry's foot; he sat up suddenly from where he had been napping on the floor. "Check this out; I was right about the papers . . . " but she trailed off when she saw Stoned!Harry's face. He was staring wide-eyed at something above and behind her, his mouth hanging open.

Dicentra wheeled around to see two figures standing behind her. She felt the blood drain from her face as she realized who they were.

"Hey, whatcha doin'?" boomed one of them. Captain Cindy strode over to the piles of parchment, recklessly grabbed a handful, and began to sift through them, tossing them randomly on the floor. Cindy was captain of the Big Bang and had a reputation as one of the most formidable denizens of Theory Bay. She made her crewmembers scrub the deck of the Big Bang with toothbrushes, tried to drown a theory she didn't like, tossed the local tavern when she encountered a theory she thought was too complicated, and spectacularly failed her anger management class. Tucked underneath one arm was her trademark Big Paddle, which everyone knew to stay clear of.

"Yeah, Dicey, what gives?" said Elkins, who sat down next to Dicentra and began to poke through the piles. Elkins was another of the more formidable denizens of the bay but for different reasons. Elkins had delivered a three-day Memory Charm Symposium in the basement of the Canon Museum, a nine-part treatise on the Crouch family saga, used words like "subsumption" and "bildungsroman" and "realpolitik" without blinking, and frequently got away with subversive readings of canon.

Dicentra finally found her voice. "You guys, put that stuff back," she squeaked.

"Back where?" said Cindy, "on the floor, where I found it? Well, OK." She opened her hand and let the parchment drop to the floor.

"Oh look," said Elkins. "Here are all those chocolate frog cards. A couple of Dumbledores, some Circes and a Merlin . . . what's all this about, Dicey? What are you doing down here."

"Nothing," Dicentra said, shortly.

"Doesn't look like nothing to me," said Cindy as she sat herself down right next to Stoned!Harry, who, to her great amusement, slid away from her. "Actually, it looks like you're trying to put together an exhibit for that dusty old display case by the men's room."

"They told us at the front desk why you were down here," Elkins said, grinning at Dicentra's startled expression.

"So it's about parchment, is it?" asked Cindy.

"Sort of," said Dicentra, relaxing only a little. "I think I've found a pattern. See, in each book, the action is kicked off by something somebody wrote." She held up the admission letter, the clipping of the Weasleys in Egypt, and the singed scrap. "In *Chamber of Secrets*, it's the handwriting on the wall that starts it all."

Elkins looked mildly impressed. "Say, you're right. Who knew?"

"What about *Order of the Phoenix*?" smirked Cindy. "Which bit of writing kicks off the action there—the Muggle newspapers Harry pulls out of the dumpsters?"

"Trick question," replied Dicentra. "*Order of the Phoenix* doesn't have a central mystery like the first four. The action is kicked off by the return of Voldemort in *Goblet of Fire*."

"What about the rest of the papers, Dicey?" said Elkins quickly, seeing Cindy's hands tighten around her Paddle.

"I figure that the other important moments are provoked by written material," she continued. "I've got it . . . well, I *had* it sorted by book . . . "

"Say no more," said Cindy, grabbing Stoned!Harry's wand and magicking the paper back into place. Without missing a beat, Elkins grabbed the stack nearest her, which contained the papers from *Philosopher's Stone*.

"Well, here's the letter that Hagrid presents to the goblins at Gringotts, authorizing the stone's retrieval from the vault," she said.

"Yeah, that's a real turning point in the story," said Cindy, barely concealing the sarcasm in her voice.

"And here are the letters between Ron and his brother Charlie when they arrange to send Norbert to Romania," Elkins continued.

"A moment so pivotal it didn't even make it into the movie," Cindy said, rolling her eyes.

"Hey, they leave pivotal scenes out of the movies all the time," protested Dicentra. "Like that one from Chamber of Secrets where they figure out that Tom Riddle was around the last time the chamber was opened, and the ones that show Harry wondering if he . . . "

"The chocolate frog cards are pretty important," interrupted Elkins, as she fanned them out in her hand.

"Yes, the frog cards are important," said Dicentra. "They are one of the clues that help the Trio figure out what is hidden under the trap door. And so are these . . . " she pulled some papers from the stack Elkins was holding. "Look, here's the one that came with the invisibility cloak, the one that says 'Use it well,' and the other one that says 'Just in case.' And this article in the Daily Prophet about the break-in at Gringotts: it says the break-in happened on July 31st, so that leads Harry to wonder if the thief was looking for whatever Hagrid took from vault 713."

"Oh yeah?" challenged Cindy. "What about the first clue: the three-headed dog? That wasn't writing."

Dicentra sat, dumbfounded; her eyes began to well up with tears.

"It's ok, Dicey," Elkins said, patting her gently on the shoulder. "You just have to adjust your theory a little. I think you're onto something. There is a preponderance of written material in the series. It's just a matter of discovering what it means."

Elkins returned to the papers in her hand. "Let's look at some more. Ok, here's the riddle for Snape's potions . . . " She held up the roll of paper with the logic puzzle. "It's the final obstacle before Harry finds the Stone . . . and what's this?" She unrolled a large piece of tissue paper. "Erised stra ehru oyt . . . ?"

"Oh, I made a rubbing of the inscription on the Mirror of Erised," Dicentra explained. "It's up in one of the dioramas upstairs."

Elkins had two pieces of paper left in her hands. One was an envelope, the other a small piece of rolled parchment.

"I've never seen those before," said Stoned!Harry in a very, very small voice as he edged away from Cindy.

"No I don't expect you would have," said Dicentra, forgetting for a moment that he was not really Harry. "The envelope is the letter that Dumbledore wrote to the Dursleys and left on the doorstep with you; the other is the note that was supposedly from the Ministry of Magic, calling Dumbledore away from Hogwarts on urgent business."

"Well, hey!" said Cindy jovially, as she put Stoned!Harry in a headlock and pulled him closer. "That looks like a good exhibit to me, eh Stoner?" She gave him a furious noogie before releasing him.

Elkins frowned. "No, I don't think we've figured this out yet. Maybe we need to group them differently. But according to what . . . ?"

For a moment, there was silence. Elkins stared at the papers in front of her, Dicentra tried not to look at Stoned!Harry, who was sullenly combing his fingers through his hair; Cindy began to balance her Big Paddle on one finger.

"By author!" Elkins said, suddenly. Stoned!Harry jumped a little at the sound of her voice. Elkins began to sort the papers and soon had them in the order she wanted.

"All right, now," said Elkins. "In this largest pile are things written by Dumbledore: the letter to the Dursleys, the letter authorizing the Stone's removal from Gringott's, and the two notes that accompanied the invisibility cloak."

"What about the Hogwarts acceptance letter?" asked Dicentra.

"Well, that was signed by McGonagall," said Elkins.

"But with Dumbledore's blessing," Dicentra persisted, "so I think it should go with his letters."

"Fine by me," said Elkins, moving the letter.

Dicentra stared at the Dumbledore pile for a moment, then gasped loudly. "Oh! I know what it is!" she said excitedly. "A long time ago I posted something on Harry Potter for Grownups about Dumbledore's role in *Philosopher's Stone*. Get it for me, will you?" she said, turning to Stoned!Harry.

Without taking his eyes off Cindy, Stoned!Harry conjured document 33289 from Jan. 12, 2002. Cindy intercepted it as he passed it to Dicentra.

"Give me that," she barked. "Lessee . . . 'I'd like to propose a theory that builds on all that's been said and then goes one step further: The spells were breakable by first-year students because Dumbledore MEANT for Harry to face Voldemort. And in fact, most of the events of *Philosopher's Stone* were engineered by Dumbledore for Harry's benefit. (Sincere apologies if this very argument has been made before, but parsing 33,000 posts to find out was a bit daunting.)'

"Ha!" she crowed. "It's the 'Sorry if this has been discussed before but . . . ' line! What a newbie!"

"Hey!" Dicentra protested, trying to retrieve the document and failing. "Everyone's a newbie once." She turned to Stoned!Harry. "Get me another copy, would you?" He obliged, and Dicentra sat back with the document, narrowing her eyes at Cindy.

"Listen to what Harry concludes after his adventure," Dicentra continued. "Harry says "'I think he sort of wanted to give me a chance. I think he knows more or less everything that goes on here, you know. I reckon he had a pretty good idea we were going to try, and instead of stopping us, he just taught us enough to help. I don't think it was an accident he let me find out how the mirror worked. It's almost like he thought I had the right to face Voldemort if I could . . . . ""

"See, Dumbledore is grooming Harry to play a particular role," Dicentra explained. "Harry isn't fully aware of what it is, but you know Dumbledore is looking at a much larger picture than Harry is."

"And that is related to these papers how?" Cindy arched her eyebrows.

"He uses these papers to assign Harry his role," said Elkins suddenly, eyes widening. "It's as if Harry were an actor in a play, but instead of seeing the whole script up front, he gets these occasional cues from backstage. Look!" She held up the Hogwarts admission letter. "What kind of change did receiving this letter effect in Harry? He went from being an ordinary kid in lousy circumstances to a wizard who belonged to a whole different world. And not just any wizard, either. He became The Boy Who Lived. New life, new role."

"Right!" said Dicentra, "but it didn't end there." She read again from the document. "'It cannot be a coincidence that Harry is with Hagrid when he recovers the Stone. Dumbledore sends Hagrid to collect Harry and get the Stone at the same time.' See, that's where this comes in," she said, holding up the letter Hagrid took to Gringotts. "Harry doesn't know it at the time, but Dumbledore is setting him up by letting him be privy to the existence of the Stone."

Elkins took the document from Dicentra and read, "'Dumbledore gave Harry the Cloak of Invisibility for Christmas, telling him to "use it wisely." What could that mean except "go roaming about the school after hours to figure out this mystery"?'

"That's right," she mused. "And he gave Harry the cloak not once but twice, both times with a mysterious note giving Harry implicit permission to use the cloak in solving the mystery. He was definitely using written materials to assign Harry his role."

"What about this?" said Cindy, holding up the letter to the Dursleys. "Fat lot of good this did. Harry was supposed to know all of this stuff but the Dursleys never told him."

"They never wanted me to get the letters from Hogwarts, either," piped up Stoned!Harry.

"Ladies and gentlemen, I think we have a function for the Dursleys," Elkins said dramatically. "Just as Dumbledore uses writing to assign Harry his role, the Dursleys suppress writing to keep Harry from fulfilling his destiny."

Cindy snorted. "Well, that's nice and all, but you've forgotten something. The item that is explicitly associated with passing out roles has nothing to do with paper or writing: the Sorting Hat."

Elkins let out her breath in a long, low hiss. Dicentra rubbed her chin thoughtfully. Stoned!Harry summoned the hat from a shelf two rows away and began to play with it.

"Well, the hat is an object in a book and is therefore a literary construct," said Dicentra, hesitantly. "So it's made up of words."

"Nice try, but no dice, Dicey," said Cindy, staring fixedly at Dicentra, who averted her gaze and pretended to be interested in her fingernails.

"You got us there," said Elkins, "but that's ok. You could always argue that the hat isn't Dumbledore's tool. After all, everyone gets sorted, and what happens between Harry and the hat is, well, between Harry and the hat. Dumbledore knows about it, but he didn't tell either the hat or Harry what to do."

"Maybe not every single thing that assigns Harry his role is written matter, but that doesn't mean the theory isn't valid," Dicentra said, regaining a modicum of confidence. "What if we find stuff in the other books to show how Harry gets his role handed to him in writing. Would that convince you at all?"

"Humph," said Cindy, crossing her arms defiantly.

"Well," said Elkins, clapping her hands cheerfully. "That sounds like a yes. On to Chamber of Secrets." She scooted the pile toward Dicentra. "Your turn."

"This pile seems a little bigger than the last," Dicentra observed.

"Longer book," snarled Cindy.

Dicentra picked up a bundle of unopened letters. "These are all addressed to Harry."

"Those are *mine*," said Stoned!Harry, lunging at them. "Gimme."

Dicentra held them out of his reach. "These are the letters that Dobby intercepted after Harry's first year at Hogwarts," she said, laughing. "Dobby never gave them to Harry, so I won't give them to you."

Stoned!Harry sat back down sulkily, grabbed the Sorting Hat, and jammed it down on his head so far it almost covered his chin.

"Another instance of someone trying to manipulate Harry by keeping written material away from him," observed Elkins.

"They're not from Dumbledore," said Cindy in a sarcastic monotone.

"They don't have to be," retorted Elkins. "The important part is that Dobby was trying to alter Harry's role by keeping the letters from him, almost an echo of what the Dursleys did to him in Philosopher's Stone."

"The Dursleys deny him writing in this book, too," said Dicentra. "They won't let Hedwig out of her cage because they're afraid Harry will send letters to his friends at 'that freak place,' as Dudley calls it."

"See if you can find things written by Dumbledore," suggested Elkins.

Dicentra shuffled through the pile and produced a handful of identical envelopes addressed to Harry and the five youngest Weasleys. "These are the letters from Hogwarts with the list of textbooks for the next year. They were all delivered to the Burrow, and Arthur observes that Dumbledore knows where Harry is."

"So Dumbledore presents Harry with his new role as a second-year student," grumbled Cindy. "Big whoop."

"Well, sometimes a letter is just a letter," replied Dicentra. "I don't think this one really counts, do you think?"

"Probably not," replied Elkins. "See if you can find writing that plays a larger role in Harry's life."

"There aren't any more from Dumbledore," Dicentra said slowly. "But here's one *for* Dumbledore." She produced a roll of parchment from the stack.

"The order of suspension from Lucius Malfoy," said Elkins. "Looks like ol' Lucius is trying to write Dumbledore's role for him."

"He *did* write it," said Dicentra. "That is, until these came along." She pulled out a handful of envelopes and parchment scraps. "I don't recognize the names of the senders, but they're all asking Dumbledore to return to Hogwarts at once. Which he does."

"Well, there you go," said Elkins triumphantly. "Harry's not the only one whose role is given to him in writing."

"No kidding," said Dicentra quietly, pulling out a small, black-covered book with a ragged puncture hole through the center.

"That's Tom Riddle's diary," said Cindy, sitting bolt upright. "Get that out of here."

"Don't worry: this is the one from the end of the book," said Dicentra, poking her finger through the hole. "Tom's not in it anymore."

"I don't care; it creeps me out. Get rid of it."

"Actually, Dicey, it kinda creeps me out, too," said Elkins, leaning away from her. "I mean, talk about having your role written for you . . . "

"I think this should be at the center of the exhibit," Dicentra continued, flipping through what was left of the pages. "Of all the written material in the series, this diary is most emblematic of one character trying to manipulate another by writing a role for that character. Poor Ginny: she just thought she had found a sympathetic interlocutor, when in reality Tom Riddle's memory was writing her a role she never would have consciously accepted."

"But did he tell her to open the Chamber through writing or did he simply control her mind while she was in a trance?" Elkins asked, still edging away from the book.

"He never explains that," said Dicentra, "but he does get her to pour her soul out to him by telling her what she wants to hear. I mean, read. So in some ways she unwittingly wrote a role for herself in the diary, too. And then later, Harry gets pulled in by Tom's writing, though Tom used writing to lie to Harry about who opened the Chamber the last time. In both cases, it was an eerie collaboration between innocence and evil that resulted in . . . "

"A lame collaboration, you mean," Cindy interrupted. "All those people were supposed to have been *killed* by the basilisk, but they were only petrified, and early on we learn that they'll eventually be healed. Yawn! And don't even get me started on that idiot Gilderoy Lockhart . . . "

"Speaking of people who write their own roles . . . " Dicentra passed the diary to Stoned!Harry, who promptly removed one of his socks and stuffed the diary into it. "Lockhart's whole identity is contained in his collected works. He had decided at some point that he wanted to play the role of the fearless, famous fighter of Dark forces, but instead of actually doing the fighting, he wrote about it, stealing experiences from others and substituting his name for theirs."

"And because it's in writing—published writing—it legitimizes his claim," Elkins added. "Writing is often much more authoritative than speech, especially when the writing comes between the pages of a bound book. People are more likely to trust what has been published than what they merely hear."

"Exactly," Dicentra said. "Once he had his supposed deeds published, he could step into his role. And once people read his books, they played their roles as the adoring crowd, further supporting his written, though fraudulent, role."

Dicentra paused to gather up the Lockhart books that Stoned!Harry had summoned while she and Elkins were speaking. She set them aside and began to sort through the pile for Chamber of Secrets again.

"Looks like writing provides the clues to solve the central mystery again," said Cindy, carefully. "That page Hermione tears out of a library book—very out of character for her, if you ask me—and the word 'pipes' that she writes on the scrap, are what clinch it eventually."

"I guess so," said Dicentra, slowly, "but then there's what Aragog said, what Tom Riddle showed, and what Moaning Myrtle told them. I'd call it pretty even between written, verbal, and visual in this case."

"Ha!" Cindy shouted. "Writing doesn't furnish even half of the clues to the mystery. I got you!"

"I don't know about that," said Elkins, who had been quietly thinking. "If we go back to the premise that Harry's role comes to him as written cues, we can find a clearer pattern. So far, we've identified the letters Dobby intercepted, the Dursleys not letting Hedwig fly, and Tom Riddle's diary . . . "

"Oh look," said Cindy dryly, as she pulled a handful of lilac-colored envelopes out of the pile, the addresses written in purple ink. "Here are all those envelopes Harry addressed for Lockhart. What does this tell us? Why, it tells us that Lockhart also assigned Harry a role . . . as cheap slave labor."

Dicentra and Elkins grinned and Stoned!Harry snorted loudly from underneath the Sorting Hat.

"Actually, Lockhart spent quite a bit of time trying to assign Harry a role" said Elkins, chuckling, "but I don't think that was exactly it. Lockhart's thematic role in *Chamber of Secrets* is the same as Colin Creevey's: to present two unsavory aspects of fame. Lockhart is the preening, self-absorbed lover of fame, and Colin is the lover of the famous. Lockhart believes that he can tutor Harry in how to be properly famous, and one of those tutoring moments is when Harry does detention addressing those envelopes. Harry isn't the only one writing in that instance: Lockhart is autographing photos of himself, something only a celebrity does. And yet on two previous occasions, Colin pesters Harry for an autograph and Harry flatly refuses. I think we can safely say that autographing photos symbolizes embracing fame, and refusing to autograph means refusing fame. In that simple act of writing—or lack thereof—we get the essence of Harry's attitude toward fame."

Dicentra applauded. "Well done, Elk! Now, here are two more letters I found while you were talking. Filch's Kwikspell letter and Nearly Headless Nick's letter from Sir Patrick Delaney-Podmore. In both cases, the letters identify the recipient as someone who cannot assume a particular role. Nearly Headless Nick's letter tells him that he is not qualified to join the Headless Hunt, and the Kwikspell letter identifies Filch as a Squib. Both Nick and Filch deeply resent the fact that they have been excluded, and both see the letters as evidence of their disgrace."

"There are only a few more pieces of paper left," Elkins said, picking them up, "but I don't know what kind of significance they have. Here we have the letter from Mafalda Hopkirk informing Harry that they know about the hovering charm and that if he does it again he'll be expelled . . . "

"That's a set-up for later events: Harry thinks he has to assume the role of renegade when he blows up Aunt Marge," said Dicentra. "And then when he produces the Patronus in Order of the Phoenix, he gets a second letter from Mafalda Hopkirk telling him he's been expelled.

"Here's Ron's Howler . . . " Elkins held up a red envelope sandwiched between two panes of glass and tied tightly with about a mile of twine.

"To showing the consequences of stealing the car," Dicentra said, "but I don't think it assigns a role."

"The note from Snape authorizing the Slytherins to use the Quidditch pitch . . . "

"That is an example of the authority of written material," said Dicentra. "Because Snape himself writes the note, it has a kind of proxy value: it's the same as if he were standing there saying it. And yet it's not assigning anyone a role."

"The note from Lockhart authorizing Hermione to check out Moste Potente Potions . . . "

" . . . same as the note from Snape . . . "

"A few clippings from the Daily Prophet. This one is about Muggles seeing the flying Ford Anglia and this other one is about Arthur Weasley getting into trouble for bewitching it in the first place . . . "

"Backstory!" Cindy shouted, brandishing her Big Paddle. "That's just backstory—information. Don't even think about making it more important than that."

"I wouldn't dream of it," said Dicentra, eyeing Cindy's paddle, "because you're right. In this case, that's all it is: backstory. But I can't promise I won't find meaning in Daily Prophet articles in the next three books."

Cindy frowned. "Are you done yet?" she asked Elkins.

"Just these two scraps of parchment with the Dursley's phone number on it."

"And I suppose you're going to tell us that they represent Harry's first tentative attempts to reconcile his Muggle and wizard worlds," Cindy said sarcastically.

"Well, yeah," said Elkins, surprised. "He's asking Hermione and Ron to call. That's more invasive than a letter."

"I just didn't want my letters to get intercepted again," said Stoned!Harry, pulling off the Sorting Hat.

"See," said Cindy. "Practical function only. No need to turn it all into this symbolic literary crap."

"Whatever," muttered Elkins.

"You've forgotten something," Dicentra blurted out. "The writing on the wall. After Tom Riddle's diary, that's the most important writing in the book."

"Oh yeah," said Elkins, her eyes glinting. "That has Biblical overtones, too."

"Biblical?" said Cindy, eyebrows arched. "I thought it was just that old saying about reading the writing on the wall, when you can see you're goin' down because you're picking up on clues from the situation."

"That saying came from an incident in the Old Testament," said Dicentra, motioning to Stoned!Harry to conjure a Bible. "It's right here in the book of Daniel, chapter 5. Belshazzar, the king of Babylon, is having a big feast with his cronies, and they're using the sacred vessels that his father took from the temple when he conquered Jerusalem. Suddenly, they see a hand appear and write something on the wall that they can't understand. They bring in Daniel, who interprets it. It says, in part, 'thou art weighed in the balances and found wanting.' That very night, the Persians conquer Babylon."

"'Enemies of the Heir, beware,' carries a similar message," explained Elkins. "It also says 'You're goin' down.' It's another example of how Rowling borrows imagery from outside sources and makes it fit her own needs."

"What does that have to do with assigning roles?" demanded Cindy.

"It forces the students to think of themselves as 'pure-bloods' and muggleborns," said Dicentra. "That's its first role-creating function. It also seems to put Harry in the role of bad guy, to the point that Harry himself wonders if he is the Heir of Slytherin. Ultimately, it launches Harry into his inevitable role as Hero Who Saves The Day."

"WooHoo!" cried Elkins. "We've made it through *Chamber of Secrets*."

"No, you haven't," said Cindy darkly. "There's one more." She grabbed Stoned!Harry's wand and wrote in the air: Tom Marvolo Riddle.

"Of course," said Elkins. "Tom created the name for his new identity by manipulating the letters of his given name. It's a unique way of using writing to create a role."

"Can we go now?" said Cindy impatiently.

"But there are three more books to go!" protested Elkins.

"Fine, you play with your papers; I'm going to the beach." Cindy got up and left the room.

Stoned!Harry relaxed visibly and Dicentra let out a slow breath. She pushed the pile for *Prisoner of Azkaban* toward Elkins. "Your turn."

"Ok, what is going on with Harry during *Prisoner of Azkaban*," she murmured to herself as she sifted through the papers.

"The threat of Sirius Black on the periphery," said Dicentra. "That's provoked by this." She held up the clipping of the Weasleys in Egypt. "Sirius assumes the role of protector when he sees Scabbers on Ron's shoulder."

"Right," said Elkins, "and Harry isn't allowed to go to Hogsmeade because of this."

She produced the unsigned permission slip. "Once again, the Dursleys function is to negate writing."

"But he does get into Hogsmeade," said Dicentra, "because of another piece of writing."

"And what a piece of writing it is," said Elkins, as she pulled a blank piece of parchment from the middle of the pile. She placed it in front of Stoned!Harry, who tapped it with his wand and swore he was up to no good. The Marauder's Map unfurled.

"It's not hard to identify this as the assignment of a role," she mused. "The twins decide to assign Harry the role of rule-breaking adventurer, so they give him this."

"And *they* had assumed that role when they first stole the map from Filch's office," added Dicentra. "A role that the original manufacturers of the map intended for anyone who possessed it."

"Possessed being the operative term," said Elkins. "There's evidence that the map can exercise a little undue influence over its owner. I can't help but think that the Twins didn't make the decision to give it to Harry by themselves."

"Let's see, what else is there?" said Dicentra. "This pile isn't very big, is it?" She looked at the birthday cards and letters from Ron, Hermione, and Hagrid; the notes from Hagrid to the Trio notifying them of Buckbeak's trial; the notice in Hogsmeade about the dementor patrols; and Neville's password list.

"Here's something," said Elkins, producing a roll of parchment. "Hermione's werewolf essay. Snape assigned the students to write about werewolves in the hopes that they would assume the role of informers when they put two and two together. But only Hermione wrote the essay, and she declined to assume the role he wanted her to take. Interesting."

"Not much written material in *Prisoner of Azkaban*, is there?" said Dicentra, a bit crestfallen.

"No . . . " Elkins said, sitting back on her heels. "But you know, there is an awful lot of *reading* going on. Think of Trelawney's class. She's trying to get them to read the future in all kinds of media: tea leaves, lines on the palm, crystal balls. And she keeps trying her hardest to assign Harry the tragic role of The Student Who Dies This Year by finding it 'written' in all manner of signs. Harry tries not to read the sign of the Grim, but he has a hard time ignoring it, and it messes with his head."

Dicentra lowered her voice. "The strongest forces that Harry has to wrest with are how the Dementors affect him and his desire for revenge against Sirius Black. Neither of those things involve writing, but don't tell Cindy."

"Don't worry Dicey," said Elkins. "The instances of writing in *Prisoner of Azkaban* make up in importance what they lack in number."

"Thanks, Elk," said Dicentra, brightening. "Ready for *Goblet of Fire*?"

"Ready," she said, pushing the pile toward Dicentra. "But you've already identified the most important instance of writing: the scrap of parchment that came out of the goblet."

"Right, this is the writing that assigns Harry his primary role in *Goblet of Fire*, but I can think of two *prolific* writers right off the top of my head: Rita Skeeter and Sirius Black."

"Oh, Rita produces an awful lot of writing," moaned Elkins.

"And all of it manipulative," said Dicentra. "But interestingly, instead of writing a role for someone to follow, she writes about people playing roles they've never assumed. Arthur Weasley as incompetent bureaucrat, Harry as tragic orphan, Hermione as, uh, 'scarlet woman.'"

"And the readers react to the unfortunate subjects of her stories as if they really had played those roles. Look at how Molly reacts to Hermione when Rita says she's toying with Harry's affections, not to mention how Draco revels in the stories about Harry crying for his mum."

"As if he didn't have enough problems," said Dicentra. "Would you say that Rita is writing Draco's role for him?"

"His role as chief irritant?" replied Elkins. "No, he's been like that from the beginning. The only person who writes his role so far is JKR. Come to think of it, we haven't seen him associated with writing much at all. Except for ferreting out articles from the Daily Prophet to use in embarrassing Harry, he's kind of writing-free."

"Hee!" giggled Stoned!Harry to himself. "She said 'ferret.'"

"But Draco did write a role once," said Dicentra, reaching for a shoebox that had fallen down with the papers. She extracted a handful of "Potter Stinks" badges. "By distributing these badges to his fellow Slyths, Draco ensures that Harry knows where his place is: at the bottom of the social totem pole. I find it significant that Harry chucks one of these at Ron. It's Harry's way of accusing Ron of playing the same antagonist role as Draco."

Dicentra fell silent for a moment.

"You said that the other prolific writer is Sirius Black," prompted Elkins.

"Oh yeah," Dicentra said, returning to the moment. "His correspondence with Harry INSERTs a suggestion of the epistolary novel genre into *Goblet of Fire*. In almost all of his letters he's flat-out telling Harry what to do. And in writing these letters, Sirius is fulfilling his long-delayed role as Harry's protector."

"But Harry puts Sirius in the protector role first," observed Elkins, "by sending him that letter telling him his scar hurt. And later, when Sirius says he is going to return to Hogwarts, Harry sends him another letter telling him it was no big deal in the hopes that Sirius won't endanger himself. So, for the first time we have an example of Harry using writing to assign a role to someone else. In this case, he's trying to get Sirius to lighten up on the protector role and concentrate more on the Accused Man In Deep Hiding role."

"Harry may have written more than that role," said Dicentra as she extracted a large roll of parchment from the pile. "Here are those phony predictions that he and Ron made up for divination class. Remember that this takes place before his name comes out of the goblet of fire. The first three things off the top of Harry's head are: being in danger of burns, losing a treasured possession, and coming off the worse in a fight. Those are the three tasks, right there. And then Harry's last prediction is his own death by decapitation."

"Yeah, you're big into that decapitation thing, aren't you Dicey?" said Elkins, "that plus Ron's tin parrot lopping off the head of Harry's rubber fish, plus Nearly Headless Nick, plus the Twins' headless hats . . . "

"Shhhh!" Dicentra hissed, pointing at Stoned!Harry, whose eyes had become wide and just a little watery. "He doesn't know."

"Ha ha, just kidding!" said Elkins brightly. "No one's getting decapitated. Least of all you, Harry."

Stoned!Harry blinked a few times and wiped his sleeve across his eyes. "Got an eyelash . . . " he muttered.

"But you have to admit it's a little spooky that he would finish up with that particular prediction," Dicentra said in a low voice.

"Not half as spooky as these," replied Elkins in the same low voice. She had a stack of letters in her hand. Dicentra didn't recognize the handwriting.

"These are the letters from Crouch Sr. to Percy, telling him how to run the department. It's another blatant example of someone handing someone else his role in writing. Percy, being Crouch Sr.'s biggest fan, went ahead and did everything he read without question. It doesn't seem like such a big deal until you remember that Crouch was under Imperius at the time. What we have is yet another Weasley unwittingly putting his trust in written material that ultimately comes from Voldemort."

Dicentra shivered. "I think I can find something creepier," she said, digging into the pile. "Ah, here it is. In his dream, Harry is riding the eagle owl that delivers this. It tells Voldemort that Crouch Sr. has been neutralized. We have to assume that Voldemort told Barty Jr. about his father's escape by owl post, too, so Voldemort wrote Barty the role of parricide. This is the evidence that he fulfilled that role."

"I can go you one better than that," said Elkins. "Look at these."

Dicentra looked. They were all addressed to Ludo Bagman. "They're the letters the twins write to Bagman, asking for their winnings," said Dicentra. "What's so creepy about that?"

"Ok, I was kidding about the creepy part. But only a little. By writing these, the twins put themselves into the role of blackmailers. I can't help but feel that they're going to flirt with more criminal behavior in the future."

Dicentra sighed. "Is that it for *Goblet of Fire*?"

"Looks like it. My turn," she said. But it took a great deal of pushing plus a magical assist from Stoned!Harry to move the tottering *Order of the Phoenix* pile toward her.

"That thing is huge," observed Dicentra.

"Of course it's huge," said Elkins. "Look at the size of the book whence it came." She looked up and down the pile of newspapers, letters, notebooks, and parchment. "Where do I start?"

Dicentra sighed. "Isn't there any way we can sort these things into smaller groups?"

"Probably," grinned Elkins. She snapped her fingers, and the contents of the *Phoenix* pile flew into the air. For a moment, it appeared that a highly localized blizzard had appeared over their heads, then the papers fluttered to the ground and settled into several small piles.

Dicentra blinked. "I didn't know you could do . . . that."

Elkins pretended not to hear her as she straightened the piles, idly humming something that sounded strangely like "Weasley Is Our King."

"Check it out: Muggle newspapers," said Dicentra, as she gingerly pulled some greasy, smelly papers off the top of one pile.

"Ewww! Where did those come from?" demanded Elkins.

"Harry went dumpster-diving in Chapter 1, remember? He was looking for any sign of Voldemort's activities," Dicentra replied.

"That's right! Instead of Harry receiving writing from others, he's looking for it himself, not only in the Muggle newspapers but also in the *Daily Prophet*." She took all of the *Daily Prophet*s from June 1995 and set them on top of the Muggle newspapers to cover their odor. "I don't know what he thought he would do if he found something."

"They were keeping me totally in the dark," Stoned!Harry loudly protested. "What else was I supposed to do?"

Dicentra and Elkins turned to stare at Stoned!Harry. He was standing over them, defiantly, wand in hand. "What are you looking at?"

"Uh, nothing," Dicentra said, not taking her eyes off him. "You just seem a little . . . different."

"WHAT'S THAT TO YOU?" Stoned!Harry turned on his heel and stormed off. They heard the clatter of cauldrons at the far end of the room before he finally settled in a corner to sulk.

Elkins mouthed the word "teenager" to Dicentra, who nodded.

"Back to the stack," Elkins said quietly, pulling out a handful of letters. They all were addressed to Harry, and they were from Ron, Hermione, and Sirius. "These are those letters they sent during the summer that made Harry so frustrated. He could tell they were all in on something but they weren't telling him. So again we have absence of writing being a driving force, only this time it doesn't come from the Dursleys—it's coming from Harry's most trusted friends."

"Which makes it doubly ironic in 'A Peck of Owls,'" adds Dicentra, "when Harry is peppered with letters and Vernon is beside himself with rage at their invading his home. "Unlike the Letters From No One, which he kept from Harry with some measure of success, he's totally powerless to stop these letters from coming. It's a sign of the increasing blurring between the Wizarding and Muggle worlds—between Harry's two modes of existence."

"Those letters are also competing with each other to assign Harry roles," observed Elkins. "The first letter, from the Ministry of Magic, tells Harry he's been expelled from Hogwarts, which would cement his future as a failed wizard. Then we get the letter from Arthur telling Harry to not yield his wand and to stay home. The next letter from the Ministry tells Harry that he's merely been suspended pending a hearing, and then Sirius tells him to not leave home. Vernon determines that Harry might be a danger to his home and tries to throw him out, but Dumbledore's Howler to Petunia intervenes on his behalf. All these pieces of writing are tugging at Harry in different directions at the same time, not unlike the conflicting emotions and other forces of adolescence that pull at him."

They heard a derisive snort from the far side of the room. Dicentra grinned. "So to respond," she said loudly, making sure her voice carried far enough, "Harry writes three identical letters and sends them to three different people. It demonstrates how Harry's psyche is becoming fragmented into ego, id, and superego, represented by Ron, Sirius, and Hermione, respectively."

Elkins raised an eyebrow. "No, it doesn't," she whispered, "and besides, you don't even believe in Freudian interpretations."

"I know. I'm just playing with his head," replied Dicentra, as a Galleon came flying toward them and landed with a resounding clatter near Elkin's right foot.

"Here, why don't you two buy a real life," came the petulant voice from across the room.

With great effort, Dicentra and Elkins stifled a good five-minutes' worth of laughter Elkins reached into the pile again and withdrew another letter, this time with Muggle stamps and addressing on it.

"The letter from Tonks telling the Dursleys about the All-England Best-Kept Suburban Lawn Competition," she said. "It also serves as a means to manipulation, as it lures the Dursleys from their house while the Advance Guard rescues Harry."

"Check these out," she added, dragging a large pile of newspapers toward her. "A whole year's worth of *Daily Prophets*—from June 1995 through June 1996."

"Geez," said Dicentra. "*Order of the Phoenix* was long, but I don't remember it mentioning all of those."

"It doesn't mention each one individually," replied Elkins, "but they all play a significant part in shaping Harry's role. Hermione rightly deduces that the remaining reporters for the *Prophet* take up where Rita Skeeter left off, characterizing him as a 'deluded, attention-seeking person who thinks he's a great tragic hero or something.' Harry may not really play that role, but most people believe that he does. The way they react to him affects the role Harry does play—that of misunderstood martyr."

"Martyr?" Dicentra said doubtfully. "Isn't that a bit melodramatic?"

"He's a teenager," Elkins said. "Everything is melodramatic to him. Only in his case, it's not an exaggeration. Voldemort's return is no small event, and not being believed about something of this magnitude is one of the factors that drives Harry's anger throughout the book."

"It also results in these," said Dicentra soberly, picking up a pile of puckered parchment. "Look at these: rolls and rolls of the same thing over and over again, 'I must not tell lies. I must not tell lies' in that creepy dark-red ink. Blood, I mean . . . " she sat the parchment down carefully, as if setting down a sleeping creature that she couldn't afford to waken.

"We don't have the most important component of this bit of writing, though," Elkins said quietly. "We don't have the back of Harry's hand."

Dicentra shivered. "That episode has Biblical overtones, too. You remember how Moses came down from the mount with the 10 Commandments engraved on two stone tablets? Well, in later scripture, the image of engraving the commandments on one's heart was a metaphor for internalizing the ethical code as opposed to giving it lip service. Proverbs 7 says 'Keep my commandments, and live; . . . write them upon the tablet of thine heart.' Then in the New Testament, 2nd Corinthians 3 uses the phrase 'written . . . not in tablets of stone, but in fleshy tablets of the heart.' Umbridge said she wanted Harry to write 'I must not tell lies' until he internalized the message, which to her meant that the words were permanently etched on the flesh of his hand. Considering that Harry *was* telling the truth, and considering the fact that she obviously enjoyed making him suffer, the whole episode makes for an extraordinarily twisted, perverse variation on the Biblical metaphor."

"What role does this writing assign to Harry?" asked Elkins.

"Umbridge is trying to make him into yet another mindless unbeliever," answered Dicentra, "and furthermore, she's showing him that she won't be challenged—that the price for questioning her version of the truth is his own blood."

"She uses the writing as a tool of coercion, then," concluded Elkins, "which goes right along with these." She picked up a stack of official-looking documents. "The Educational Decrees: with each decree she tightens the thumbscrews a bit more; with each one, she extends the range of her power while severely curtailing the power of others. Because these are documents from the Ministry, she only has to post them around the school to assert her new status."

"That clipboard she writes on while inspecting the teachers is another means of coercion," said Dicentra. "Whatever she writes in her notes is considered to be the Truth, at least as far as she's concerned. And she uses this concocted 'Truth' to sack Trelawney and Hagrid, and to do who knows what else."

"Aren't you guys finished yet?" boomed Cindy as she bounced into the room.

Elkins and Dicentra exchanged glances. "Almost," said Elkins.

"And?"

"We've discovered that it *is* rather common for the characters in the Potterverse to quite literally write roles for each other, and sometimes for themselves," explained Dicentra.

"But we've got one more thing to determine," said Elkins. "I wonder if we can find a common theme to these roles, perhaps on a book-by-book basis."

Dicentra poked idly through the piles for a moment. "In *Philosopher's Stone*, Dumbledore writes Harry's role to introduce him to the Wizarding World and to Voldemort," she said slowly.

"Initiation, then," said Elkins. "And in *Chamber of Secrets*, the prominent examples of role-writing concern transforming the self into a written work and vice versa."

"*Prisoner of Azkaban* is about escape," said Dicentra. "Sirius escapes prison because of the *Daily Prophet* article, and Harry escapes Hogwarts using the Marauder's Map."

Elkins paused for a moment. "The writing in *Goblet of Fire* seems to emphasize false roles. Harry wasn't supposed to be a Triwizard Champion, and all those Rita Skeeter articles paint Harry in a very false light."

"And in *Order of the Phoenix*," concluded Dicentra, "it's coercion." Elkins nodded.

"Tell me this, though," challenged Cindy. "Did JKR do this on purpose or are you just reading too much into the books again?"

"I very much doubt that JKR consciously planned to use writing in this way," said Dicentra, "but that doesn't matter. If we can see it, it's there."

"Reading too much into it. I thought as much. So what are you going to call your exhibit?"

"I think I'll call it 'Scriptwriting for Pleasure and Profit: The Power of the Written Word in *Harry Potter*.'"

"That's a stupid name," said Cindy. She swaggered over to where Stoned!Harry was sulking and poked him with her paddle. "Hey, Stoner! Get up! We need another body for volleyball." She grabbed his robes, pulled him to his feet, and dragged him protesting from the room.

"Oh, would you look at the time," said Elkins, checking her watchless wrist. "I've got another seminar to give over at the Canon College on the Crouch Family Saga." She jumped to her feet and ran out of the room.

Dicentra sat alone amid the stacks of papers. Rising slowly, she extracted a wand from her robes and magicked the parchment blizzard into the air again. "Come on," she said wearily. "We've got a display to put together." And she sloped out of the room, trailing papers, parchment, and letters in her wake.

Bonnie May, a.k.a. Dicentra spectabilis, is a technical writer in Salt Lake City, Utah. Her academic credits include Bachelor and Masters degrees in Spanish literature from Brigham Young University and most of a Ph.D. (all but dissertation) in Spanish Literature from Cornell University. She began to read Harry Potter during the summer of 2001 and finished Harry Potter and the Goblet of Fire *during Thanksgiving holiday of that year. On Dec. 26, 2001, she Googled "Harry Potter," discovered the Lexicon, linked to HPforGrownups, and joined. At HPforGrownups, she is a List Elf, curator of Inish Alley (HPfGU acronyms), co-curator of Hypothetic Alley (wild theories cooked up in Theory Bay), a Sirius Apologist, keeper of the Sirius FAQ, and slayer of Jealous!Ron.*

Appendix

Incidents of Writing in the *Harry Potter* Series
(Page numbers refer to Scholastic editions)

Philosopher's Stone

016—Dumbledore: Letter to Dursleys about Harry
034—McGonagall: Acceptance letter
073—Dumbledore: Letter authorizing Stone's removal
102—Chocolate frog cards
141—*Daily Prophet (DP)*: Gringott's break-in
202—Dumbledore: "Use it well"
206—Erised inscription
219—Chocolate frog card; Flamel
236—Charlie: "I'll take Norbert"
261—Dumbledore: "Just in case"
267—Owl from "MoM"
285—Potion riddle

Chamber of Secrets

007—Dursleys don't allow letters to Hermione & Ron
018—Letters intercepted by Dobby
020—Mafalda Hopkirk: One more and you're expelled
043—List of school materials goes to Burrow
043—Lockhart's books (throughout)
078—*DP*: Ford Anglia seen by muggles
087—Molly: Ron's howler
097—Harry won't sign autographs
106—Harry won't sign autographs
111—Snape: Slytherins have Quidditch pitch
120—Harry addresses envelopes for Lockhart
124—Nick can't be in Headless Hunt
127—Kwikspell Letter
138—Writing on the wall: "The Chamber of Secrets has been opened . . . "
163—Permission to check out *Moste Potente Potions*
221—*DP*: Arthur in trouble for enchanting the Ford Anglia

231—Tom Riddle's Diary
233—Diary insinuates itself in Harry's mind
240—Harry writes in Diary
262—Order of Suspension for Dumbledore
290—Page from book: "pipes"
293—"Her skeleton will lie . . . "
314—Riddle's anagram name
341—Harry: phone number to Ron and Hermione

Prisoner of Azkaban

001—Harry writes an essay under the covers
008—Birthday card, clipping from Ron
011—Card & letter from Hermione
014—Note from Hagrid about book
014—Unsigned Permission slip
037—*DP*: Harry reads about Sirius Black on bus
107—Tea leaves
186—Werewolf essay from Snape
191—Marauder's Map
199—Notice of Dementor's patrol in Hogsmeade
217—Buckbeak's trial notification
223—No card with Firebolt
249—Neville's passwords
271—Gran Longbottom's howler
362—*DP*: Sirius's copy of Ron's article
432—Note from Sirius; signed permission slip

Goblet of Fire

029—Harry: tells Sirius about scar
030—Molly: invites Harry to QWC
035—Ron: "Dad got tickets"
036—Harry: "See you at 5"
056—Cauldron-bottom report
146—Rita: rumors of bodies, Arthur not forthcoming
151—Howlers to MoM making claims for damaged tents, etc.
152—Twins to Ludo: "Pay us back" (multiple)
203—Rita: alarm at Mad—eye's
221—Ron & Harry's divination predictions
226—Sirius: "I'm coming north"

Order of the Phoenix

080—Secret plans on kitchen table
103—Lockhart's guide to pests
111—Black family tapestry
126—Harry's guest badge at Ministry
130—Flying memos
134—Memo about changed venue for hearing
138—Percy takes notes
140—Charges against Harry
161—Ron makes prefect
185—Luna's *Quibbler*
190—*Quibbler* articles
222—Twins' advert for test subjects
232—Snape's potion ingredients on board
239—Umbridge's Course Aims
259—Bowtruckle sketch
266—"I must not tell lies"
274—"I must not tell lies"
280—Harry's cryptic note to Sirius
287—*DP*: Sturgis Podmore article
296—Percy's letter to Ron
299—Hermione corrects Sinistra's essays for Ron and Harry
306—*DP*: Umbridge is High Inquisitor
309—Snape's potions grades
347—Jinxed list of DAs
351—Ed. Decree 24: No clubs
359—Sirius: "Today, same time, same place."
383—Potions book: recklessness
389—Books in Room of Requirement
404—Weasley Is Our King badges
415—Ed. Decree 25: High Inquisitor can override staff punishments
447—Umbridge's clipboard
501—Homework planner from Hermione
509—Lockhart autographs
511—Lockhart fan mail
543—*DP*: DEs escape from Azkaban
546—*DP*: Death of Bode
551—Ed. Decree 26: No non—course-related info to students
558—Wanted poster in Hogsmeade of 10 DEs
565—Rita's interview in the *Quibbler*
578—Owls in support of Harry
581—Ed. Decree 27: anyone with *Quibbler* will be expelled

584—Enchanted poster of Harry's cover shot in Common Room
617—List of DAs; "Dumbledore's Army," not "Potter's"
619—Percy's note-taking
624—Ed. Decree 28: Umbridge is Headmistress
641—Snape's DADA OWL
656—Career advice notice; leaflets
673—Approval for whipping
725—History OWL
780—Label on prophecy: SPT to APWBD
845—*DP*: Voldemort is back
858—Note from Sirius with mirror
862—Luna's request for her stuff

Mythology and Magical

Systems

Lord Voldemort's Gift for Spreading Discord and Enmity:
The Challenge of Evil in Harry Potter

Richard C. Burke

I'm interested today in the ways in which J. K. Rowling steadily increases the power and the extent of evil across the five Harry Potter books. I'll be giving my definition of evil; then I'll discuss the various evils in the five books and trace their escalation through *The Order of the Phoenix*. After that, I'll look at Voldemort's nature and power, then at Harry and his confrontations with evil, and finally at the effects of all this evil on the readers.

Key to understanding evil in these books is the recognition that J. K. Rowling very successfully combines story elements that are perfectly familiar to most readers—characters, incidents, and concerns that nearly every child recognizes from his or her own life—with elements that are less mundane, more mysterious, more mythical in their origins and their resonances. While quidditch, for example, is just another school sport and History of Magic another subject, the Mirror of Erised and Voldemort have no simple parallels in everyday life. Rowling's evils are both mythical and mundane, and both sorts increase in prominence and power, at least through the first four books, making each one darker and more ominous than the ones that preceded it. As the books grow more disturbing, they also become richer, more complex, and more thought-provoking.

First, now, a definition of evil. Or two definitions, actually. Considered as a *personal characteristic*, evil can be defined as a willingness to disregard, or even welcome, another's pain in pursuit of one's own pleasure. Considered as an *effect*, evil is unjustifiable human suffering as a result of the willing act of a thinking creature. Traditional religious beliefs sometimes ascribe the origins of evil to a transcendent power, but modern philosophers locate the origins within thinking individuals (see Lara).

The cruelty of people like the Dursleys and the Malfoys is mundane evil; Voldemort's is mythical. As Mary Midgley argues in her lectures on wickedness, evil can be passive as well as aggressive—"a general kind of failure to live as we are capable of living" (7)—and so one need not set out to enslave the world to be evil.

The prominence of evils great and small plays a large part in creating the emotional and moral richness of all five novels. But in *The Sorcerer's Stone*, the greatest wickedness *brackets* most of the story and leaves the rest of it to lesser evils. Voldemort is defeated before the novel begins. True, he has just tried to kill a baby and has succeeded in killing its parents, so we're made aware of powerful evil right at the start. But the dead parents were strangers to us, the villainous wizard has lost nearly all his power, and the lesser evil of the Dursleys immediately draws our attention in a new direction. The emphasis falls, not on the dead and the defeated, but on "Harry Potter—the boy who lived!" (*Sorcerer's Stone* 7).

Throughout much of *The Sorcerer's Stone*, Harry encounters the sort of mundane evils that we might all experience: the stupid prejudice of the Dursleys, the snobbish taunts of Malfoy, the bitterness of Filch, the vindictiveness of Snape. All this nastiness results from one form or another of *egotism*, from a willingness to disregard the well-being of another in order to benefit oneself. It causes Harry frustration and emotional pain and reminds him (and us) of his powerlessness in the face of them. But it is evil he can *endure*; it won't destroy him. The Dursleys are the worst of the lot, because they go beyond inflicting pain—Malfoy's forte—and actually seek to deny Harry his identity and any knowledge of his parents. Making him sleep in the closet beneath the stairs is an outrage, sure to infuriate young readers, but the Dursleys do deeper, more serious injuries by regarding Harry as worthless and keeping secret his wizard identity.

The Dursleys, Malfoy, Filch, and Snape are disagreeable, even cruel, but unquestionably human. Voldemort, even when we first learn of him, is a different sort: truly pitiless and diabolical, more monstrous than human, a man transformed by evil. But in *The Sorcerer's Stone*, Voldemort has virtually no power and almost no life, and he can do nothing without the willing, even eager assistance of Professor Quirrel. His evil is intense and undiminished, but impotent and contained.

Harry Potter and the Chamber of Secrets steps up the evil a bit. The villain now is Voldemort's teenage self, Tom Riddle. He has no willing accomplice like Quirrel, but instead uses young Ginny Weasley, whom he cruelly manipulates by playing on her loneliness and anxieties.

The second book adds to the mundane evils by including both the ridiculously egotistical Gilderoy Lockhart, who chooses to abandon Ginny to her death in order to preserve his reputation, and the vicious Lucius Malfoy, who plants Tom Riddle's enchanted diary among Ginny Weasley's books for his own political purposes (he tries to get Dumbledore fired for the same purposes).

The Chamber of Secrets also introduces a particular type of wizard prejudice: the hatred of wizards like Hermionewith muggle parents. It even has its own racist slur, "mudblood." In *Sorcerer's Stone*, all of the really *serious* evil appeared to be linked to the seductive power of Voldemort. The existence of this bigotry reveals that the wizard world, which is in many ways the stuff of children's dreams, includes a deeply ingrained social evil.

The third book, *Prisoner of Azkaban*, retains all the old problems. And it introduces the dementors. These non-human Azkaban guards bring a new and eerie kind of evil to the stories which, like Voldemort, does not have a direct human equivalent in ordinary life. Unlike mountain trolls, giant spiders, and other natural evils which don't *need* to inflict pain on human beings, the dementors purposefully torment their victims, draining away happiness and replacing it with anguish, guilt, and despair: "They infest the darkest, filthiest places, they glory in decay and despair, they drain peace, hope, and happiness out of the air around them . . . . If it can, the dementor will feed on you long enough to reduce you to something like itself . . . soul-less and evil" (*Azkaban* 187). Like Voldemort, the dementors present Harry with an ominous and essentially mysterious challenge that he cannot simply *endure*, as he does the likes of Malfoy and Snape. He must fight back or be conquered.

What's more, because they work by leaving one with the worst that is in him or her, the dementors emphasize the presence within *every*one of pain, weakness, longing, and a capacity for evil. Like Malfoy, with his snotty attacks on Ron's poverty and Hermione's prominent teeth, they remind us that everyone in Harry's world has personal sources of unhappiness and discontent that no amount of good fortune can wholly erase and no skill at wizard spells can readily correct.

Besides introducing the dementors, *The Prisoner of Azkaban* also recounts the hateful treachery of Peter Pettigrew. If Quirrel was a weak-minded fool and Ginny Weasley an exploited victim, Pettigrew is the self-serving betrayer of Harry's parents, the murderer of some dozen people, and the would-be killer of Harry. Like other Death Eaters in subsequent novels, he demonstrates Voldemort's power to bring out the worst in his followers. And just as Voldemort has taken away Harry's parents, Pettigrew has robbed him of his godfather, leaving Harry at the mercy of the Dursleys.

Before moving on to the fourth book, I'd like to observe that the conflict with evil in the first three books has an innocent parallel in quidditch. Like all team sports, quidditch presents one with a controlled and ultimately harmless "evil"—the opposing team. The players *fight* for victory, the fans yearn for the enemy's defeat, and every new event in a match can be understood in moral terms, to the extent that one team is regarded as *good* and the other as *bad*. In their quidditch matches, Harry and the Gryffindor team prove their worth by facing and overcoming their opponents. The sporting events of the first three books are all good clean fun.

Then in *The Goblet of Fire*, where evil pervades so much of the wizarding world, the Triwizard Tournament replaces quidditch, and Harry's difficulties increase greatly: besides his opponents, he faces the tournament's three main challenges: the dragons, the lake, and the maze. And ultimately, Voldemort and young Barty Crouch turn the sporting contest into a very real battle.

This transformation—and subversion—of sports parallels the change in evil's power and extent in the fourth book. In *The Goblet of Fire*, the power and extent of evil escalate dramatically. Evils that are less than Voldemort's but greater than young Malfoy's now appear everywhere. The *Daily Prophet,* notable earlier only for its amusing animated photos, is now the home of Rita Skeeter and her pointlessly cruel articles. After one of them attacks Hermione as Harry's heartbreaker, she gets loads of hate mail, revealing an unsuspected mean streak in the general wizarding public. The jovial Ludo Bagman cheats Fred and George by paying them with worthless leprechaun gold. Cornelius Fudge, the Minister of Magic, reveals himself to be cowardly and irresponsible. The Death Eaters torment a family of muggles after the Quidditch World Cup. The hitherto spontaneous torments meted out by Draco Malfoy become formalized with the production of the badges that say "Potter Stinks." Frank Bryce is killed in the Riddle House; Mr. Crouch is killed by his own son; Cedric Diggory is killed at a casual command from Voldemort. We learn that Death Eaters tortured Neville Longbottom's parents with the Cruciatus Curse until they went permanently mad. And we see that human sympathy, which ought to be a bulwark against evil, can be dangerously misleading, when we watch the pathetic but utterly appropriate spectacle of young Barty Crouch being dragged off to Azkaban.

Worst of all in *Goblet of Fire*, of course, is the return of Voldemort to full life and considerable power. In the book's terrific climax, he may not be able to kill Harry, but hereafter he will be a threat to the entire wizarding world such as he has not been since before the first book began: " . . . we are all facing dark and difficult times," Dumbledore warns at the end of the book (724).

The transformation—or exposure—of Cornelius Fudge efficiently represents the transformation of the wizard world in *Goblet of Fire*. Rowling says that "Harry . . . had always thought of Fudge as a kindly figure, a little blustering, a little pompous, but essentially good natured. But now a short, angry wizard stood before him, refusing, point-blank, to accept the prospect of disruption in his comfortable and ordered world . . . " (707). That comfortable and ordered world has appealed to readers and given the books some of their charm. Now it's in serious danger.

Harry Potter and the Order of the Phoenix does not substantially expand the range or power of evil. Rather, it dramatizes at great length many of the *consequences* of evil. Again and again, characters endure fear, anger, confusion, distrust, violence, and isolation, as well as social fragmentation at every level from the Weasley family on up to the whole wizarding world.

Harry scarcely enjoys a moment's pleasure in *Order of the Phoenix:* irritation, doubt, frustration, desperation, and fury dominate his dealings with friends as well as enemies, and he is constantly yelling. The Weasley's endure the smug hostility of Percy. Harry and his friends come face to face with the madness of Neville's parents and Lockhart. The Dementors abandon their duties at Azkaban. And after several favorite characters come near to death, Sirius Black actually dies, leaving Harry bereft.

Rowling doesn't provide much new evil here, beyond the wickedly self-righteous Dolores Umbridge. Cornelius Fudge isn't really an evil man but rather a man who cannot cope with evil. A more interesting development is the presentation of James Potter, Harry's father, as a self-important fifteen-year-old with a capacity for cruelty equal to Malfoy's.

The fifth book's refusal to present new and more powerful forms of evil serves the series well. *The Order of the Phoenix* portrays a world where evil increasingly harms people, behaviors, attitudes, and institutions. The charming world of the first book has deteriorated: the fifth book offers relatively few pleasures as the wizards' world threatens to collapse before Voldemort's onslaught.

Rowling provides small comforts: the self-reliance and cooperation of the students in "Dumbledore's Army," the long-delayed success of Ron as a quidditch player, the emergence of Neville Longbottom as a capable opponent of Voldemort, and—above all—Dumbledore's even-tempered yet fully committed efforts to lead the battle against evil. But the predominant mood of *Order of the Phoenix* is grim.

Well, now for Voldemort.

Late in *Goblet of Fire*, Harry thinks, "It was Voldemort . . . it all came back to Voldemort" (607). But evil in these books neither begins nor ends with Voldemort; it is in the nature of things. Basilisks, boggarts, giant spiders, and grindylows reflect the darker side of things, as do the dangerous books that Ron mentions in *Chamber of Secrets*: "there was one that burned your eyes out. And everyone who read *Sonnets of a Sorcerer* spoke in limericks for the rest of their lives" (*Chamber of Secrets*, 230-31). The students at Hogwarts have to study Defense Against the Dark Arts every year, implying that they have a great deal to defend themselves against. But these nasty little menaces are generally marginalized and inconsequential. Serious injuries are more likely to occur on the quidditch field, and those are quickly cured by Madam Pomfrey, leaving the casual reader with the impression that the students have little to fear beyond "he who must not be named."

But Voldemort embodies evil in a way that none of the other characters do, not even the dementors. Except for the dementors, the other evil figures in the books are basically ordinary people. They may be thoroughly stupid and nasty, but they are identifiably human all the same. Voldemort, on the other hand, comes not from everyday life but from the realm of myth and archetype: he's an embodiment of evil, glorying in his wickedness and unwilling to make any accommodation whatsoever with any power other than his own. He can be surrendered to or destroyed, but he cannot be made good—as the prophecy implies in *Order of the Phoenix*. In *Sorcerer's Stone*, Professor Quirrel explains Voldemort's ideas about evil: "There is no good and evil, there is only power, and those too weak to seek it" (291). Of course one can have power without seeking to use it against innocent people (as Dumbledore shows). But Voldemort links goodness with weakness, thus making goodness a vice and evil a virtue. Rita Skeeter, Snape, and the Dursleys do evil in the confidence that they are doing right. Voldemort alone rejects the very ideas of right or good, and instead pursues power with an unrestrained appetite. There is nothing beyond himself that he regards with anything but contempt. Perhaps that is why he alone, of all the human characters in the book, reveals no trace of an indication that he is capable of being redeemed.

Like others in these books, Voldemort's evil is inseparable from his egotism. And like others, his evil seeks to dehumanize his victims, not just cause pain or thwart desires. The Dursleys and Rita Skeeter dehumanize their victims, imposing a harmful and restrictive identity on them. Tom Riddle—the young Voldemort—violates Ginny Weasley's integrity, making her commit vicious acts around Hogwarts and allowing her to think she is going mad. And in the end, he plans to draw the life force from her, which will enable him to escape from the diary but which will kill her. The adult Voldemort consciously and continually seeks to dehumanize *every*one.

Voldemort threatens not so much the ruin as the enslavement of the wizard world. His origins may be in myth, but he operates on a smaller scale than the forces of evil in, say, Diane Duane's *So You Want To Be a Wizard* or Susan Cooper's *The Dark Is Rising*, books in which annihilation rather than enslavement appears to be the ultimate threat. The ruin he has in mind is more mundane than apocalyptic: more Nazi oppression than Hiroshima obliteration. The potential destruction that looms at the end of *So You Want To Be a Wizard* may be a more cosmic horror, but the threat that has emerged by the end of *Goblet of Fire* is likely to strike the reader with a greater immediacy and likelihood.

The concluding chapters point towards the dreadful possibility of a world trapped in monstrous servitude to Voldemort. Lesser evils that appeared throughout the book (and the Death Eaters are the most villainous of these) show that evil is already more extensive than we may have thought. Despite Dumbledore's plans and exertions at the very end, Voldemort seems to be in the ascendant—or about to be. And things do not improve in *The Order of the Phoenix*.

And now we ask, what of Harry Potter? What of goodness?

Harry's stature, both within the novels and with readers, depends largely on the stature and power of those who oppose him. He is famous from infancy for having survived Voldemort's attack. And he wins the reader's sympathy early on for enduring life with the Dursleys. In each of the books, he proves himself to be heroic by directly fighting evil characters, even at the risk of death.

In several respects, he is the typical boy hero of a school novel: he has engaging friends, is good at sports, gets into scrapes, studies with eccentric teachers, and copes with school bullies, all the time showing that his heart is both large and warm. All of this is important to his popularity with readers, because it helps create our ready identification with his point of view: we quickly learn to see that whatever is good for Harry is *good*, and what is bad for Harry is not.

As Bruno Bettleheim has observed, children—and older readers, I assume—do not respond to or identify with *goodness* itself but with the character who wins their sympathy (9). Harry does nothing to lose our sympathy; he isn't the sort of boring goody-goody that Hermione appears to be in the early days, still less the insipid hero of "improving books." Evil with his prickly adolescence in *Order of the Phoenix*, there is no evil in him. For one thing, he lacks the ego for it. For another, he is profoundly good at heart.

Coping with Malfoy, the Dursleys, Snape, and the like (as well as triumphing in his quidditch matches) establishes Harry's strength of character in the everyday realm, the one in which *we* live. His climactic confrontations with evil at the end of each book reveal his extraordinary courage and virtue and elevate him to a genuinely heroic status. If in the first instance he is the hero of traditional school novels, in the second he is a fairy tale hero, proving his worth by battling evil.

Until *Goblet of Fire*, Harry has important help when he bravely faces evil in the climactic scenes: from Dumbledore in *Sorcerer's Stone*, and from Fawkes, the phoenix, in *Chamber of Secrets*. In the climax of *Prisoner of Azkaban*, he gets plenty of help from Sirius Black, Lupin, Dumbledore, Hermione, and Ron (as well as from himself, thanks to a little time travel).

And in each of these first three books, Harry goes willingly in pursuit of the evil characters. But in *Goblet of Fire*, he has no choice. Voldemort brings Harry to him using the portkey. In fact, Harry's been relentlessly manipulated towards this encounter throughout the whole book—an act of evil that abridges his freedom. This change shows how greatly Voldemort's power has increased, and with it, Harry's vulnerability.

But Harry's courage and strength of will are equal to the challenge. Despite the shock of finding himself face-to-face with Voldemort, despite the injury to his leg from the spider in the maze, and the pain he endures from a Cruciatus Curse, and the certainty that he is going to die, Harry resists: "He was going to die like Cedric . . . and there was nothing he could do about it . . . but he wasn't going to play along. He wasn't going to obey Voldemort . . . he wasn't going to beg" (*Goblet of Fire*, 661). At first, this may look like nothing more than a tough-guy determination not to show weakness; in fact, Harry is refusing to make any *compromises* with evil. Voldemort responds with an Imperius Curse, which should take complete control of Harry's will, and still he resists.

Harry escapes Voldemort's *Avada Kedavra* curse and death through a bit of luck (a.k.a.: authorial manipulation): because his wand and Voldemort's share feathers from the same phoenix, the Reverse Spell effect stops the spell each casts at the other. The events that follow allow Harry to escape, but they're quite independent of any qualities that Harry might possess. They remind us that, for all his power and will, Voldemort is not in complete control: like Harry and all others, he operates within a world he cannot yet dominate, and it is apparently not yet evil enough to facilitate his schemes.

Harry escapes thanks to external circumstances, but he shows his heroic nature when he risks his life to bring Cedric's body back to Hogwarts. It isn't enough to survive an encounter with evil; Harry actively does good as well.

By refusing to collapse in the presence of Voldemort, Harry proves himself to be a mythic hero as well as a hero of a more mundane sort. He faces both kinds of evil and beats both kinds—or, for the time being, copes with and survives both kinds. Harry manages to do so again in *The Order of the Phoenix*, where he once again goes willingly into battle against the enemy, and does so with the greatest array yet of support, demonstrating the importance of cooperation in the confrontation with evil.

Finally, how does this escalation of evil affect us readers? For one thing, all that evil highlights the existence of at least as much goodness. For another, the collisions with evil, whether great or small, create potent emotional stimuli: Harry's orphan-state helps us sympathize with him right away; I suspect that most children reading the book want to smack Malfoy, yell at Snape, demolish the Dursleys, and commit any number of outrages against Professor Umbridge. And Harry's triumphs provide the satisfaction of a conflict favorably resolved. Furthermore, as we know, Harry's triumphs in the face of evil are empowering for children. The character they identify with has faced down evil and come away triumphant. As Natalie Babbitt has said of such confrontations, "We are attracted by the hero, who faces the evil, who may even dance on its teeth and still survive. For the hero, of course, is us. These stories . . . act out encounters with disaster. Many characters will be mauled, burned, drowned, or drawn and quartered, but not the hero—not *us* . . . " (177).

The evil in the Harry Potter books *has* to escalate, intensify, and spread if it is to be consequential. A story should not create the impression that everyone who is good is finally untouchable, that evil is for *other* people. If, to use an analogy, Gryffindor always wins the house cup at the end of the year, the victory eventually loses meaning. If Voldemort is always squashed like a bug, he's not a sufficient villain. In *The Goblet of Fire*, Voldemort is restored, and his power expands in *The Order of the Phoenix*. His wickedness is greater than ever, and other evils in this world are more visible than ever. And Harry Potter, older, braver, and facing a more desperate situation than before, must be more heroic than ever in the face of these evils.

Richard Burke is a Professor of English at Lynchburg College in Virginia, where he is currently chair of the faculty. He regularly teaches courses in Victorian, Romantic and 17th century English literature, as well as children's literature. His professional activities include publications on Trollope, Dickens, Wordsworth, Marvell and Shakespeare, and presentations on such subjects as Japanese literature, Victorian wills, the Oz books, Harry Potter, and Philip Pullman's "His Dark Materials" trilogy. His sons are aged 11 and 12.

Children's Literature or Adult Classic?
Harry Potter & The Great Tradition

Dr. Paige Byam

A slightly revised version of this article will be published in Issue 54 of Topic: The Washington and Jefferson Review.

In his 1948 essay, "The Great Tradition," F. R. Leavis set out to "discriminate" among the field of English novelists. He wants to distinguish

> the few really great—the major novelists who count in the same way
> as the major poets, in the sense that they not only change the possibilities
> of the art for practitioners and readers, but that they are significant in
> terms of the human awareness they promote; awareness of the
> possibilities of life.

I don't want to contest Leavis' project or his choices—other scholars have taken on those quarrels—but rather to show how the Harry Potter series fits the criteria Leavis admires as "great."

When I started looking at *Harry Potter* from an academic perspective after the first two novels in the series had been published, very little had been written about the books. For anyone paying attention, it was very clear that *Harry Potter* had engaged a new generation of readers, especially among the elementary-school-age crowd. However, it was apparent that adults were also reading *Harry Potter* in huge numbers, and I became interested in this aspect of the series—as well as eagerly anticipating each book in the series from a reader's standpoint.

Interestingly, the cult status of *Harry Potter* among adults has drawn much criticism since that time. Many debates, inside of the academy and out, have focused on whether or not *Harry Potter* is "just" a children's book, and whether it has literary merit. This controversy erupted most spectacularly in the *NY Times'* handling of *Harry Potter* on its "Best Seller List."

Because the huge, long-term success of *Harry Potter* placed books in the series atop the list and left no room for books aimed strictly at adult readers, the *NYT* decided to put *Harry Potter* into a "new" children's category. Commenting on this decision in July of 2000, Charles McGrath, the editor of the *Book Review* stated:

> The sales and popularity of children's books can rival and, in the case
> of the Harry Potter books, even exceed those of adult books . . . . With
> a separate children's list we can more fully represent what people are
> reading, and we can clear more room on the adult list for adult books.
> ("New York Times")

Some regarded this as attempt to quash adult interest in *Harry Potter* by sending out a message to readers that it is really children's fiction. Also, placement on the new children's list did a disservice to the series by not reflecting how many copies each book sold each week compared to adult best-sellers.

At the very least, the *NYT* decision to create a separate children's bestseller list was a strategy to shift attention away from the Harry Potter series. At this point in time, July 7, 2000, "one or more of the three books in the J. K. Rowling Harry Potter series [had] commanded spots on the adult fiction bestseller list for 81 weeks to date" ("New York Times"). Removing Harry Potter from the adult bestseller list was a marketing decision designed to obscure the fact that *Harry Potter* was still outselling top adult fiction and that no other children's book approached it in sales at the time.

The *Harry Potter* series not only deserves the attention it is getting because of its imaginative qualities and compelling storyline, but also because of its literary merits. I will argue here that the *Harry Potter* series fits well into "the great tradition" of British novels that F. R. Leavis has described, and that the *Harry Potter* series is rooted specifically in the historical British novel tradition.

Perhaps it's the sense of "fun" and the comedic element that we encounter—especially in books 1-4 of the series—that makes some people think that *Harry Potter* isn't for adults. In many cases, the problems and even tragedies that Harry encounters are resolved or diminished and not left for readers to ponder as in many other classic British novels. While this pattern of resolution is less typical of "adult" classics, it shouldn't be used as a reason for knocking the *Harry Potter* series out of the "adult" fiction category.

Another reason some critics think *Harry Potter* is not for adult readers is because the hero is not grown up. True, the character of Harry is an adolescent—as are Jane Eyre, Pip, and Esther Summerson when we first meet them, to name a few. As of yet, the series hasn't followed Harry to adulthood, but this shouldn't be a "requirement" for adult fiction either. Furthermore, with the publication of *Harry Potter and the Order of the Phoenix*, Rowling has introduced us to a "new" Harry—one who is entering turbulent teen years and experiencing all the angst, doubts, and troubles that we see in "classic" British novels.

In fact, the *Harry Potter* novels can be linked to many novelistic and literary traditions, including the Gothic tradition in literature, the mystery, the Bildungsroman, and the heroic quest, to name a few. These connections to classic literature can be seen from the beginning of the first novel: Harry is Christ-like in his status of being marked from birth by Voldemort and destined for greatness since he has "saved" the wizarding world. His life is also parallel to a hero such as King Arthur who is raised away from danger or attention until he is of age or ready for challenges. King Arthur is raised in Sir Kay's shadow, not realizing that he is special—King Uther Pendragon's son—until he inadvertently pulls the sword from the stone. In a similar way, magic pulls Harry from his life as an underling with the Dursleys when he comes of age to be educated.

The Gothic elements in *Harry Potter* also link the novel to many 19th-century British novels. Trappings such as the castle-school architecture, the threat of enclosure, the magic, and the supernatural, as well as the notable similarities in Gothic elements (e.g.: crime, deformity, murder, blood, miracles, armored knights, the mark, dreams and visions, lineage, the stranger motif, the "foreign" realm) are prevalent in the texts. In addition, in *Harry Potter* we find the psychological aspects of the interior Gothic that we find in 19th-century British novels such as Charlotte Brontë's *Jane Eyre*, Charles Dickens' *Great Expectations* and *Bleak House*, and Emily Brontë's *Wuthering Heights*.

A central issue that links *Harry Potter* to these "great tradition" novels is the figure of the orphan. The orphan is a common feature of the Bildungsroman, or novel of education or development, where a character must develop in society, and find his or her own way in the world. The figure of the orphan is often used in developmental novels, since an orphan can act outside of the social norm because his/her "normal" family structure is absent. Therefore, the orphan can be exposed to unusual circumstances and is freer to act within them than a "normal" protagonist would be. The orphan has audience appeal because he or she is alone in the world and has often suffered great trauma; the reader thus usually sympathizes with the character and roots for him/her. Harry Potter lives with his aunt, as do Jane Eyre and Esther Summerson (although she doesn't know it), while Pip lives with his sister. Each of these children has a family connection to their lodgings, but each is living in misery because of how they're treated. They are often deprived of food (as in the cases of Harry and Pip) and enclosed both literally (Harry in the cupboard; Jane in the Red Room) and psychologically by their "families." They must endure cruel behavior: Harry is beaten by his cousin Dudley, Jane is struck by her cousin John, and Pip is physically abused by his sister, Mrs. Joe.

In the lives of these protagonists, there is usually a turning point that coincides with a coming of age. At this point in many of the novels, there is an interruption of the characters' lives and often a direct intervention by an outside force. In *Harry Potter*, letters descend in multitudes upon the Dursley's household and Hagrid arrives to rescue Harry and take him to Hogwarts; in *Jane Eyre*, the doctor who treats Jane after her experience in the Red Room recognizes Jane's predicament and recommends schooling, so Jane is sent to Lowood; in *Great Expectations*, Pip receives notice that he is to be educated to be a "gentleman." There is an element of the fairy tale rescue in these novels, and the protagonists are then pushed to embark on a different course of education or development.

In the various worlds into which these characters are thrust, all of their "norms" are stripped away and they must learn to survive by their innate abilities. They must use their inner strength to "read" the situations and circumstances that they encounter. On one level, the different "worlds" that the protagonists encounter help prepare them to re-enter society in a more adjusted way. Harry learns to negotiate between the Muggle world and Hogwarts; Jane must experience and emerge from the worlds of Gateshead, Lowood, Thornfield, Moor House, and Ferndean before she is through with her quest; and Pip must leave the world of Joe and Mrs. Joe and come to terms with Miss Havisham and Magwitch before he gains understanding.

It is also significant that at this point different religions or philosophies are often introduced to the protagonists. Harry learns to tap into his own powers, train his magic, and understand the relationship between the world of the Muggles and the wizarding world. He must use his wits to decipher the new world he encounters at Hogwarts, learn to avoid characters like Draco Malfoy, and follow in his parents' footsteps, although he is uncertain of their path. Similarly, Jane Eyre must find the different possibilities for living available in the Christian world that she inhabits—from the hypocrisy of Gateshead and Lowood to the cold, doctrinaire religious interpretation of St. John Rivers to the fairy tale "reality" of Ferndean. Pip must learn to understand and reject the empty life of Miss Havisham and Estella. Throughout their ordeals, each central character must learn what *not* to be.

In this stage of their education, each protagonist must solve a mystery or decode an enigma in order to proceed, just as the reader must unravel, solve, and come to terms with each problem confronting the central character along the way. Harry Potter must come to terms with "He-who-must-not-be-named"/Voldemort and solve the "riddle" of Tom Riddle; Jane Eyre must discover Rochester and his secret and uncover the identity and relevance of the madwoman in the attic; Pip must be open to learning that his benefactor is Magwitch the convict—who is Estella's father—and not Miss Havisham.

In another crucial novelistic motif, the character or characters to be unraveled are, like the protagonist, orphans. Each serves as a literary double or Doppelganger of the protagonist. The psychological double does what the other character would like to and acts on similar impulses; the Doppelganger represents a spirit that can adapt its form (as Voldemort literally does). The double and Doppelganger functions represent a possible future for each protagonist.

The Doppelganger motif is prevalent in most "great tradition" novels. In *Jane Eyre*, Bertha and Jane are psychological doubles in any number of ways, from drawing blood from their victims, to seeing their images in the glass, to their association with fire, and their connection with Rochester. In *Great Expectations*, Pip must come to terms with his dawning awareness of his role as a gentleman—such as in the scene when he sees his shoes through Estella's eyes and recognizes how they place him in a specific social class. Perhaps his greatest challenge is to acknowledge his psychological and literal connection with Magwitch, the banished criminal. Moreover, Orlick's assault on Mrs. Joe is often interpreted as an acting out of Pip's psychological desire, just as Bertha's burning of Thornfield acts out Jane's own subliminal desires. We learn from Hagrid that Harry's subliminal wishes take tangible form in magic—his revenge on Dudley is manifested in Harry's unwitting release of the boa constrictor at the zoo.

In *Harry Potter*, Tom Riddle/Voldemort is a double for Harry—both are parseltongues, the Sorting Hat would have liked to place Harry in the Slytherin House where Riddle lived, Harry can identify with Riddle's diary, they have "twin" wands, and Harry is privy to many of Voldemort's thoughts through the scar that Harry received from him. This is developed even further in *The Order of the Phoenix* when Harry and Voldemort seem to be in each other's minds.

The protagonist orphans learn key information about themselves from their orphan doubles, but then they must sift through their various inheritances. In *Jane Eyre*, Jane must learn from Bertha—her rival and simultaneous double and antithesis—and decide how she needs to negotiate her place in Rochester's world. At the same time, she is given her inheritance from her uncle. Pip must come to terms with the identity of his benefactor, the role of love in his life, and the contagion of love that pervades his world. The "secret" and "tainted" money from Magwitch that helps Pip also reveals the social hypocrisy that underlies the social strata that Pip must negotiate.

In the *Harry Potter* series, Harry must keep trying to understand the literal and psychological scar that Voldemort inflicts upon him, he must deal with his fame, and he must learn to traverse two worlds. Harry has tangible things such as his unexpected fortune in wizarding currency, as well as the unanticipated advantage of the invisibility cloak and the Marauders' Map to help him, but these tools only *lead* him toward understanding, they do not produce it.

The final message in each text involves what the central character learns in each narrative. In *Jane Eyre*, Jane must learn how to bring unarticulated passions to the surface, but may ultimately sublimate her understanding in the "Reader, I married him" ending; and Pip must deal with what it means to be a gentleman beyond the obvious trappings that money can buy. In the *Harry Potter* series, Harry learns of friendship and must recognize enemies, power, and a life beyond his own.

While some of these issues have been tied up neatly in books 1-4 of the series, in *The Order of the Phoenix*, Harry's growth—in literal age and in psychological depth approaching adulthood—also makes the perspective of the book more complicated. Harry is learning that nothing is as simple as it seems: relationships are complicated and require work, communication, and acceptance to endure. Sirius' death shows Harry that he, again, must rely on himself and go on alone psychologically, although supported by loyal friends like Ron, Hermione, and Dumbledore. Understanding and forgiving James Potter's childhood weaknesses of vanity and cruelty may be a way for Harry to understand and conquer his anger and rashness eventually.

The similarities drawn here between *Harry Potter* and other novels in the Bildungsroman tradition are just a beginning. In offering a sketch of the similarities, I hope more scholars recognize *Harry Potter* as the legitimate British novel that it is in terms of literary merit. It is hard to recognize a prophetic novel in its own time, especially since the *Harry Potter* series is not yet complete. Whether or not Harry matures or learns to deal with the coming-of-age adversities that Jane Eyre and Pip ultimately overcome is yet to be seen—although *The Order of the Phoenix* shows more progression this way. Readers want the ending, and the fact that *Harry Potter* is currently in flux adds to the critics' feeling that *Harry Potter* is not "worthy" of being identified as "adult" fiction; the fact that J. K. Rowling is not finished writing unsettles many critics who want to "place" the Harry Potter novels.

A final note: many critical or academic readers have been reluctant to embrace the series because of its popularity and because of what they see as the crass commercialization of serial publication. However, it is worth noting that *Great Expectations* was published in a serial form that has similarities to *Harry Potter*. Additionally, the market was a driving force in Dickens' writing of *Great Expectations*, and Dickens ended up writing two different endings to the text in an effort to please his audience. This shows that the "Great Tradition" has never been divorced from commercial considerations; critics are wrong to dismiss the *Harry Potter* series because of its popularity.

Although we have yet to see the "resolution" of the *Harry Potter* series, its literary connections to Gothic, mystery, and the Bildungsroman make the books worthy of literary analysis in the "great tradition" of the British novel. Ultimately, the *Harry Potter* series is too important and too popular to be defined exclusively as either children's or adult fiction, in part because it represents the revival of Leavis' "Great Tradition."

Works Cited

Brontë, Charlotte. *Jane Eyre*. New York: Penguin, 1981.

Brontë, Emily. *Wuthering Heights*. 1847. New York: Penguin, 1981.

Dickens, Charles. *Bleak House*. 1853. New York: W. W. Norton, 1977.

_____. *Great Expectations*.

Leavis, F. R. "The Great Tradition." 1948. In *The Great Tradition: A Study of the English Novel*. Garden City, N. Y.: Doubleday, 1954.

"The New York Times Book Review to Debut Children's Bestseller List." Friday, July 7, 2000. July 14, 2003. http://www.writenew.com/2000/070700_nytimes_children.htm

Rowling, J. K. *Harry Potter and the Chamber of Secrets*. New York: Scholastic, 1999.

_____. *Harry Potter and the Goblet of Fire*. New York: Scholastic, 2000.

_____. *Harry Potter and the Order of the Phoenix*. New York: Scholastic, 2003.

_____. *Harry Potter and the Prisoner of Azkaban*. New York: Scholastic, 1999.

_____. *Harry Potter and the Sorcerer's Stone*. New York: Scholastic, 1997.

Dr. Paige Byam is Associate Professor of English at Northern Kentucky University. Courses she teaches include "The Gothic in Literature and the Arts," "The British Novel," and "Mystery, Murder, and Mayhem in Literature and Film." She and her husband, Steve Gores, live in Cincinnati with their four Harry Potter fans: Hal, Jasper, Hugh, and Simon.

Narratorial Control:
Harry Potter Joins The Three Investigators

Ernelle Fife

J. R. Rowling's ongoing Harry Potter series and Robert Arthur's Alfred Hitchcock and The Three Investigator series seem worlds apart. Rowling's first books in the Potter series are smash hits both with her intended audience of juvenile readers and with younger children, older teens, and even adults. Arthur's The Three Investigators series began in 1964, and while never as successful as the Nancy Drew series or The Hardy Boys series, it did span over twenty-five years with five different authors and generated two sequels. It has been translated into over two dozen languages, and became the blueprint for similar mystery series in countries from Germany to Saudi Arabia to Japan. Its readership is intensely loyal, generating dozens of fan sites world wide. Both series work for the target juvenile audience primarily for narratological reasons: each author creates a narrator who controls how the reader reads, inviting the reader to become the narratee, a active participant in the story as the narrative progresses. Both Arthur and Rowling create narrators who control the process of reading, turning the juvenile reader into the narratee.

There are several differences between the two series beyond the obvious one of magic. Arthur in his original six books depicts a world of three ordinary boys living in southern California, not the fantasy world of English witches and wizards. Additionally, while most of the action in the Potter series takes place in the Hogwarts School of Witchcraft and Wizardry, The Three Investigators series is set during school breaks.

However, these two series do share several important narratological features. Both sets of juvenile protagonists mirror the juvenile reader in numerous ways. Both series are character, not plot, driven: while the stories certainly are filled with action, suspense, and danger, the choices that the protagonists make are always more significant. Secondly, teamwork and perseverance are key elements, morals in fact: even though the Potter series focuses on one boy, his escapades once he arrives at Hogwarts include his closest friends, Ron Weasley and Hermione Granger, who become more and more involved in Harry's life both at school and with his Muggle relatives. These characteristics or morals, teamwork and perseverance, are the key to the success of both sets of protagonists, to Hogwarts, as the Sorting Hat reveals (OP 204-07), the group from Dumbledore's Army who set off to rescue Sirius, and the Order of the Phoenix, though Sirius has great difficulty working within a team. His attitude mirrors Harry's in the fifth book. Harry, is, after all, fifteen, a difficult age best characterized by the country singer Kenny Chesney as possessing "a typically bad attitude," being brave, crazy, and mostly young.

Both series also share the technique of wordplay: word games or puzzles are major plot devices in Arthur's *The Mystery of the Stuttering Parrot*, *The Mystery of the Green Ghost*, and *The Secret of Skeleton Island*; in addition to clues embedded in character names such as Malfoy, Draco, Sirius, Prongs, and Lupin, *Harry Potter and the Sorcerer's Stone* has mirror writing and the potions riddle, *Harry Potter and the Chamber of Secrets* invites the active reader to solve the riddle of Tom Marvolo Riddle's name, and *Harry Potter and the Goblet of Fire* has a Sphinx riddle. Furthermore, both narrators indirectly present information needed to solve riddles, challenging protagonist and reader to determine what information is significant. In *The Mystery of the Fiery Eye* at their first meeting the young man seeking his hidden inheritance reveals to the Three Investigators, and the reader, that one reason his name is Augustus is because he was born in August; his birth date happens to be the clue needed to decipher his uncle's will. In *Harry Potter and the Order of the Phoenix* the narrator emphasizes Firenze's lesson that portents and prophecies can easily be misread, even by centaurs (604). Perhaps Voldemort marked the wrong wizard, or perhaps Neville has been marked in a less visible way, for as Madam Pomfrey notes, "thoughts could leave deeper scarring than almost anything else" (847). Something for readers to puzzle over waiting for book 6.

Finally, both narrators "hook" the juvenile reader immediately in the first book and continue to control the reader's response so that he or she becomes the narratee, an active reader participating in the narrative along with the protagonists. The primary appeal of both series is its focalizer, the character through whose eyes and mind the reader sees. The focalizer of the Harry Potter series is almost always Harry; the focalizer of the Three Investigators series is always one of the three boys, Jupe, Pete, or Bob.

In all of The Three Investigator books the three boys operate as a team, with each member possessing unique abilities and attributes. Jupiter Jones is the organizer and team leader; he is the most observant and logical and possesses near total recall of everything he reads. Bob Andrews does the necessary research, primarily because of his library job, and keeps the case notes. Pete Crenshaw does the legwork, frequently rescuing the others by his courage, tenacity, and physical strength, as well as "an instinct like a built-in compass for going in the right direction" (VT 88). He does tend to panic when faced with what appears to be the supernatural, but he always comes through, in Jupiter's words, "with bravery and perfect timing" (SP 168). Each boy trusts the other two, all working together as a team, with Jupe as the unquestioned leader, as the narrator makes clear: "Neither Bob nor Pete was happy about following Jupe's instructions, but he was head of the firm and they did what he said" (VT 141). It is this trust in each other that makes this team so successful, just as Harry, Ron, and Hermione trust each other and their different talents and skills in reaching the sorcerer's stone (280-87) and in their later adventures.

Harry is not an exceptionally bright wizard or a fast learner. He is best at flying and excels as a Seeker in Quidditch. Ron comes from a poor and large wizard family, so he must make do with his brothers' castoffs. While Ron shows greater promise in *Harry*

Potter and the Order of the Phoenix, becoming Prefect and eventually a fair Keeper, he is, like Pete, the least intellectual of the three. Hermione is the brains of the bunch, a fast and retentive reader who enjoys research and study. At first the boys regret her being in Gryffindor, but her knowledge and magic abilities rescue them from trouble on several occasions, although her bossy nature annoys the boys, and possibly the reader. She is remarkably like Jupiter who also annoys some readers.

In addition to the commonality of friendship and teamwork, both writers include another moral—perseverance. Few adolescents succeed at everything or even anything without diligence, practice, and patience, character traits that seem to be uncommon in post-modern literature or in contemporary society which may explain the initial adult criticism of the Potter books as "too long." Both narrators describe challenging obstacles which the protagonists do not always initially surmount. For example, Harry takes three years to lead his Quidditch team to victory and needs help to figure out the tasks for the Triwizard Tournament; in Arthur's *The Secret of Terror Castle*, the boys twice flee in terror from the supposedly haunted castle before returning to unmask the all-too-human ghosts.

Furthermore, the protagonists are not always correct. Each narrator describes situations where the protagonists are wrong and in such a way that the reader frequently makes the same mistake. Arthur's narrator ensures that the boys and the reader misjudge characters in *The Mystery of the Whispering Mummy, The Mystery of the Green Ghost*, and *The Secret of Skeleton Island*. The reader also falsely assumes that Jupiter has correctly deduced the hiding place of the stolen jewelry in *The Mystery of the Vanishing Treasure* and interpreted the coded message in *The Mystery of the Fiery Eye*. Rowling's narrator tricks the reader into ignoring Quirrell and thinking that Snape is after the Philosopher's Stone although the narrator has previously drawn the reader's attention to Quirrell "looking very peculiar in a large, purple turban" (122). Both Harry and the reader believe that Professor McGonagall will expel Harry for flying after Madam Hooch ordered the students to remain on the ground (SS 149). The protagonists and the reader falsely assume that Draco is Sytherin's heir, overlooking Ginny's increasingly problematic behavior; that Sirius Black did betray the Potters and escaped Azkaban to kill Harry, ignoring Scabbers' deterioration and the detail of his missing toe, and misinterpreting the actions of both Crookshanks and the Sneakoscope; that Harry's "dreams about corridors and locked doors" have no connection with Voldemort's search for a weapon (96) despite repeated linkages through Harry's scar. Neither narrator enlightens the reader as to the reality of the situation, allowing the reader either to make the same mistakes as the protagonists or to figure things out correctly. For example, because the focalizer, Harry, forgets that Sirius gave him a way to communicate, the narrator does not mention this device until Harry finds it, too late. An active reader, one who has become the narratee and does not identify with the focalizer, is more likely to remember Sirius's gift and so fault Harry for responding irrationally after the Avision@ of Voldemort torturing Sirius.

Both narrators also create a sense of powerlessness; the juvenile reader does not have the authority or power of adults. The three investigators need others to provide transportation around southern California; the boys have won the use of a rental car and driver, but when Jupiter fails to convince the rental agency's owner to abide by the contest rules, he has no option but to accept the owner's terms (FE 16). Juvenile readers are under the authority of their parents and teachers just as the three investigators are always under their parents' or guardians' authority and Hogwarts students are under the authority of their teachers, even when such authority seems capricious or prejudiced, Professors Snape and Umbridge being the prime examples. When Bob complains that "'Adults don't like to listen to kids when their minds are made up'" (SI 129), he could be describing Professors Snape, Trelawny, and especially Umbridge, that symbol of evil education administrators everywhere. This failure of adults (Muggle, magical, and academic) to listen explains Harry, Ron, and Hermione deciding to save sorcerer=s stone themselves (267-70) and why Hermione and Harry must use the Time-Turner to save Sirius Black (PA 392-93). Arthur's narrator notes that "adults, of course, were neither frequently reasonable nor logical" (FE 16), an accurate, though restrained, assessment of the Muggle Dursleys, the wizard Cornelius Fudge who refuses to believe Harry's testimony regarding Voldemort's return, and rule-bound Percy.

Both authors do provide at least one adult authority figure who is trustworthy, who listens and judges the protagonists fairly. Hitchcock respects the boys after they solve their first case and even recommends their detective agency to others (SP, WM, FE). The Rocky Beach police chief listens and provides assistance on numerous occasions (SP, GG, VT). Professor McGonagall listens and comes to respect Harry, Ron, and Hermione, particularly Hermione, as does Dumbledore though he proves fallible in *Harry Potter and the Order of the Phoenix*.

To combat adult authority the adolescent protagonists frequently employ what Lissa Paul calls "feminine strategies," using cunning or trickery instead of violence to solve a problem. I find the term "feminine strategy" sexist, not to mention confusing since boys are using it most often in these books, so I use the term "powerless strategy." Arthur's narrator describes one such example of powerless strategy: soon after introducing the three boys, he notes that Jupiter's guardians assign chores to the boys whenever they see them, so in "self-defense Jupiter had, bit by bit, arranged the piles of various types of junk so they hid his workshop from sight" (TC 8). Later, armed with their newly printed business cards, Jupe maneuvers his way into Alfred Hitchcock's office by pretending to be Hitchcock's nephew (TC 17-18) and then proceeds to trick him into introducing their case if they find a real haunted house for Hitchcock's next movie (18-20). And after all what is magic but a creative, imaginative, non-violent solution to a particular problem, such as shrinking a sweater one doesn't want to wear (SS 24) or flying up to a roof to avoid a fight (25). Powerless strategy also includes compromise, such as when Jupiter wants to preserve his independence in the face of the chauffeur's insistence on performing all of his duties (TC 15), or when Harry needs his uncle's permission to visit the village near Hogwarts (PA 20).

Both narrators recreate the protagonists' frustration and sense of helplessness when confronted with unreasonable adults, such as when Jupiter's advice is repeatedly ignored in *The Mystery of the Vanishing Treasure* and *The Secret of Skeleton Island* or when Hagrid is arrested and Dumbledore leaves, when Buckbeak is "executed," or when even Dumbledore can not save Sirius by waving a magic wand.

However, these limitations can be turned to one's advantage. Jupiter creates the Ghost-to-Ghost Hookup because they lack the resources to trace a missing person: each boy calls five friends who each call five friends asking for information. Even with duplications, within hours thousands of children are looking for the missing person. An interesting side effect is that adults suddenly find that the phone is useless: Bob's mother is unable to reach any of her church friends, getting twelve busy signals in a row (ST 49). The powerless have become powerful. Harry's Invisibility Cloak and the Weasley twins' Maurader Map perform similar functions. The best example so far is Hermione's formation of Dumbledore's Army, the group of students Hermione convinces Harry to teach practical Defense Against the Dark Arts techniques in defiance of Umbridge's Ministry-approved theory.

Additionally, both authors faithfully capture a common feature in adolescent life—the bully, a rich, spoiled, rude and obnoxious only child. Arthur creates Skinny Norris, a boy just old enough to drive and with enough money to attract a few equally stupid followers. He is introduced through the boys' conversation as little more than a pompous irritant (TC 28), and the narrator later verifies this assessment (TC 87-88). His bullying, like Draco Malfoy's until the fifth book, is confined mostly to verbal harassment, but he does interfere with several investigations and helps to kidnap Bob and Pete. Rowling gives Harry two bullies; the first is his cousin, Dudley, whose only exercise seems to be punching people (SS 20). Hogwarts has a wizard bully as well. When Draco Malfoy first appears, no overt judgment is necessary by the narrator because the reader compares him to Dudley:

> "My father's next door buying my books and mother's up the street looking at wands," said the boy. He had a bored, drawling voice. "then I'm going to drag them off to look at racing brooms. I don't see why first years can't have their own. I think I'll bully father into getting me one and I'll smuggle it in somehow." *(77)*

The narrator follows this speech merely by commenting that Harry was strongly reminded of Dudley, and with good reason. Draco Malfoy bullies anyone not loyal to Slytherin House or the Malfoys, ridiculing the Weasleys, tormenting Neville, and insulting Hermione.

Arthur's first volume, *The Secret of Terror Castle*, creates the series' blueprint just as Rowling's *Harry Potter and the Sorcerer's Stone* does. Arthur includes an introduction by Alfred Hitchcock who was then an established figure whose movies and TV show were at the time the ultimate in terror but still acceptable for an adolescent audience. Hitchcock's introduction explicitly draws a parallel between The Three Investigator series and his cinematic and television productions: "I seem to be constantly introducing something. For years I've been introducing my television programs. I've introduced motion pictures. And I've introduced books of mystery, ghost and suspense stories for my fans to shiver with" (*Terror Castle* vii). Arthur's connecting his series with Hitchcock's movies and television shows promises a good suspenseful story with the potential for ghosts or other supernatural elements. Arthur fulfills this promise with mysteries solved, threats resolved, and dangers overcome. The character of Hitchcock also provides a hook for the next story, as when at the end of *Terror Castle*, he suggests the investigators find a friend's lost stuttering parrot. Rowling hooks the reader through Harry telling his friends at the end of *Harry Potter and the Sorcerer's Stone*, "I'm going to have a lot of fun with Dudley this summer . . . " (309). The reader is left to imagine Dudley's comeuppance, considering he was last seen with a pig's tail (96). At the end of *Harry Potter and the Goblet of Fire* Dumbledore's words foreshadow the Order of the Phoenix and Hagrid's giant escapade in *Harry Potter and the Order of the Phoenix*. However, some potentialities have yet to materialize, such as Dumbledore's suggestion that Pettigrew owes a debt to Harry and Snape's trustworthiness and role as a Death-Eater.

A major difference between Arthur's and Rowling's hooks is that not only do the introductions "by that master of suspense Alfred Hitchcock" hook potential readers (Ishkander 129), but they also provide brief background information in subsequent books for readers new to the series limiting the necessary exposition by Rowling's narrator which becomes somewhat burdensome in *Harry Potter and the Goblet of Fire*.

Early on in Arthur's first story comes the first example of the narrator drawing the reader into the text by creating a mini-mystery, inviting the reader to play investigator figuring out the puzzle. Bob's mother relays Jupe's message, a message that she, the adult, can not understand: "'Green Gate One. The presses are rolling'" (TC 5). To help the reader in this first puzzle, the narrator explicitly explains the message later on, informing the reader that Green Gate One is one of four secret entrances into the junkyard and that Jupiter had repaired a junked printing press (7-8). The narrator will leave later mysteries to the reader to solve, along with, or ahead of the three investigators, just as Harry and the reader wonder what important secret could be inside the "grubby little package" Hagrid retrieves from the high security vault (SS 76). Rowling's narrator also provides clues, and even though the story is usually told through Harry as focalizer, the narrator still emphasizes or highlights significant information. For example, when Dumbledore restricts access to a section of Hogwarts, Harry laughs at his words, as well the reader might. However, Percy comments to Harry that the warning is "odd," and that Dumbledore has not enlightened the prefects as to the reason for this restriction (SS 127). The active reader might wonder if the secret package is there, an idea that does not occur to Harry until after the encounter with Fluffy when Hermione, the only one who does not panic, notices that the dog was guarding a trapdoor (162).

Rowling's narrative style emphasizes Harry Potter, as he is the primary focalizer—the character through whose eyes the reader sees the other characters and events—while Arthur's narrator follows each investigator in turn whenever the team separates. For example, in *The Mystery of the Fiery Eye* the narrator follows Bob to the library where he becomes the focalizer so that the reader learns what he learns when he learns it (71-74). In contrast, Rowling's narrator does not follow Hermione in *Harry Potter and the Chamber of Secrets* when she rushes off to the library to verify her theory as to the monster's identity (255), but instead remains with Harry as the focalizer, so that both he and the reader believe Hagrid's giant spider is the evil monster (249) until he and Ron re-discover the information Hermione had found (290). However, the narrator does drop a hint when describing that the voice sounds like "ice-cold venom" (120), venom being associated more with snakes than with spiders.

Thus the protagonists in both series have problems that the juvenile reader either personally experiences or at least is familiar with—the school bully; balancing chores or school work and fun; and convincing adults that they are intelligent and dependable. They overcome the obstacles imposed upon them and the ones they create themselves. But the most significant attribute of both series is the narratorial control that actively involves the juvenile reader in the story, hooking the reader into attempting to solve the mystery along with the protagonists. Each narrator controls both the pace and the amount of information given to the reader. Information is given as needed, a technique that creates narratorial gaps, unanswered questions to be puzzled over by the reader who chooses to become an active participant in the story instead of remaining a passive onlooker. In other words, the reader becomes part of the story, the narratee who attempts to figure out the mystery.

Works Cited

Arthur, Robert. *The Mystery of the Green Ghost.* Alfred Hitchcock and The Three Investigators Series. New York: Random House, 1965.

_____. *The Mystery of the Fiery Eye.* Alfred Hitchcock and The Three Investigators Series. New York: Random House, 1967.

_____. *The Mystery of the Stuttering Parrot.* Alfred Hitchcock and The Three Investigators Series. New York: Random House, 1964.

_____. *The Mystery of the Vanishing Treasure.* Alfred Hitchcock and The Three Investigators Series. New York: Random House, 1966.

_____. *The Secret of Skeleton Island.* Alfred Hitchcock and The Three Investigators Series. N New York: Random House, 1966.

_____. *The Secret of Terror Castle.* Alfred Hitchcock and The Three Investigators Series. New York: Random House, 1964.

Chambers, Aiden. "The Reader in the Book." Rpt. *Children's Literature: The Development of Criticism.* Ed. Peter Hunt. London and New York: Routledge, 1990. 91-114.

Chesney, Kenny. AYoung.@ *No Shoes, No Shirt, No Problems*. BMG Entertainment, 2002.

Cockrell, Amanda. AHarry Potter and the Secret Password: Finding Our Way in the Magical Genre.@ Whited 15-26.

Doughty, Terri. ALocating Harry Potter in the >Boys=Book= Market.@ Whited 243-57.

Dresang, Eliza T. AHermione Granger and the Heritage of Gender.@ Whited 211-42.

Farmer, Joy. AThe Magician=s Niece: The Kinship between J. K. Rowling and C. S. Lewis.@ *Mythlore* 88 (Spring 2001): 53-64.

Griesinger, Emily. AHarry Potter and the >Deeper Magic=: Narrating Hope in Children=s Literature.@ *Christianity and Literature* 51.3 (Spring 2002): 455-82. Rpt. *Gale Literature Resource Center*. 5/23/2003 <galenet.galegroup.com/servlet>.

Grimes, M. Katherine. AHarry Potter: Fairy Tale Prince, Real Boy, and Archetypal Hero.@ Whited 89-122.

Hunt, Peter. *Criticism, Theory, and Children's Literature*. Oxford and Cambridge, Mass: Basil Blackwell, 1991.

Iskander, Sylvia Patterson. "Arabic Adventurers and American Investigators: Cultural Values in Adolescent Detective Fiction." *Children's Literature* 21 (1993): 118-31.

Lacoss, Jann. AOf Magicals and Muggles: Reversals and Revulsions at Hogwarts.@ Whited 67-88.

Lewis, C. S. *An Experiment in Criticism*. 1961. Canto ed. pb. Cambridge: Cambridge UP, 2002.

————. *The Four Loves*. 1960. San Diego: HarvestBHarcourt, 1988.

McVeigh, Dan. AIs Harry Potter Christian?@ *Renascence: Essays in Values in Literature* 54.3 (Spring 2002) 197-214.

Mendlesohn, Farah. ACrowning the King: Harry Potter and the Construction of Authority.@ Whited 159-81.

Natov, Roni. AHarry Potter and the Extraordinariness of the Ordinary.@ Whited 125-39.

Paul, Lissa. "Enigma Variations: What Feminist Theory Knows About Children's Literature." *Signal* 54 (1987): 186-201.

Pharr, Mary. AIn Medias Res: Harry Potter as Hero-in-Progress.@ Whited 53-66.

Pinsent, Pat. AThe Education of a Wizard: Harry Potter and His Prodecessors.@ Whited 27-50.

Robertson, Judith P. AWhat Happens to Our Wishes: Magical Thinking in Harry Potter.@ *Children=s Literature Association Quarterly* 26.4 (2002): 198-211.

Rollin, Lucy. AAmong School Children: The Harry Potter Books and the School Story Tradition.@ *The South Carolina Review* 34.1 (Fall 2001): 198-208.

Routledge, Christopher. AHarry Potter and the Mystery of Ordinary Life.@ *Mystery in Children=s Literature From the Rational to the Supernatural*. Eds. Adrienne E. Gavin and Christopher Routledge. New York: Palgrave, 2001. 202-20.

Rowling, J. K. *Harry Potter and the Chamber of Secrets*. New York, Scholastic, 1999.

————. *Harry Potter and the Goblet of Fire*. New York, Scholastic, 2000.

————. *Harry Potter and the Order of the Phoenix*. New York, Scholastic, 2003.

————. *Harry Potter and the Prisoner of Azkaban*. New York, Scholastic, 1999.

_____. *Harry Potter and the Sorcerer=s Stone*. New York, Scholastic, 1997.

Steege, David K. AHarry Potter, Tom Brown, and the British School Story: Lost in Transit?@ Whited 140-56.

Thompson, Deborah. ADeconstructing Harry: Casting a Critical Eye on the Witches and Wizards of Hogwarts.@ *Beauty, Brains, and Brawn: The Construction of Gender in Children=s Literature*. Ed. Susan Lehr. Portsmouth, NH: Heinemann, 2001. 42-50.

Trites, Roberta Seelinger. "The Harry Potter Novels as a Test Case for Adolescent Literature." *Style* 35.3 (Fall 2001) 472-488.

Tucker, Nicholas. AThe Rise and Rise of Harry Potter.@ *Children=s Literature in Education* 30.4 (Dec 1999): 221-34. Rpt. *Gale Literature Resource Center*. 5/23/ 2003 <galenet.galegroup.com/servlet>.

Whited, Lana A., ed. *The Ivory Tower and Harry Potter: Perspectives on a Literary Phenomenon*. Columbia and London: U of Missouri P, 2002.

_____ and M. Katherine Grimes. AWhat would Harry Do? J. K. Rowling and Lawrence Kohlberg=s Theories of Moral Development.@ Whited 182-208.

Zipes, Jack. AThe Phenomenon of Harry Potter, Or Why All the Talk?@ *Sticks and Stones: The Troublesome Success of Children=s Literature form Slovenly Peter to Harry Potter*. Ed. Jack Zipes. New York: Routledge, 2000. 170-89.

http://www.thrillingdetective.com/3invest.html
http://www.bookloversden.com/series/boys_children/3inv.html
http://www.palacecreations.com/3inv.html
http://www.threeinvestigators.com/SD.html
http://www.tunneltwo.com/secrets/
http://www.3investigators.homestead.com/files/t3ihome.htm

Ernelle Fife is an Assistant Professor in the Department of English at SUNY-New Paltz. She has a Master's in cellular immunology from Northwestern University and a Ph.D. in English literature from Georgia State University. Her specialization is 18th-century British literature, especially the interdisciplinary field of medicine and literature. She was a fellow at the 2002 National Institute of Humanities "Medicine, Literature, and Culture" Institute at Hershey Medical Center. Her paper on gender and midwifery, "The Discourses of Professionalism in 18th-century Midwifery," will appear in the British journal Women's Writing, *in the upcoming special issue: "Sex, Sexuality, and the Body." She has given numerous papers on 18th-century midwifery treatises and plague narratives, Madeleine L'Engle's mythology, and filming Jane Austen's ironic narrator. She was also a lecturer in 2001 for the Center for Life Enrichment program in Highlands, North Carolina on the Harry Potter series to an audience of grandparents. She is currently developing a senior-level course in Classic Juvenile Fantasy Literature for English majors and English/Education majors at SUNY-New Paltz.*

Harry Potter: A Universal Hero?

Michéle Fry

Jack Zipes describes Harry Potter as "one of the mythical chosen heroes [who is] called upon by powers greater than himself to rescue his friends and the world from diabolical evil. He is [. . .] the little guy who proves he's bigger than life";[1] whilst David Colbert describes Harry Potter as "a very familiar type of hero".[2] In this paper I intend to look at how much J. K. Rowling's characterisation of Harry Potter conforms to the universal mythical hero archetype, and how far she has subverted this archetype.

Since Western culture emerged in its own right, the hero story has always been with us, and the adventure story, concerning the hero's quest, has appeared in countless forms such as folk tales and legends, adult thrillers and children's stories.[3] Northrop Frye argues that romance, when it acquires a literary form, tends to consist of a series of "minor adventures" that lead up to a "major [. . .] adventure". This major adventure is the quest, and the successful quest is the "complete form of romance", and as such it has three main stages:

> the stage of the perilous journey and the preliminary minor adventures; the crucial struggle, usually some kind of battle in which either the hero or his foe, or both, must die; and the exaltation of the hero.[4]

Any quest that involves conflict requires two central characters—a hero (protagonist) and an enemy (antagonist)—and whilst the enemy may be a mere mortal with nothing extraordinary about him (or, less usually, her), Frye comments that "the nearer the romance is to myth", the more likely the enemy is to possess "demonic mythical qualities" and the more "attributes of divinity" will be possessed by the hero.[5] Given the fact that Lord Voldemort's demonic qualities are becoming increasingly apparent with each new volume, and the fact that the novels are strong on mythical qualities, Harry Potter must, it seems, be more divine than is yet apparent. Frye, in *The Secular Scripture*, states that the hero's success depends on his own courage, but also on things given to him, such as noble blood, unusual strength, or a "destiny prophesied by an oracle".[6] On these grounds Harry's success is assured: he has noble (wizard) blood; he has a destiny in the shape of the prediction made by Professor Trelawney which is revealed for the first time in *The Order of the Phoenix*, and which indicates that Harry is the "one with the power to vanquish the Dark Lord".[7] This unspecified and as-yet unmanifested power could be the unusual strength mentioned by Frye. In *The Anatomy of Criticism*, he observes that romance's central form is dialectical—that is, everything is focused on the conflict between the hero and his enemy, with the sympathies of the reader being "bound up with the hero".[8] Thus the villain may be seen as a representation of the "lower world['s]" demonic powers, whilst the hero is a representation of the "mythical Messiah or deliverer" who comes from an upper world.[9] Frye distinguishes romance from myth by the power of action associated with the hero: his power is essentially human in the romance, but divine in the myth.[10] Whilst all Harry's manifest powers are human (assuming magic to be neither demonic or divine since both sides wield it), he is regarded as a deliverer by much of the wizarding world. He is expected to defeat Voldemort, having already given the wizarding world a ten year respite from Voldemort. This, often unvoiced, expectation has led Harry, albeit unwillingly, to develop something akin to a saviour mentality. This has been noticed by both his allies and his enemies: Ron accuses Harry of acting the hero following his completion of the second Triwizard Tournament task in *The Goblet of Fire*, whilst Hermione says he has a "saving people thing" in *The Order of the Phoenix*, and later Lucius Malfoy tells Bellatrix Lestrange that Harry has a love of heroics.[11]

Margery Hourihan says that the "conceptual centre" of the hero story contains a set of binary oppositions which she terms "dualisms"; these ascribe certain qualities to the hero, and an opposing set of qualities to his enemy.[12] Frye, who had earlier suggested a similar idea about opposing qualities, associates the qualities of "spring, dawn, order, fertility, vigour and youth" with the hero, whilst the qualities of "winter, darkness, confusion, sterility, moribund life and old age" are associated with the villain.[13] Hourihan lists some of the dualisms which have been identified, among them are reason and emotion, male and female, order and chaos, human and non-human, and mind or soul and body.[14] It is Hourihan's belief that the meanings which a reader draws from a hero story are dependent upon these related binary oppositions. However, as Hourihan observes, whilst these oppositions express the inherently dualistic nature of Western thought, a dualism is more than a mere dichotomy since one of the terms in a dualism is always constructed as inherently superior in contrast to the other.[15] From the hero tales which emerged during the Christian era a further pair of signifiers, "good" and "evil", can be included, with "good" being located on the side of reason. Such a location is a powerful reinforcement of the sense of the innate inferiority of "wild, emotional, female chaos" as against "civilised, rational male order".[16]

In popular hero stories, particularly those aimed at children, the most simplistic dualism implied in the story is this opposition of good and evil; frequently in such novels, as Hourihan notes, the terms 'good' and 'evil' "mean little more than 'us' and 'them'", so that the hero is only good by definition, and his opponents are only evil because they oppose him.[17] Frye, meanwhile, observes that the characters of a romance follow the same "general dialectic structure" as the story itself, which results in a lack of complexity or subtlety in the characters who are either in favour of the quest, or opposed to it.[18] The characters who assist in the quest are then "idealised as simply gallant or pure", whilst those who obstruct it are "caricatured as simply villainous or cowardly".[19] As a consequence of such simplification, the "typical character in romance tends to have his[/her] moral opposite confronting him[/her], like black and white pieces in a chess game".[20] Rowling does not fall into this trap—her characterisation of the major players in her novels, is less simplistic: as one of her characters, Sirius Black, points out to Harry "the world is not divided in good people and Death Eaters".[21] People are more complex than that, and it is possible to be a corrupt government official, such as Dolores Umbridge, without being a Death Eater, or whole-heartedly supporting Voldemort.

Marie-Louise von Franz says that in the classic fairy tales, the hero is rarely shown as an ordinary human being; for example, if a lion approaches the hero, he promptly kills it without pausing to consider what must be done.[22] Franz quotes Max Lüthi's observation that fairy tale heroes are "abstract figure[s] and not at all human".[23] This means that the hero is either pure white, or pure black, with no shades of grey anywhere; his reactions are stereotypical, in that he kills the lion, rescues the damsel and shows no fear of the "old woman in the woods".[24] This makes him "completely schematic".[25] In this respect, Harry Potter has no resemblance to the hero of classic fairy tales. As I will show later, Rowling represents Harry as feeling fear, doubt, pain, loneliness, sadness and anger; thus he is clearly not an abstract figure, but a very human young man. Rather than being a fairy tale hero, he is nearer to being the hero of an epic or saga. Meanwhile, Julia Eccleshare believes that as the series has progressed, Harry Potter has become less of an ordinary child, and more of a legendary hero; she sees Harry as Arthur to Professor Dumbledore's Merlin, particularly in the way that Harry spends time alone with Dumbledore, learning new things about both his enemy and himself.[26]

Hourihan notes that Joseph Campbell, in his "seminal work", *The Hero With a Thousand Faces*, recognises that the hero story concentrates on male development; that is, the progress made by the male psyche towards wholeness, enlightenment, and above all, maturity. Whilst other characters are included in hero stories, it is only their impact upon the hero that is shown.[27] This is true even of the *Harry Potter* novels; although (as I have argued elsewhere[28]), Hermione Granger is essential to Harry's success, her story is revealed only in relation to Harry's story. Hourihan believes that the perception which the reader of the hero story gains of both the world within the story, and the events which take place in that world, comes either from the point of view of the hero, or that of an admiring narrator, who foregrounds him so that his evaluations and perspective are imposed on the reader by the story.[29] The reader's sympathies towards, and perceptions of, characters and events are manipulated by the narrative point of view in the story. In a first-person narrative the events of the story are filtered through the consciousness of the character telling the story, whereas the point of view in a third-person narrative is less obvious or consistent, and events are "focalised" through one or more characters' consciousness. This results in the reader's view of the other characters, and of the events which occur, being influenced by the focalising character's attitudes.[30]

A narrative stance, by selecting and filtering the information that is presented to the reader, implies that certain kinds of human activities have greater (or lesser) significance/value. Thus, an "overwhelming concentration [. . .] on physical action and conflict" in hero tales will relegate creativity, emotion, imagination and domestic relations/activities to the margins of the story.[31] This is less true of Rowling's novels: whilst she does not place significant emphasis on domestic relations and activities (except, perhaps, with respect to the Weasley family), she does show the reader Harry's feelings and emotions. The reader sees him crying on at least two occasions: when he talks with Dumbledore in the hospital wing near the end of *The Philosopher's Stone*, and when he is talking to Lupin, whilst he is learning the Patronus Charm in *The Prisoner of Azkaban*.[32] Harry is also frequently seen displaying anger, and occasionally the way he expresses that anger is childish, such as when he and Ron fall out over Harry's entry into the Triwizard Tournament in *The Goblet of Fire*, or when Harry throws away his birthday chocolates from Ron and Hermione in *The Order of the Phoenix*.[33] His anger at Sirius' death which is directed at Dumbledore toward the end of *Phoenix* verges on a temper tantrum.[34] Rowling does not relegate emotion to the margins of her novels—Harry's are not the only emotions portrayed and whilst the instances are too many to list here, recent examples include Cho's frequent tears over the death of Cedric Diggory, and Sirius' impatience at having to remain at Grimmauld Place in *Phoenix*.[35]

Hourihan observes that since the narrative of the hero tale is presented from the point of view of the hero, and since the foreground of the tale is occupied by that hero, "the reader is invited to share his values and admire his actions" even when they are not necessarily admirable.[36] The insistence on the hero's "central importance [. . .] in the scheme of things" means that his opponents are not seen as "people with complex motivations of their own", but as mere villains whose "fate" is either domination of the entire world or their own destruction.[37] Here, too, Rowling subverts the hero tale and explains some of Voldemort's motivations: during the course of the novels some of the background to Voldemort's character has been filled in, and the reader is shown why he hates non-wizards (Muggles) and from where some, at least, of his lust for power derives. Harry (and the reader) learns in *The Chamber of Secrets* that Voldemort's Muggle father left his witch mother on learning her nature, before Voldemort was even born. This meant that Voldemort had to be brought up in a Muggle orphanage after his mother died giving birth to him.[38] Voldemort cannot forgive his father for this betrayal, and the reader is told in *The Goblet of Fire* that Voldemort killed his father and his paternal grandparents by way of revenge whilst he was still a teenager.[39]

Hourihan believes that since the events of the hero story are "focalised through [the hero's] consciousness and the reader's perceptions are focused upon him", the result is that the hero's "qualities are foregrounded and valued" whilst other characters' qualities are overlooked or marginalised.[40] Thus the reader is expected to admire action, skill, courage and determination, whilst qualities such as sensitivity, creativity and self-doubt are not given a place in the world of the hero.[41] Again, Rowling does not entirely conform: Harry's self-doubts are made plain in his comments to both Hagrid and Ron early in *The Philosopher's Stone*.[42] Harry's sympathetic nature is also made clear in his response to Ron's embarrassment over his family's lack of money,[43] and to Neville's parental situation;[44] in addition, Harry's concern for Sirius' well-being is made clear in *The Goblet of Fire*,[45] and his reactions to the news that both Professor Lupin and Hagrid are only part-human indicate his sensitivity.[46]

I now want to take a closer look at how Harry Potter conforms to or subverts the hero archetype, particularly as described by Hourihan. It is Hourihan's belief that the direction of the hero tale and the order in which events occur are a consequence of the hero's ambition, will, rationality, activism and world view.[47] Rowling demonstrates most strongly in *The Goblet of Fire* that Harry Potter is not only often not in control of events, but is frequently at the mercy of the will of others who are stronger than him, and particularly of Voldemort. Although Harry fantasises about entering and winning the Triwizard Tournament, he is (for once) prepared to obey the rules and intends to respect the new ruling that only students who are 17 or older may participate; when his name unexpectedly comes out of the Goblet of Fire, ensuring his participation, Harry is as stunned as anyone.[48] It is not until nearly the end of *The Goblet of Fire* that the reader is shown that Voldemort, through his servants Peter Pettigrew and Barty Crouch Jr, has been directing Harry's actions in order to bring Harry to himself for the "re-birthing" process.[49] Similarly, Voldemort influences Harry's action in *The Order of the Phoenix* through the psychic/magic link that Harry's scar has created. Voldemort is a Legilimens, that is he is able to extract feelings and memories from a person's mind, and he discovers that Harry's scar facilitates this skill.[50] Voldemort uses this to direct Harry's dreams, leading him to believe that Sirius Black has been trapped by Voldemort in the Department of Mysteries at the Ministry of Magic. Harry reacts to this as Voldemort knows he will, by rushing off to save Sirius, thus playing into Voldemort's hands since he needs Harry to acquire the record of Professor Trelawney's prediction concerning them both.[51] Voldemort, like Lucius Malfoy, knows that Harry has a "saving-people thing".

Hourihan says that the hero sees opposition to himself as "evil, or [. . .] inferior" and he "struggles to subdue" this opposition because his "mode is domination", domination of his enemies, his friends, the environment, and even of his emotions and weaknesses.[52] Whilst it is true that Harry wants to subdue Draco Malfoy, particularly with regard to the undisguised hatred he has for wizards of Muggle parentage, he has not, so far, shown much desire to try to dominate his friends. He, Ron and Hermione work as a team wherever possible, and he lets Ron or Hermione take the lead when they obviously know more than he does, for example, when Ron leads them through the gigantic chess game in *The Philosopher's Stone*,[53] or when Hermione takes the lead in preparing the Polyjuice Potion in *The Chamber of Secrets*.[54] Nor does Harry always make a noticeable effort to dominate his emotions and weaknesses: his displays of anger towards others, especially Snape and Malfoy,[55] are a feature of all the published books. He also "blows up" his uncle's sister, Marge, in a fit of anger in *The Prisoner of Azkaban*,[56] and he displays intense anger, hatred even, towards Sirius Black before he discovers the truth about who was responsible for betraying James and Lily Potter to Voldemort.[57] His seething anger throughout *The Order of the Phoenix* boils over frequently and he loses his temper with Ron and Hermione more than once, before badly losing his temper with Dumbledore; the latter results in the destruction of a table and several magical objects belonging to Dumbledore.[58]

Hourihan describes the hero's relationships as "typically adolescent" which is literally true in the case of Harry Potter, but she goes on to say that for the hero, his heroic purpose is of greater importance than his personal relationships.[59] This is not so true of Harry: the value he places on his personal relationships is demonstrated on many occasions with regard to Ron and the whole Weasley family, Hermione, Hagrid, Sirius, and to a lesser extent, with Professors Lupin and Dumbledore. Throughout *The Goblet of Fire* Harry worries almost constantly about Sirius' safety, whilst the breakdown of his friendship with Ron causes him pain, even though he is too proud (or maybe too stubborn) to make the first move to repair the breakdown.[60] Harry considers the Weasleys his favourite family—he is delighted when Molly and Bill Weasley visit him at Hogwarts on the day of the final task of the Triwizard Tournament instead of the Dursleys,[61] and he is touched when Mrs Weasley tells Sirius that Harry is as good as being her son.[62] Hourihan goes on to note that the "hero is usually very conscious of his dependence on the support of his friend who often provides [. . .] his only emotional warmth in a seemingly hostile, or at least, unwelcoming world".[63] This is true for Harry, who is clearly very conscious of the importance of his friends' support, and although he is embarrassed by Mrs Weasley's extra hug when she sees him and the others off at Kings Cross in *The Prisoner of Azkaban*, he is also "really quite pleased";[64] he is similarly grateful for her hugs after his encounter with the returned Voldemort in *The Goblet of Fire*.[65]

Hourihan observes that the hero, historically, has opposed the darkness and notes that the task of the hero in early legends is to "defeat the forces of chaos, fear and ignorance", thus ensuring that the state, together with the "realm of civic order and rational behaviour" survive.[66] Whilst it is unnecessary to have an in-depth knowledge of Greek mythology in order to find meanings in these myths, the "images of light and strength on the one hand and stifling darkness on the other, make their impact with minimum context".[67] Jung talks of the requirement of the hero to "overcome the monster of darkness",[68] and Rowling certainly combines the light/dark and good/evil dualisms in a meaningful manner—Lord Voldemort is often referred to as the Dark Lord[69], and all of Harry's encounters with Voldemort, or his minions, take place after dark.[70] Voldemort can certainly lay claim to being a force of "chaos, fear and ignorance", and it is Harry's task to defeat him in order to ensure the survival of both the Muggle and wizarding worlds. Roz Kaveny notes that the Dark Lord of fantasy "aspire[s] to be the Prince of this world", and this is clearly Voldemort's goal.[71]

Hourihan describes the hero as "a man of action" and says that the nature of the hero is expressed in action: his courage, skills, determination and dominance all come to the fore since he is neither creative nor contemplative.[72] Whilst it is true that Harry is not creative in the strictest sense, he is resourceful and his strategies for overcoming obstacles, defeating his opponents, and achieving his goals are, generally, well thought out, even when he is reacting swiftly to events as they happen. Hourihan believes that the commitment of the hero to action results in violence becoming a natural, immediate response, and she notes that the hero is marked out by his warrior status, that is, his ability to destroy his people's enemies.[73] In this respect, Harry is not yet a great warrior— he has not destroyed his people's enemies, not even Voldemort, and when opportunities to do so have arisen, he has mostly preferred to see his enemies handed over to justice instead. When Harry has the opportunity to kill Sirius Black, whom he believes betrayed his parents to Voldemort years earlier, he lacks the resolution to do so.[74] Similarly, when Sirius Black and Professor Lupin decide to kill Peter Pettigrew, who has confessed to being the real traitor, Harry intervenes insisting that Pettigrew should be sent to Azkaban instead.[75] In *Phoenix*, Harry wants to kill Bellatrix Lestrange after seeing her kill Sirius Black, but he does not succeed, in spite of using one of the Unforgivable Curses. Lestrange tells Harry that his "righteous anger" alone is not sufficiently powerful enough to use the curse effectively—"You need to *mean* them . . . You need to really want to cause pain—to enjoy it.".[76] Harry does not appear to want to cause pain, and he does not enjoy it when he does: whilst he deliberately causes pain to Professor Quirrell in order to prevent him from stealing the Philosopher's Stone for Voldemort, he never expresses enjoyment of it.[77] Harry does use violence to destroy the Basilisk which inhabits the Chamber of Secrets, but he does so in defence of himself and Ginny Weasley, not to mention the Muggle-born students whom the Basilisk has been attacking. He also destroys the preserved memory of Tom Riddle (Voldemort), but he does so to prevent Riddle/Voldemort from continuing to use his old diary to manipulate others.[78]

Hourihan next explores the way the hero treats the "wild things": dragons, wolves and other beasts, "human beasts" and ogres; she says that the triumph of the hero over these wild things demonstrates patriarchy's mastery. Harry Potter fails to exert any mastery over any of the "wild things" he encounters: instead of slaying dragons, he helps to protect Hagrid's pet dragon, Norbert, and although he encounters a dragon in the first task of the Triwizard Tournament, he does not even attempt to use magic on it, choosing instead, to outwit it by other skills.[79] Similarly, Harry develops a closer-than-usual student-teacher relationship with Professor Lupin, who is a werewolf, and he counts Hagrid, who is revealed to be a half giant, as a good friend.[80] He treats the various other wild things which he encounters with caution, and sometimes even respect; such creatures include the Centaurs and three-headed dog in *The Philosopher's Stone*, giant spiders in *The Chamber of Secrets*, Hippogriffs in *The Prisoner of Azkaban*, and unicorns, a Sphinx, and Hagrid's "Blast-ended Skrewts" in *The Goblet of Fire*. His dealing with other part—or non-humans (aside from Hagrid and Professor Lupin) are always equalising or respectful: the house-elves Dobby and Winky are not belittled or mistreated by Harry, as they are by many adult wizards in *The Chamber of Secrets* or *The Goblet of Fire*.

Hourihan observes that whilst the world population contains more than 50% of women, who often play a crucial role in the cultural and social lives of communities, and who work alongside men, these facts are not accurately reflected in hero myths.[81] Women appear infrequently, and the majority appear only in a domestic setting as mothers or wives; of the few women whom the hero encounters outside the domestic setting, the majority perform extraordinary feats and possess "amazing powers": they are sirens, goddesses, evil witches or fairy godmothers.[82] Hourihan sees women less as "characters" and more as "symbols of events in the hero's psyche".[83] The narration of the hero tale from the point of view of the hero means that women are seen only in relation to their involvement with the hero's quest; consequently, women appear to have little significance to the hero. However Rowling, as I have discussed elsewhere, has created at least one strong, significant female character: Hermione has an essential role in Harry's continuing quest to defeat Voldemort, even more so than Ron, although the latter does get to play a bigger role in *The Order of the Phoenix*, and is even allowed to do things without Harry, such as when he becomes a Prefect. Rowling is developing Hermione's character and role in much the same way as she is developing Harry's character, and whilst it is true that Hermione has an expository role throughout, she is also frequently beside Harry during the action.

Hourihan categorises the women who appear in hero tales into four groups: mothers; witches and bitches; brides; and goddesses, fairy godmothers and others, and I will look at each of these groups in turn. Mothers who preside over the home from which the hero sets out on his quest tend to appear at the opening of hero tales and, occasionally, again at the close when they welcome the hero back home; invariably these mothers are characterised as nurturing and good, occasionally as saint-like.[84] On occasion the hero's "good and loving mother" has died at his birth, or dies early in the tale; consequently the hero's severance from her when he embarks on his quest is doubled, and he has to overcome this "central psychic lack" or remain a child emotionally.[85] Harry's mother dies when he is little more than a year old, and although Harry's loss affects him emotionally, he is not weaker for it; as his thoughts about Neville's parental situation show, his loss gives him compassion for others.[86] Also, the affection that others, such as Professors Dumbledore and Lupin, Sirius and Hagrid, hold for his parents gives Harry strength, courage and determination.

Any discussion of the women whom Hourihan terms "witches and bitches" is going to be complicated with regard to the *Harry Potter* novels as almost all the women portrayed are witches. However, Hourihan is also referring here to those women who are often termed *femme fatales*.[87] These are the women who have "escaped" from the domestic setting and are "loose in the wilderness"; they are considered dangerous because they will threaten the self-control, purposefulness and rationality of the hero by tempting him, usually sexually.[88] This is less of an issue for Harry Potter; Rowling has largely steered clear of any hints of sexual involvement—Harry's brief relationship with Cho Chang never gets beyond a kiss. Similarly, the sexually alluring Veela, the Bulgarian team's mascots at the Quidditch Cup Final, are led to demonstrate their "ugly" side, thus ensuring that Harry is not distracted from his Triwizard Tournament tasks by the half-Veela Fleur Delacourt;[89] and since few of Voldemort's female supporters have been revealed yet, there is less concern that such women might tempt Harry or lead him astray. Although Harry does meet one of Voldemort female Death Eaters, Bellatrix Lestrange, who has escaped from Azkaban, her appearance is no longer as beautiful as it was when Harry watched her trial in Dumbledore's Pensieve, so she is not much of a *femme fatale*. However, she might conceivably be described as a bitch, particularly with regard to the way she taunts Harry when they meet at the Ministry of Magic.[90] Brides have yet to make any appearance in Rowling's novels, presumably since Harry and his friends are still below the legal age of marriage.

In some hero tales, females who are maternal (or quasi-maternal), that is autonomous, strong women, appear to help the hero when he is most in need of assistance in his quest.[91] These goddesses and fairy godmothers tend not to fit in so easily with the hero tale's ideology of male dominance and female subordination, as such "meek domestic creatures" as Mrs Darling (in *Peter Pan*), do.[92] The older women, frequently substitute mothers, who appear occasionally in contemporary hero tales for children, are there to help the hero complete his quest; whilst they are significant to the plot, they tend, asserts Hourihan, to be undeveloped and unconvincing characters—like the goddess Athene, they "naturalise the concept of women's inherently ancillary role".[93] Although Mrs Weasley is a maternal character, she is being developed somewhat over the course of the series of novels. However she has yet to play a significant role in aiding Harry to complete his quest, in spite of her role in Dumledore's Order of the Phoenix.

In conclusion, then, Harry Potter has definite pretensions to being considered an archetypal mythic hero, but Rowling has subverted many of the elements of the hero archetype so that he is not the all-conquering hero described by Hourihan. He has many human qualities, some of which may prove to be serious weaknesses, but whether Harry will be able to turn them into strengths remains to be seen.

Michèle Fry is from Oxford, England. She has worked in both computer programming and administration, but is now working as a freelance writer. She has a degree in Computer Programming but recently undertook a second B.A. degree in English with History. She discovered the Harry Potter books one afternoon when browsing in a bookshop for something to read as an "antidote" to her first year examination revision reading. During the final year of her B.A., she wrote a paper on the Harry Potter novels, "Heroes and Heroines: Myth and gender roles in the Harry Potter Books." This was considered to be original enough to merit publication, and it appeared in the 2001 issue of The New Review of Children's Literature and Librarianship *(Taylor Graham Publishing). She also presented a version of this paper at the Harry Potter Convention in Västerås, Sweden in May 2001. Currently Michèle is working on a book,* From Heroine to Lady-Hero: Gender and Heroism in Modern Fantasy Fiction, *about female protagonists in late 20th century fantasy novels (including the Harry Potter novels).*

The Dangers of Dynamics: Transport in the Harry Potter Series

Steven J. Gores

Many readers have noted the ways in which J. K. Rowling limits the presence of the Muggle world in her magical novels: Harry's experience with Muggledom is claustrophobically confined to the Dursley home. This means that Harry rarely goes anywhere except to school via King's Cross train station. Whereas the portions of the Harry Potter series that represent Harry in the world of Muggles are remarkably static, Harry Potter's experiences in the magical world are extremely dynamic: he and/ or others are constantly in motion, travelling by one device or another. In contrast to his magical friends and his Muggle family, Harry is defined, as a traveller, one who occupies a liminal space between Muggle and magical worlds.

Within the Harry Potter series, travel is not just an index of which world we are in, magical or Muggle—it is treated as a theme of its own, offering the characters opportunities for both marvel and danger. For instance, Harry's rather innocuous, if marvelous, first trip on the Hogwart's train in Book I is balanced by Harry and Ron's near-fatal use of Mr. Weasley's enchanted car to make the same trip in Book II. There appear to be three principal methods of magical travel: enchanted objects, floo powder, and Apparation. Mr. Weasley's flying Ford Anglia is, of course, an enchanted object, as are the brooms that are famously used in playing Quidditch. So, too, are the port keys used in Books IV and V to transport groups of wizards. Use of any of these objects automatically entails the possibility of injury.

The first enchanted travel object appears in the novels along with Harry's first appearance: as a baby, he arrives at the Dursley household via Sirius Black's flying motorcycle, driven by Hagrid. This begins Harry's characterization as a traveller. It also announces the association of travel with danger and deviance. Dumbledore, who witnesses Harry and Hagrid's arrival, is surprised at the motorcycle's appearance. The motorcycle is not only huge and very loud—contrary to the discretion expected in magical intrusions in the Muggle world—but also seems dangerous as it "fell out of the air and landed on the road in front of them" (I.14).

Harry's next encounter with magical travel does not occur until he is summoned to Hogwarts. When Hagrid finally rescues Harry from the Dursleys, after all of Mr. Dursley's attempts to avoid contact with the magical world, Hagrid enchants their boat so as to make it self-propelled.

This seems innocuous, but Hagrid admits that he is not supposed to do magic, so even this simple act is a deviation. Actually getting to Hogwarts involves travelling on the Hogwart's train, which seems to be a normal, if antiquated, steam-powered train: "A scarlet steam engine was waiting . . . . Smoke from the engine drifted over their heads" (I.93-4). The engine's old-fashioned appearance is reiterated in the train's carriages, which is divided into old style compartments where groups of as many as six students are seated together. The train leaves King's Cross at 11 AM and does not arrive at Hogwarts until dark, which is certainly a normal travel time, according to Muggle standards. In other words, although this train's platform and route are concealed from Muggles, everything else about it follows Muggle norms, down to the pistons that power it (III.81).

Brooms are the first enchanted travel objects to which Harry is introduced at school. Initially, Harry and his fellow first years are very cautious about brooms, in part because Fred and George Weasley warn them that the school brooms "started to vibrate if you flew too high, or always flew to the left" (I. 146). In his first lesson on broom riding, Harry speculates that brooms, "like horses, could tell when you were afraid" (I. 146). This seems to be true, for Neville, who is both afraid of his broom and afraid of not being able to fly alongside his peers, cannot control his broom:

> Neville was rising straight up like a cork shot out of a bottle . . . . Harry saw . . . him gasp, slip sideways off the broom and—Wham—a thud and a nasty crack and Neville lay facedown on the grass in a heap. His broomstick was still rising higher and started to drift lazily toward the forbidden forest and out of sight (I. 146).

The fact that the broom continues to rise and then heads away to the forbidden forest seems to confirm that, as Harry noted, enchanted brooms seem have a mind or will of their own and, like an ornery horse, will take advantage of those not fit or skilled enough to control them. Like the enchanted car, Harry's broom nearly causes his death when it is magically manipulated later on in Book I.

However, while dangerous, the broom is also a source of marvel and a necessary aid for Harry. In Book IV, during the Quidditch World Cup, the Bulgarian seeker Victor Krum performs a maneuver called the "Wronski Feint" that both demonstrates his amazing flying ability and sidelines his Irish counterpart. All the quidditch fans— Bulgarian and Irish—are bowled over by Krum's skill with his broom, and Ron very nearly worships him, buying a Krum figurine and dogging him in hopes of obtaining his autograph. Krum and Harry are, to some degree, doubles: Harry, like Krum, is known for his natural flying ability, and later in Book IV, Rita Skeeter's *Daily Prophet* article names the two of them as rivals for Hermione's attentions. It is no coincidence that, when Harry must face the first task of the Tri-Wizard tournament, he summons his "Firebolt" to lure and then evade the Hungarian Horntail dragon. Once he is on his broom, he no longer feels panicky facing the dragon; instead, he calms himself by comparing the task to a quidditch game, and by developing a strategy for overcoming his opposition. For Harry, flying is both natural and necessary, his strongest skill that he can rely upon to get him through difficult circumstances.

Other enchanted travel objects, such as Mr. Weasley's car, offer less opportunity for skill and more for danger. When Harry and Ron borrow it to get to Hogwarts, it simply gives up flying just as they arrive, and they end up plummeting out of the sky toward what they imagine to be their deaths. They end up crashing into the Whomping Willow and are nearly killed by the tree. Once free of the Willow, the car essentially ejects them and flies, like a wild animal, into the forbidden forest:

> *The car . . . had reached the end of its tether. With two sharp clunks, the doors flew open and Harry felt his seat tip sideways: next thing he knew he was sprawled on the damp ground. Loud thuds told him that the car was ejecting their luggage from the trunk . . . Then, dented, scratched, and steaming, the car rumbled off into the darkness, its rear lights blazing angrilyi* (II.76).

Neither Harry nor Ron are able to control this beast-like car, and they are likewise unable to control the aftereffects of their voyage. Because the car is an unauthorized enchanted vehicle, and because its flight was observed by many Muggles, Harry and Ron's trip not only endangers them physically, but endangers their status as students and Mr. Weasley's job at the Ministry of Magic.

If brooms *seem* like animals in that they require skill in order to ride them, the car is *truly* like a wild animal in that it acts on its own volition and is in control of its passengers. When Harry and Ron enter the forbidden forest to consult the giant spider Aragog, the enchanted car comes to their rescue, Apparently having observed their peril: "Mr. Weasley's car was thunder down the slope, headlights glaring, its horn screeching, knocking spiders aside . . . [it] screeched to a halt in front of Harry and Ron and the doors flew open" (II.279). The car's heroic efforts on their behalf underscore the fact that it is an enchanted travel object that is wild, or independent of wizarding control, and therefore both a source of marvel and potential danger.

The Knight bus, in contrast to Mr. Weasley's car, is a vehicle that, despite its frightening qualities, is a regular and official part of the wizarding world. It is, as the conductor announces, "emergency transport for the stranded witch or wizard" (III.33). When Harry accidentally flags the bus down, he is nearly run over by it:

> *There was a deafening BANG, and Harry threw up his hands to shield his eyes against a sudden blinding light—With a yell, he rolled back onto the pavement, just in time. A second later, a gigantic pair of wheels and headlights screeched to a halt exactly where Harry had just been lying* (III.33).

Things are not much better when he mounts the purple triple-decker bus and it begins to move again—the driver does not pay any attention to the Muggle streetscape that his bus hurtles through:

Ernie didn't seem to have mastered the use of a steering wheel. The Knight Bus kept mounting the pavement, but it didn't hit anything; lines of lampposts, mailboxes, and trash cans jumped out of its way as it approached and back into position once it had passed (III.36).

This frightening prospect, along with the incredible lurches the bus makes as it somehow hops longer distances, makes the passengers "very pleased" to leave the bus (III.41). At least one seems to have been made ill by the bus's reckless progress. This happens again in *Harry Potter and the Order of the Phoenix* when Harry, Hermione, and the Weasleys travel back to Hogwarts by the Knight Bus after Christmas break. Ron is at first excited to ride the bus, then he is very eager to leave it; a "Madam Marsh" leaves first, but only after being very sick. Finally, the fact that the conductor and driver sometimes don't know exactly where they are suggests that this mode of magical travel, like Mr. Weasley's Ford Anglia, is a bit out of the control of its operators.

Port keys, in contrast to other enchanted objects, do not require skill, and using them does not normally result in injury. This is perhaps reflected in their prosaic appearance: a musty old boot transports the Diggorys, Weasleys, and Harry and Hermione to the Quidditch World Cup in Book IV; a teakettle in Dumbledore's office takes the Weasleys and Harry to Mr. Weasley's bedside in St. Mungo's in the middle of Book V; and the head of a statue transports Harry back to Hogwarts from the Ministry of Magic near the end of Book V. Moreover, travelling by port key is Apparently quite a passive experience—one just touches the port key and is transported. Nonetheless, like the use of other enchanted travel objects, it is not an instantaneous means of travel but is instead quite dynamic:

Harry felt as though a hook just behind his navel had been suddenly jerked irresistibly forward. His feet left the ground; he could feel Ron and Hermione on either side of him, their shoulders banging into his; they were all speeding forward in a howl of wind and swirling color; his forefinger was stuck to the boot as though it was pulling him magnetically onward and then—His feet slammed into the ground; Ron staggered into him and he fell over; the Portkey hit the ground near his head with a heavy thud. Harry looked up. Mr. Weasley, Mr. Diggory, and Cedric were still standing, though looking very windswept; everybody else was on the ground (IV.73-4).

This is clearly a very visceral travel experience, and not necessarily a pleasant one. Jerked forward as if by a hook, banging into others uncontrollably, slamming into the ground, and being nearly hit in the head, Harry seems fortunate to arrive at the Quidditch World Cup without injury. Also, nearly every port-key traveller ends their journey by falling flat on the ground. Thus, in addition to its potential physical effects, this form of travel is certainly humbling.

Floo powder enables travel by fire to any fireplace connected to the floo network; though more commonly used than port keys, it has some difficulties. Harry's first experience travelling by floo powder nearly makes him ill:

> *It felt as though he was being sucked down a giant drain. He seemed to be spinning very fast—the roaring in his ears was deafening—he tried to keep his eyes open but the whirl of green flames made him feel sick—something hard knocked his elbow and he tucked it in tightly, still spinning and spinning—squinting through his glasses he saw a blurred stream of fireplaces and snatched glimpses of the rooms beyond—his bacon sandwiches were churning inside him—he closed his eyes again wishing it would stop, and then— He fell, face forward, onto cold stone and felt the bridge of his glasses snap* (II.49).

No permanent damage is done, but Harry's glasses are broken, and he is quite sooty, dizzy, and bruised. This mode of travel seems to approximate the experience of the rider on a very poorly maintained Muggle carnival ride.

Moreover, Harry's inexperience with floo powder results in him missing his destination and winding up lost. Instead of delivering him to that center of wizard commerce, Diagon Alley, the floo network lands him nearly in the arms of his enemies the Malfoys; because he has uttered an unclear destination upon stepping into the fireplace, he ends up in "Knockturn Alley," home of shops devoted to the dark arts (II.49-54). While the Weasley boys think this is cool, Knockturn Alley is clearly a place of danger for Harry.

In Book IV, the Weasleys attempt to use floo powder to travel to the Dursley's house, where they end up trapped in a bricked-up fireplace and must blast themselves out. Like using enchanted objects, floo powder and port keys are physical modes of travel, despite the fact that travellers using such means seem to enter a different dimension, travelling unseen to their destination.

The final magical means of travel is Apparation, which allows wizards and witches to travel instantaneously from one location to another. Apparation is the only method of travel in the wizarding world that does not seem to involve the physical feeling of movement; it is perhaps analogous to transporter travel in *Star Trek*. In Book IV readers find out that a license is required to Apparate because of the danger of leaving some body parts behind while moving instantly from one place to another. Hogwarts is the only location in which Apparation is impossible, perhaps because most of the student body is underage, but also because of security concerns at the school.

However, even normal foot travel within the precincts of Hogwarts can be dangerous, due not only to lurking monsters and Filch's enforcement of the curfew, but also to moving staircases and changing hallways:

> *There were a hundred and forty two staircases at Hogwarts: wide, sweeping ones; narrow, rickety ones; some that led somewhere different on a Friday; some with a vanishing step halfway up that you had to remember to jump. There were doors that wouldn't open*

unless you asked politely, or tickled them in exactly the right place, and doors that weren't really doors at all but solid walls just pretending. It was also very hard to remember where anything was, because it all seemed to move around a lot (1.131-2).

In other words, while the Professors and students at Hogwarts are generally confined to non-magical forms of transport within the school grounds, the building itself moves and reconfigures.

Any kind of movement, transport, or change in the magical world of Harry Potter is fraught with potential for both good and evil. While this may seem daunting, the alternative is clearly not acceptable: the miserably safe and static imprisonment of the Dursley household, the only representation of Muggle life that this series offers readers.

Steven Gores is Associate Professor of English at Northern Kentucky University. He and his wife, Paige Byam, live in Cincinnati with their four Harry Potter fans: Hal, Jasper, Hugh, and Simon.

All This Magic Makes My Brain Ache[1]

Roger Highfield

Now let's get one thing straight. I don't think of myself as a Pottermaniac. True, I did write the first book on the science of Harry Potter. And I love JKR's books. But I have never resorted to the use of a wand, even in anger. I do issue curses, but not of the occult variety. And, although I did wear a sixteenth century uniform at school, and gown and mortar board at university, I have never donned a pointy hat. Ever. But as I discovered at Nimbus 2003, eccentric apparel only scratches the surface of what lurks in the die-hard HP 'fandom.'

When in January I was asked to be a VIP speaker at the world's first adult symposium on Harry Potter, (named after the legendary racing broomstick), it seemed a bit of a hoot. But as I read the programme in detail on my transatlantic flight, I began to have misgivings. Sessions included: 'sexuality, protest, elves and white womanhood," "Imperial Harry: Race, J.K. Rowling, and the Postcolonial Context", and "Emeric Switch on Gender; Harry and Hermione's Transgendered Heroism."

At Orlando airport, I was greeted by Renee Antoine, 23, who had driven with friends overnight from Dayton, Ohio, to help run the conference. Her day job was working with disturbed teenagers but, typical of the people I was to meet, was also one of the many thousands of Potter devotees who contribute mega-bits and bytes of Potter material to the internet every day.

Nimbus was an roots up meeting of enthusiasts conceived and developed by the 'online fandom'. It was born in a Yahoo adult discussion site on Harry Potter and highly populated by those who write derivative fan fiction, run 'shipping' sites (to discuss 'ships, such as Harry's relationship with Hermione) and even 'slash' sites, which focus on same-sex relationships such as Harry/Ron—a particular favourite among the Japanese. Delegates flew in from afar—America, the UK, Australia, India and the Philippines.

In the wet heat of the airport car park, my heart sank when I saw that Renee's red minivan had been vandalised. It was coated in graffiti. As we got closer, I could make out various slogans: 'I (heart) Harry', 'Honk if you love Harry Potter' and 'Gryffindor Chasers'. All the idea of her friends, apparently.

I climbed inside with another VIP speaker, Judith Krug, director, Office of Intellectual Freedom, at the American Library Association. What was she doing there? 'My office

---

[1] This paper is the original version of the article that Roger Highfield wrote on July 22, 2003 about his experiences at Nimbus – 2003.

keeps track of books that have been challenged in schools and libraries. The Harry Potter series is the number one on our list for the fourth year running.'

Far-right and fundamentalist Christian groups who take a literal-minded reading of the Bible have an equally literal-minded view of Hogwarts witchcraft and wizardry. They have fought, notably in a recent Arkansas court case, to remove these 'occult books' from the shelves. 'The Dursleys are mean,' one complained. ('You don't say! was Krug's reply) Another suggested that Potter's potions promoted drug use.

'Some people believe that only truth gets into print,' Krug laughed, noting that her two year old grandchild can easily tell the difference between a story and real life, 'There are adults who can't make that distinction. There's a group who feel that just by reading Potter, you will become a witch.' Krug is a fan of the meeting and of the books, which have 'brought an entire generation of young people back to reading.'

In Disney's magic kingdom, Renee dropped us off in the Swan, a monster of a hotel that reminded me of one of Saddam's palaces. Within its gloomy air conditioned interior, the 'fandom' was gathering. A queue of around two hundred people, mostly women in their 20s and 30s, snaked down a corridor from the registration desk. The excitement was palpable. There was a magical Mallory Towers feel to the proceedings. It was hard to know what the adjoining meeting of mortgage experts would make of this lot.

Some wore schoolgirl's outfits. Many had academic gowns. And a fair few wore the full witch regalia, complete with scarf, broomstick, wand and pointy hat (velvet, flashing LEDs, stuffed animal—take your pick). There were robes, some red, others silken and shimmering. One had made a coordinated lilac witch's outfit with sequins. And there were plenty of home-made T shirts: 'Chudley Cannons', 'What would Draco do?', 'Padfoot Forever (a reference to Sirius Black) and 'Slytherins are sexy.'

The latter moved me to select the sly Slytherin colour—green—for my name tag. (Besides, all Hollywood villains are Brits. And I am a hack, after all). Now initiated into the Potter coven, I was greeted by Penny Linsenmayer, a Houston lawyer and one of the organisers, as revealed by their badges, sashes and purple lanyards.

The meeting brought together Trekkie-like enthusiasm, net heads with names such as Lilac, Mariner and Caius Marcius, dry-as-dust academe and daft stunts. The latter included an auction of a blue Ford Anglia, a 'taste of the UK' expedition, and vote for the worst official merchandise—a close run thing between Harry underpants and a Troll bogey glue gun.

Penny straddled these worlds. She supports a 'shipping site' which explores the relationship between Harry and Hermione and was going to give a paper on the geography of Harry Potter. Not just the easy stuff, such as the location of Privet Drive, but key Pottermaniac obsessions, notably the site of Godric's Hollow, where Harry's parents were killed. Her exclusive revelation: it has to be in Wales, Cornwall or the West Country. She came over all serious. It is going to be controversial, she warned.

I checked out the wizard merchandise, located in a room dubbed 'KumpulsieveAlley'. There was relatively little mass marketed Potter junk. There were capes, waistcoats, jewelry floppy velvet hats, magic tricks and a deserted stand extolling the joys of UK tourism. Even competing wand manufacturers. On one side was Alivan's, self-styled master wand makers, run by Dave Wedzik, who offers a line of 35 dollar wands, rising to a 65 dollar customised ebony variety. 'We have had the occasional person ringing to say my wand does not work,' he shrugged, as I waved his black wand about (nothing happened). 'I honestly don't know what to say.' As for phoenix feathers, 'it has been difficult to find them lately. We get calls on that too.'

At the other end of the Alley was rival company Whirlwood, born when the artist Gary Hall made a wand for his little boy. He proudly showed me 'Dumbledore's ceremonial wand', a 300 dollar affair complete with brass handle. His rival, Wedzik, is 'the wandmaker who must not be named,' he hissed. As we gossiped, Gary handed out 'Barbie wands'—better known as toothpicks. But he stopped for a moment, bewitched by a striking young Puerto Rican, Bianca Belezon from Miami's South Beach, as she patrolled past us. Bianca was armed with a walkie talkie and carried a black sash marked with 'security' in silvery lettering. She did not seem concerned by evangelical protests, or Warner brother spies (tireless in their efforts to guard their copyright) but told me she was scanning for 'dark wizards'.

Many of the six hundred or so Pottermaniacs who met in Orlando had corresponded for years online. The first big event of the meeting was marked by the occasional whoop, when they met for the first time and could talk, rather than swap emails. I bumped into a fellow Brit. Susan Hall, an intellectual property lawyer from Cobbetts Solicitors, Manchester, who had become sucked into the 'Potterverse' when she began to exchange emails on magical law with another lawyer in Florida.

She was to give a paper on justice in the wizarding world. Tell me more, I asked. Susan launched into a long account of how wizard and Muggle law were once closely linked before 1692 and the introduction of the Statute of Wizarding Secrecy, when they moved apart. Now, the wizarding world has a system of 'bastard client/patronage networks', akin to what happened in the later Roman Republic.

She was particularly vexed by *The Order of the Phoenix* (referred to at the meeting as The Big Book), where Harry, a minor, was tried by a full criminal court with no adult or even legal representation. 'It is a textbook example of bad practice,' she said. What do her colleagues think? She winced, suggesting that not all her peers shared her enthusiasms.

Wiseley, she pointed out that the sceptics should realise that wearing Mickey T shirts and other Disney merchandise was altogether sadder. 'I have just spent two days in Disneyland and I arrive here and see people wearing funny hats—that they had made themselves! I thought, thank god, normal people at last.' It is easy to mock the Pottermaniacs, but as she made clear, Nimbus 2003 fizzed with home brewed fantasy, a rare thing in the land where dreams are usually bought off the shelf.

The evening ended with the first conference session, where the organisers were to analyse the personas of a group of key characters (the Marauders), the first of many intense discussions about Rowling's books. To ululations, the event was launched by Gwendolyn Grace, Minister of Magic (aka Lee Hillman, self-confessed common or garden pagan ('I

DON'T believe in Satan' she later told me). Ebony Thomas took the part of James Potter 'the sexiest dad in the world' (huge cheer). Carlisle Kraft, a New Jersey librarian, talked up the persona of Peter Padfoot (aka Wormtail). This Death Eater, she sneered, had descended from being Voldemort's right hand man to a 'squealing James Potter Fanboy' in the latest book. She was greeted by boos as the Minister implored the mob to 'be nice'.

The evening ended with a Californian 'acoustic punk' group, the Switchblade Kittens, who delivered their 'Ode to Harry Potter.' For some reason, I found myself being talked by Susan Hall into playing Quidditch. How? What about broomsticks? I went to bed wondering what I had let myself into. And how a British chap wearing a suit who waffled about science would fare among the die-hard fandom.

Six AM the next day my phone rings. 'Have a magical day,' intones the automated wake up call. My talk is soon after breakfast. The venue is almost full. Can we create three headed giant dogs, become invisible or whiz around a network of fireplaces with the help of floo powder? (yes-ish, thanks to GM, adaptive camouflage and quantum teleportation). The audience seemed enthusiastic. The chap from *Time* magazine was there. So was the woman from the *Orlando Sentinel*. And several of my academic peers. Plus a teenage woman who would not stop asking questions about ghosts. My book sold out. But the fandom had deserted me. There was not one pointed hat to be seen as I discussed owl mail, dragons and levitating frogs.

Prowling around outside were some of the die-hard fans who I had failed to enchant. Itching to find out more about them, I found myself talking to one of the two Draco Malfoys (Harry's enemy at Hogwarts) that I had spotted at the meeting. 'I got the blond hair and I love Draco,' declared Kayla Georgiafancis, a 19 year old fan fiction writer. 'And I'm bad,'she added. Like her peers, she was keenly awaiting a session on 'Draco redeemed'. 'I rewrote Philosopher's Stone from Draco's point of view and I got a lot of people sympathetic to him by doing that.'

Another was Sara Pierce of Tennessee, a 14-year-old in a fetching witch outfit who looked like a shy version of Hermione. No, she protested. 'I am just coming as me.' As she clutched a pile of books on black magic (a few of her collection of 200 or so), she denied that Potter fosters a belief in the occult, as her grandmother had constantly told her. 'It is the stupidest idea I have ever come across. I just like magic. And I believe in God.' In an odd twist of fate, I would encounter these two fans later that day, during a test of my mettle and resolve.

After Krug delivered a stirring defence of the First Amendment at lunch, I saw a huge crowd gather outside the 'Great Hall'. I slipped in, a sole suit among the costumed fandom. A bespectacled Brit ex public schoolboy who now lives in New York was one of the stars. With a plastic golden snitch hanging around his neck, and rainbow glitter in his gelled hair, he launched a discussion on the slash genre: 'Romantic relationships between members of the same sex who are not in an explicitly stated relationship within an opus,' he explained But there was a limit to how explicit this twenty-something wanted to be. Because his grandmother reads the Telegraph, 'and doesn't know,' he politely asked me to call him by his web name, 'Queer as John.'

'I'll be playing with Draco's wand,' announced fellow panellist Dave Wang, a Delaware mathematics teacher. It is obvious, he told the whooping throng, that 'Draco wants Harry.' Kate Tanski, who has studied the slash genre for her honours project, bemoaned how academics did not seem to understand the thrill of her research. 'It's hot.'

Slash is mostly enjoyed by heterosexual women. On this point, Dr Bridget Cowlishaw of Florida Atlantic University was refreshingly candid: 'I read slash for the sex.'. As a teacher, she was particularly taken by Snape/Harry. Then she upped her academic cred by explaining how male-male sex 'subverts the patriarchal system' and the genre gives readers ownership of a book as much as a writer.

This kind of session was poles apart from academic offerings. Legal eagles jokingly admitted to speaking the 'US dialect of Parseltongue (snake language). Teachers assessed the Hogwarts curriculum ('room for improvement ') and pondered whether the books followed the Gothic tradition or were influenced by Jame Austen or Stoic philosophy. Dr Philip Nel of Kansas State University defended the books against attacks by A S Byatt and others. And Dr Alice Trupe, who teaches writing, pointed out that Harry, like other characters, 'is severely constrained by a history of which he is largely ignorant, replete with class prejudices, racism, economic disparity and exploitation.'

My mind was beginning to be boggled. Sidharth Jaggi talked of 'ontological displacements' (something to do with Platform 9 and three quarters) while John Granger, author of The Hidden Key to Harry Potter and the only Potter professor (from the online Barnes and Noble University), explained how the Potter books 'offer initiation, not into the occult, but rather into the symbolist world view of revealed faiths and the dominant symbols and doctrines of traditional Christianity.'

An interview in *Bitch: Feminist reponse to Pop Culture*, once derided JKR's 'little European white boy hero.' Not so, the meeting was told by literature graduate Emily Anderson: Hermione is intelligent, bossy, brave and logical, revealing masculine traits, while Harry 'displays more qualities traditionally associated with feminism.'

'By making Harry the undisputed hero . . . Rowling is celebrating femininity, depicting female power ans overpowering male power, even if that female power is embodied in a male character.' Then Amy Miller tried to convince us that there are many Jewish teachings in the Potter books and 'parallels to Hitler, genocide and racism as well'. Enough!

Until this point, I had succumbed to the all embracing enthusiasm for all things Potter. The meeting had been great fun. But there was no avoiding it. Quidditch cometh.

At six PM, and feeling somewhat queasy, I joined a noisy throng in one of the huge ballrooms where six hoops had been erected, three at each end. It was, I was later told, the biggest ever Muggle Quidditch match. My team was the Cape Canaveral Kestrals. As a 'beater', one of two in each team armed with rubberised bats, I was supposed to defend the team from 'bludgers' and whack them at our opponents.

Fans have discussed endlessly how to bring Quidditch to life. Some versions involve unicycles. Others require juggling. Never broomsticks, alas. I should have realised that this was going to be a complex affair. The evening 's MC, Chris Dickson, a mathematics graduate from Oxford who works on web sites, took several minutes to read out the rules.

The first match took for ever. At first, I really could not work out what was going on. Gradually, among the couple of dozen Muggles milling about on the pitch, I could discern three games: glorified basketball by chasers with a red ball (quaffle) to score ten points for each pass through a hoop; a hunt by a seeker for a little yellow ball (instant victory if you got the golden snitch—but it had to be the right one, since dummies were being carried hither and thither); finally a target competition where I and the other beaters had to whack black balls at rival players to knock them out of action for ten seconds. The crowd was encouraged to count them out.

By the time the first match was over, we had lost one of our team. Liz O' Reilly of Hull University decided she would rather mug up on her forthcoming talk on 'Perceptions of Childhood and Adult Child Relations in Harry Potter. 'By the time our match came around, we had also been deserted by our most important member, the Seeker. What losers! Lacking the chutzpah of our rivals, it took some time to find a replacement. Finally, one came forward: Sara Pierce, the 14 year old fan I had met earlier. It took some persuading to get her to take off her gown.

My fellow beater was unimpressed when I explained that I was hopeless at sports. This was not false modesty but hard fact, I said, as he rolled his eyes. I forgot how Americans find this British habit of talking things down annoying. They have a good point. We tied on our fetching blue and silver ribbons to distinguish us from the enemy. There was now no doubt we were playing in America, after we were asked to sign a waiver so we could not sue if a bludger broke an arm, or a Snitch took someone's eye out.

Our rivals, the Miami McCaws, had some serious looking basketball players. We were doomed. Among them was Draco (Kayla Georgiafancis), who leered at me in character. I spent much of my time ineffectually swinging at the ball and stumbling about. And when I did connect, the referee told me off for hitting the bludger too hard. I reckon I hit my own team more often than the enemy. It was not going very well. Sara grabbed yet another snitch. They were usually dummies and there was little suspense. However, after a confused pause, we found that we had won, much to our opponent's amazement—and our's too.

Very satisfactory. Our honour preserved, we could now go to a nearby nightclub to help celebrate the birthday of FictionAlley, one of the fan fiction sites sponsoring the meeting. It was not to be. The bespectacled MC declared that we had a strong score and, still out of breath, we found ourselves facing by far the most impressive team, the Orlando Ospreys. We were through to the Grand Final. A teenage girl introduced us as the losers. Draco shook her fist at me menacingly from the sidelines. Like something out of the pages of Potter, we were a depleted Gryffindor against a mighty Slytherin. We had no chance. The Telegraph photographer, Stuart Conway, looked on in pity.

By now most of the audience had melted away to the night club and we played on in near silence. After three minutes and two seconds, the snitch was caught. The Seeker was Sarah. After a brief, astonished, pause, the Kestrels did a little victory dance and the Ospreys looked on, aghast. I am now the proud bearer of a commemorative scroll, thanks to my small contribution to a historic victory of the Cape Canaveral Kestrals.

Minutes later, the heavens opened and the night sky lit up with a spectacular electric storm. As we left the hall in high spirits, our MC, Chris, turned to me and gave his verdict on our victory, the fastest of the tournament. It had been a 'fairytale ending.'

Indeed it had.

Dr. Roger Highfield is the Science Editor of The Daily Telegraph which has published several thousand of his articles since he first joined the newspaper in 1986. He studied chemistry at Oxford University where for his doctorate he became the first person to bounce a neutron off a soap bubble. With the BBC, he has organised mass experiments that have involved hundreds of thousands of people. He has also run an annual science writing competition and a host of other events, from science parties to a seminar on the science of chocolate at the Royal Institution. He is a regular broadcaster on the BBC and has won several awards for journalism, including four Glaxo science writing awards, two for medical journalism, and one British Press Award. He is also a member of the Royal Society Science in Society Committee.

Dr. Highfield is the author of two highly praised books: The Physics of Christmas (Can Reindeer Fly?) (UK edition), which was in the top 30 Christmas bestsellers in the UK; and The Science of Harry Potter: How Magic Really Works. He is coauthor of three other books: The Arrow of Time, a bestseller which has been translated into over a dozen languages; The Private Lives of Albert Einstein, which has been translated into half a dozen languages; and Frontiers of Complexity.

Imagination at Work:
Harry Potter and Stoic Virtue

Edmund M. Kern

J. K. Rowling develops an essentially Stoic moral philosophy through the ethical dilemmas in which she places Harry Potter, dilemmas requiring him to think in complex ways about right and wrong. In considering her ethic, banish once and for all the common stereotype of the Stoic who is unemotional, tediously puritanical, and blindly indifferent to enjoyment and grief. Although early Stoic works do contribute to this stereotype, Rowling's characters are anything but unfeeling and embrace life to the fullest. Her version of Stoicism is admittedly an updated one, providing full attention to emotional development, but nonetheless one whose chief virtue is old-fashioned constancy. Harry's resolution in the face of adversity is the result of conscious choice and attention to what is and is not within his control. He cultivates himself in order to help others. Harry worries about who he *is*, but realizes that what he *does* matters most. In fact, the stories *focus* on Harry's self-fashioning and the moral decisions that go into it, elaborating, along the way, upon several key Stoic themes such as fatalism, endurance, perseverance, self-discipline, reason, solidarity, empathy, and sacrifice. Rowling's accomplishment, blending imaginative wit and serious contemplation of virtue, is astonishing. By putting her imagination into play, she puts her imagination to work.

A foreboding permeates Harry's life. He senses quite accurately that he has some frightful enemies and that he is the target of vengeance. Despite some cheery optimism, Harry has a pronounced sense of fatalism—that is, he recognizes how events unfold around him, drawing him into circumstances not of his own making. In precisely this way, Rowling introduces the Stoicism so central to the moral system at work in her series. She gives Stoic fatalism a clear voice in the characters mentoring Harry, along with its Stoic antidotes. In the first book we find Dumbledore observing:

> "Nevertheless, Harry, while you may only have delayed his return to power, it will merely take someone else who is prepared to fight what seems a losing battle next time—and if he is delayed again, and again, why, he may never return to power." (*Harry Potter and the Sorcerer's Stone* 298)

By the fourth book, these sentiments are echoed in the plain language of the groundskeeper Hagrid:

"Knew he was goin' ter come back," said Hagrid . . . . "Known it fer years, Harry. Knew he was out there bidin' his time. It had ter happen. Well, now it has, an' we'll jus' have ter get on with it. We'll fight. Migh' be able ter stop him before he gets a good hold." (*Harry Potter and the Goblet of Fire* 718-19)

This view of fatalism running throughout Rowling's series is not wholly out of character with the ancient Stoics' understanding of the problem, derived from their conception of "nature." For them, nature is the unfolding of a providential design (fate or fortune) that shapes both events and human norms. The essence of this design is reason, which, according to the Stoics, is precisely what humans find within themselves through therapeutic self-examination. Nature thus places within humans the ability to live according to its plan, and thereby find fulfillment, through the exercise of practical reason. Seneca's depiction of human life as a combination of both fate and free will might clarify this view: "Good men toil, spend and are spent, and willingly; they are not dragged along by Fortune but follow her and keep in step. If they knew how, they would have outstripped her" ("On Providence" 41). Seneca's point is that even the best of us cannot hope to do better than understanding the nature of the realities confronting us and making our own desires conform to them.

It is worth remembering that the Stoics are not counseling passivity. Rather, they recommend a particular kind of engagement with the world, an active and rational constancy through the cultivation of virtue that renders them indifferent to external concerns. Such concerns are the source of neither harm nor greatness. We can see this idea at work in a passage from Seneca's essay, *On Constancy*:

> The wise man can lose nothing. He has everything invested in himself, he trusts nothing to fortune, and his own goods are secure, since he is content with virtue, which needs no gift from chance, and which, therefore, can neither be increased nor diminished . . . . Fortune can snatch away only what she herself has given. ("De Constantia Sapientis" 1:61)

Again, Epictetus makes a similar point in a somewhat skeptical description of the uses of divination to foretell the future (which is particularly appropriate to an examination of Harry Potter):

> First clearly understand that every event is indifferent and nothing to you, of whatever sort it may be; for it will be in your power to make a right use of it, and this no one can hinder . . . . Come to divination [when] no opportunities are afforded by reason or any other art to discover the matter in view. (*Enchiridion* 30)

Epictetus is suggesting that divination is simply one tool among many for assessing the future—and clearly the least important among them. More significant, however, is the implication that whatever the future may have in store, the individual who remains constant will meet it with confidence. Both Seneca and Epictetus counsel contentment with virtue and the need to adapt to maintain it. Boldness and audacity play no role in this scheme, because they have little relation to inner contentment.

In the Harry Potter books, we see this theme in persistent reminders that Harry deals successfully with things beyond his power. Other than Voldemort's threat upon Harry's life, the most obvious example is Harry's acceptance of the Dursleys' cruelties. But he also learns, for example, that wands choose their wizards, that the Sorting Hat will decide his fate at Hogwarts, that death cannot be denied, and that, as Hagrid points out, everything seems to happen *to* him regardless of his own actions. Of course, as a Stoic counterpoint, Hagrid, Dumbledore, and Sirius—his most important mentors—counsel Harry to remain constant and to have little concern for glory (which he sometimes entertains but always represses). They encourage him not to worry about things beyond his control, to accept adverse circumstances while adapting to them, and to realize that choices make people who they are.

Two particularly good examples of the tensions between fatalism and moral constancy can be seen in episodes involving Firenze the centaur and Professor Trelawney the divination teacher. Centaurs, as a group, read the stars to see what is "foretold," and then meekly accept it, choosing not to get involved in others' affairs. But Firenze sets himself against evil "because the planets have been read wrongly before" (*Sorcerer's Stone* 259). Trelawney, in contrast, always misreads the signs in her efforts to foretell the future but does nothing about it. Both she and her subject are revealed as fraudulent, and the wisest characters ignore her predictions. She does manage to get it right twice, but, tellingly, she does so unconsciously in a trance-state that she cannot later recall. These episodes pit active engagement against passivity and clearly suggest that the former is the best course of action—within reason. If one follows fate, one must not tempt it.

Harry, of course, consciously acts out his fate, like Seneca's "good men," in each of the central challenges put to him. He also prefers reason, like Epictetus, to "any other art" when assessing the nature of realities confronting him. In contrast, Harry's nemesis Voldemort tries to deny fate to his own loss and humiliation. His first words to Harry, "see what I have become" (*Sorcerer's Stone* 293), reveal the extreme depths of his folly. What is Voldemort's pursuit of the sorcerer's stone other than an attempt to deny everyone's ultimate fate—death? Harry's constancy, in contrast, is emblematic of his Stoic wisdom. Harry's heroism, thus inflected, is neither bold nor audacious.

Portrayals of the many disappointments confronting Harry should suggest to readers that his constancy coexists with at least two additional Stoic virtues. For if fate bestows both generosity and calamity, endurance and perseverance are necessary tonics for warding off the effects of adversity. Epictetus writes the prescription against disappointments in this manner:

> Remind yourself of what nature they are . . . . If you have a favorite cup, that it is
> but a cup . . . if it is broken, you can bear it; if you embrace your child or your wife,
> that you embrace a mortal—and, thus, if either of them dies, you can bear it.
> (*Enchiridion* 18)

This easy juxtaposition of cups and family members is pretty rough medicine, but it is intended to suggest that bearing loss is necessary rather than easy. Unfortunately, life provides many disappointments, because vice is so pervasive in human affairs.

Stoics concede that there is enough evil in the world to justify a perpetual anger, but for this very reason, they will not allow vice in others to affect their own inner tranquility. Marcus Aurelius reminds us why when he writes, "it is madness to expect inferior men to do no wrong, for this is to desire the impossible." But he goes in a different direction in another passage, noting, "men are born for each other's sake. So either teach people or endure them" (*Meditations* 118 and 84). The Stoics thus counsel a kind of detachment from the world as a means of surviving its many disappointments, but they do so within the context of a cosmopolitan and egalitarian ethic. Anger will mislead, but endurance and perseverance will bring good counsel: patience in the fight against evil. For this reason, it is worth calling attention to Chrysippus's definitions of courage, which he relates to endurance and perseverance, rather than daring or bravado: it is "scientific knowledge of matters requiring persistence" or "a tenor of the soul fearlessly obedient to the supreme law [reason] in enduring and persisting" (Long and Sedley 1:192).

If we keep these ideas in mind, we can thus see the source of Harry's own courage in his acceptance of circumstances he did not choose. Harry survives life with the Dursleys, the loss of his parents, the animosity of Snape, serious injuries, the depravity of the dementors, competition in the Triwizard Tournament, Cedric's death, and Voldemort's promised threats upon his own. Most telling, Harry manages to thrive as an increasingly self-possessed individual despite such profound adversity. He endures and perseveres. Harry's particular form of heroism, as Chrysippus would see it, results from his conscious willingness to do so.

Harry's moral growth is dependent upon his increasing self-awareness. This consciousness emerges because of the self-discipline and capacity for reason that comes with age, two virtues highly valued by the Stoics. Epictetus makes the point by way of analogy:

> Do not, like children, be now a philosopher, then a publican, then an orator, and
> then one of Caesar's officers. These things are not consistent. You must be one man,
> either good or bad. You must cultivate either your own reason or else externals;
> apply yourself to things within or without you—that is, be either a philosopher or
> one of the mob. (*Enchiridion* 28)

Stoics thus place a high value upon reason and a concomitant self-discipline, seeing them as essential to a successful life—as essential to happiness.

In fact, as I argued earlier, the Stoics claim that nature gives humans the capacity to live according to its design through reason. As Cicero reports, Chrysippus saw reason as godly: "For he says that divine power resides in reason and in the mind and intellect of universal nature" (Long and Sedley 1:323). In order to be happy, it is incumbent upon humans to use reason to bring themselves into accord with nature's design. We can see this clearly in Stobaeus's outline of Stoic definitions of the purpose, or "end," of life:

> Zeno represented the end as: "living in agreement." This is living in accordance with one concordant reason, since those who live in conflict are unhappy . . . . Cleanthes, his first successor, added "with nature," and represented it as follows: "the end is living in agreement with nature." Chrysippus wanted to make this clearer and expressed it thus: "living in accordance with experience of what happens by nature." (Long and Sedley 1:378)

Reason thus leads to knowledge of the most important things in life. Epictetus provides a concise explanation of the workings and benefits of practical reason in discussing the value of particular pleasures:

> If you are dazzled by the semblance of any promised pleasure, guard yourself against being bewildered by it; but let the affair wait your leisure, and procure yourself some delay. Then bring to your mind both points of time . . . [when you enjoy it and when you later reproach yourself] . . . and set before you, in opposition to these, how you will rejoice and applaud yourself if you abstain. (*Enchiridion* 33)

Epictetus is not implying pleasures are not worth pursuing; he is instead suggesting they be in accord with true happiness—with nature, with reason. In a moral treatise, Plutarch brings up the Stoics and makes the same point, by way of negative example:

> It is called irrational whenever an excessive impulse which has become strong and dominant carries it [the soul] off towards something wrong and contrary to the dictates of reason. For passion is vicious and uncontrolled reason which acquires vehemence and strength from bad and erroneous judgment. (Long and Sedley 1:394)

When Seneca asks, "What is best in man?" he answers without hesitation, "Reason: with this he precedes the animals and follows the gods . . . . Perfect reason is called virtue and it is identical to rectitude" (Long and Sedley 1:395).

Reason thus leads to true nobility. Directed outward, its exercise makes humans vigilant, discerning, and committed to the truth. Cultivated internally, it liberates the self and leads to a better understanding of personal capacities. This rational self-discipline makes philosophy a way of life. Harry embodies a true nobility because of his indifference to "externals" and through his "living in accordance with experience of what happens by nature." Both are made possible by higher levels of reason and self-discipline. Harry consistently maintains an active agency in the face of constraining circumstance, and he persistently chooses what is right over what is easy.

Rowling communicates the importance of reason and self-discipline in a number of ways throughout her series. The earliest palpable examples include sharp juxtapositions between Harry and Dudley Dursley. The latter's books go untouched and he is in possession of too many video games. Harry, in contrast, reads diligently each summer and engages in more worthwhile activities. Hermione's intellect and her willingness to use it also serve to emphasize the significance of rational engagement with the world. Throughout Harry's stories, in fact, central characters seek information, discuss their options, and assess the decisions they reach. They may not be philosophers, as Epictetus would have it, but they are not members of the unthinking mob either.

Numerous examples of this theme can be found throughout Rowling's books. Harry and Hermione, in particular, have a knack for seeing things that others can't. Lupin and Sirius consistently pursue the truth, even if they sometimes falter or arrive at insights late in the process. McGonagall teaches prudence and precision. And Dumbledore embodies a life of learning, intellect, and discipline.

Much of Harry's growth consists of learning to avoid extremes. When he enters into a reckless rage, as he does several times in *Harry Potter and the Prisoner of Azkaban*, he soon overcomes it. Free to wander Diagon Alley, in the same book, he exercises a lot of self-control. Feeling sorry for himself, he considers the plight of others. Made aware of his weaknesses, he cultivates—with the assistance of others—his prowess, daring, deduction, and ability to cope with danger to compete in the Triwizard Tournament. Most important, again and again, Harry sees himself as personally diminished when he realizes that he has done something wrong. A number of characters counsel him in the ways of prudence. Lupin calls attention, for Harry's benefit, to his own reckless and thoughtless actions as a youth. Cautioning awareness, Sirius encourages the careful accumulation and analysis of information. Even the false Moody teaches vigilance through harsh lessons to foster knowledge of what is at stake.

Of course, Dumbledore models reason and self-discipline most consistently of all. He counsels Harry to be prepared before the Mirror of Erised, reminds him to keep busy rather than brooding in times of uncertainty, and encourages not only curiosity but caution. At the end of *The Sorcerer's Stone*, Dumbledore speaks oracularly of truth as a beautiful but terrible thing, something that might be withheld but which should not occasion lies. It is significant that Harry finds guidance in the headmaster's reactions to events.

Harry thus learns the lessons of rationality and self-control. This ability is signaled subtly near the end of *The Goblet of Fire*, when Harry, Ron, and Hermione consider the aftermath of horrible events:

> He felt as though all three of them had reached an understanding they didn't need to put into words; that each was waiting for some sign, some word, of what was going on outside Hogwarts—and that it was useless to speculate about what might be coming until they knew anything for certain. (717)

The moral is clearly that any action taken out of ignorance is unwise. Sensing future dangers, in good Stoic fashion, Harry, Ron, and Hermione take stock of themselves and the situation confronting them.

One of the chief hallmarks of the Harry Potter books is Harry's activity on behalf of others. This may seem strange given the Stoics' emphasis upon indifference to events in the world, but their conception of individual autonomy never implies surrendering to evil. It implies exactly the opposite. In light of this fact, self-sufficiency is always balanced by a strong commitment to others through the virtues of empathy, solidarity, and sacrifice. Stoic ethics are cosmopolitan and egalitarian.

Stoic treatments of empathy take many forms, but we can quickly assess their implications in the writings of Hierocles. For this reason, his views are worth quoting at length:

Each one of us is as it were entirely encompassed by many circles, some smaller others larger, the latter enclosing the former on the basis of their different and unequal dispositions relative to each other. The first and closest circle is the one which a person has drawn as though around a centre, his own mind. For it is virtually the smallest circle, and almost touches the centre itself. Next [extending outward, come circles including] . . . parents, siblings, wife, and children . . . . uncles and aunts, grandparents, nephews, nieces, and cousins . . . . other relatives . . . local residents . . . fellow-tribesmen . . . fellow-citizens . . . people from neighboring towns . . . fellow-countrymen. The outermost and largest circle, which encompasses all the rest, is that of the whole human race . . . . It is incumbent upon us to respect people from the third circle as if they were those from the second, and again to respect our other relatives as if they were from the third circle . . . . The right point will be reached if, through our own initiative, we reduce the distance of the relationship with each person. (Long and Sedley 1:349)

Hierocles, thus, gives much fuller form to Marcus Aurelius's claim that "we were born for each other's sake" (*Meditations* 116).

In practice, such Stoic empathy seeks to recognize the human dignity in every person. The implication is that, if individuals are responsible for and to themselves in their cultivation of virtue, they must also recognize this potential in others. Reason demands, therefore, that their own safety is of no greater value than the safety of others. Stoics thus recognize the virtuous potential in reacting to tyranny, but their goals are always limited to the cultivation of human potential. Their politics are thus built, like their educational ideals, upon the universal value of human dignity and a belief in its preservation through self-government. Indifferent, as individuals, to worldly distinctions, Stoics espouse a similar politics that is anti-sectarian and anti-nationalist. It implies universal citizenship.

This view of human solidarity is dependent upon an empathetic imagination that replaces the emotional intensity of compassion—which can lead to cruelty as well as kindness—with a more powerful (at least according to the Stoics) rational recognition of radical human equality. Thus, pity and sympathy, as forms of compassion, become suspect, but empathy and mercy—arrived at through reason—can lead to a similar imaginative extension of the self, while skirting the inherent dangers associated with impulsive, emotional responses.

This empathetic imagination, therefore, can lead to an incredible willingness among some Stoics to sacrifice themselves in the name of reason. Note how Epictetus formulates the problem:

When, therefore, it is our duty to share the danger of a friend or of our country, we ought not to consult the oracle as to whether we shall share it with them or not. For though the diviner should forewarn you that the auspices are unfavorable, this means no more than that either death or mutilation or exile is portended. But we have reason with us; and it directs us, even with these hazards, to stand by our friend and our country. (*Enchiridion* 30-31)

Only death or mutilation or exile? Since within the Stoic scheme of things, life is ultimately less important than virtue, in some instances, self-destruction becomes the necessary means of self-preservation. Remember, however, Stoics never encourage rash behavior of any sort, let alone the taking of one's own life. Only a proper assessment of circumstance occasions self-sacrifice.

It is difficult to read the Harry Potter books without noticing the emphasis they place upon the virtues of empathy, solidarity, and sacrifice. Although Harry often enough finds himself in danger without pursuing it on his own, in both *The Sorcerer's Stone* and *Harry Potter and the Chamber of Secrets*, he consciously chooses to put his own life at risk on behalf of others. In *The Prisoner of Azkaban* and *The Goblet of Fire*, Harry finds himself in difficult circumstances and, yet, willingly assumes greater risks in order to correct an injustice and to show mercy upon the survivors of a murder victim. Harry's empathy, the imaginative extension of himself, provides the justification.

A particularly good illustration of the importance of empathy, solidarity and sacrifice is found in *The Prisoner of Azkaban*, because, within it, we find the motivation that implicitly underlies so much selfless behavior in Harry's stories: the protection of innocent life. I have in mind an interchange between Sirius Black and Peter Pettigrew:

> "Sirius, Sirius, what could I have done? The Dark Lord . . . you have no idea . . . he has weapons you can't imagine . . . . I was scared, Sirius, I was never brave like you and Remus and James. I never meant it to happen . . . . He-Who-Must-Not-Be-Named forced me—"

> . . . "He—he was taking over everywhere!" gasped Pettigrew. Wh— what was there to be gained by refusing him?"

> "What was there to be gained by fighting the most evil wizard who has ever existed?" said Black, with a terrible fury in his face. "Only innocent lives, Peter!"

> "You don't understand!" whined Pettigrew. "He would have killed me, Sirius."

> "THEN YOU SHOULD HAVE DIED!" roared Black. "DIED RATHER THAN BETRAY YOUR FRIENDS, AS WE WOULD HAVE DONE FOR YOU!" (374-5)

In this short, yet poignant, passage we encounter the empathy so necessary to acting on behalf of others. Sirius imagines the effects of evil and subordinates his own sense of self to them—despite his less-than-Stoic rage. Perceiving a larger threat, he determines that his own safety is irrelevant. In contrast, Pettigrew displays his incapacity to imagine the suffering of others. Fearing for his life, Pettigrew expressly indicates that he is incapable of extending himself beyond his own skin. From this illustration emerges a number of themes: circumstances beyond an individual's control must be met with resolve; they provide no justification for acting immorally; evil must be resisted regardless of cost; and death is preferable to treachery or submission.

Needless to say, many additional episodes illustrate self-denial. Whether we consider Ron's sacrifice in defense of the Sorcerer's Stone, Sirius's continuing loyalty to Harry, or Cedric's sense of fairness, we see that an empathetic connection to others motivates moral behavior. What makes such episodes in the Harry Potter books so striking is that they seldom result from emotional sentimentality. Reasoned assessments of what is right usually prompt them, even if sympathy or compassion sometimes plays a role. Harry always acts out of solidarity rather than a sense of obligation; other characters do as well. This is important, because obligation can imply a relationship between persons who are unequal in status. Solidarity, in contrast, carries no such connotation. It is therefore important to note that Harry never condescends even when he works on Dobby's behalf, regrets the relative poverty of the Weasleys, consoles Hagrid, or rescues Fleur's sister from the merpeople. Even if we do not consider the overt attention paid to prejudice and bigotry in Harry's stories, we can see that their hero always displays an egalitarian ethic. Given Dumbledore's anti-sectarian challenge to the assembled students of Hogwarts at the end of the *Goblet of Fire*, it seems a safe bet to assume we'll see more of the same in the future.

In an important sense, understanding Harry's moral decisions is dependent upon understanding how he copes with frustration. In other words, we must see how well he balances his own desires against the world's demands. This question of balance is the central challenge posed by Stoic philosophy, and it is one that Harry answers frequently. Frustrations cannot be avoided entirely, because their sources are beyond an individual's control, but responses to reality's habit of intruding in undesirable ways can be shaped through Stoic virtue. Only such mental preparedness can keep adverse circumstances from spinning out of control and drawing the individual along with them into a debilitating anger, grief, or anxiety, which have the potential to make matters worse and no ability to change circumstance.

Seneca offered the following parable to explain both the workings of fate and the fruitlessness of overly emotional responses to them:

> An animal, struggling against the noose, tightens it . . . there is no yoke so tight that it will not hurt the animal less if it pulls *with* it than

if it fights *against* it. The one alleviation for overwhelming evils is to endure and bow to necessity. (qtd. in de Botton 108)

Isn't Seneca implying that it's not even worth trying to fight back? In a commentary on this passage in *The Consolations of Philosophy*, best-selling author Alain de Botton provides an answer:

> Seneca's point is more subtle. It is no less unreasonable to accept something as necessary when it *isn't* as to rebel against something when it *is*. We can as easily go astray by accepting the unnecessary and denying the possible, as by denying the necessary and wishing for the impossible. It is for reason to make the decision. (109)

Reason thus ultimately strikes the balance between individual desire and unrelenting reality. Ambiguities certainly persist, but it is our own "distinctive freedom" to choose our attitudes towards them.

Early in the Potter series, we find a perfect illustration of how the Stoics understand the relationship between desire and reality, in *The Sorcerer's Stone*, when Dumbledore explains the powers of the Mirror of Erised:

> "Now, can you think what the Mirror of Erised shows us all?"

> Harry shook his head.

> "Let me explain. The happiest man on earth would be able to use the Mirror of Erised like a normal mirror, that is, he would look into it and see himself exactly as he is. Does that help?"

> Harry thought. Then he said slowly, "It shows us what we want . . . whatever we want . . . "

> "Yes and no," said Dumbledore quietly. "It shows us nothing more or less than the deepest, most desperate desire of our hearts . . . . However, this mirror will give us neither knowledge or [*sic*] truth. Men have wasted away before it, entranced by what they have seen, or been driven mad, not knowing if what it shows is real or even possible.

> "The Mirror will be moved to a new home tomorrow, Harry, and I ask you not to go looking for it again. If you ever *do* run across it, you will now be prepared. It does not do to dwell on dreams and forget to live, remember that." (213-14)

Later in the book, we also find how striking the balance between desire and reality applies to moral decisions.

It is no mere coincidence that when Harry again sees himself in the Mirror, he sees himself as he is, in possession of the Stone. He obtains it (thanks to Dumbledore's magic), not because he intends to use it, but because he intends to protect it from misuse, an intention that has motivated his actions right from the start. For in exercising his distinctive freedom to choose his attitude towards fate, Harry is as unrelenting as the realities beyond his control. He finds the right thing to do when confronted with conditions that he cannot escape. When Dumbledore muses to Harry in the hospital wing, "You *did* do the thing properly, didn't you" (297), he is speaking about more than Harry's investigative powers. Before the Mirror, in Voldemort's malevolent presence, Harry accepts what is necessary, without denying what is possible. He strikes the Stoic balance, and not for the last time.

From **The Wisdom of Harry Potter: What Our Favorite Hero Teaches Us About Moral Choices** *by Edmund M. Kern. pp. 19, 32-33, 89-93, and 107-119 (slightly revised and abridged). Amherst, NY: Prometheus Books. Copyright ©2003 by Edmund M. Kern. Reprinted with permission.*

List of Works Consulted

Antoninus, Marcus Aurelius. *The Meditations*. Translated by G. M. A. Grube. Indianapolis: Hackett Publishing, 1983.

Botton, Alain de. *The Consolations of Philosophy*. New York: Pantheon Books, 2000.

Epictetus. *The Enchiridion*. Translated by Thomas W. Higginson. Indianapolis: Bobbs-Merrill, 1955.

Long, A. A., and D. N. Sedley, eds. and trans. *The Hellenistic Philosophers*. Vol. 1. New York: Cambridge University Press, 1987.

Nussbaum, Martha C. *The Therapy of Desire: Theory and Practice in Hellenistic Ethics*. Princeton, N.J.: Princeton University Press, 1994.

Nussbaum, Martha C. *Upheavals of Thought: The Intelligence of Emotions*. New York: Cambridge University Press, 2001.

Rowling, J. K. *Harry Potter and the Chamber of Secrets*. New York: Scholastic Press, 1999.

Rowling, J. K. *Harry Potter and the Goblet of Fire*. New York: Scholastic Press, 2000.

Rowling, J. K. *Harry Potter and the Prisoner of Azkaban*. New York: Scholastic Press, 1999.

Rowling, J. K. *Harry Potter and the Sorcerer's Stone*. New York: Scholastic Press, 1998.

Seneca. "De Constantia Sapientis." In *Moral Essays*, translated by John W. Basore. New York: G. P. Putnam's Sons, 1928.

Seneca. "On Providence" In *The Stoic Philosophy of Seneca*. Translated by Moses Hadas. Garden City, N.J.: Doubleday, 1958.

Edmund M. Kern is the author of The Wisdom of Harry Potter: What Our Favorite Hero Teaches Us About Moral Choices, which was published by Prometheus Books in September 2003. He received his Ph.D. in Early Modern European History from the University of Minnesota, and he is currently Associate Professor of History at Lawrence University in Appleton, Wisconsin, where he has taught since 1992. His essays and reviews on the history of witchcraft and religious culture have appeared in several periodicals and anthologies, including The Sixteenth Century Journal, The Journal of Ecclesiastical History, The Austrian History Yearbook, The Journal of Interdisciplinary History, The Witchcraft Reader, edited by Darren Oldridge, and Infinite Boundaries, edited by Max Reinhart. He has served as a media consultant on witchcraft and witch-hunting, historical and modern paganism, and the roots of Halloween. In addition to continuing work on other projects, he is completing Witchcraft and the Confessional State, a book on religion and politics in European witchcraft-trials.

Where in the World?
The Geography of Harry Potter

Penny Linsenmayer & Steve Vander Ark

I.   INTRODUCTION

With the exception of the 2-3 years spent in Porto, Portugal, Joanne Rowling has spent her life in various locales in the United Kingdom. Fortunately, the locations that have figured in Rowling's life are easily pinpointed on muggle maps. The locations that pop up in her writing are sometimes harder to pin down. J. K. Rowling admits to being a great collector of "names." Some place names appear to have inspired her writing (sometimes figuring in the novels as names for characters, for example). Some of the places in the Potterverse are unplottable and do not exist on muggle maps (though we're prepared to take some guesses). Others can be located on muggle maps easily enough based on information given in Rowling's books or interviews and chats that she has given over the years. In all cases, the information included herein is solely based on the opinions and guesswork of its muggle authors.

II.   J. K. ROWLING'S WORLD

Arbroath, Scotland (www.undiscoveredscotland.co.uk/arbroath)

Peter Rowling and Anne Volant met on a train from King's Cross station in London en route to a military posting in Arbroath, Scotland in 1964. A very old port city, Arbroath is perhaps most well-known for being the site of the Declaration of Arbroath on 6 April 1320. From the Arbroath Abbey (founded by 1174), a group of supporters of Robert the Bruce petitioned Pope John XII to pressure English King Edward II to recognize Robert the Bruce as the legitimate King of Scotland. Arbroath is a trading port and has long had a thriving fishing industry.

Tufnell Park (North London)

On 14 March 1965, Peter Rowling and Anne Volant were married at All Saints Parish Church on Fairmead Road in the Tufnell Park vicinity, near where Stan and Frieda Volant lived. Available biographical information does not indicate whether the Volants lived there until their deaths or moved elsewhere.

Wimbourne Minster: Wimbourne Minster is a village in southern Dorset near the village of West Mors, where Rowling's paternal grandparents, Ernie and Kathleen Rowling, had a grocery store business for many years. West Mors and Wimbourne Minster are both in the vicinity of Bournemouth, a sizeable coastal Dorset town just northwest of the Isle of Wight. Rowling's beloved grandmother, Kathleen Rowling, died in 1974 in Poole, near Bournemouth.

Yate (www.yateonline.co.uk)

Although she has stated in interviews that she was born in the village of Chipping Sodbury, Rowling's birth record records her birth at Yate General Hospital on 31 July 1965. Rowling and her family lived in this village to the east of Bristol until the late 1960s (sometime between her sister Dianne's birth in 1968 and 1970). The name of the village derives from the Saxon "giete" or "gete," which means a gateway into the forest area. At that time, southern Gloucestershire was covered by woodlands and forest areas. It had evolved into a pastoral agricultural area by the middle of the 19th century. The Yate coal mines (at their height from 1830-1890) serviced Bristol's industrial development. Nearby Chipping Sodbury is a more attractive village than current-day Yate, with its attractive 17th century buildings and upscale shopping. Chipping Sodbury ("chipping" means "cheeping" or buying/selling) is an old market town.
[BW_Lexicon]

Winterbourne (www.winterbourne.freeuk.com/ludwell.htm)

The Rowling family moved to this village to the northeast of Bristol sometime in 1970 and lived here until 1974. Rowling first attended school in the Winterbourne primary school. The Potter family were neighbors to the Rowlings in this village in the early 1970s. The village derived its name from Bradley Brook, a brook that used to burn or dry up in the wintertime. After Henry III's "Disafforestation Act" in 1228, the native forests were cleared and agriculture became the main-stay of the village economy (wheat, flax and barley in particular). Stone quarrying and coal mining were also carried out in this vicinity.

Tutshill (www.ukvillages.co.uk)

The Rowling family moved to this small village across the Severn River from Bristol in 1974. Rowling spent the remainder of her childhood at Church Cottage in Tutshill. Tutshill is in Gloucestershire, right at the border between England and Wales (Chepstow, a short mile downhill from Tutshill, is in the Gwent county of Wales). Tutshill is situated right at the edge of the legend-filled Forest of Dean and between the confluence of the Rivers Wye and Severn. In an interview, Rowling affirmed that

Hagrid's accent is "West Country", based on her childhood experiences in this area of England.

The **Forest of Dean** (www.fweb.org.uk/dean) is one of England's last remaining ancient forests, and it was designated as a National Forest in 1938. Bordered on the southeast by the River Severn and on the west by the River Wye (which also forms the border with Wales), this forest is rich with legends that would likely been of interest to young Joanne Rowling. Rowling attended the Wyedean Comprehensive in the nearby village of **Sedbury**.

Exeter

Rowling attended the University of Exeter (www.ex.ac.uk), taking a degree in French and Classics in 1987. Rowling studied abroad in Paris for a year (1985-86).

Clapham (London)

After finishing her studies at the University of Exeter, Rowling took a flat in Clapham with some friends for some unknown period of time.

Manchester, England (www.manchester.com)

Rowling followed her long-term boyfriend from her Exeter days to Manchester in 1990. It was on a train delay from Manchester back to London that Rowling first had the inspiration for Harry Potter and began to plot out the novels.

- o **Didsbury:** a suburb of Manchester. Rowling booked herself a hotel room at the Bournville Hotel in Didsbury after a particularly nasty row with her boyfriend and spent that weekend in Didsbury inventing the sport of Quidditch.

Porto, Portugal

Rowling taught English in Porto, moving there in 1991 after her mother's death (30 December 1990). She met Jorge Arantes, her first husband, in a bar in Porto in March 1992. They were married on 16 October 1992 in Porto. Her daughter Jessica was born in Porto on 27 July 1993. She fled Porto with baby Jessica in November 1993, settling in Edinburgh near her sister Di.

Edinburgh, Scotland

Rowling moved to Edinburgh to be near her sister in late 1993. She taught French and began writing the Harry Potter novels in earnest in Edinburgh. Her first flat in

Edinburgh was in Leith. She was able to move into a nicer neighborhood, Hazelbank Terrace, in 1998, shortly after *Harry Potter and the Philosopher's Stone* was published.

III.   *MUGGLE WORLD GEOGRAPHY*

Albania—It was to the forests of Albania that Voldemort fled after his defeat of October 31, 1980. He lived there for eleven years, biding his time, waiting to return. He was temporarily "rescued" by Quirrell in about 1990. He returned to Albania in 1991, living there until the summer of 1994 when he was again rescued: this time by Wormtail. Bertha Jorkins' second cousin lives there. In the early 1990s, Albania's thickest forests were located in the central and northern mountain ranges, with the southern areas of the country being mostly deforested. The North Albanian Alps includes the most rugged part of the country's landscape, and this area is both heavily forested and sparsely populated.,

Crouch is the name of a small village in Kent.

Dudley—Located 9 miles west of Birmingham in Worcestershire, the "Black Country" is centered around this town. This highly-industrialized area is notorious for pollution and general atmospheric bleakness.

Dursley is a Gloucestershire village located approximately 25 miles north of Bristol. Situated on the edge of the Cotswolds escarpment, above the Vale of Berkeley and the River Severn, it is a picturesque village. Interestingly, a local manor house bears the name of Owlpen Manor.

Fenland: Founder Salazar Slytherin originally came from "fen," and the Fenland is an area of low-lying, very flat land (some of it below sea-level) in eastern England. Although nearly all of it is now drained and is a very fertile agricultural area, historically it was a place of marshes extending as far as the eye could see and well beyond. The counties included in the Fenland are: Cambridgeshire (almost all of it), Huntingdonshire (all of it), parts of west Norfolk, south Lincolnshire and part of north Bedfordshire. Drainage has resulted in shrinking of the soil, to the extent that some rivers, notably much of the Norfolk part of the Great Ouse, flow well above the surrounding land and are contained only by massive earthen embankments. The Isle of Ely, miles from the sea, is so-named because it was an island in the surrounding miles of fens. Incidentally, a fen is an alkaline marsh, distinguishing it from a bog which is always acidic.

Egypt: Bill Weasley worked as curse breaker for Gringotts Wizarding Bank in Egypt, taking a desk job with what presumably must be Gringotts' corporate headquarters in London in mid-1995.

Errol is the name of a village in Scotland, near Perth.

Flitwick (pronounced without the "w") is a village in Bedfordshire. See www.flitwick-village.org.uk for further details.

Glen: Rowena Ravenclaw, one of the four founders of Hogwarts, hailed from "glen" according to the Sorting Hat. Glen is a Scottish term for valley.

Ilfracombe—This resort town on the northern coast of Devon was the scene of an infamous attack on a beach filled with Muggles by a rogue Welsh Green dragon in 1932. A disaster was averted by a vacationing wizarding family.

King's Cross Station, London—Designed as the Great Northern Railway's London terminus by the architect Lewis Cubitt, the structure was built in 1851-2. It was erected on the site of a former smallpox and fever hospital. The train shed is faced with a yellowish brick screen which fronts onto Euston Road and features a central 120 ft high clock tower in Italianate style, with 9 ft diameter clock dials. On either side, there are large arched windows over the fronts of the two big arched train sheds (71 ft high, 800 ft long).

Rowling has confirmed, however, that she was thinking of **Paddington Station** but wrote King's Cross by mistake. Paddington Station opened in 1854. Marylebone Station was used for the Hogwarts Express departure scenes in the Harry Potter films. **Marylebone Station** is London's smallest rail station and opened in 1899.

Moor—A moor is a broad tract of open land, often high but poorly drained, with patches of heath and peat bogs. Of the heather moorland in the United Kingdom, most of it lies in North Yorkshire, Wales, Cumbria and Dartmoor. For further information about moors, see: http://www.moorlandassociation.org/. Godric Gryffindor hailed from "wild moor" according to the Sorting Hat, and could accordingly have been from the Yorkshire region, as well as Wales, Cumbria or Dartmoor.

Romania—Charlie Weasley is studying dragons in Romania. For further information, see: http://www.homestead.com/BlueMoonMarket/Files/Hogwarts/RomDragCen-ter.html

Snape is the name of two separate villages in England. Further details about the village of Snape located in the county of Suffolk can be found at www.snapevillage.org.uk.

Surrey is a county southwest of London. Heaths, commons and woodlands abound in the area and much of the county is devoted to agriculture. The market towns and villages of the area are nestled among the lakes and forests.

Wiltshire is home to the Malfoy family. A large county which is the starting point of the "West Country," Wiltshire stretches from the expansive plains of Salisbury in the south to the picturesque hills and valleys of the area north of Swindon. At this point, Wiltshire is rapidly turning into Oxfordshire and reaching the lovely world of the Cotswolds. The landscape varies as starkly as the towns of Wiltshire. Wiltshire includes Stonehenge and the Avebury Stone Circle, as well as nine white chalk horses carved into hillsides.

IV. *WIZARDING WORLD GEOGRAPHY*

A. HARRY'S WORLD

Azkaban—The Wizarding World's prison, Azkaban, is located on an island in the north of the North Sea. Although it seems implausible to many readers that Sirius swam ashore in the northern reaches of Scotland, journeyed all the way down to Surrey in the far south of England and then made the same journey back north to Hogwarts, this is apparently exactly what happened. When asked if Azkaban was instead in the southern part of the North Sea given Black's detour to see Harry in Surrey, Rowling emphasized again that Azkaban is located in the north of the North Sea (Scholastic chat, February 2000).

Beauxbatons: The location of Beauxbatons is unplottable, though several possible locations have been theorized by fans. Many believe that the school is located in Andorra, an autonomous principality nestled amongst the peaks of the Bas Pyrenees mountain range in southern France and northern Spain. Historically, the Bas Pyrenees have been called "The Magic Mountains." Many other fans have argued that Beauxbatons must be located in the former Bourbon Empire region (Madame Maxime's giant flying horses only drink single-malt whisky).

Burrow, The: The Burrow is situated near the village of Ottery St. Catchpole. Several wizarding families live in the vicinity of Ottery St. Catchpole: the Weasleys, the Lovegoods, the Fawcetts and the Diggorys.

The village of Ottery St. Mary (**http://www.eastdevon.net/ottery/**) is located in Devon, just to the east of Exeter, where Rowling attended university, and is almost certain to be the source of the Burrow's nearest village. The village of Chudleigh (perhaps the model for the Chudley of the Chudley Cannons Quidditch team) is located just to the west of Exeter. Birthplace of poet Samuel Taylor Coleridge (*Rime of the Ancient Mariner*), Ottery St. Mary has a rich history. Each year, the village inhabitants celebrate Pixie Day on the Saturday closest to the summer solstice. Local folklore holds that pixies once controlled the village prior to the establishment of the church and that the pixies, in an effort to retain their power, cast a spell on some monks to prevent their returning to the village with church bells. The monks became disoriented as a result of the spell, heading for the cliffs of the coast and certain doom, when one monk's foot was pierced with a thistle and he cried out "God bless my soul and Saint Mary." The pixies were banished to the outskirts of town to Pixie's Parlor (a magical place located on the east bank of the River Otter).

Noting that the Weasleys, Harry and Hermione took muggle taxis to King's Cross from the Burrow in GoF, some people have suggested that the Burrow cannot be located in Devon at all, as the cost of taxis would have been prohibitive. Others believe that the nexus of Ottery St. Mary and Chudleigh, on either side of Rowling's university life, cannot be ignored and the transport by taxis was simply a logistical goof on Rowling's part.

Diagon Alley: Tapping just the right brick in the wall behind the Leaky Cauldron pub in London ("Three up . . . two across . . . ") will reveal an archway which is a portal into Diagon Alley, a long cobbled street where is to be found a strange and exciting assortment of shops and restaurants.

You can view a more detailed accounting of the shops of Diagon Alley at The Harry Potter Lexicon: **http://www.hp-lexicon.org/w_pl_diagon.html**

Durmstrang: Durmstrang is unplottable and several possible locations have been debated over the years. Noting the similarity between the school's name and the German words *sturm* and *drang* (storm and stress), the German literary movement, some people have argued that Durmstrang must be located in Germany. It could be located in the Alps (Switzerland) since Viktor Krum mentions flying over lakes and mountains. However, no location in Germany or Switzerland is north enough for the extremely cold weather or shortness of days Krum describes. Durmstrang could be located in Norway, though it would need to be located in the far northern reaches of Norway to experience the degree of cold weather and short winter days described by Krum. Another possible locale might be Russia as the weather would be sufficiently cold to justify fur capes as part of the school uniforms. This location might also be the logical choice for students from Krum's native Bulgaria and other Eastern European countries. Further, the area surrounding Murmansk in Northern Russia contains numerous lakes (which conforms to Krum's description). Latvia is yet another strong possibility for Durmstrang's location.

Godric's Hollow: Bowman Wright of Godric's Hollow invented the Golden Snitch for Quidditch games here sometime between 1350-1400. *See* the separate attachment entitled "Godric's Hollow" for an overview of various theories on its location.

Grimmauld Place, No. 12: Unplottable and hidden away behind a fidelius charm, between two shabby London Muggle houses, is 12 Grimmauld Place. It was given by the only surviving heir, Sirius Black, as headquarters for The Order of the Phoenix beginning in the summer of 1995. For further information, see The Harry Potter Lexicon at **http://www.hp-lexicon.org/grimmauld.html**

Leaky Cauldron: The Leaky Cauldron is a small, shabby-looking inn on Charing Cross Road, London, sandwiched between a big book shop and a record store. For further details about the Leaky Cauldron, visit The Harry Potter Lexicon at: **http://www.hp-**

lexicon.org/w_pl_diagon.html#Leaky%20Cauldron. *See also* the HPforGrownups Topical Essay on Geography which includes some "field research" by London residents and tourists (concluding that The Leaky Cauldron must be just south of Oxford Street): http://www.hpfgu.org.uk/faq/

Little Hangleton: Located approximately 200 miles from Little Whinging, Little Hangleton is likely located somewhere in Yorkshire, especially given the "Little" and "Greater" appellations. It could, however, still be 200 miles to the west of Little Whinging or even 200 miles to the northwest (Wales). It cannot, however, be located 200 miles to the south or east of Little Whinging. Little Hangleton is the location of the Riddle House, where Tom Riddle killed his father, Tom Riddle Sr., and his grandparents in the summer of 1944. It is also the location of the graveyard where Voldemort regained a body (June 24, 1995).

Little Whinging, Surrey: A quiet, perfectly normal suburb of London, where you'll find the quiet, perfectly normal residence at Number 4, Privet Drive. Little Whinging is also the location of a zoo that the Dursley family visited on Dudley's eleventh birthday.

Ministry of Magic: The Ministry of Magic has its offices in London, underground and not far from the centre or financial district of central London (also approximately four Tube stops from the Tube stop nearest to 12 Grimmauld Place). For further information about the Ministry of Magic, visit The Harry Potter Lexicon at: **http://www.hp-lexicon.org/w_ministry.html**

St. Mungo's Hospital for Magical Maladies—Located in central London and hidden magically in a manner similar to Diagon Alley.

B. HOGWARTS & ENVIRONS

Hogsmeade—The only totally wizarding village in Britain, Hogsmeade is located near Hogwarts School of Witchcraft and Wizardry.

Hogwarts: Hogwarts School of Witchcraft and Wizardry is located some eight or nine hours by train, to the north of London. Rowling has confirmed that the school is located in Scotland (B&N chat, September 1999). One HPforGrownups member researched latitude, longitude and sunset times on Sept 1st and on June 6th, 1993, the days of major events in Prisoner of Azkaban, and concluded that Hogwarts was likely in the vicinity of Aberdeen specifically. For a detailed reference of various possible locales for Hogwarts, see:

http://www.homestead.com/BlueMoonMarket/Files/Hogwarts/hogwarts1.htm

For a detailed textual description of what canon tells us about Hogwarts castle and its environs, please see The Harry Potter Lexicon at:

http://www.hp-lexicon.org/atlas-h.html

C. QUIDDITCH

Appleby Arrows (Quidditch Team, Britain & Ireland League): based in northern England according to QTTA.

Ballycastle Bats (Quidditch Team, Britain & Ireland League): based in Northern Ireland according to QTTA.

Bigonville Bombers (Quidditch Team, Luxembourg, European League):

Braga Broomfleet (Quidditch Team, Portugal, European League):

Caerphilly Catapults (Quidditch Team, Britain & Ireland League): Welsh Quidditch team

Chudley Cannons (Quidditch Team, Britain & Ireland League):

Falmouth Falcons (Quidditch Team, Britain & Ireland League): must be based near Falmouth, England

Fitchburg Finches (Quidditch Team, Massachusetts, North American League)

Gimbi Giant-Slayers (Quidditch Team, Ethiopia, African League)

Gorodok Gargoyles (Quidditch Team, Lithuania, European League)

Grodzisk Goblins (Quidditch Team, Poland, European League)

Haileybury Hammers (Quidditch Team, Canada, North American League)

Heidelberg Harriers (Quidditch Team, Germany, European League)

Holyhead Harpies (Quidditch Team, Britain & Ireland League): very old Welsh team according to QTTA.

Kenmare Kestrels (Quidditch Team, Britain & Ireland League): Ireland-based according to QTTA.

Kopparberg to Arjeplog, Sweden (annual broom race): according to QTTA (pgs 3-4)

Montrose Magpies (Quidditch Team, Britain & Ireland League)

Moose Jaw Meteorites (Quidditch Team, Canada, North American League)

Moutohara Macaws (Quidditch Team, New Zealand, Australia & New Zealand League)

Patonga Proudsticks (Quidditch Team, Uganda, African League)

Pride of Portree (Quidditch Team, Britain & Ireland League): Isle of Skye, Scotland

Puddlemere United (Quidditch Team, Britain & Ireland League)

Queerditch Marsh: where Quidditch originated (QTTA, page 7)

Quiberon Quafflepunchers (Quidditch Team, France, European League)

Stonewall Stormers (Quidditch Team, Canada, North American League)

Sumbawanga Sunrays (Quidditch Team, Tanzania, African League)

Sweetwater All-Stars (Quidditch Team, Texas, North American League): small town in West Texas

Tarapoto Tree-Skimmers (Quidditch Team, Peru, South American League)

Tchamba Charmers (Quidditch Team, Togo, African League)

Thundelarra Thunderers (Quidditch Team, Australia and New Zealand League)

Toyohashi Tengu (Quidditch Team, Japan, Asian League)

Tutshill Tornados (Quidditch Team, Britain & Ireland League): Tutshill, Gloucestershire, England

Vratsa Vultures (Quidditch Team, Bulgaria, European League)

Wigtown Wanderers (Quidditch Team, Britain & Ireland League): a "borders" team according to QTTA

Wimbourne Wasps (Quidditch Team, Britain & Ireland League)

Woollongong Warriors (Quidditch Team, Australia & New Zealand League)

D. FANTASTIC BEASTS

Antipodean Opaleye: dragon breed native to New Zealand.

Borneo—home to the Acromantula (eight-eyed spider capable of human speech). A colony of Acromantula have been illegally established in Scotland, in the Forbidden Forest near Hogwarts.

China: home to the Chinese Fireball dragon breed and phoenixes.

Cornwall: the place where pixies are most commonly found.

Dorset: together with southern Ireland, Dorset is home to the porlock, a creature that serves as a guardian of horses.

Egypt is also one of the three natural homes for the phoenix and is the home to the sphinx.

Greece: the place of origin for the following beasts: the Chimaera (a monster with a lion's head, goat's body and dragon tail); the griffin (lion's body and eagle's head and front legs); and the manticore (head of a man, body of a lion and scorpion tail)

Hebrides: home to the Hebridean Black dragons

Hungary: home to the Hungarian Horntail breed of dragons

India: one of the three natural homes for phoenixes

Isle of Drear: unplottable island off the northernmost tip of Scotland and home to the quintaped, a carnivorous beast with a low-slung body and five legs with club feet.

Loch Ness, Scotland: home to the world's largest kelpie

Norway: home to the Norwegian Ridgeback dragon breed (Baby Norbert)

Peru: home to the Peruvian Vipertooth dragon breed

Romania: home to the Romanian Longhorn dragon breed (Charlie Weasley is studying dragons in the wild in Romania)

Sweden: home to the Swedish Shortsnout dragon breed

Tibet: home to the yeti

Ukraine: home to the Ukrainian Ironbelly dragon breed

Wales: home to the Common Welsh Green dragon breed

Penny Linsenmayer was a moderator of HPforGrownups, one of the longest running and largest Harry Potter discussion lists on the Internet, for over three years and now assists with the HP Lexicon. She is one of Nimbus—2003's Programming Committee co-chairs. She lives in Houston, Texas with her husband and and two childrenr. She has a B.A. in History and English (summa cum laude) from Texas Tech University and earned her law degree at The University of Texas School of Law. She practiced corporate and securities law for nearly nine years and is now, in addition to being a full-time stay-at-home mother, involved in various writing projects relating to the life and works of Laura Ingalls Wilder. She enjoys reading, genealogy and scrapbooking in her spare time.

Steve Vander Ark is a K-8 library media specialist from Grand Rapids, Michigan. He is also a freelance writer and columnist, as well as being the resident director for Caledonia Community Players. Steve is probably best known in fandom as the creator and editor of The Harry Potter Lexicon, a reference web site devoted to the book series; the Lexicon was awarded the Site of the Month award by J.K. Rowling herself in July, 2004. Steve has been involved with fandoms for many years, beginning with his first Star Trek convention back in 1975. He's served as president of various fan clubs and other fan organizations over the years. Steve used to be just an inch or two shy of six feet tall, but now he isn't sure if he is shrinking or if his 14-year-old daughter with the long blonde hair is really getting that tall.

The Heroic Quest:
Harry Potter and Myth

Jeff Morgan

In order to classify J.K. Rowling's *Harry Potter and the Sorcerer's Stone* as a myth, there must be some agreement on what a myth is. If Rowling's novel consists of certain elements that exist in other works that have been categorized as myth, then her novel must receive due consideration as a modern myth. The repetition of certain elements has been a cornerstone of mythical studies for years. In *The Golden Bough*, Sir James George Frazer points out startling similarities between myths of different times and cultures to assert "the essential similarity of man's chief wants" (824). In the concluding chapter of his great work, he emphasizes "order as the underlying principle of all things" (825). If we look at the heroic quest as a particular type of mythical story, the similarities and the order of the elements within these type of stories suggest one of those chief wants, namely to characterize a hero. Harry Potter is one of these heroes, and his quest in Rowling's first novel has striking similarities between other heroic quests of mythology.

Connecting Harry Potter to other heroes from the mythical past is not a stretch. Rowling's hero seems to be a part of what Carl Gustav Jung would call man's collective unconscious, "a sphere of unconscious mythology whose primordial images are the common heritage of mankind" (664). Rowling characterizes her hero with the same primordial images evident in classic Greek myth, Arthurian legend, or, for a more modern example, J.R.R. Tolkien's *The Hobbit*. She also creates a heroic quest that follows a similar order like that seen in the classics. We may catalog the characteristics and actions of the heroes from these heroic quests and discover Jung's "universal hero myth," which "always refers to a powerful man or god-man who vanquishes evil in the form of dragons, serpents, monsters, demons, and so on, and who liberates his people from destruction and death" (79). If Rowling conjures up similar primordial images and develops a plot structure that follows a similar path as the heroic quests before Harry Potter, then there is no reason to not consider Harry Potter a modern myth.

To some such a comparison may seem astounding, but in "The Structural Study of Myth," Claude Levi-Strauss notes "the astounding similarity between myths collected in widely different regions." He uses "astounding" because "in the course of a myth, anything is likely to happen" (810). He goes on to compare this apparent contradiction to a similar one in language. Similar sounds may appear in different languages. However, though the sounds may be the same, these same sounds may evoke different meanings. Therefore, Levi-Strauss claims that meaning in myth, as in language, depends on the combination of the elements, or the points of similarity we may find. In other words, the plot or story makes the meaning.

The heroic quest lends itself comfortably to an analysis of plot. Though time will not permit a discourse on all the possible variables, an analysis of plot structure in heroic quests from Greek myth to Arthurian legend and extending into more modern myth such Tolkien's *The Hobbit* will reveal a similarity in the combinations of elements which comprise the plots of these various mythologies. Levi-Strauss claims that myth "is static," with "the same mythical elements combined over and over again" (40). By listing the elements, we can map out a certain structure and meaning found in heroic quests, and ultimately discover that J. K. Rowlings *Harry Potter and the Sorcerer's Stone* fits comfortably into the structures and meanings of heroic quests seen from different sources. To be sure, there are logical patterns to myth, and Rowling assumes the role of bricoleur, recycling the heroic quest for a modern myth, the Harry Potter story.

Perhaps the best starting point to begin mapping the elements that comprise a heroic quest would be the hero's birth. In Greek mythology, several of her greatest heroes have rather unusual beginnings. Greek heroes tend to be raised away from their fathers. Hercules and Perseus are sons of Zeus, who, in each case, descends from the heavens and impregnates a mortal. After the immaculate conception, he ascends to Mt. Olympus, leaving the child fatherless. Though mortals step into father roles, early home life is hardly untroubled. Jealous Hera tries to kill Hercules, and Perseus, though originally taken in by a kind fisherman, eventually falls into the fatherly realm of the kind fisherman's cruel brother, who, falls in love with the boy's mother, but despises the boy. Subsequently, the cruel brother devises a plan to kill our young hero. In addition, though no sons of Zeus, Jason and Theseus still have unusual beginnings. They are both raised away from their true fathers. Jason was secretly sent away from his home after his father was overthrown by his nephew, and Theseus was raised by his mother far from his father's kingdom in Athens.

Arthurian legend continues this thread with the unusual beginning of the once and future king. In fact, the boy's conception is remarkably similar to the birth of Hercules. Zeus transformed himself into Alcmena's husband, Amphitryon, and visited her while her true husband, a general, was away fighting. Arthur's true father, King Uther, had Merlin transform him into the Duke of Cornwall, who was away fighting, so that he could have his way with the Duke's wife, Ygraine. Merlin only agreed to the plea with the stipulation that the wizard would get the offspring of the union, which would be Arthur, who was subsequently taken by Merlin and left with Sir Ector to be raised under his care as a squire to Sir Ector's biological son, Kay.

The hero of Tolkien's *The Hobbit*, Bilbo Baggins, continues in this vein of early characterization that portrays mythical heroes with origins in broken families and helps create a hero archetype. Bilbo is isolated from many of the other Bagginses on his father's side, who are primarily jealous of his inheritance of his father's home. His father married a hobbit from the Took family, which was reputed to have fairy connections and was confirmed as having an adventurous streak, undesirable traits that further distanced Bilbo from many other Bagginses. Bilbo's mother and father never enter the narrative, and Bilbo is characterized as having inherited "something a bit queer in his makeup from the Took side" (3). The early exposition of *The Hobbit* characterizes Bilbo as a solitary figure who is a bit unusual compared to the general population of hobbits.

Rowling's characterization of Harry Potter's unusual beginnings resembles that of these previously mentioned characters, allowing him to fit within a Jungian archetype. Harry's parents were wizards killed by an evil wizard named Voldemort. Other wizards protective of Harry leave him under the care of his mother's sister and her family. They are not wizards. They despise wizards. They fear Harry may follow in his parents' footsteps, so they keep him ignorant of his past and raise him with cruel favoritism toward their own son.

From these unusual beginnings, these archetypal heroes come to an age at which they must fulfill a kind of destiny. At his eleventh birthday, Harry Potter receives his invitation to attend Hogwarts, a school of wizardry that the young boy must save from evil. He appears to be the appointed one to do so based on his survival of Voldemort's attack and the mark he bears to signal that miraculous survival. Similarly, Bilbo Baggins seems destined for some kind of greatness. Gandalf, a great wizard, arrives at his door to invite him on an adventure which, no matter how hard he tries, he cannot refuse. Bilbo is to accompany thirteen dwarves on a quest to regain stolen treasure. Bilbo joins this group as the lucky number and the burglar, or, as Gandalf remarks, "[he] will be when the time comes" (19).

Working back to Arthurian legend, Arthur also appears to be destined for greatness. Always a legitimate heir to a throne, Arthur, though, is never aware of such a destiny until he pulls the sword from the stone. Then, he fulfills a prophecy that marks him as the king who would unite all of Britain. This sense of a predetermined world also permeates Greek myth, which follows a like course with its heroes with the likes of Jason, whose return to reclaim his rightful kingdom is foretold by the oracles, or Perseus, whom the Delphic oracles have claimed will kill the king. Even Odysseus, because of the favoring he receives from the goddess Athena, appears destined to return to Ithaca and to rule her. In each case, the hero seems destined to rule a world and/or save a world. Harry must save Hogwarts. Bilbo must save the dwarves from the certain failure of regaining their riches and kingdom without the hobbit's help. Arthur must save Britain and rule her. And, Greek heroes must return to their rightful kingdoms and slay usurpers. In a larger sense, these are the quests of these heroes.

However, in order to fulfill these larger destinies, our heroes often must go on quests that will prove their rightfulness for whatever greatness fate has in store. The heroic quests of Greek mythology particularly emphasize often grueling tests that no man might accomplish alone and, thereby, stress the need for help, which Greek heroes are frequently receiving, as in the case of Odysseus. The help may not always come from gods, for Jason has his crew and Harry his classmates; however, it is almost always supernatural, lending more credence to the notion that the destiny of mythological heroes is predetermined. Perseus and Jason are illustrative of this pattern in the heroic quest. In order to gain the head of Medusa and bring it to Polydectes as a wedding gift, a quest which the king hoped would kill the young man, Perseus receives help from Hermes, Athena, and the Hyperboreans. Jason, in his quest to return to his homeland with the Golden Fleece that would, at least as he was told, restore greatness to that kingdom, receives help from Hera and Medea.

Likewise, more modern myths involving heroic quests grant their heroes some supernatural help, although the help is less ethereal and more down to earth, a natural progression of a realistic world. Arthur has Merlin and his Knights of the Round Table. Bilbo has Gandalf and the dwarves, and Harry has Dumbledore and most of the faculty and staff at Hogwarts.

In fact, most of the heroes on these heroic quests encounter some equally supernatural obstacles along the way. Harry Potter's ultimate obstacle is Voldemort, the evil wizard who killed Harry's parents but couldn't kill Harry. Among other things, Voldemort wants control of Hogwarts. In order to accomplish his goals, he needs the sorcerer's stone, an amazing work of alchemy which proffers eternal life to its beholder. Until he can get his hands on the stone, Voldemort must rely on others for help. In Rowling's first book, this is namely Professor Quirrel. A good example of his efforts to undermine Harry's power, which threatens Voldemort's desires, is during the quidditch match in which Quirrel curses Harry's broom and almost causes Harry to fall to his death.

These obstacles heroes face point to the difficult nature of any quest. Bilbo must face goblins, giant spiders, wargs, and ultimately a dragon before his quest is through. As the diminutive hero encounters these obstacles and successfully gets beyond them, he grows in his leadership skills. To unite Britain, Arthur must first overcome a series of rogue knights and kings who refuse to accept his democratic policies. Still, once successful on that front, another obstacle rears its ugly head. With peace comes an antsy nest of knights who begin behaving in much the same way as the rogue knights of before. This is when Arthur devises the quest for the Holy Grail as, basically, a scheme to keep these warriors busy with something constructive. All the while, Arthur must contend with the obstacle of the Orkney faction and face his most difficult challenge, the affair between Lancelot and Guinevere that presents the greatest threat to Camelot.

The Greek heroes also face numerous obstacles on their individual quests. In his quest to return home to Ithaca, Odysseus must leap over too many hurdles to list. Hercules must perform his famous twelve labors as his penance for the rash murder of his wife and children. Jason encounters a host of troubles on his way to Colchis to gain the Golden Fleece, and he runs into significant problems once there.

To get beyond these obstacles, heroes have help from gods and other supernatural characters, but they also, for the most part, have special weapons that aid them. Odysseus has his great bow which only he can bend and arm. Theseus has his father's sword. Perseus has an arsenal. He has a special sword, a shield that can work as a mirror to avoid the stare from Medusa that can turn one to stone, winged sandals, a magic wallet, and cap of invisibility. Arthur has Excalibur. Bilbo has Sting and the ring. Harry has, most notably, his wand and the invisibility cloak.

By identifying the elements which comprise particular myths, we can also identify particular meanings. Based on the kinds of similar elements found in heroic quests through the centuries, and based on the larger quest that is common to most of these heroic quests, it becomes evident that, in the Jungian sense of a collective consciousness, there is an archetype for a leader. Since J. K. Rowling has characterized Harry Potter with many of the same formal elements as seen in other heroic quests, her great character may enter the pantheon of other mythic heroes who enter into the human perception of what it means to be a leader. The timing of the Harry Potter phenomenon is curious. Jung writes that art "is constantly at work educating the spirit of the age, conjuring up the forms in which the age is most lacking" (666). In that light, the Harry Potter myth works as a reminder of what kind of leaders we need now. These mythic leaders tend to come from unusual beginnings, to be enshrouded in destiny, to be receptive to whatever help they can get, to be tested and matured as leaders through a series of obstacles, and to be on quests that involve the tenuous future of the societies in which they live. Through these stories we come to a better understanding of what it takes to lead. Levi-Strauss writes that myth "gives man . . . the illusion that he can understand the universe and that he *does* understand the universe" (17). We need Harry Potter.

In the end, there is one last common trait these heroes share, the return home. It is usually far from a ticker-tape parade. After twenty years of struggle that includes ten years of fighting in the Trojan War and ten years trying to return to Ithaca, Odysseus finally makes it home, only to discover that his home has been overrun by suitors to his wife and crown. When Jason returns home with the Golden Fleece, he expects to be king. He is never crowned. He finds his parents dead, and he becomes involved in a scandal that draws the ire of Medea, who then kills his wife and sons. Perseus has two homecomings, each grim. He first returns to the island ruled by Polydectes only to find his mother hiding in fear of the cruel king. So, he uses the head of Medusa to turn Polydectes to stone. Then, his mother decides to return to the home of her son's birth in an attempt to reconcile with her father, but he has disappeared. He finally did turn up at a discus tournament, during which an errant throw by Perseus decapitates him.

The grim returns do not end with the Greeks. Arthur returns from an assault on Lancelot's castle in France only to find that his own son, Mordred, has taken over and made advances on the queen. In a final battle, father and son slay one another as prophesized. Arthur is then taken across the waters to Avalon where he would remain until Britain needs him again. Bilbo's story ends similarly, with him on a ship to the Undying Lands, but that is in *The Lord of the Rings*. In *The Hobbit*, Bilbo returns to his home after helping the dwarves regain their treasure only to find that his cousins are auctioning off his possessions and securing his home.

As for Harry Potter, after saving Hogwarts from the evil designs of Voldemort, Harry must return for the summer to the Dursleys. However, it is only a temporary discomfort. He will return to Hogwarts for his second year of schooling there. Actually, Harry Potter's quest is not nearly over yet. In essence, his characterization is no further along than Arthur's in the first book of T. H. White's *The Once and Future King*. At Hogwarts, Harry has demonstrated great leadership skills in various quests, but his education will continue until he graduates; then, he may very well join the ranks of mythic heroes who not only save their worlds, but rule them as well.

Works Cited

Frazer, Sir James George. *The Golden Bough*. New York: MacMillan, 1951.

Jung, Carl Gustav. *Man and his Symbols*. New York: Doubleday, 1964

_____. "On the Relation of Analytical Psychology to Poetry." *The Critical Tradition*. Ed. David H. Richter. New York: Bedford, 1989. 656-666.

Levi-Strauss, Claude. *Myth and Meaning: Cracking the Code of Culture*. New York: Schocken, 1979.

_____. "The Structural Study of Myth." *The Critical Tradition*. Ed. David H. Richter. New York, 1989. 869-877.

Tolkien, J.R.R. *The Hobbit*. New York: Ballantine, 1997.

Jeff Morgan lives in Boynton Beach, Florida with his wife, Dana, and their son, Colin. He chairs the English Department at Lynn University in Boca Raton, where he has taught the last four of his 22 years in teaching. Having earned his B.A. from Ohio University, his M.A. from Pan American University, and his Ph.D. from Case Western Reserve University, Dr. Morgan was able to transform the culmination of his studies, his dissertation on Sarah Orne Jewett, into a book, Sarah Orne Jewett's Feminine Pastoral Vision: The Country of the Pointed Firs, *recently published by the Edwin Mellen Press. His poetry can be found in* The Pen, Love's Chance, *and* Hadrosaur Tales, *and his recent return to poetry has garnered him an editorial position with* Florida English, *a publication of the FCEA. The obsessive appetite his son has demonstrated for all things concerning mythology, legend, and folklore has led to his creation of a mythology course and his participation in the conference.*

Harry Potter and the Western Occult Tradition

Kiri Aradia Morgan, M. A.

I. The Story

It is important to remember that we are trying to tell a story. As a writer of both fanfiction and original fiction, I try never to forget that. Stories are true and facts are true, but stories and facts are not true in the very same way. The truth of facts is verifiable, objective, scientific; the truth of stories is in the heart. The Western Occult Tradition, like the Harry Potter novels, contains a certain amount of objective historical truth, a great deal of myth, and a lot of invention. Like all true stories, its value is ultimately subjective. It is a story about God, a story about Good, a story about Evil, a story about Love, a story about War, a story about Class, and ultimately, a story about human beings: the ways they differ, and the ways they are alike. The story of Harry Potter is about the same things, so it shouldn't surprise anyone if the cosmology should seem to overlap a bit.

Joanne Rowling says that she hasn't studied the Western Occult Tradition, but as science and what we now think of as magick were one and the same in the Western world before the Enlightenment, perhaps what has crept into her novels is merely that part of the Western Occult Tradition which has become a part of the mythology of our postmodern world. I do not know, nor do I claim to know, what Rowling has read or why she read it. Nonetheless, as an occultist on the cusp of the twenty-first century, I see my own world mirrored in Rowling's world, and it is a marvelous fun-house mirror. I want to tell you what I see there, in the hopes that my experience of this wonderfully fun and often exasperating creation can illuminate and broaden your own and deepen your enjoyment of it.

II. Hogwarts and the Wizarding World

The Western Occult Tradition today and the wizarding world of the Potterverse have both inherited the class conflicts of the middle ages that led to the division between high and low magick. High magick is the magick of the ceremonial magician who uses a wand and many other tools devoted solely to magick to do spells, often in sophisticated language, perhaps even in an ancient or foreign tongue, in the company of other well-trained, initiated magicians. Low magick is the magick of the country folk, done in everyday language, with tools that may have many purposes, handed down in the home and family and clan. Some people like to say that high magick is that which is done to unite the caster with God and the universe, and low magick is done with the intent of making everyday life work better, but historically, spells of both kinds are found in both categories. In the Potterverse, high magick would be that which is taught at schools like Hogwarts, Beauxbatons and Durmstrang, and low magick would be that which is learned by the hags, who aren't permitted to own wands, and the very ordinary folk we see in the streets of wizarding London, people as far below impoverished gentry like the Weasleys as the Weasleys are below the Malfoys. Hogwarts may be the only wizarding school in all of Great Britain, yet we see a fair number of people in wizarding Britain whom it is difficult to imagine ever having attended Hogwarts.

Ceremonial magicians and low magicians (hedge-witches, hags, cunning men and the like) have always had trouble getting along. In the Middle Ages, ceremonial magicians came from the wealthiest families, attended universities, took degrees in the natural sciences, and were loudly and proudly Christian. Nicolas Flamel and his wife Perrenelle, who were real people, are perfect examples of this type of magician. While it isn't known how well Flamel's Philosopher's Stone actually worked—he did live to be nearly one hundred years old, which was certainly no mean feat in the fifteenth century—the churches he endowed with his gold are all over Paris today. Very few of these people were ever in any danger from the Church, although some of them, like Giordano Bruno and Galileo Galilei, paid the price for wandering too far from accepted doctrine. Most of the people who were executed for witchcraft in the Middle Ages were common folk, so it's not too terribly surprising that Binns tells us the persecutions had a fairly low impact on the survival of the wizarding world, which seems to be very concerned with matters of bloodline and class. One doesn't see a lot of evidence that people who practice folk traditions are represented in the Hogwarts student body; one sees the pureblood ceremonialists, such as the Malfoys and the Blacks, the impoverished gentry who intermarried freely with Muggle-borns and Muggles, such as the Weasleys, and a lot of Muggle-born and half-blood students.

Hogwarts seems to have two functions: to educate the children of the middle and upper classes of the wizarding world and prepare them for careers in its governance, given the importance of Ministry testing and career counseling in the lives of its students, and also to ensure that Muggle-born wizards and witches (at least the most talented ones) are properly educated and brought into wizarding society. There seems to be considerable distrust in the wizarding world between humans and nonhuman users of magick and there is quite a bit of political tension with regard to Hogwarts' role in properly indoctrinating future wizards and witches, as witnessed by the continual conflict between Albus Dumbledore, Lucius Malfoy and the pureblood elite, and the Ministry, represented by such persons as Dolores Umbridge and Percy Weasley.

Hogwarts' House system falls out very neatly when laid out in correspondence to the Four Elements of the Western Occult Tradition and their correspondences. Gryffindor, whose weapon is a Sword and whose colors are red and gold, whose virtue is bravery, corresponds neatly to the element of Fire. Ravenclaw, whose virtue is intelligence, corresponds to the element of Air, and Hufflepuff, whose virtues are loyalty and hard work, corresponds to the element of Earth. Slytherin, whose virtue is willfulness, corresponds to the element of Water. It is to be noted that all four elements are necessary for the health and safety of the world and to complete the Great Work. Similarly, the Sorting Hat continually reminds us that House Slytherin is important and that there is a reason it hasn't been abolished, even though Rowling hasn't seen fit to show us any of Slytherin's virtue. The magickal weapon of Water is the cup or the cauldron—the Potions Master's cauldron, and the Grail of immortality, about which more will be said later.

The subjects Hogwarts students study are not the Trivium and Quadrivium of the medieval university, while we do see them studying astronomy, we don't see any mention of grammar, rhetoric, logic, or music. However, many of these disciplines do correspond to modern occult disciplines. Arithmancy, for instance, corresponds to gematria and numerology, methods of discovering a thing's essential meaning through unraveling its numbers. The use of herbs, or Herbology, and the making of potions, are important to both ceremonial magicians and low magicians, and form the basis of the advanced art of alchemy.

Divination is taught, but not shown to be very effective. Rowling seems to have a bias against the notion that the future can be accurately predicted (a bias shared by much of the modern occult community), and also seems to not much care for mysticism, as only the Death Eaters and Albus Dumbledore are ever allowed to be mystical.

Also, the students are taught about nonhuman magickal creatures and their role in the magickal world. Some of these are well-known to us from mythology and folklore, such as unicorns and pixies; others, such as Blast-Ended Skrewts, Crups, and Kneazles, are Rowling's inventions. Students are allowed to bring 'familiars' to Hogwarts, although these cats, birds, and toads seem to function mainly as pets and helpers rather than actually assisting in the practice of magick, as familiars have traditionally been believed to do.

Finally, there are the restricted magickal teachings, such as the Animagus transformation, clearly very similar to the acts of Norse and Celtic shamans who had spells which enabled them to take the forms of animals, usually bears or ravens, and Legilimency and Occlumency, which seem to be very similar to Victorian Theosophical notions of mesmerism and New Age teachings about thought transference.

III. Voldemort and the Death Eaters

Surprisingly, given that this is a fantasy series, the only mysticism ever hinted at is that of the Death Eaters, and the hints are extremely oblique. Rowling doesn't tell us very much about the Death Eaters' beliefs, but we can infer a few things from the symbolism. The name "Voldemort" means "flight from death", and the Dark Mark is a symbol that dates at least to the seventeenth century, where we see snakes crawling through skulls in the German text *Chymische Hochzeit Christiani Rosencreutz*, translated into English as "The Chemical Wedding of Christian Rosenkreutz". In this text the snake is a symbol of Gnosis, or enlightenment, and the victory of the enlightened soul over Death. The belief that Death can be conquered by magickal knowledge goes back to the ancient world, to the first centuries of the Common Era, and has its origins in Gnosticism, a belief system that strongly influenced early Christianity, though it was eventually denounced as a heresy. The Cathari, the Knights Templar, and other sects persecuted by the Church during the Middle Ages all had Gnostic beliefs and practices in common.

Gnosticism was not just one, but many, religious traditions, and all of them were somewhat obsessed with purity and purification: not purity of blood, but spiritual purity. It was believed that the material world was hopelessly corrupt and that it could only be redeemed by the gnosis, or arcane knowledge, necessary to remake it in a pure form, without Death. Most Gnostic religious groups, Christian or pagan, were peaceful and ascetic. However, some were not, engaging in every kind of shocking behavior there was. Some of them, for instance, engaged in sex magick and blood ritual—the use of sexuality as a method of raising power, and also the use of sexuality to overturn conventional notions of morality and human relationships. Blood and violence could also be used for this purpose, as the world was already hopelessly corrupt and unjust.

This might sound familiar to readers of the Harry Potter series, if they think about it a little. The sex is absent, but the violence is not, and it seems quite obvious that Voldemort wishes to take over the world and remake it, with himself and his chosen ones as its rulers.

IV. Mysticism

Rowling, as a writer, doesn't seem to be very comfortable with mysticism. Like modern occultists who preface their ritual writings with statements that they don't believe in actual deities, merely in 'thought forms' or 'energies' or 'archetypes', and astrologers who are chary of prediction, she doesn't mention religion at all. There are no churches in Hogsmeade. It seems likely that a large proportion of the wizarding world would be nominally Christian (albeit somewhat Gnostic and heretical) given the historical bent of ceremonial magicians such as Flamel, John Dee, and Giordano Bruno, and also given the large number of Muggle-borns who are presumably mostly from families of orthodox mainstream religions, but we never, ever hear about it.

Certainly the wizarding world is not neo-Pagan, no matter what the majority of fanfiction writers would like to believe—if only because neo-Paganism is a collection of largely invented religious traditions that owe their existence to Theosophy, a Victorian melange of spiritist Christianity and Hindu teaching; the Golden Dawn, a ceremonial magickal order that turned away from Christianity and incorporated classical pagan imagery; Thelema, a religion based in the writings of Gnostic Aleister Crowley, and Gerald Gardner's Wicca, which, despite all of the claims that it is an ancient religion, is actually a mixture of ceremonial magick, Thelema, and folk or low magick teachings that Gardner had learned from a number of sources.

Rowling's discomfort with and distaste for divination is made fairly clear in the character of Sybill Trelawney, and the Death Eaters, who are the villains, use more mystical symbolism than anyone else does. The only other character who speaks in mystical terms is Albus Dumbledore, whose bizarre behavior is sometimes reminiscent of Taoist sages and Zen teachers, who offers up his possessions to be destroyed by an angry Harry in the conclusion of *Order of the Phoenix*, and who insists that Voldemort's failure to understand that "there are worse things than Death" will be his downfall.

The Department of Mysteries hints at some sort of scientific approach to mysticism, and also to the Ministry's inherent hostility to mysticism, as all Mysteries must be neatly classified, locked up, and kept away from the general public, who might actually do something with them. One does occasionally wonder what the message of this series with regard to censorship will eventually be; we are shown time and again that adults lock up necessary books, teachers withhold needed information (and are then surprised when students return the favor), and the Ministry attempts to control access to wands, access to knowledge, and access to foreknowledge. One also wonders, since somebody does seem to know something about what happens after death, why the Death Eaters have not been told, as it would seem that this would put an end to the rationale for the things that they do.

V. Conclusions?

It's hard to make conclusions about a series that hasn't been concluded. This paper has been completely rewritten in the past three weeks. Rowling gets further and further away from the historical occult and uses more and more of her own inventions with every book, which isn't a bad thing at all, as the story she is trying to tell is her own. A lot of my impressions of the Potterverse have been reinforced, much to the surprise of more Gryffindor-oriented fans of my acquaintance, and yet I am, if possible, even more confused than I was before about the message of the series and the relationship of its magick to historical, real-world magick.

But let us not forget that we are all telling stories, and that the very best stories are true—but not, necessarily, factual.

Kiri Aradia Morgan, also known as Azalais Malfoy, is an associate member of the occult fraternity OTO (Ordo Templi Orientis) and has an M.A. in Medieval History, specializing in mysticism and the history of science. She is also the author of the fan fiction series House of Ill Faith *and a major contributor to the Lightningwar Potterverse historical collaborative fiction RPG on LiveJournal.*

Technology Meets Magic

D.A. Patterson

A rthur Weasley loves Muggles' technology, although he does not understand it *(CoS* 29). He collects the large, British ecklectrical plugs *(GoF* 45), and he clearly does not understand how the fellytone works, despite Harry's giving him lessons, *(CoS* 37, *OotP* 766) any more than his son Ron does *(CoS* 250—1; *PoA* 9).

Most wizards who venture into the Muggle world find some of the technology baffling: 'Hagrid kept pointing out perfectly ordinary things, like parking meters and saying loudly, "See that, Harry? Things these Muggles dream up, eh?"'*(PS* 52). Nevertheless, witches and wizards are great users of technology, from Dumbledore's Put-Outer *(PS* 12, *OotP* 57), to the Hogwarts train. Rowling's magical world is defined in terms of technological advancement, epitomized by the continually improving models of Quidditch brooms, rather than by the ritual worship of some great power, which makes Rowling's magic quite different in kind from the magic of the past.

Much of the technology within the magical world is either medieval, such as writing with quills on parchment, or 19th—century, such as using megaphones (c. 1878) and trains (commercial passenger trains 1838). Except for the added bewitchment of the object, the wizard world uses what advocates of third-world sustainable development call low to middle technologies. For instance, Hagrid knits *(PS* 52). Mrs. Weasley knits *(PS* 147). Hermione can only knit well with bewitched needles, but she does try without *(OotP* 230). Hagrid has a crossbow *(PS* 104, and Ch. 15, *passim* Other Potter books *passim*), although clearly, had he not left school in his third year at Hogwarts, he might have been able to use spells to tie people up with cords *(PS* 209), make them rigid—as even first-year Hermione is able to do *(PS* 198)—or he might, occasionally be able to perform one of the unforgivable curses, which seem to be acceptable against spiders *(GoF* Ch. 14). Harry is able to perform the Cruciatus curse by year 5 against Bellatrix Lestrange, whether or not it is illegal against a Death Eater *(OotP* 715). Considering that he has a soft heart and thus Bellatrix can overcome it, even a Muggle crossbow would probably have been more effective.

Clockworks of an elaborate kind, supported no doubt by a magical lubricant, form the beginnings of the middle technologies. Upon first entering Dumbledore's office, Harry is struck by '[a] number of curious silver instruments [which] stood on spindle-legged tables, whirring and emitting little puffs of smoke'; we do not yet know what they do, although we watch Dumbledore use one of them in *The Order of the Phoenix*! (OotP 415)—but they sound very much like bewitched eighteenth-century clockworks from this description *(CoS* 154). Similarly, we know that Diagon Alley has at least one shop selling 'telescopes and strange silver instruments' *(PS* 56). Possibly the middle technologies include the odd clock that the Weasleys have in the Burrow and the wizard radio *(CoS* 31), and Dumbledore's watch with 12 hands but no numbers *(PS* 15, *OotP* 722). Certainly trains, self-directed Gringotts carts, Ford Anglias and other flying cars *(OotP* 446-7) would be the upper end of middle technologies. One middle technology that *sounds* very high tech is the Omnioculars used at the Quidditch World Cup to provide the special sports effects *we* see on the ecklectrically run television, yet they are merely binoculars with extra knobs on *(GoF* 86, 90, 96).

What still remains interesting in this area of research is the dark-side's level of magical technology vs. the white (Albus) side of technology. So far, the most advanced dark technomagical devices we have seen are the middle-to-low level devices in the House of Black's parlour cupboard *(OotP* 107-9). These include a biting silver snuffbox, containing Wartcap powder, an 'unpleasant-looking silver instrument, something like a many-legged pair of tweezers, which scuttled up Harry's arm like a spider when he picked it up, and attempted to puncture his skin,' and a 'music box that emitted a faintly sinister, tinkly tune when wound, and they all found themselves becoming curiously weak and sleepy, until Ginny had the sense to slam the lid shut.' These items seem very comparable to Albus Dumbledore's objects on spindle-legged tables, kept out in the open, when Blacks' objects are closed up in a cupboard. So far, at least, we have seen no high-tech evil, even as advanced as omnioculars.

Although wizard technology sounds a bit behind the times, it moves on. In 997, for instance, or thereabouts, the four founders of Hogwarts had employed the technology of a hat to hold their abilities in choosing children to be placed in the appropriate houses, allowing the character of the houses to continue in perpetuity (fully explained in *GoF* 156—7). The hat is a technology, as well as a fashion, in that this sorting hat has a brim—a mechanism to keep off sun and rain. While the Cretans seemed to have had some kind of brimmed hats about 1500 BCE, and some kind of flat anti-sun basket was worn on the head about the same time that Ollivander's Wands was established *(PS* 63), most Greeks, Romans and Byzantines seemed to have forgotten the brimmed hat, and it was reinvented or remembered in the later Middle Ages.

Is this hat any technological advancement? Well, as the earliest witch recorded is the Witch of Endor, 1 Samuel, Chapter 28, the approximate date of which is possibly somewhere after 1055 BCE (Hull)[2] the chances are she did not have a brimmed hat, unless she had a Cretan cousin.

Only in the 16th century did the hat begin to be worn indoors, and the combination of the very tall crown with the wide brim, seems to have been mainly 17th century. Either the use of a 17th—century style hat in the 10 th century is anachronistic, or the

---

[2]   Modern theologians, notably in the *New Catholic Encyclopaedia* (2003), will not give any dates for the Witch of Endor, and sites I found on the Internet varied all over the BCE timeline, so I resorted to the 1890 chart created by Edward Hull where a person can find a date all the way back to Adam. Hull was no wish-washy modern scholar unable to make up his mind!

founders of Hogwarts had better luck than Prof. Trelawney in predicting the future. (Laver 23—24, 60, 83, 94)

The Crossbow was used for hunting as early as the 4th century A.D., and in war before the year 1000 (Tarassuk 145). So Hagrid's use of this instrument at Hogwarts coincides nicely with the founding of Hogwarts, but is well after the beginnings of wizardry, and thus shows the adaptation of a new technology for the wizarding world. So far, however, we have no indication that this is a magical technology like the candle that seems to be able to sputter in the sockets of Moaning Myrtle's toilet for a very long time (*CoS* 118), or the floating candles in the Great Hall. Similarly, books are an indication that wizard technology moves on. At the time of the Witch of Endor, the scroll, such as the Dead Sea Scrolls, would have been the technology for reading and writing, either in papyrus form in the warm places near Egypt, or in parchment, following the development by the Greeks in Pergamon of a surface for cooler climates. The codex, the book as we now think of it, was a random-access method of organising text rather than the sequential organisation of the scroll. The codex is an invention of the late classical period, somewhere, again, about the period of the founding of Ollivander's wands. But, of course, the wizarding world has added magical features, as described eloquently by Ron when he warns Harry about picking up the very deceitful and magical Riddle diary.

> *'Dangerous?'* said Harry, laughing. 'Come off it, how could it be dangerous?'

> 'You'd be surprised,' said Ron, who was looking apprehensively at the book. 'Some of the books the Ministry confiscated—Dad's told me—there was one that burned your eyes out. And everyone who read *Sonnets of a Sorcerer* spoke in limericks for the rest of their lives. And some old witch in Bath had a book that you could *never stop reading*! You just had to wander around with your nose in it, trying to do everything one-handed.' (CoS, 172)

The book as we know it is a technology that Socrates eschewed in *Pheadrus* because one could not talk to it to ask it questions (Plato). We, on the contrary, eschew Riddle's diary because we *can* talk to it and ask it questions. Times do move on. Another fascinating, related technology is the Marauder's Map worthy of a paper entirely to itself (*PoA* 143).

The Magical folk seem to have no particular aversion to borrowing Muggle technology and making it magical when they find it appropriate, such as the train, porcelain tea pots, binoculars, and flying cars.[3] (Unless, of course, Muggles are borrowing Wizard

---

[3]   The Ford Anglia is a difficult bit of technology that raises the question of what forms technology. Mostly it appears to be a charmed, mechanical device. But the Ford Anglia is more like a transfigured dog: where does a charm end, and a transfiguration begin? The Wizard Chess pieces (*PS* 146–7, 204–6) as compared with the flying keys (202–3) show a similar difficulty.

technology, but we have no evidence so far that this is the case.) Only some kinds of technology seem absurd to the Magical World, such as telephones and parking meters, and these are absurd only because the Magical world already has the picture phone in the fireplace, and travel without cars, using portkeys or Apparating. Sometimes the use of technology or fashion is part of the disguise of the magical world so that Muggles do not find out about it. Such disguise includes the fashion or technology of trainers and jeans. The Hogwarts train may have started as this kind of disguise, but then the train may have grown out of date without the wizarding world noticing, probably because witches and wizards outlive most Muggles by a long chalk. Dumbledore, we know, is very old, although we do not know his precise age from the books.[4] His friend Nicholas Flamel who has attained the age of the beast, 666 (although this number is carefully avoided by one and all), seems not to have drawn too much attention; he seems merely somewhat older than others, not horrifying as the Wandering Jew was described, for instance, in Maturin's *Melmoth the Wanderer*, who must keep moving so that no one will notice how old he has grown. People living to great ages would help stretch the life of old technologies.

Purely wizard technology seems mainly, but not exclusively, connected with Quidditch, because Muggles do not play it. For instance, the snitch is a replacement of the bird who could not be so easily controlled (Whisp, 10-5). Broom technology has moved on from the Muggle broom, but does not seem to be *originally* a wizard technology. The broom must have begun as a piece of technology used to fly because it would seem normal in the house of an old woman who would ordinarily not have any other means of transport than her own two feet. Although broomstick games seem to have begun in 962, there is no indication in *Quidditch Through the Ages* that broom designs were progressing from that time. But then brooms began to improve, probably with the advent of curling, a Scottish sport invented not far from Hogwarts in the 16th century ("History"). Quidditch players, however, seem to have adopted brooms from the Muggle world until the 19th century, when advancements began of a purely wizard nature. These mainly involving hidden mechanisms for flight or comfort, such as the Cushioning Charm by Elliott Smethwyck in 1820 (Whisp 47). Other purely wizarding technology unconnected with Quidditch include the Sneakoscope, the Secrecy Sensor, and the Foe-Glass. Although doubtless Muggle spies and special forces organisations would like such devices, wizards seem to have developed this technology exclusively.

What is the purpose of wizard technology beyond the obvious social satire on our own obsession? We have several reasons provided in the books in a direct way. One is that certain kinds of magic are not permitted to the young because they are inexperienced or because the magic is dangerous. Percy has to finish school before he can get a license to apparate, although Fred and George manage to pass their tests before they leave school, possibly because they are especially handy with charms. Presumably to create

---

[4]   A BBC Potter Quizz gives his birthdate as 1840, where this date comes from, I certainly do not know <http://news.bbc.co.uk/cbbcnews/hi/quiz/newsid_2380000/2380653.stm> (5 April 2003).

some barrier around Hogwarts to keep out dark magic, apparating is forbidden into Hogwarts. Some wizards never attain the skill levels to do apparating—they splinch or fear splinching—as Arthur Weasley points out *(GoF* 63—64). Apparating over long distances is untrustworthy, and so for long distances (Whisp 48), wizards use brooms, as did Charlie Weasley's friends when they collected Norbert the Norwegian Ridgeback from the Astronomy Tower *(PS* 176). More practically, we see people who have not developed their magical abilities or who are ill, like Lupin, taking portkeys *(GoF, OotP* 722) into and out of Hogwarts, or using the Knight Bus or Hogwarts train. And presumably the squib Filch would never be able to do any of the magical things expected of a wizard if technology were not available. Technology supports witches and wizards who are less skilled for various reasons, and everyone seems to start out with little or no skill.[5]

Part of what we all find comforting, charming, and endearing about these stories is that the mighty witches and wizards start off as school children, nearly as helpless as the Muggle readers, unable to change matchsticks into needles. These tyro magical folk must struggle with books. Some children discover that they are squibs or nearly squibs, but some gradually grow into truly powerful wizards. It would appear that some particularly talented witches or wizards can bewitch objects in ways to convey power to those with little or no power, and hence the use of magical technology. It appears that there is a science of experimental magic connected with this development. The Committee on Experimental Charms is run by Gilbert Wimple who still has the horns on his head to show how advanced he is in allowing himself to be used as a guinea pig (First mentioned in *CoS* 34; *GoF* 79). We know little of what this committee does, and its name never appears in the lift at the Ministry of Magic. Wimple may be the person who certifies new Quidditch brooms or omnioculars,[6] or they may be patented by the Ludicrous Patents Office, which seems to be within the Department of Magical Games and Sports *(OotP* 119).

A difficult question is whether using these magical, technological objects is, in fact, doing magic at all. In the book *The Chamber of Secrets*, Harry is disturbed that he will be unable to practice Quidditch on his broomstick during the summer because Uncle Dursley has locked his Nimbus 2000 in the cupboard under the stairs *(CoS* 8—9), whilst he knows equally well that he is forbidden to do magic himself because of the law against underage magic, which catches up with him, of course, when Dobby levitates the Dursley pudding (20-21). Yet, flying the Ford Anglia is not doing under-age magic when the Weasley boys use it to pick up Harry.

---

[5] Peter Appelbaum sees this use of technology as part of the gundam child's method of stretching powers, and he is doubtless correct, but as a magical technology, it has a multiplying technique of the power of the technology, and a change in the meaning of magic that I don't see Appelbaum as addressing directly (especially 28, 31, 40, 43, 45, 47).

[6] We know that the Quidditch-broom magic is extremely powerful because when Quirrell interferes with Harry's Nimbus 2000 at the Gryffindor—Slytherin match, Hagrid says, 'Can't nothing interfere with a broomstick except powerful Dark magic—no kid could do that to a Nimbus Two Thousand' *(PS* 140).

> "Oh, this [flying the car] doesn't count," said Ron. "We're only borrowing this, it's Dad's, *we* didn't enchant it" *(CoS* 24).

Some confusion exists over the exact infraction that Harry and Ron committed in missing the Hogwarts train and flying the car—was the problem underage magic, misuse of a Muggle artifact, or simply being seen?

Constant reference is made to the advantage that children from wizard families have in knowing some magic or about magical things already. But are these children doing magic, or using the technology invested in magical objects? The Weasleys fly their brooms in a field near the Burrow without repercussions *(CoS* 39). Much is made in the *Philosopher's Stone* of Malfoy and Finnegan flying brooms as children. By the time we meet wizard babies in campgrounds outside the Quidditch World Cup, we have magic in the hands of all kinds of children, seemingly with no implied violations: possibly the baby poking a slug with a wand, turning it into something the size of a salami was too young to be blamed for doing magic *(GoF* 75), but a small girl has a toy broom she can use to skim a foot or so off the ground—surely this is sanctioned activity, if a flying broom is manufactured in a child's size *(GoF* 75). So are the underage attendees of the World Cup who have bought miniature Quidditch stars to march around in their hands, and luminous rosettes that squealed the players' names doing magic, or just possessing an object that does the magic without their participation? It would appear that the magic is in the object.

Consider the whole point of Arthur Weasley's Misuse of Muggle Artefacts Office. Ron explains its workings to Harry using a specific example:

> 'It's all to do with bewitching things that are Muggle-made, you know, in case they end up back in a Muggle shop or house. Like, last year, some old witch died and her tea set was sold to an antiques shop. This Muggle woman bought it, took it home and tried to serve her friends tea in it. It was a nightmare—Dad was working overtime for weeks[. . . .]The teapot went beserk [sic] and squirted boiling tea all over the place and one man ended up in hospital with the sugar tongs clamped to his nose. Dad was going frantic, it's only him and an old warlock called Perkins in the office, and they had to do Memory Charms and all sorts to cover it up . . . .' *(CoS* 28-29)

The old woman of this story is just a Muggle, and so the magic was in the tea service, not in anything she did or said.[7] This is an important point in that it alters the foundation of magic from a metaphysical point of view. We can see this clearly by a very brief look at well documented witchcraft from both witch trials and from literary sources.

---

[7] The Maurauder's map can also be used by anyone if it is not wiped clean.
'"Right" said George briskly, "don't forget to wipe it after you've used it—"
"—or anyone can read it," Fred said warningly.' *(PoA,* 144).

As we know from many instances in the Potter books, one is born a witch or wizard, usually by inheritance, but occasionally by genetic aberration. But at the time of the great witch trials of the 16th and 17th centuries, the courts obtained confessions, through torture, that told us that becoming a witch was just as the judges believed before hearing any evidence: witches and wizards were not born, but created by a compact, usually signed in blood, with the devil (Calef 34, 65; Boulton [i]; W.P. 13; *Compleat Wizard* 177 [*sic*=129]; Davis 6; *History* 21; *True* 10). This Faustian compact is was not a view held during the early history of witchcraft, but it was the view that eventually persisted. The fact that there were families of witches was simply the devil's luck, not a genetic connection.

In addition, as Sharpe eloquently points out, the terms 'witchcraft' and 'necromancy' had class associations: the lower classes made a pact with the devil and sold their souls when they were taught what to do by the devil himself. The upper classes practiced necromancy and magic, and they could acquire these skills through reading books (14). Apparently Faust may have sold his soul, but John Dee (a real person) could practice white magic by not selling his soul—merely by reading books.

Once the compact was made, the magic was achieved through invoking an evil spirit through ritual, worship, and incantations. It appeared that people believed that acquiring the ability to do witchcraft came immediately, full-blown, with the signing of the bloody contract. One added spells to one's repertoire, but not increasing skill.

Taking as a very detailed example of one of Harry's skills from what purports to be a genuine, magical, ceremonial source, *The Key of Solomon*, a late 19th—century compilation of genuine kabala materials, based on 'historical manuscripts' in the British Museum, we can see that the method of becoming invisible required some very low-tech assembling of materials, but much ritual movement, prayer and writing (de Laurence 45—46). It used image magic, making a figure of wax as a talisman, offering it to the 12 or 15 gods invoked in the prayers said, and then through holding the talisman in the left pocket one becomes instantly invisible. The talisman is then buried until invisibility is needed again. Whilst the wax image is an object, it is somewhat incidental to the business. The prayers and rituals performed to please the devil make one invisible. Were this skill taught in Hogwarts, we might expect that the student would become slightly translucent, or fuzzy around the edges until the student acquired full skill. Dumbledore, the most powerful wizard of his age, needs no special device, even a waxen image, to become invisible. But Harry, who has not yet attained the skill to become invisible himself, can obtain that power through the technology of the magical cloak used previously by his father. This cloak is not an offering to some outside spirit, and no invocation of anyone else's power is required. In fact, no wand needs to be used, and no spell needs to be said. Apparently one can purchase the cloak, although Ron claims they are extremely rare. The power is in the technology itself.

Although witches do not seem to improve in their abilities to perform spells in the 16th and 17th centuries, they do have different abilities one from another. Ben Jonson's several plays that make fun of magic, and Marlowe's *Dr. Faustus*, which treats magic seriously most of the time, at least, suggest that the different levels of magic are obtained through invocation of spirits, some of whom have more power in the hierarchy of magical spirits than others.

Notably, *The Devil is an Ass* credits white magic to very inferior devils. Likewise, *Witchcraft Farther Display'd* describes the orders and degrees of evil spirits that witches can use to do different kinds of work, some of which might be mistaken for white magical deeds (Bragge 13). Once again, this is a late view, one created after the learned had decided that all magic came only from contracting with the devil. Probably the Witch of Wapping was more usual, in that she was both good and bad *(Witch* 3).

The conclusion of most later commentators is that witches and wizards have no skills. Several of the trials of witches portray these women as stupid dupes of the devil's (E.G. 6, Cooper 210). And whilst Faustus, as depicted by Marlowe, is intended to be a great magus involved in necromancy, it seems that he gives up his soul merely to do parlour tricks and fly about, and might be considered nearly as funny as Ludo Bagman, and not as good as Fred and George Weasley, if the loss of his soul were not so serious a matter.

The witch trials, until skepticism about the truth of magic eventually takes over, (e.g., Ady) were printed to prove that all magic is evil and in league with the devil. Even magic beneficial to people is dangerous, because, like smoking marijuana, it leads inevitably to the hard stuff.

Rowling's magic is different in kind.

It is a set of skills and abilities, linked to genetic inheritance,—not a religion—that can be invested in technology, even to the exclusion of the use of a wand or words. Whilst the greatest wizard of the age can be invisible without a cloak, fly without a broomstick, and see through invisibility cloaks without a mechanical eye, those without abilities can use magical technology to do many of these things. Thus we have two consequences: the first is the *possibility* of a kinder and gentler world where the Neville Longbottoms and Argus Filches of the magical world need not be entirely useless or helpless compared with the Albus Dumbledores; and the second is that because the use of magic is possible to everyone without reliance on a spirit with its own agenda, good magic and bad magic are a moral choice. The small voice in Harry's head does not come from the devil or anyone else who must be believed in, and it cannot steer him into Slytherin if he does not want to be there.

Works Cited

HARRY POTTER BOOKS AND ABBREVIATIONS

GoF. Rowling, J.K. *Harry Potter and the Goblet of Fire.* Vancouver: Raincoast, 2000. (and Adult Edition, Bloomsbury and Raincoast, 2000).

CoS. Rowling, J.K. *Harry Potter and the Chamber of Secrets.* London: Bloomsbury, 1998. (and Adult Edition, 1999)

OotP Rowling, J.K. *Harry Potter and the Order of the Phoeni*x. Vancouver: Raincoast Books, 2003

*Po*A. Rowling, J.K. *Harry Potter and the Prisoner of Azkaba*n. Vancouver: Raincoast, 1999. (and Adult Edition), London: Bloomsbury, 1999.

PS. Rowling, J.K. *Harry Potter and the Philosopher's Ston*e. London: Bloomsbury, 1997. (and Adult Edition, 1998.)

Whisp, Kennilworthy. *Quidditch through the Age*s. Vancouver: Raincoast, 2001.

OTHER WORKS

Ady, Thomas. *A Candle in the Dark: or, a Treatise Concerning the Nature of Witches & Witchcraft: Being Advice to Judges, Sheriffes, Justices of the Peace and Grand-Jury-men, what to do, before they passe Sentence on such as are Arraigned for their Lives, as Witches.* London: Printed for R.I. to be sold by Tho. Newberry at the three Lions in Cornhill by the Exchange. 1656. Thomason Tracts. 131.E.869[5].

Appelbaum, Peter. "Harry Potter's World: Magic, Technoculture, and Becoming Human." *Harry Potter's World: Multidisciplinary Critical Perspective*s. Ed. Elizabeth El Heilman. New York: RoutledgeFalmer, 2003. *The Apprehension and Confession of Three Notorious Witches. Arreigned and by Iustice Condemned and Executed at Chelmes-forde, in the Countye of Essex, the 5. Day of Iulye, Last Past. 1589. With the Manner of Their Diuelish Practices and Keeping of Their Spirits, Whose Fourmes Are Heerein Truelye Proportioned.* [London : E. Allde, 1589]. *Early English Books 1475-1640* 952:19.

[Boulton, Richard.] *A Compleat History of Magick, Sorcery, and Witchcraft; Containing, I. the Most Authentick and Best Attested Relations of Magicians, Sorcerers, Witches, Apparitions, Spectres, Ghosts, Daemons, and Other Preternatural Appearances. II. A Collection of Several Very Scarce and Valuable Tryals of Witches, Particularly That Famous One, of the Witches of Warboyse. III. An Account of the First Rise of Magicians and Witches; Shewing the Contracts They Make with the Devil, and What Methods They Take to Accomplish Their Infernal Designs. IV. A Full Confutation of All the Arguments That Have Ever Been Produced Against the Belief of Apparitions, Witches, &C. With a Judgment Concerning Spirits, by the Late Learned Mr. John Locke.* 2v. London: Printed for E. Curll at the Dial and Bible, J. Pemberton at the Buck and Sun, both against St. Dunstan's Church in Fleet-Street; and W. Taylor at the Ship in Pater-noster-Row, 1715-16. Price of the Two Volumes 5s. The Eighteenth Century ; reel 5389, no. 5.

[Bragge, Francis.] *Witchcraft Farther Display'd. Containing I. an Account of the Witchcraft Practis'd by Jane Wenham of Walkerne, in Hertfordshire, since Her Condemnation, upon the Bodies of Anne Thorn and Anne Street, and the deplorable Condition in which they still remain. II. An Answer to the Most General Objections Against the Being and Power of Witches: With some Remarks upon the Case of Jane Wenham in particular, and on Mr. Justice Powel's Procedure therein. To Which Are Added, the Tryals of Florence Newton, a Famous Irish Witch, at the Assizes Held at Cork, Anno 1661; as also of Two Witches as the Assizes Held at Bury St. Edmonds in Suffolk, Anno 1664, before Sir Matthew Hale, (then Lord Chief Baron of the Exchequer) Who were Found Guilty and Executed.*

London: Printed for E. Curll, at the Dial and Bible against St. Dunstan's Church in Fleet-Street, 1712. Price 6d. Where may be had, The Tryal and Proceedings at Large Against Jane Wenham, at Hertford-Assizes. Price 6d. The Eighteenth Century; reel 8262, no.02

Calef, Robert, 1648-1719. *More Wonders of the Invisible World: Or, the Wonders of the Invisible World, Display'd in Five Parts. Part. I. an Account of the Sufferings of Margaret Rule, Written by the Reverand* [sic] *Mr. C.M. P. II. Several Letters to the Author, & c. and His Reply Relating to Witchcraft. P. III. The Differences Between the Inhabitants of Salem Village, and Mr. Parris Their Minister, in New-England. P. IV. Letters of a Gentleman Uninterested, Endeavouring to Prove the Recieved* [sic] *Opinions about Witchcraft to Be Orthodox. With Short Essays to Their Answers. P. V. a Short Historical Account of Matters of Fact in That Affair. & to Which Is Added, a Postscript Relating to a Book Intitled, the Life of Sir William Phips. Collected by Robert Calef, Merchant, of Boston in New-England. Licensed and Entred According to Orde*r. London: Printed for Nath. Hillar, at the Princes-Arms, in Leaden-Hall-street, over Against St. Mary-Ax, and Joseph Collyer, at the Golden-Bible on London-Bridge, 1700. *Early English Books, 1641-1700*; 18:15.

The Compleat Wizzard [sic]*; Being a Collection of Authentic and Entertaining Narratives of the Real Existence and Appearance of Ghosts, Demons, and Spectres: Together with Several Wonderful Instances of the Effects of Witchcraft. To Which Is Prefixed, an Account of Haunted Houses, and Subjoined a Treatise on the Effects of Magic.* London: Printed for T. Evans, No. 54 in Paternoster Row. 1770. The Eighteenth Century; reel 1933, no. 03.

Cooper, Thomas, fl. 1626. *The Mystery of Witch-craft. Discouering, the Truth, Nature, Occasions, Growth and Power Therof. Together with the Detection and Punishment of the Same. As Also, the Seuerall Stratagems of Sathan, Ensnaring the Poore Soule by this Desperate Practize of Annoying the Bodie: with the Seuerall Vses Thereof to the Church of Christ. Very Necessary for the Redeeming of These Atheisticall and Secure Times.* By Thomas Cooper. London : Printed by Nicholas Okes, 1617. *Early English Books, 1475-1640*; 1133:04.

Davis, Ralph, of Northampton. *An Account of the Tryals, Examination and Condemnation, of Elinor Shaw, and Mary Phillip's (Two Notorious Witches,) Northampton Assizes, on Wednesday the 7th of March 1705, for Bewitching a Woman, and Two Children, Tormenting Them in a Sad and Lamentable Manner till They Dyed. With an Account of Their Strange Confessions, about Their Familiarity with the Devil and How They Made a Wicked Contract.* London: Printed for F. Thorn, near Fleet street. [1705]. The Eighteenth Century ; reel 7228, no.13 de Laurence, L.W. ed. *The Greater Key of Solomon: including a clear and precise exposition of King Solomon's Secret Procedure, Its Mysteries and Magic Rites. Original Places. Seals, Charms and Talismans.* Translated from Ancient Manuscripts in the British Museum, London. By S. Liddel MacGreagor Mathers. Chicago: The de Laurence Company, c. 1916, rpt. Hackensack, NJ: Wehman Bros. [c. 1974].

E. G, gent. *A Prodigious & Tragicall History of the Arraignment, Tryall, Confession, and Condemnation of Six Witches at Maidstone, in Kent, at the Assizes There Held in July, Fryday 30. This Present Year. 1652. Before the Right Honorable, Peter Warburton, One of the Justices of the Common Pleas. Collected from the Observations of E.G. Gent. (A Learned Person, Present at Their Conviction and Condemnation) and Digested* by H.F. Gent. To Which Is Added a True Relation of One Mrs. Atkins a Mercers Wife in Warwick, Who Was Strangely Caried Away from Her House in July Last, and Hath Not Been Heard of Since. London: Printed for Richard Harper, in Smithfield, 1652. Thomason Tracts: 103:E.673[19]

Greater London Council. *John Joseph Merlin: The Ingenious Mechanick*. [An exhibition catalogue of objects and trade cards related to Merlin's clockwork mechanisms and musical instruments.] London: The Iveagh Bequest, Kenwood, Greater London Council, 1985.

Hansen, Chadwick. *Witchcraft at Salem*. New York: George Braziller, 1969. *The History of the Lancashire Witches. Containing the Manner of Their Becoming Such; their Enchantments, Spells, Revels, Merry Pranks, Raising of Storms and Tempests, Riding on Winds, &c. The Entertainment and Frolicks Which Happened Among Them. With the Loves and Humours of Roger and Dorothy. Also. A Treatise of Witches in General Conducive to Mirth and Recreation. The Like Never Before Published.* [London?, 1785?]. The Eighteenth Century: reel 642, no. 5.

[Hull, Edward] *The Wall Chart of World History*. [facsimile of *Deacon's Synchronological Chart of Universal History*, London: C.W. Deacon, 1890] rpt. London: Bracken, 1990.

Jonson, Ben. "The Devil is an Ass," *Four Jacobean City Comedies*. Ed. Gamini Salgado. London: Penguin, 1975, 188—310.

Jonson, Ben. "The Alchemist," *English Drama 1580—1642*. ed. C. F. Tucker Brooke and Nathaniel Burton Paradise. Boston: Heath, 1933, 573-623.

Laver, James. *A Concise History of Costume*. London: Thames and Hudson, 1979.

Marlowe, Christopher. "The Tragical History of Doctor Faustus," *Christopher Marlowe: The Complete Plays*. London: Penguin, 1986.

Magomastix, Hieronymus. *The Strange VVitch at Greenvvich, (Ghost, Spirit, or Hobgoblin) Haunting a Wench, Late Servant to a Miser, Suspected a Murtherer of His Late VVife: with Curious Discussions of Walking Spirits and Spectars of Dead Men Departed, for Rare and Mysticall Knowledge and Discourse, by Hieronymus Magomastix. April 24. 1650. Imprimatur.* John Dovvname. London : Printed by Thomas Harper, and are to be sold by John Saywell, at the Greyhound in Little Britaine, 1650. Thomason Tracts; 92:E.600[15].

Morton, Peter and Barbara Dähms. "The Metaphysics of Witchcraft: The Trial of Tempel Annake 1663" a paper presented in a Humanities Colloquium, Mount Royal College, Calgary, Alberta, Canada, 20 March 2003.

Perkins, William, 1558-1602. *A Discourse of the Damned Art of Witchcraft; So Farre Forth as it Is Reuealed in the Scriptures, and Manifest by True Experience. Framed and Deliuered by M. William Pirkins* [sic], *in His Ordinarie Course of Preaching, and Now Published by Tho. Pickering Batchelour of Diuinitie, and Minister of Finchingfield in Essex. Whereunto Is Adioyned a Twofold Table; One of the Order and Heades of the Treatise; Another of the Texts of Scripture Explaned* [sic], *or Vindicated from the Corrupt Interpretation of the Aduersarie.* [Cambridge] : Printed by Cantrel Legge, printer to the Vniuersitie of Cambridge, 1608. *Early English Books, 1475-1640*; 725:7 Plato. *Phaedrus*. Trans. by B. Jowett. 20 March 2003. <http://ccat.sas.upenn.edu/jod/texts/phaedrus.html>.

Royal Caledonian Curling Club. "History of the Game" *Royal Caledonian Curling Club*. 15 March 2003. <http://www.royalcaledoniancurlingclub.org/dyncat.cfm?catid=1995>

Sharpe, James. *Instruments of Darkness: Witchraft in Early Modern England*. Philadelphia: U of Pennsylvania P, 1997.

Tarassuk, Leonid and Claude Blair, eds. *The Complete Encyclopedia of Arms & Weapons: The most Comprehensive Reference Work Ever Published on Arms and Armor from Prehistoric Times to the Present with over 1,250 Illustrations*. New York: Simon and Schuster, 1979.

Thomas, Keith. *Religion and the Decline of Magic: Studies in Popular Beliefs in Sixteenth and Seventeenth-century England*. London: Weidenfeld and Nicolson,1971. *A True and Full Relation of the Witches at Pittenweem. To which is added by way of Preface: An Essay for proving the Existence of Good and Evil Spirits, relating to the Witches at Pittenweem, now in Custody with Arguments against the Sadducism of the Present Age*. Edinburgh: Printed by John Reid Junior, and are to be Sold at his Printing House in Labortown Wynd. 1702.

W. P. *The History of Witches and Wizards: Giving a True Account of All Their Tryals in England, Scotland, Sweedland, France and New England; with Their Confession and Codemnation. Collected from Bishop Hall, Bishop Morton, Sir Matthew Hale, Dr. Glanvil, Mr. Emlin, Dr. Horneck, Dr. Tilson, Mr. Baxter, Mr. Hodges, Corn. Agrippa. By W. P.* London: Printed for C. Hitch and L. Haws, at the Red Lion in Paternoster Row; and R. Ware at the Bible and Sun, Ludgate Hill; H. Woodgate and S. Brook in Paternoster Row; S. Crowder, in Paternoster Row. [1760?]. The Eighteenth Century: reel 5155, no. 2.

The Witch of Wapping. Or an Exact and Perfect Relation, of the Life and Devilish Practises of Joan Peterson, that Dwelt in Spruce Island, near Wapping; Who Was Condemned for Practising Witch-craft, and Sentenced to Be Hanged at Tyburn, on Munday the 11th. of April, 1652. Shewing, How She Bewitch'd a Child, and Rock'd the Cradle in theLikenesse of a Cat; How She Frighted a Baker; and How the Devil Often Came to SuckHer, Sometimes in the Likeness of a Dog, and Other Times like a Squirrel. Together, withthe Confession of Prudence Lee, Who Was Burnt in Smithfield on Saturday the 10th. ofthis Instant for the Murthering Her Husband: and Her Admonition and Counsel to All Her Sex in General. London: printed for Th. Spring. 1652. Thomason Tracts; 101:E.659[18].

Diana Patterson teaches English, Publishing History, and Technical Communications, and team teaches in an Engineering course, at Mount Royal College, Calgary, Alberta, Canada. She has a Ph.D. in English from the University of Toronto, and an M.A. in the History of the Book from the University of London. Before becoming an academic, she was a computer software technical writer. Her areas of research include the history of the technical book in Canada, and the history of wastepaper bindings in 18th and early 19th century Britain. She collects editions of Harry Potter, and served on the organizing team for 2004's ConventionAlley in Ottawa.

Within the Pantheon?
Harry Potter and the Epic Question

Mary Pharr

As an academic, I have been intrigued by the Harry Potter series for some time now. As a staunch if conventional supporter of creative freedom, I find that neither the theological controversies associated with the books nor the inconsistencies of their cinematic adaptations especially concern me. But the question of Harry's place within the literary pantheon haunts me. While most of my professional colleagues seem more bemused than inflamed by this question, I feel like a cross between the unnamed governess entangled in the eerie events of *The Turn of the Screw* and a Hogwarts student caught by nature's call in Moaning Myrtle's bathroom: that is, I know that something definitely out of the ordinary is all about me, but I can't quite make it out.

Repeatedly, however, I have been on the verge of what I thought was clear vision. As early as *Chamber of Secrets*, I had begun to see the Potter series as an epic in the making, and I have since then several times used Rowling's books as examples of the postmodern epic *mentalité*. My theory is based on J. B. Hainsworth's assertion that while heroic poems "celebrate, affirm, and confirm something; they do not, as the epic can and does, explore and question at the same time as they celebrate" (6). Spinning through time and format from ancient oral poetry to contemporary prose fiction and reflexive mass media, the epic yet retains what I see as its dual purpose: to celebrate human conduct—especially heroic conduct—even as it ponders the cost and complexity of such conduct. By this theory, Harry Potter, whose expanding heroism is becoming both essential to his society and intricate in its design, may be moving toward an epic destiny.

Presented in a number of undergraduate classes and in campus and professional presentations, my argument has met with near universal success, but it's the "near" part that's become the problem. While students and audiences seem to appreciate my linking of Harry Potter to the likes of Achilles and Beowulf through the use of traditional devices, character analogies, and heroic archetypes, an unnamed but clearly respected reader for a university press flat out rejected this same thesis when I used it as the linchpin for my chapter in the anthology *The Ivory Tower and Harry Potter*. Among other objections, the reader said that I could not identify the Potter series as an epic-in-the-making because I had not dealt with the issue of the "high seriousness" of the epic genre. Admittedly stung, I had to ask myself some somber questions. Had I been fooling myself and my middlebrow audiences into an interpretation of the epic that inadvertently degraded what Hainsworth justly describes as "the longest-lived and most widely diffused of all literary forms" (3)? Could it really be that the Potter series and my thesis fell so far below epic standards in the "seriousness" area that we were both intellectually irretrievable? Was I just a P. T. Barnum—or far worse, a Jerry Springer—capitalizing on the postmodern disregard for value systems as a means of calibrating literary worth? Here were questions not so easily ignored, not even by my Full Professor's ego. Although I did salvage the *Ivory Tower* chapter thanks to a patient editor and a refocusing of my thesis, to this day I continue to ponder the reader's objection even as I also continue to esteem Rowling.

To begin with, I find myself considering the "seriousness" issue in the light of the humor for which the Potter series is renowned. However much it delights readers of all ages, such humor may be disavowed as essentially foreign to the epic *zeitgeist*, with its somber atmosphere of struggle and sacrifice. Yet such a blanket disavowal can be overstated. After all, even the *Iliad* has some humor in it: consider the book depicting the gods brawling with one another in an Olympian travesty of the War at Troy. The humor of this episode is too cruel to be comic, perhaps, but it must have delighted Homer's Hellenic audience as they envisioned the endless banquet of the gods turned topsy topsy-turvy. In our own determinedly egalitarian society, Harry's juvenile pranks that repeatedly defy external authority may strike a similar chord with readers who fantasize stepping outside the narrow lines of bureaucratic regulation. Nonetheless, no epic can sustain such a perspective as its primary point of view: the stakes involved in any crisis demanding true heroism simply become too high to be laughed away. In the early books of Rowling's series, the humor is appropriate to Harry's age and schoolboy station; book by book, however, the humor is thinning out and repositioning itself to the background. By *The Order of the Phoenix* it has become the primary province not of Harry but of joke shop owners-in-development George and Fred Weasley. As for Harry, he's moving from adolescent horseplay toward his adult destiny. That movement brings up a second issue. Like so much else in contemporary life, the Potter controversy is presently pinpointed by its location on a list. That is, as if in acknowledgment of the unnamed reader's position, Rowling's series has for some time now been relegated to a seemingly permanent position at or near the top of the hitherto nonexistent Children's Bestsellers List at the *New York Times*, indicating not only its massive popularity but also its placement by cultural critics within the respected *and* restricted field of the *Bildingsroman*, the novel of education and a mainstay of children's literature. As I've already indicated, Harry's often hazardous quest for an extraordinary education is certainly a *rite de passage* moving him toward adulthood, but his growth is also inextricably linked to a larger quest toward a stature that will isolate him from most other adults.

I tend to see that quest through a series of analogies with other literary characters, and though an analogy is only as good as its associative links, such connections are what create the archetypal web upon which the epic sensibility depends. Thus, I find myself connecting Harry with Gilgamesh, the mythical king of Uruk who may well be the oldest extant epic hero; and with Dante, the reflexive shadow of the real Dante Aligheri who serves as protagonist in the great Medieval epic, *The Divine Comedy*. What can such honored literary figures have in common with this "Children's List" character? More than first supposed, I believe. For one thing, like Gilgamesh and Dante, Harry journeys—literally and figuratively—toward knowledge of a unique and powerful authority within himself: for Gilgamesh the authority is that of a demigod, for Dante that of a poet, and for Harry that of a magician. More significantly, perhaps, from the epic perspective, all three also learn the limitations of that authority: hard knowledge teaching Gilgamesh that the demigod cannot return life to his boon companion Enkidu, teaching Dante that not even poets as great as Virgil and Homer can avoid God's judgment, and teaching Harry that no wizard has enough magic to rescue first Cedric Diggory and later Sirius Black from undeserved death. M. Katherine Grimes has pointed out that Harry "loses any illusion that he will emerge unscathed by his horrible grand adventures" when Cedric is killed "on Harry's watch" (104). One year later, the death of Sirius—with Harry, Dumbledore, Snape, and Sirius himself all bearing some responsibility—hits Harry even harder as he loses his closest link to the father he never knew.

Yet in his losses, Harry paradoxically gains a dimensionality that opens him up to potential epic status, to the ironic grandeur of extra-human authority within the all-too-human confines of mortality. He may—indeed, does—vanquish Voldemort repeatedly, but now he knows that he cannot save everyone—perhaps not even himself. At the end of his fifth year at Hogwarts, Harry learns the grim prophecy that he is presumed to be the one who "must be either murderer or victim" of Voldemort (*Phoenix* 849)—a vision of tragedy as much as of glory. Like those who came before him, Harry must struggle with the guilt, the dread, and the hubris wrought by his knowledge of himself—more frightening than the whispers of the Sorting Hat on his first day at Hogwarts.

There's something else about Harry's burgeoning authority and knowledge: it leaves him prey to solitude and misinterpretation. Here is another connection to epic heroes, whose stature and power make them too different from the general run of humanity to fit comfortably into its social norms. Small wonder that many readers of the *Iliad* prefer Hector, with his familial values and understandable failings, to Achilles, with his deific ties and overwhelming force. For as Thomas Van Nortwick has said of Achilles, "what makes him great is also what isolates him" (44), and even Achilles' fellow Greeks are more in awe than admiration of him. As for a less egotistical epic hero like Beowulf, who is lauded at his death as "the man most gracious" (l. 3180) (literally, the "mildest of men" in Old English), he is still bound more by who he is rather than whom he protects. After all, Beowulf has no immediate family when he dies defending the Geats, most of whom prove themselves completely unworthy of him. Yet none of that matters. Beowulf, like Achilles, must be himself—and so must Harry. Famous before he knew his own name, Harry is, like Achilles' shield, like Beowulf's sword, and like his own scar, unique and, therefore, not easily incorporated. The Dursleys hide him in a cupboard because he's different, while most of his classmates (occasionally even Ron and Hermione) cheer him one day and snub him the next. These alternating waves of adulation and rejection suggest that Harry may never entirely fit within any social cluster. In fairness, Rowling may have conflicted feelings about this lack of social acceptance, and she has used Harry's best friends and his mentors to mitigate it. In *Goblet of Fire* she modified it further by giving the adolescent Harry the warmth of a romantic interest in Cho Chang— but that warmth is gone (at least temporarily) by the end of *Phoenix*. Without parents, godfather, or girlfriend, Harry on the verge of manhood is alone more than not, and the absence of any compassionate blood ties in his life seems to me another indication that he is moving toward an epic destiny.

But what is that destiny? I have no secret knowledge of the conclusion to the series. And even if I choose to assume that its close will emulate the ancient theme of an ephemeral victory of order over disorder (a victory achieved at great cost and one that cannot last longer than the mortality that earned it), I must still deal with the fundamental issue of the writing itself. Over the millennia, many would-be Homers have tried to create epics out of the great events of their mythology, their history, their own imagination; only a handful of such efforts are remembered. Is Rowling, that most accessible of writers, good enough stylistically or thematically to merit serious literary consideration? Stylistically, perhaps her case must be reviewed not within Homeric guidelines (wherein she—like virtually every other writer of our age—falls pitifully short) but instead in a postmodern context. For if the blind bard's work was chanted to a primarily preliterate audience, Rowling's series is designed for an audience that may fairly be described as postliterate, bored by print. "I don't like to read," says the ten-year old cited in a *World Literature Today* article. But then this same youngster describes her experience with the Potter books as the exception to her antipathy: "When my teacher says that it [is] time to stop reading, me and my classmates would groan" (qtd. in Beach and Willner 102). In an era of visual texts and electronic narratives, Rowling is somehow able to reach even this grammatically dysfunctional (meaning quite normal) child. That may not make Rowling a classical *rhapsode*, but it does merit legitimate attention.

Thematically, however, is she just a snappy storyteller or is she able to make her audience meditate on the nature of the universe, on its vast possibilities in relation to human identity and action? No one can offer more than a tentative opinion to this question until the Potter series concludes—but I can say now that Rowling is good enough to have made me think about such issues through her first several books. From a somewhat different literary perspective, Roni Natov speaks of the best of "adventure stories" as negotiating between the "reckless pace of the narrative" and the "meditative pockets that provide the space and time to turn inward—to affirm our sense that something memorable is happening to us, something we can retrieve later, after the book is ended" (134). Natov finds Rowling truly adept at such negotiation, and I can only echo her appreciation.

I appreciate as well the unknown reader, who has made me admit that my sense of this series is as speculative as it is analytical. I still have my facts: Rowling does employ a cascade of traditional epic characteristics, parallels, and references—everything from beginning her series *in medias res* (in the midst of the plot) to frequent use of the *deus ex machina* device (divine, or in this case, wizardly intervention) to the inclusion of catalogues of fantastic creatures (everything from house-elves to thestrals). By themselves, however, I now admit that such a cascade is nothing more than a list of conventions, but when combined with the transcendent creative spirit of her work, the list becomes a web whose strands suggest—as I hope I have done in this paper—that Harry carries not just the Potter name but a much larger, more meaningful identity within him. Herein I sense the prime recognition that is vital to the epic perspective. Harry's not just Professor Dumbledore's successor and Lord Voldemort's doppelganger; he is—more and more—the hope for the future of his society. I think that, inexorably, Harry is moving toward something very large, perhaps a destiny wherein the freedom—the survival—of both magicians and Muggles hangs in the balance.

All epic heroes represent the fears of desperate reality translated into the visions of narrative fantasy. Harry's own representation of hope is, I believe, increasingly timely and appealing—no small accomplishment in the world of Rowling's readers, a cynical world that yet dotes on fantasy, indulging in it through every possible medium. In a culture obsessed with the *faux* "authenticity" of reality TV and virtual reality, of digital effects and identity theft, we may need the honest fantasy of the Potter books.

So am I deluding myself in speculating on the dimensionality, the "high seriousness" as it were, of a series still referenced by many critics as child's play? Well, the seriousness does seem to me to be within the Potter novels, but initially, it scarcely dared to speak its name. In *Goblet of Fire* and especially in *Phoenix*, however, I believe that Rowling has found the voice with which to express epic intensity. As for the series' admittedly postmodern protagonist, Harry will likely never exhibit the complexity of Odysseus—but neither does the *Chanson's* Roland, and few deny his epic status. If he continues to journey as he has thus far, Harry Potter will, I think—or, perhaps more precisely, I *hope*—end not just as a child's version of old mythology but more as a pop-cultural version of epic heroism, a fitting figure for our time and place.

Works Cited

Beach, Sara Ann, and Elizabeth Harden Willner. "The Power of Harry: The Impact of J. K. Rowling's Harry Potter Books on Young Readers." *World Literature Today* 76.1 (Winter 2002): 102-106.

Beowulf. Trans. Seamus Heaney. NY: Norton, 2000.

Grimes, M.Katherine. "Harry Potter: Fairy Tale Prince, Real Boy,and Archetypal Hero." Whited 89-122.

Hainsworth, J. B. *The Idea of Epic*. Berkeley: U of CA P, 1991.

Natov, Roni. "Harry Potter and the Extraordinariness of the Ordinary." Whited 125-139.

Rowling, J. K. *Harry Potter and the Order of the Phoenix*. NY: Arthur A. Levine-Scholastic, 2003.

Van Nortwick, Thomas. *Somewhere I Have Never Travelled: The Second Self and the Hero's Journey in Ancient Epic*. NY: Oxford UP, 1992.

Whited, Lana A., ed. *The Ivory Tower and Harry Potter: Perspectives on a Literary Phenomenon*. Columbia: U of MO P, 2002.

Mary Pharr is Professor of English at Florida Southern College. She has written and presented extensively in the areas of speculative film and fiction. Coeditor of The Blood Is the Life: Vampires in Literature (Popular Press, 1999), she is also more recently the editor of Fantastic Odysseys (Praeger, 2003).

The Pleasure & the Pain of the Scar: Harry Potter as a Popular Culture Icon

Anne Frances N. Sangil

Quidditch. Nimbus 2000. Golden Snitch. Diagon Alley. Floo powder. Mad Eye Moody. Caput Draconis. Alohomora. Wingardium Leviosa. Avada Kedavra. If you do not have a clue as to what those words mean, then the question I must ask is: what are you doing here in this symposium? All these words form part of the Harry Potter universe and, along with many other terms and expressions contribute to the formation of the ultimate signifier—Harry Potter.

Who is Harry Potter? Why is Harry Potter so popular? How has Harry Potter evolved from a mere literary persona into a significant cultural icon? A few facts are in order. In the textual universe, everyone knows who Harry Potter is. He is a wizard in training at Hogwarts School of Witchcraft and Wizardry. He is the son of the late James and Lily Potter. He is a friend to Ron Weasley and Hermione Granger. A godson to Sirius Black. A pest of a student to Prof. Severus Snape. A Quidditch Hero to all the Gryffindor students. He is bane to Lord Voldemort. Harry Potter is the boy who lived.

Outside the HP universe, it is also quite impossible to find a muggle who is not at all aware of the HP phenomenon. We are all too familiar with the conception of this boy wonder. Harry Potter is the brainchild of J.K. Rowling, a former struggling mother on public assistance who would often hang about in coffee houses where she would write about this little boy with a curious lightning-bolt scar on the forehead. The rest, as they always say, is history. Or herstory if we speak of Rowling. Or harrystory, if we speak of the worldwide phenomenon. There are more than 200 million Harry Potter books in print worldwide. All books in the series have received various awards and recognition from different award-giving institutions like the Scottish Arts Council, the Booksellers Association, the Federation of Children's Books Group, etc. The books also broke many publishing records, for instance, Harry Potter and the Order of the Phoenix, the 5th in the promised septology, has the top advance sales in history: it was Amazon.com's bestseller two hours after it became available for pre-ordering, and at 8.5 million copies, holds the record of having the largest first printing ever. Harry's story is published in at least 50 languages from Albanian to Zulu and has made its creator one of the wealthiest women in Britain. With a movie franchise and merchandise tie-ups, Harry Potter's success is indisputable. Capping this phenomenon is the birth of Tanya Grotter and many other wannabes who wish to cash-in on Harry's galleons.

Obviously, Harry has been welcomed in the public arena. The verdict: bring in the magic. The boy is brilliant.

Harry Potter has successfully embedded himself in popular consciousness and has conjured a powerful magic that will ensure his place in popular culture. He has become an icon.

But what, exactly, are icons? What is our relationship with icons? What meanings do we assign to icons? Why do we continue to create icons?

> "A letter? Really, Dumbledore, you think you can explain all this in a letter? These people will never understand him! He'll be famous—a legend—I wouldn't be surprised if today was known as Harry Potter day in the future—there will be books written about Harry—every child in our world will know his name!"
>
> —Professor Minerva McGonagall

Harry Potter and the Sorcerer's Stone

Traditionally, icons are associated with religious artifacts, particularly crucifixes, pictures of saints, rosaries, and sculptures of holy beings in various sizes and poses. Charged with sacred meanings, these icons are meant to be worshipped and valued; steeped with cultural significance, these artifacts reflect the ideals and the beliefs of the community that cherishes and empowers such icons. But an icon is not just a function of religion. It connotes many intersecting avenues such as myth, magic, rituals and traditions.

The usual dictionary definition of icon [from the Greek eikon, also ikon] is a "sacred image." But icons are more than images. According to Marshall Fishwick,

> Icons are images and ideas converted into three dimensions. They are admired artifacts, external expression of internal convictions, everyday things that make every day meaningful.

> Icons are cultural ciphers. They help us to de-cipher, or unlock, the mystery of our attitudes and assumptions. As objects they can be approached objectively; but people who believe in them also operate on an emotional level—the level of love and reverence[1].

In the HP universe, every wizard and every witch know the celebrity that is Harry Potter. His story is stuff of legends. Orphaned as a child, he was the only one who was able to defeat the evil Dark Lord Voldemort, not once but several times in the course of the series: first as an innocent boy, second as a 12-year old young man battling against a memory of a younger Tom Riddle, and third as a 14 year old wizard versus a resurrected foe. He has become a revered symbol of what is good and powerful in the magical

434

world. Every little thing he does is magic. Every move worthy of a headline in the Daily Prophet. Even his scar has become celebrated, for this is the proof of Harry's very being, a testimony to Harry's wizarding powers. Literally, Harry is marked for life.

Outside the text, Harry Potter works his magic in a not so different manner. Muggles may not be able to literally shake his hand but people do line up to buy his books and watch his movies. Youngsters buy his pillows and tack his pictures and posters on their bedroom walls (so much like fastening pictures of saints on walls). Kids drink from his mug, write with his pen (quills are available even for muggles), wear his Gryffindor scarf, and play his games via different platforms like Playstation, X-Box and GameBoy. We have HP avatars (literal icons) on our desktops with matching HP screensavers. And I'm sure, very sure that some enterprising muggle right now is experimenting on a few potions that will hopefully defy gravity so he/she can finally make a prototype of the best broomstick ever—the Firebolt. Most of us have perhaps read the news about the 21-year-old woman in Madrid who set her house ablaze in an attempt to brew her own kind of magic[2]. Unfortunately, she used ingredients like toothpaste and surgical alcohol (obviously muggle elements) in her effort to imitate the boy wizard. This dismal display of potion making would have surely incensed Professor Severus Snape (Perhaps next time HP books will have to carry a blurb on the dust jacket—"Don't try this at home folks!").

As an icon, Harry Potter has transcended himself from a mere literary figment of the imagination (seriously, there are material significations of Harry's presence) into something that has become an object of our reflection. He has objectified a segment of human experience, real or imagined. Something of our corporal or imaginative experience has been turned into an object to aid us in our attempts in making sense of our environment, and ultimately, of ourselves.

Harry Potter is an Everyman, our Everyboy. He represents us in our ideal state. As muggles trying to go about our daily lives, we struggle with many obstacles: there are Draco Malfoys, dementors and Whomping Willows that are always out to get us. And just like Harry, we try to fight them off. And hopefully, just like Harry, we will always prevail. Harry has become an icon for our potentiality. The scar has served (and continues to serve) its purpose. It's wicked!

But icons are not static entities. They come and go in our lives, as icons lose and gain significance according to our life situations. Iconic meanings do vary from one person to another, the same way Harry Potter's relevance varies depending on the critical stance of a reader. As Fishwick claims, "Your insight might be my oversight; your icon my kitsch . . . . The operative word for icon is still magic."[3]

Yet magic is not all good and dandy. As we all know, there is also the practice of the Dark Arts which shows us the other side of magic. The same way goes for the study of Harry Potter. He too has his own share of condemnation. Whether it is promoting witchcraft or sexism, Harry has been targeted left and right by people of different persuasions: marxism, feminism, religious fanaticism, and many other—isms. One important view regarding Harry Potter was raised by Tammy Turner-Vorbeck who claims that Pottermania induces commodity fetishism. According to her:

> The infringement of consumerism on child culture is particularly evident in the mass marketing of Harry Potter products . . . the proliferation of these items constitute a blatant exploitation of the genuine excitement for children's literature that stems from children's true interests. In an effort to create more profits for its shareholders, conglomerates, such as AOL Time Warner, which holds distribution rights to Harry Potter products, supersaturate the marketplace with every conceivable spin-off product . . . .

> The insidious nature of all this is that these corporations not only own a segment of popular culture through their control of the commodity but also they created the fetishism—the need, the desire, and the very market—for that commodity! Such commodity fetishism is even modeled in the Harry Potter books themselves as the children among the characters long to purchase particular kinds of brooms and trading cards[4]

This viewpoint is not without basis. Just looking at the overwhelming records of the books and everything Harry Potter related will prove how the market has used this little boy to generate maximum profit. Have we really been hoodwinked by the capitalist machine yet again? Just like bottled holy water, is Harry Potter doomed to be for sale?

My answer: no.

What many people, neo-marxists or otherwise often fail to see is the other side of the magic. It's not just the magic of economics that is at work here. There is also the magic of semiotics which is always at work in popular culture. John Fiske calls this "the art of making do." What is profitable may not be necessarily cultural. And according to Fiske, "it is the people who finally choose which commodities they will use in their culture."[5] This is an empowering idea for unlike other notions, this does not assume a pure commodification of people into victimized, willing dupes of capitalism. It allows the people, the populace that makes up popular culture to have a say, to find relevance in their culture amidst a capitalist environment. This is where resistance comes in. And where there is resistance, there is power being fought. And what is this power? This is the power over the cultural product, in this case, the cultural icon that we have imagined for ourselves.

> Every act of consumption is an act of cultural production, for consumption is always the production of meaning. At the point of sale the commodity exhausts its role in the distribution economy, but begins its work in the cultural. Detached from the strategies of capitalism, its work for the bosses completed, it becomes a resource for the culture of everyday life.[6]

In the capitalist arena, the public is seen as a passive audience waiting to be manipulated by the dominant power bloc. But this arena is not the end all of our everyday life. Popular icons are not mere metaphors for dollar, pound or peso signs as mass cultural theorists are wont to propose. These icons are created by the people to serve a purpose. In itself, an icon is inadequate. It is never a self-sufficient signifier of some significance. Rather, an icon is a provoker of meanings and pleasures, of relevance and ideals. As a popular text, an icon is completed only when people take it up and integrate it into their everyday culture.

This is the cultural magic of Harry Potter. When we see the scar, how many of us really see the dollar sign and hear the ka-ching of the cash register as opposed to the number of people who see the scar as a reminder, not for Harry, but for ourselves of ourselves. The scar may be a link to Harry's tragic past, but for us, it is our remembrall that will always remind us of our journey towards self-realization. Just as Harry constantly struggles to find his place in the magical world, thus a seeker in both the literal and the figurative sense, we too try to seek our own magic.

The pleasure and the pain

> "It was agony to touch a person marked by something so good."
> —Prof. Albus Dumbledore
> *Harry Potter and the Sorcerer's Stone*

Amidst the seeming 'pain' imposed by the capitalists to the consumers in the former's relentless campaign towards an enormous return of investment, the latter, from being a commodified, homogenized entity now becomes a producer, a producer of meanings and pleasures.

Fiske said that popular culture is the culture of the subordinate who resent their subordination. How is this reflected in the realm of Harry Potter? How do the readers (consumers) manifest this resentment in relation with the power play in both the literary and filmic texts (readers/viewers as willing participants in the fantasy narrative) and in the economic and political situations they find themselves in (outside of the text)? What are the possible meanings created by the consumers in their attempt to subvert the pain-inducing economy of the capitalists? How do the consumers (now producers of meanings) work against the center of economic power and authority?

This is where pleasure comes in. Readers as icon makers participate in the Harry Potter world out of a sense of pleasure, not out of pressure. It is not out of coercion but of conviction. People do line up in bookstores and cinema houses waiting for their dose of Harry Potter magic, but that doesn't stop there. From mere receivers, they become co-creators in this phenomenon. They create unofficial websites and post lengthy arguments on unendorsed message boards. They criticize the film adaptations up to the minute details. They compose Harry Potter ringtones for their mobile phones. They design Harry Potter animes and write fan fiction. They even have slash stories with matching images sometimes lifted from the films. They manipulate photographs, create 'what if' scenarios, and make their own short films—all these without the financial backing of Time Warner, Scholastic or Bloomsbury Press. Prior to the release of the Order of the Phoenix, fans were in a state of collective suspense and anxiety that they consumed even little rumors about the book. I for a fact know someone who wrote such rumors and spread it via cyberowls, just for the fun of it. Obviously, they do not limit themselves with what is being provided for them. They go an extra mile by using the master icon in creating their own Harry Potter-inspired universes.

Yes, it is quite painful to buy the merchandise, but remember, fans can always break their eyeglasses and secure it with Scotch tape if they want to.

Clearly, pain isn't everything, is it Mr. Potter?

Nachbar, Weiser and Wright claim that the fundamental functions of popular icons are part of the function of popular culture itself: "to create order out of chaos, to help us define what is important, to serve as tangible reminder of our origin and destiny, to ease our sense of isolation or aloneness, to evoke and resolve human problems, to give significance to the world around us." [7] Without a doubt, Harry Potter as an icon is all that and perhaps more. As a literary character, Harry always saves the day, finds courage within him when there is none outside of him, consciously tries to find his place in his world, and in the process, learns more about his capabilities and limitations, and thus ends up truly knowing himself. This act of seeking his full potential inspires us readers to do the same, to come to the full awareness of our own magic. As an icon, Harry mirrors back to us not what we want to see, but what we want to become.

When we see the scar, we are reminded of not just the story behind it, but also the story that lies ahead.

We see through Harry, in both meanings of the phrase. First, we see through Harry, the same way Harry and his friends see through Nearly Headless Nick. We see Harry thoroughly, inside and out. We see him completely, all the way. We know him that much because we know ourselves that much.

Second, we see through Harry, we see via Harry. Harry has become our agent, our seer/seeker. When Harry looks at the Mirror of Erised and sees the deepest desires of his heart, we see ourselves and the deepest desires of our hearts. What Harry sees, we also see. And when Harry sees himself, we see ourselves.

We see through Harry.

Harry Potter is more than a literary character. He symbolizes something else for the reader. He communicates the belief of many people. He represents our attitude. He is an accurate reflector of our concerns. For some he may be a symbol of great power. For others a symbol of commodity fetishism and cultural hegemony. And for most of us, he is an image of what we greatly desire: ourselves, complete knowledge of ourselves.

That is truly the function of an icon.

Whatever the meaning we choose to ascribe to this icon, the fact is, Harry Potter as an icon has minimized the difference between text and life, between pleasure and pain, between magic and reality.

To be able to read an icon, Nachbar and company suggest that we ask the following questions:

- What myths and beliefs are suggested by the icon?
- Does the icon have magical powers?
- What is its history?
- What ritual behavior is associated with the icon? And
- What does the icon mean to you?[8]

We know the many myths and beliefs suggested by Harry Potter. We are familiar with the magic he is able to conjure (whether economic or cultural). We are aware of Harry's history, the harrystory. The fanaticism, the collective hysteria over the books, the rush to the cinema houses to see the film adaptations, the fascination for game cards, game boards, and GameBoys, the communal gatherings online—all these are rituals we willingly participate in.

But what does this icon mean to you?

Quidditch. Nimbus 2000. Golden Snitch. Diagon Alley. Floo powder. Mad Eye Moody. Caput Draconis. Alohomora. Wingardium Leviosa. Avada Kedavra. If you know what those words mean, then my dear witches and wizards, you know how to answer that fifth question.

Works Cited

Primary Texts:

Rowling, J.K. Harry Potter and the Sorcerer's Stone. New York: Scholastic, Inc., 1997.
_____. Harry Potter and the Chamber of Secrets. New York: Scholastic, Inc., 1999.
_____. Harry Potter and the Prisoner of Azkaban. New York: Scholastic, Inc., 1999.
_____. Harry Potter and the Goblet of Fire. New York: Scholastic, Inc., 2000.

Secondary Texts:

Fishwick, Marshall and Ray B. Browne. Eds. Icons of Popular Culture. Ohio: Bowling Green University Popular Press, 1970.
Fiske, John. Reading the Popular. Boston: Unwin Hyman, 1989.
_____. Understanding Popular Culture. Boston: Unwin Hyman, 1989.

Heilman, Elizabeth E. Ed. Harry Potter's World: Multidisciplinary Critical Perspectives. New York: RoutledgeFalmer, 2003.
Nachbar, Jack, Deborah Weiser, and John Wright. Eds. The Popular Culture Reader. Ohio: Bowling Green University Popular Press, 1978.

Anne Frances N. Sangil is Assistant Professor in the Department of Literature at De La Salle University where she teaches film criticism, popular culture, art appreciation, and Philippine and world literatures. She is currently writing her dissertation on Filipino filmmaker Mike de Leon and auteur theory for a Ph.D. in Literature. Ms. Sangil is also a member of Popular Culture Association, and presently serves as circulation manager of the new internationally refereed journal American Studies-Asia *published by DLSU Press Inc.*

Harry Potter vs. Other Fantasy Novels

Andrew Seeger

Well, the wait is finally over, and Book 5, *Harry Potter and the Order of the Phoenix*, is out. Many avid readers have undoubtedly already finished this latest tome of Harry and friends' latest exploits, but the wait has been excruciating, forcing Potter fans to be patient . . . and to perhaps see what else was out there while they were waiting for the next volume to be published.

Authors and publishers have gladly done what they could to fill this void in the months between J. K. Rowling's novels, and while there have been numerous pale imitations, there have also been numerous worthy efforts made in the field of children's literature. With the overwhelming success of the Harry Potter novels and films, there have been a vast number of new books aimed at the same core audience. Some of these are by well-established children's authors, some by new writers, and some by authors best known for adult-oriented fare who are now taking their shot at a new market. Furthermore, there have been changes in the market and reception of such works, with fancier (and more expensive) versions of books being published. In the face of all these developments, there have also been changes made to the established bestseller lists.

One of the marvels of the Harry Potter novels which is the reading craze they brought about. It has often been discussed by the media how these books have turned children of all ages back to reading amidst all of the high-tech distractions of movies, television, the internet, and videogames. Droves of fans have shown up for midnight sales of the latest volumes in the Potter saga, and in the meantime, children (and adults alike) have been discovering other books and other authors. While there have naturally been some poor imitations and rip-offs by second-rate hack writers, there have also been some shining examples of good books. While it could be debated to what extent, if any, the books discussed here, or any others, have been influenced by Pottermania, there's no denying that these writers have an excellent sense of timing. And if there is any hint of imitation, that is, after all, the sincerest form of flattery.

This presentation will examine this phenomenon and some of the books that have appeared in the wake of J. K. Rowling's novels, including Lemony Snicket's *A Series of Unfortunate Events* series, Eion Colfer's *Artemis Fowl* books, Cornelia Funke's *The Thief Lord*, and Clive Barker's *Abarat*. While there are also examples I could have discussed by Alice Hoffmann, Amelia Atwater-Rhodes, Joyce Carol Oates, Isabel Allende, Michael Chabon, and others, time only allows for a few, so I have chosen some of what I consider to be the best.

*   *   *

Once a mainstay of children's literature, orphans are now back in style. The surviving son of Lily and James Potter has brought back the tradition of novels dealing with the exploits of an orphan, albeit a wizardly one. As in many of the books of yore, this parentless protagonist must overcome all kinds of neglect and mistreatment to find his own way in this world. As we all know, Harry has endured all kinds of horrible things while growing up in the home of his uncle, aunt, and cousin.

In a similar vein, Lemony Snicket's *A Series of Unfortunate Events* books chronicle the trials and tribulations of the Baudelaire orphans—Violet, Klaus, and Sunny—as they are shuttled from one family to another, beginning with their distant relative, the sinister Count Olaf, who tries to steal the family fortune which the orphans are to inherit. When the nefarious plot is discovered, the children are rescued at the last moment, primarily by their own ingenuiety and luck, and in no way thanks to the efforts of the inept Mr. Poe, the executor of their parents' will. In subsequent books, the children are brought to the homes of various people who agree to take them in, sometimes well-meaning but flawed individuals, other times Count Olaf and his cohorts. In each book, the Count uses all means of trickery and deceit to come at the Baudelaire fortune.

At first glance, *The Bad Beginning* and the other volumes of *A Series of Unfortunate Events* might seem quite derivative of the Potter novels. On the cover picture, Klaus looks like a Harry wannabe, with his round spectacles. The three Baudelaire siblings could also be compared to the trio of Harry, Hermione, and Ron, but these books are original in both their stories and their characters—even if Violet and Hermione do share a love for books.

Utterly unlike the Potter novels, Lemony Snicket's books are written in a rather tongue-in-cheek style, while still drawing the reader in and making him or her care really about the fate of the Baudelaire children. The back cover of each book has a letter from the author, warning potential readers of the unhappy events, such as the following (*The Bad Beginning*, back cover):

Dear Reader,

I'm sorry to say that the book you are holding in your hands is extremely unpleasant. It tells an unhappy tale about three very unlucky children. Even though they are charming and clever, the Baudelaire siblings lead lives filled with misery and woe. From the very first page of this book when the children are at the beach and receive terrible news, continuing on through the entire story, disaster lurks at their heels. One might say they are magnets for misfortune.

In this short book alone, the three youngsters encounter a greedy and repulsive villain, itchy clothing, a disastrous fire, a plot to steal their fortune, and cold porridge for breakfast.

> It is my sad duty to write down these unpleasant tales, but there is nothing stopping you from putting this book down at once and reading something happy, if you prefer that sort of thing.
>
> With all due respect,
> Lemony Snicket

A further characteristic unique to these books is the author's defining of possibly unfamiliar words. This is done in a humorous manner as well, so that even readers who understand the words can enjoy it, such as the following example from Book 2, *The Reptile Room* (79):

> All afternoon, the three children had sat and worried in the Reptile Room, under the moc   king stare of Stephano and the oblivious—the word "oblvious" here means "not aware that Stephano was really Count Olaf and thus being in a great deal of danger"—chatter of Uncle Monty.

Finally, the books in *A Series of Unfortunate Events* have no magical or supernatural occurrences at all. In fact, the children usually figure out all of the Count and his gang's schemes, as well as how they were pulled off, much like an Ann Radcliffe novel or a Scooby-Doo episode.

Another tale of orphans is Cornelia Funke's *The Thief Lord*, in which brothers Prospero and Bo run away to Venice after the death of their parents. Their only living relative is their aunt, Esther Hartlieb, their mother's sister, who only wants to adopt the younger child, Bo, as she really only wants a cute little cherub to raise. She has no real love or affection for either of her nephews, much like a certain family we all know at number four, Privet Drive.

Beyond this similiarity, however, *The Thief Lord*, a novel originally in German, shares little in common with the Potter novels. Sure, there's the close-knit friendship that Prosper and Bo develop with a gang of thieves, which includes a clever girl, Hornet, but otherwise this is the tale of a bunch of kids surviving on the streets of Venice, eluding a detective who is searching for Bo on behalf of his aunt, and various other exploits.

Magic doesn't seem to play a part in the story, at least not until halfway through the book, when the young thieves discover that the object they've been contracted to steal is the missing part to a legendary and supposedly magical carousel. However, this is the only appearance of magic in the entire book, and its significance is relatively small, even if it does have a great effect on several of the characters.

Unlike the Potter novels and *A Series of Unfortunate Events* books, *The Thief Lord* seems to be a stand-alone book with little likelihood of further volumes. The same cannot be said of Eion Colfer's *Artemis Fowl*, a series which already consists three books.

Artemis Fowl is also a young thief, a twelve-year-old mastermind. He is not an orphan, exactly, but at the beginning of the first book, we find out that his father, the patron of a crime family, is missing, and his distraught mother is bedridden, a nervous wreck since her husband's disappearance. Thus he is able to act on his own accord, like the orphans in *The Thief Lord*, and must figure many things out without the help of his parents, like the protagonists in all of the other books. Also, like Harry Potter, he seems to have singularly amazing abilities, which the prologue of the first book hints at (1):

> How does one describe Artemis Fowl? Various psychiatrists have tried and failed. The main problem is Artemis's own intelligence. He bamboozles every test thrown at him. He has puzzled the greatest medical minds, and sent many of them gibbering to their own hospitals.
>
> There is no doubt that Artemis is a child prodigy. But why does someone of such brilliance dedicate himself to criminal activities? This is a question that can be answered by only one person. And he delights in not talking.

This tale of thievery is rife with magic, beginning in the first chapter where Artemis and his faithful servant/bodyguard, Butler, travel to Ho Chi Minh City to obtain a copy of a fairy's Book. His plan to obtain a bunch of fairy gold using secrets from this magical tome goes awry, and he comes up against the LEPrecon Unit, a police force of the supernatural world.

Like the Potter novels, there is some more base humor, such as the description of how Mulch Diggums, a tunnel dwarf, burrows through earth and rock. He unhinges his jaw to eat through the ground, and without getting too explicit here, let me just say that there is also a way that he expells said earth and rock out of his system. There is also plenty of wordplay, similar to Rowling's books, with magical items and forces, as in the name of the police force of the magical realm (31-33):

> Holly Short was lying in bed, silently fuming. Nothing unusual about this. Leprechauns in general were not known for their geniality. But Holly was in an exceptionally bad mood, even for a fairy. Technically she was an elf, fairy being a general term. She was a leprechaun too, but that was just a job.
>
> . . .
>
> The fairy suited up, zipping the dull-green jumpsuit up to her chin and strapping on her helmet. LEPrecon uniforms were stylish these days. Not like that top-o'-the-morning costume the force had to wear

back in the old days. Buckled shoes and knickerbockers! Honestly. No wonder leprechauns were such ridiculous figures in human folkore. Still, probably better that way. If the Mud People knew that the word "leprechaun" actually originated from LEPrecon, an elite branch of the Lower Elements Police, they'd probably take steps to stamp them out. Better to stay inconspicuous and let the humans have their stereotypes.

Besides offering often amusing descriptions of things of the supernatural world, the *Artemis Fowl* books also share with the Potter books the two overlapping worlds of our everyday, mundane exisitence, and a magical realm. In spite of these similarities, however, the books do not seem to have copied all that much out of Potter's world, other than that they feature a young hero—or in this case, something of an anti-hero (he is a criminal mastermind, after all)—who ventures into a magical world unseen by most people.

The last book I wish to consider is the first in a series, even though that only becomes clear once on has finished the first book. This is Clive Barker's *Arabat*. While this is not his first foray into children's literature (that was *The Thief of Always*), it does seem to have more in common with the Potter novels.

Candy Quackenbush, the main character, isn't an orphan, but she often wishes she were rid of the parents she has. Her father is an an unemployed and abusive alcoholic, and her mother simply tries to stay out of his way. Neither one pays much attention to Candy, so she has no qualms leaving them behind when the mysterious Sea of Izabella suddenly appears on the plains outside of her hometown of Chickentown, Minnesota.

Like Harry, Candy quickly adjusts to all of the amazing places she visits and magical beings she meets, including her very first encounter with someone from the Arabat (45):

> Candy let out a yelp of shock at the sight of the stranger. And then, once the shock had worn off, she started to laugh. The man—whoever he was—was wearing some kind of Halloween mask, or so it seemed. What other explanation could there be for his freakish appearance? His left eye was round and wild, while his right was narrow and sly, and his mouth, framed by a black mustache and beard, was downturned in misery.
>
> But none of this was as odd as what sprouted from the top of his head. There were large downy ears, and above them two enormous antlers, which would have resembled those of a stag except that there were seven heads (four on the left horn, three on the right) growing from them. Heads with eyes, noses and mouths.
>
> . . . These heads sprouting from the antlers were *alive*, and they were all staring at Candy the way their owner was staring at her: eight pairs of eyes all studying her with the same manic intensity.

Once Candy crosses the Sea of Izabella and arrives in the Abarat, a vast archipelago where every island is a different hour of the day, she is faced with an overwhelming number of incredible creatures. Anyone familiar with Barker's œuvre knows his wild imagination, such as in the *Hellraiser* films (or books they are based on). Besides being a talented writer he is also a gifted artist, and the books contains over 100 paintings illustrating the beings and places Candy finds in the Abarat.

Later into the novel, it becomes apparent that Candy has some inherent magical ability, much like Harry Potter. She is able to help in conjuring a glyph to escape without ever having studied the wizardly arts, and when she does so, it feels natural to her, almost as if she had done it before. However, Candy's adventures seem to harken back to fantasy novels where the otherwordly hero, or heroine, suddenly appears to save the world.

*   *   *

All of the books that I have considered here share some affinity with the Potter novels, and all of them have been very popular, presumably with many of the same people who have been reading Rowling's books. Most bear the mark of the Potter influence, although none are simple copies, like some books that have popped up around the world (http://politics.slate.msn.com/id/2084960):

> If you're a serious Harry Potter fan, you finished *The Order of the Phoenix* over the weekend and are already impatient for the sixth book. While you wait (and wait) for it, how about trying some of the international versions of Potter? In China last year, it was easy to buy the unusual Potter sequel *Harry Potter and Leopard-Walk-Up-to-Dragon*, in which Harry encountered sweet and sour rain, became a hairy troll, and joined Gandalf to re-enact scenes from *The Hobbit*. The book, while credited to J.K. Rowling, wasn't authorized or written by her, but that didn't prevent it from selling like butterbeer.

This online article goes on to describe other shameless plagiaristic endeavours, some of which have actually sold well before running into something called copyright law, including the Russian tale of Harry's Slavic twin, *Tanya Grotter and the Magic Double Bass*. "Tanya rides a double bass, sports a mole instead of a bolt of lightning, and attends the Tibidokhs School of Magic" (ibid). This book has already sold over a million copies!

Regardless of the intrinsic value and/or literary quality of these knock-offs, there is no denying that they are shamelessly cashing in on the Harry Potter craze. The books that I have discussed here, however, bear the mark of Potter without carrying any shame of cheap imitation. They are tales worthy of sharing shelf space with Rowling's novels and can help fill that seeming eternity as we eagerly await Book Six.

Works Cited

Barker, Clive. *Abarat*. New York: HarperCollins Children's Books, 2002.

Colfer, Eoin. *Artemis Fowl*. New York: Hyperion Books for Children, 2002.

Funke, Cornelia. *The Thief Lord*. New York: Scholastic, 2002.

Snicket, Lemony. *The Bad Beginning* (Book 1). New York: Harper Collins, 1999.

Snicket, Lemony. *The Reptile Room* (Book 2). New York: Harper Collins, 1999.

Wu, Tim. *Harry Potter and the International Order of Copyright: Should* Tanya Grotter and the Magic Double Bass *be banned?*
(http://politics.slate.msn.com/id/2084960)

Andrew Seeger is a graduate student and doctoral candidate in Modern Languages & Literatures at the University of Nebraska in Lincoln. He is currently finishing up his dissertation on connections between English & German Gothic literature of the late 18th and early 19th centuries. He intends to graduate with a Ph.D. (German, Spanish & English) in December 2003. He is also finishing his first year in a tenure-track position as an Assistant Professor of International Studies at Auburn University in Montgomery, Alabama.

His many interests include literature and film of many different genres, including fantasy, science fiction, horror, gothic, and comics. He has given presentations on many different aspects of the Fantastic at conferences in Atlanta, Boston, and Fort Lauderdale, on topics as diverse as Kafka, Borges, Lovecraft, Stephen King, J.K. Rowling, "Buffy", and the "X-Files."

Platform 9-3/4 and Sundry Barriers: Ontological Displacements in the Harry Potter Series

Sudha Shastri

'But Hogwarts *is* hidden,' said Hermione, in surprise, 'everyone knows that . . . well, everyone who's read *Hogwarts: A History*, anyway.'

'Just you, then,' said Ron. 'So go on—how d'you hide a place like Hogwarts?'

'It's bewitched,' said Hermione. 'If a Muggle looks at it, all they see is a mouldering old ruin with a sign over the entrance saying DANGER, DO NOT ENTER, UNSAFE'.

(*Harry Potter and the Goblet of Fire*, 148)

As the title of my paper suggests, I propose to pursue some ontological interpretations of the wall(k)-through barrier to Platform 9-3/4, which is the starting point for not only Harry's journeys to Hogwarts School of Witchcraft and Wizardry, but also the various adventures in his growth as a wizard. The ostensible wall that becomes a doorway into a world of wonder and awe—co-existing invisibly with the world of Muggles—is an appropriate trope for J.K. Rowling to create her own brand of magic: magic that makes the impossible possible, by straining limits so that they give way to another, presumably richer, dimension of experience.

At the outset let me define 'ontological displacement' as I deploy it in this paper. Ontological displacement occurs whenever a world is projected whose laws of Physics flout those of the phenomenological world (of Muggles) with impunity. To take an instance, the unidirectional movement of time in the sequence Past—> Present—> Future is natural to the Muggle-world. The creation of an event or situation wherein this sequence can be reversed or changed in any other way is an ontological displacement, and it produces an ontological disorientation for the reader.

Platform number 9-3/4 is thus, for the purposes of my argument, a launch pad for a close look at the operation of ontological borders/boundaries/barriers in the *Harry Potter* series and the ways in which these barriers are overcome. A related question that I shall ask is: to what effects are ontological margins unsettled? Some of the effects that I shall examine are semantic (the ways in which we as readers create meaning out of these phenomena; the meaning is usually symbolic) while other effects are narratological (the ways in which narrative counters like plot or narrative perspective are affected).

MOVING PHOTOS AND PORTRAITS

An early indication of the collapse of the wall between the two ontologically incompatible realms of Muggles and Magicians comes in the moving photographs that amaze Harry (and the reader, who identifies with Harry). This happens soon after Harry has taken the train from Platform 9-3/4. Seated aboard the Hogwarts' Express, and in the process of making friends with Ronald Weasley, Harry picks up a pack of Chocolate Frogs and chooses a card from the pack. He finds himself staring at a man's face on the back of the card, with half-moon glasses, a long crooked nose and silver beard and hair. This, he learns, is the picture of Albus Dumbledore, the Headmaster of Hogwarts. Harry turns the card over and reads the write-up describing Dumbledore as "the greatest wizard of modern times", "particularly famous for his defeat of the dark wizard Grindelwald in 1945" among other achievements, and a lover of "chamber music and tenpin bowling" (77). When Harry turns the card over he finds "to his astonishment, that Dumbledore's face had disappeared" (77). The reader, who is as surprised as Harry, is familiarised with the physics of the world of magic as Ron responds nonchalantly: "Well, you can't expect him to hang around all day" (77).

The motif of moving pictures reappears in the newspaper photographs accompanying the reports on the attack on Gringotts' bank, and later in the photo album gifted to Harry by Hagrid. This motif continues in *The Prisoner of Azkaban*, where Percy accuses Ron of having dropped tea on the photo of his girlfriend, Penelope. "She's hidden her face under the frame because her nose has gone all blotchy . . . " (56). And in *The Order of the Phoenix*, Mad-Eye Moody urges the people in the back row of a photograph to come forward so that Harry can take a good look at them (158).

For the reflective reader, combined with amazement is the knowledge that the phenomenon of ontological disorientation is arguably the most effective means of producing magic. We are introduced to the domain of magic as a world where photographic images move freely and independently within their frames, much as their real-life originals do in life, but without a one-to-one correspondence between each other.

How are we supposed to respond to ontological disorientations such as the above? What questions do we ask in our endeavour to understand the laws of this new world? What would be relevant, and what, irrelevant questions?

At first glance, Ron's comment seems to suggest that Dumbledore is actually there on the reverse of the card. If he is, then can he see Harry as well? Is the process of 'seeing', two-way?

The answer seems to be a loud affirmative in *The Order of the Phoenix*, where the portrait of Sirius Black's mother, now dead, shrieks aloud when alerted to the presence of the members of the Order of the Phoenix. All it takes to rouse her from her 'still' portrait self to one of hoarse yelling is a noisy disturbance. She is difficult to quieten, as Lupin and Mrs Weasley discover when they "tried to tug the curtains shut over the old woman, but they would not close and she screeched louder than ever, brandishing clawed hands as though trying to tear at their faces" (74). She saves her more choice abuses for her son whenever her eye falls on him, for she considers him "the shame of her flesh" (74) for consorting with Muggle-lovers. Push the logic a little ahead, and we are faced with the frightening question, 'what if she tells (anyone who counts, say Fudge) about the Order?' Rowling does not pursue this line of reasoning in the plot, but an actively imaginative reader can find a source of suspense herein.

The issue of seeing is a relevant question, since sight is one of the main faculties that is subjected to ontological displacement by Rowling. The magical world can exist because the Muggle-world cannot see it. Take Number 12, Grimmauld Place, in *The Order of the Phoenix*. Or the epigraph to this paper. I will come back to this idea at the end of my presentation.

So, is Dumbledore actually there? Or is it just his image? What does being an image mean within the ontological scheme of *Harry Potter*, since clearly it does not mean the same thing that it does to us Muggles? Is an image interchangeable with its original?

If Dumbledore is not 'himself' there on the back of the card, then a characteristically Muggle question might be: 'which of the two is the *real* Dumbledore?'—a question that would come very naturally into the mind of a reader who has read *The Goblet of Fire*, and knows that the resolution of the plot of this book rests on raising this question with respect to Alastor (Mad-Eye) Moody.

Rowling implicitly addresses this question—of real and counterfeit—when she shows the images as being authentic to the spirit of their originals. Inside the world of *Harry Potter*, then, this is what it means to speak of an image as though it were real. So for instance, in *The Chamber of Secrets*, vain Professor Gilderoy Lockhart 's office is 'adorned' by his photographs. As Harry enters the office, he notices "a flurry of movement across the walls; [Harry] saw several of the Lockharts in the pictures, dodging out of sight, *their hair in rollers*" (emphasis mine, 107). Later, Harry's photographic 'self' resists the attempts of Lockhart's photographic 'self' to drag it into centre-stage of the photo. Presumably, then, the images are likely to behave in a manner in which their originals typically behave. But the images are not themselves interchangeable with the originals.

By logical extension, the figures in the portraits are also mobile like the photographic images. A portrait of the Fat Lady guards the Gryffindor Common Room. *The Philosopher's Stone* features a scene where Hermione goes out at night to warn Harry and Ron, but is unable to come back in, as the Fat Lady has gone on a night-time visit; and Hermione finds herself facing an empty painting (116). In *The Prisoner of Azkaban* the Fat Lady flees when Sirius Black attacks her; note how the ontological divide is thrown up between 'real' (life) and 'picture' (image) in the words used to describe her recovery. She is reported to be "expertly restored" (199)—a verb natural to the world of art rather than life.

During her brief absence in this book, the portrait of Sir Cadogan occupies the Watchdog's post. Sir Cadogan has made an earlier appearance in the same book while helping Harry, Ron and Hermione find their way to Professor Trelawney's first Divination class. Offering to act as their guide, he leaps enthusiastically from portrait to portrait, causing, expectably, confusion and alarm *within* these other portraits, as he charges across. Harry and his friends follow him from this side of the ontological frame.

Sir Cadogan belongs to the world of magical art, which makes it natural for him to jump from one painting frame to another, reappearing "in front of an alarmed group of women in crinolines, whose picture hung on the wall of a narrow spiral staircase" and so on until finally "popping his head into a painting of some sinister-looking monks" (*The Prisoner of Azkaban* 78).

In *The Order of the Phoenix*, it is a medieval Healer who pursues Ron in St. Mungo's hospital. Asserting that Ron has "a bad case of spattergroit", "the Healer pursued him through six more portraits, shoving the occupants out of the way" (449).

JOURNEYS INTO MIND AND MEMORY

Moving images and portrait figures thus indicate a failure of ontological boundaries to restrict. The fluidity that they symbolise is taken a step further by Rowling in creating larger ontological violations, which produce the effect of magic through journeys into the mind and memory.

The two ontological adventures I wish to consider under this rubric are Harry's visits to the worlds of:

a) Tom Riddle's memory via his diary in *The Chamber of Secrets*, and
b) Dumbledore's reflections and Snape's memory via the Pensieve in *The Goblet of Fire* and *The Order of the Phoenix* respectively.

Harry's entry into Riddle's memory through the diary in *The Chamber of Secrets*, engineered by Riddle himself, is an experience calculated to mislead him. Riddle 'lives Harry through' a scene where Hagrid is seen to be nurturing a monster in his room, which Riddle tries to destroy. Riddle thus 'selects' a 'memory' for Harry, which, if Harry were to believe on the strength of his sensory impressions (and not discriminated by his own knowledge of Hagrid's character) would invert the truth and result in Voldemort's triumph.

The Very Secret Diary of Tom Riddle which engineers the plot of *The Chamber of Secrets* is slipped into Ginny Weasley's cauldron by Lucius Malfoy at the beginning of the story; through this diary, Riddle aka Lord Voldemort takes possession of Ginny

Weasley's mind—and later her body and soul. Eventually the diary finds its way into Harry's possession. At first the diary seems unexciting, with nothing but blank pages. However as Harry starts writing in it, it—or rather Tom Riddle—writes back to him. Within minutes Riddle tells Harry that in his schooldays at Hogwarts, the chamber of secrets had indeed been opened, that he had caught the person who had opened it, and that the person had been expelled. Riddle adds that Harry need not take his word for it, that Harry can see for himself what happened on that night.

In one of the most brilliant ontological sleights-of-hand in the *Harry Potter* series, Rowling transports Harry from the magical world of Hogwarts into the world of the mind, by giving him access into the mind of Riddle, albeit at Riddle's discretion. Harry's journey into the memory of Riddle enables Rowling to take the narrative to symbolic levels, where the essentially abstract notion that the past can cast long shadows, and the positive value of the need to be rid of a potentially dangerous past, are conveyed as important messages to the reader. Ontological displacement enables Rowling to transfer concepts and values from the realm of abstractions to the realm of events. And Harry's literal visit to the past is appropriately made through the memoir, the genre that represents memory.

So the moral is: memory, if fed repeatedly, can cause a 'coming-back-to-life'; such is the power of thought. Ginny unwittingly performs the task of insistent recall for Tom Riddle, which enables him to emerge into Harry's world through the frame of the diary. While it is true that Harry has the advantage of viewing the past from the future, when he 'enters' the memory that Riddle chooses for him, his questionable advantage ends there. Harry's participation in this past becomes self-destructive, not just because it is scripted by Riddle, who assigns to him the role of 'fooled spectator', but also because in the larger sense, Harry is divorced from the continuity and flow of time which confers meaning on events. Having seen just the part where Hagrid has secreted a monstrous animal, Harry can be pardoned for initially believing that Hagrid had access to the chamber of secrets. This is just what Tom Riddle wants him to believe.

To make a semantic extrapolation from this episode, then, Harry's ontological excursion in *The Chamber of Secrets* is a test: of his wits, his faith in Hagrid, and his own ability to discriminate; which he passes, despite having been totally at Riddle's mercy.

The interestingly named 'Pensieve' in *The Goblet of Fire* imaginatively charts another ontological boundary between the reality of the phenomenological world and the reality of the mind, where the thoughts and musings (pensés) of Dumbledore become accessible to Harry with the clarity and reality-effect of personal experience. While waiting in Dumbledore's office for him to return from inspecting the school grounds, Harry finds a stone basin with odd carvings around the edge; he does not know it yet, but this basin is the equivalent of Tom Riddle's diary, and will draw him into its world as effortlessly as Riddle's diary did.

There is this difference, though; Riddle meant to lure Harry and trap him for his own devious purposes; the Pensieve however has no ulterior motives. It merely 'happens' to present to him the various trials conducted by Barty Crouch (Senior) in his attempts to convict the Death Eaters. It simultaneously functions as coincidence within the plot, as Harry witnesses the trial of young Barty Crouch, who, posing as Mad-Eye Moody, is his deadliest enemy in this book.

A curious Harry looks into the Pensieve, "expecting to see the stone bottom of the basin—and saw instead an enormous room below the surface of the mysterious substance" (*The Goblet of Fire* 507). As he leans further, his nose makes contact with the substance in the basin, Dumbledore's office gives "an almighty lurch" (508), and Harry is thrown forward and sucked into a dark whirlpool which gives way to a bench on which he finds himself seated, a spectator of the trials.

Of the three trials that Harry sees, the most vital to his own understanding is that of young Barty Crouch. He sees Barty condemned, and taken away by the Dementors. In other words, what he witnesses is a corroboration of the public knowledge about young Barty Crouch, which is that he is taken back to Azkaban—and dies there. That young Barty is not dead but active in a most evil manner is the knowledge that will help Harry in this book, but this knowledge is not only denied to him, the opposite of this knowledge is reinforced. As in the case of Riddle's diary, Harry is not allowed to gain practically from his experience in the Pensieve, since what he sees only seems to reinforce the death of young Crouch. At best, then, this episode only helps him identify the impostor Moody as Barty Junior, when the effect of the Polyjuice potion wears off.

Thus, Harry's experience in the two foregoing instances (Riddle's dairy and Dumbledore's recollections) takes him towards a higher domain of knowledge, which, however, he seems unable to access and implement in a practical manner, and which in fact appears to lead him astray.

Whereas, Harry's foray into the Pensieve in Snape's office in *The Order of the Phoenix* becomes an eye-opening experience of a mortifying nature. While learning Occlumency, Harry travels into the Pensieve in Snape's absence only to see, for himself, that his father James was just the insensitive, vain and arrogant man that Snape always accused him of being. This is one experience that Harry will not forget in a hurry, since it involves a drastic re-assessment of the important people in his life: his parents, his godfather and his most-hated teacher, Professor Snape.

How do these instances of ontological skewing affect the narrative? Plot-wise, the instances from *The Chamber of Secrets* and *The Goblet of Fire* contain the seeds of an alternative direction to the progression of the story, raising questions such as: could Hagrid have opened the Chamber of Secrets? After all, he does have a monster-fixation; and he was expelled from Hogwarts. It seems to fit. However Rowling eventually rules out this likely detour in the plot of *The Chamber of Secrets*. With the Pensieve, what she does is to give the narrative an entirely new uncharted path to pursue (young Barty Crouch did not die, after all), and uses the episode to fool the reader (along with Harry, who are for the main part together) by ostensibly reaffirming Barty's death. As for *The Order of the Phoenix*, the Pensieve reaffirms (for the reader) Dumbledore's faith in

Snape, by revealing the vulnerabilities that he has not quite recovered from, so much so that he needs to hide them from Harry.

TIME AND AGAIN

A more proactive control over time is enabled for Harry in *The Prisoner of Azkaban*. By far the most ontologically resistant barrier that Harry successfully overcomes with Hermione's help is that of time. If *The Chamber of Secrets* disrupts temporal ontologies by allowing Voldemort's past to catch up with Harry's present through memory, the reverse is achieved in *The Prisoner of Azkaban*, where the present takes a trip back to the past, makes the necessary alterations, and comes back to itself. Going back in time to set things right—which is also the philosophy advocated by Dumbledore of giving a second chance—is not only the ultimate fantasy; it is arguably the most empowering possibility presented to mankind, if used with integrity, and the most constructive of promises held out by ontological collapsing.

Within the world of magic, the flow of time seems largely to obey the same rules as it does in the Muggle world, barring a few isolated exceptions. Until, that is, Rowling brings the time-turner into *The Prisoner of Azkaban*. Hermione uses it routinely for all of a year to attend all the courses she has signed up for, whose timetables would otherwise conflict. But the dramatic potential of the time-turner comes to the fore only when she and Harry turn to it in a final, desperate bid to rescue Sirius Black from the Dementors.

The drama begins after Macnair has ostensibly executed Buckbeak, and Sirius has been locked in Professor Flitwick's office to await the kiss of the Dementors. Harry and Hermione frantically assert that Sirius is innocent, but only Dumbledore is willing to believe them. Even he, however, is unable to help them in any way, beyond telling them that they need more time. It is up to Hermione and Harry then, to go back in time to before Buckbeak's execution, so that they can rescue it, and use it in turn to rescue Sirius.

Fraught with great excitement, the return to three hours past (back to 8:55 p.m. from 11:55 p.m. on the sixth of June) in order to undo some acts, and complete some that were left undone, transforms the sombre and gloomy mood of the narrative to an upbeat one. Since Buckbeak's execution was not seen by Harry and his friends, but only inferred by them from the sound of the executioner's swing of the axe (which, it appears when they return to the past, was a swish in anger at the escape of the beast), the retrieval of Buckbeak alive into the narrative is achieved credi(ta)bly by Rowling.

Besides turning a story heading for a tragic resolution to one with a happy ending, this ontological disruption through time is also used by Rowling to dispel a mystery created in the first account of the three hours from Buckbeak's execution to Sirius's imprisonment. The first time round, Harry is unable to fight the Dementors off with his feeble Patronus and reconciles himself to their kiss when all of a sudden, he sees someone send a very powerful Patronus across the lake, which chases the Dementors away. The second time round when Harry relives this segment of his past (from the other side of the lake), he is extremely curious to see who sent that Patronus, for the figure had looked so very familiar that he had supposed it to be his dead father, James Potter.

Making sure that he does not violate the time-turning rule about not being seen, Harry runs as fast as he can to the edge of the lake, hoping to catch a glimpse of his father.

> But no one came. Harry raised his head to look at the circle of Dementors across the lake. One of them was lowering its hood. It was time for the rescuer to appear—but no one was coming to help this time—
>
> And then it hit him—he understood. He hadn't seen his father—he had seen himself—
>
> Harry flung himself out from behind the bush and pulled out his wand.
>
> 'EXPECTO PATRONUM!' he yelled.
>
> (The Prisoner of Azkaban 300)

As Dumbledore would say later in the same book, of the bond between Harry and Wormtail, "This is magic at its deepest, its most impenetrable" (311).

One of the most ontologically challenging ideas that this event throws up is that of the past containing the seeds of an alternative future—of, in fact, several parallel futures. The first time that Harry faces the Dementors, the course of events leads to the capture of Sirius Black and, one assumes, his inevitable death. And yet, it appears that time works in a circular fashion, because, already, an event from the 'second-time' experience has INSERTed itself into this 'first-time' experience. Indeed the former's presence is integral to the latter; which is paradoxical, to say the least; not to add illogical and mind-boggling, since the two time-sequences lead to completely different endings. For one, the second-time sequence of events vetoes a very important event of the first-time experience by enabling the escape of Buckbeak from Macnair. Yet the two sequences also seem to draw from each other by intersecting at vital nodes.

SPACE

"Time and space matter in magic, Potter," says Snape in *The Order of the Phoenix* (469). Rowling bends space in her versatile imagination such that the venues of magic lie adjacent to the most ordinary Muggle venues. Indeed, what makes the ontological dislocations so fascinating in the *Harry Potter* series is Rowling's suggestion that the world of magic is found *within* the world of restrictive reason, and overlaps it in the unlikeliest places. A disused telephone booth, with several missing planes of glass, is, as Harry finds, the entry point to the Ministry of Magic. When Mr. Weasley dials the number, the "floor of the telephone box shuddered. They were sinking slowly into the ground. Harry watched apprehensively as the pavement seemed to rise up past the glass windows of the telephone box until darkness closed over their heads" (*The Order of the Phoenix* 116).

Similarly, the entrance to St Mungo's Hospital is guarded by a dummy in a deserted department store called Purge & Dowse Ltd. A Muggle woman passing by is heard to remark to her friend, that this place is "never open" (*The Order of the Phoenix* 427). But when Tonks whispers to the dummy, she gets a tiny nod in return. "Harry glanced around at the jostling crowd; not one of them seemed to have a glance to spare for window displays as ugly as those of Purge & Dowse Ltd; nor did any of them seem to have noticed that six people had just melted into thin air in front of them" (*The Order of the Phoenix* 427). Thus Rowling tantalises the child in her reader by hinting that if we cannot see magic, it is quite our fault.

Place in the world of wizardry is an idea, oftentimes. When Harry needs a room to conduct his classes in defence against the dark arts, Dobby tells him about the Room of Requirement. It is located behind a wall, and would appear to anyone who walked past the wall three times, *concentrating hard on what they needed*. Harry and his friends follow Dobby's instructions and find, on their third round, that a highly polished door had appeared in the wall. It opens into a room lined with bookcases, cushions instead of chairs, and shelves with sneakoscopes secrecy sensors and a foe-glass: in short, just the room that the DA needed for their purposes. Rowling also reminds the readers that this room has been foreshadowed in *The Goblet of Fire*, by having Harry recall that Dumbledore had mentioned a room that had filled itself with chamber pots when he had desperately needed a bathroom. Space and magic thus work toward empowerment in the form of a room that adapts its identity to the needs of the person who wants it desperately. And though it is 'behind a wall', it cannot be located on a map, it can only be located on need. "Sometimes it is there, and sometimes it is not, but when it appears, it is always equipped for the seeker's needs" (*The Order of the Phoenix* 343).

Rowling's brand of magic is rarely spectacular display; her magic is subtle. In a perhaps singular instance, the two converge in the death of Sirius in *The Order of the Phoenix*. Sirius is fighting Bellatrix Lestrange in the room with the archway and veil in the Department of Mysteries that had so fascinated Harry, when a jet of light from her wand fells him. As he falls, he falls behind the veil, never to return. Magic here is a combination of the literal and the connotative as Sirius disappears, *with his body*, and rather appropriately, behind what is clearly the veil separating the worlds of life and death.

Earlier, Harry had been curious to see what lay behind the veil, but could see nothing, although he did get the feeling that there was someone behind it while it fluttered continuously.

> 'Can't anyone else hear it?' Harry demanded, for the whispering and murmuring was becoming louder; without really meaning to put it there, he found his foot was on the dais.

> 'I can hear them too,' breathed Luna, joining them around the side of the archway and gazing at the swaying veil. 'There are people *in there*!'

> 'What do you mean, "*in there*"?' demanded Hermione, jumping down from the bottom step and sounding much angrier than the occasion warranted, 'there isn't any "*in there*", it's just an archway, there's no room for anybody to be there. Harry, stop it, come away—'
>
> (*The Order of the Phoenix* 683)

After Sirius dies, only Luna Lovegood, who has also lost a parent, can offer fleeting comfort to Harry at the end of the book to the effect that those whom they loved were there just behind the veil; they had not gone away. As Dumbledore tells Harry in *The Prisoner of Azkaban*, even death cannot take away from us those whom we truly love (312).

OF SIGHT AND INSIGHT

I have thus far endeavoured to show some ontological displacements in the *Harry Potter* series. My list however is by no means exhaustive, but it is time to conclude. I shall end by returning to the role of sight, which I raised in the section on moving figures.

The question whether seeing is two-way is both valid and significant for a study of Rowling's ontological distortions. For it is sight that becomes a major target of innovation in the *Harry Potter* stories. Consider *The Goblet of Fire*, for instance, where Harry watches the drama unfolding inside the Pensieve without a single member of his audience observing his presence. Or *The Chamber of Secrets*, where inside Tom Riddle's diary, Harry is able to watch Riddle, Hagrid and the teachers, but they cannot see him intruding from the future. *The Chamber of Secrets* is an interesting example since here Harry is enabled to watch them because of Riddle's stage-managing of this scene. This phenomenon creates a hierarchy of levels of seeing and knowledge, with worlds embedding and embedded, resulting in a Chinese-box structure.

Rowling endows the faculty of sight with the connotations of power and the effect of magic when she makes it a position of advantage. At the same time, she also proffers the idea that the ability to see is not fluke; it need not be a random distribution of talents, even within the magical world. Seeing is conditioned by experience—so Luna Lovegood and Harry Potter can see the thestrals because they have seen death close at hand.

I shall conclude with an example of ontological displacement of 'seeing' that has both semantic and narratological significance. This is the Fidelius charm, which was used for the protection of Harry's parents from Voldemort. It is, in Professor Flitwick's words,

> 'An immensely complex spell . . . involving the magical concealment of a secret inside a single, living soul. The information is hidden inside the chosen person, or Secret-Keeper . . . As long as the Secret-Keeper refused to speak, You-Know-Who could search the village where Lily and James were staying for years and never find them, *not even if he had his nose pressed against their sitting-room window!'*
> (*The Prisoner of Azkaban*, emphasis mine, 152-53)

Everyone in the magic world mistakenly assumes Sirius Black to have been the Potters' Secret-Keeper, who then betrayed them. It is only at the end of this book that his innocence is proclaimed, and even then only to a small group of people. Larger, ethical issues like loyalty, betrayal and trust are thus prefigured in the implications of 'magical' seeing.

Works Cited

Rowling, J. K. *Harry Potter and the Philosopher's Stone*. London: Bloomsbury, 1997.
_____. *Harry Potter and the Chamber of Secrets*. London: Bloomsbury, 1998.
_____. *Harry Potter and the Prisoner of Azkaban*. London: Bloomsbury, 1999.
_____. *Harry Potter and the Goblet of Fire*. London: Bloomsbury, 2000.
_____. *Harry Potter and the Order of the Phoenix*. London: Bloomsbury, 2003.

Sudha Shastri is currently an Assistant Professor in English in the Department of Humanities and Social Sciences, Indian Institute of Technology, Bombay, India. Her doctoral dissertation on intertextual theory, with specific reference to twentieth-century literary interactions with the Victorian period, was published under the title Intertextuality and Victorian Studies *by Orient Longman in 2001. Her current research interests include postmodern fiction and narratology, besides intertextual operations. Her other main interest is Indian classical music, and she is a trained vocal singer.*

The Hero's Progress: Harry Potter's Discovery of Identity withing J.K. Rowling's Hierarchical World

Alice L. Trupe

An important function of children's literature is its ability to provide a sympathetic hero that children can identify with, enabling them to feel empowered through his or her victories. J. K. Rowling's books may be identified as heroic quests because they bring their hero face to face with a threatening arch-villain who represents evil incarnate. The Harry Potter books may also be classified as school novels, given their setting and the time frame of each novel in the series—although the adventures encountered by heroes in this genre are usually smaller in scale than the archetypal conflicts between good and evil into which Harry is drawn. School novels, however, do present a world that is shaped by and reflects the class values of the larger society in which the school is located, and the Harry Potter series is no exception. Furthermore, school novels present a culture and value system peculiar to the school that is paramount in shaping students' values and loyalties. Harry Potter's heroism, moreover, is enacted within a contemporary multiracial fantasy world in which team sports generate international competition and the media is omnipresent. A complicating factor in Harry's development is his celebrity, which is hidden from him until he sets off for school at age eleven, and his fame generally proves to be more of a handicap than an asset, since it ensures that most of his acts, his blunders, and his emotions attract glaring publicity. The blending of the various elements of the heroic quest, the school novel, and the fantasy genre, within the context of contemporary media-dominated society, thus creates a unique set of circumstances for playing out the heroic conflict between the forces of good and evil within a hierarchical, multiracial world of economic disparity that in some ways espouses egalitarian values and in other ways conserves rigid socioeconomic classes.

From early in the series, Harry's possibilities for agency have seemed limited by the forces that shape his world. In the fourth book, *Harry Potter and the Goblet of Fire*, Harry seems to have few opportunities for real choice; many of his actions are controlled by others, and especially by those allied with the forces of evil. *Harry Potter and the Order of the Phoenix*, in contrast, opens up Harry's scope for action in new ways, despite the efforts of his protectors, masters, and allies to proscribe or circumscribe significant action against evil. A framework for understanding the shifting power relations within Harry Potter's world may be found in Michel Foucault's analysis of power. By examining the ways in which fifteen-year-old Harry and his friends begin to challenge and subvert the institutions that attempt to maintain existing hierarchies and power relations, we may raise some questions as to what the series is telling its readers about the possibilities for heroic action in a world in which power is vested in institutions and groups rather than in good or evil individuals of larger-than-life proportions.

At the outset of the series, Harry Potter embarks on his wizarding career as though experiencing a second birth. Discovery of his true nature and status empowers him, even at age eleven, when he is modest and nervous about his newfound identity, not yet touchy about his status. Discovery of his heritage gives Harry a new conceptual framework for understanding the odd incidents that have accompanied intense emotion. He also learns that he has wealth and fame—in this he resembles one of Dickens' orphans, come to self-discovery along with success—and he finds fellows who share his abilities and mentors who will help him develop them. His life is transformed when he is invited to Hogwarts, just as his sense of self is transformed. Like a hero embarking on a quest, Harry leaves behind the familiar and goes forth to meet new challenges that will initiate him.

However, discovery of his heritage brings Harry a darker body of knowledge as well: his surviving his parents acquires new significance when he learns they were Voldemort's victims rather than accident victims. Dark hints of Voldemort's power and hints of inevitable confrontation engage him in a search for better understanding of his family and wizardry. And furthermore, Harry has stepped into a world of loyalties, prejudices, and power relations that he is ill equipped to understand. Information about his past, his enemy, and his powers is doled out to him in small amounts, almost grudgingly. Moreover, this is a world in which Harry has been a celebrity since infancy, and it is because he is a celebrity, one who is in danger from the arch-evil of his world, that he has been exiled by benevolent authorities from his birthright and subjected to an imprisoning and abusive childhood with those who neither love him, value him, nor tell him the truth. In this world of power struggles, constant surveillance and publicity, and control of knowledge and individual action, Harry makes strenuous efforts to play the hero's part.

Harry embarks on his school career, and his career as Voldemort's nemesis, from a position both privileged and de-privileged. Many aspects of his situation and certain abilities and powers prepare him for hero status. However, many factors hem him in, narrowing the range of actions possible to him:

1) the claustrophobic Wizarding world that has promised new possibilities is a world permeated with surveillance and control, from owls that find one anywhere and portraits that can report on one's activities to Aurors with all-seeing eyes and dementors that feed on one's very emotions;

2) class prejudices, economic inequalities (even ruthless oppression, in the case of House-Elves), and sometimes virulent racism (particularly against Muggles

and mixed-ancestry wizards, half-giants, and werewolves) control social relations within Hogwarts and manipulate its policies and staffing by permeating Hogwarts' supervision, with the Ministry of Magic's playing an ever more conspicuous role;

3) Harry's celebrity status (like J. K. Rowling's) further hems him in: his scar makes him always recognizable (as well as reveals and reminds him of his intimate connection with Voldemort); younger students fascinated with his fame embarrass him, and publicity seekers like Gilderoy Lockhart exploit his fame to advance their own; his emotions, distorted beyond recognition, become public property through the press; and his truth-telling is dismissed as attention-seeking;

4) and access to necessary, useful information is limited: Harry needs to understand ongoing conflicts and alliances shaped by his father's actions, needs to know about prophecies that concern him, needs to understand specific magical tools and weapons, needs to practice magical skills in a school that seems set on withholding knowledge.

Not only do these historical and social factors continually constrain Harry, but a loving network of concerned adults, including the Weasleys, Sirius, Hogwarts teachers, Ministry officials, and the kindly headmaster Dumbledore, attempt to control him and restrict his actions. This benevolent, apparently well-intentioned restriction, in the name of protection, serves only to hamper Harry when the contest between good and evil forces is played out as a contest for control over Harry: Voldemort wants Harry's knowledge, Harry's strength, Harry's mind, Harry's life. Given the importance of the contest, you'd think Harry could at least get a little information! It is no wonder that he has grown angry and frustrated. Yet even when Harry gets special instruction—trained to conjure a Patronus for defense against dementors, scheduled for special lessons in Occlumency—the knowledge he most needs (knowledge of his place in the Wizarding world and the world as a whole) and the skills he needs in order to survive, to protect his mind and body as well as his actions from control and exploitation—vital information is withheld by the most powerful forces in his world.

Thus Harry keeps trying to act the traditional hero, vanquishing evil with the power of good, on the basis of limited knowledge, within a disenchanted postmodern world. Is his heroism mere celebrity? Does he merely enact a hero's role in the glare of publicity—a bit like living in *The Truman Show*? Can he achieve heroic status, succeed in reaching wisdom by winning through the trials set him? Or is Harry's subjectivity the product of an array of forces—political, social, economic, historical—that mold his actions in predictable ways that reproduce existing power relations? Is it possible to *be*, or to *become*, a hero, taking initiative, acting out of talent and resources of character like courage and wisdom?

We can read the Harry Potter series very differently, depending upon whether we see it as an heroic quest with a romantic hero who comes to knowledge and adulthood through a series of escalating challenges that bring the hero back home no longer innocent but fully initiated in adult wisdom or as an updated school story in which the protagonist successfully weathers a series of scrapes that test and mold his courage and character, threatening expulsion as the worst imaginable punishment but ultimately endorsing his class values of daring, resourcefulness, loyalty, and honesty, and affirming bonds of friendship that we anticipate will last for life.

When the fourth book in the series, *Harry Potter and the Goblet of Fire,* was published, it was easy to interpret Harry's position as bound entirely by history—his family's history, his inheritance of magical objects and genetically transmitted athletic ability, his gifts from parents (self-sacrificing love) and his enemy, or evil double (Parseltongue, a mystical linking of minds and powers through wound and wand), as well as a history of uneasy race relations between the Muggle world and the world of magic. One might conclude that the possibilities for heroic action are significantly diminished by the realities of the contemporary, disenchanted world in which this heroic fantasy is set. Harry's actions in *Harry Potter and the Order of the Phoenix,* on the other hand, may incline a reader to look more fully at the school story tradition again, although this updated, postmodern school story plays out in a world of unrelenting publicity and celebrity, surveillance, and contest over what counts as knowledge.

A useful framework for analysis is offered in Michel Foucault's "The Subject and Power." In this essay, Foucault describes power struggles between opposing groups in society, including parents' struggle for control over children, and the relationship between children and their teachers may be seen to be characterized by power struggles. Furthermore, in Harry's world, several adults take a parental role toward him, most noticeably Dumbledore, Sirius Black, and Molly Weasley. Foucault identifies six characteristics of such power struggles.

1) They are "transversal," occurring universally, under any form of government or economic structure. (329-30)

One might, then, find these power struggles in fantasy worlds as well as in the whole range of real-world societies, anywhere where parent-child relationships exist.

2) These struggles have vital effects, in determining who has power over bodies, health, life and death. (Foucault 330)

The struggles in Harry's world revolve around children's living spaces and their safety at home or at large in London or Hogsmeade, and they result in children's near-death [experiences? near-deaths?], paralysis or coma, and even death.

3) The power struggles are "immediate" struggles with those close to the individual, and no ultimate resolution is expected. (Foucault 330)

Harry struggles against his guardians and the Hogwarts teachers who function as parent-substitutes, with no resolution, and this lack of resolution contrasts with his confrontations with Voldemort, which do end somewhat conclusively, however temporarily, in each novel.

4) They "question the status of the individual" and are struggles against institutional control of the process of individualization. (Foucault 330)

Rowling's novels revolve around Harry and his assertion of his individualism, even within the community of wizards in which he is delighted to find himself and an explanation for his difference from the Dursleys.

5) They are "struggles against the privilege of knowledge, . . . an opposition against secrecy, deformation, and mystifying representations imposed" upon subject groups. (Foucault 330-331)

Harry and his friends continually challenge their teachers, parents, and enemies in their quest for knowledge that is withheld from them. From the beginning of the series, Harry seeks information about his past; in each novel, he must grow in skill to confront his enemy, and to do so, he must combat secrecy and disinformation surrounding his and his parents' history and Voldemort's Death-Eaters' past and present machinations.

6) Finally, these power struggles "revolve around the question 'Who are we?'"; the struggle to define identity occurs in challenges institutionally imposed abstractions and definitions. (Foucault 331)

Harry's growth from childhood to young adulthood throughout the series revolves around discovery and formation of identity, often in rebellion against the defining power of his world's institutions.

In J. K. Rowling's series, then, we see that Harry is engaged in the struggle of the young with their elders, both mentors and enemies, for control of knowledge. In order to analyze power relations and understand how power functions within any setting, Foucault tells us, we need to look at the following things:

1) "*The system of differentiations* that permit one to act upon the actions of others";
2) "*The types of objectives* pursued by those who act upon the actions of others";
3) "*Instrumental modes*" of maintaining power (such as the threat of violence, economic disparities, or rules, surveillance, etc.).;
4) "*Forms of institutionalization*" (including traditions, laws, fashions), which may be complex;
5) "*The degrees of rationalization*"; that is, power has processes for expanding, organizing, and achieving change within its specific context. (Foucault 344-45)

As this list suggests, "Power relations are rooted in the whole network of the social." (Foucault 345) The conflict over power and knowledge is clearer in *Harry Potter and the Order of the Phoenix* than in any of the earlier books.

In *Order of the Phoenix*, we see Harry deprived of privacy, disciplined through a formal state trial, and finding his freedom to act both inside and outside of Hogwarts increasingly limited. Both press innuendo and Snape's instruction in Occlumency invade his privacy. He is plagued by nightmares that may or may not bring truth, he is threatened with mind control, and he is seeing things (the frightening bat-winged Thestrals) that perhaps only crazy people see. He is isolated from his friends as they are incorporated into a benevolent protective network that Harry finds smothering, and their achievements and maturity are formally recognized in their appointment as Prefects, creating a significant status gap. Furthermore, his usual opportunities for subversion and the ordinary heroism he achieves on the Quidditch field are circumvented. Rules and laws are created for the specific purpose of barring Harry and other students from access to the knowledge they need to survive in their world as the Ministry of Magic plays its most invasive role to date in Hogwarts' governance. Yet Harry feels impelled to act, finally, whether or not he has sufficient knowledge to act.

And when he acts, Harry seizes the institutional tools for control of knowledge and turns them to his own advantage.

- He uses the Pensieve to acquire additional knowledge of the past.
- At Hermione's instigation, "Harry Potter tells all" to Rita Skeeter, using the power of the press to restore his damaged credibility.
- Harry responds to his friends' request to meet secretly and uses the knowledge he has obtained through experience to train them in wielding their wands to practical purposes rather than accept the limitations imposed on their learning by their teachers.
- He makes use of his wealth, funding Fred and George's rebellion against the constraints of Hogwarts, and he "employs" them to create diversions.
- He literally seizes his fate when he takes control of the prophecy concerning him, and this important action signals the unwillingness of the young to have their destinies controlled by their elders, even though the words of the prophecy are not lost because they are still known to Dumbledore.
- And, ultimately, he forces apology and concession from Dumbledore that love does not entitle caring adults to restrict the knowledge of those dependent on that care, especially when such restriction endangers them.

These actions mark a significant point of departure from Harry's earlier demonstrations of courage and wizarding talent. After all, his earlier successes have come largely through the gifts and help of others: the Invisibility Cloak inherited from his father, Ron's and Hermione's intelligence and steadfast loyalty, the ability to speak

Parseltongue, the phoenix Fawkes' powers, the friendship of Lupin and Sirius, the Marauder's Map, the sometimes misguided efforts of Dobby, the secrets that Hagrid betrays, the bond between Harry's and Voldemort's wands, and even Harry's own inherited physical ability at Quidditch, the stack of inherited gold at Gringotts, and the protection afforded by his mother's love and even his Muggle aunt's family loyalty. While these gifts gave Harry successes in the face of escalating encounters with Voldemort and his minions in the first four books, helping him to play the role of a hero, his more convincing displays of agency come as he learns to use institutional values, policies, and instruments to lead his friends into the very bowels of the institutions and engage in life-and-death struggle without the knowledge or implicit permission of the adults.

In *Harry Potter and the Order of the Phoenix,* then, we see the most significant steps into adulthood. But the adulthood of Harry and his friends is still threatened by the deepening shadow of Voldemort's evil power. Harry must continue to learn as much as he can, as rapidly as he can, to ensure his continued survival, and, while the Minister of Magic's willful blindness has been rebuked in this book, we know that institutions are still in place, and institutions resist dramatic change. But not only will the institutions of Harry Potter's world obstruct heroic action. As Harry and his friends grow in knowledge and sophistication in the ways of their society, there is real danger that they will simply be co-opted and will themselves reproduce the conditions of power, taking their own positions in the existing structures of power and perpetrating their own petty tyrannies over the younger, the weaker, the less privileged. But, if we are optimists and romantics, we may find ourselves hoping that Harry Potter will truly become a hero, not only vanquishing the evil villain but using the power that knowledge brings him to remake the institutions that are shaping him and his friends.

Works Cited

Foucault, Michel. "The Subject and Power." *Power.* Ed. James D. Faubion. Trans. Robert Hurley et al. *Essential Works of Foucault 1954-1984.* Vol. 3. Series ed. Peter Rabinow. New York: The New Press, 2000. 326-48.

Rowling, J. K. *Harry Potter and the Goblet of Fire.* New York: Arthur A. Levine Books, 2000.

_____. *Harry Potter and the Order of the Phoenix.* New York: Arthur A. Levine Books, 2003.

Alice Trupe teaches writing courses and Young Adult literature at Bridgewater College in the Shenandoah Valley of Virginia, where she lives in an old farmhouse with several cats. She has enjoyed fantasy literature since she first learned to read. She also enjoys nineteenth-century novels and Elizabethan drama.

The Heroic Journey and Harry Potter: An Examination of J. K. Rowling's Use of the Monomyth in the Harry Potter Series

Antoinette F. Winstead

Following in the tradition of C. S. Lewis and J. R. R. Tolkien, J. K. Rowling has, through the Harry Potter Series, created a collection of high-adventure and fantasy novels that exemplify the heroic journey as outlined by Joseph Campbell in his book *The Hero with a Thousand Faces*, thus proving her to be a twenty-first century mythmaker. She has modernized the mythic tale and updated the structure and form through which the myth is expressed by setting her stories in a world that is both mythic—full of magical creatures and witches—and realistic—suburban Britain and boarding school, thus creating a world that one can recognize, yet discover at the same time.

To truly appreciate Rowling's talent as a mythmaker, one need only compare her novels to Joseph Campbell's diagram of the mythical adventure. There are three distinct stages of adventure for the mythical hero. They are as follows: the departure, the initiation, and the return. While all parts associated with the three stages are not used, Rowling does typically utilize what Joseph Campbell terms "the Call to Adventure" (49, "the Road of Trials" (97), "the Meeting with the Goddess" (109) and the "the Freedom to Live." Her usage of Campbell's heroic journey is exemplified in *Harry Potter and the Sorcerer's Stone*, the first novel in the Potter Series. Rowling skillfully maneuvers Harry Potter through each stage of this mythical journey, successfully manipulating the archetypal struggle of man against himself so that it reflects the self-identity and coming of age crisis that so many adolescents face by placing it within the larger context of good versus evil, thus creating the adventure.

According to Edward C. Whitmont:

> In order to effect a constructive and lasting change in our lives we
> must strive toward a transformation of potentially disturbing or
> disruptive complexes by reaching their archetypal cores. (73)

This is exactly what the myth does. It forces the hero to change by sending him on a self-finding mission. In fact, the mythical journey, as used by Rowling, is nothing more than a search for inner peace or, in the case of Harry Potter, a search for identity outside of the one imposed on him by society. In order to find his true identity, Harry Potter must embark on a mythic adventure that begins in *Harry Potter and the Sorcerer's Stone* with his "call to adventure."

The Harry Potter series is essentially the story of an orphan boy's quest for his identity and place, a boy who has "dreamed and dreamed of some unknown relation coming to take him away" (Sorcerer's Stone 30). It is in many ways the typical "Oliver Twist" story line except for one thing: Harry Potter is no ordinary boy. In fact, the series, in regard to the orphan myth, and the fact that Harry is no ordinary boy, might actually be more akin to the "King Arthur" legend in that Harry has unique abilities that are unknown to him, until he gets his "call to adventure." His unique abilities, however, are eluded to in the beginning of *Harry Potter and the Sorcerer's Stone,* not only by the "curiously shaped cut, like a bolt of lightning" on his forehead (15), but also by the fact that although just a baby, "people meeting in secret all over the country [of England]" toasted him saying, "To Harry Potter—the boy who lived" (17). However, before Harry can embark on his quest for identity and place, he must first be summoned by someone who has the "power of destiny" (Campbell 52).

Campbell points out that in every mythical journey there is a moment when the hero gets "the call to adventure" (49). This call comes from a "figure that appears suddenly as [a] guide, marking a new period, a new stage, in the biography" of the hero (55). In the case of Harry Potter the person who has the power over his destiny is Rubeus Hagrid.

Harry, like every mythic hero, is endowed with a particular talent that makes him invaluable to the "guide." Harry's talent is that he is a wizard, and not just any wizard. He is the wizard that the evil Voldemort could not kill; in fact, when Voldemort attempted to kill Harry, his "power somehow broke" (Rowling 12), which is why Professor McGonagall predicts that "in the future—there will be books written about Harry—[and] every child . . . will know his name" (13). Of course, all this is unknown to Harry until Hagrid shows up at exactly midnight on his Harry's eleventh birthday. Hagrid's entry into Harry's life is heralded by a raging storm and the sound of "the sea, slapping hard on the rock" (45) Uncle Vernon has taken the family to in order to avoid the mysterious letters Harry has been receiving. Hagrid, "a giant of a man" (46), literally crashes into Harry's life, bringing with him not only happy birthday greetings, but also what Harry wants most: to be taken away from the Dursleys.

The "call to adventure" leads Harry to London and Diagon Alley where he is inundated with the wonders of the wizarding world and learns of his fame, then on to Hogwarts where he encounters Albus Dumbledore. Dumbledore, in the tradition of Merlin and Gandalf, is Harry's "supernatural aid" or helper (Campbell 69). He is a figure representing the "benign, protecting power of destiny" (71). He guides Harry to the next phase of his adventure by offering him a safe environment, Hogwarts, in which he can discover not only his wizarding talents, but also his history and how he fits into the wizarding world.

Dumbledore, "considered by many the greatest wizard of modern times", (Sorcerer's Stone 102) serves as the "threshold guardian" (Campbell 77). The threshold guardian is the one who pushes the hero into "the regions of the unknown" (79). Dumbledore does this overtly and subtly. He overtly pushes Harry first with the mysterious letters by owl post then, when at last they meet, by feeding him tidbits of information about Voldemort, which prepares Harry over the series of books for his numerous encounters with the evil wizard. Dumbledore's subtle pushes include giving Harry "an invisibility cloak" (Sorcerer's Stone 201), which leads to Harry's discovery of the mirror of Erised, through which, as Dumbledore explains, one is able to see "the deepest, most desperate desire of our hearts" (213). In Harry's case it is his mother and father. And while this is a seemingly innocent encounter with a magical mirror, one learns that nothing involving Dumbledore is ever innocent or serendipitous, as one finds with Fawkes, Dumbledore's pet phoenix, and the penseive, which holds his "excess thoughts" (Goblet of Fire 597).

While Dumbledore serves as the main "threshold guardian," he is not the only "helper." Harry also has Ron Weasley and Hermione Granger who help to translate and guide Harry through his new surroundings, as does Hagrid and later in the series Dobby, Remus Lupin, and Sirius Black. Armed with Dumbledore, Hagrid, Ron and Hermione, Harry is ready to cross the threshold into the world of the unknown, which literally begins when he steps "through the archway" into Diagon Alley (Sorcerer's Stone 71). And thus begins Harry's initiation into the wizarding world.

The "initiation" sequence of the mythic journey involves a series of trials that the hero must overcome in order to return to the known world. The first trial that the hero encounters represents "only the beginning of the long and really perilous path of initiatory conquests and moments of illumination" (Campbell 109).

What is interesting about the Harry Potter Series is that each book contains a series of trials that Harry must overcome, while each book in and of itself represents an individual trial. For example, Harry's first trial is the sorcerer's stone mystery, which leads to his first battle with Voldemort; the second trial is the snake in the chamber of secrets and another encounter with Voldemort as Tom Riddle; the third trial involves the dementors and an encounter with Wormtail, one of Voldemort's evil helpers; the fourth trial is the maze and yet another encounter with an even more powerful and dangerous Voldemort; and the fifth trial is not only Voldemort's possible possession, but his own willfulness. Again, while each book in the series represents an individual trial, within each book is a series of reoccurring trials leading up Harry's "conquests and moments of illumination" (Campbell 71), which is best exemplified in *Harry Potter and the Sorcerer's Stone*.

The series of "mini-trials" that leads to Harry's confrontation with Voldemort in *Harry Potter and the Sorcerer's Stone* begins with the perception of greatness, bestowed upon him by the wizarding world. This perception in turn leads to hostile encounters with characters like Draco Malfoy and Severus Snape, who "didn't [just] dislike Harry—he hated him" (136). These encounters within themselves are trials in that Harry must learn to control his emotions and not let them get the best of him, especially in moments where his celebrity is thrown in his face, such as when Snape snaps, "fame, clearly isn't everything" (137). This perception of celebrity is Harry's greatest hurdle, which subsequently leads to his first trial.

Harry's first trial comes when he meets Draco Malfoy and must decide whether or not to join forces with him or stick with Ron Weasley, an obvious underdog. By choosing Ron, Harry has chosen the path of good over evil, distinguishing himself as a leader and not a follower, which proves critical in subsequent books. It would be just as easy for Harry, a celebrity in the wizarding world, to join up with "pure bloods" and take his place amongst the elite in society, but he makes a deliberate choice, thus sealing his fate as an avenger. This also serves as the first time that Harry actually has a choice about his path. Up to this point, various forces, such as Dumbledore, have guided him. However, although he chooses to befriend Ron and live his life at Hogwarts as a Gryffindor, it is still fate guiding his life.

Harry's second trial involves his parents—a reoccurring trial—and his overwhelming sense of loss and disconnection because of this loss. His overwhelming loss leads to his three-night obsession with "the Mirror of Erised," a magnificent mirror, "as high as the ceiling, with an ornate gold frame, standing on two clawed feet," which reflects what he most wants to see: his mother and father. While this mirror provides him with the immediate gratification of seeing his parents, Dumbledore points out that "men have wasted away before it, entranced by what they have seen, or been driven mad, not knowing if what it shows is real or even possible" (213). Dumbledore then imparts upon Harry the greatest bit of wisdom he is to receive and that is that "it does not do to dwell on dreams and forget to live" (214), which is perhaps an allusion to Harry's dreams of being rescued by an unknown relative. The mirror is taken away and Harry no longer has access to it; however, its removal does not stop him from thinking about it or dreaming about "his parents disappearing in a flash of green light" (215). To rid himself of this nightmare, he must overcome his final trial of the book: his life as a loner.

Before coming to Hogwarts, Harry was a loner, relying solely on his own abilities. The third and final trial in *Harry Potter and the Sorcerer's Stone* is comprised of overcoming five obstacles: (1) Fluffy, a three-headed dog, guarding a trapdoor; (2) Devil's Snare, a magical strangling plant; (3) charmed keys; (4) a live chessboard; and (5) seven bottles of liquid, one of which can kill and one of which will let him "Move ahead" through the door of fire. Harry, however, does not overcome these obstacles on his own. It is only with the help of Hermione and Ron that he finds success, which shows his growing maturity and movement away from isolation. From here, Harry can enter what Campbell calls "the belly of the whale" (90).

The "belly of the whale" for Harry occurs in a chamber with his nemesis, Voldemort. The hero is swallowed up by the abyss of the unconscious and must face himself. It is here that "the hero goes inward to be born again" (91). But to be born again the hero "must put aside his pride, his virtue, beauty, and life, and bow or submit to the absolutely intolerable" (108), which is death of the ego. Because a true "transformation can occur only when we have gone beyond the personal dimension to the universal" (Whitmont 73), Harry must relinquish his selfish obsession with the Mirror of Erised, allowing him the ability to defeat Voldemort. For the first time since discovering the mirror, Harry no longer sees his parents' reflection, but rather he sees "himself exactly as he is" (213) . . . "pale and scared-looking" (292). It is a true image, not an imagined one, and now that he has seen himself, he is free to see a less selfish, ego driven reflection of himself with the sorcerer's stone—his boon. Having overcome this last hurdle, Harry is now ready to embark on the "ultimate adventure" (Campbell 109).

"When all the barriers" of self have been overcome, then the hero is ready for the "mystical marriage" with the "the Queen Goddess of the World" (Campbell 109). The goddess is "mother, sister, mistress, bride . . . the incarnation of the promise of perfection . . . who was known to us, and even tasted, in the remotest past" (111). The goddess also represents the union of everything that was good and bad in the hero's past. Harry's "goddess" is his mother, who was murdered trying to save his life. His increasing need to avenge her murder is what fuels his drive for vengeance, which becomes more pronounced in *The Prisoner of Azkaban*.

The final stage of the mythic journey is the hero's return to the known. Harry, because of his encounter with Voldemort, and his subsequent success, is able to rise from "the belly of the whale" with his boon—his life and the sorcerer's stone. And while Harry has won this particular battle, he has only "delayed his [Voldemort's] return to power" (298). However, on the positive side, Harry has gained insight into his past and overcome his some of his isolationist tendency. He is gradually finding out how he fits into universal scheme of things, and, in the process, is slowly gaining that peace he longs for.

Campbell states that:

> The goal of the myth is to dispel the need for [false images of self]
> such life ignorance by effecting a reconciliation of the individual
> conscious with the universal will. And this is effected through a
> realization of the true relationship of the passing phenomena of time
> to the imperishable life that lives and dies in all. (238)

Rowling's Harry Potter series as exemplified in *Harry Potter and the Sorcerer's Stone* shows how one boy, Harry Potter is able to successfully shed the false images imposed on him by both the muggle and wizarding societies. Rowling accomplishes this feat by using the classic form of the myth. She is truly a twenty-first century mythmaker.

Works Cited

Campbell, Joseph. *The Hero with a Thousand Faces*. 3rd. ed. New Jersey: Princeton UP, 1973.

Rowling, J. K. *Harry Potter and the Goblet of Fire*. New York: Scholastic Press, 2000.

_____. *Harry Potter and the Sorcerer's Stone*. New York: Scholastic Press, 1998.

Whitmont, Edward C. The Symbolic Quest: Basic Concepts of Analytical Psychology. New York: Putnam's, 1969.

Antoinette Winstead moved to San Antonio, Texas in 1977 where she remained until she graduated from San Antonio College in 1985 with an A.A. in Theater. She continued her studies in New York City and received a B.F.A. from New York University (1987) in Film/Television Production and a M.F.A. from Columbia University (1989) in Film. She is currently a full time Associate Professor of Communication Arts, English and Theater and the Communication Arts Program Head at Our Lady of the Lake University in San Antonio, Texas, where she also received a M.A. in English Literature in 1995. She has written four screenplays, two plays, several short stories and poems. She has completed two novels and is currently working on a third. Her poetry has been published in such journals as The Poet Magazine, ViAztlan, Inkwell Echoes, *and* Cross Currents. *In 1997, she published twelve poems in* A Garland of Poems: a Collection from Ten Female Poets. *Her primary interests are writing and film, but she also enjoys theater. From 1993 to 1995, she directed seven plays, one of which she also wrote—*One Drink Too Many—*and one of which she also choreographed—*Forever Free.

Biographies and Summaries

Biographies of Additional Speakers

Below are the biographies for those panelists and presenters whose papers and presentations were not able to be included in this Compendium; biographies were current as of July, 2003; where an updated biography was provided, it has been included here.

Connie Neal
Author of *What's a Christian to do with Harry Potter?* and
The Gospel According to Harry Potter

Connie Neal is first and foremost a grateful servant of Jesus Christ. After receiving her B.A. in Communication from Pepperdine University, she invested ten years as a youth pastor, then began a ministry of speaking and writing in 1989 which continues today. She has been married to her husband, Pat, since 1979, and they have three children (ages 18, 13 and 12) and reside in the Sacramento, California area.

Connie's signature book is *Dancing in the Arms of God* (Zondervan Publishers). She teamed up with her daughter (and illustrator), Casey, to create a Young Women of Faith girl's journal (for ages 8-12) entitled *Hey! This is Me!* She is sought after by both secular and Christian audiences regarding the intersection between Christianity and pop culture with her books: *What's a Christian to Do with Harry Potter?* (WaterBrook Press, 2001) and *The Gospel According to Harry Potter* (Westminster John Knox Press, 2002). Her next work will be released in the summer of 2003 titled: *Walking Tall in Babylon: Raising Children to Be Godly and Wise in a Perilous World.*

Philip Nel

Dr. Philip Nel is an Assistant Professor of English at Kansas State University, where he teaches courses in children's literature, including one devoted to Harry Potter. He is the author of *J.K. Rowling's Harry Potter Novels: A Reader's Guide* (2001) and *The Avant-Garde and American Postmodernity: Small Incisive Shocks* (2002). His next book will be *Dr. Seuss: American Icon* (forthcoming in 2004).

Ari Rapkin
Computer Graphics Software Engineer,
Industrial Light & Magic

Ari Rapkin began working at Industrial Light & Magic in 1998. For two years, Rapkin was a member of the Production Software team, providing support and development for a variety of graphics software systems. In 2000, she joined the Software R&D department's Simulation group. Her contributions to ILM's software include fluid & smoke simulation for films, including *Pearl Harbor* and *The Mummy Returns*, and cloth and flesh simulation for films such as Jurassic Park III, Star Wars: Episode II *"Attack of the Clones,"* and *A.I. Artificial Intelligence*. Rapkin is currently continuing development of the cloth simulation system for use in several upcoming films including *The Hulk, Van Helsing* and *Harry Potter and the Prisoner of Azkaban.*

Although born in Los Angeles, Rapkin has lived mostly on the East Coast. She grew up in Wilmington, Delaware and attended The Johns Hopkins University in Baltimore, where she received a B.A. in mathematics. Her graduate education began with a program in gifted education at the University of Virginia, where she also earned a Master's degree in computer science. Later she went on to obtain an M.S. in computer science at Carnegie Mellon University, graduating in 1997.

SPEAKERS & PANELISTS:

Irina Achildiyev

Can Draco Malfoy Be Redeemed? (Panelist)
Binghamton University, Binghamton, New York (undergraduate student)

Ms. Achildiyev is presently surprising no one but herself by still being an undergraduate student at Binghamton University, pursuing a degree in something-or-other, which she will deny to the end is going to be the English language. Most of the time, she avoids studying and being a productive member of Muggledom by escaping into young adult fantasy books, writing (most recently, obscene amounts of slash fan fiction), and over-analyzing fictional characters and their love-lives. She defends this by saying it prepares her for the "real world" by enumerating all that it isn't. Yet.

Emily Anderson

Emeric Switch on Gender: Harry and Hermione's Transgendered Heroism

Ms. Anderson graduated from Susquehanna University with a B.A. in literature and minors in women's studies, classical studies, and philosophy in December 2002. She is currently deciding where to attend graduate school, where she will work towards a Ph.D. in contemporary women's fiction.

Nancy Carstensen

Harry Potter Library Events Workshop
Oceanside Public Library, Oceanside, California (Children's Librarian)

Ms. Cartensen is a graduate of San Diego State University, and is currently one of the Children's Librarians at the Oceanside Public Library in California, and serves special guest liaison, volunteer coordinator, and co-chair of Sponsorship and fundraising for Lumos, HP Education Fanon's 2006 event. She has been the project coordinator for many large events and fundraisers, including the *Starcon* Sci-Fi conventions and last year's 2-day *Fantasy Faire: Harry Potter & Friends*. A lifelong fan of science fiction and fantasy, she is an avid Harry Potter fan and memorabilia collector, which her family & friends happily indulge at every opportunity!

Cassandra Claire
Can Draco Malfoy Be
Redeemed? (Panelist)

Cassandra Claire is a 20-something freelance writer and editor. Cassie lives in New York with her cat, Simon, and ArtisticAlley.org moderator, Ali Wildgoose, in The Avocado.

Bridget Roussell Cowlishaw
Coming out of the Cupboard: Slash in the Harry Potter Fandom (Panelist)
Florida Atlantic University, Boca Raton Florida (Assistant Professor of English)

Bridget R. Cowlishaw received her Ph.D. from the University of Oklahoma English Department in 1998. She was an Assistant Professor of English at Florida Atlantic University in Boca Raton for five years, where she taught literary and language theory, and is now an Assistant Professor in the Department of English & Languages at Northeastern State University in Oklahoma. Dr. Cowlishaw has published analyses of popular culture texts in the *Journal of Popular Culture*, the *Journal of American and Comparative Cultures*, and forthcoming in *Prospects: An Annual Journal of American Cultural Studies*. She comes to Nimbus—2003 because she is currently working on a manuscript about Harry Potter online fan fiction.

Vicki Dolenga
Coming out of the Cupboard: Slash in the Harry Potter Fandom (Panelist)

Also known as Morrigan, Ms. Dolenga has a bachelor's degree in Communications with a minor in Women's Studies from Loyola University Chicago (she also has a master's degree but it's in a geek thing) and has presented at a number of conferences, including BiWest 98 in San Diego, CA. She joined the Harry Potter fandom in November 2001 and began writing slash fan fiction soon afterwards. She is the Headmistress and owner of RestrictedSection.org, an NC-17 Harry Potter fan fiction archive, and a former moderator for the Nocturne Alley roleplaying game, both of which include slash pairings.

Eliza Dresang

Hermione Granger and Issues of Gender in the Harry Potter Books and Films
Censorship, Book Banning and the First Amendment (Panelist)
Florida State University, Tallahassee, Florida (Professor, Information Studies)

Eliza T. Dresang, Professor of Information Studies at Florida State University and former Director of Library and Technology Services in the Madison, Wisconsin School District, places her interest in the Harry Potter books in the context of many years of professional experience, teaching, and research in the field of children's and young adult literature. Dresang's long term professional involvement with children's literature includes chairing the American Library Association's 2004 Newbery Award Committee, the 2002 Pura Belpré Award Committee, and serving as a member of numerous other children's literature award committees.

The Harry Potter books serve as examples of the type reading net-generation youth enjoy, described in her book *Radical Change: Books for Youth in a Digital Age* (H.W. Wilson, 1999). Rowling's books experience censorship such as that described in her book *School Censorship in the 21st Century* (with John S. Simmons, International Reading Association, 2001) and other recent articles and interviews appearing in national and international media. She is an advocate for children as capable and in need of connection, rather than innocent and in need of protection, which she will speak to in light of legal concerns at Nimbus—2003.

Gender studies and multicultural issues in relation to children and their reading are of particular interest to Dresang. She wrote a chapter, "Hermione and the Heritage of Gender" for the recently published *The Ivory Tower and Harry Potter* (edited by Lana Whited, University of Missouri Press, 2002), and will address this topic in relation to all five books and the two movies at Nimbus—2003. She also conducted an in-depth study of award-winning Hispanic children's literature, published in 2000. She has taught university-level courses dealing with gender and other multicultural issues since 1990.

Carole Estes

Moony, Wormtail, Padfoot and Prongs: Marauder's Panel (Sirius Black)

Carole Estes is the Site Logistics Coordinator for Nimbus—2003, and will serve as AV Coordinator for 2005's The Witching Hour. She's been involved in the fandom since March 2000, when, in a moment of extreme boredom, she picked up her son's copy of *Harry Potter and the Sorcerer's Stone*. After reading *Harry Potter and the Prisoner of Azkaban*, she became addicted to the character of Sirius Black and the rest is history. She reads and writes fan fiction, and is best known for her collaboration with Penny Linsenmayer (Programming Co-Chair) on *A Sirius Affair*. In real life, Carole is a 40-something consulting hydrogeologist, living in Florida, with her husband and three boys. She has a B.S. in Oceanography and an

M.S. in Geology and can be found online when not working, taking care of the kids, doing laundry, reading, or even occasionally sleeping.

Katherine Grimes
Publishing on Potter: Dodging the Bludgers (Moderator)

Katherine Grimes is associate professor at Ferrum College, where she has directed the First-Year Experience program for six years. She holds a bachelor's degree in English and psychology from Catawba College, a master's degree in English from the University of North Carolina at Chapel Hill, and a doctorate in English with a major in twentieth century British and American literature from the University of North Carolina at Greensboro.

She is especially interested in maturation fiction and wrote her dissertation on absent mothers in Southern literature. In addition to her essay "Harry Potter: Fairy Tale Prince, Real Boy, and Archetypal Hero" in *The Ivory Tower and Harry Potter*, edited by Lana A. Whited, she has published articles in *The Companion to Southern Literature*, edited by Joseph M. Flora and Lucinda H. McKethan, as well as in Collier's CD-ROM encyclopedia and Masterplots series. She is especially interested in literature of the South and work by African American writers.

Anita Helmbold
Harry Potter: Can Any Wisdom come from Wizardry? (Panelist)
Taylor University College, Edmonton, Alberta, Canada
(Associate Professor of English)

Anita Helmbold is an Associate Professor of English at Taylor University College, a small, Christian liberal arts college in Edmonton, Alberta, Canada. She first become interested in the Harry Potter books a couple of years ago when they were recommended to her by a friend, and she quickly become hooked. She has just finished teaching a course on Magical Traditions in British Literature, which looked at legends of Merlin, King Arthur and the holy grail; famous literary Renaissance magicians, such as Dr. Faustus and Prospero; and the use of magic in modern fantasy literature, including, but not limited to, the Harry Potter series.

James Inman
Harry Potter and Popular Culture: From the Italian Renaissance to Star Wars
University of South Florida, Assistant Professor of English

James A. Inman is Assistant Professor of English at the University of South Florida in Tampa, Florida, where he directs the writing center and coordinates the professional and technical writing program. A longtime fan of the Harry Potter books, James is currently working on projects about digital tools in cultural contexts, the rhetoric of online matchmaking, and cultural artifacts in Disney theme parks.

Dawnellen Jacobs
Harry Potter: Can Any Wisdom come from Wizardry? (Panelist)
California Baptist University

DawnEllen Jacobs is beginning her 12th year at California Baptist University as a Professor of Modern Languages and Literature after teaching English and math in middle school and high school. She currently serves as the Graduate Program Director for the MA English. DawnEllen received both her M.A. and Ph.D. in Comparative Literature from the University of California at Riverside. She is a regular presenter at teacher conferences and workshops, including NCTE and ASCI and has authored numerous program and accreditation documents for CBU programs. She has been recognized in Who's Who among American Teachers. Her collegial interests include the integration of faith and learning and mentoring female faculty.

Sidharth Jaggi
Platform 9 3/4 and Sundry Barriers: Ontological Displacements in the Harry Potter Series (Proxy Presenter)
California Institute of Technology (Ph.D. student)

Mr. Jaggi (B. Tech., Indian Institute of Technology-Bombay, 2000; M.S., California Institute of Technology, 2001) is currently pursuing his Ph.D. in Electrical Engineering from the California Institute of Technology, Pasadena, California. Sidharth realizes the futility of trying to compress a life into the confines of a three-sentence-biographical sketch. He therefore invites those who are interested in learning more about him to check out his website at http://jaggi.caltech.edu

Sarah Kelman
Will Cease and Desist Cease to Exist?: The Effects of *Eldred v. Ashcroft* on Harry Potter Fan Sites
University of Georgia School of Law (Law Student)

Ms. Kelman is a rising 2L at the University of Georgia School of Law. She earned her M.A. in Film Studies from the University of Wisconsin-Madison in May 1999 and her B.A. in Russian Area Studies from the University of Georgia in 1997. Her research interests include intellectual property, constitutional law, and the law's effect on personal freedoms. This summer she is interning at the Georgia Department of Corrections Legal Office.

Mary LeGrow

Cloaks and Cauldrons: An Anti-Stereotypical Analysis of Wizarding Fashion

Mary LeGrow is a former professional model and now owns the Wonderland Costume Shop. Ms. LeGrow has been a production and show costumer for three years, earning a substantial number of awards at convention competitions around the country, as well as having done photo shoots for Savannah College of Art and Design's catalogues. In addition to costume design and modeling, Ms. LeGrow is a published comic artist and free-lance illustrator.

Kimberly Lowe

Examining Writing Style: Learning from J.K. Rowling's Writing Style
Oppenheimer, Wolff & Donnelly, L.L.P., Minneapolis, Minnesota

Ms. Lowe, an attorney in Minneapolis, practices law in the corporate finance and business transactional arena. Prior to practicing law, Ms. Lowe worked for a communication and training firm where she wrote speeches for executives from many Fortune 100 companies and training publications and presentations. Ms. Lowe received her J.D. from Boston College Law School. She graduated, *summa cum laude*, with an Honors B.A. in English and Economics from the University of Detroit. Ms. Lowe currently volunteers as a Guardian ad Litem, a Residential Business Leader at a business emersion camp for high school students and as a business mentor for several high school students. Ms. Lowe has been the recipient of several scholastic awards, including: Presidential Scholar, Howard Walsh Award for Outstanding English Scholar and Outstanding Economics Scholar. In connection with her volunteer activities, Ms. Lowe has been the recipient of an Unsung Hero Award from *City Business,* a Minneapolis business paper and a Volunteer Service Award from BestPrep, a non-profit organization dedicated to teaching business and economic fundamentals to students in grades first through twelfth.

Meredith McCardle

Parseltongue for Non-Native Speakers: A Legal Tutorial for Fanfic Writers, Fan Artists and Website Hosts

Meredith McCardle is a recent graduate of Boston University School of Law and is currently spending all of her time and energy studying for the bar exam. She has been researching issues related to copyright law and fan fiction for the past two years and published an article on the subject, "Fan Fiction, Fandom and Fanfare: What's All the Fuss?," in the Spring 2003 issue of the Boston University Journal of Science and Technology Law.

Kendra Nuckels
Slytherins, Smoke and Shadows: The Secret Life of Severus Snape (Panelist)
The Wizarding World: Past, Present and Future (Panelist)

Resmiranda Miller (Kendra Nuckels) was raised by wolves, and is a recent college graduate of the University of Tulsa, where she majored in Sociology and minored in History. She is most well-known for her fan fiction series, *The Shadows Trilogy*, and spends her days writing. She lives in Texas, and is currently working on her second novel.

Liz O'Reilly
Perceptions of Childhood and Adult-Child Relations in Harry Potter
Hull University, England (postgraduate student)

Ms. O'Reilly is a postgraduate student and Graduate Teaching Assistant at Hull University, England. Her PhD title is: 'Representations of Childhood & Adulthood in Contemporary Children's Literature: Roald Dahl, Anne Fine, JK Rowling & Diana Wynne Jones.'

Sarah Marie Parker-Allen
Strangers in a Strange Land: How the Muggleborn
are a Powerful Force for Social Change

Sarah Marie Parker-Allen is 22 years old, and is about to graduate from The Ohio State University with a degree in Political Science, with an emphasis in Eastern Europe/ former Communist nations. She works for Disneyland in Anaheim, California, and enjoys lining up for weeks just to see Star Wars movies at Grauman's Chinese Theatre in Hollywood (for charity).

She first discovered Harry Potter as a conscript—reading *Harry Potter and the Prisoner of Azkaban* to her little brother in 2000—and went on to read the other three books over the course of two days. She is a recent convert to the Harry Potter fan fiction community, and has published three short stories on FictionAlley under the user ID "Lloannna," including her own version of Hermione's infamous political tract regarding the treatment of house elves.

Kathleen Robinson
Harry Potter and Popular Culture: From the Italian Renaissance to Star Wars
University of South Florida (Graduate Student)

Kathleen Robinson is pursuing a master's degree in comparative literature at the University of South Florida in Tampa, Florida, and she also serves as a writing center consultant at the University of South Florida's St. Petersburg campus.

Aja Romano
Can Draco Malfoy be Redeemed? (Moderator)

Aja (pronounced "Asia") is a resident of Bloomington, Indiana, she reviews theatre and occasionally completes a double major in Voice and English at Indiana University. She joined the fandom a few months before the release of *Harry Potter and the Goblet of Fire*, and has been actively putting off real life to play in it for just over a year and a half. While in the fandom, she has served as a Niffler for FictionAlley Park, and as a moderator for the Guns & Handcuffs web site, as well as the Yahoo!Group Draco_101. She owns the fan fiction list Armchair_Slash and its discussion forums, as well as Nraged, the livejournal community for the discussion of the Nocturne_Alley rpg, of which she is also a member. She is perhaps best known for her opinions on the subject of Trilogy Slash. While not all that fond of the pairing in general, she admits that there is some slight merit to the idea of H/D in *Draco Veritas*.

Suzanne Scott
Celluloid Polyjuice: The Filmic Transfiguration of Harry Potter into Infallible Hero
University of Southern California, School of Cinema and Television
(Graduate Student)

Ms. Scott is currently obtaining her Masters degree in Critical Studies at the University of Southern California's School of Cinema and Television, with an emphasis in Cult Media. Her undergraduate work, also in Cinema Studies, was done at New York University's Tisch School of the Arts. Recently, she has presented work on Harry Potter at the Southwest American Culture Association/Popular Culture Association, as well as work on Buffy the Vampire Slayer at the first global "Vampires: Myths and Metaphors of Enduring Evil" conference in Budapest. Future research includes a dissertation surrounding issues of (re)authorship within the multimedia expanse of the Harry Potter phenomenon.

Mary Shearer
Pottermania Brag 'n' Swap Meet
Cameron Public Library, Cameron, Wisconsin (Public Library Director)

Ms. Shearer is a small town Public Library Director in Cameron, Wisconsin. She came to library sideways after a stint as a substitute teacher, having received her college degree in her mid-thirties from Hamline University in St. Paul, Minnesota where she majored in English with an emphasis on Women's and American literature. She has been coaching high school forensics for the last ten years, and her love of books, along with her communication skills, fit the bill nicely for running a small town library.

In the fall of 2001, her daughter persuaded her to read *Harry Potter and the Sorcerer's Stone* aloud to the family, which led her to what will probably be a lifetime love affair with all things Potter. She developed a course called "Pottermania" for the local University of Wisconsin campus's Kids Kollege program, which was very successful and continues to be a popular draw for the program. In addition to her "Potter problem" (for which they have yet to develop a twelve-step program) she enjoys being a musician and acting for her area community theater troupe, as well as spending time with her husband Monty, and their children Luke, 13 and Erika, 10 on the beautiful Wisconsin lakes.

E. Stone Shiflet
Harry Potter and Popular Culture: From the Italian Renaissance to Star Wars
University of South Florida
(Ph.D. student)

E. Stone Shiflet is a doctoral candidate in the Department of English at the University of South Florida in Tampa, Florida, where she coordinates the writing center and is completing a dissertation exploring metalanguage in the American justice system. Stone and her son Gantt are avid Harry Potter fans.

Heidi Tandy
Parseltongue for Non-Native Speakers: A Legal Tutorial for Fanfic Writers,
Fan Artists and Website Hosts
Miami Beach, Florida (Attorney)

Ms. Tandy is a 30-something intellectual property & internet lawyer in Florida, and serves as President of FAWC, the 501(c)(3)entity behind FictionAlley.org. She obtained her undergraduate degree from the University of Pennsylvania, and her J.D. from American University; since 1995, she has practised intellectual property and internet law in New York and Florida. She is also an editor for The Leaky Cauldron and serves as an advisory board member for HP Education Fanon.

Kate Tanski
Coming out of the Cupboard: Slash in the Harry Potter Fandom (Panelist)
Lawrence University, Appleton, Wisconsin (recent graduate)

Ms. Tanski is a 22-year-old yaoi fangirl who found her way into the Harry Potter fandom by chance, and has since devoted an absurd amount of time incorporating Harry Potter and the Harry Potter fandom into her academic coursework. She served as a panelist for the Lawrence University Harrison Symposium for Humanities and Social Sciences in May 2003 with a paper titled "'But Harry Isn't Gay!'—Controversy and Sexuality in Harry Potter Fanfiction," and was also awarded honors at graduation for her undergraduate thesis "Harry Potter and the Age of the Internet: Community and Conflict in the Harry Potter Fandom." Graduating in June 2003 with an English Major, she is undecided on whether to continue her work on Harry Potter in graduate school, or to find a small island where no one has heard of Harry Potter fan fiction and live out the rest of her days in seclusion.

Amy Tenbrink
Parseltongue for Non-Native Speakers: A Legal Tutorial for Fanfic Writers,
Fan Artists and Website Hosts
Minneapolis, Minnesota (attorney)

Ms. Tenbrink is an attorney in the Denver area, and currently serving as one of three co-chairs for The Witching Hour, HP Education Fanon's 2005 event (http://www.hp2005.org). She received her Bachelor of Science from the University of Southern California, graduating *magna cum laude* with a major in music industry and a minor in political science. Ms. Tenbrink received her J.D. *cum laude* from the Georgetown University Law Center. While at Georgetown, she served as administrative staff for the *Georgetown Journal of Legal Ethics* and as a teaching assistant for the Family Advocacy Clinic, where she represented special education children. She developed an expertise in censorship and the First Amendment while researching her paper, "Parental Advisory Labels: Will the responsible party please stand up?" Ms. Tenbrink has a background in intellectual property, having worked in entertainment law for two years and later for the Department of Justice's Computer Crime and Intellectual Property Section of the Criminal Division. Today, she spends less time meeting the members of Tool and chasing down computer hackers than she does researching issues liability under the Communications Decency Act and drafting agreements for the sale of lime spalls. When not working, she can usually be found running, serving on the board of a theatre group, beta reading fan fiction or ghost managing a rotisserie baseball team.

Ebony Thomas
Imperial Harry: Race, J.K. Rowling and the Postcolonial Context
The Wizarding World: Past, Present and Future (Moderator)
Moony, Wormtail, Padfoot and Prongs: Marauder's Panel (James Potter)
Wayne State University, Detroit, Michigan (Graduate Student)

Ebony Elizabeth Thomas holds bachelor's and master's degrees in English, and is currently a Ph.D. candidate in the same. She teaches creative writing, composition, and selected topics in literature to students on the high school, undergraduate, and graduate levels in her native city of Detroit, Michigan. Her many research interests include children's literature, multicultural education, and postcolonial studies.

Ebony AKA AngieJ, her alter ego, is the author of the post-Hogwarts fan fiction duology *Trouble in Paradise* and Paradise Lost, a former List Elf and FAQer at the HPforGrownups Yahoogroup, a founding Moderator for FictionAlley, and First Mate of the HMS Pumpkin Pie.

Rebecca Tushnet

Parseltongue for Non-Native Speakers: A Legal Tutorial for Fanfic Writers, Fan Artists and Website Hosts
New York University School of Law (Assistant Professor of Law)

Professor Tushnet is an assistant professor at Georgetown School of Law, specializing in intellectual property. Previously, she clerked for Chief Judge Edward R. Becker, U.S. Court of Appeals for the Third Circuit, and for Associate Justice David H. Souter, and practised intellectual property law at Debevoise & Plimpton. Her website is http://www.tushnet.com.

Dave Wang

Coming out of the Cupboard: Slash in the Harry Potter Fandom (Panelist)

Mr. Wang teaches high school mathematics, coaches volleyball, and chairs the Mathematics Department at St. Andrew's School in Middletown, Delaware. A lifelong fantasy and science fiction fan, he discovered the world of Harry Potter in July 2002 and immediately saw that Harry and Draco belong together. He writes fan fiction under the pseudonym Stormwynd.

Karin Westman

When Harry Met Jane: The Legacy of Austen in Rowling's Harry Potter
Kansas State University, Manhattan, Kansas (Assistant Professor of English)

Dr. Westman is an Assistant Professor of English at Kansas State University. She has published *Pat Barker's Regeneration: A Reader's Guide* (Continuum, 2001) and articles on A.S. Byatt, J. K. Rowling, and Virginia Woolf.

Lana A. Whited

Publishing on Potter: Dodging the Bludgers (Panelist)
Ferrum College, Ferrum, Virginia (Professor of English)

Dr. Whited is editor of *The Ivory Tower and Harry Potter: Perspectives on a Literary Phenomenon* and has also presented on Harry Potter at meetings of the Popular Culture Association of America and the Children's Literature Association. Dr. Whited earned a Ph.D. in English at the University of North Carolina at Greensboro. She teaches English and journalism at Ferrum College in Virginia's Blue Ridge Mountains and writes a weekly column on media issues for roanoke.com. Dr. Whited's essay "Naturalism's Middle Ages: The Evolution of the American True-Crime Novel, 1930-1960" appears in *Twisted from the Ordinary; Essays on American Literary Naturalism* (edited by Mary Papke, University of Tennessee Press, 2003).

Schedule of Panels, Papers and Presentations

9:00-10:00 p.m.

MOONY, WORMTAIL, PADFOOT AND PRONGS: MARAUDERS' PANEL

Lee Hillman (Moderator, Remus Lupin); Carole Estes (Sirius Black); Carlisle Elizabeth Kraft (Peter Pettigrew), Ebony Thomas (James Potter)

This session is sponsored by
Carole Estes

To whet our appetites for the amazing and varied programming on Friday and Saturday, this panel discussion highlights the Nimbus—2003 mascots: The Marauders. Topics will range from individual questions about each of James, Peter, Remus, and Sirius, as well as questions that address their relationships during school, before James's death, and after Sirius's escape from Azkaban.

8:30 a.m.

TECHNOLOGY MEETS MAGIC
Dr. Diana Patterson
This session is sponsored by
Rob Ihinger and Peg Kerr.

From omnioculars to the Hogwarts train, Rowling's books are filled with magical technology. Dumbledore's office seems to be full of it on spindly tables, and yet Arthur Weasley and Hagrid express their amazement at Muggle technology. This paper explores some of the reasons for, and the progress of, wizard technology. The paper compares Rowling's notions of where magic inheres with the notions used in discussions of 16th and 17th century magic in order to show how the use of technology changes the meaning and purpose of magic. (25 minutes)

PLATFORM 9 3/4 AND SUNDRY BARRIERS: ONTOLOGICAL DISPLACEMENTS IN THE HARRY POTTER SERIES
Sidharth Jaggi, proxy presenter for Dr. Sudha Shastri

This paper looks at the operation of boundaries in the 'Harry Potter' series; the ways in which these limits are transgressed; and to what effects they unsettle ontological margins. This presentation will primarily describe the various means and tools that Rowling deploys to distort ontological stability. Examples include: the moving photographs and portraits that amaze Harry, his journey back to the past with Hermione in the third book, and his entry into the memory of Dumbledore through the Pensieve in the fourth book. This motif is conveyed as a process of overcoming (rather than violating) barriers in the pursuit of knowledge and experience, and is anticipated right at the entry-point to the world of magic, when Harry is required to walk through a wall in order to reach the platform from where he will take the Hogwarts Express. This paper will also raise questions regarding the effect of such boundary-crossings, and if and how they contribute to the definition of magic in the Harry Potter books. (25 minutes)

WHAT MAKES A PROFESSOR BEHAVE LIKE SNAPE?: LITERATURE, MARKETING AND THE CRITICAL BACKLASH AGAINST HARRY POTTER
Dr. Philip Nel (Featured Speaker)

This presentation will take up the question of why so many who specialize in children's literature have found fault with the series, and will in particular answer Jack Zipes' question, "How is it possible to evaluate a work of literature like a Harry Potter novel when it is so dependent on the market conditions of the culture industry?" The answer, this paper proposes, lies at the intersection of three competing discourses: the law, capitalism, and aesthetics. (50 minutes)

ONCE UPON A TIME-TURNER: A HISTORY OF THE HARRY POTTER FANDOM (PANEL DISCUSSION)
Mai Pucik (Moderator), Amy Gordanier and Madeline Klink

This session is sponsored by
FictionAlley.org eMentors

Fandoms, or online fan communities, are rapidly-evolving places and the case of Harry Potter is no exception. Though it dates back only four years, our fandom has undergone many changes, from its genesis as arena for young readers to meet and trade ideas and stories to its current sprawling incarnation as a writing, drawing, and theorizing base for thousands of fans of all netsurfing ages. Mai Pucik ("Firebolt", "Tinderblast"), Amy Gordanier ("Amy G."), and Madeline Klink ("Flourish") explore trends of the past, present, and possible future of the Harry Potter fandom, including the rise of "epic" fan fiction, the turnover of popular character pairings and the changes in the treatment of throwaway characters and other offhand textual references. No experience of the fandom is required. (50 minutes)

PARSELTONGUE FOR NON-NATIVE SPEAKERS: A LEGAL TUTORIAL FOR FANFIC WRITERS, FAN ARTISTS AND WEBSITE HOSTS

Amy Tenbrink, Rebecca Tushnet, Meredith McCardle and Heidi Tandy

This session is sponsored by

The Ultimate Unofficial Guide to the Mysteries of Harry Potter

Our presentation shall be addressed to two decidedly distinct segments of fandom members—first, those fan fiction writers and fan artists who, in the course of their unique creative process, may find themselves in need of assistance with Parseltongue, and second, the web site hosts, who face their own singular set of challenges. On behalf of interested fan fiction writers and fan artists, we will address the following poisonous topics: Copyrights; Trademarks; the First Amendment (including, ahem, obscenity); Rights of Privacy and Publicity; Defamation; and Plagiarism and Ethics. We will also impart a small lesson in Expecto Patronum (that is, in those not-too-rare occasions when a fandom member is confronted by a Dementor cloaked as a cease and desist letter). Web site hosts will be instructed in the areas detailed above, but they will also be introduced to their own set of venomous themes: Patents and Trade Secrets; Incorporation and Limited Liability; Charitable Organizations; Solicitation; and the most odious of all—Taxes! (110 minutes)

9:30 a.m.

THE SCIENCE OF HARRY POTTER: HOW MAGIC REALLY WORKS

Dr. Roger Highfield (Featured Speaker)

As illuminating as it is enchanting, The Science of Harry Potter sheds light not only on Harry Potter's magical realm, but on the magic that is taking place in labs and science classrooms in our own Muggle world. With the success of Harry Potter and Lord of the Rings, interest in magic spells, charms and potions has never been greater. Drawing on the help of more than 100 leading scholars around the world, Highfield is able to both explain and entertain at the same time, making the remarkable world of magic even more real to all those who want to believe. (50 minutes)

HARRY POTTER: ARE THEY CHILDREN'S BOOKS?

Carlisle Elizabeth Kraft, Evelyn Browne and Mai Pucik

This session is sponsored by

Patricia Spotanske

Historically, there is support for Harry Potter as a children's book series. The books follow the structure of an English boarding-school tale, and had they been released prior to the 1950s, there is no doubt they would have automatically been shelved in children's sections in libraries. However, literary times have changed. Most importantly, the young adult genre is growing, and the lines between children's and young adult books are becoming increasingly blurred. Most librarians have seen parents push the Harry Potter books on their children because they are so heavily marketed by the media as a children's series, without regard for what a young child actually can read and comprehend. While a child can read the books and take them at face value, is that what we want kids to learn about reading? Also, what about the books' value as read-alouds? Both sides of the issue (for and against the books being marketed to children) will be discussed. (50 minutes)

THE IMPORTANCE OF BEING RON (PANEL DISCUSSION)
Catherine Tosenberger (Moderator), Debra Duncan and Susan Faust

This will take the form of a round table, with the moderator acting as discussion coordinator. Audience participation will be encouraged, although the panelists will contribute the bulk of the discussion. Emphasis will be placed on literary readings of Ron—as an example of "the sidekick," as an archetypical knight, as an ambassador/representative of the wizarding world for Harry and Hermione, as the entryway to the "ideal" family, and so forth. Some discussion will be given to the Ron/Hermione ship, but as that topic is being covered in-depth by another panel, this discussion will be kept to a minimum. (50 minutes)

10:30 a.m.

CENSORSHIP, BOOK BANNING AND THE FIRST AMENDMENT (PANEL DISCUSSION)
Judith Krug, Dr. Eliza Dresang and Amy Tenbrink

This session is sponsored by
Kristine Twesme

Ever since the release of Harry Potter and the Sorcerer's Stone, people have tried to have the Harry Potter books banned, usually from educational institutions such as schools and libraries. The increase in the books' popularity has only heightened this controversy. As more and more children read the books through their school or library, more and more groups—most notably some conservative Christians in the United States and some religious groups in other countries who object to J.K. Rowling's discussion of witchcraft and wizardry—seek to have the books banned, claiming the subject matter is inappropriate. This panel will discuss the legal issues surrounding book banning, with particular reference to Harry Potter, including the recent District Court case striking a school's restriction on its students' access to the Harry Potter series. (50 minutes)

THE HISTORICAL OCCULT IN THE WORLD OF HARRY POTTER
Azalais Malfoy (aka Kiri Aradia Morgan)

An exploration of the real-world occult symbolism and historical figures who appear in the Harry Potter books. Covered topics will include Nicolas and Perenelle Flamel, the Philosopher's Stone, the possible meanings of the Dark Mark, 'eating Death', and the correspondences of the four Houses to the four alchemical elements. The nature of some of the disciplines which are taught at Hogwarts will also be covered, and then the floor will be thrown open to discussion and speculation about the past and future of the Potterverse. (50 minutes)

HARRY POTTER AND POPULAR CULTURE: FROM THE ITALIAN RENAISSANCE TO STAR WARS
Dr. James Inman, Kathleen Robinson and E. Stone Shiflet

This session is sponsored by
Etakyma

In this panel, three presenters will explore the intersections of Harry Potter, both in books and films, and popular culture texts as old as the Italian Renaissance and as contemporary as the Star Wars film series. The presenters will focus on discourse and imagery in Harry Potter adventures, emphasizing the way connections can be forged that help scholars understand more about the scholarly capital of J.K. Rowling's works. After detailed presentations, each featuring handouts and resources for attendees, the presenters will invite attendees to join them in an interactive discussion about other popular culture influences. (50 minutes)

FANWORDS: THE EVOLUTION OF FANDOM VERNACULAR IN THE HARRY POTTER FANDOM
Mai Pucik

This session is sponsored by
Armchair Slash

Every activity that involves socializing among its hobbyists will eventually develop its own distinctive vocabulary. Once limited to niche magazine publications and the rare hobbyist gathering, the arrival of the Internet allowed wide-ranging and frequent contact between hobbyists as never before. In the case of Harry Potter fans, the vast size of the fan community allowed particular vocabulary to appear not only for the fandom as a whole, but for individual sites, mailing lists, and other places where fans interact. This paper examines the evolution and spread of vernacular in various regions of the Harry Potter fandom, with examples. (25 minutes)

AFFINITY AND LEXICAL CHOICE IN THE FAN COMMUNITY
EVELYN BROWNE

This session is sponsored by
HPforGrownups

In my study of the usage of Japanese loanwords in the Live Journals (weblogs, online diaries) of 23 Harry Potter fans, half of whom are also fans of Japansese anime and/or manga, the most telling predictor of the use of such loanwords was whether the user is a fanfic writer. Writers must market their work by showing their adherence to the community aesthetic, which is at odds with the favored aesthetic of Japanese-media based fan fiction. Readers, having less status to maintain within the fandom, are much freer and more inventive in their use of borrowings, as are writers who set themselves in opposition to the stylistic norms of the fandom. Other topics I consider in this paper include the creation of a fandom's norms, the role of the "fannish butterfly," and overt and covert prestige in the fan writing community. (25 minutes)

11:30 a.m.

THE PAIN AND THE PLEASURE OF THE SCAR: HARRY POTTER AS A POPULAR CULTURE ICON
Anne Frances N. Sangil

Harry Potter as a cultural text is a site of struggle. On the one hand there is the ever ubiquitous dominance and power of a capitalistic bloc determined to continually lure the consumers into consuming everything and anything HP-related: books, films, soundtracks, Playstation games, calendars, even apparel in the form of round spectacles held together by Scotch tape. This is the political economy of Harry Potter. The commodities are produced and distributed by a profit-motivated industry that follows only its own economic interests. But on the other hand, there is also Harry Potter within the realm of popular culture. Amidst the seeming 'pain' imposed by the capitalists to the consumers in the former's relentless campaign towards an enormous return of investment, the latter, from being a commodified, homogenized entity now becomes a producer, a producer of meanings and pleasures. These consumers turned producers create the Icon that is Harry Potter. (25 minutes)

THE DANGER OF DYNAMICS: TRANSPORT IN THE HARRY POTTER SERIES
Dr. Steven J. Gores

Many readers have noted the ways in which J. K. Rowling limits the presence of the Muggle world in her magical novels: Harry's experience with Muggledom is claustrophobically confined to the Dursley home. Whereas the portions of the Harry Potter series that represent Harry in the world of Muggles are remarkably static, Harry Potter's experiences in the magical world are extremely dynamic: he and/or others are constantly in motion, travelling by one device or another. Travel, however, is not just an index of which world we are in, magical or Muggle—it is treated as a theme of its own, offering the characters opportunities for both marvel and danger. For instance, Harry's rather innocuous, if marvelous, travel experience on the Hogwart's Express is balanced by Harry and Ron's near-fatal use of Mr. Weasley's enchanted car to make the same trip. Floo powder, an apparently conventional means of transport in the magical world, almost lands Harry in the arms of his enemies. Harry's Nimbus, upon which he performs great aerodynamic feats, is also nearly manipulated to cause his death. Any kind of movement, transport, or change in the magical world of Harry Potter is fraught with potential for both good and evil. (25 minutes)

HARRY POTTER VERSUS OTHER FANTASY TALES
Dr. Andrew Seeger

With the overwhelming success of the Harry Potter novels and films, there have been a number of new books aimed at the same core audience. Some of these are by well-established children's authors, some by new writers, and some by authors best known for adult-oriented fare who are now taking their shot at a new market. Furthermore, there have been changes in the marketing and reception of such works, with fancier (and more expensive) versions of books being published and with changes made to the established bestseller lists. This presentation will examine these phenomena and some of the recent books that have appeared in the wake of J. K. Rowling's novels, including Lemony Snicket's "A Series of Unfortunate Events" series, Eion Colfer's "Artemis Fowl" books, Cornelia Funke's The Thief Lord, Michael Chabon's Summerland, as well as books by Clive Barker, Alice Hoffmann, Amelia Atwater-Rhodes, and others—not only as novels, but also the editions that have come out and how they have been marketed. (30 minutes)

PRISONER OF AZKABAN: A CASE AGAINST THE DEATH PENALTY
Dr. Joy Morgenstern

This session is sponsored by
HPforGrownups

In Harry Potter and the Prisoner of Azkaban, Harry, in an action atypical for the standard hero of myth, does not kill Sirius Black, his supposed enemy, to avenge the death of his loved ones when provided with an opportunity to do so. In addition, he later refuses to allow Black and Remus Lupin to kill his true enemy, Peter Pettigrew. Nevertheless, his actions are presented as heroic, and Harry is portrayed as moral because he will not let Lupin and Black become killers. This paper interprets the plot of Harry Potter and the Prisoner of Azkaban as a political argument against the death penalty, and examines the ways in which J.K. Rowling uses Harry's feelings and decisions (and, to a lesser extent, Lupin's and Black's) as metaphors for the various political arguments surrounding the death penalty debate. (30 minutes)

12:00 p.m.

HARASSING HARRY: THE "DEMONIZING" OF THE HARRY POTTER SERIES
Judith Krug, Director of the Office of Intellectual Freedom,
American Library Association

Uncommonly popular with children, parents, educators and readers of all stripes, the Harry Potter books have attracted the attention of critics as well as fans. For four years running, the books have been the most frequently banned and challenged titles in the country. Judith F. Krug, director of the American Library Association's Office for Intellectual Freedom, will discuss the Harry Potter phenomenon and the unprecedented attempts to censor it, in the context of censorship and intellectual freedom in our schools and libraries. (90 minutes)

1:30 p.m.

EDUCATION AT HOGWARTS: A CLOSER LOOK
Linda McCabe, as proxy presenter for Peter Gow

This session sponsored by
Rob Ihinger and Peg Kerr

In many ways the novels in J.K. Rowling's Harry Potter series reflect the conventions of schoolboy (and—girl) novels dating back to the Victorian era, but the setting, Hogwarts School, is also a highly specialized institution serving a distinct community with unusual and particular needs. For educators, the essential questions about Hogwarts revolve around the nature of the educational program as it is designed to educate children for all conditions of life in the wizarding world. This study will address the nature and efficacy of that program. In other words, what makes Hogwarts, as Rubeus Hagrid asserts, "the finest school of witchcraft and wizardry in the world," and what makes Albus Dumbledore "the greatest headmaster Hogwarts ever had"? Based loosely on evaluative methodologies drawn from independent secondary school accreditation guidelines from both the United Kingdom and the United States, this inquiry will focus on three aspects of Hogwarts School of Witchcraft and Wizardry: School Culture, Curriculum and Instruction, and

Administration and Governance. A fourth category, "Unanswered Questions," will include questions and concerns relating to the education of young witches and wizards in general, looking at issues not specifically addressed in the Rowling oeuvre. (50 minutes)

JUSTICE IN THE WIZARDING WORLD
Susan Hall

This session is sponsored by
The Garks

Although the magical society depicted in the Harry Potter novels has certain elements and institutions that have close parallels in contemporary UK society (for example, the Ministry, the school examinations system, the press), the justice system (if it can be called that at all) applicable to wizards does not in any real sense parallel its Muggle equivalent. So notable are the divergences between the justice system in the wizard world and that which applies in contemporary England that it can only be seen as a deliberate theme. This presentation will draw specific attention to the treatment of justice, crime and punishment in the world of Harry Potter and contrast it to the contemporary English equivalents (with consideration of European law to the extent relevant). It will go on to consider the societal pressures which could have created such a divergence. In particular, the existence of a system of bastard client/patronage networks in the Wizard World (loosely corresponding to the model from the later Roman Republic) is in itself inimical to the development of a legal system based on the principles of equality before the law. Furthermore, the successive states of emergency through which the wizard world seems to have passed during the course of the second half of the twentieth century, and the historic and ongoing need for secrecy as to the world's very existence, are likely both to have strengthened the client/patron system and, independently, contributed to the repressive, partial and arbitrary regime which passes for a justice system for witches and wizards. (50 minutes)

DON'T TELL THE GROWNUPS: SUBVERSION IN HARRY POTTER TEXT AND FANDOM
Catherine Tosenberger

This session is sponsored by
RestrictedSection.org

Roman Jakobson noted that folklore can display and embody two competing dynamics: the conservative and the subversive. Conservative folklore reinforces the beliefs and norms of the dominant culture, while subversive folklore mocks, undermines, complicates, or overturns the received wisdom of that culture. In the Harry Potter fandom, some of the most exciting developments and activities are taking place at the fringes, where fans are forging new developments and relationships of text that subvert the "received wisdom," not only of canon interpretation, but of fans' interaction with the text itself. Slash is the most visible of these "subversive" acts, but it's only the tip of the iceberg: stories about incest, BDSM, intergenerational relationships, and other controversial subjects flourish as well. In addition, the proliferation of Harry Potter RPGs may be the most radical development of all—fans ENTER INTO the text, in an interactive format, and transform it as a group effort. This presentation will focus on this shadowy radical fringe of fandom, and explore the subversive techniques of these happily non-mainstream writers and roleplayers. (50 minutes)

BUT THAT'S THE TITLE ON THE MANIFESTO!: LABOR AND CLASS CONCERNS IN HARRY POTTER
Wendy A.F.G. Stengel

This session is sponsored by
The Humanists of Florida Association

Kings and peasants. Masters and servants. In-group and out-group. Classist explorations are hardly new in British fiction. However, with the phenomenal interest in J. K. Rowling's Harry Potter books, the class explorations are firmly in the hands of children, teens, and adults around the world. While protestors decry the possibility of a mistaken mystical message seeping into children's minds, stronger political messages are coming through: Class is nothing. Laborers deserve respect.

As a starting point, this paper will explore Dobby, the house elf. It is tempting to view Dobby's storyline simplistically: "Slavery is bad." However, the issue resonates on many more levels, especially since for most of the target audience, slavery itself is seen as a historical, American concern—Britain may have had serfs, but slaves? Clearly, there is more going on. Harry and Hermione have similar mud-bloody backgrounds—each grew up with Muggles around—but have very different levels of political awareness. Harry treats Dobby decently, Hermione becomes a firebrand for labor rights. Other sympathetic characters beg for them not to challenge the status quo. Springing from that foundation will be an exploration of the laborers in the series, from shopkeepers to groundskeepers to teachers, and how the children of the series relate to each. (25 minutes)

S.P.E.W./SPEW OR HERMIONE SPEWS A BADGE
Bharati Kasibhatla

This paper explores opposition to Hermione's subversive campaign for elf welfare. The title of the paper points to the translation of S.P.E.W. into spew, indicating the venom and verbiage that Hermione is supposedly spewing in her 'obsessive' reaction to the enslavement of elves in Harry Potter and the Goblet of Fire. The resistance to Hermione's

S. P. E. W. takes many forms, ranging from the insistence that the elves like being enslaved to the belief that elves are not really enslaved at Hogwarts. I argue that the hostility to S. P. E. W. is an expression of the anxiety that Hermione is challenging Dumbledore's established system at Hogwarts, which the text projects as democratic in contrast to Voldemort's dictatorial politics. Hermione's radical potential lies in her challenge to Dumbledore, and concomitantly to Harry's heroic narrative, which draws sustenance from Dumbledore's wisdom. (25 minutes)

2:30 p.m.

WILL CEASE AND DESIST CEASE TO EXIST?: THE EFFECTS OF *ELDRED V. ASHCROFT* ON HARRY POTTER FAN SITES
Sarah Kelman

Intellectual property law troubles Harry Potter fan websites. The recent Supreme Court decision in *Eldred v. Ashcroft* upheld a 1998 copyright term extension. Thus, rights holders will have firmer support for cease and desist letters used to intimidate Harry Potter fan sites. However, the decision may undermine other limiting laws like the Digital Millennium Copyright Act. (50 minutes)

Harry Potter Library Events Workshop
Nancy Carstensen

This session sponsored by
Linda DeNell

Want to put on a successful Harry Potter event at your library or business? Find out how to choose special guests, find local talent, and cultivate media connections and sponsors? From small parties to multi-day extravaganzas, Children's Librarian Nancy Carstensen shows you the key elements to a winning program. Lots of handouts, ideas and a special 'make & take' craft! (50 minutes)

COMING OUT OF THE CUPBOARD: SLASH IN THE HARRY POTTER FANDOM (PANEL DISCUSSION)
John Walton (Moderator), Bridget Roussell Cowlishaw, Vicki Dolenga, Kate Tanski and Dave Wang

This session is sponsored by
Victoria Powers

What is slash? Beyond the background of the genre, what has it come to represent in Harry Potter and other fandoms? From defining the term and discussing its subtextual implications, the panel will move on to the evolution of slash specifically in the Harry Potter fandom, including reactions to slash and the ways in which popular fan fiction (such as the Draco Trilogy) have been "slashed," creating subtext of its own. The panel will also explore sexuality and slash, through such theories as the 'feminisation' argument and relevance of the sexuality of slashers, and the extent to which slash as a medium provides a forum or platform for GLBT issues. (50 minutes)

IMPERIAL HARRY: RACE, J.K. ROWLING AND THE POSTCOLONIAL CONTEXT
Ebony Thomas

This session sponsored by
Anne Sjursen

J.K. Rowling's unique blending of fantasy with the classic boarding school story incorporates features from genres of British literature which were irrefutably informed by imperialist thought. One of Rowling's primary thematic concerns in the Harry Potter series is the subtle refutation of long-entrenched notions of class, ethnicity, and race. However, in the very process of subverting this authoritative metadiscourse, upon occasion Rowling resorts to some of the selfsame rhetoric that her narrative critiques and challenges.

This topical analysis will include the following:

- "I Didn't Know Dean Was Black!": The Role of the Racialized Other in Harry Potter
- Necessary Enslavement or Involuntary Servitude?: The Problem of the House-Elves
- The Monster Bash: Werewolves, Giants, and Other Misunderstood Beastly Beings
- Of Mud and Blood: Issues of Racial Purity and Ethnic Cleansing in the Wizarding and Muggle Worlds
- Which Magic?: The Quidditch World Cup, the Triwizard Tournament, and the Global Position of Post-Imperial Britain

(25 minutes)

SEXUALITY, PROTEST, ELVES AND WHITE WOMANHOOD: HERMIONE AND S.P.E.W.
Laurie Barth Walczak

In Harry Potter and the Goblet of Fire, Hermione Granger forms S.P.E.W., the Society for the Promotion of Elfish Welfare, to fight for the equal rights of house elves, who are in essence the slaves of the magical world. Hermione takes up the house elves' cause with tenacity and verve, but she does not play the role of the abolitionist for long. As her friendship with Viktor Krum develops, Hermione loses interest in the plight of the house elves. Hermione's relationships to the elves change as she commences her passage into white womanhood; her protest is forgotten when she becomes preoccupied with her new friend. This paper will explore—and deconstruct—the intersections of slavery, whiteness, and femininity in the Harry Potter series, paying particular attention to Hermione and her identity as a Muggle-born witch, a civil rights leader, and a young woman with several admirers. (25 minutes)

3:30 p.m.

TANYA GROTTER: A HARRY POTTER KNOCK-OFF OR PARODY?
Mark Hooker

The appearance of the Russian Tanya Grotter books caused a furor as reviewers and lawyers compared them to the Harry Potter books, and threats of legal action filled the air. This presentation will assist the reader in making up his or her own mind about whether Tanya Grotter is a knock-off or a parody, by offering a summary of the Tanya Grotter books. No knowledge of Russian, or Russian folklore and literature is necessary to enjoy this presentation. Knowledge of the Harry Potter books, on the other hand, will be extremely helpful. Be sure to bring your sense of humor. (50 minutes)

POTTERMANIA BRAG 'N' SWAP MEET
Mary Shearer

This session is sponsored by
Linda DeNell

A forum in which educators, librarians and parents can gather to share stories about and ideas for Potter-themed programming in their libraries, classrooms and homes. Participants are encouraged to bring hand-outs, and the atmosphere will be informal, with a moderator on hand to keep track of time. (25 minutes)

CLOAKS AND CAULDRONS: AN ANTI-STEREOTYPICAL ANALYSIS OF WIZARDING FASHION
Mary LeGrow

Ms. Mary LeGrow, a professional model and costumer and owner of the Wonderland Costume Shop, will discuss the costume choices and designs used to enhance the story and character developments seen in the Harry Potter films. The how and why of wizarding fashion will be discussed, as well as the director's use of certain design elements and fabrics to separate the wizarding world from the Muggle world. Ms. LeGrow will also analyze the use of costuming as a way of defining certain character personalities, such as Professor Snape, Lucius Malfoy, Professor Lockhart and others. Audience participation in this lecture is preferred and attendees are encouraged to share their ideas on the costume choice and selection for each character, setting or mood. Free sample patterns for House robes will be distributed while supplies last, so please show up on time! (25 minutes)

CAN DRACO MALFOY BE REDEEMED? (PANEL DISCUSSION)

Aja Romano (Moderator), Irina Achildiyev, Cassandra Claire, Carlisle Elizabeth Kraft, Catherine Tosenberger

This session is sponsored by
Victoria Powers

He has been compared to Adolph Hitler, Mr. Darcy, and the Vampire Lestat. He inspires rampant hatred and fervent loyalty. His character transformation through fan fiction is both a unique fandom phenomena and the source of heated debate. Is his redemption in canon a foregone conclusion or a lost cause better left to the realm of sympathetic fans? Join us as we examine the furor surrounding the powder keg otherwise known as Draco Malfoy, and find out. (50 minutes)

Strangers in a Strange Land: How the Muggleborn are a Powerful Force for Social Change

Sarah Goff, proxy presenter for Sarah Marie Parker-Allen

This session is sponsored by
HPforGrownups

There is a continual flow of new members to the magical community, who have not been indoctrinated into its social patterns and who have not been raised with its basic assumptions: the Muggle-born. These people can, and do, provide a powerful force for social change within the community, along with those who recognize their value and support them (the Muggle-aware). The evidence of Muggle influence abounds throughout the community. Without the influence of the Muggle-born, the magical world would be in jeopardy of becoming isolated, stagnant. Persons of Muggle heritage provide more than just additional DNA for the biological preservation of the community—they are the continual wind of change, charting the direction of the community's future. (50 minutes)

4:30 p.m.

EXAMINING WRITING STYLE: LEARNING FROM J.K. ROWLING'S WRITING STYLE
Kimberly Lowe

This session is sponsored by
danielradclifferocks.com

This presentation will examine writing style using JK Rowling's Harry Potter novels as a benchmark. Writing well is more than just piecing together grammatically correct sentences; well written prose reflects the choices a writer makes with respect to point of view, characterization, tone and even sentence structure. This presentation will include: (1) a discussion of the various aspects of writing style, including tone, pacing, plot, structure, language usage, point of view, narrative voice, characterization, style and intentional departures from the rules of grammar for stylistic impact; (2) a discussion of how JK Rowling utilizes these fundamental tools of writing in her body of work; and (3) a critical review of selected fan fiction to illustrate how the elements of writing style have been or can be better used by writers of fan fiction. (50 minutes)

THE GREAT TRADITION AND HARRY POTTER
Dr. Paige Byam

This presentation will cover the Harry Potter as part of the Gothic tradition, drawing on elements of the classic novel and using Gothic trappings as well. Harry Potter's popularity and contemporary appeal is directly related to its connection with commonly known Gothic trappings such as castles, labyrinths, doubling of characters and worlds, magic, and appearances of the supernatural. Other elements in Rowling's series can also be construed as transformations of Gothic conventions: crime, enclosure, deformity, murder, blood, miracles, armored knights, the mark, dreams and visions, hidden lineage, the stranger motif, the 'foreign' realms. The massive popularity of the Harry Potter series (as well as its label as children's literature) has masked its very traditional aspects. In many ways, J. K. Rowling's works revive forms of the Gothic novel for an international, modern readership. (25 minutes)

When Harry Met Jane: The Legacy of Austen in Rowling's Harry Potter
Dr. Karin Westman

This session is sponsored by
The Tito Family

In "J.K. Rowling's Bookshelf" (2001), Rowling claims Jane Austen as one of her favorite authors, having already cited Austen's Emma as "the most skillfully managed mystery I've ever read" ("Let me tell you a story," 2000). In her own novels, Rowling's debt to Austen reaches beyond her borrowing Mrs. Norris from Mansfield Park to name Filch's cat. Like Austen, Rowling favors a narrative style which relies upon limited omniscient point of view to restrict the readers' experience of the story to one character's view of the world. As readers, we only gradually realize the degree to which our perspective on the wizarding world is shaped primarily by Harry's perspective, just as Emma's limitations prevent our knowledge of Frank Churchill and Jane Fairfax's engagement. This narrative style emphasizes the development of Harry's character, as it does Emma's, allowing us to follow his responses to the wizarding world as they range from awe and fear, to delight and frustration. While several critics of the novels claim them to be only plot—"And then, and then, and then" (Hensher, The Independent, 25 Jan 2000)—Rowling's narrative style reminds us that character, as well as a well-crafted plot, is one of the pleasures of the novels and one of its strengths. (25 minutes)

Other Voices, Other Common Rooms
Meghan Mercier

Woe betide any non-Gryffindor Hogwarts students during Harry Potter's seven years at school. Their House will never win the Quidditch or House Cup. Fan fiction writers have done much to humanize Slytherins, Ravenclaws, and the much maligned Hufflepuffs. There are both fictions parallel to the novels, and fictions that focus on characters that are only marginal such as Susan Bones, Pansy Parkinson, Millicent Bulstrode, or Percy Weasley. Other fictions that center on our favorite Gryffindors incorporate characters from other Houses that are more than just names during a Sorting. Come and join a discussion among various House and character advocates, and we'll celebrate fictions that expand the scope of the wizarding world as these do, and generally toot the horns of the smart, hardworking, and ambitious (who aren't all nerdy, dull, or evil) in defiance of the brave. (50 minutes)

The Geography of Harry Potter
Penny Linsenmayer and Steve Vander Ark

This session is sponsored by
HPforGrownups

This presentation will explore various known locales connected to the Harry Potter books, including London, Surrey, and Albania. We will also examine theories as to the potential locales of other Potterverse places, based on clues in the books and Rowling interviews (such as Hogwarts, Azkaban, Godric's Hollow and The Burrow). Finally, the presentation will cover locales with names that served as inspiration to Rowling in her novels, even if not as place names (such as the villages of Dursley, Flitwick and Snape). (50 minutes)

8:30 a.m.

ONLINE WRITING WORKSHOPS: FANFICTION AS A SPRINGBOARD INTO IMPROVING TECHNIQUE AND ORIGINAL CREATIVE WRITING
Dr. Catherine Schaff-Stump

This session is sponsored by
sugarquill.net

In her capacity as a writer, Dr. Schaff-Stump has been involved with an on-line writing workshop, and has become interested in the commonalities and differences in the creative processes and critiquing of fan fiction and original character fiction. This presentation will discuss those commonalities and differences, as well as demonstrate the set-up of an on-line writing workshop and an actual session of a workshop. (50 minutes)

LORD VOLDEMORT'S GIFT FOR SPREADING DISCORD AND ENMITY: THE RISE OF EVIL IN HARRY POTTER
Dr. Richard Burke

This session is sponsored by
The Ultimate Unofficial Guide to the Mysteries of Harry Potter

The Harry Potter books confront the hero with a potent and relentless evil force: Lord Voldemort. But part of the dramatic power of these novels comes from the presence of various other evils in addition to Voldemort. Read in order, the books grow increasingly compelling as the evil within them spreads and deepens. Besides the elemental evil of

Voldemort, the books contain the mundane evils of the Dursleys, Malfoy, and Snape, whose worst behaviors result from the contemptuous willingness to make others suffer, which is at the core of evil. Rowling uses athletics in all four books as a revealing parallel to Harry's confrontation with evil. The Quidditch matches that are so prominent in the first three novels provide a safe sort of surrogate for the battle with evil: one's favored team struggles to vanquish an enemy in controlled circumstances where little besides emotion is at stake. But in Harry Potter and the Goblet of Fire, where Voldemort's evil is spreading, Quidditch is replaced by the Tri-Wizard Tournament, which Voldemort manipulates into a truly deadly competition. (25 minutes)

THE HERO'S PROGRESS: HARRY POTTER'S DISCOVERY OF IDENTITY IN J.K. ROWLING'S HIERARCHICAL WORLD
Dr. Alice Trupe

At first glance, Harry Potter seems to be a likable, average boy whose pleasant exterior conceals some traditional English qualities and values that raise him to the status of hero in the face of extraordinary challenges: courage, resourcefulness, honor, fairness. He epitomizes the good, opposed to the evil epitomized in Voldemort, in a classic epic conflict between good and evil. Yet closer examination of the conditions that shape Harry's choices and actions reveal that he, like other characters, is severely constrained by a history of which he is largely ignorant, replete with class prejudices, racism, and economic disparity and exploitation. The hierarchical world of Hogwarts reproduces the values of the hierarchical magical realm in which it exists. Ultimately, the conflict at the heart of the series may be read as a class conflict between a dominant privileged wizarding class and all other races and classes. (25 minutes)

ALCHEMY, DOPPELGANGERS AND THE IRONY OF RELIGIOUS OBJECTIONS TO HARRY POTTER
John Granger (Featured Speaker)

Each Potter novel and the series as a whole are built on parallel structures of a hero's journey and the alchemical work. This presentation focuses on the neglected alchemical symbols and meaning in the books. Expect, in addition to a quick course in what alchemy is and isn't (it's not what your chemistry teacher or New Age buddy says it is), to learn: the alchemical elements in the structure of each book and the series (how the names of Black, Snape, Dumbledore, and Hagrid identify them as stages in the creation of the Philosopher's Stone—and why Ron and Hermione are ciphers for sulfur and quicksilver, the alchemical reagents); the possible interpretations (and misinterpretations) of alchemy via Eliade, Jung, and Burckhardt; the use of alchemy in English literature from Chaucer and Shakespeare to Lewis and Tolkien; why every character has a narratological shadow or 'doppelganger' and the importance of this echo of 19th century Gothic romances in understanding Harry and his friends (and enemies!); the differences between psychological and symbolist (or 'spiritual') understanding of the books; and the irony of Christian objections to the books and their unwitting witness to the psychological power and spiritual impact on Harry Potter readers, old and young, of Ms. Rowling's alchemical artistry. (50 minutes)

CANON, INTERPRETATION AND THE ALTERNATE UNIVERSE: NAVIGATING THE FANDOM SAFELY (PANEL DISCUSSION)
Debra Duncan (Moderator), Peg Kerr, Barbara Purdom and Steve Vander Ark

This session is sponsored by
Etakyma

What is the Harry Potter canon? Whether you're an armchair Auror, a writer of fan fiction, or critically analyzing the books, you must confront this question. The panelists will discuss these questions and more, including: Should the U.S. editions, the schoolbooks, interviews or the movies qualify as canon? What makes a particular interpretation worthy of serious consideration? Can fan fiction be analyzed as an interpretation of canon? Why are some fans concerned that reading fan fiction *taints* the canon? (50 minutes)

9:30 a.m.

OPHELIA'S QUILL PEN: HOW WRITING FANFICTION EMPOWERS WOMEN AND GIRLS
Catherine Danielson

This session is sponsored in memory of
Janice Scott

We live in a media-saturated culture. Magazines, television shows, and films constantly bombard us with images and messages that always tell us what we should be, but rarely what we could be, and still less what we have the power to become. But what happens when we turn the paradigm around? What happens when we become, not passive consumers, but active creators? That's the story of fan fiction, and above all of fan fiction set in the Harry Potter universe, which appeals to more first-time fanfic readers and writers, and more young female writers, than any other. Come prepared to learn and discuss the fascinatingly subversive nature of fanfic, and the brave new world of fanfilms and fangames. Also, see the premiere of filmmaker Cathy Danielson's new animated short, "Ophelia's Quill Pen!" (50 minutes)

Harry Potter: A Universal Hero?
Michèle Fry

This session is sponsored by
HPforGrownups

Jack Zipes describes Harry Potter as "one of the mythical chosen heroes [who is] called upon by powers greater than himself to rescue his friends and the world from diabolical evil. He is [. . .] the little guy who proves he's bigger than life"; whilst David Colbert describes Harry Potter as "a very familiar type of hero." In this paper I intend to look at how much J. K. Rowling's characterisation conforms to the universal hero archetype, and how far she has subverted this archetype. It is intended that this paper will complement my last published paper "Heroes and Heroines: Myth and Gender in the Harry Potter Books" (New Review of Children's Literature and Librarianship, 2001). (25 minutes)

Within the Pantheon: Harry Potter and the Epic Question
Dr. Mary Pharr

The question of Harry Potter's place in the literary pantheon is a query not easily answered. Defined by many critics as a Bildingsroman, Rowling's schooldays series may actually be extending itself into something larger—but only if it can prove its seriousness, its ability to make its readers meditate on the universe beyond its narrative. If it does so prove itself, the Potter books may end as not just a child's version of old mythology but as a postmodern version of epic heroism, its title character a fitting figure for our time and culture. (25 minutes)

Harry Potter: Witchcraft? Pagan Perspectives
Lee Hillman, Amy Vezza and John Walton

Everyone hears a great deal about the Christian controversy over the Harry Potter books. Occasionally a pagan group pipes up, usually to praise the books, sometimes to criticise them. What is paganism, how does it relate to Harry Potter, and what kinds of things do pagans have to say about the books' take on magic, morals, and myth? (50 minutes)

Sail on Good Ship: Shipping Debate

Sarah Goff (Moderator); Susan Faust (Lead Debater: Ron/Hermione); Emily Bytheway (Debater: Ron/Hermione); Sara Goetz (Lead Debater: Harry/Hermione); Linda McCabe (Debater: Harry/Hermione)

This session is sponsored by
Bake a Nimbus Pie/Pumpkinpie.org

This moderated debate will square off two of the most popular romance pairings in the Harry Potter fandom: Ron/Hermione versus Harry/ Hermione. (50 minutes).

10:30 a.m.

THE HEROIC JOURNEY AND HARRY POTTER
Dr. Antoinette Winstead

Focusing primarily on Harry Potter and the Sorcerer's Stone, this paper examines how, J. K. Rowling has, through the Harry Potter series, created a collection of high-adventure and fantasy novels that exemplify the heroic journey as outlined by Joseph Campbell in his book The Hero with a Thousand Faces, thus proving her to be a twenty-first century mythmaker. (25 minutes)

THE HEROIC QUEST: HARRY POTTER AND MYTH
Dr. Jeff Morgan

Levi-Strauss claims that meaning in myth, as in language, depends on the combination of the elements, or the points of similarity we may find. An analysis of plot structure and characterization in heroic quests from Greek myth to Arthurian legend and extending into more modern myth such as Tolkien's The Hobbit will reveal a similarity in the combinations of elements which comprise the plots and characterizations of these stories. J.K. Rowling's Harry Potter and the Sorcerer's Stone has certain similarities with other heroic quests in mythology, allowing her first novel to take the stand with them in the arena of mythology and the heroic quest. (25 minutes)

KEEPING IT IN THE FAMILY: THE WEASLEYS, THE MALFOYS AND CANON AND ITS DIS(MAL)CONTENTS
Catherine Tosenberger

The Weasleys and the Malfoys, as the two most prominent wizarding dynasties within the Harry Potter canon, occupy a central place in a narrative that is so deeply concerned about belonging. What, then, does it mean to be a Weasley or a Malfoy, both in canon and fanon? Particular emphasis will be placed upon fan fictional incest narratives, as a working example of genre reinscription, in this case the Gothic or Gothic-Romantic. With that in mind, these stories, by enshrining a subversive or pathological family dynamic as a central theme, explicitly articulate the tensions between the public, external interactions of the families, and the private, interior relationships among family members, and illuminate broader issues of each family's representation within the fandom. (50 minutes)

HARRY POTTER: CAN ANY WISDOM COME FROM WIZARDRY?
Dr. David Isaacs (Moderator); Emily Bytheway, Dr. Anita Helmbold,
Dr. Helen Huntley, Dr. Dawnellen Jacobs

Prof. David Isaacs of California Baptist University (CBU) will present an overview of the Harry Potter controversy, giving the main arguments against Harry Potter, to provide a foundation for discussion. Opening statements will include such sources as Richard Abanes, Gene Veith and Charles Colson. Emily Bytheway of Brigham Young University will build on this and respond to some of the critics' claims that Harry Potter is anti-religious and full of witchcraft. Professor Anita Helmbold of Taylor University College will demonstrate that the books' endorsement of an ethic rooted in concern for the well-being of others more accurately reflects Christian ethical principles than does the strictly rule-based morality which some critics have castigated the series for failing to propagate. Professor DawnEllen Jacobs, also of CBU, will compare critiques of Rowling with those of C.S. Lewis's Narnia series. Those who object to Rowling, she will demonstrate, forget there was a similar reaction to Lewis; ironically, Lewis's works are most often held up as examples of great literature, worthy of inclusion in any canon of Children's Literature. Helen Huntley of CBU will conclude with an analysis demonstrating that children are much wiser than adults perceive. With the written word, children's imagination goes only as far as the child can accept; in visuals, however, the presentation may go beyond the child's limits. Reading, therefore, is the perfect way for a child to understand he/she has the same ghosts in the imagination as others; reading is the perfect way to guide a child into decision making, both critical and creative. As Lewis Mumford wrote, in sadness, of his son: "When we took away the folk and fairy tales, we took away St. George, but we left the dragon!" (90 minutes)

Publishing on Potter: Dodging the Bludgers
Dr. Katherine Grimes (Moderator); Dr. Giselle Anatol, John Granger, Dr. Edmund Kern, Connie Neal, Dr. Philip Nel, Dr. Lana Whited

This session is sponsored by
HPforGrownups

Five years into the Harry Potter phenomenon, it is abundantly clear that, for writers assembling books about J. K. Rowling's work, the path to publication is both as unusual and as potentially dangerous as Dorothy's journey to Oz. In an e-mail to Lana Whited in March 2002, a representative of the Christopher Little Agency wrote, "For your information, we do not approve companion books based on the [Harry Potter] series." It is unlikely that authors of any other secondary sources have experienced such unusual interaction with the copyright holders of the primary material. Nevertheless, authors and editors have persisted in analyzing J. K. Rowling's work in books of several kinds, including reader's or teacher's guides, volumes of critical essays, biographies of Rowling, and discussions of morality and theology in the series. Nearly all these books bear on their covers a stamp declaring them "Not approved or authorized by J. K. Rowling or Warner Brothers." Authors or editors will discuss their own experiences publishing on Potter, with particular attention to any "bludgers" they had to dodge due to the resistance of Rowling's official representatives. The focus of the discussion will be on two questions: To what extent can the copyright holders of literary works control published discussion of those works? What is the effect of such attempts to control the published discussion of Harry Potter? (90 minutes)

11:30 a.m.

CELLULOID POLYJUICE: THE FILMIC TRANSFIGURATION OF HARRY POTTER INTO INFALLIBLE HERO
Suzanne Scott

This paper argues that the adaptations of the Harry Potter canon from fiction to film are significant in terms of their exclusion/alteration (rather than reenactment/realization) of specific sequences, thereby serving to re-author the series' titular protagonist and the metatext at large, be it literary or cinematic. "Celluloid Polyjuice" examines the repositioning of Harry from reluctant to infallible hero, both in terms of the impact on the forthcoming films/books and the Hollywood tendency to deproblematize literary protagonists, via textual analysis of scenes and marketing strategies of Chris Columbus' adaptations. (30 minutes)

PERCEPTIONS OF CHILDHOOD AND ADULT-CHILD RELATIONS IN HARRY POTTER
Liz O'Reilly

This paper will concentrate on the nineteenth-century polarisation of children as either 'Angels' or 'Devils', and how these ideas can be related to the Harry Potter novels. In particular, it will explore the attitudes of adult characters towards the children in their care. The Dursleys view Harry as a 'devil' and their own child, Dudley, as an 'angel'. Their attitude towards Harry embodies the view of a child as something evil—their treatment of him can be seen to stem from fear. This fear centres on his magical powers—therefore, could the magical world be seen, in some ways, to represent childhood itself, with its potential to expose adult fallibility and threaten the social order? However, if the Dursleys fear childhood itself, why do they not view Dudley as evil? Dudley is the idolised 'angel' child—yet this can also be seen as a (more subtle) form of repression and control. Therefore, the sentimentalisation of Dudley may stem from the same fear of disruption which causes the Dursleys' harsh treatment of Harry. The Weasleys, in contrast, can be seen to provide a middle-ground between the two extremes, viewing their children as a 'normal' combination of good and bad. These children are neither sentimentalised nor treated harshly, and consequently are able to develop in their own individual ways. (30 minutes)

12:00 p.m.

CREATING DIGITAL COSTUMES AND ENVIRONMENTS FOR FEATURE FILMS
Ari Rapkin, Computer Graphics Software Engineer, Industrial Light and Magic

In recent feature films, computer-generated characters have evolved from mere background extras to leading players. We'll look at the need for computer-generated characters, the challenges of creating them, and the technology & techniques developed to meet those challenges. We'll pay particular attention to computer-simulated clothing, taking a tour through the clothing simulation system used for Jedi robes and other clothing in STAR WARS: EPISODE II "Attack of the Clones," followed by an in-depth look at the process of designing and simulating Dobby's pillowcase costume. We'll conclude with a brief discussion of issues and solutions for upcoming films. (90 minutes)

1:30 p.m.

IMAGINATION AT WORK: HARRY POTTER AND STOIC VIRTUE
Dr. Edmund M. Kern

In her Harry Potter series, J. K. Rowling develops an essentially Stoic moral philosophy through the ethical dilemmas in which she places Harry and his friends, dilemmas requiring them to think in complex ways about right and wrong. In considering this ethical system, banish once and for all the common stereotype of the Stoic who is unemotional, tediously puritanical, and blindly indifferent to enjoyment and grief. Although early Stoic works do contribute to this stereotype, Rowling's characters are anything but unfeeling and embrace life to the fullest. Her version of Stoicism is admittedly an updated one, providing full attention to emotional development, but nonetheless one whose chief virtue is old-fashioned constancy. Harry's resolution in the face of adversity is the result of conscious choice and attention to what is and is not within his control. He cultivates himself in order to help others. Harry worries about who he is, but realizes that what he does matters most. In fact, the stories focus on Harry's self-fashioning and the moral decisions that go into it, elaborating, along the way, upon several key Stoic themes such as fatalism, endurance, perseverance, self-discipline, reason, solidarity, empathy, and sacrifice. Rowling's accomplishment, blending imaginative wit and serious contemplation of virtue, is astonishing—an apt term for a work on witchcraft. In fact, creativity and ethics coexist quite easily in Harry's adventures. Their author offers her readers not only an exciting world, but also one troubled by problems; she provides not only the promise of triumph over evil, but also guidance on how to meet it through thoughtful attention to right and wrong. By putting her imagination into play, she also puts her imagination to work. (50 minutes)

HERMIONE GRANGER AND ISSUES OF GENDER IN THE HARRY POTTER BOOKS AND FILMS
Dr. Eliza Dresang

This session is sponsored by
Penny Linsenmayer

Hermione, by name, has a long literary legacy and historical heritage. In 428 B.C.E., Euripides captured her from Greek mythology and placed her in the drama Andromache. St. Hermione from the Christian Bible was martyred at Ephesus. In a more contemporary setting, a slightly familiar-seeming Hermione appears in the poet and novelist, H.D.'s Hermione and in D.H. Lawrence's Women in Love, described by one essayist as "wanting to know everything 'intellectually' and control everything." Drawing upon her literary antecedents as appropriate to lend understanding, Hermione Granger, heroine in the Harry Potter books, is analyzed from the point of view of postmodern feminist literary theory. To what extent does J.K. Rowling let her character fall prey to perpetuating stereotypes, some of which stretch across thousands of years, and to what extent does she allow Hermione to invent her own independent image as she grows and matures? What will be the heritage of gender that Hermione passes on to readers now and in the future? Is she a pawn for the male characters or a principal actor on her own? How does the character of Hermione fare when she moves from the printed page to the screen? Although the answer cannot be complete after only five of seven books and two of possibly seven films have appeared, a considered study of Hermione's developing inner strength, social conscience, and problem-solving abilities meshed with her initial external "squealing" and her perceived "bossy" nature may provide perspective about what lies ahead. Some evidence from J.K. Rowling's stated perception of the character she refers to as herself will provide background for this in-depth analysis of Hermione Granger. (50 minutes)

THE SEVEN DEADLY SINS/SEVEN HEAVENLY VIRTUES: MORAL DEVELOPMENT IN HARRY POTTER
Peg Kerr

This session is sponsored by
HPforGrownups

This presentation grows out of a series of essays prepared for the HPforGrownups Yahoogroup, tracing the 7 Deadly Sins and 7 Heavenly virtues in Rowling's work. Critics of the Harry Potter series fault Harry for lying and disobeying authority, but in fact, Harry's story is about the acquisition of a moral education, specifically in learning how to handle an alternate technology (i.e, power (magic)) responsibly. Topics touched upon may include the role of the Dursleys in the series, Maslow's hierarchy of needs, Dumbledore's educational approach, and the moral ramifications for Harry and other characters of the tragic events of the Halloween night when Harry's parents died. Audience participation encouraged. (50 minutes)

SLYTHERINS, SMOKE AND SHADOWS: THE SECRET LIFE OF SEVERUS SNAPE (PANEL DISCUSSION)
Madeline Klink (Moderator), Meghan Mercier and Kendra Nuckels

This session is sponsored by
Emerson Spartz

Severus Snape: love him or hate him, you have to be intrigued by him. This panel will explore fanon interpretations of Snape's character and how far they are supported by canon, discuss Snape's appeal, and analyze several commonly held theories about his past and future. (50 minutes)

2:30 p.m.

TALKING ABOUT HARRY: THE FAIRY TALE AND BUILDING MORAL CHARACTER
Gina Burkart

The fantasy world has been used to enchant and teach children moral lessons for centuries. Harry Potter is really nothing new—in fact Harry Potter is essentially a modern-day fairy tale. By looking at the elements and use of the fairy tale as well as consulting with moral theorists Lawrence Kohlberg, Jean Piaget, and Martin Hoffman, you will realize that Harry Potter and my book, A Christian Parent's Guide to Harry Potter, are useful tools for developing moral character in children. (25 minutes)

EMERIC SWITCH ON GENDER: HARRY AND HERMIONE'S TRANSGENDERED HEROISM
Emily Kathryn Anderson

This session is sponsored by
Bake a Nimbus Pie/Pumpkinpie.org

Superficially, a feminist reader would be likely to lament the fact that Hermione, who is clearly the most intelligent and assertive of the three main characters, often ends up playing a supporting role to Harry, even when a majority of the problems are solved by her. This presentation will demonstrate that while Hermione clearly identities as a female, she possesses more of the qualities of a male archetypal hero than does Harry. She is assertive in and out of the classroom, she is extremely logical (she is the one who solves Snape's potion riddle in Sorcerer's Stone), she is commandeering and bossy, and often displays more bravery than Harry or Ron (she is the only person confident about the use of the Polyjuice Potion in Chamber of Secrets). Conversely, Harry displays more qualities traditionally associated with femininity. He is soft-spoken, polite, and insecure about his abilities both socially and as a wizard. Although he repeatedly displays bravery at the end of the novels, the majority of the books illustrate his fearfulness (the spotting of the Grim in Prisoner of Azkaban, his trepidation when he sees the dragons in Goblet of Fire).

This presentation will argue that Rowling is placing the psyche of a stereotypical and socially acceptable male in the body of Hermione, and a stereotypical and socially acceptable female's psyche within the body of Harry. By making Harry the undisputed hero at the end of each novel, Rowling is celebrating femininity, depicting female power as overpowering male power, even if that female power is embodied in a male character. However, by celebrating conventional female character traits in the body of a male, Rowling is creating a radical transgendered hero, one that is not entirely male or female. By depicting two characters whose behavior conflicts with their prescribed gender roles, Rowling is questioning the merit of a social system that assigns behavior expectations based on biological sex. Harry and Hermione both represent a type of transgendered consciousness, where they adopt the personality traits and characteristics that best suit them, ignoring dichotomous definitions of "male" and "female." For this reason, Rowling's vision of gender is more libratory than many critics have credited her for. (25 minutes)

Jewish Perspectives on Harry Potter
Amy Miller

What's a nice Jewish boy like Harry Potter doing in a place like this? Believe it or not, there are many Jewish teachings in the Harry Potter books, many of them cited by Dumbledore (although I'm sure he's unaware of how Jewish he is, too). There are parallels to Hitler, genocide, and racism as well. We will cite Torah and other biblical passages that address magic, discuss the occult in Judaism, how JKR could have been a member of the Workman's Circle (a Jewish society devoted to socialist and workers' ideals), and how Harry might even be a "lamed-vovnik"! (25 minutes)

The Wizarding World: Past, Present and Future
Ebony Thomas (Moderator); Kendra Nuckels and Steve Vander Ark

This session is sponsored by
Yasmin Cameron, winner of the Jumper Tandy Birth Pool

We know that Hogwarts School of Witchcraft and Wizardry was founded nearly 1000 years before the start of canon. We know that Nearly Headless Nick celebrated his 500th Deathday in 1492. We know that Hermione Granger was born on September 19, 1980. We know that Marcus Flint was a seventh year twice. However, there are still many things that we don't yet know. How has the publication of Harry Potter and the Order of the Phoenix supported or refuted fan assumptions about important events in the series? What about information from author interviews and the Rowling-sanctioned timeline included on the Chamber of Secrets DVD-ROM? What might the post-Book Seven edition of Hogwarts, A History look like? Have Rowling's "Flints" and inconsistencies regarding dating of events and character ages affected the story, and if so, how? Has the wizarding world changed over the centuries since the International Compact mentioned in Fantastic Beasts and Where to Find Them? Where can we place the adult characters on the series timeline? If Harry and his friends are to be the history makers of their generation, then can we as fan readers predict the impact of their legacy? In this session, Steve Vander Ark of the Harry Potter Lexicon, post-Hogwarts fan fiction author Ebony AKA AngieJ, and university student Kendra Nuckels discuss the timeline of the wizarding world. (50 minutes)

3:00 p.m.

GREENHOUSES ARE FOR GIRLS; BEASTS ARE FOR BOYS?: GENDER CHARACTERIZATION IN HARRY POTTER
Sarah Goff

Since the rise to fame and widespread popularity of J.K. Rowling's Harry Potter series, detractors have attacked the books for promoting gender stereotypes. Critics claim the books are sexist and chauvinistic, portraying stereotyped dominant-male and supporting-female characters. This presentation will examine gender characterization in Harry Potter, focusing on themes used to create male and female paradigms. Specifically, this presentation will explore how Rowling delineates gender through naming—including themes of flora and fauna, the power of perspective and narrative voice. Rowling uses individual interests and talents, such as affinity for Herbology, Magical Creatures, and Flying to delineate gender distinctions. This presentation will dissect and discuss the mechanisms by which gender is shaped to show how Rowling has created unique and well-rounded characters that transcend gender boundaries. (25 minutes)

SCRIPTWRITING FOR PLEASURE AND PROFIT: THE POWER OF THE WRITTEN WORD IN HARRY POTTER
Bonnie May

This session is sponsored by
FandomWank

The protagonist of Don Quixote is a man who, after reading dozens of chivalric novels, decides to take on a new identity based on the conventions of these novels. In Madame Bovary, the protagonist imagines that her life is, or ought to be, patterned after the novels she reads. Many classic novels have used this same technique—the characters in a book mimic the roles that they read in books or see in the theater.

The world of Harry Potter is replete with books as well, yet none of them are novels. None of the characters, least of all Harry himself, attempts to assume a role from a story written by someone outside the Potterverse. However, the characters nevertheless find themselves manipulated into taking on roles written by other characters in the Potterverse. From the Hogwarts acceptance letter to the scrap of parchment from the Goblet of Fire, Harry and Potterverse populace are continually handed fragments of a "script" that their fellow characters have devised for them. (25 minutes)

The Gospel According to Harry Potter, & Other Good News for Harry Potter Fans
Connie Neal (Featured Speaker)

While some insist the Harry Potter books are filled with witchcraft, Connie Neal shares how she looked at the same stories and found the Christian gospel. Using quotes from C.S. Lewis and J.K. Rowling on what people find in fantasy writing (some of which the author never intended), Neal takes a lighthearted look at the joy of sharing personal insights on beloved stories and how to handle people who insist Harry is "of the devil" in a friendly way. (50 minutes)

3:30 p.m.

It's Not Easy Being Hermione: Harry Potter and the Paradox of Girl Power
Meghan Mercier

In the days leading up to the release of the film of Sorcerer's Stone, I saw a TV interview with Emma Watson, in which she seemed excessively anxious to differentiate herself from Hermione Granger. I thought, "hey, don't bite the hand that feeds you!" but after that I began to pay attention to the treatment of Hermione (and Watson) in the movie and the press. I discovered a disturbing trend . . . so if Hermione is one of your favorite things about the Potter books, hear me out: she is much diminished in the transition to the screen. (25 minutes)

Narratorial Control: Harry Potter Joins the Three Investigators
Dr. Ernelle Fife

Ostensibly, the ongoing Harry Potter series and The Three Investigator series are worlds apart. Both series work because each author creates a narrator who controls how the reader reads, inviting the reader to become a active participant in the story as the narrative progresses, a process aided by the protagonists being mirrors of the adolescent reader. This presentation will investigate this narratorial control, responding to Peter Hunt's appeal for literary critics to study how narrative functions in children's stories.

Why narrative appeals, how the storyteller tells her or his story, what keeps us turning the page, how to recognize what is important for the narrative (What we need to know as opposed to what is nice to know), must be the concern of theoretician and practitioner alike. Both series are character, not plot, driven; the stories certainly are filled with action, suspense, and danger, but the choices the protagonists make are always more significant than what happens to them. Secondly, teamwork and perseverance are key elements in both series. Furthermore, each set of adolescent heroes face challenging obstacles that they do not always initially surmount. (25 minutes)

The Witching Hour—2005

In early October, 2005, The Witching Hour, the second event by HP Education Fanon will commence in Salem, Massachusetts. We expect a thousand atttendees—they will have a chance to don their cloaks, grasp their wands, tote their magical texts and Apparate to the Historic District of Salem for five days of magic and merry-making, text and context, craft and criticism.

Like Nimbus—2003, The Witching Hour will explore the Harry Potter books and culture through academic examination and discussion, as well as through some fun fan convention elements. The main component of The Witching Hour will be nearly three days of formal academic presentations, panels and round tables and more than three days of workshops, round tables and booths that focus on writing and art.

We will begin on the evening of Thursday, October 6, 2005, with a float in Salem's annual Hallowe'en Parade, a Welcome Banquet, and Tom and Harry: From Similar Beginnings, an introductory panel on the lives of Tom Riddle and Harry Potter. Three full days packed with formal academic programming, art and writing workshops, individual and team games, a gallery and a multitude of intellectual opportunities, festivities and events will follow, and on Monday morning we'll say goodbye after awarding the House Cup.

The focus—or spirit, if you will—of The Witching Hour is an exploration of the darkness within each of us, the choices that may turn our paths and the moral ambiguity that confounds us. JK Rowling delves deeply into these themes in the Harry Potter books, and we feel the time is right for their study and exploration. There can be no more fitting place to conduct this exploration than Salem, Massachusetts. Salem has a colored past, the result of the terror-filled year of 1692 when her residents, stirred on by a hysterical girl and their own bigotry, hanged nineteen people and jailed countless others in a terrifying display of intolerance and mistrust. Salem has overcome this tragedy, and has used this terrible history to become a town that celebrates acceptance. Every year during October, beneath the merriment of celebration, Salem keens for her past, decorating the town, but leaving the hanging grounds bare. Only stones, trees and remnants of offering candles remain on the space where those deaths occurred, a sober reminder of how our choices can come to define us.

Similarly, there is a new starkness in the Harry Potter series. The bleakness emphasized in *Harry Potter and the Order of the Phoenix* has injected a tone into the books as a whole and the fan community; there is a sense of loneliness, of emptiness, a feeling that things are not quite what we thought them to be. It is at this time—when the Harry Potter world has turned grey—that we need to look at our perceptions of morality, the choices we face, and the many paths that lie before us. Academic presentations offered at The Witching Hour will allow attendees to explore these perceptions. As Harry stands on this cusp of indecision, balancing on the knife edge between life altering choices, we look to examine what makes JK Rowling's characters choose the way they do—either giving in to the darkness crowding their souls or pushing it back—and why we as readers and people choose to deal with our own potential for darkness the way we do.

For more information (including a schedule, venue information, academic programming, surprises and convention events), please visit our website at www.witchinghour.org, or e-mail help@witchinghour.org in order to receive our monthly newsletter. Then pack your trunk, don your cloak, and make your way to the "Portkey"!

If you'd like to be notified of the release of our Call for Papers on October 31, 2004, please sign up to receive the electronic version of The Witching Hour's official newspaper, The Oracle, by e-mailing updates@witchinghour.org If you have questions regarding a potential submission, please e-mail Catherine Tosenberger, our Chair of Formal Programming, at cat@witchinghour.org.

Lumos! 2006

With a whirl of the wand and a hearty chant of "Lumos!" Harry Potter fans are welcomed to the bright lights of Las Vegas as HPEducation Fanon gets ready to present our first event west of the Rockies.

From July 27 through 30, 2006, Las Vegas, Nevada—the Muggle "City of Lights"—will play host to Lumos 2006: A Harry Potter Symposium. Through a "Back to School" theme, academic presentations and panels, including special workshops for educators and librarians, will mesh with Water Quidditch, magical Night School casses, live chess and other events. The event will welcome proposals from academics and enthusiasts who wish to focus on areas ranging from literary analysis, psychology and legal studies to fandom culture, fanfiction and fanart.

"Lumos 2006 will offer a fun, educational atmosphere that's exclusively Harry Potter," says Debbie McLain, the event's Minister of Magic. "From British food all weekend long, to Butterbeer in the hotel's Irish pub, attendees will be completely immersed in J.K. Rowling's unique and magical universe."

In keeping with the theme, conference planners intend to fill the host hotel with "Hogwarts" feel. There will be house tables in the Great Hall, a Common Room for all four houses that will showcase school spirit with their house banners, and a library in the Art Gallery to browse a variety of Potter-themed books—including this one!

This meeting is still early in the planning stages and continues to staff and evolve. Anyone wishing to join in the planning process, or to volunteer at the event itself, may sign up at http://groups.yahoo.com/group/vegasroomofrequirement/.

For additional information as it is released, please visit Lumos 2006: A Harry Potter Symposium's website at http://www.lumos2006.org/.

Endnotes

Notes from Justice in the Wizarding World

[1]   P.271

[2]   see, for example *Goblet* p.124 Hermione complains that Crouch treats Winky the house-elf as though she "wasn't even human": Ron retorts, "Well, she's not". In *Azkaban* his response to Lupin is "'*Get away from me werewolf*'" (p.253) and in *Goblet* he expresses the wizarding prejudice against giants: "'They're just vicious, giants'" (p.374).

[3]   Hagrid is imprisoned in Azkaban on the basis that the Minister of Magic has "*Got to be seen to be doing something. If it turns out it wasn't Hagrid, he'll be back and no more said.*" (p. 193) "No more said" is interesting, suggesting as it does that those imprisoned without trial should be thankful if their incarceration proves purely temporary. There is no suggestion that civil actions for wrongful imprisonment or the like might be available to the innocent victim in such circumstances.

[4]   P.16

[5]   *Goblet*, p.161

[6]   *Chamber* p.27

[7]   *Goblet* p. 329

[8]   *Phoenix* p.342

[9]   *Goblet* p.119

[10]   *Phoenix* p.639

[11]   Goblet p.390

[12]   p. 81

[13]   p. 174

[14]   *Beasts* p.*xii*

[15]   *Beasts* p. *xv*

[16]   p. 247

[17]   As for example Alec Dossetor does, in his unpublished essay *Expecto Patronus - or how the Wizarding World really works*

[18]   Although we learn for the first time in *Phoenix* that the wizarding high court is called the Wizengamot, we learn at the same time (p.90) that Dumbledore has apparently been demoted from his position as Chief Warlock, either by or on the instigation of the Ministry.

[19]   *Phoenix* p.138

[20]   p.518

[21]   *Beasts* p.*xv*

[22]   p.7

[23]   *Chamber* p.115 "There is not a shred of evidence that Slytherin ever built so much as a secret broom cupboard". But Binns must have known about the Chambers being opened

during the Dippet headship, and the circumstances in which his fellow ghost, Moaning Myrtle, came to be killed.

[24] *Chamber* p.21

[25] *Beasts,* p.*xvi*

[26] The same practical concern applies to taking Muggle born children at Hogwarts. Their parents/guardians and possibly other friends and relations become perforce aware to some degree of the existence of the magical world and its institutions. We never find out what excuse *Hermione's* parents find to explain her absence at a school no-one in their circle will ever have heard of, or how she answers when family friends enquire "And what GCSEs are you taking, dear?"

[27] *Stone* p. 61

[28] *Chamber* p, 231. Actually, since it is clear from *Goblet* p.8 that the elder Tom Riddle was financially somewhat of a catch, whereas his wife seems to have been without friends and family, it is entirely possible that the sequence of events was pregnancy resulting in a hurried marriage, and that the feeling he had been trapped into matters contributed to his reaction to her revelation. Although since we know nothing about Mrs Riddle's moral character, this may be casting unfair aspersions upon her.

[29] *Stone* p. 93

[30] *Chamber* p.*181*. The dating of the school year relies on its being 50 years before the deathday party of Nearly Headless Nick, which occurs at Hallowe'en 1992. Prefects are chosen in their fifth school year (*Phoenix*).

[31] *Chamber* p. 182. There is no evidence Tom Riddle senior was aware she had, indeed, died, although he might have obtained an annulment on presumption of death any time after about 1933.

[32] She would have had grounds on the basis of his desertion, or it is possible he might have convinced a Muggle court that her assertions of magical ability evidenced insanity, or argued for cruelty.

[33] Although the Finnigans could, theoretically, be either Catholics from Northern Ireland or Irish immigrants to Great Britain, Seamus's accent (particularly as portrayed in the films but as depicted phonetically in the books) justifies the assumption that the Finnigans originate from and are still resident in Eire. The Quidditch League is played between British and Irish teams, suggesting that the events of 1916-22 did not impact upon wizarding boundaries.

[34] P. 89

[35] [1942] AC 624

[36] Those interested may wish to know that *HMS Thetis* was raised from the sea-bed, refitted, and served with distinction in the Battle of the Atlantic under the name *HMS Thunderbolt* before being torpedoed and sunk on March 14th 1943.

[37] Five being usual.

[38] p. 633-634

[39] [1968] All ER 874

40 L.P. Hartley *The Go Between* 1953

41 Which is scarcely unreasonable, given the flagrant corruption and abuse of power that characterises the Ministry and its officials.

42 I am indebted to Alec Dossetor and Pamela Maddison for their assistance in clarifying the thoughts developed about the client/patron relationships over numerous discussions during the preparation of this paper.

43 For comparatively "modern day" fictional examples of bastard patronage in operation, the first chapter of Mario Puzo's *The Godfather* (1969) is illuminating, as is O'Casey's *Shadow of a Gunman* (1923) in which the neighbours mistaken assumption that Donal is a Republican terrorist is accompanied by demands on him (as their natural patron) to provide services to them as clients.

44 First published London, 1814. It contains an example of breath-taking snobbery worthy of the Malfoys. A powerful patron and political leader is puzzled by the defection of one of his leading aristocratic supporters into a rival patronage network. It is discovered that the reason for the defection is that the patron made the mistake of sealing a letter to the aristocrat with a gummed wafer—to be moistened before application like our ordinary envelopes—instead of using sealing wax. The aristocrat defected because he could not bear to be associated with someone who could "Stoop to send me his spittle".

45 Sherlock Holmes, while usually avoiding taking the law into his own hands, in *The Adventure of Charles Augustus Milverton*, commits a burglary and witnesses a murder, being able to identify the murderer. He declines to assist the police in the investigation, stating *"there are certain crimes which the law cannot touch and which therefore, to some extent, justify private revenge" (The Penguin Complete Sherlock Holmes,* (Penguin, 1981) p.582. This tradition is carried through by Sayers' Lord Peter Wimsey (*The Unprincipled Affair of the Practical Joker* and *The Unsolved Puzzle of the Man With No Face* in *Lord Peter Views The Body* (Penguin, 1963) include law-breaking to combat crimes the law cannot touch, and allowing murderers to escape because of the nature of their victims. Both Christie's Hercule Poirot and Gladys Mitchell's Dame Beatrice Adela Lestrange Bradley go even further in direct illegal action.

46 As we only learn in *Phoenix* p.90 when he has been deprived of these honours.

47 Another example of failure in respect of separation of powers, of course. The International Confederation are the supra-legislative body concerned with the international wizarding communities and keeping member countries' individual laws in line with the Statute, and the Wizengamot is the Wizarding High Court. This year the UK has been forced to abolish the judicial function of Lord Chancellor because it is believed that it is improper for a judge to have a role in interpreting laws which that judge may have played a political part in drafting or promulgating. No such scruples apparently apply in wizarding society.

48 *Goblet* p.142-3. Ironically, of course, the "cover-up" plays straight into the hands of Barty Crouch Junior. That, together with way Amos Diggory allows his prejudices against house-elves to prevent him interrogating Winky effectively, and the unquestioned power Mr Crouch senior possesses to take the interrogation out of Ministerial hands altogether, are of

course contributory causes to Cedric Diggory's death. Voldemort kills him, but it is the corruption of the Ministry that puts the weapon in Voldemort's hand.

[49]   The 1965 Ban on Experimental Breeding in the case of Blast-ended Skrewts (*Beasts p.xix*) and the Warlocks Convention of 1709 in the case of dragons (*Stone* p. 169).

[50]   *Stone* p. 68. As Hagrid at this point is not in fact permitted to have a wand at all the complex of laws he must have broken hardly bears thinking about. And for Muggle purposes it was almost certainly an assault occasioning grievous bodily harm, too.

[51]   Well, strictly speaking, up to 1994. *Azkaban* p.257.[1] The Animagi are James Potter, Sirius Black, Peter Pettigrew and Rita Skeeter.

[52]   *Goblet* p. 192 and p.203

[53]   p. 39

[54]   A fuller description of this point can be found in my essay *Harry Potter and the Rule of Law*, published in *Reading Harry Potter: Critical Essays* ed. Giselle Liza Anatol (Praeger, 2003).

[55]   *Azkaban* p.155

[56]   Chapter 2

[57]   p.136

[58]   p.125—Arthur explains it is "not allowed" for him to come to the hearing with him.

[59]   p. 137

[60]   p. 658

[61]   *Goblet* p.198

[62]   And it does appear the more likely of the two options.

[*]   In the British edition the text is slightly different: "*I'm not doing this for you. I'm doing it because I don't reckon my dad would've wanted his best friends to become killers—just for you.*"

Notes from And That's The Title on the Manifesto:

[1]   They were both also thought to be frivolously interested in nothing but clothing.

[2]   "Well, they hardly ever leave the kitchen by day, do they?" said Nearly Headless Nick. "They come out at night to do a bit of cleaning . . . see to the fires and so on . . . I mean, you're not supposed to see them are you? That's the mark of a good house-elf, isn't it, that you don't know it's there?" (*Goblet of Fire*, p.491, US version)

[3]   Marxist theory also speaks to the Weasley's lack of concern: "[Political economy] confines itself to systematizing in a pedantic way, and proclaiming for everlasting truths, trite ideas held by the self-complacent bourgeoisie with regard to their own world (Marx, in Engels)."

[4]   Thankfully, this intellectual shift has a historical precedent: A Victorian lady, accused of treating her maid as a slave, said "To compare the feelings of English ladies towards their maids with those of slave-holders towards their slaves is just one of those extravagances which none but the ignorance of a volunteer reformer would have ventured on (Linton, *Mistresses*)."

[5]   The fact that she has just recently bound herself to his son complicates matters; though the world views her as both freed and disgraced, she is still bound magically to the family.

6   In particular, its historical legacy of slavery.

7   "What caste is to India and race is to the United States, class is to Britain." (Wagner)

8

Notes from Harry Potter: Witchcraft? Presented as part of the Pagan Perspectives Panel

1   Sabbats are the four days that coincide with the Solstices and Equinoxes each year. Esbats coincide with the full moon each month. Sabbats are commonly considered the most powerful days to perform ritual; esbats are considered more routine occasions, but still more powerful than other times of the month.

2   "To one as young as you, I'm sure it seems incredible, but to Nicolas and Perenelle, it really is like going to bed after a very, very long day. After all, to the well-organized mind, death is but the next great adventure" (Rowling, Harry Potter and the Sorcerer's Stone, 121).

Notes from The Seven Deadly Sins / Seven Heavenly Virtues: Moral Development in Harry Potter

1   Alan Jacobs, "Harry Potter's Magic." *First Things* 99 (January 2000) 35-38.

2   This paper is a further development of a series of essays written on the Seven Deadly Sins and Seven Heavenly Virtues, first written and posted at the Yahoo Group Harry Potter for Grownups. See http://groups.yahoo.com/group/HPforGrownups/files/Essays/ESSAYS%20-%20Peg%20Kerr/

3   Citations to the texts of Rowling's work refer to the American hardback editions.

4   This quotation is taken from the table in "the Proceedings of the Conference on Psychology and the Process of Schooling in the Next Decade: Alternative Conceptions", Editor Maynard C. Reynolds. Kohlberg's contribution was entitled "The concepts of Developmental Psychology as the Central Guide to Education: Examples from Cognitive, Moral, and Psychological Education." The document is further marked "A publication of the Leadership Training Institute/Special education, sponsored by the Bureau of Educational Personnel Development, U.S. Office of Education". See *http://www.xenodochy.org/ex/lists/moraldev.html*.

5   A.S. Byatt. "Harry Potter and the Childish Adult." *New York Times*, July 11, 2003.

6   See, for example, Chapter 12 of C.S. Lewis's *Mere Christianity* ("The Cardinal Virtues").

7   Thomas Hobbes, *The Leviathan* I 13.

8   See, for example, C.S. Lewis, *Mere Christianity*, Chapter One ("The Law of Human Nature").

Notes from What's A Nice Jewish Boy Like Harry Potter Doing In A Place Like This?

1   Yiddish: a "human being," a person who behaves in a righteous and caring manner.

2   The two Hebrew letters, lamed and vov, have a numeric value of 36, which is double chai

(18), Hebrew for "life." The rabbis teach that the Holy One does not destroy the world because of 36 righteous people, but we do not know who they are. These people are pure of heart.

3 The Workman's Circle is a secular Jewish society that has socialist ideals. In Yiddish, its name is Arbeter Ring.

4 In Hebrew, the Jewish Bible is called "tanach" and is called the "old testament" by non-Jews. It is divided into three parts—the torah, the prophets and the writings; in Hebrew, torah, n'vi-im and k'tuvim, respectively. By taking the first letter of each word, the acronym is tanach.

5 The torah is the first five books of tanach.

6 Exodus 22:18

7 Leviticus 19:26

8 Hebrew: "The Name"; we do not know the Holy One's name

9 Deuteronomy 18:10-11

10 It is now thought that Saul suffered from bi-polar disorder, which would explain his apparent mood swings and incongruous behavior.

11 The word "gematria" is believed to be derived from the Greek words, *geo*, meaning "earth," and *metria*, meaning measure.

12 Hebrew: from the root "to receive." Traditionally, Jewish men over the age of 40, with a lifetime of torah and Talmud study and experience behind them, were allowed to receive the teachings from an expert kabbalist.

13 *Harry Potter and the Philosopher's Stone*, p. 51

14 Jewish dietary laws. Kashrut comes from the Hebrew word kasher, which means fit or proper.

15 http:// www.circle.org/wcwho.html

16 One is forbidden to mistreat widows and orphans several times in the torah, beginning with Exodus 22:21.

17 A Roman soldier approached Rabbi Hillel and demanded that the rabbi teach him the torah while the rabbi stood on one leg. Rabbi Hillel stood on one leg and said, "What is hateful to you, do not do to another person. That is the whole torah. All the rest is commentary. Go and learn it."

18 Yiddish: compassion

19 Yiddish: literally, a "good soul"

20 In Hebrew, "pikuach nefesh"

21 Moses Maimonides (1135-1204 C.E.), "Mishneh Torah"

22 *Harry Potter and the Order of the Phoenix*, p. 646

23 *Harry Potter and the Chamber of Secrets*, chapter 16

24 *Harry Potter and the Prisoner of Azkaban*, chapter 17

25 *Harry Potter and the Goblet of Fire*, chapter 26

26 ibid, chapter 31

27 *Harry Potter and the Order of the Phoenix*, chapter 1

28 Deuteronomy 30:19-20

29 Micah 6:8
30 From the tamudic tractate Pirke Avot (teachings of the sages) 1:14
31 Pirke Avot 2:6
32 *Harry Potter and the Goblet of Fire*, p. 628
33 *Harry Potter and the Order of the Phoenix*, chapters 32-38
34 Yiddish: craziness
35 Yiddish: foolishness

Notes from Harry Potter: A Universal Hero?

1   Zipes, Jack *Stick and Stones: The Troublesome Success of Children's Literature from Slovenly Peter to Harry Potter* (Routledge: New York and London, 2001), 175
2   Colbert, David *The Magical Worlds of Harry Potter: A Treasury of Myths, Legends and Fascinating Facts* (Penguin: London, 2001), 155
3   Hourihan, Margery *Deconstructing the Hero: Literary Theory and Children's Literature* (Routledge: London, 1997), 2
4   Frye, Northrop *Anatomy of Criticism: Four Essays* (Princeton University Press: Princeton New York, 1957), 187
5   *ibid.*
6   Frye, Northrop *The Secular Scripture: A Study of the Structure of Romance* (Harvard University Press: Cambridge, Mass. and London, 1976), 67
7   Rowling, J K *Harry Potter and The Order of the Phoenix* (Bloomsbury: London, 2003), 741
8   Frye, *Anatomy of Criticism*, 67
9   *ibid.*
10 *ibid.*, 188
11 *The Goblet of Fire*, 437; *The Order of the Phoenix*, 646-7, 690
12 Hourihan, 15
13 Frye, *Anatomy*, 188
14 Plumwood, Val *Feminism and the Mastery of Nature* (Routledge: London and New York, 1993) 42-3, cited in Hourihan, 17
15 Hourihan, 16
16 *ibid.*, 17
17 *ibid.*, 32
18 Frye, *Anatomy*, 195
19 *ibid.*
20 *ibid.*
21 *The Order of the Phoenix*, 271
22 von Franz, Marie-Louise *The Interpretation of Fairy Tales* (revised ed.) (Shambhala: Boston and London, 1996), 17
23 Lüthi, Max *Die Gabe im Märchen und in der Sage* Inaugural dissertation (Bern, 1943) cited in *ibid.*, 17

24   von Franz, 17

25   *ibid.*

26   Eccleshare, Julia *A Guide to the Harry Potter Novels* (Continuum: New York and London, 2002), 88

27   Hourihan, 38

28   See Fry, Michèle 'Heroes and Heroines: Myth and Gender in the Harry Potter books', *New Review of Children's Literature and Librarianship 2001*, pp. 157-67

29   Hourihan, 38

30   *ibid.*

31   *ibid.*, 39

32   Rowling, J K *Harry Potter and The Philosopher's Stone* (Bloomsbury: London, 1997), 217; Rowling, J K *Harry Potter and The Prisoner of Azkaban* (Bloomsbury: London, 1999), 178

33   Rowling, J K *Harry Potter and The Goblet of Fire* (Bloomsbury: London, 2000), 273, 280, 294; *The Order of the Phoenix*, 13

34   *The Order of the Phoenix*, 725-36

35   *ibid.*, 402, 273 respectively.

36   Hourihan, 41

37   *ibid.*

38   Rowling, J K *The Chamber of Secrets* (Bloomsbury: London, 1998), 231

39   *The Goblet of Fire*, 561

40   Hourihan, 41

41   *ibid.*

42   *The Philosopher's Stone*, 47, 66, and 75-6 respectively

43   *ibid.*, 75-6

44   *The Goblet of Fire*, 527-8; *The Order of the Phoenix*, 453-5

45   *ibid.*, passim.

46   *The Prisoner of Azkaban*, 308-10; *The Goblet of Fire*, 373-4

47   Hourihan, 58

48   *The Goblet of Fire*, 239-40

49   *ibid.*, 565-71, 587-600

50   *The Order of the Phoenix*, 468-71

51   *ibid.*, 641 ff.

52   Hourihan, 58

53   *The Philosopher's Stone*, 204-6

54   *The Chamber of Secrets*, 120-1, 157-63

55   See, for example, *The Prisoner of Azkaban*, 209-10, 265, 285 for Harry's anger towards Snape, and *The Goblet of Fire*, 262, 632 for Harry's anger towards Malfoy.

56   *The Prisoner of Azkaban*, 25-8

57   *ibid.*, 157-9, 183, 249-51

58   *The Order of the Phoenix*, 726

59   Hourihan, 78

60   *The Goblet of Fire*, 254-5, 277-8

[61] *ibid.*, 25, 534-5

[62] *The Order of the Phoenix*, 85

[63] Hourihan, 79

[64] *The Prisoner of Azkaban*, 58

[65] *The Goblet of Fire*, 620

[66] Hourihan, 89

[67] *ibid.*

[68] *Jung on Mythology* (ed.) Robert A Segal (Routledge: London, 1998), 132

[69] *The Goblet of Fire*, 584-5; *The Order of the Phoenix*, 468-75

[70] *The Philosopher's Stone*, 197-8; *The Chamber of Secrets*, 219-40; *The Prisoner of Azkaban*, 244-78; *The Goblet of Fire*, 538, 552-81; *The Order of the Phoenix*, 676 ff.

[71] Clute, John and John Grant (eds) *The Encyclopaedia of Fantasy* 2e (Orbit: London, 1999), 250

[72] Hourihan, 96

[73] *ibid.*, 98

[74] *Harry Potter and the Prisoner of Azkaban*, 249-52

[75] *ibid.*, 275

[76] *The Order of the Phoenix*, 715

[77] *The Philosopher's Stone*, 213-4

[78] *The Chamber of Secrets*, 233-4

[79] *The Philosopher's Stone*, 172-6; *The Goblet of Fire*, 304-11

[80] *The Prisoner of Azkaban*, 115-8, 174-80, 308-10; *The Goblet of Fire*, 373-4

[81] Hourihan, 156

[82] *ibid.*

[83] *ibid.*

[84] *ibid.*, 161

[85] *ibid.*, 163

[86] *The Goblet of Fire*, 52/-8; *The Order of the Phoenix*, 453-5

[87] *ibid.*, 174

[88] *ibid.*

[89] *The Goblet of Fire*, 101

[90] *The Goblet of Fire*, 516

[91] Hourihan, 167

[92] *ibid.*

[93] *ibid.*, 174

Notes from The Pleasure & the Pain of the Scar: Harry Potter as a Popular Culture Icon

[1] *Icons of Popular Culture* (Ohio, 1970), p.1.

[2] "*Harry Potter's Fan Magic Attempt Sets House Ablaze*," July 10, 2003. Yahoo! News.   **http://story.news.yahoo.com/news?tmpl=story&u=/nm/20030710/od_nm/fire_dc_1**

[3] *Icons of Popular Culture* (Ohio, 1970), p.1.

4   *"Pottermania: Good, Clean Fun or Cultural Hegemony?"* in Harry Potter's World: Multidisciplinary Critical Perspectives (New York, 2003), pp.17-18.

5   *Reading the Popular* (Boston, 1989), p.4.

6   *Understanding Popular Culture* (Boston, 1989), p.35.

7   *The Popular Culture Reader* (Ohio, 1978), p.93.

8   Ibid.

Printed in the United Kingdom
by Lightning Source UK Ltd.
106058UKS00005B/79-84